*What They Said*
*in 1975*

# What They Said In 1975

## The Yearbook of Spoken Opinion

•

Compiled and Edited by

ALAN F. PATER

and

JASON R. PATER

MONITOR BOOK COMPANY, INC.

COPYRIGHT © 1976 BY MONITOR BOOK COMPANY, INC.

SEVENTH ANNUAL EDITION

Printed in the United States of America

Library of Congress catalogue card number: 74-111080

ISBN number: 0-9600252-8-6

*To*

*The Newsmakers of the World . . .*

*May they never be at a loss for words*

# *Preface to the First Edition (1969)*

Words can be powerful or subtle, humorous or maddening. They can be vigorous or feeble, lucid or obscure, inspiring or despairing, wise or foolish, hopeful or pessimistic . . . they can be fearful or confident, timid or articulate, persuasive or perverse, honest or deceitful. As tools at a speaker's command, words can be used to reason, argue, discuss, cajole, plead, debate, declaim, threaten, infuriate, or appease; they can harangue, flourish, recite, preach, discourse, stab to the quick, or gently sermonize.

When casually spoken by a stage or film star, words can go beyond the press-agentry and make-up facade and reveal the inner man or woman. When purposefully uttered in the considered phrasing of a head of state, words can determine the destiny of millions of people, resolve peace or war, or chart the course of a nation on whose direction the fate of the entire world may depend.

Until now, the *copia verborum* of well-known and renowned public figures—the doctors and diplomats, the governors and generals, the potentates and presidents, the entertainers and educators, the bishops and baseball players, the jurists and journalists, the authors and attorneys, the congressmen and chairmen-of-the-board—whether enunciated in speeches, lectures, interviews, radio and television addresses, news conferences, forums, symposiums, town meetings, committee hearings, random remarks to the press, or delivered on the floors of the United States Senate and House of Representatives or in the parliaments and palaces of the world—have been dutifully reported in the media, then filed away and, for the most part, forgotten.

The editors of *WHAT THEY SAID* believe that consigning such a wealth of thoughts, ideas, doctrines, opinions and philosophies to interment in the morgues and archives of the Fourth Estate is lamentable and unnecessary. Yet the media, in all their forms, are constantly engulfing us in a profusion of endless and increasingly voluminous news reports. One is easily disposed to disregard or forget the stimulating discussion of critical issues embodied in so many of the utterances of those who make the news and, in their respective fields, shape the events throughout the world. The conclusion is therefore a natural and compelling one: the educator, the public official, the business executive, the statesman, the philosopher—everyone who has a stake in the complex, often confusing trends of our times—should have material of this kind readily available.

These, then, are the circumstances under which *WHAT THEY SAID* was conceived. It is the culmination of a year of listening to the people in the public eye; a year of scrutinizing, monitoring, reviewing, judging, deciding—a year during which the editors resurrected from almost certain oblivion those quintessential elements of the year's *spoken* opinion which, in their judgment, demanded preservation in book form.

*WHAT THEY SAID* is a pioneer in its field. Its *raison d'etre* is the firm conviction that presenting, each year, the highlights of vital and interesting views from the lips of prominent people on virtually every aspect of contemporary civilization fulfills the need to give the *spoken* word the permanence and lasting value of the *written* word. For, if it is true that a picture is worth 10,000 words, it is equally true that a verbal conclusion, an apt quote or a candid comment by a person of fame or influence can have more significance and can provide more understanding than an entire page of summary in a standard work of reference.

The editors of *WHAT THEY SAID* did not, however, design their book for researchers and scholars alone. One of the failings of the conventional reference work is that it is blandly written and referred to primarily for facts and figures, lacking inherent "interest value." *WHAT THEY SAID,* on the other hand, was planned for sheer enjoyment and pleasure, for searching glimpses into the lives and thoughts of the world's celebrities, as well as for serious study, intellectual reflection and the philosophical contemplation of our multifaceted life and mores. Furthermore, those pressed for time, yet anxious to know what the newsmakers have been saying, will welcome the short excerpts which will make for quick, intermittent reading—and rereading. And, of course, the topical classifications, the speakers' index, the subject index, the place and date information—documented and authenticated and easily located—will supply a rich fund of hitherto not readily obtainable reference and statistical material.

Finally, the reader will find that the editors have eschewed trite comments and cliches, tedious and boring. The selected quotations, each standing on its own, are pertinent, significant, stimulating— above all, relevant to today's world, expressed in the speakers' own words. And they will, the editors feel, be even more relevant tomorrow. They will be re-examined and reflected upon in the future by men and women eager to learn from the past. The prophecies, the promises, the "golden dreams," the boastings and rantings, the bluster, the bravado, the pleadings and representations of those whose voices echo in these pages (and in those to come) should provide a rare and unique history lesson. The positions held by these luminaries, in their respective callings, are such that what they say today may profoundly affect the future as well as the present, and so will be of lasting importance and meaning.

ALAN F. PATER
JASON R. PATER

*Beverly Hills, California*

# Table of Contents

# About the 1975 Edition . . .

During the preparation of *WHAT THEY SAID* each year, it often becomes apparent that certain key words seem to be especially associated with a particular year. And 1975 was no exception.

The word "assassination" was suddenly being used: assassination of Saudi Arabian King Faisal; attempted assassinations of U.S. President Ford; Central Intelligence Agency alleged assassination plots against foreign leaders.

The word "bribe" came to be associated with the world of big business and multinational corporations: bribes to foreign governments; revelations of illegal contributions (a form of bribe) during the 1972 U.S. Presidential election campaign.

"Bankruptcy" was a word used for the first time in connection with a major city: in this case, the virtual bankrupt City of New York.

Although the war in Indochina ended in 1975, it spawned a word that may be remembered long afterward: *Mayaguez*, the U.S. merchant ship seized by the new Communist government in Cambodia.

"Malpractice" was a word that agitated the medical profession as well as the consumer, because physicians were faced with ever-increasing rates of insurance premiums and patients would inevitably have to pay higher medical fees.

---

The Editors of *WHAT THEY SAID* again this year thank those educators, librarians and others who have given encouragement and offered suggestions on improving the series. All comments are of course welcomed, and any ideas deemed practical and worthy will be considered for forthcoming volumes.

---

With no intention of being a complete news summary of 1975, following are some of the happenings reflected in many of this year's quotations . . .

*Commerce:*

Revelations of overseas bribes paid by U.S. businesses, as well as illegal domestic political contributions, made headlines and prompted investigations of multinational companies.

*Crime:*

The Federal Bureau of Investigation was criticized for past illegal or unethical practices. Gun control and capital punishment continued as two controversial issues.

*Education:*

The lowering of standards in education was debated during the year, partly as a result of a drop in college-entrance examination scores. The merits of grading were discussed, and liberal-arts vs. vocational education received attention.

# WHAT THEY SAID IN 1975

*Environment:*

The effect of growth on the environment was an important ecological topic in 1975.

*Energy:*

Oil and gas rationing, imported vs. domestic petroleum, energy independence, fuel prices and nuclear power shared the spotlight in this ever-more-important category.

*Foreign Affairs:*

Detente continued as the most-discussed topic in the foreign field, but other areas of debate included Congressional vs. Presidential authority over foreign affairs, Secretary of State Kissinger's power and influence, and the effect on U.S. foreign policy of the Communist victory in Indochina.

*Intelligence/Spying:*

More disclosures of Central Intelligence Agency activities, including alleged assassination attempts on foreign leaders, culminated in Congressional investigations and calls for more oversight of the Agency.

*Government:*

Dispute continued throughout the year on such subjects as government spending, the bureaucracy and public confidence. Also discussed was decentralization of power from Federal to state units, and the President's veto power.

*Labor/The Economy:*

This again was one of the year's most talked-about and widely felt areas of national importance, with inflation, recession and unemployment the three by-words of the economy. National economic planning was offered by some as a possible future necessity and rejected by others as a dangerous and unworkable system.

*Law/The Judiciary:*

Judges' salaries, plea-bargaining and the expanding jurisdiction of courts were significant areas of discussion.

*National Defense:*

Should U.S. defense spending and expansion go down as detente progresses? This was one of the year's most controversial questions.

*Politics:*

While the furor of Watergate officially ended in 1974, the subject proved to be an on-going subject of debate throughout 1975. There were assassination attempts on President Ford, which sparked discussion on campaign methods, such as wading into crowds and "flesh-pressing." The forthcoming 1976 Presidential election began to set the stage for much campaign rhetoric to come.

*Urban Affairs:*

The inability of New York City to meet its financial responsibilities, with bankruptcy on the horizon unless aided by the Federal government, made news headlines in 1975.

*Africa:*

Angola's independence from Portugal, and the subsequent civil war for control of the country, sparked debate on whether the U.S. should aid the pro-West faction in response to Soviet and Cuban backing of the Communist group.

*Americas:*

There were allegations of past U.S. Central Intelligence Agency assassination plots against Cuban Premier Fidel Castro. The question of sovereignty over the Panama Canal was as yet unresolved.

*Asia:*

U.S. President Ford visited Communist China for the first time. American arms aid to Pakistan resumed. Prime Minister Indira Gandhi declared a state of emergency in India and took virtually total power.

*Indochina:*

The war came to an end as U.S. support for South Vietnam and Cambodia was terminated in the face of increasing Communist military successes. Communist forces took control of those two countries and of Laos. The new Cambodian government seized a U.S. merchant ship, the *Mayaguez,* and touched off an incident in which U.S. forces were brought in and the ship recovered.

*Europe:*

Socialists and Communists continued to vie for power in Portugal following 1974's coup. U.S. arms cut-off to Turkey, as a result of that country's Cyprus policy, created a rift between the two governments. Spain's long-time ruler, Francisco Franco, died; Juan Carlos was installed as King.

*Middle East:*

A Sinai agreement between Egypt and Israel was ratified. The Suez Canal was re-opened. King Faisal of Saudi Arabia was assassinated; King Khalid assumed leadership.

*United Nations:*

The General Assembly voted to condemn Zionism as racist. New United States Ambassador Daniel Moynihan caused a stir with his frank and often critical assessments of the world and of the UN.

*Medicine:*

A frenzy over ever-increasing malpractice insurance premiums culminated in a doctor strike in California. A few celebrated cases brought to the fore the subject of prolonging the life of terminal or incurable patients.

# WHAT THEY SAID IN 1975

*Stage:*

A musicians strike temporarily closed virtually all Broadway musicals.

*Television:*

The new "family hour" concept brought both praise (a step in the right direction, with networks controlling violence and sex on their own) and derision (a form of censorship that may be unconstitutional).

*Sports:*

Football's reserve clause was struck down by a Federal judge.

## *Editorial Treatment*

### ORGANIZATION OF MATERIAL

Special attention has been given to the arrangement of the book—from the major divisions down to the individual categories and speakers—the objective being a logical progression of related material, as follows:

(A) The categories are arranged alphabetically within each of three major sections—

| | |
|---|---|
| Part One: | "National Affairs" |
| Part Two: | "International Affairs" |
| Part Three: | "General" |

In this manner, the reader can quickly locate quotations pertaining to particular fields of interest (see also *Indexing*). It should be noted that some quotations contain a number of thoughts or ideas—sometimes on different subjects—while some are vague as to exact subject matter and thus do not fit clearly into a specific topic classification. In such cases, the judgment of the Editors has determined the most appropriate category.

(B) Within each category, the speakers are in alphabetical order by surname, following alphabetization practices used in the speaker's country of origin.

(C) Where there are two or more quotations by one speaker within the same category, they appear chronologically by date spoken or date of source.

### SPEAKER IDENTIFICATION

(A) The occupation, profession, rank, position or title of the speaker is given as it was *at the time the statement was made* (except when the speaker's relevant identification is in the past, in which case he is shown as "former"). Thus, due to possible changes in status during the year, a speaker may be shown with different identifications in various portions of the book, or even within the same category.

(B) In the case of speakers who hold more than one position or occupation simultaneously (or who held relevant positions in the past), the judgment of the Editors has determined the most appropriate identification to use with a specific quotation.

(C) Nationality of speakers is normally not given unless this information is of interest or relative to the quotation(s).

### THE QUOTATIONS

The quoted material selected for inclusion in this book is shown as it appeared in the source, except as follows:

(A) *Ellipses* have been inserted wherever the Editors have deleted extraneous or overly long words or passages within the quoted material used. In no way has the meaning or intention of any quotation been altered. *Ellipses* are also used where they appeared in the source.

(B) *Punctuation and spelling* have been altered by the Editors where they were obviously incorrect in the source, or to make the quotations more intelligible, or to conform to the general style used throughout this book. Again, meaning or intention of the quotations has not been changed.

(C) *Brackets* ([ ]) indicate material inserted by the Editors or by the source to either correct obvious errors or to explain and/or clarify what the speaker is saying.

(D) *Italics* have sometimes been added by the Editors where emphasis is clearly desirable.

Except for the above instances, the quoted material used has been printed verbatim, as reported by the source (even if the speaker made factual errors or was awkward in his choice of words).

Special care has been exercised to make certain that each quotation stands on its own merits and is not taken "out of context." The Editors, however, cannot be responsible for errors made by the original newspaper, periodical or other source, i.e., incorrect reporting, mis-quotations or errors in interpretation.

## DOCUMENTATION AND SOURCES

Documentation (circumstance, place, date) of each quotation is provided as fully as could be obtained, and the sources are furnished for all quotations. In some instances no documentation details were available; in those cases only the source is given. Following are the sequence and style used for this information:

> Circumstance of quotation, place, date/Name of source, date: section (if applicable), page number.

> Example: *Before the Senate, Washington, Dec. 4/The Washington Post, 12-6:(A)13.*

The above example indicates that the quotation was delivered before the Senate in Washington on December 4. It was taken for *WHAT THEY SAID* from *The Washington Post,* issue of December 6, section A, page 13. (When a newspaper publishes more than one edition on the same date, it should be noted that page numbers may vary from edition to edition.)

(A) When the source is a television or radio broadcast, the name of the network or local station is indicated, along with the date of the broadcast (obviously, page and/or section information does not apply).

(B) One asterisk (*) before the (/) in the documentation indicates that the quoted material was written rather than spoken. Although the basic policy of *WHAT THEY SAID* is to use only *spoken* statements, there are occasions when written statements are considered by the Editors to be important enough to be included. These occasions are rare and usually involve Presidential messages, Presidential statements released to the press and other such documents attributed to a person in high governmental office.

(C) Two asterisks (**) after the (/) indicate the speaker supplied the quotation to *WHAT THEY SAID* directly.

INDEXING

(A) The *Index to Speakers* is keyed to the page number. (For alphabetization practices, see *Organization of Material,* paragraph B.)

(B) The *Index to Subjects* is keyed to both the page number and the quotation number on the page (thus, 210:3 indicates quotation number 3 on page 210); the quotation number appears at the upper right-hand corner of each quotation.

(C) To locate quotations on a particular subject, regardless of speaker, turn to the appropriate category (see *Table of Contents*) or use the detailed *Index to Subjects.*

(D) To locate all quotations by a particular speaker, regardless of subject, use the *Index to Speakers.*

(E) To locate quotations by a particular speaker on a particular subject, turn to the appropriate category and then to that person's quotations within that category.

(F) The reader will find that the basic categorization format of *WHAT THEY SAID* is itself a useful subject index, inasmuch as related quotations are grouped together by their respective categories. All aspects of journalism, for example, are relevant to each other; thus, the section *Journalism* embraces all phases of the news media. Similarly, quotations pertaining to the U.S. Presidency, Congress, revenue-sharing, etc., are together in the section *Government.*

---

MISCELLANEOUS

(A) Except where otherwise indicated or obviously to the contrary, all universities, colleges, organizations and business firms mentioned in this book are located or based in the United States; similarly, references to "national," "Federal," "this country," "the nation," etc., refer to the United States.

(B) In most cases, organizations whose titles end with "of the United States" are Federal government agencies.

---

SELECTION OF CATEGORIES

The selected categories reflect, in the Editors' opinion, the most widely-discussed public-interest subjects, those which readily fall into the over-all sphere of "current events." They represent topics continuously covered by the mass media because of their inherent relevance to the changing world scene. Most of the categories are permanent; they appear in each annual edition of *WHAT THEY SAID.* However, because of the transient character of some subjects, there may be categories which appear one year and are not repeated.

SELECTION OF SPEAKERS

The following persons are *always* considered eligible for inclusion in *WHAT THEY SAID:* top-level officials of all branches of national, state and major local governments (both U.S. and foreign), including all United States Senators and Representatives; top-echelon military officers; college and university presidents, chancellors and professors; chairmen and presidents of major corporations; heads of national public-oriented organizations and associations; national and internationally known diplomats; recognized celebrities from the entertainment and literary spheres and the arts generally;

sports figures of national stature; commentators on the world scene who are recognized as such and who command the attention of the mass media.

The determination of what and who are "major" and "recognized" must, necessarily, be made by the Editors of *WHAT THEY SAID* based on objective personal judgment.

Also, some persons, while not recognized as prominent in a particular professional area, have nevertheless attracted an unusual amount of attention in connection with a specific issue or event. These people, too, are considered for inclusion, depending upon the circumstances involved.

## SELECTION OF QUOTATIONS

The quotations selected for inclusion in *WHAT THEY SAID* obviously represent a decided minority of the seemingly endless volume of quoted material appearing in the media each year. The process of selection is scrupulously objective insofar as the partisan views of the Editors are concerned (see *About Fairness,* below). However, it is clear that the Editors must decide which quotations *per se* are suitable for inclusion, and in doing so look for comments that are aptly stated, offer insight into the subject being discussed, or into the speaker, and provide—for today as well as for future reference—a thought which readers will find useful for understanding the issues and the personalities that make up a year on this planet.

---

## ABOUT FAIRNESS

The Editors of *WHAT THEY SAID* understand the necessity of being impartial when compiling a book of this kind. As a result, there has been no bias in the selection of the quotations, the choice of speakers or the manner of editing. Relevance of the statements and the status of the speakers are the exclusive criteria for inclusion, without any regard whatsoever to the personal beliefs and views of the Editors. Furthermore, every effort has been made to include a multiplicity of opinions and ideas from a wide cross-section of speakers on each topic. Nevertheless, should there appear to be, on some controversial issues, a majority of material favoring one point of view over another, it is simply the result of there having been more of those views expressed during the year, reported by the media and objectively considered suitable by the Editors of *WHAT THEY SAID* (see *Selection of Quotations*). Also, since persons in politics and government account for a large percentage of the speakers in *WHAT THEY SAID,* there may exist a heavier weight of opinion favoring the political philosophy of those in office at the time, whether in the United States Congress, the Administration, or in foreign capitals. This is natural and to be expected and should not be construed as a reflection of agreement or disagreement with that philosophy on the part of the Editors of *WHAT THEY SAID.*

# *Abbreviations*

The following are abbreviations used by the speakers in this volume. Rather than defining them each time they appear in the quotations, this list will facilitate reading and avoid unnecessary repetition.

| | |
|---|---|
| ABM: | antiballistic missile |
| ADA: | Americans for Democratic Action |
| AFL-CIO: | American Federation of Labor-Congress of Industrial Organizations |
| ANC: | African National Council |
| ANZUS: | Australia-New Zealand-United States security treaty |
| BBC: | British Broadcasting Corporation |
| CAB: | Civil Aeronautics Board |
| CIA: | Central Intelligence Agency |
| CSU: | Chicago State University |
| DH: | designated hitter |
| EC: | European (Economic) Community |
| EPA: | Environmental Protection Agency |
| ERA: | Equal Rights Amendment |
| ESP: | extra-sensory perception |
| FAA: | Federal Aviation Administration |
| FBI: | Federal Bureau of Investigation |
| FCC: | Federal Communications Commission |
| FDR: | Franklin Delano Roosevelt |
| FHA: | Federal Housing Administration |
| FNLA: | National Front for the Liberation of Angola |
| FTC: | Federal Trade Commission |
| GAO: | General Accounting Office |
| GDR: | German Democratic Republic (East Germany) |
| GM: | General Motors Corporation |
| GNP: | gross national product |
| HEW: | Department of Health, Education and Welfare |
| HMO: | health maintenance organization |
| IBM: | International Business Machines Corporation |
| ICC: | Interstate Commerce Commission |
| ILO: | International Labor Organization |
| IRA: | Irish Republican Army |
| IRS: | Internal Revenue Service |
| ITT: | International Telephone & Telegraph Corporation |
| ITV: | Independent Television Network |
| KGB: | Soviet secret police |
| LDC: | less-developed countries |
| LEAA: | Law Enforcement Assistance Administration |

# WHAT THEY SAID IN 1975

| | |
|---|---|
| MAC: | maximum allowable cost |
| MIA: | missing in action |
| MPLA: | Popular Movement for the Liberation of Angola |
| NAACP: | National Association for the Advancement of Colored People |
| NASA: | National Aeronautics and Space Administration |
| NATO: | North Atlantic Treaty Organization |
| NATPE: | National Association of Television Program Executives |
| NBA: | National Basketball Association |
| NCAA: | National Collegiate Athletic Association |
| NFL: | National Football League |
| NFLPA: | National Football League Players Association |
| NOW: | National Organization for Women |
| NRA: | National Rifle Association |
| NSF: | National Science Foundation |
| OAS: | Organization of American States |
| OAU: | Organization of African Unity |
| OEO: | Office of Economic Opportunity |
| OPEC: | Organization of Petroleum Exporting Countries |
| PBS: | Public Broadcasting Service |
| PLA: | Palestine Liberation Army |
| PLO: | Palestine Liberation Organization |
| PTA: | Parent-Teachers Association |
| SALT: | strategic arms limitation talks |
| SAM: | surface-to-air missile |
| SAT: | Scholastic Aptitude Test |
| SEC: | Securities and Exchange Commission |
| SMU: | Southern Methodist University |
| TEE: | Trans-Europe Express |
| UHF: | ultra high frequency (television) |
| UN: | United Nations |
| UNITA: | National Union for the Total Independence of Angola |
| U.S.: | United States |
| U.S.A.: | United States of America |
| U.S.S.R.: | Union of Soviet Socialist Republics |
| VD: | venereal disease |
| VHF: | very high frequency (television) |
| WFL: | World Football League |

---

Party affiliation of United States Senators, Congressmen and Governors—

| | |
|---|---|
| C: | Conservative-Republican |
| D: | Democratic |
| I: | Independent |
| R: | Republican |

# The Quote of the Year

*"I am convinced that Americans, however tempted to resign from the world, know that it cannot be done. The spirit of learning is too deeply ingrained. We know that, wherever the bell tolls for freedom, it tolls for us."*

**—GERALD R. FORD**

*President of the United States; at University of Notre Dame, Notre Dame, Ind., March 17.*

# PART ONE

# National Affairs

# The State of the Union Address

*Delivered by Gerald R. Ford, President of the United States, to a joint session of Congress, House of Representatives, Washington, January 15, 1975.*

Mr. Speaker, Mr. Vice President, members of the 94th Congress and distinguished guests:

Twenty-six years ago, a freshman Congressman, a young fellow with lots of idealism who was out to change the world, stood before Sam Rayburn in the well of the House and solemnly swore to the same oath that all of you took yesterday—an unforgettable experience, and I congratulate you all.

Two days later, that same freshman stood at the back of this great chamber—over there someplace—as President Truman, all charged up by his single-handed election victory, reported as the Constitution requires on the State of the Union.

When bipartisan applause stopped, President Truman said:

"I am happy to report to the 81st Congress that the State of the Union is good. Our nation is better able than ever before to meet the needs of the American people and to give them their fair chance in the pursuit of happiness. It is foremost among the nations of the world in the search for peace."

Today, that freshman member from Michigan stands where Mr. Truman stood and I must say to you that the State of the Union is not good.

## America's Problems

Millions of Americans are out of work. Recession and inflation are eroding the money of millions more. Prices are too high and sales are too slow.

This year's Federal deficit will be about $30-billion; next year's probably $45-billion. The national debt will rise to over $500-billion.

Our plant capacity and productivity are not increasing fast enough. We depend on others for essential energy.

Some people question their Government's ability to make hard decisions and stick with them. They expect Washington politics as usual.

Yet, what President Truman said on January 5, 1949, is even more true in 1975.

We are better able to meet our people's needs.

All Americans do have a fairer chance to pursue happiness. Not only are we still the foremost nation in the pursuit of peace, but today's prospects of attaining it are infinitely brighter.

There were 59 million Americans employed at the start of 1949. Now there are more than 85 million Americans who have jobs. In comparable dollars, the average income of the American family has doubled during the past 26 years.

Now, I want to speak very bluntly. I've got bad news, and I don't expect much, if any, applause. The American people want action and it will take both the Congress and the President to give them what they want. Progress and solutions can be achieved. And they will be achieved.

My message today is not intended to address all of the complex needs of America. I will send separate messages making specific recommendations for domestic legislation, such as the extension of general revenue sharing and the Voting Rights Act.

The moment has come to move in a new direction. We can do this by fashioning a new partnership between the Congress on the one hand, the White House on the other, and the people we both represent.

Let us mobilize the most powerful and most creative industrial nation that ever existed on this earth to put all our people to work. The emphasis on our economic efforts must now shift from inflation to jobs.

## Tax Reduction

To bolster business and industry and to create new jobs, I propose a one-year tax reduction of $16-billion. Three-quarters would go to individuals and one-quarter to promote business investment.

This cash rebate to individuals amounts to 12 per cent of 1974 tax payments—a total cut of $12-billion with a maximum of $1,000 per return.

I call on the Congress to act by April 1. If you do, and I hope you will, the Treasury can send the first check for half the rebate in May and the second in September.

The other one-fourth of the cut, about $4-billion, will go to business, including farms, to promote expansion and to create more jobs. The one-year reduction for businesses would be in the form of a liberalized investment tax credit increasing the rate to 12 per cent for all business.

This tax cut does not include the more fundamental reforms needed in our tax system. But it points us in the right direction—allowing taxpayers rather than the Government to spend their pay.

Cutting taxes, now, is essential if we are to turn the economy around. A tax cut offers the best hope of creating more jobs. Unfortunately, it will increase the size of the budget deficit. Therefore, it is more important than ever that we take steps to control the growth of Federal expenditures.

## Federal Spending

Part of our trouble is that we have been self-indulgent. For decades, we have been voting ever-increasing levels of Government benefits—and now the bill has come due. We have been adding so many new programs that the size and the growth of the Federal budget has taken on a life of its own.

One characteristic of these programs is that their cost increases automatically every year because the number of people eligible for most of the benefits increases every year. When these programs were enacted, there is no dollar amount set. No one knows what they will cost. All we know is that whatever they cost last year, they will cost more next year.

It is a question of simple arithmetic. Unless we check the excessive growth of Federal expenditures or impose on ourselves matching increases in taxes, we will continue to run huge inflationary deficits in the Federal budget.

If we project the current built-in momentum of Federal spending through the next 15 years, state, Federal and local government expenditures could easily comprise half of our gross national product. This compares with less than a third in 1975.

I've just concluded the process of preparing the budget submissions for fiscal year 1976. In that budget, I will propose legislation to restrain the growth of a number of existing programs. I have also concluded that no new spending programs can be initiated this year, except for energy. Further, I will not hesitate to veto any new spending programs adopted by the Congress.

As an additional step toward putting the Federal Government's house in order, I recommend a 5 per cent limit on Federal pay increases in 1975. In all Government programs, tied to the Consumer Price Index—including Social Security, Civil Service and military retirement pay, and food stamps—I also propose a one-year maximum increase of 5 per cent.

None of these recommended ceiling limitations, over which Congress has final authority, are easy to propose, because in most cases they involve anticipated payments to many, many deserving people. Nonetheless, it must be done. I must emphasize that I am not asking to eliminate, to reduce, or to freeze these payments. I am merely recommending that we slow down the rate at which these payments increase and these programs grow.

Only a reduction in the growth of spending can keep Federal borrowing down and reduce the damage to the private sector from high interest rates.

Only a reduction in spending can make it possible for the Federal Reserve System to avoid an inflationary growth in the money supply and thus restore balance to our economy. A major reduction in the growth of Federal spending can help dispel the uncertainty that so many feel about our economy, and put us on the way to curing our economic ills.

If we don't act to slow down the rate of increase in Federal spending, the United States Treasury will be legally obligated to spend more than $360-billion in fiscal year 1976—even if no new programs are enacted.

These are not matters of conjecture or prediction, but again a matter of simple arithmetic. The size of these numbers and their implication for our everyday life and the health of our economic system are shocking.

I submitted to the last Congress a list of budget deferrals and recisions. There will be more cuts recommended in the budget that I'll submit. Even so, the level of outlays for fiscal year 1976 is still much, much too high. Not only is it too high for this year, but the decisions we make now will inevitably have a major and growing impact on expenditure levels in future years. I think this is a very fundamental issue that we, the Congress and I, must jointly solve.

### Foreign Oil

The economic disruptions we and others are experiencing stem in part from the fact that the world price of petroleum has quadrupled in the last year. But, in all honesty, we cannot put all of the blame on the oil exporting nations. We, the United States, are not blameless. Our growing dependence upon foreign sources has been adding to our vulnerability for years and years. And we did nothing to prepare ourselves for such an event as the embargo of 1973.

During the nineteen-sixties, this country had a surplus capacity of crude oil, which we were able to make available to our trading partners whenever there was a disruption of supply. This surplus capacity enabled us to influence both supplies and prices of crude oil throughout the world. Our excess capacity neutralized any effort at establishing an effective cartel, and thus the rest of the world was assured of adequate supplies of oil at reasonable prices.

### Surplus Capacity

By 1970 our capacity, our surplus capacity, had vanished, and as a consequence the latent power of the oil cartel could emerge in full force.

Europe and Japan, both heavily dependent on imported oil, now struggle to keep their economies in balance. Even the United States, our country, which is far more self-sufficient than most other industrial countries, has been put under serious pressure.

I am proposing a program which will begin to restore our country's surplus capacity in total energy. In this way, we will be able to assure ourselves reliable and adequate energy and help foster a new world energy stability for other major consuming nations.

### Future Energy Difficulties

But this nation and, in fact, the world, must face the prospect of energy difficulties between now and 1985. This program will impose burdens on all of us with the aim of reducing our consumption of energy and increasing our production. Great attention has been paid to the considerations of fairness, and I can assure you that the burdens will not fall more harshly on those less able to bear them.

I am recommending a plan to make us invulnerable to cutoffs of foreign oil. It will require sacrifices. But it—and this is most important—it will work.

I have set the following national energy goals to assure that our future is as secure and as productive as our past:

First, we must reduce oil imports by one million barrels per day by the end of this year and by two million barrels per day by the end of 1977.

Second, we must end vulnerability to economic disruption by foreign suppliers by 1985.

Third, we must develop our energy technology and resources so that the United States

GERALD R. FORD

has the ability to supply a significant share of
the energy needs of the free world by the end
of this century.

*Short-Term Measures*

To attain these objectives, we need immediate action to cut imports. Unfortunately, in the
short-term there are only a limited number of
actions which can increase domestic supply. I
will press for all of them.

I urge quick action on the necessary legislation to allow commercial production at the Elk
Hills, Calif., Naval Petroleum Reserve. In order
that we make greater use of domestic coal resources, I am submitting amendments to the
Energy Supply and Environmental Coordination Act which will greatly increase the number
of power plants that can be promptly converted
to coal.

Obviously, voluntary conservation continues
to be essential, but tougher programs are
needed—and needed now. Therefore, I am using
Presidential powers to raise the fee on all imported crude oil and petroleum products.

Crude oil fee levels will be increased $1 per
barrel on Feb. 1, by $2 per barrel on March 1
and by $3 per barrel on April 1. I will take
action to reduce undue hardship on any geographical region.

*Long-Term Actions*

The foregoing are interim administrative
actions. They will be rescinded when the
broader but necessary legislation is enacted.

To that end, I am requesting the Congress to
act within 90 days on a more comprehensive
energy tax program. It includes:

• Excise taxes and import fees totaling $2
per barrel on product imports and on all crude
oil.

• Deregulation of new natural gas and enactment of a natural gas excise tax.

• I plan to take Presidential initiative to
decontrol the price of domestic crude oil on
April 1.

• I urge the Congress to enact a windfall
profits tax by that date to ensure that oil producers do not profit unduly.

The sooner Congress acts, the more effective
the oil conservation program will be and the
quicker the Federal revenues can be returned to
our people.

I am prepared to use Presidential authority
to limit imports, as necessary, to guarantee
success.

I want you to know that before deciding on
my energy conservation program, I considered
rationing and higher gasoline taxes as alternatives. In my judgment, neither would achieve
the desired results and both would produce
unacceptable inequities.

A massive program must be initiated to increase energy supply, to cut demand and provide new stand-by emergency programs to
achieve the independence we want by 1985.

The largest part of increased oil production
must come from new frontier areas on the
outer continental shelf and from the Naval
Petroleum Reserve No. 4 in Alaska. It is the
intent of this Administration to move ahead
with exploration, leasing and production on
those frontier areas of the outer continental
shelf where the environmental risks are acceptable.

Use of our most abundant domestic resource—coal—is severely limited. We must strike
a reasonable compromise on environmental
concerns with coal. I am submitting clean air
amendments which will allow greater coal use
without sacrificing clean air goals.

I vetoed the strip-mining legislation passed
by the last Congress. With appropriate changes,
I will sign a revised version when it comes to
the White House.

I am proposing a number of actions to
energize our nuclear power program. I will submit legislation to expedite nuclear leasing and
the rapid selection of sites.

In recent months, utilities have canceled or
postponed over 60 per cent of planned nuclear
expansion and 30 per cent of planned additions
to non-nuclear capacity.

Financing problems for that industry are
worsening. I am therefore recommending that
the one-year investment tax credit of 12 per
cent be extended an additional two years to
specifically speed the construction of power
plants that do not use natural gas or oil. I am

6

also submitting proposals for selective reform of state utility commission regulations.

To provide the critical stability for our domestic energy production in the face of world price uncertainty, I will request legislation to authorize and require tariffs, import quotas or price floors to protect our energy prices at levels which will achieve energy independence.

### Energy Conservation

Increasing energy supplies is not enough. We must take additional steps to cut long-term consumption. I therefore propose to the Congress:
- Legislation to make thermal efficiency standards mandatory for all new buildings in the United States.
- A new tax credit of up to $150 for those homeowners who install insulation equipment.
- The establishment of an energy conservation program to help low-income families purchase insulation supplies.
- Legislation to modify and defer automotive pollution standards for five years which will enable us to improve new automobile gas mileage by 40 per cent by 1980.

These proposals and actions, cumulatively, can reduce our dependence on foreign energy supplies to three to five million barrels per day by 1985.

To make the United States invulnerable to foreign disruption, I propose stand-by emergency legislation and a strategic storage program of one billion barrels of oil for domestic needs and 300 million barrels for national defense purposes.

### Energy Alternatives

I will ask for the funds needed for energy research and development activities. I have established a goal of one million barrels of synthetic fuels and shale oil production per day by 1985 together with an incentive program to achieve it.

I have a very deep belief in America's capabilities. Within the next 10 years, my program envisions:

- 200 major nuclear power plants.
- 250 major new coal mines.
- 150 major coal-fired power plants.
- 30 major new refineries.
- 20 major new synthetic fuel plants.
- The drilling of many thousands of new oilwells.
- The insulation of 18 million homes.
- And the manufacturing and the sale of millions of new automobiles, trucks and buses that use much less fuel.

### We Can Do It

I happen to believe that we can do it. In another crisis—the one in 1942—President Franklin D. Roosevelt said this country would build 60,000 military aircraft. By 1943, production in that program had reached 125,000 aircraft annually. They did it then. We can do it now.

If the Congress and the American people will work with me to attain these targets, they will be achieved and will be surpassed.

### Taxes

From adversity, let us seize opportunity. Revenues of some $30-billion from higher energy taxes designed to encourage conservation must be refunded to the American people in a manner which corrects distortions in our tax system wrought by inflation.

People have been pushed into higher tax brackets by inflation, with consequent reduction in their actual spending power. Business taxes are similarly distorted because inflation exaggerates reported profits resulting in excessive taxes.

Accordingly, I propose that future individual income taxes be reduced by $16.5-billion. This will be done by raising the low-income allowance and reducing tax rates. This continuing tax cut will primarily benefit lower- and middle-income taxpayers.

For example, a typical family of four with a gross income of $5,600 now pays $185 in Federal income taxes. Under this tax-cut plan, they would pay nothing. A family of four with a gross income of $12,000 now pays $1,260 in

7

Federal taxes. My proposal reduces that total by $300. Families grossing $20,000 would receive a reduction of $210.

Those with the very lowest incomes, who can least afford higher costs, must also be compensated. I propose a payment of $80 to every person 18 years of age and older in that very limited category.

State and local governments will receive $2-billion in additional revenue sharing to offset their increased energy costs.

To offset inflationary distortions and to generate more economic activity, the corporate tax rate will be reduced from 48 per cent to 42 per cent.

### Global Economics

Now, let me turn, if I might, to the international dimensions of the present crisis. At no time in our peacetime history has the state of the nation depended more heavily on the state of the world. And seldom if ever has the state of the world depended more heavily on the state of our nation.

The economic distress is global. We will not solve it at home unless we help to remedy the profound economic dislocation abroad. World trade and monetary structure provides markets, energy, food and vital raw materials—for all nations. This international system is now in jeopardy.

### International Cooperation

This nation can be proud of significant achievements in recent years in solving problems and crises. The Berlin agreement, the SALT agreements, our new relationship with China, the unprecedented efforts in the Middle East—are immensely encouraging. But the world is not free from crisis. In a world of 150 nations, where nuclear technology is proliferating and regional conflicts continue, international security cannot be taken for granted.

So let there be no mistake about it: International cooperation is a vital factor of our lives today. This is not a moment for the American people to turn inward. More than ever before, our own well-being depends on America's determination and America's leadership in the whole wide world.

We are a great nation—spiritually, politically, militarily, diplomatically and economically. America's commitment to international security has sustained the safety of allies and friends in many areas—in the Middle East, in Europe, in Asia. Our turning away would unleash new instabilities, new dangers around the globe which, in turn, would threaten our own security.

At the end of World War II, we turned a similar challenge into an historic opportunity and, I might add, an historic achievement. An old order was in disarray; political and economic institutions were shattered. In that period, this nation and its partners built new institutions, new mechanisms of mutual support and cooperation. Today, as then, we face an historic opportunity. If we act, imaginatively and boldly, as we acted then, this period will in retrospect be seen as one of the great creative moments of our nation's history.

The whole world is watching to see how we respond.

### Global Effects of U.S. Economic Recovery

A resurgent American economy would do more to restore the confidence of the world in its own future than anything else we can do. The program that this Congress passes can demonstrate to the world that we have started to put our own house in order. If we can show that this nation is able and willing to help other nations meet the common challenge, it can demonstrate that the United States will fulfill its responsibility as a leader among nations.

Quite frankly, at stake is the future of the industrialized democracies, which have perceived their destiny in common and sustained it in common for 30 years.

The developing nations are also at a turning point. The poorest nations see their hopes of feeding their hungry and developing their societies shattered by the economic crisis. The long-term economic future for the producers of raw materials also depends on cooperative solutions.

### Relations with Communists

Our relations with the Communist countries are a basic factor of the world environment. We must seek to build a long-term basis for co-existence. We will stand by our principles; we will stand by our interests; we will act firmly when challenged. The kind of world we want depends on a broad policy of creating mutual incentives for restraint and for cooperation.

### Military Strength

As we move forward to meet our global challenges and opportunities, we must have the tools to do the job.

Our military forces are strong and ready. This military strength deters aggression against our allies, stabilizes our relations with former adversaries and protects our homeland. Fully adequate conventional and strategic forces cost many, many billions—but these dollars are sound insurance for our safety and for a more peaceful world.

### Diplomacy

Military strength alone is not sufficient. Effective diplomacy is also essential in preventing conflict and building world understanding. The Vladivostok negotiations with the Soviet Union represent a major step in moderating strategic arms competition. My recent discussions with the leaders of the Atlantic Community, Japan and South Korea have contributed to our meeting the common challenge.

### President's Foreign Power

But we have serious problems before us that require cooperation between the President and the Congress. By the Constitution and tradition, the execution of foreign policy is the responsibility of the President.

In recent years, under the stress of the Vietnam war, legislative restrictions on the President's ability to execute foreign and military decisions have proliferated. As a member of the Congress, I opposed some and I approved others. As President, I welcome the advice and cooperation of the House and the Senate.

But, if our foreign policy is to be successful, we cannot rigidly restrict in legislation the ability of the President to act. The conduct of negotiations is ill-suited to such limitations. Legislative restrictions intended for the best motives and purposes can have the opposite result, as we have seen most recently in our trade relations with the Soviet Union.

For my part, I pledge this Administration will act in the closest consultation with the Congress as we face delicate situations and troubled times throughout the globe.

When I became President only five months ago, I promised the last Congress a policy of communication, conciliation, compromise and cooperation. I renew that pledge to the new members of this Congress.

### Summary

Let me sum it up:

America needs a new direction which I have sought to chart here today—a change of course which will:

● Put the unemployed back to work.

● Increase real income and production.

● Restrain the growth of Federal Government spending.

● Achieve energy independence.

● And advance the cause of world understanding.

We have the ability. We have the know-how. In partnership with the American people, we will achieve these objectives.

As our 200th anniversary approaches, we owe it to ourselves, and to posterity, to rebuild our political and economic strength. Let us make America, once again, and for centuries more to come, what it has so long been—a stronghold and a beacon light of liberty for the whole world.

Thank you.

# The American Scene

**Helen Delich Bentley**
*Chairman,*
*Federal Maritime Commission*

1

America is not perfect—let that be said right here and now. We have a long way to go in this country, and it may take us another 200 years to approximate our goal. But let it also be said that America is so far the closest thing to perfection the world has ever seen—and I challenge anyone, right here and now, to disprove that statement. We may be worried about the rising cost of food—but not many of us, in this day and age, go hungry. Few other countries can say that about themselves. We may be concerned about the high rate of unemployment—but where else do those who refuse to work own cars and color television sets? We may have problems in our educational system; but what other nations guarantee their citizens a right to a higher education, in many cases free of charge? In America, virtually anyone can go to college. There are scholarships, fellowships, grants-in-aid, student loans. Many companies—and the government—even provide tuition and/or textbook expenses so that employees can upgrade their education. I suggest to those who don't appreciate America that they take a look at some of the alternatives. I just returned recently from a trip to Europe, during which I visited East Berlin. And let me tell you—just passing through the several checkpoints and seeing the restrictions that were placed on certain members of the visiting party who were West Germans was enough to make my blood run cold. It might not be a bad idea for some of our severest critics to visit a Communist country just one time. For once is all it takes to make a believer out of even the most ardent skeptic.

*Before Maryland Society of the Sons of the American Revolution, Annapolis, Oct. 18/ Vital Speeches, 11-15:73.*

**Christopher S. Bond**
*Governor of Missouri (R)*

2

The Soviet Union is a great nation with even more territory than ours; rich in natural resources and with 250 million capable people. The U.S.S.R. has had more than 50 years to fully implement a national system of socialism without hindrance or interference. We [in the U.S.] could be just like them, but it would take a little doing on our part. We'd have to start by cutting our paychecks 75 per cent; move 60 million workers back to the farm; abandon two-thirds of our steel-making capacity; destroy 40 million television sets; tear up 14 of 15 miles of highway; junk 19 out of 40 autos; tear up two-thirds of our railroad track; knock down 70 per cent of our houses; rip out nine of 10 telephones. Then, all we'd have to do is find a capitalist country willing to sell us wheat on credit to keep us from starving! Double, even triple, our troubles and we Americans still are better off than any other people on earth.

*Quoted in an address by W. F. Rockwell, Jr., chairman, Rockwell International/\*\**

**Edmund G. Brown, Jr.**
*Governor of California (D)*

3

There is a limit to the good things we have in this country. We're coming up against those limits. It's really a very salutary exercise to learn to live with them. Everybody looks for politicians to come up with the solutions to the society's problems. It really is a rather totalitarian urge if you analyze it. Maybe the answer is the Ten Commandments.

*Interview, Los Angeles/Time, 12-8:18.*

**R. Manning Brown, Jr.**
*Chairman,*
*New York Life Insurance Company*

4

The polls tell us that people generally are uncertain about our free system and its ability to accommodate change. There is, we read, a disheartening loss of faith in government, in business and in the will and the ability of leaders to work for the common good. From the near bankrupt condition of many states, cities and municipalities, to the stalling, log-rolling tactics at the Federal level, it is clear that all is not as right as it can be. And business, no less than government, is being challenged to think new ideas for these new times. At the moment, the public jury is still out as to whether or not we can meet this critical test. I would like to address myself to this current mood of uncertainty and doubt—not to defend the status quo, but rather to suggest, on the eve of our Bicentennial, that we the people can and will succeed . . . We would have to be totally blind to reality if we didn't recognize that the American system, with all its shortcomings, is still alive and intact. And it will remain so as long as people of good-will are willing to work to retain it.

*At President's Council, San Francisco, Sept. 2/Vital Speeches, 9-15:722.*

### Art Buchwald
*Newspaper columnist*
                                                                    *1*

. . . no matter what you read in the newspapers or see on television, I assure you that we're all going to make it. For 200 years this country has muddled through one crisis after another, and we have done it without changing our form of government. It seems like centuries ago, but it is less than a year, that a President of the United States [Richard Nixon] was forced to resign from office under the darkest of clouds and he was asked to leave the office because he lied to the American people. I was at the White House that night to hear his resignation speech, and what impressed me more than anything else was that, while one leader of our country was resigning and another was taking his place, I did not see one tank or one helmeted soldier in the street, and the only two uniforms I saw that night were two motorcycle policemen who were directing traffic on Pennsylvania Avenue. Two hundred million people able to change Presidents overnight without one bayonet being unsheathed. I believe that any

country in the world that can still do that can't be all bad.

*At Vassar College commencement/ The New York Times, 6-8:(4)17.*

### Willard C. Butcher
*President, Chase Manhattan Bank, New York*
                                                                    *2*

Business has been told many times that it needs to sell itself to America. I disagree. Business must sell America to America—its strengths, its greatness, its potential for creating the most humane and prosperous society on earth. In short . . . we must sell America on the value of its liberties and individual freedoms.

*Before Economic Club, Chicago, Feb. 20/ Vital Speeches, 4-1:373.*

### Otis Chandler
*Publisher, "Los Angeles Times"*
                                                                    *3*

[On recent events such as the Communist take-overs in Cambodia and South Vietnam; Watergate, the energy crisis, recession, the Middle East, etc.] : It is hard for anyone to take this much this fast, and particularly for Americans, who are used to winning, and winning big, in everything and in every place . . . But this does not mean that we have to go and hide our heads in the sand and say to hell with the rest of the world. What this means to me is that this country, after 200 years, has arrived at adulthood. We have come of age. We are no longer the biggest kid on the block. Like any adult, we must expect some hard knocks, some defeats and occasional setbacks. But let us not sit around feeling sorry for ourselves like we are now doing.

*Before William Allen White Foundation, University of Kansas, April 30/ Los Angeles Times, 5-1:(1)22.*

### John B. Connally, Jr.
*Former Secretary of the Treasury of the United States; Former Governor of Texas (D, now R)*
                                                                    *4*

Right now we are a nation tossed around like a cork at sea. We are without direction. Once again—as often in the past—we must assert control over our destiny. To do this we don't

# WHAT THEY SAID IN 1975

## (JOHN B. CONNALLY, JR.)

need a man on horseback. But we do need an act of national will, rising up from the people, strong enough to be felt in the Congress and the Executive Branch. If Congress and the President come together and challenge us to effort and sacrifice, they will find us ready. But we can't rally to a program of action that does not exist. And that is what the Bicentennial celebration is all about. There will be parades and learned symposia and all manner of other celebrations over the next year. That will be all to the good. But what history will record about our Bicentennial is how we answered this question: In the face of grave economic problems and grave threats to our security, did we have the maturity and vigor and sense of community to pull back from the brink and to prove that the Americans of 1976 were worthy of their heritage? I, for one, believe we are; but *if* we are, we've got to prove it.

*At World Trade Week convocation, New York/*
*The Dallas Times Herald, 6-1:(B)3.*

## Alistair Cooke
*Journalist, Historian*
1

There's something wonderful—and crass—about the American conviction that this country is unique. That's nonsense, of course, but it makes people attempt the unattemptable. We don't tend to live a middle ground; we lurch between apathy and euphoria. Shortly after I came here [from his native England in the 1930s], H. L. Mencken said to me, "Well, Cooke, you'll find this country will exasperate you, it will disgust you, it will enrage you and it will amuse you; but it's a nine-ring circus and you'll never be bored!" Of course, he was absolutely right.

*Interview, New York/"W":*
*a Fairchild publication, 3-7:8.*

## Edward L. R. Elson
*Chaplain of the United States Senate*
2

O God, our creator, redeemer and judge, we beseech thee to forgive those national sins which so easily beset us: our wanton waste of soil and sea, our squandering of energy, our desecration of natural beauty, our heedlessness

of scars of nature left to those who come after us, our love of money, our contempt for small things and our worship of big things, the loneliness of life in big cities, the dull complacency of small towns, the degeneracy of our culture, our bad manners, and our indifference to suffering—for these wrongs done and for right things left undone, good Lord, forgive us.

*Before the Senate, Washington/*
*The Wall Street Journal, 3-20:16.*

## Sam J. Ervin, Jr.
*Former United States Senator,*
*D—North Carolina*
3

It is impossible to over-magnify the value of the First Amendment to society, government and individuals. The freedoms it protects compel society to respect the fundamental rights of individuals, enable government to rule wisely, permit individuals to become everything they are capable of becoming, and make our other freedoms living realities rather than empty verbal dreams.

*San Francisco Examiner & Chronicle,*
*2-16:(This World)2.*

## Gerald R. Ford
*President of the United States*
4

In unhappy times and unpopular wars, Americans accept the challenge. No generation of Americans has failed to accept the necessary sacrifices of the day. I am convinced we will not fail ourselves or future generations . . . [Solutions to today's problems] will require the same hard work and tenacity required to wage a successful revolution, establish a working government, carve a civilization out of wilderness, produce the greatest industrial machine ever, and develop the highest standard of living of any nation in the world. [To honor the past,] we must hand this magnificent experiment in self-government on to future generations, free and strong.

*At National Bicentennial Conference,*
*Washington, Feb. 25/The Dallas Times Herald,*
*2-25:(A)1.*

5

I have heard much too much from people who say everything is falling apart, how the quality of life in America is sliding downhill, how the dollar is worthless, how muggers and murderers have driven everyone behind locked doors, and how even the President of the United States should stop visiting public places and seeing the American people [for fear of assassination]. I have had it with that attitude. I did not take the sacred oath of office to preside over the decline and fall of the United States of America. I most emphatically reject the scenario of pessimism.

*Before National Federation of Republican Women, Dallas, Sept. 13/ The Washington Post, 9-14:(A)8.*

1

I see the great challenge of our next hundred years as the advancement of individual independence, of specific steps to safeguard the identity of each and every American from the pressures of conformity. The pressures close in upon us from many quarters—massive government, massive management, massive labor, massive education, massive communication and massive acquisition of information. To meet this challenge, we still need a positive and passionate commitment to law, to learning and to liberty.

*At dedication of Stanford University Law School, Sept. 21/The New York Times, 9-22:13.*

**John H. Glenn, Jr.**
*United States Senator,*
*D–Ohio*

2

The mood [in the U.S.] is somewhat frightening. I don't think I've ever seen people so uneasy, so unsure about the future. Never in my life have I seen people as uncertain about where we are going and how we are going to get there and what kind of country we are going to have for our children.

*Interview, Washington/Los Angeles Times, 1-21:(2)7.*

**Mills E. Godwin**
*Governor of Virginia (D)*

3

[If America] stands as the last hope of freedom in the world ... then let us first be ourselves the voices of freedom, the pur-

veyors of hope, the channels for charity and, above all, the fountains of faith. [America needs] men and women who can articulate the true meaning of America at a time when an alien philosophy of collectivism seems to be in the ascendancy. We have been backed into the trap of appearing to be defenders of the status quo, whereas the collectivists extol themselves as revolutionaries. [But] if we believe that the central thread of history has been mankind's long, slow struggle to be free, a struggle toward individual worth and dignity, then Americans are the revolutionaries of our time.

*At Randolph-Macon College graduation, Ashland, Va., June 1/ The Washington Post, 6-2:(C)6.*

**Louis Harris**
*Public-opinion analyst*

4

The American people may have low confidence in politics, politicians, government at all levels, the White House, the Congress and the U.S. Senate, but they have not lost hope. They do not feel that we are a doomed giant of a nation in the last throes as other empires of the past, where corruption is rife, where the disease of disintegration has reached an advanced stage and where desperation reigns. A solid 95 out of every 100 Americans believe in our system of pluralistic democracy. But, above all, they want it to work.

*At Senate hearing, Washington/ The Washington Post, 11-5:(A)26.*

5

We have found the American people distinctly of a mind, of late, of insisting that their leadership level with them out in the open on just how serious the problems are confronting us as a nation ... If given a choice between seriously trimming their material lifestyles or enduring more cycles of double-digit inflation and high levels of unemployment, they find that decision relatively easy. By 77 per cent to 8 per cent, they would opt for cutting back in their material life-styles. These are significant results, for they signal the enormous change that is taking place in our country. Simply put, it means in the future that the three-bathtub and three-car syndrome is

# WHAT THEY SAID IN 1975

*(LOUIS HARRIS)*

disappearing from American life. People no longer aspire to sitting in front of a table and heaping more and more physical acquisitions onto a pile of things they own. Instead, they are seeking, yearning and even crying out for a different kind of existence.

*At Sentry Insurance Company, Concord, Mass./*
*The Wall Street Journal, 11-18:20.*

**Jesse A. Helms**
*United States Senator, R—North Carolina*    1

We are still the greatest and most powerful nation in the world. Yet we now feel constrained to add that word "still" in the phrase as though there are creeping doubts, nagging insinuations we have passed the apex of our history.

*Before Americanism Educational League,*
*Beverly Hills, Calif., Feb. 3/*
*Los Angeles Herald-Examiner, 2-4:(A)13.*

**James Jones**
*Author*    2

[On returning to the U.S. after having lived in Europe]: Being away has given me a different perspective. Americans don't know how lucky we are. This is still the best system in the world . . . We're trying to solve problems here. We're trying to deal with technology, to give everybody some living space. I think America is very exciting. I think writers should celebrate life more than we do.

*Interview, Sagaponack, N.Y./*
*The New York Times, 8-1:23.*

**Henry A. Kissinger**
*Secretary of State of the United States*    3

We [in America] sometimes seem uncertain of our future, disturbed by our recent past, and confused as to our purpose. But we must persevere for we have no other choice. Either we lead, or no one leads; either we succeed, or the world will pay for our failure. It is the glory of our nation that when challenged we have always stepped forward with spirit and a will to dare great things. It is now time to do so again, and in so doing to reaffirm to ourselves and to the world that this generation of Americans has the integrity of character to carry on the noble experiment that began two centuries ago.

*Before National Press Club, Washington,*
*Feb. 3/The New York Times, 2-4:3.*

**Edward H. Levi**
*Attorney General of the United States*    4

It is not necessarily a reproach that our society has not fulfilled all its aspirations . . . The good society must have ideals beyond its attainment.

*At dedication of law-school building,*
*University of Nebraska/*
*Los Angeles Times, 5-23:(2)7.*

**Richard W. Lyman**
*President, Stanford University*    5

The urge to legislate in haste and repent in leisure—not just on the part of the Congress, but on the part of the people who elect the Congress—is greater now than at any time since the early 1930s, in a nation that doesn't know quite what it wants but is terribly impatient with what it has.

*The Wall Street Journal, 11-11:20.*

**Rod MacLeish**
*Senior commentator,*
*Westinghouse Broadcasting Company*    6

Americans tend to dwell more on their patriotism than most other people. Yet its proclaimers cannot explain exactly what it is they *do* love. The divisions are such in this country that they can hardly claim it is their fellow Americans. The heedless misuse of the landscape makes it doubtful that it is the geography we all love. That leaves the ideas upon which the country is based. Yet we quarrel about the various meanings of the Constitution and entertain grave doubts about the Bill of Rights—except when the rights described apply to us personally. Last summer, in Philadelphia, I went to see that neat chamber in Independence Hall where the Declaration of Independence and Constitution were written. In reading the Declaration, I was struck, most of all, by its ending: "And for the support of this Declaration . . . we *mutually pledge to each other* our

Lives, our Fortunes and our sacred Honor." It is that sense of pledging *to each other* that we have lost—that 18th-century sense, as real now as it was then, that we are all in this thing together. If, in some way, we could regain that feeling of mutuality, our proclamations of patriotism would be a lot more tangible.

*The Reader's Digest, July:/18.*

**William Lee Miller**
*Professor of political science, and
director of the Poynter Center,
Indiana University*
                                    1

Each people has its own particular role to play in the story of mankind. We [in the U.S.] have ours. And if we do have an unusual circumstance in that we are a large democratic nation, coming out of Europe at a lucky moment, during which we have developed and sustained a constitutional existence for what will soon be 200 years, without a break, an existence which survived a bitter civil war—well, that is, indeed, a very important part of the perennial, continuing human story. Europeans, above all, are aware of the difficulties of constructing a constitutional republic and keeping it going through assassinations, civil wars, world wars. So they do appreciate what the United States is and what it means to the rest of the world. They do not obscure—nor should we— either the good or the evil things we have done as a nation—and I include in the latter the Bomb, the Vietnam war, putting Japanese in concentration camps, slavery. Those were evil. But we do stand for something better, and we have acted on that, and, to a great extent, we have brought it off, we have embodied the democratic ideal in a living, complex, heterogeneous society. We should not let anyone dismiss that.

*Interview, Indiana University/
The Center Magazine, July-Aug.:68.*

**Richard B. Morris**
*President-elect, American Historical
Association; Professor of History,
Columbia University*
                                    2

Much of the world still looks to the United States for leadership in so many areas. To take a few: in the peaceful use of the atom; in

directing resources and controlling the environment in ways that are beneficial to the whole earth, not to America alone. Surely, to be an American does not mean that we should turn our back on our world obligations. Benjamin Franklin once expressed the hope that the knowledge of the rights of man would prevail world-wide some day, and that a time would come when a philosopher might set his foot anywhere on its surface and say, "This is my country." Franklin personified pride in nation in the best sense—a love for America and a conviction that it would be a world standard-bearer of humane progress.

*Interview/
U.S. News & World Report, 7-7:45.*

**Bill Moyers**
*Former Press Secretary to the President
of the United States (Lyndon B. Johnson)*
                                    3

[Addressing college students]: I find a growing number of people [in the U.S.] who question whether anything matters, whether anything works, whether anyone listens, whether anyone cares. As many of you must, I find myself afraid, cantankerous, bewildered, often hostile, often gracious, battered by a hundred new sensations every month and filled with the sense that we are either on the verge of the worst of times or the best of times. I vacillate, as I suspect you do, between the determination to change society and the desire to retreat into the snuggeries of myself and my family. [What America must beware of] is defeatism, the nothing-can-be-done disease. In that kind of environment it becomes every man for himself, and catastrophe is inevitable. [But] I've seen too many Americans coping with the unexpected, coping with the tragic, coping with the extraordinary, coping with the evil, the perfidy and the suffering and still holding on to their irreducible humanity, to their grace, to their humor. I've seen too many of them to believe that this is yet a lost race.

*At University of Texas/Parade, 5-11:12.*

**Edmund S. Muskie**
*United States Senator, D—Maine*
                                    4

There is so much negative in all that we read and all that we say and all that we hear about

# WHAT THEY SAID IN 1975

*(EDMUND S. MUSKIE)*

our country, about the disappointments around the world, about the frustrations here at home ... that what we really need is a feeling of confidence that we can deal as a united country with these problems. We are very strong in all respects, from the tangible to the intangible and spiritual values that our country has subscribed to for 200 years. I think we can deal with every one of these problems about which we disagree and deal with them effectively and move forward into tomorrow. I believe that. I think that the basic instinct of the American people in this time of frustration is consistent with that.

*TV-radio interview, Washington/*
*"Meet the Press,"*
*National Broadcasting Company, 4-13.*

## David Packard
*Chairman, Hewlett-Packard Company* 1

I'm convinced that democracy will continue in America. I don't think the problems we're facing today are as serious as some of the problems this country faced over the past 200 years. I see no reason to be concerned about the vitality of democracy today. It will change and be adaptable to meeting changing situations. But I think we've demonstrated here, particularly in the last two or three years, that our democracy has a great resilience and a great strength. I'm confident it will survive all challenges.

*Interview/U.S. News & World Report, 7-7:50.*

## Norman Podhoretz
*Editor, "Commentary" magazine* 2

We are living in a culture in which the degradation of American culture by Americans has become the common wisdom.
*Before American Jewish Committee, New York,*
*May 4/The New York Times, 5-5:4.*

## James Reston
*Vice president and columnist,*
*"The New York Times"* 3

The main difference in America is that, unlike the political masters in Moscow and Peking, who conceal and suppress the facts, America is now grappling with ... conflicts in the open, as a free people should. There is not a single human relationship that is not being carefully analyzed in this country today—whether of husband to wife, parents to children, employers to employees, teachers to students, preachers to parishioners. It is a tremendous challenge to a free society at a very difficult time. But my faith, indeed my conviction, is that we will meet it, if we can hold together at home.

*Lecture, Auburn University/*
*Quote, 4-27:393.*

## Richard A. Riley
*President,*
*Firestone Tire and Rubber Company* 4

I hear about material shortages, unemployment, energy crises, the decline in automotive production, the scarcity of investment money, inflation, recession, over-population, food shortages and many others. You cannot help but hear them. But I also listen to and hear about continued growth in automotive registrations, about declines in inflation rates, some return of confidence in the investment market, the prospects of new energy sources, the promise of peaceful coexistence and many stories of accomplishment ... Favorable things are music to our ears. But they are not music unless we hear them. Do you hear what I hear? I hear all kinds of things full of hope and confidence, determination and success, and I hear them just as clearly as I hear the doomsday cries. When I hear the talk of an impossible energy crisis, of world famine, of total moral bankruptcy, of depression, of the U.S. becoming only a market economy, I always wonder how the positive can be ignored. What is the positive? All such prophecies forget or downgrade our proven ability to cope with problems. How can history be ignored? We have had problems before and we solved them. I firmly believe that to go along with the fatal predictions is to downgrade American ingenuity. We were founded in the midst of adversity. We have survived every kind of problem, and we will continue to survive as long as we believe in the system that has served us so well, as long as we believe in the problem-solving ability of our people, and as long as we allow the system to function as it is intended.

*At Earthmoving Industry Conference, Peoria, Ill., April 15/Vital Speeches, 6-1:500.*

**Dean Rusk**
*Professor of international law, University of Georgia; Former Secretary of State of the United States*
1

I'm an optimist in the long run. Americans have a way of doing at the end of the day what they don't want to do at noon.

*Interview, Bethlehem, Pa./ The National Observer, 4-12:4.*

**James R. Schlesinger**
*Secretary of Defense of the United States*
2

There is some tendency among our fashionable classes, first, to raise questions about whether power in itself is not immoral and, secondly, whether it is appropriate to fight for the values of the West—whether those values are even defensible. So I think that our basic problem as a nation is not our physical strength or our stance. It is a question of reviving the underlying moral stamina and the internal fiber of this nation, as well as of other free-world nations.

*Interview, Washington/ U.S. News & World Report, 5-26:24.*

**Eric Sevareid**
*News commentator, Columbia Broadcasting System*
3

There is a somewhat top-lofty theory now that America is teetering between decadence and vitality. There is an odor of decadence . . . hanging over the public scene—the preoccupation with the sex lives of public persons, the phenomenon of convicted criminals finding big audiences for their books and lectures, cinematic thieves pictured as sympathetic heroes, wide readership for the literary narcissism of failures and neurotics. But underneath the surface scene lie the vitality, the healthiness, the faith in the law, respect for responsibility, belief in the original purposes of the country. The performance in that [House Judiciary]

Committee [investigating Watergate] one year ago and the reaction to it proved that these ingredients in the complicated mix of the American character are still in place.

*CBS News commentary/ The Christian Science Monitor, 8-5:31.*

**James N. Sites**
*Special Assistant to the Secretary (Public Affairs), Department of the Treasury of the United States; Chairman, Economic Policy Board*
4

I feel we Americans can solve almost any problem as long as we manage to retain those priceless incentives to work, to produce, to achieve, to excel. And we will surely fail once they are lost.

*At San Francisco State University commencement, May 24/San Francisco Examiner & Chronicle, 5-25:(A)7.*

**Howard K. Smith**
*News commentator, American Broadcasting Company*
5

All we [in America] need to master our sea of troubles is some good, hard, creative thought and argument, and then the will to activate the ideas that result from that. And for that, above all, we need the underlying sense that we are not enemies, fighting one another to the death. We are workers side by side in the same vineyard and with the same purpose. As 200 years ago against a common foreign foe, now against our domestic troubles, only in unity is there strength. In these coming, trying years, we need to embrace more ardently than ever the symbol of our common endeavor, the flag.

*Before the House, Washington, June 14/ The Christian Science Monitor, 6-23:31.*

**Al Ullman**
*United States Representative, D—Oregon*
6

Unless we slow down and take stock of our real situation—not the dreams that appear in advertisements—we're not going to take the Constitution and a free economy into the next century. The critical question is, how long will it take us to change our old ways? How long will it take us to repaint the American dream?

*(AL ULLMAN)*

How many years before the longest car and the thickest carpet are no longer measures of the nation's health? ... Our scientists have been warning us for years that we have created a throw-away society based on all the wrong assumptions. And we were wrong, our teachers and leaders were wrong. We just assumed we were right. They were painful lessons. It's a jolt to the American psyche to become suddenly aware that we've reached the ceiling—that growth has its limits—that fortune has its peak.

*At Gonzaga University commencement,*
*May 11/The Christian Science Monitor, 5-22:10.*

### George C. Wallace
*Governor of Alabama (D)*      1

Don't ever underestimate the will and tenacity of the average citizen of this country. They're going to get angry and they're going to get frustrated, and they're going to change some things, maybe, at the ballot box; but they're still going to fly that flag ... I think that much of the loss of confidence that has come about has been superficial and has come more in the minds of some of our so-called intellectuals than it has in the average man. Now, he's mad about some things. He's mad about taxes; he's mad about all of that. But when he gets good and mad as a mass, that's when he's going to wind up helping straighten the country out in the proper manner.

*Interview, Montgomery, Alabama/*
*The New York Times Magazine, 4-27:48.*

### Robert Penn Warren
*Author*      2

... we Americans—for both good and bad—have a contempt for the past. We set out to make a radically new kind of nation, in all ways, and our successes, beyond all expectation, have encouraged us to agree with Henry Ford that "history is bunk."

*Interview/U.S. News & World Report, 7-7:49.*

### Lowell P. Weicker, Jr.
*United States Senator, R—Connecticut*      3

[On the U.S. after the 1976 Bicentennial]: What about 1977? Will there be one less starving child? Will there be one less homeless black? Will there be one less old person dying of polluted air? Will there be one less car and one more train? Will there be one less parent screaming racial hate at children? Will there be one less closed-door session of government? Will there be one less rifle and one more tractor? The number of times we say "yes" to those questions will gauge our patriotism.

*At University of Maine commencement/*
*The New York Times, 5-24:26.*

### Caspar W. Weinberger
*Secretary of Health, Education and*
*Welfare of the United States*      4

Our country was built by people of energy, daring and ingenuity—the Edisons, the Wright brothers, the Helen Kellers, the Fultons, the Carnegies, the great musicians and artists, and countless others brimming with dreams and filled with the courage to reach out and realize those dreams, whatever the odds. Their kind of daring was nurtured in a social climate that rewarded risk-takers and practical visionaries. If we now proceed mindlessly to change that climate to one favoring a faceless gray egalitarianism, we will have lost all that has made America great and enabled us to help so much of the world. The real social agenda of America, still unfinished, is to discover and reward excellence wherever we find it—under a black skin, a white skin, in a female or male, in a Catholic, a Jew, a Protestant, or an agnostic. That is the real purpose of equal opportunity. If we fail to see this as our real agenda, we risk delivering our destinies over to the cold and lifeless grip of a distant egalitarian government whose sole purpose is to ensure an equally mediocre existence for everyone, achieved at the cost of personal liberty.

*Before Commonwealth Club, San Francisco,*
*July 21/The National Observer, 8-2:2.*

### Billy O. Wireman
*President, Eckerd College*      5

For 25 years following World War II, America's strategy and values were clear. The objective was growth. Communism was the enemy. Education was the religion. The lubricants were money, Western will, technology and ingenuity. The pie was ever-expanding, and American power—economic, political, military, diplomatic—was inexhaustible. "We will bear any burden," [President] John Kennedy promised at his inspirational inauguration, "to ensure the survival . . . of liberty." We now know that the philosophic and economic underpinnings of that strategy are coming unstuck. Present growth rates, according to the Club of Rome, will exhaust the world's non-renewable resources in 70 years. We have better relations with Communist Russia and China than we do with India, the world's largest [ex-] democracy. Our blind faith in education has been painfully shattered, and we have learned, hopefully, that money and technology alone cannot answer that nagging, persistent yearning in the human soul for fulfillment and meaning. The expanding-pie myth has led, in economist William Janeway's words, to a government with "responsibilities in excess of available resources." Finally, rather than being all-

powerful, America must, to an unprecedented degree, respect what Jefferson called "the decent opinions of mankind." The old strategy, then is historically spent, intellectually exhausted and to borrow a word from our recent unhappy past, "inoperative." But, unfortunately, we have not formulated a new strategy to deal with new realities. Therein lies the heart of the problem. As we approach the third American century, we are suspended in time, aloof from reality, spending money we do not have. We continue to hold out infinite human expectations in a finite world of finite resources. We continue to act as if the demands of what Daniel Bell calls the "revolution of rising entitlements" can be met, when we all know they cannot. By refusing to tax sufficiently to support social legislation and national defense, we mortgage our children's precious future to crippling interest payments. In short, we are the epitome of the "Now Generation"— tomorrow be damned.

*St. Petersburg, Fla./*
*The National Observer, 11-1:13.*

# Civil Rights

**Joseph R. Biden, Jr.**
*United States Senator, D—Delaware*    1

[Arguing against the busing of school-children for racial balance]: Examining the concepts we used to rationalize busing six or seven years ago, they now seem to me to be profoundly racist. Busing is harmful for several reasons: First, busing, in effect, codifies the concept that a black is inferior to a white by saying, "The only way you can cut it educationally is if you're with whites." I think that's a horrible concept. It implies that blacks have no reason to be proud of their inheritance and their own culture. Second, busing violates the cardinal rule that the American people pose for their elected officials. They'll forgive our vice. They'll forgive our avarice. They'll forgive our greed. They expect it. But the one thing they don't expect—and won't tolerate—is not using good old common sense. The reason, in my opinion, why there's such a vociferous reaction to busing today in both black and white communities is that we're not using common sense. Common sense says to the average American: "The idea that you make me part of a racial percentage instead of a person in a classroom is asinine." In addition, busing also is damaging because it spends on transportation money that could be better spent on new textbooks and other educational improvements.
*Interview/*
*U.S. News & World Report, 10-20:33.*

**Theodore M. Black**
*Chancellor,*
*New York State Board of Regents*    2

[On the busing of schoolchildren for racial balance]: We continue to impose upon the American people drastic and unwelcome changes in their children's daily school lives when we are still not certain that the rationale for these changes—the theory that black children will perform better scholastically when they are taught together with white children—is really valid.
*Before New York State School Boards*
*Association, Rochester, Oct. 21/*
*The New York Times, 10-22:18.*

**Andrew F. Brimmer**
*Visiting professor, Harvard University*
*Graduate School of Business Administration;*
*Former member, Federal Reserve Board*    3

This is what it will take to improve the lot of blacks, Indians, people of Oriental and Spanish descent, and the other "left out" groups: an enormous investment in skills. That can be financed only by outside help—mainly, the Federal government. Clearly, these minorities themselves cannot, through their own savings, finance an investment in skills of the magnitude required. Also, there has to be a reawakening in this country—among whites as well as among blacks and other minority groups—of interest in equality. If these things happen, I see no reason why economic equality should not be achieved. So I'm optimistic.
*Interview/U.S. News & World Report, 7-7:50.*

**Edward W. Brooke**
*United States Senator, R—Massachusetts*    4

[On the violence generated against court-ordered busing of schoolchildren for racial balance]: Change never comes easily. I didn't expect—and I don't believe anyone else did—that we were going to desegregate the public-school system in this country without some violence. Unfortunately, there was racial violence when we integrated public conveyances. I remember when we integrated drugstores in Washington there was violence. I don't know of any racial changes taking place in this country that have not occurred with violence and often bitterness as a by-product. It's a tragic fact of life that can't be denied.

*Interview/*
*U.S. News & World Report, 10-20:34.*

**Edmund G. Brown, Jr.**
*Governor of California (D)*
1

The fact is, unless we find a way to integrate this society, then this civilization is not going to make it. We cannot live half black and half white. We are one people.

*Television interview, Sacramento, Oct. 3/*
*Los Angeles Herald-Examiner, 10-4:(A)6.*

**John H. Bunzel**
*President, California State University,*
*San Jose*
2

[Arguing against race and sex quotas in education, employment and politics]: The absolute equalitarians believe that justice requires equality not at the beginning of a race, but at the end. They want the minority or female runner to be given more than equal treatment with the White male runner. It is as if they were asking the scorekeeper to insure that the minority or female runners win a certain percentage of the races. That is the worst form of condescension. It is also a distorted definition of equality. It carries with it the principle that in order to make some people equal, we must use the authority of the state to make others unequal.

*Before Commonwealth Club, San Francisco,*
*Feb. 14/Los Angeles Times, 2-15:(1)20.*

**Ernest Q. Campbell**
*Professor of sociology and dean of the*
*graduate school, Vanderbilt University*
3

[On busing of schoolchildren for racial balance]: The goals sought by large-scale busing are highly desirable, but the negative consequences of busing are larger than we thought. It turned out that it misfired, but it was worth trying ... It is important to remember that when we talk about school effects on learning, we are not talking about the strongest effects. The important things are those which happen outside of school. What the advocates of busing did not see from the beginning is that any gains

are not going to be major. That point became largely obscured and lost as busing became "the" remedy ... The real problem with busing is that the gains are not commensurate with the costs. There are losses that go with making it terribly inconvenient for children and parents to get from home to school. There is the loss of informal contact with teachers and classmates in non-school settings. Your classmates become people you only see at school.

*Interview, Nashville, Tenn./*
*The Christian Science Monitor, 7-30:10.*

**Julian M. Carroll**
*Governor of Kentucky (D)*
4

Forced busing [of schoolchildren for racial balance] is damaging educational quality, contributing to white flight, disrupting community and family life, wasting important state and local resources and creating special problems of law enforcement. It is [a] hope that has failed and failed miserably.

*Before Senate Judiciary Committee,*
*Washington, Oct. 28/*
*The New York Times, 10-29:32.*

**Kenneth B. Clark**
*Former professor of psychology,*
*City University of New York*
5

[On integration and the busing of schoolchildren for racial balance]: To ask whether white and black children should attend school together is to ask whether it's possible for a democratic society to arrange for justice and decency in the face of massive social resistance.

*Newsweek, 9-15:52.*

**James S. Coleman**
*Sociologist, University of Chicago*
6

Integration isn't losing any support, but, as I see it, the strategies are basically producing resegregation, unfortunate strategies that are the outgrowth of court cases. We need an approach that is more stable, because if integration is going to come to exist in this country, we have to devise ways where after two or three years of integration we won't end up with resegregation ... There were two components to integration. First, there was the

# WHAT THEY SAID IN 1975

*(JAMES S. COLEMAN)*

basic Constitutional protection that eliminated segregation based on state action, North and South. Then there was individual action manifested in white flight. As long as the court dealt with the first component, it was okay. But then it got into the other realm beyond the protection of Constitutional rights. It attempted to eliminate all facets of segregation—not only that arising from state action, but that which arose from individual action. That is where it went wrong, because it is not set up to counter every individual action. The tools the court had to eliminate individual action were such blunt and coercive tools that they were inappropriate for desirable social ends. The court doesn't have the means to do that. It doesn't have the funds and resources to provide holding power to make the schools stable. It could institute a policy of desegregation, but only the kind of policy with a short life expectancy.

*Interview, Chicago, June 3/*
*The New York Times, 7-7:25.*

## Dan Dodson
*Scholar-in-residence,*
*Southwestern University*     *1*

...what do we mean by institutional racism? Let's start by saying what we think it is not. Institutional racism is not prejudice, although prejudice may or may not be involved in it. Prejudices are personal and private. Racial prejudice, while deplorable, is one's right. Institutions, on the other hand, do not have attitudes. They have policies and practices, some fully stated and defended, others often subtle and unconscious, which block opportunity for people because of their race or ethnicity ... Institutional racism is any institutional policy or practice which gives one ethnic group of the community an advantage over the others.

*At symposium, Dallas/*
*The Dallas Times Herald, 6-5:(B)3.*

## Sam J. Ervin, Jr.
*Former United States Senator,*
*D–North Carolina*     *2*

A lot of people accuse me of being sort of a split personality, opposing civil-rights bills and

standing for civil liberties. I think my position on the civil-rights bills was perfectly consistent. The trouble with every civil-rights bill is that it takes away from everybody, including the people it's supposed to benefit—rights just as precious as those it undertakes to give to one segment of the population. For example, I think that a man with an investment in a business has an inherent right to say who he will hire and fire and not have this regulated by some civil-rights crusader in a Federal bureaucracy.

*Interview, Morganton, N.C./*
*Los Angeles Times, 11-16:(1)13.*

## Vivian Henderson
*President, Clark College*     *3*

As important as they are, race-relations problems are overriden by the problems of economic class distinctions. The black person's problem is hardcore class distinction.

*At Leadership Conference on Civil Rights,*
*Washington, Jan. 27/*
*The Washington Post, 1-28:(A)2.*

## Herbert Hill
*National labor director, National*
*Association for the Advancement of*
*Colored People*     *4*

There are some who argue that [job] seniority is a vested right. This, of course, is sheer nonsense. The argument that white men have a prior right to a job and that black people must wait until there is full employment before they too can work is the essence of the racist mentality.

*At NAACP convention, Washington, July 1/*
*The New York Times, 7-1:11.*

## Benjamin F. Holman
*Director, Community Relations Service,*
*Department of Justice of the United States*     *5*

I'm really concerned, even though we can find means to hold down the tension, that we haven't reached a solution to this [racial conflict] in the North, and not even in the South. What we're doing now isn't working. The more we integrate, the more whites move to the suburbs. Maybe it's time to look at the whole process, the value of integration ... I'm not saying we've reached the point the Kerner

Commission predicted, that society is pulling apart. But young minority kids are not so docile any more, either. There is racism there. They don't like Whitey.

*The Dallas Times Herald, 8-10:(A)29.*

**Hubert H. Humphrey**
*United States Senator, D—Minnesota*
1

I am opposed to massive forced busing [of schoolchildren] solely for the purpose of racial balance on a quota basis. No parent, black or white, wants his child to have an inferior education. It makes no sense to bus a child from a good school to a poor school. It makes sense to bus a child from a poor school to a better school. It makes better sense to improve schools in all neighborhoods.

*TV-radio interview, Washington/*
*"Meet the Press,"*
*National Broadcasting Company, 11-2.*

**Jesse L. Jackson**
*Civil-rights leader; President, PUSH*
*(People United to Save Humanity)*
2

The strategic role of blacks is such that all the others find us necessary, they need us. We must make sure we are useful and not used up. But we're dealing from a position of powerlessness. Arabs and Jews deal with each other on a business level. Jews and Africans deal with each other on a business level. Africans and Arabs deal with each other on a business level. But none of them deal significantly with blacks. Black relations with all of them is symbolic rather than substantive.

*Chicago/The New York Times, 1-5:(1)43.*

3

The opposite of segregation is not integration. Martin Luther King didn't dream about a completely integrated world. He knew this was a pluralistic society and that ethnics tend to keep an identity. It's not a contradiction.

*Los Angeles Times, 1-20:(1)2.*

4

[During the 1960s, the civil-rights] struggle was based upon caste questions, questions of color. People could use public accommodation facilities. People could ride buses. We [blacks] could not. We were disenfranchised solely on color. It was clearly a black and white question. Now we're fighting more a class question. We have the right to go to any school in America but we can't pay the tuition. We have the right to move into any neighborhood in America but we can't get a mortgage. In the last era of the movement, the disenfranchised were the blacks, the colored. Now the disenfranchised are the have-nots, the unemployed, the hungry.

*Interview, Chicago/San Francisco*
*Examiner & Chronicle, 2-16:(A)21.*

5

[Urging job quotas during layoff periods]: No one can honestly deny that blacks, Chicanos, Puerto Ricans and women have been victims of discrimination in hiring and are today disproportionately unemployed. We contend that the quota principle does not represent reverse discrimination as [AFL-CIO president] George Meany projects. Rather, it is a serious effort at correcting the fact of disproportionate unemployment among these sectors of the population. We have no quarrel with the seniority principle, but neither should it be considered a sacred or inflexible formula. The quota principle should be defended as the primary formula until unemployment among blacks and Spanish-speaking and others is reduced to the national level of unemployment.

*At labor breakfast, Chicago, Sept. 25/*
*The New York Times, 9-28:(1)67.*

**Maynard H. Jackson, Jr.**
*Mayor of Atlanta*
6

I think more black and white people are coming together . . . On the other hand, some areas have become more anxious. In that regard, I think the sophisticated kind of racism we see in the North is becoming manifest in the South.

*Interview/*
*The Christian Science Monitor, 5-1:16.*

**Daniel James, Jr.**
*Lieutenant General, United States Air*
*Force; Commander-designate, North*
*American Air Defense Command*
7

These young [black] people today, suffering all these obstacles to equality—b-u-l-l! Most of

23

# WHAT THEY SAID IN 1975

their obstacles are illusionary. You can vote. You can go to any school you want to. Most of them are making a career out of being black. They don't know what suffering is. I hate to see kids going back, trying to pretend they have to do this all over again. These black kids aren't fighting any battles today—they're going back over plowed ground. All they need to do is solidify the gains that have been made.

*Interview, Scott Air Force Base, Ill./*
*The Washington Post, 7-21:(A)1.*

**Edward M. Kennedy**
*United States Senator, D—Massachusetts*     *1*

The Founding Fathers did a magnificent job, but failed on the matter of race. Now we live with failure. We have to get national leadership on the race matter. Look what we have to face: [Alabama Governor George] Wallace. He's going into the Massachusetts [Presidential] primary with considerable strength ... The tragedy is, black and white parents have identical interests: good education, safe schools. The number of students entering college each year from South Boston High, white, and Roxbury High, black, is awfully low. And the parents are at each other's throats. That's tragedy. They have common interests.

*Interview, Washington/*
*Los Angeles Times, 7-15:(2)5.*

**Clarence E. Lightner**
*Mayor of Raleigh, North Carolina*     *2*

I think from here on out our problem is not so much one of integration as it is of economics. If we get to the point where everyone can make a fair and decent living, integration takes care of itself.

*Interview/*
*The Christian Science Monitor, 5-1:16.*

**Peter MacDonald**
*Chairman, Navajo (Indian) Tribal Council*     *3*

Since the treaty of 1868, our [Indians'] biggest enemy has been government programs, the Federal bureaucracy, the paternalistic effort to run our lives. For years only Indians suffered from the bureaucratic hand. Now all of us [in the country] share that problem.

*News conference, Los Angeles, Dec. 9/*
*Los Angeles Herald-Examiner, 12-10:(A)13.*

**Carl McCall**
*New York State Senator*     *4*

[On why he, a black, supports the busing of schoolchildren for racial balance]: I went to Roxbury Memorial High School [in Boston]. I graduated in 1954. In those days the school was predominantly white, Jewish. The white parents were well-organized and active. They made the school system responsive, and it was a good school. That experience made the difference for me. My family was on welfare. I got a scholarship at Dartmouth, and then at the University of Edinburgh for a master's degree in divinity. It was a unique, rich experience, that school [Roxbury]. And what bothers me is that those experiences don't seem to be available now in Boston ... We have to do what we can, and busing seems to be it. Yes, the [anti-busing] reaction is troubling. People are reacting to a lot more than busing—to the feeling of being pushed around, of being neglected while the blacks are helped—but busing is a symbol. What we need is better relations between the black community and white working-class people. But that is a long-term thing, and in the meantime do you say to the black community, "Wait"? For how long?

*Interview/The New York Times, 9-15:21.*

**George S. McGovern**
*United States Senator, D—South Dakota*     *5*

[On the busing of schoolchildren for racial balance]: Do we want integration or segregation? If busing is the wrong answer, what is the right answer? ... What substitute will integrate the schools, and how, and when, and at what cost? Busing is the one way to pay the bill for the ancient regime of racism. There may be other ways, but none of them will be painless or priceless.

*At Democratic Issues Convention,*
*Louisville, Ky., Nov 23/*
*The Christian Science Monitor, 11-24:24.*

**George Meany**
*President, American Federation of*
*Labor-Congress of Industrial Organizations*  1

[On whether white labor-union members should make sacrifices to help blacks]: To say that I've got some responsibility to make up for discrimination that took place 125 years ago is nuts. And it's completely against human nature. How would you feel if you worked in a factory and you had 15 years seniority and you had a contract. And you felt that you had to take care of your kids and your family and you were told that because you were white you were going to be disposed of in favor of the fellow with 15 years less seniority. I don't buy that at all.

*At Press luncheon, Washington/*
*The Washington Post, 8-31:(A)6.*

**James G. O'Hara**
*United States Representative, D—Michigan*  2

I think the university, not for itself alone, but for all of the society in which it lives, must gently but firmly reassert the proposition that sex, race, color, national origin and creed are completely irrelevant to job qualifications, and that the way to end the practice of taking them into account is to end it—not simply to look for a new set of victims ... I don't have an easy answer to the question, "How do we prove that the university is obeying the law?" The law does not mandate that 51 per cent of the faculty or administrative staff shall be women, or that 14 per cent shall be black, or 5 per cent of Spanish-speaking ancestry, any more than it mandates that 49 per cent must be men, or 86 per cent shall not be black. The law does not, in short, mandate results. It mandates that discriminatory practices be avoided. It does not mandate "proportionate representation," but it does mandate an end to giving preferences to one sex or one race over another without regard for motives. And more than incidentally, the law does not specify which race or which sex may not be given preference; it says unequivocally that none can be.

*Before American Council on Education,*
*San Diego, Calif./*
*The Wall Street Journal, 6-17:18.*

**J. Stanley Pottinger**
*Assistant Attorney General, Civil Rights*
*Division, Department of Justice of the*
*United States*  3

It's true that the political atmosphere has become one of caution and opposition to busing [of schoolchildren for racial balance]. But I don't want to give the impression that the atmosphere influences how we enforce the law. The Justice Department still has to do its duty regardless of the atmosphere. If segregation exists in schools due to deliberate plan or design, that is a violation of law.

*Interview, Washington/*
*The Dallas Times Herald, 10-19:(A)18.*

**Vincent Reed**
*Acting Superintendent of Schools*
*of the District of Columbia*  4

There are two things we have to do immediately. We've got to stop telling people the system can't be managed. It can. And we've got to stop telling our children they can't learn because they're black, poor or both. They can learn. We don't want them using racism as a crutch and an excuse. Now, we all know racism exists in this country—that's no secret. But the fact is our students have got to be able to achieve in spite of racism and poverty. If you tell them long enough that they can't learn because of what they are, they'll begin to believe it themselves. Malcolm X said if you want to convince a man he's lazy, just keep telling him he's lazy. That's the kind of psychology blacks have been subjected to for years. I don't buy it.

*Interview, Washington/*
*The Washington Post, 11-17:(A)1.*

**Wilson Riles**
*California State Superintendent*
*of Public Instruction*  5

[On busing of schoolchildren for racial balance]: ... some sociologists, educators and people of good-will have taken the position that black children can't learn unless they sit with whites. The people who have promoted this, in my opinion, are wrong. The fact of the matter is that the most important variable that we

# WHAT THEY SAID IN 1975

*(WILSON RILES)*

know about is not color, but socio-economic status. Children who come from lower-income families tend to do less well in school than children who are better off. To become blinded by color in this has gotten us into trouble. My position regarding integration by bus or other means is this: Wherever it's reasonable and feasible, fine. But if you're going to recommend extreme measures that have a mechanistic and racial basis, I think it's nonsense. How are you going to integrate places like Washington, D.C., where white children are in a small minority? We are going to be much better off concentrating on the problem of providing youngsters with an equal education wherever they are going to school.

*Interview, Washington/*
*U.S. News & World Report, 9-1:57.*

1

[Criticizing the busing of schoolchildren for racial balance]: The concept that black children can't learn unless they are sitting with white children is utter and complete nonsense ... Give a person an opportunity to get a job and access to move, where he wishes to move, and you deal with the problem. He can move to Beverly Hills or Encino. But to say you're going to pick youngsters up on 111th Street in Watts and bus them to Encino [28 miles] in order to integrate them—that's where I get off. The minorities are not going to be happy with it, the majorities are not going to be happy with it, and I see no educational value in that nonsense unless you equip the bus with a television set and a teaching machine.

*News conference, Washington, Sept. 8/*
*Los Angeles Times, 9-9:(1)6.*

**Bayard Rustin**
*Executive director,*
*A. Philip Randolph Institute*

2

[Saying seniority of white employees should not be disregarded by employers when hiring black employees]: We are unalterably opposed to any change in the seniority system. I've never yet met a black man with high seniority who would agree to let a newly hired black

woman take his job in case of layoff, even if the woman got the job because of past discrimination against women. We blacks cannot expect whites to respond differently. [Setting aside seniority would destroy unions, because] no union could exist without maintaining lines of seniority; [a break in the seniority system would] only lead to violent disorders, to whites and blacks fighting in the streets.

*Before National Urban League, Los Angeles,*
*May 23/Los Angeles Times, 5-24:(2)1.*

**Joe D. Waggoner, Jr.**
*United States Representative, D—Louisiana*

3

I've always believed in equal opportunity for all Americans ... I've got as many black friends as most people have. You know, what people never have really understood about Southerners, there's always been more mutual respect one for the other, black or white, or between blacks and whites, than people have ever understood. We never have had the bitterness that some people have portrayed us to have.

*Interview, Washington/*
*The New York Times, 2-25:62.*

**George C. Wallace**
*Governor of Alabama (D)*

4

[Arguing against busing of schoolchildren for racial balance]: ... the people in Boston, black or white, ought to be able to go to whatever school they want to go to. If the black people from Roxbury want to transfer to some other place, they ought to be able to transfer, and they ought to give them a ride over there, and vice versa. But nobody ought to be made to go out of his district if he doesn't want to go, or if his parents don't want him to go. Open the schools up to everybody and provide quality education and let the people choose ... Who in the world ever invented a law that you've got to have a quota system and you've got to have a certain number of Chinese- and Japanese-Americans here, and a certain number of black and white Americans here? That's a lot of folderol.

*Interview, Montgomery, Alabama/*
*The New York Times Magazine, 4-27:45.*

*1*

... people in the deep South have never been against people because of race, and one reason we've had better relations in our schools is that our fight in the beginning was never against black people, except a few militants here on both sides; it was against big government. Otherwise, why would any black vote for me like they did before? ... I've been working with black people ever since I've been Governor from '63. They just didn't haul off and all of a sudden vote for me. I pick up the paper and find endorsements of this black Mayor and this black judge. I never had to sit down and make any agreements and deals, as they're called.

*Interview, Montgomery, Alabama/*
*The New York Times Magazine, 4-27:47.*

**Caspar W. Weinberger**
*Secretary of Health, Education and*
*Welfare of the United States*
*2*

Today most of the deliberate segregation has been dealt with, and we have fallen into a statistical approach to school desegregation. There is too much emphasis on numbers and racial balance. Often, this has no regard for the education of the child or the quality of the school.

*Interview/*
*U.S. News & World Report, 8-11:25.*

**Kevin H. White**
*Mayor of Boston*
*3*

Eighty per cent of the people in Boston are against busing [of schoolchildren for racial balance]. If Boston were a sovereign state, busing would be cause for revolution. No sovereign government can enforce a law if 80 per cent of those who are asked to comply do not support it. Busing is probably the most inflammable domestic issue in America today. And I think that many other cities would react the same way as Boston has if the same kind of busing program were imposed on them ... I am for integration and against forced busing, and those positions are not mutually exclusive. Now, I mean to be fair, but there is something wrong with busing. It tends to disrupt one of the natural, wholesome, sustaining, substantive contributions to the stability of a city—firm

neighborhoods. My own feelings are that, as desirable as racial integration may be, busing is not the best vehicle for it. It breaks up the cohesiveness of the neighborhoods and it compromises parental prerogative to send their children to a nearby neighborhood school.

*Interview, Washington/*
*U.S. News & World Report, 4-7:41, 42.*

**Roy Wilkins**
*Executive director, National Association*
*for the Advancement of Colored People*
*4*

Some people are arguing that the Negro has nothing to celebrate in this [U.S.] Bicentennial. He has everything to celebrate. He has overcome all kinds of obstacles; if he cannot celebrate, no American can.

*San Francisco Examiner & Chronicle,*
*11-30:(This World)2.*

**Margaret Bush Wilson**
*Chairman, National Association for*
*the Advancement of Colored People*
*5*

[Saying the word "colored" in the title of the NAACP refers to people of all colors] : If I handed you a Kennedy half-dollar and asked you to get me a package of colored paper, you would have no trouble knowing what I mean. It's paper of all the colors of the rainbow. That's what colored means. I would in no way think of changing the initials NAACP. They are initials that are respected, well-known and, in some places, even feared.

*Interview, St. Louis/*
*The Dallas Times Herald, 4-18:(D)5.*

*6*

[On those who criticize busing of schoolchildren for racial balance] : We in the NAACP understand full well that the foundations for more democratic living are established and maintained through a system of universal free public education. ... consequently, the sophisticated attempts to use educational and behavioral science data to support the premise that public schools make little difference in the achievement of equality is malicious mischief and ought to be branded as such.

*At NAACP convention, Washington, June 30/*
*The Washington Post, 7-1:(A)6.*

# WHAT THEY SAID IN 1975

**Andrew Young**
*United States Senator,*
*D—Georgia*                                    1

Ten years from now, white people will realize that the best thing that happened to their kids is that they were bused [to racially balance the schools]. If it were not for integration, we'd have culturally deprived white kids and culturally deprived black kids.

*On 20th anniversary of civil-rights movement,*
*Montgomery, Alabama/*
*San Francisco Examiner & Chronicle,*
*12-7:(A)13.*

**Coleman A. Young**
*Mayor of Detroit*                              2

I don't believe you will solve anything by busing [of schoolchildren for racial balance] in Detroit where 70 per cent of the students are black. Cross-district busing, which I favored as a state Senator, serves only to focus attention on the inequities in the funding of schools. [If students are forced to commute between] Dearborn and Duffield School, which I attended, it would be an exchange of hostages.

*Before University of Detroit Law School*
*Student Bar Association/Human Events, 3-1:3.*

**Robert H. Anderson**
*President, W. T. Grant Company*
1

You open a store in the morning. It's a dark, cold place. Even when you put on the lights, it's only a lighted, cold place until the people who work there warm it up, make it come alive. And it's the merchandise presentation, too. Is it warm, cold, alive, dead? Within three minutes after entering the store, a complete stranger can tell whether a "merchant" lives there or not.
*Interview/The New York Times, 5-11:(3)7.*

**Abdel Rahman al-Atiqi**
*Minister of Finance and Oil of Kuwait*
2

[The American] press has written about the threat to the U.S. from the invasion of oil money. Let me reply. First, if we do not have a place to invest our money, how can there be recycling of petro-dollars as U.S. officials advocate? Second, you [the U.S.] have worried about your balance of payments and that problem is helped when our money is placed in your country. Finally, attempts to restrict investment in the United States seem strange. After all, American companies and citizens invest outside the United States a hundred times what we place in your country.
*Interview/U.S. News & World Report, 9-29:72.*

**Dewey F. Bartlett**
*United States Senator, R—Oklahoma*
3

The oil industry has been discredited in the minds of many people . . . I think one of the problems in Washington—because oil and energy are so important—is that there's a dearth rather than an excess of people who are knowledgeable in energy . . . One of the problems today that some people try to convey is the feeling that those people connected with oil are somehow more evil than those who are not. My conviction is that people in the oil industry are

just as honest and just as dishonest as newspapermen, politicians, college presidents and everybody else. I have no prejudice against them.
*The Washington Post, 1-8:(A)9.*

**Marylin Bender**
*Financial news reporter,*
*"The New York Times"*
4

. . . I wouldn't want to live like so many people at the top [in business]. Power rushes to the head. So many people there only talk among themselves, only say what they want to hear. How can people in power sense the quality of the information they're getting? Many of them go to work in their chauffeur-driven cars, dictating and not even glancing out the window. I wouldn't give up the subway. Horrible as it can be, it's one essential way to keep in touch with the pulse of the streets. So many of these people never see, never feel anything but power. How can they know anything? In a way, one can feel sorry for them.
*Interview, New York/*
*"W": a Fairchild publication, 10-17:5.*

**Edward M. Benson**
*Executive vice president,*
*Atlantic Richfield Company*
5

I don't think illegal [political] campaign contributions—or any other type of corporate misconduct—are widespread. But even a small amount is bad. They stick out like a sore thumb, undoing what the business community has worked at for years. I think it's appalling.
*Los Angeles Times, 5-4:(1)1.*

**William Bernbach**
*Chairman, Doyle, Dane, Bernbach,*
*advertising*
6

My personal feeling is anybody can be a big hit in this business [advertising] if he meets

# WHAT THEY SAID IN 1975

two requirements. He has to have a new path and he has to be able to run fast down that path. You can never operate on a formula to make advertising because the second time you use the formula it isn't fresh any more. The first principle is to do things in ways they were never done before.

*The Washington Post, 3-23:(K)2.*

**W. Michael Blumenthal**
*President,*
*Bendix Corporation* 1

Business executives are professional people, but there is nothing in business life that corresponds to the bar associations, the American Medical Association or the American Society of Architects. Why, then, should business people not set up an association dedicated to defining and maintaining the standards of their profession? Such a group would deal with concrete questions of business ethics—not as an advocate defending business right or wrong; not from the view of a trade or industry association or on the basis of a concern for consumer relations, which the better business bureaus are already doing; nor, finally, in terms of a commitment to the economic and fiscal policies that are deemed to be in the interests of industry. Instead, it would focus on devising new ethical-behavior codes to which all business would be expected to subscribe. The founding members of this new group could be leaders from the business community, but it would draw as well on lawyers, the clergy, statesmen, philosophers and others whose views would represent the moral concerns of society as a whole. This, indeed, would be the very point of the new departure—that it would be, and would be seen to be, operating on behalf of society as a whole.

*At University of Detroit/*
*The New York Times, 5-25:(3)1.*

**Harold Bridges**
*President,*
*Shell Oil Company* 2

[On U.S. companies having to pay overseas bribes in order to do business in foreign countries] : Why did [they] pay? I would think because of an exaggerated view of how important their investment was in that country and a misassessment of how much they were needed, quite frankly . . . Now, this is an easy thing to say because you have to be sorry for those guys, because the guy who started it was dead or maybe retired and the problem has been that they have continued to do something and it takes more guts to stop doing something that somebody started than it does never to start at all.

*Interview, Washington/*
*The Washington Post, 8-10:(G)2.*

**Edmund G. Brown, Jr.**
*Governor of California (D)* 3

Too often people point to the infirmities of government, but they neglect the obeseness of business—you know, the tax breaks, the subsidies, the welfare for the privileged. Businesses have to start doing their part. They all want government to provide jobs. Businesses ought to start providing jobs. If they wouldn't pay such inflated salaries to their executives they could hire a few more people.

*Los Angeles Times, 9-2:(1)24.*

**James L. Buckley**
*United States Senator,*
*C–New York* 4

If the anti-business bias continues to grow, if the regulatory mentality is allowed to expand and tighten still further the Federal grip on almost every facet of our economic life, I fear we may soon reach the point of no return in our drift into a state-controlled economy.

*Before American Association of*
*Petroleum Geologists, Dallas, April 8/*
*The Dallas Times Herald, 4-9:(E)2.*

**Arthur F. Burns**
*Chairman, Federal Reserve Board* 5

. . . a great deal of emphasis is put by members of the economics profession in all camps on the stock of money; and, in my judgment, they are looking at the wrong thing, or they are emphasizing the wrong thing. Far more important than the stock of money is the willingness to use the existing stocks. The high dynamic variable in the business cycle is not the stock of money but the rate of turnover of money, the willingness to use the existing stock, and this depends basically on the state of confidence . . . If you examine the historical record, you will find that in the first year of recovery it is the rate of turnover of money that shoots up dramatically in contrast to the change in the existing stock. Now, that is the critical variable—the willingness to use money. And if we at the Federal Reserve Board, and if I personally, differ to some degree from other economists, this may be the main source of the difference. I pay a lot of attention to velocity. Other economists either neglect it or pay much less attention to it.

*Before Senate Banking Committee,*
*Washington, May 1/*
*U.S. News & World Report, 5-19:50.*

**Earl L. Butz**
*Secretary of Agriculture of the*
*United States*
1

There's no reason in the world to believe that a large, rigid bureaucracy staffed with people having little at stake other than their personal pensions would be able to solve today's problems any better than private enterprise. Endless committee meetings won't drill through the rock to reach new oil reserves. Study groups won't build ships to take food to other people who need it. Welders build ships. Farmers grow crops. Wildcatters find oil. Individual business people keep commerce rolling. They all do it for a profit motive—to keep commerce rolling.

*At businessmen's luncheon, Pepperdine*
*University, Malibu, Calif./*
*The National Observer, 7-19:7.*

2

[On why the U.S. doesn't hike the export price of its agricultural products for a greater financial return]: We could do that, I guess. But it has not been our policy to establish cartel prices. That would mean a two-price system—a high one for exports and a lower one for domestic use. That would be asking the farmers to subsidize the American consumer by accepting a lower-than-competitive price for

that share of produce consumed domestically, which is three-fourths of our feed grain, nearly all of our livestock, two-fifths of our wheat and half our soybeans. I don't think we should gouge buyers of U.S. farm exports. They are selling well and are our Number 1 source of foreign exchange. The total of farm exports in the last fiscal year that ended June 30 was a record $21.6-billion—$12-billion more than agricultural imports. This 12-billion-dollar favorable balance is the primary way we pay for a vast array of goods and services we enjoy that foreigners produce, and the basic way that we maintain the value of the American dollar abroad.

*Interview/*
*U.S. News & World Report, 8-11:39.*

3

The loudest critics of scientific and mechanized agriculture are those who never had to drag themselves out of bed on the third morning of haying season with hands so sore they could hardly hold a dinner fork, let alone a pitchfork . . . The general public must learn what is at stake when they hear the young radical or a jaded politician talk about the need to go more slowly in applying scientific techniques to agriculture. In the past it has been too easy to stand at the cocktail party and let the criticisms go flying by, never opening our mouths to speak the truth. Silence is a luxury agriculture can no longer afford . . . Mankind can either lie down and give up, or we can use all of our productive skills and knowledge to work for a better future. We can hide our heads in the comforting sands of an imaginery past, or we can move agriculture ahead to meet the increasing food needs of tomorrow.

*Before Allied Chemical Company, liquid*
*fertilizer division, Miami/*
*The National Observer, 9-13:14.*

**Geoffrey Chandler**
*President, British Institute of*
*Petroleum; Director, Royal Dutch/*
*Shell Group*
4

[Saying the oil industry's negotiating role is coming to an end]: The arguments for this role,

# WHAT THEY SAID IN 1975

*(GEOFFREY CHANDLER)*

and the arguments against government-to-government negotiation, with its potential for entangling political issues with oil, are as strong as ever and remain evident to governments and industry alike. But the growth of equity participation by OPEC countries and the unilateral setting of prices have brought this role to a close.

*The New York Times, 2-2:(1)38.*

**Frank Church**
*United States Senator, D—Idaho* 1

[On corporate flaunting of the law] : We have found: ITT secretly offering the CIA a million dollars to prevent [the late Salvador] Allende, lawfully elected by the people of Chile, from becoming President; like the longshoremen refusing to load wheat [bound for the Soviet Union], this giant corporation sought to usurp for itself the right to determine the course of American foreign policy. Exxon parceling out $27-million in political contributions in Italy in return for economic favors from the government. Gulf Oil doling out $4-million in illegal corporate contributions in Korea. Northrop paying an agent $450,000 to bribe Saudi Arabian generals. United Fruit slipping the President of Honduras $1.2-million to lower the export tax on bananas. Lockheed admitting illegal payments to government officials in countries around the globe ... in Europe, in Asia, in the Middle East and in the Far East, amounting to many million of dollars. All of this wrongdoing is acknowledged by straight-faced executives who say they had to break the law to get the business. The excuse, after all, is written plainly in the adage, "When in Rome ..." But the excuse is hollow. The bad habits of Rome were brought home to America. The roster of companies that made illegal corporate contributions to the [former President Richard] Nixon compaign in 1972 include such luminaries as American Airlines, 3-M, Northrop and Gulf. And the list has only commenced to be exposed. Perhaps the most depressing aspect of this corporate lawlessness is that it is authorized at the highest levels. These corrupt practices are not aberrations en-

gineered by underlings. They are company policy. Contempt for the law has come to preside in the boardrooms of our largest companies.

*Before Commonwealth Club, San Francisco/*
*San Francisco Examiner & Chronicle,*
*10-5:(A)17.*

**Harold van B. Cleveland**
*Vice president, First National City Bank,*
*New York* 2

A return to fixed or relatively stable [monetary] exchange rates on a global scale ... if ever it occurs, will occur only under some form of dollar standard. For the United States is the only country large enough to lead a system of this kind. And the U.S. dollar remains the only international currency that is used widely enough to serve again as the key currency of a global fixed-rate system ... History suggests that, after a period of floating, the world tends to come back to fixed exchange rates when stable monetary conditions in the leading countries have been restored. This happened in the mid-1920s and again toward the end of the 1930s. It happened in the late 1950s. It could happen again.

*At Conference Board of Canada financial*
*conference, Toronto/*
*The Wall Street Journal, 9-23:22.*

**Alan Coleman**
*Professor of financial management,*
*Southern Methodist University* 3

The history of great societies is invariably linked with the value of their money—the integrity of their financial systems. The debasement of currency eventually debases the political basis of the society itself.

*At financial conference, Dallas, March 18/*
*The Dallas Times Herald, 3-19:(D)13.*

**John B. Connally, Jr.**
*Former Secretary of the Treasury of the*
*United States; Former Governor of Texas*
*(D, now R)* 4

There was a great hue and cry when a number of American businesses reported that individuals in some nations have customarily extracted payola and political contributions in return for permission to do business. No one applauds corruption wherever it occurs, but I submit that in too many cases American business enterprises overseas have had to use fang and claw to stay in operation because they get so little support and encouragement and help from their own State Department. We have helped make it that way, as a national policy of many years' duration, and we cannot escape the responsibility.

*Before National Federation of Republican Women, Dallas, Sept. 13/ The Dallas Times Herald, 11-26:(B)5.*

*1*

[Proposing a guaranteed annual payment to every registered voter, financed by the corporate taxes collected by the Federal government]: Let's assume you rebate the corporate taxes on a per-capita basis to every registered voter of 18 years or older. First, it seems to me that it would permit you to cut out a great many Federal social programs of all types. It would obviously cause a revamping and a reworking of the entire social-program structure, which desperately needs to be done . . . It also gives every citizen of this country a new awareness of what a corporation is. It also would inject a competitiveness among people to make every corporation as productive as possible and as profitable as possible. But first, you would have to put a 50 per cent limit on the taxes of a corporation. It pays less now, about 48 per cent. But you just have to put a limit because if it's going to be rebated, people get a little bit voracious. But then when people realize that the more profitable the corporation, the more rebate they're going to get, then everybody working for any corporation, large or small, is going to be very careful. They're not going to be wasteful. They're not going to be dogging it. They're going to increase their productivity an incredible amount. This will make goods and services produced in this country enormously competitive because they're going to want their corporation to pay this 50 per cent tax, because it will just mean that much more rebated. [In a relatively short period of time,] you'd get a productivity increase in the range of 5-to-7 per cent. We have

to somehow provi'  some incentive for the American workman.

*Interview, Houston/ Los Angeles Times, 10-8:(1)10.*

**C. Marshall Dann**
*Commissioner, Patent & Trademark Office of the United States*

*2*

[Criticizing a movement in Congress to give the government exclusive rights to patents arising from Federally funded research and development programs]: Now, if you had a problem to solve which required inventive technical solutions, you would think that, in addition to supplying whatever funds were available, the one thing you would try to do would be to provide all the incentives possible. [Despite this,] there are strong voices in Congress more concerned with dividing up the rights in whatever technology we have or may create than in providing the best climate for the creation of new technology . . . The more important the technological goal, whether it be energy, the environment, medicine or anything else, the more important become the incentives which patents provide.

*Interview, Los Angeles/ Los Angeles Times, 3-4:(3)10.*

**Justin W. Dart**
*Chairman, Dart Industries*

*3*

. . . I certainly feel very strongly that we as business people have to tell our story to the many publics which make up the American audience. We are doing it horribly. We must activate, catalogue and orchestrate the many instruments we have, and get on with telling our story. We are in an almost desperate position. People don't understand us. They don't want to understand us. And we don't help them to understand us. This is the Number 1 problem of American business as far as I am concerned. If we don't change our image, we're up the river.

*Interview/Nation's Business, June:52.*

**James W. Davant**
*Chairman, Paine, Webber, Jackson & Curtis, Inc.*

*4*

At the end of 1971, after years of steady growth, 32.5 million Americans owned shares

# WHAT THEY SAID IN 1975

*(JAMES W. DAVANT)*

in corporations and investment companies. In 1972, the shareholding population dropped by 800,000. In 1973, another 800,000 individuals dropped out. If this trend continues, the individual American investor will be extinct in a generation. His disappearance would repeal centuries of progress toward wider public participation in the process of capital formation. It began with an invention called the stock corporation. Public participation grew fastest and best in America. Our system, in time, made it possible for an individual to buy a share of stock as readily as he could buy a suit of clothes. And millions did. But now, individuals are withdrawing from direct participation in our capital markets by the hundreds of thousands . . . The downward trend in independent investing has become self-perpetuating. The decline in the number of individual investors decreases the apparent need for brokers. And, in turn, the dwindling number of brokers further weakens our industry's capacity to present the option of investing independently to individuals. This should be a matter of serious national concern. The independent investor's expanding participation is essential to the resumption of economic growth, the efficiency of our capital markets, and perhaps even to the survival of what we call free enterprise.
*Before Executives Club, Chicago, Feb. 28/*
*Vital Speeches, 5-1:429.*

## Robert H. Dean
*Chairman, Ralston Purina Company* 1

Probably the single most important factor we [at Ralston Purina] emphasize is the individual [employee]. We're far from perfect, but we consistently try to have a climate throughout management that ensures the individual a right to contribute to the organization, to share in the challenge, to share in the success, and to be rewarded for it. This reward must be fair in the monetary sense, but equally important is job satisfaction. This is what will really make a corporation go. I've seen organizations so constructed that people have to fit into slots. We've gone the other way. Our organization is built around our people and their skills. As a result,

we are in a constant state of flux or adjustment, as our people develop and come along.
*Interview, St. Louis/*
*Nation's Business, October:50.*

## John Z. DeLorean
*Former vice president and general manager,*
*Chevrolet Division,*
*General Motors Corporation* 2

The present salary structure among top corporate officers is archaic and completely inconsistent with our business enterprise system as it is today. Executives are employees, not owners; and I've known some who thought entrepreneur was something on the menu in a French restaurant. People who own or start a business, and have a personal stake in its success or failure, should get a bigger slice of the reward than those who are chosen from among many to run it for a little while.
*Before National Postal Forum/*
*The Wall Street Journal, 1-14:14.*

## Tom Dillon
*President, Batten, Barton, Durstine &*
*Osborn, advertising* 3

. . . my picture of advertising is that it is a tool. You cannot evaluate a tool, particularly a specially constructed one, without knowing for what purpose it is intended. Only when you know the purpose is it likely that you can evaluate whether the tool will accomplish it. The campaign that is designed to bring salesmen to their feet in a sales meeting will not necessarily bring 18- to 34-year-old housewives into the store. The 30-second boffo gag that brings down the house at the awards dinner may not be as well received by a man with a bad head cold. The commercial that is designed to break the bank of a specific testing method may be designed to do just that and nothing else. I do not wish to quarrel at this point as to which purposes of advertising are more valid than other purposes. I should like to suggest that the surest road to advertising mediocrity is for a corporation to be vague and ill-defined in determining the precise purpose for which it intends to use the advertising tool. Nor do I assume that corporations consciously couch their advertising purposes in vague and conflicting terms. If they do so, it is not because of any lack of intelligence or general cussedness on the part of the management of corporations. It is simply because successful businesses are not likely to be run by people who have devoted most or all of their time to the actual creation of advertising.

*Before Adcraft Club, Detroit, April 18/*
*Vital Speeches, 6-1:492.*

## Paul Rand Dixon
*Commissioner, Federal Trade Commission*
1

What we do at the FTC is popularly styled "consumer protection," but I think that done properly it is just as much protection of businessmen. There is a fundamental unity of interest between consumers and businessmen when it comes to the matter of credibility in advertising. Without it the capacity of our economy to grow must be fatally impaired.

*Before National Association of Chain*
*Drug Stores, Washington, Jan. 22/\*\**

2

Being against deceptive and unfair trade practices is like being against sin. You hardly ever run into anyone who professes to be in favor of deceptive and unfair trade practices. The only difficulty is that not everybody agrees on what should be considered "deceptive" or "unfair." Just as not everyone agrees on what constitutes sin.

*At consumer seminar, University of*
*Tennessee, Nashville, Jan. 29/\*\**

## William H. Donaldson
*Dean-designate, Graduate School of*
*Organization and Management,*
*Yale University*
3

I think the lines between the private and public sectors are blurring more and more. Business has to interface with government increasingly, and government is more and more involved with business. It's just a fact of life and not necessarily bad.

*Interview, New York, Sept. 30/*
*The New York Times, 10-1:1.*

## Edward S. Donnell
*Chairman, Montgomery Ward & Company*
4

The selection of key executives who can work in top corporate, middle management and other profit centers is critical to a company's success. It is also essential to properly manage one's assets and to recognize what is achievable within the financial capability of your company. In the go-go years of the 1960s, we saw many companies make acquisitions that are now serious liabilities, because these elements were not given proper consideration. I think it is vitally important for managers to understand financial limitations, to understand the parameters in which they are operating.

*Interview, Chicago/*
*Nation's Business, November:46.*

## B. R. Dorsey
*Chairman, Gulf Oil Corporation*
5

Any move on the part of the government to take over traditional industry functions would only compound our present problems. To put this into a current perspective, there are those who, in their exasperation of the present energy situation, have suggested that the government nationalize the oil industry. I would point out that, in 1974, the sales volume of some 40 of the largest American oil companies was slightly over $200-billion. This is equivalent to two-thirds of present total Federal expenditures. Thus, any take-over move would result in an unprecedented and unmanageable increase in the fiscal domain of the Federal government. The result would be chaotic. It is clear that the solution to our problems is not the acquisition by government of traditional industry functions, and certainly not the acquisition by industry of traditional government functions. The solution is the continual refinement of the organizational capabilities in both sectors so that each can do its own job more capably. Given assurance of such separation of responsibilities, both government and industry will continually welcome constructive criticism and reasonable investigation; indeed, these are necessary to prevent the bureaucracy in either sector from becoming complacent and entrenched.

*At Texas Christian University, May 2/*
*Vital Speeches, 6-15:544.*

# WHAT THEY SAID IN 1975

## (B.R. DORSEY)

*1*

[On foreign bribes paid by U.S. companies in order to do business overseas] : There is no universal ethical absolute. You know that morals, customs, standards, values, principles and attitudes vary all over the world. What is immoral to some is perfectly correct to others. What is onerous to one culture may be perfectly proper and decent to another. What is unacceptable in one society may be the norm in another.

*Before Senate Subcommittee on Multinational Corporations, Washington/ The Christian Science Monitor, 11-5:18.*

## Lewis A. Engman
### *Chairman, Federal Trade Commission*

*2*

This nation's antitrust laws were designed to promote and preserve competition. They were enacted because both theory and experience suggested that competition was the public's best guarantee against exploitation, whether through price gouging or shoddy merchandise. The simple notion which underlies those laws has been the guiding principle of the Federal Trade Commission for more than half a century now, and the integrity of its logic has survived all challenges. We do not mean to suggest that there are not instances in which the outcome of the marketplace can be improved upon by giving recognition to competing social or political objectives. We believe that competition is simply the standard, the touchstone, the frame of reference against which those who espouse some alternative method of pricing and resource allocation must argue their case. For the record requires that the burden of proof be theirs.

*Before Senate Antitrust and Monopoly/ Subcommittee, Washington, Feb. 18/\*\**

## Gerald R. Ford
### *President of the United States*

*3*

[On government regulation of business]: Regulations do not automatically expire when they have outlived their usefulness. There is no systematic pattern of review; and even when it is acknowledged that changes are warranted, procedural delays often result in obsolete rules remaining in force for years. While the intention of regulation is to protect consumers, it sometimes does just the opposite. In many cases, the reduction or elimination of existing regulations would result in lower prices for the consumer and open new opportunities for business. In other industries, where there is inadequate competition, regulation should continue, but it is the job of government to ensure that such necessary regulation is administered efficiently and fairly.

*Before Chamber of Commerce of the United States, Washington, April 28/ Nation's Business, June:34.*

*4*

Although most of today's [government] regulations affecting business are well-intentioned, their effect, whether designed to protect the environment or the consumer, often does more harm than good. They can stifle the growth in our standard of living and contribute to inflation . . . We cannot eliminate all regulations. Some are costly but essential to public health and safety. Let us evaluate costs and benefits. The issue is not whether we want to control pollution. We all do. The question is whether added costs to the public make sense measured against actual benefits. As a consumer, I want to know how much the tab at the front-door check-out counter is raised through the back door of regulatory inflation. And as President, I want to eliminate unnecessary regulations which impose a hidden tax on the consumer. Over a period of 90 years, we have erected a massive Federal regulatory structure encrusted with contradictions, excess and rules that have outlived any conceivable value.

*Before National Federation of Independent Business, June 17/ U.S. News & World Report, 6-30:26.*

*5*

[On government regulation of business]: Starting from point zero not quite a century ago, the Federal government now employs over 100,000 people whose sole responsibility is the writing, reviewing and enforcing of some type of regulation. One hundred thousand people whose principal job is telling you how to do your job. It's a bureaucrat's dream of heaven, but it's a nightmare for those who have to bear the burden.

*Before business leaders,*
*Sacramento, Calif., Sept. 5/*
*Los Angeles Times, 9-6:(1)2.*

**Carol Tucker Foreman**
*Executive director, Consumer*
*Federation of America*
1

Companies see consumerism as "something we should be doing" but not as something to be taken all that seriously. I don't believe that many, if any, consumer-affairs professionals are powerful enough to influence corporate or public policy.

*The National Observer, 8-9:15.*

**Jay W. Forrester**
*Professor of management, Massachusetts*
*Institute of Technology*
2

The corporation has gotten bigger. We've put corporations together into conglomerates, into multinational corporations with the idea that somehow or other the problems of the individual corporation will be absorbed and handled by a bigger unit. I think it's becoming progressively more clear that the big unit is getting unmanageable, and that's not working.

*Interview, Washington/*
*The Washington Post, 6-8:(C)5.*

**David Foster**
*Chairman and president,*
*Colgate-Palmolive Company*
3

Good management requires imagination to plan ahead, leadership by example, and being suspicious. Never think things are all they seem to be on the surface. Dig deeply for the problem areas. Never be satisfied with mediocre performance. Also, know your business intimately. Let other people go into details and then make them give you, in concise form, the recommendations that should guide your decisions . . . you need the courage to make decisions, right or wrong. You need industry and devotion to the job you're presently in—not to the next one. And it's essential that you have

the ability to work with people and that you avoid company politics. Another thing: Intuition plays a great part . . . There is no point in losing sleep once a decision is made. The time to lose sleep is before you make the decision. A wrong decision should never stop or delay your next one. The higher you go up the executive ladder, the fewer your bad decisions should be, thanks to your experience with making both good ones and bad ones.

*Interview, New York/*
*Nation's Business, August:48.*

**Betty Furness**
*Consumerist*
4

For all you do about passing and enforcing [consumer] laws and trying to persuade industry to do the right thing, no matter what practices are changed or what laws are passed, if people don't know about them, they are at a disadvantage. The problem of getting information to the people is a tough one, and I have known since the day I started in this business how to get information to the people: You do it on television; it is the only place to do it.

*Interview, New York/*
*The Christian Science Monitor, 2-10:8.*

**John Kenneth Galbraith**
*Professor of economics, Harvard University*
5

There is no question that much of the talk about free enterprise is fraudulent. Most people recognize how quickly a concern like Lockheed, Penn Central, Rolls-Royce or the big New York brokerage houses convert to socialism when the alternative is bankruptcy. People of impeccable capitalist instincts seem to have no hesitation in seeking out the government when the alternative is losing their shirts.

*Interview/People, 7-7:37.*

**Ray Garrett, Jr.**
*Chairman, Securities and Exchange Commission*
*of the United States*
6

The SEC expects every corporate director to do his duty, but we are not willing to try to tell him exactly what his duty is in every situation in which he finds himself. We are, however,

# WHAT THEY SAID IN 1975

*(RAY GARRETT, JR.)*

willing to say, indeed are eager to say, that we expect directors to take seriously what the law has in fact long required of them ... [The problem is] that practices have become careless, and the idea has been lost that directors of publicly held companies have a prudent or reasonable-man duty to investors to provide full and accurate information, and otherwise to cause the company to comply with the Federal securities laws. We propose to encourage the performance of that duty by appropriate actions ... It means adequate examination into the materials the directors are asked to approve ... Most of all, it means remembering that a director's duty is to investors, and not to the individuals who make up management.

*U.S. News & World Report, 2-3:75.*

*1*

[On corporations paying bribes for political or business purposes and the resultant falsification of financial records]: It is central to our whole financial-reporting apparatus that accounts not be deliberately false, even in relatively small amounts. To the extent a business or company is dependent upon the making of illegal, and therefore necessarily secret, expenditures, the quality of earnings is obviously affected. The degree of hazard injected by this clandestine and illicit underpinning may vary considerably from case to case, but we are not likely to be swayed by arguments as to the improbability of getting caught.

*San Francisco Examiner & Chronicle, 6-8:(C)10.*

## Harold S. Geneen
*Chairman, International Telephone & Telegraph Corporation*    *2*

Multinational corporations are playing a major role as links between societies. They create jobs, promote balance of trade, and spread technology and management know-how. Such achievements are far more enduring than the imagined fears that world corporations seem to have evoked in some quarters in the past.

*At ITT annual meeting, Charlotte, N.C., May 7/ The Washington Post, 5-8:(E)13.*

## Henry B. Gonzalez
*United States Representative, D–Texas*    *3*

This forthcoming speculation in gold will not build houses or buy stocks and bonds; it will not finance the needs of industry, of people, or of the government. It will only reinstate the ancient myth of gold.

*Quote, 1-12:25.*

## James R. Greene
*Senior vice president, Manufacturers Hanover Trust Company, New York*    *4*

After some prodding from the Securities and Exchange Commission and Congress, a number of leading American firms have admitted to paying bribes and operating political slush funds overseas. This is not, as *Fortune* [magazine] has pointed out, "back alley" stuff, but the calculated deeds of highly responsible and respected executives ... I do not agree with those who say international businessmen face a terrible, insoluble, moral dilemma: to lose business if they do not make a shady payment, but to risk losing the respect of the United States public and governmental authorities if they do. I cannot accept the proposition that profits are the only measure of our performance, or that managers who achieve good results by unscrupulous dealing should be rewarded. In the longer run, a reputation for integrity and honesty in all our dealings, wherever in the world they take place, is a critically important part of our competitive mix. The only sure guide in this admittedly murky area of business ethics is to do abroad what we are required to do at home. Only in that way, it seems to me, can we be assured of retaining the support of the American public and their elected representatives. True, we have not always done what is required by law and regulations here in the United States. But at least we do not attempt to excuse these violators by saying everyone is doing the same. My conclusion is that we must take this same hard-nosed approach to business dealings overseas—first, because it is the right thing to do; second, it is what the American people expect of us.

*Before Netherlands Chamber of Commerce in the United States, New York, Sept. 17/ Vital Speeches, 10-15:25,27.*

**Tom Hanna**
*Vice president, Motor Vehicle*
*Manufacturers Association*
1

In bargaining [between business and government], both sides give, both sides gain. The result is compromise—not everything we wanted, but not everything we didn't want, either.

*Before Motorcar Dealers Association of Southern California, Indian Wells, Calif./ Los Angeles Times, 4-28:(3)8.*

**Fred R. Harris**
*Former United States Senator,*
*D—Oklahoma*
2

I'm for enforcement of the antitrust laws and to break up these monopolies; and I'm for ending special subsidies for private gain—right now they amount to $94-billion a year to the Lockheeds, the Penn Centrals, the timber interests, the oil and gas crowd, directly or indirectly. That's a kind of Robin Hoodism in reverse. It takes from people who have to work for a living, which is about 90 per cent of the people, and it turns it over to the super-rich and the giant corporations. If we take the rich off welfare, we can get America back to work . . .

*Interview/*
*The Christian Science Monitor, 5-12:34.*

**Philip A. Hart**
*United States Senator, D—Michigan*
3

In theory we have a free-enterprise economy. But in fact, in each of our basic industries, a handful of corporations calls the shots, immune from the pressures of competition.

*Quote, 3-9:218.*

4

In 15 years we have not made even a dent in the task of redistributing wealth in this nation. Some 200 corporations still control most of the wealth. Until we do something about that appalling concentration of power—power that even overwhelms the Congress at times—we will be able to do little to improve matters for the poor.

*At Congressional Black Caucus hearing/ The New York Times, 6-6:20.*

**Alfred Hayes**
*President,*
*Federal Reserve Bank of New York*
5

[On a proposed organization modeled after the Reconstruction Finance Corporation of the 1930s]: I can see real merit in an examination of the need for some new form of public institution designed primarily to provide capital to corporations suffering unusual financial stress or corporations engaged in programs of great importance to the solution of major national problems, such as energy and transportation, when adequate capital is not obtainable from private sources.

*Before New York State Bankers Association/ The New York Times, 2-23:(3)13.*

6

Certainly, the last decade's devastating inflation, culminating in a severe recession, has served as a reminder, if we need one, that monetary policy alone is no answer to the nation's economic problems; but it has also pointed up the crucial importance of having a wise monetary policy, as free as possible from day-to-day political pressures.

*At luncheon in his honor, New York, June 5/ The New York Times, 6-6:41.*

7

[On the reputed capital shortage]: I've never quite understood that term. There is always a good deal of capital around, and the problem is to bring it together in a marriage with a profitable investment need.

*The New York Times, 10-10:55.*

**Luther H. Hodges, Jr.**
*Chairman, North Carolina National Bank*
8

I have less religion, less family, less quality of life, less of a lot of things because I am willing to make a commitment to participate in running a company.

*Business Week, 10-6:56.*

**Jerome W. Hull**
*Chairman, Pacific Telephone &*
*Telegraph Company*
9

. . . the free-enterprise system in this country is in mortal peril. [Businessmen have allowed

39

# WHAT THEY SAID IN 1975

*(JEROME W. HULL)*

themselves] to be painted as greedy profiteers, a sort of ruling class that is responsible for most of the ills and frustrations of our society ... The answer is that the American public is not greatly educated—they are stupid and naive about how our system works ... Businessmen must work to get people elected who recognize and understand the free competitive system.

*Before California Bankers Association,*
*Los Angeles, May 16/*
*Los Angeles Times, 5-19:(3)10.*

## Hubert H. Humphrey
*United States Senator, D—Minnesota*    1

I think the Democrats are good for business ... We are good for it because every businessman knows that they do much better when the Democrats are in power. The big-businessmen frequently feel [that] if they belong to the country club and they are big business, they have got to be Republicans. I don't mind them saying they are Republicans, but for their own good and their own stockholders' good, they ought to vote Democratic.

*TV-radio interview, Washington/*
*"Meet the Press," National Broadcasting*
*Company, 11-2.*

## Frank N. Ikard
*President, American Petroleum Institute*    2

[There] seems to be a total misunderstanding of the role of profit on the part of many in Congress and the public. Without profit, no business can grow. Without profit, consumer needs can't be met.

*The New York Times, 2-2:(1)38.*

3

[On proposals to break up the petroleum industry]: Each tired, disproven argument for divestiture is being trotted out anew. But there is a difference this time. Only last month, in a vote on the floor of the Senate, 45 Senators voted for a provision that would make the breaking up of oil companies the law of the land ... The advocates of divestiture include many whose real aim is to provide Federal management of the oil industry ... But this would only bring higher prices, uncertain supply of domestic oil and gas, plus the inefficiencies inherent in government involvement ... We must reach our neighbors, our customers, even our critics. They must learn there is no advantage to anyone if the oil industry is shattered. We must remind them that once the radical surgery is performed, the damage cannot be corrected. You cannot unring a bell.

*Before American Petroleum Institute,*
*Chicago, Nov. 10/*
*The New York Times, 11-11:43.*

## Henry M. Jackson
*United States Senator, D—Washington*    4

For the past six years, the Republican Administration has been tilting in favor of big business, the large corporations, the people who can take care of themselves. And the little people—little business, the elderly, the young, across the board—have been the ones who have been taking the beating. And I think we need to change that tilt. I want to change that tilt to help these people. I'm not against big business. I'm for the profit motive. I'm for incentives. But what is needed is to redress the balance, to tilt back in favor of those who need the help, because that will help the whole country.

*Television broadcast announcing his candidacy*
*for the 1976 Democratic Presidential*
*nomination, Feb. 6/*
*The Washington Post, 2-7:(A)1.*

## J. K. Jamieson
*Chairman, Exxon Corporation*    5

[On the recent increase in retail gasoline prices]: What began to emerge, starting gradually a few years ago and accelerating ever more rapidly, was not a new spirit of collusion between the oil companies and the governments of OPEC. It was rather the assertion of power and control over production and prices by the member countries themselves. This is what caused the huge increase in prices and acted as a magnet which drew energy prices everywhere up to new levels. The startling fact is that revenues to the OPEC governments from crude oil now average about 24¢ per gallon as compared with 2¢ per gallon a few years ago. Our oil companies' own upstream earnings from the same crude oil meanwhile continue at less than 1¢ per gallon; and even if all downstream profits are thrown in as well, we come up to only 2.4¢ per gallon. If collusion has existed, the effect of the collusion has been completely one-sided.

*At American Bankers Association Trust Conference, Miami, Jan. 28/ Vital Speeches, 2-15:279.*

**Reginald H. Jones**
*Chairman, General Electric Company*      1

There is a strange perversity in the air today, and it is hard to understand. Our companies with overseas operations—our main strength in world-wide economic competition—are under attack precisely when they are a growing source of income and employment in the United States, and a force for economic and social progress around the world. The forces of isolationism are advancing precisely when interdependence among the nations is so clearly a necessity if humankind is to survive. The clamor against export programs is rising even as other nations, made desperate by the rising cost of imported oil, are stepping up their export subsidies. And our few incentives for capital investment are attacked as "loopholes" precisely when we face a capital shortage that threatens to perpetuate inflation, stagnation and unemployment. We can no longer take for granted our old privileged position as the most productive and prosperous nation in the world. If we want to maintain our leadership—and all the benefits that flow from it—then we will have to abandon old illusions and face up to the challenges of a new world.

*At Wharton School, Philadelphia, June 4/ Vital Speeches, 8-1:613.*

     2

Uninformed critics have so perverted the meaning of the word "profits" in the public mind that it has come to mean something like "undeserved income" or "the exploiter's unjust reward." One of my associates has even suggested that we stop using the word "profits," regardless of accounting tradition. Almost half of what are called profits are really the government's take from the operators of a business—

the corporation's income tax. The part paid out in dividends is really "interest on equity"—a fee paid for the use of people's savings, essentially no different from interest paid on loans. And the remainder—the profits reinvested in the business—are just as well called "business savings" or "reinvested earnings." The advantage of calling these costs of operation by their right name is that people understand such things as taxes, interest, earnings and savings, because they are all part of the family budget. But nobody in the family thinks in terms of profits. They are considered something alien, received only by the undeserving businessman.

*At National Association of Manufacturers' Congress of Industry, New York/ The Wall Street Journal, 7-14:8.*

     3

[The problem] centers on the ability of companies to raise money to expand and modernize and keep a jump ahead of competition. The economists refer to this process as capital formation. A country's economy grows and flourishes when people set aside a part of what they earn to invest in facilities and technology that will make the nation still more productive. A generation ago, the U.S. led the world in capital investment, and we pulled out ahead in terms of production and national wealth. But that's no longer the case. Since World War II, we have been emphasizing the good life—high consumption and expansion of government services—at the expense of savings and investment. We've been building up demand and ignoring the supply side, the producer sector. We've lost touch with a basic formula for success.

*Interview/Nation's Business, December:16.*

**Thomas E. Kauper**
*Assistant Attorney General, Antitrust Division, Department of Justice of the United States*
     4

Obviously, you won't cure all of our economic ills by repealing fair-trade legislation. But you will do two things: You will allow the free market to serve the consumer in the manner it should; and you will allow the firm hand of the law to fall once more upon those manufacturers

# WHAT THEY SAID IN 1975

and retailers who now, with state permission, are reaching into the pockets of consumers after dollars they could never hope to obtain under totally free market conditions.

*Before Senate Antitrust and Monopoly Subcommittee, Washington, Feb. 18/ The Washington Post, 2-19:(E)10.*

## Arthur F. Kelly
*President, Western Airlines*　　　　　*1*

Too many of my peers are carried away on an ego trip. A chief executive has lots of power and authority. It's a heady experience. If he's not careful, he grows to believe he's the only one who can make decisions. Surprisingly, that happens to many chief executives. They bottle-neck their companies, and I've noticed it especially in the airline business. The ego trip can go so far that a man reaches retirement age and he doesn't have a replacement ready. He has persuaded himself that the company cannot survive without him, and he hopes that the board of directors will come to him and say, "We know you have reached retirement age but please stay on, because we need you." If I'm different it's because I try not to be a bottle-neck. I encourage decision-making all the way down the line. There are plenty of replacements ready to take over when *I* reach retirement age.

*Interview, Los Angeles/ Los Angeles Times, 5-18:(Home)55.*

## James S. Kemper, Jr.
*President, Kemper Insurance Companies*　　*2*

One of the most disturbing aspects of our economic picture is that much of the press, and those politicians who look for highly visible and politically vulnerable targets, find it profitable to attack corporate management and to make "business" the scapegoat for economic problems. Of course, business needs to be regulated; its activities require surveillance in the public interest, as do those of labor unions and even consumer organizations. But it is a disservice to the national welfare and the welfare of the average citizen to deliberately create distrust of the corporate system and its managers, instead

of directing our attention to the imperative need to exercise the economic discipline necessary to a healthy economy.

*At CPCU Insurance Day Conference, Washington, March 19/ Vital Speeches, 5-1:428.*

## Richard C. King
*President, Los Angeles World Trade Center; Chairman, Center for International Business*　*3*

... in the field of international business, it's not the formal contractual aspect of business that's important. What is important is understanding that you're doing business with people of different cultures, of different value systems. They make decisions differently, and you have to understand that in order to get along harmoniously and successfully. I've had 25 years experience in business with the Russians, Japanese, Chinese and Germans. They're all different. They approach business schemes differently. They have a different sense of priorities. And since today we have a world of multinational corporations and world-wide operations, with markets, currencies and finances totally trans-national and multinational in structure, there is a need for a totally different kind of employee. Ones in the past could just know their trade; today they can't.

*Interview, Los Angeles/ Los Angeles Herald-Examiner, 1-7:(B)1.*

## Eugene Klein
*Former chairman, National General Corporation; Owner, San Diego "Chargers" football team*　　　　*4*

... when I was selling encyclopedias door to door and going to college at night, I often heard people complain that there's no opportunity left in America, and my standard response was "nonsense." That's still my response. Opportunity is always around us, always within reach. The key to making the most of it is to have some ability, plus a willingness to pay the price for success ... It's so steep that most people give up. In almost any career it may mean working 20 hours a day, neglecting family and friends. It may mean years and years of living on airplanes, sleeping in strange motels night after night, putting up with poor food in bad restaurants, always thinking about your wife and kids, missing them but seldom seeing them. Perhaps none of it sounds terribly rough in mere conversation, but in reality it's an enormous price to pay. The loneliness, the discomfort, the sweat and tears and sacrifice all become an emotional burden that grows heavier and heavier as you keep climbing the mountain toward business success.

*Interview, Los Angeles/*
*Los Angeles Times, 10-5:(Home)33.*

**Virginia H. Knauer**
*Director, Federal Office*
*of Consumer Affairs*

1

I would maintain that there is a clear distinction between the public interest and the consumer interest. In my view, the public interest entails the whole spectrum—from producer to distributor to consumer. The consumer interest represents the ultimate purchaser of the product. There are times when, in the public interest, the consumer interest must give way.

*Before Pennsylvania Electric*
*Association, Pittsburgh/*
*The National Observer, 10-11:13.*

**Philip Kotler**
*Professor of marketing,*
*Northwestern University*

2

Being dynamic . . . consumerism is pulling in many new directions all the time. Yet in the large picture, there does appear to be a new and very important "societal phase" emerging. Back in the late 1960s and early 1970s when consumerism first burst on the scene, it focused mainly on product durability and integrity. While these are still leading considerations, consumerism is now going beyond that and getting into the effect of products and services on our quality of life. If you smoke, then I want you to go to another part of the theatre, bus, plane or train. Or if you drive a big car, that means you are polluting my air, and I may not like that. Who knows—in some future millennium this may lead to smokeless cigarettes or noise-free jackhammers.

*Interview/Business Week, July 28:43.*

## COMMERCE / INDUSTRY / FINANCE

**R. Heath Larry**
*Vice chairman, United States*
*Steel Corporation*

3

Much of what the tax law required us to show as "profits" are not "profits" at all—they are what's "left over" after accounting for the *real* costs of producing our products and services. Yet, our profits are being adjudged "huge" or "fantastic" or "obscene" in the eyes of some headline writers, union leaders, academicians and politicians! Too bad they aren't equally impressive to the sophisticated investors—who seem overly aware of what I have just been pointing out.

*Before Chamber of Commerce, Grove City, Pa./*
*The Wall Street Journal, 2-28:12.*

**Mary Wells Lawrence**
*Chairman, Wells, Rich, Greene, advertising*

4

Isn't it ironic that just as women have pushed our way into the pipeline of business and are popping out as managers, vice presidents and presidents-to-be, American business is being shot down? . . . Many of my agency's commercials can't be run today because of new laws and regulations. Cigarettes can't be advertised on television at all, for example, and the Food and Drug Administration has told Alka-Seltzer it could advertise only for a limited range of problems . . . Shortages of capital and materials, back-to-back recessions, inflation, and government movement into business operations have created frustration, anger, confusion and a kind of wary watchfulness in business now . . . I suggest the possibility that the government will be managing all major industries in the U.S. in a few years. Pretty soon the private sector will be reduced to health-food stores, barber shops, pet stores and umbrella stands.

*Before Sun Oil Co. employees at program*
*honoring International Women's Year,*
*Dallas, Nov. 17/*
*The Dallas Times Herald, 11-18:(C)5.*

**Edward H. Levi**
*Attorney General of the United States*

5

The antitrust laws are enormously important to our country, to industry. Part of their impor-

43

# WHAT THEY SAID IN 1975

*(EDWARD H. LEVI)*

tance is that they keep aloft the ideal of the competitive system. They also keep aloft the ideal that this is a country which is not so controlled by any few concerns that one would think they have political domination. It's not solely an economic issue. If the ideal is pressed too hard, and the notion of effective enforcement through legislative changes or supervision of industry is pushed too hard, the antitrust laws, instead of being for free enterprise and competition, become regulatory devices themselves. One of the things about the antitrust laws is that they're so important you mustn't expect too much from them. You can't claim repeatedly that they're going to revolutionize the world. Yet they have revolutionized the world. They've been effective in the United States and they're extremely important.

*Interview, Washington/*
*U.S. News & World Report, 6-30:33.*

## Theodore Levitt
*Professor, Harvard Business School* 1

You must have experience to make good judgments [in the corporate world]. Business is not like physics, where you have culture heroes at 26. Just knowledge isn't enough.

*Business Week, 10-6:64.*

## Walter J. Levy
*Energy economist* 2

The major oil companies will continue to be the most important technical and marketing force in most of the world for a long time. Their technical competence and logistical services can only be replaced at great risk to those who eliminate them.

*The New York Times, 2-2:(1)38.*

## John V. Lindsay
*Former Mayor of New York* 3

Those who preach to us today about the glory of individual initiative conveniently ignore the over-weening grasp of the marketplace of multinational institutions, run from private executive suites, that hold more power than most foreign governments. Only government action can monitor their conduct and ensure protection for the millions of individuals they deal with.

*At Bicentennial Forum, Boston/*
*The Christian Science Monitor, 7-15:27.*

## Louis B. Lundborg
*Former chairman, Bank of America* 4

Profit has to be the businessman's primary objective. Without profit, there is no possibility of anything else.

*Los Angeles Times, 5-4:(1)5.*

## Frank R. Lyon, Jr.
*Senior vice president and general counsel,*
*Union Carbide Corporation* 5

. . . businessmen cannot be effective in promoting free enterprise and contributing to the public good if they are concerned only about reducing government regulation and if their response to every new proposal is to cry "socialism." We must recognize that in the free market, as in the everyday lives of individuals, liberty does not mean license. There are areas in which it is appropriate for government to intervene. It is as important for business, as it is for private individuals, that government prohibit business conduct which is harmful to society— conduct which impinges upon the rights and welfare of our citizens. In these areas, the question is not whether government should intervene, but whether our lawmakers and regulators are selecting the wisest, most effective form of intervention. The answer to that question must start with an objective analysis of the real nature of our problems, real condition of our society.

*Before West Virginia Manufacturers*
*Association, White Sulphur Springs, Oct. 2/*
*Vital Speeches, 11-15:84.*

## Stanley Marcus
*Chairman, Neiman-Marcus stores* 6

[On revelations of U.S. firms having to pay overseas bribes to do business in foreign countries]: I reject the cynical attitude of former Treasury Secretary John Connally who said recently that too many U.S. enterprises overseas have had to use "fang and claw" to operate because the U.S. State Department gives them little or no support . . . America is supposed to stand for something special in this world. We're not supposed to get down in the mud with the other nations; we're supposed to be a beacon for other nations to follow. How do I answer those who say that payola is sometimes necessary to do business overseas? My answer is that you have to pay for a code of ethics, and it doesn't come cheap.

*At University of Nebraska, Omaha/*
*The Dallas Times Herald, 11-26:(B)5.*

**Margaret Mead**
*Anthropologist*
1

In this country, we have never been upset when there is no relationship between the advertising and the facts. People live in an ad. Products are designed to look nice and thus be easy to sell. There is no concern for durability and value.

*Quote, 7-13:649.*

**George Meany**
*President, American Federation of*
*Labor-Congress of Industrial*
*Organizations*
2

[On the AFL-CIO's petroleum-industry proposals which some say are akin to nationalization] : I don't think this is the worst thing that could happen. If the oil companies keep behaving the way they are—conducting their business in complete disregard of the interest of the American people—I think nationalization is inevitable some day.

*Miami Beach/*
*The Dallas Times Herald, 2-24:(D)6.*

3

The question of what to do about the [U.S.] wheat sales [to the Soviet Union] and what they are doing to American consumers is a problem for the President [Ford] . . . I have no proposals to make, except to say to him: "Mr. President, you should do something about this. We got ripped off in 1972, we are about to get ripped off again, and you should see that we don't get ripped off." I've got some ideas . . . we should tell the Soviet Union, "You cannot deal with private American citizens until we in

the United States of America, as a government, are allowed to deal with private Soviet citizens." Even up—you know, give and take.

*News conference, Washington/*
*U.S. News & World Report, 9-8:50.*

**Randall Meyer**
*President, Exxon Company, U.S.A.*
4

[Criticizing government standards imposed on business and its products] : Leaders in business must conceptualize and formulate practical alternatives which provide the needed benefits without the cost of sacrificing individual freedom. The businessman must propose and support changes that respond to the real problems of the real world in which he lives. Problem-solving and constructive innovation are what business is all about.

*At Texas Christian University School of Business, Oct. 7/The New York Times, 10-8:53.*

**Clinton Morrison**
*Chairman, Chamber of Commerce of the*
*United States; Vice chairman, First*
*National Bank of Minneapolis*
5

I feel we have got to give the businessman his head. Let's unfetter him so he can innovate, create and, importantly, reap the rewards that will encourage further innovation and progress. If businesses are not allowed to make profits, then they cannot attract the additional capital that is required to move our commercial system forward. Let's not forget that commerce is everybody's business. It plays a vital role in giving the citizens of this country a quality of freedom, a quality of life, that is unrivaled in the world.

*Interview, Minneapolis/*
*Nation's Business, May:60.*

**Thomas A. Murphy**
*Chairman, General Motors Corporation*
6

In our favor, the American people, by and large, are not against profits *per se* . . . What people *are* against is a system of priorities that would place profits above more important considerations—such as product integrity, humane working conditions, minority opportunities, clean air and water—and even above religious

# WHAT THEY SAID IN 1975

*(THOMAS A. MURPHY)*

and ethical values . . . The trouble is that large numbers of Americans apparently believe that businessmen are not reasonable, that businessmen are willing and able to sacrifice most moral or humanitarian considerations in the blind pursuit of profit . . . That misunderstanding, I strongly believe, is what is behind so much anti-business feeling today. And if we value our free-enterprise system, we must do what we can to clear it up. It will not be an easy job. Profits are so basic to the continued existence of a private business that it is almost impossible to imagine a system of business priorities that does not place them near the top . . . That is why it is so common to hear profit described as the Number 1 objective of every business. It is an over-simplified answer given to an unfair question. Actually, the objectives of a legitimate business are so closely intertwined and mutually dependent that it is impossible to break them off and arrange them in a neat row of easily distinguishable priorities . . . I think we must couple our answer with a clear statement that profit is neither the first nor the last of a responsible businessman's objectives—but it is central to his ability to meet any other business or business-related objective.

*Before Chamber of Commerce, Flint, Mich./*
*The Wall Street Journal, 7-31:8.*

1

Our economic system, founded with our nation 200 years ago, has come more and more under government control. Very conspicuously in the marketplace, the government, by mandate and edict, is substituting its sovereignty for that of the individual consumer. Government, rather than the buying public, is increasingly determining the kinds of products and services offered for sale; and government regulations are influencing their costs and consequently their prices. What is of greatest concern is that each intrusion of government—because it takes decision-making power away from the individual consumer—diminishes his economic freedom.

*Before National Association of*
*Accountants/Nation's Business, August:11.*

## Ralph Nader
*Lawyer; Consumer advocate*

2

You cannot have innovation, competition and consumer protection as long as you have the private energy cartel we have in this country. Our antitrust laws have been on the books for decades. They should be enforced, specifically by deconcentrating the oil industry, getting rid of the vertical integration which is possessed by no other industry that I know of, and, through the forces of competition, getting prices lowered.

*At Energy Outlook and Global*
*Interdependence conference/*
*The Center Magazine, March-April:34.*

3

More consumer information is being disseminated. For example, the press nowadays reports faulty products by brand name, and company abuses by corporate name, far more freely than 15 years ago. I remember when newspapers would refer to a particular car only as a "medium-size, rear-engine automobile." People these days can be more on their guard when they go into the marketplace. They are more willing to organize against what they view as injustices. They are more inclined to judge a politician by his stand on consumer issues. Not so long ago, a consumer issue was anathema to a politician; you'd walk in with a problem and he'd walk out the back door. As to things we have actually accomplished, for example, I think lives are being saved and injuries prevented by improvements in auto safety. You don't get as easily ramrodded by a steering column, and if you want to use a seat-belt shoulder harness, you can. Also, a number of unsafe or worthless drugs can no longer be sold. The public also is more aware of nutrition, more skeptical about the food they buy. That's tied to the fact that 12 million home gardens have been started in this country in the past two years . . . As to inflation, that used to be an issue tied to banking and fiscal policy, but now it's very much part of consumer concern—part of the consumer movement. I'd say we are seeing the arduous beginnings of a much more accelerated consumer participation in economic and regulatory decisions at all levels, right up there with corporations.

*Interview/*
*U.S. News & World Report, 10-27:29.*

**James J. Needham**
*Chairman, New York Stock Exchange*
1

Capital is what makes capitalism work. And capital is what we are going to need—in ever-increasing quantities—to keep capitalism working in this country in the years ahead. But capital is not going to rise like some modern phoenix from the ashes of debt-ridden corporations. It will have to be coaxed out of the hands of millions of people who can afford to undertake the necessary risks. And that can be done only if potential investors are offered the prospects of reasonable, legitimate rewards based on success and profitability. If Congress and the Administration really expect to roll back inflation and turn recession into progression, they will have to set the forces of government at work to encourage a massive flow of private savings into productive business investment. And the best vehicle for starting those funds flowing is incentive-oriented tax policy.

*Before The Conference Board, New York,*
*Feb. 19/Vital Speeches, 3-15:341.*

2

This is a country of small businesses, not large ones. The reason we have been so successful, economically, in our 200-year history is because of the ease of entry for people into business, and their ability to raise capital either by borrowing money or by selling stock. Now I have the feeling that as a result of the tight money of recent years, the depressed economy and the scarcity of capital, that the nation is going to suffer five or 10 years down the road because new technology won't have been developed. Where are the Xeroxes and the IBMs of the future going to come from?

*Interview, Washington/*
*U.S. News & World Report, 12-22:71.*

**Gaylord Nelson**
*United States Senator, D—Wisconsin*
3

. . . the national small-business community consists of 97 per cent of approximately 13

million U.S. enterprises. These firms furnish 52 per cent of all private employment, 43 per cent of the business output and one-third of the gross national product. They are the traditional source of local and national economic growth. . . . more than one-half of all major inventions have come from small business and individual inventors. The giant companies of today began as small business firms; and new small businesses of today are producing the advanced integrated circuits, mini-computers, hand-held calculators and computer-peripheral equipment that have kept world leadership in these industries in the United States. These are illustrations of what small, independent business can do, if they are treated equitably under government policy and not crowded out of the marketplace by unfair competition from giant monopolies and conglomerate businesses . . . Those of us in Congress who are concerned with the preservation and strengthening of small enterprise are alarmed at the weakness and disrepair of the free-enterprise system in this country. Our basic aim must be to recreate a climate in which small business can flourish. We must seek to foster conditions under which small firms can attract capital for new ventures and accumulate earnings for growth; where they can compete in the marketplace with some protection against predatory monopolistic practices; where they can grow to be regional and national competitors; where it is still possible to preserve their independence and where the traditional American dream of business ownership can continue to be fulfilled.

*Before National Society of Public*
*Accountants, Oct. 30/\*\**

**Walter J. Neppl**
*Executive vice president,*
*J. C. Penney Company*
4

Today's consumer is skillful at recognizing quality. She knows what is good and worth owning. Above all, she perceives inefficiency and unnecessary additives as old-fashioned, as undesirable and out of phase with her no-nonsense and necessary new life-styles.

*U.S. News & World Report, 7-14:20.*

# WHAT THEY SAID IN 1975

**Constance E. Newman**
*Commissioner, Federal Consumer*
*Product Safety Commission*                                    1

Product safety is not a stimulating subject. The central reason is that we are all Walter Mitty with regard to product safety, imagining ourselves to be more invincible than we actually are. Somehow to raise questions about the safety of a product is not bold, forthright behavior. We fail to recognize that by not asking questions, we might be taking risks in buying certain products or in using them in certain ways. . . . we tend to assume that the things we buy *are* safe. Otherwise, we reason, how could they reach the marketplace? And so we approach our purchasing with the rather naive assumption that all products are safe. This assumption is reinforced by our Walter Mitty-like nature, with its twin aspects of imagined derring-do and desire to avoid unpleasant realities.

> *Before American Advertising Federation/*
> *The National Observer, 7-5:17.*

**Geoffrey Nunes**
*Vice president, Lenox, Inc.*                                   2

[Arguing against repeal of fair-trade laws]: When we put our trademark on our products [china, jewelry], we put our reputation on the line. What is wrong with our putting our price on it at the same time? If the consumer doesn't like our price, he doesn't have to buy our ware; certainly we can all agree upon that. But why can't we also agree that a discounter should not be allowed to use our product as a loss leader and debase our reputation built up over all these years?

> *Before Senate Subcommittee, Washington/*
> *Los Angeles Times, 4-18:(1)17.*

**Edward I. O'Brien**
*President, Securities Industry Association*                    3

Capital is among our most essential national resources. Like energy resources, it must be conserved and developed. The securities industry is doing its part by working to improve the depth and the liquidity of securities markets and encouraging greater participation by individuals, but we cannot do the jobs ourselves.

We need to join with corporate leaders and other concerned Americans to launch an all-out attack on our nation's capital problem . . . If we can restore meaningful incentives for investors, particularly individuals, and generate the investment capital this country so desperately needs, we can achieve the socio-economic goals that everyone seeks—full employment of labor, full utilization of industrial capacity, gains in productivity to equal or surpass those of our international competitors, and continued growth in the American standard of living under the free-enterprise system that has brought a better life to more people for a longer time than any other economic system.

> *Before Commonwealth Club, San Francisco,*
> *Aug. 8/Vital Speeches, 9-15:731.*

**Olof Palme**
*Prime Minister of Sweden*                                      4

Rather than lay off and stop producing, we will help industry with government financing [during recessions], if it continues producing for inventory. Repeatedly we have seen that, when the boom comes, manufacturers don't have sufficient product to sell. Now part of our reserve of foreign exchange is in inventories. We tried this the last time the economy declined and it worked well. The companies made very large profits because when the economy and prices went up they had inventories to sell. This is one way in which the government can help private enterprise overcome the fluctuations of the business cycle.

> *Interview, November/*
> *Business Week, 12-22:26.*

**Norman Podhoretz**
*Editor, "Commentary" magazine*                                 5

If people will not produce for profit, experience has shown they will not produce at all. The only way to attack poverty is to promote productivity and growth.

> *Before American Jewish Committee, New York,*
> *May 4/The New York Times, 5-5:4.*

**T. Rowe Price**
*Investment counsellor*                                         6

I'm very worried about the great U.S.A. and the capitalistic world. You can have everything

48

else right, but if inflation makes your currency go to nothing, all those right things are meaningless. Only a miracle—by which I mean Europe, Japan and the U.S. agreeing on an international monetary system backed by gold—could make me optimistic about the future.

*Interview, Baltimore/*
*Money, December:51.*

**William Proxmire**
*United States Senator, D—Wisconsin*
1

In 1950, profits represented 15.6 per cent of national income compared to employees' compensation, which was 64.1 per cent that year, or four times profits. In the ensuing 25 years, profits fell steadily. Last year—viewed by many as a superyear for profits—they were only 9.2 per cent of national income compared to 75.1 per cent for employee compensation. So last year employee compensation was more than eight times profits. In other words, profits are now about half as large a proportion of wages and salaries as they were 25 years ago . . . We have suffered a drop in real wages in the past year for tens of millions of Americans. In the past year, the American farmer has suffered a cruel squeeze from rising costs, just as the farm prices that represent his income have fallen. Six and a half million Americans are out of work. We are and should be acutely aware of this. But we should not lose sight of the fact that for 25 years corporate profits have been falling in relation to other income shares in our economy, and it would be foolish and counter-productive for us to adopt any policy designed to penalize them further.

*Human Events, 2-1:4.*

**Ronald Reagan**
*Former Governor of California (R)*
2

[Criticizing strict government controls on business]: We have all heard that if you build a better mousetrap the world would beat a path to your door. Today if you build a better mousetrap, the government comes along with a better mouse.

*Cullman, Alabama, March 21/San Francisco*
*Examiner & Chronicle, 3-23:(B)5.*

3

If present trends toward government regulations continue, the free-enterprise system will cease to exist within 25 years. Business and industry in America are regulated by government more than in any other country where the free-enterprise system is allowed to exist. Eventually we are going to live in a society where everything that is not compulsory will be prohibited. The truth is that we are becoming less and less of a government by elected officials and more a government of middle-echelon bureaucrats who cannot be removed by the voters.

*At convention of public accountants,*
*Dallas, June 20/Los Angeles*
*Herald-Examiner, 6-21:(A)3.*

**Donald T. Regan**
*Chairman, Merrill Lynch, Pierce,*
*Fenner & Smith, Inc.*
4

[On competitive brokerage rates]: Many members of the financial community have spent most of the past two years proclaiming the fearful destruction which would sweep the financial district if the anti-competitive walls of Wall Street were breached. Despite the dire predictions, it looks like . . . the Street can continue to prosper. [Although there may be fewer firms on Wall Street as a result of the unfixing of brokerage rates,] I don't think we should grieve about it . . . I'm not sure that Wall Street is the most efficient place. Firms will go out of business and firms will merge. But a more efficient business will emerge.

*Before New York Financial Writers*
*Association, June 26/*
*The New York Times, 6-27:47,50.*

5

[On recent revelations of illegal domestic corporate political contributions and foreign payoffs]: I don't think that what has been revealed is necessarily true of all business; but unless you have a pro-business attitude, it would be hard for people to be convinced otherwise. [Rather than government legislation, the problem requires] corporations and the individuals managing them to get together on an individual company basis, state what the

# WHAT THEY SAID IN 1975

*(DONALD T. REGAN)*

ethical line will be for that company, and then make sure that subordinates adhere to that line or are released.

*Interview, New York/*
*The Washington Post, 7-20:(G)3.*

**Henry S. Reuss**
*United States Representative, D–Wisconsin*          1

[Saying the government should form corporations to compete with private companies]: What I would like would be to keep the great monopolies on their toes by giving them a little government competition . . . I'd like to see a government corporation drilling for off-shore oil. That way you could see that the environment wasn't threatened and then you could make available that off-shore oil to the existing oil companies . . . Let [the Federal Reserve Board] consider whether it shouldn't have a . . . nationalized bank in which they could show the rest of the banking industry that it is possible to run a bank as a service to the people of the United States . . . [We should take] a first step to making free enterprise and capitalism really work. Where it gets constipated, I favor a good swig of vitamins to set it at being competitive again.

*Interview, Washington, March 9/*
*Los Angeles Times, 3-10:(1)5.*

**John J. Riccardo**
*President, Chrysler Corporation*          2

[On government regulation of business] : . . . before government sets any standards, it should be certain the country needs them. It should be certain industry has the know-how to meet them. And it should know how much they will cost and what the benefit will be. And that should be self-evident. Apparently it is not . . . We [in business] have a responsibility to demand that the regulators show us their facts and justify their conclusions. We should object loudly when the evidence shows a given course of action will be counter-productive and wasteful of the country's resources. And based on our own practical experience, we should propose realistic alternatives. This may bring us

criticism for the short term. But if so, then that is the price we have to pay. Business does not meet its larger responsibilities to society by doing only what is easy, convenient and popular.

*Before Michigan Association of Certified*
*Public Accountants/*
*The New York Times, 7-20:(3)12.*

**W. F. Rockwell, Jr.**
*Chairman, Rockwell International*          3

Traditionally the United States has always been the most productive country in the world. We could, and we did, turn out more goods and better goods and at less cost than any other country. That was a primary reason why we achieved such a high standard of living in America. But things have changed. Our productivity growth rate is decreasing. At this moment, according to the magazine *U.S. News & World Report,* we are in last place, in terms of productive growth, among the major industrial nations of the world . . . We have lost control of the inputs. We can no longer, for example, depend on either the cost or the supply of our energy. Oil and natural gas are being apportioned, and industry ranks very low on the distribution list. A shortage of energy in a factory is a ruthless destroyer of productivity. We know, too, that we can no longer depend on a constant cost for materials. As we spend more for materials, we have less for new machine tools, for new facilities. All of these impact on productivity. Nothing is stable; everything is unstable; and that instability is a direct threat to productivity. We˙ must convince our employees that unless we produce more at less cost we can't raise incomes, and they can't maintain the American standard of living. An employee who is producing more is not enriching the shareowners. He's adding to the funds available that can be plowed back into new equipment and new buildings that, in turn, permit him to increase his income. . . . a corporation is not an evil monster seeking to devour, but a part of America, with real property, real machinery, real buildings, a part of America which makes possible employment for 85 million Americans.

*At Gantt Memorial Awards, New York,*
*Feb. 25/\*\**

1

Emerging nations which desperately need foreign capital and technology to promote their economic growth are cutting this off with nationalization. They've effectively discouraged the "have" nations from investing in the "have not" nations. They're stunting their own ability to manufacture; they'll have to depend on imports, but how will they pay for them without a domestic base of production and jobs? Other emerging countries have taken or are taking steps to restrict access—through near-prohibitive prices—to their natural resources. Such unrealistic pricing is forcing many other countries back to the old strategy they had adopted in earlier times when tariffs were riding high around the world—the strategy of self-sufficiency. But, to any nation, self-sufficiency in everything is an impossible dream. Self-sufficiency was the will-o-the-wisp that was discredited two generations ago. We thought we'd moved into a more enlightened era when each nation would concentrate on those goods it is best able to produce competitively, when free trade would open up the world as one market, when prices could then be lowered due to increased volume, and when every nation would enjoy more abundance and higher employment. These reasonable concepts are as valid today as ever. But they've been shelved in favor of concepts that are based not on reason but emotion—selfishness, suspicion and hatred. These are not the emotions that promote peace. And in this climate we stand to lose far more than the free flow of commerce. We stand to lose peace as well. What can we do about all this? I think our present Administration in Washington can do something about it through its trade negotiators. Our American Congress can do something about it. And the American people can do something by letting our Administration and our Congress know how we feel. Nor do I think the approach that Americans take should be limited to sweet reasonableness. I think the time has come for this country to be a little less benevolent. In our negotiations with other countries we need to tell it like it is—that Americans are tired of making all the sacrifices and taking all the blame.

*Before World Trade Association of Philadelphia, Sept. 17/**

## COMMERCE / INDUSTRY / FINANCE

**Robert V. Roosa**
*Partner, Brown Brothers Harriman & Company, bankers*

2

...the insistence on growth, and rapid growth, has become so widespread as completely to outrun the supply capabilities of the world economy. This is not to accept the Club of Rome's discouraged view that the world is nearing the asymptotic limits for growth, but it is to recognize, as the grain of truth in their impressive analysis, that there is a problem of pace. Supply may not have absolute limits, but there does have to be an effective mobilization of capital and labor and technology—within the constraints of social and environmental requirements—in order to expand the supply of the world's goods and services. And that mobilization has just not been able to keep up with the accelerating pace of world-wide demand.

*Before Atlantic Institute for International Affairs, Munich/ The Wall Street Journal, 4-15:20.*

**William V. Roth, Jr.**
*United States Senator, R—Delaware*

3

The large number of major companies identified as having made illegal political contributions in the country, or having paid bribes in other countries to obtain special favors, is dismaying. It is as damaging to the reputation of American business as Watergate has been to American government. I know it can be argued that under-the-table political contributions and bribes are standard practices in many other countries, but the same can be said of the Watergate crimes which toppled the Nixon Administration, which forced the resignation of an American President. It will not wash with the American public. These incidents cast a cloud over the character and credibility of corporations which can only be removed by forthright actions to insure that they do not recur . . . It is extremely difficult to establish an effective code of behavior or international mechanism for multinational business operations. But American corporations are the pacesetters in the world marketplace and it is not asking too much to expect them, by their example and leadership, to be a powerful force

# WHAT THEY SAID IN 1975

*(WILLIAM V. ROTH, JR.)*

in raising the standards of business conduct around the world.

*Before Manufacturing Chemists Association, Washington, Oct. 14/ Vital Speeches, 12-1:101.*

## Thomas A. Rothwell
*General counsel, Marketing Policy Institute*     1

[The fair-trade law is] one method of ensuring standard prices at retail. Large segments of the nation's goods and services are marketed pursuant to such standard retail pricing arrangements. The nation's press, including the periodicals, conventionally market their wares by way of a standard pricing system. Its benefits and advantages are well understood by those responsible for the marketing of such commodities.

*Los Angeles Times, 4-18:(1)17.*

## Robert W. Sarnoff
*Chairman, RCA Corporation*     2

[On U.S. companies having to pay overseas bribes in order to do business in foreign countries]: Actually, the existence of some of these practices may testify less to the power and influence of the companies concerned than to their own vulnerability. That such payments can be a condition of doing business in a foreign land suggests at least a mutual responsibility. Some of these cases appear to be clear-cut transgressions. But it is not always easy to walk a straight path through the maze of different laws and customs encountered in various countries.

*News conference, London, Oct. 7/ Los Angeles Times, 10-8:(3)12.*

## Chauncey E. Schmidt
*President, First National Bank, Chicago*     3

For the U.S. business and financial community, the area of East-West trade is still—to use the German expression—*neuland*. As such, it involves many new experiences and challenges, demanding the same spirit of adventure and innovation that made international expansion such an exciting part of banking in the 1950s and 1960s. Now, however, there is

clearly more at stake. With the ideological positions on both sides frozen, the success or failure of detente must be measured primarily in economic and financial terms. Once again, as happens so often throughout world history, it is up to the traders, merchants and financiers to bring people closer together, by establishing the kind of viable economic ties which will pave the way for future political understanding.

*Before Organization for International Economic Relations, Vienna, June 19/ Vital Speeches, 8-15:656.*

## Irving S. Shapiro
*Chairman, E. I. du Pont de Nemours & Company*     4

I think there are people in government who distrust business. Not all people, but many. They distrust the profit motive; they think businessmen are in business solely to make money and have no regard for anything else. I think for example, to take an illustration, if the Federal Energy Office had on its staff some people who knew the energy business, and we didn't get tied up in knots about conflicts of interest, which I think are illusory, they could do a much better job in solving the energy problem than we are now doing. What I would hope for would be that industry and government could have an easy means of communication so that the facts that industry has can be considered by government. Industry does not want to make government policy, but it would like to have government policy made on the basis of known facts.

*TV-radio interview, Washington/ "Meet the Press," National Broadcasting Company, 4-20.*

## Lawrence Shepard
*Economist, University of California, Santa Barbara*     5

Fair-trade laws are anti-competitive, anti-social and only work against the consumer. Their benefits are far outweighed by the deficits, which include encouragements for higher prices.

*At fair-trade laws hearing, Los Angeles, Jan. 6/Los Angeles Herald-Examiner, 1-6:(A)2.*

**William E. Simon**
*Secretary of the Treasury of the*
*United States*

*1*

When we restore our prosperity, as we will, we must not sacrifice it again on the altar of big government. We can no longer afford the practice of living off our inheritance while mortgaging our future . . . One of my saddest experiences in public life is to see businessmen trooping into Washington day after day, hat in hand, seeking shelter from the storm under a government umbrella. Tariffs, subsidies, quotas, handouts, bailouts—I've seen them all, and none of them is worth its ultimate cost. They all lead to sacrificing our freedoms for a falsely perceived security.

*Before Commonwealth Club,*
*San Francisco, Feb. 28/*
*Los Angeles Times, 3-1:(1)4.*

*2*

There have been criticisms that floating [of monetary exchange rates] is chaotic, that it removes "discipline," that it has contributed to the most serious inflation in recent history, and more recently that it is impeding world trade. While I have heard the assertions, I have not seen the evidence. In fact, I believe the situation is almost entirely the reverse. Had the world attempted to maintain par values in the face of the dramatic upheavals of the last two years, we would have had chaos, crisis, trade and capital controls and a far more severe world inflation. Floating has prevented the export of inflation and has enabled some countries to sustain much lower rates of inflation than their neighbors.

*Before Congressional Subcommittees,*
*Washington, July 21/*
*The New York Times, 7-22:43.*

*3*

One of the saddest experiences of my public life has been to watch as some of our business leaders act perfectly contented when profits are rolling in, but the moment there's a cloud on the economic horizon, they come running to Washington looking for a subsidy.

*Before Houston Chamber of Commerce,*
*Dec. 11/The Washington Post, 12-13:(B)9.*

**Howard K. Smith**
*News commentator,*
*American Broadcasting Company*

*4*

The first third of the century, business ran things, electing politicians, passing its laws at will. Discredited in the Depression, business in the '30s had to accept laws making organized labor co-equal. In the second third, labor was able to elect politicians and pass its laws. In the final third, now, the consumer is knocking on the door. It began in the '60s as a grass-root movement with [consumerist] Ralph Nader as symbol. The bill [to create a consumer-advocacy agency inside the government] means it has become a tide that is forcing its way inside government itself. The present bill will wreak no miracles. But when the flood seeps—as it will with its growing force into wage and price negotiations, tax reform, all the things that share out the national pie—America will have a changed power structure. The special interests will be displaced by the public interest—for the consumer is all of us.

*ABC News commentary/*
*The Christian Science Monitor, 6-3:35.*

**James E. Smith**
*Comptroller of the Currency of the*
*United States*

*5*

. . . I would like to say this for the [banking] industry: We have been through a period where our economy grew at an abnormal and probably unhealthy rate. It ought to be no surprise that banks increased in size during that period. But at the same time we saw a near-collapse of the financial markets, sporadic performance from the commercial-paper market, and, to put it very bluntly, the only game in town to finance the economy's needs has been the commercial banking system. And I would say to some that, rather than damning the system, we ought to be grateful that it has been around to fulfill these financing requirements, or I dare say that the economy—which is in a dreadful state today—would be in an even-more-dreadful state.

*Interview, Washington/*
*U.S. News & World Report, 2-17:45.*

# WHAT THEY SAID IN 1975

## A. A. Sommer, Jr.
*Commissioner, Securities and Exchange*
*Commission of the United States*                    1

[On SEC efforts to have corporations disclose details of what some people feel have been questionable overseas payments, bribes, etc.]: At this moment there is reason to believe that substantial segments of American enterprises may be jeopardized by disclosure of the circumstances under which they have been established and maintained. Relentless requirement that any questionable payments be now disclosed in detail may result in impairment of the value of investment abroad, political upheavals and serious consequences for American enterprises ... In some instances, what we call bribery is not even illegal overseas. If, nonetheless, that is conduct Congress thinks American enterprises should not engage in, then it should so decree. [But] burdening disclosure, and the processes of the SEC with the responsibility of making these determinations ... is, in my estimation, the wrong way to proceed.
*At Wharton School, University*
*of Pennsylvania, June 24/*
*The Washington Post, 6-25:(D)7.*

## William I. Spencer
*President, Citicorp (First National*
*City Bank, New York)*                               2

The banking system today is in far better shape, contributes far more to society and is far sounder than it was in the green-eyeshade days that so many long for ... To suggest that banking, in the interest of serving the public adequately and safely, stuck to the practices of generations ago would be like insisting that aviation, for the sake of safety, stuck with the Ford Trimotor, or medicine, for the sake of health, reject every innovation since President Herbert Hoover.
*Before financial analysts, Denver, March 7/*
*The New York Times, 3-8:35.*

## Arthur R. Taylor
*President, CBS, Inc.*                                3

...many people in business, particularly senior executives, have worked their way up inside the corporate structure and within the business community, shielded to a great extent from public scrutiny and criticism ... Unlike politicians or public advocates, their professional skills usually tend to be directed inward, toward their companies, rather than outward toward the public. A middle-level corporation executive generally will not have to undergo the same rough-and-tumble give-and-take in the public arena, from people who do not understand how business works, that his or her counterpart in politics might have to. And when he or she gets to the top, and becomes a captain of industry, that isolation will be even further enforced by a protective staff.
*Before Financial Executives Institute,*
*New Orleans/*
*The Washington Post, 12-14:(F)7.*

## R. W. Taylor
*Vice president, Lockheed Aircraft*
*Corporation*                                         4

Mostly I believe in putting every individual under me in a position where he can do his best job. Aerospace is a complex business; you can have 20,000 people working on a single project. My role is to tell a guy the importance of what he's doing by showing him how one function fits into the whole. That improves performance, and that's how I've gotten results.
*Interview/Business Week, 10-6:60.*

## Preston Robert Tisch
*President, Loews Corporation*                        5

Twenty years ago we were bewitched by the concept of corporate "image." It was innocent enough in the beginning. It makes perfect sense to find out as accurately as possible what the public thinks about a company or a product, to respond to public priorities, to correct misconceptions, to present oneself to the public accurately. But then we began to perceive that image could be shaped [separately] from reality—that an image could be shaped independently of reality. A dozen years ago, a professional [political] campaign manager boasted that he could elect anyone to any public office given only a sufficient budget and a solemn pledge from the candidate to keep his mouth shut. Business began to concern itself not with how to present itself to the public most accurately, but whether to maintain a "high profile" or a "low profile." We began to think more about the impact of alternative synthetic images than with the authenticity of our image. And so we in business—whether we like it or not or whether we deserve it or not—find ourselves bracketed in the public consciousness with the politicians and planners who make decisions in secret, who shade the truth, who view public opinion as something to be managed and manipulated . . .

*Before Executives' Club, Chicago/*
*The Washington Post, 11-12:(A)26.*

## Lynn Townsend
*Chairman, Chrysler Corporation*

1

[On his recently announced decision to retire as chairman]: I can't remember a day or week when I wasn't making decisions that would have an impact on this entire company. I never remember a period of relaxation when I wasn't concerned with some element of business. I do believe we ask more of an individual than we should when we ask him to bear the brunt of these decisions for an extended period of time. Ten years is long enough for a chairman or president.

*Interview, Detroit/Time, 7-21:46.*

## Alexander B. Trowbridge
*President, The Conference Board*

2

In my opinion, bribery as a way of business life does not exist in this country. There are, there have been, and there probably always will be individual cases in which somebody takes what he thinks is the easy way out. When such people get caught and their acts are publicized, the public gets the impression that unethical practices are far more prevalent than is really the case . . . I know of many cases—and there have been some big and serious ones—in which individual judgments were made by people who came to regret them. But these instances simply underline the fact that paying bribes and passing big sums of money under the table just doesn't work. It doesn't work ethically, and it doesn't make sense from a business point of view, because once you get started you get

increasingly bogged down in quicksand. Today's contract or tomorrow's business deal, if you have to get it that way, will be more trouble than it's worth.

*Interview/U.S. News & World Report, 7-14:28.*

3

[On criticism of foreign investment in the U.S.]: For years we've gone around the world convincing countries that free entry of American private capital into their economies would be beneficial to those economies. I find it a little hard to see the tables turned and all of a sudden change our basic approach to the free flow of capital . . . The recent upsurge in foreign investment in this country is a mark of confidence in the U.S. economy as a place to invest for the long-term future. It hasn't been overwhelming in any sectors that we can identify. It's been sizable in some parts of the country and in some particular industries, but nowhere has the percentage of ownership reached a point at which alarm bells should go off. If we expect our capital and our economic investments to be welcomed overseas, we must be willing to accept foreign investment here at home.

*Interview/U.S. News & World Report, 7-14:30.*

## Rawleigh Warner, Jr.
*Chairman, Mobil Oil Corporation*

4

[Criticizing Congress for removing the percentage oil depletion allowance from most domestic oil production]: The problem is that on the one hand [Congress] professes to recognize the need for additional safe and secure oil in this country, but on the other hand has taken action that can only work against the achievement of that objective. Many in Congress still seem to feel that crippling the United States petroleum industry is somehow going to benefit the public.

*At Mobil shareholders meeting,*
*San Diego, Calif., May 1/*
*The New York Times, 5-2:48.*

## James H. Weaver
*United States Representative, D—Oregon*

5

[Saying a Federal export board should be established to supervise sale of U.S. grain

# WHAT THEY SAID IN 1975

*(JAMES H. WEAVER)*

abroad]: ... the U.S. is not getting the best possible price for its grain. Four years ago, wheat and oil were bringing about the same price in world markets. Today, oil costs three times as much as wheat. This allows the Russians, who are exporters of oil, to make a killing with high-priced oil, then come in and buy our wheat and other grain at prices that are cheap by comparison. We should make the Soviet Union pay as much for our grain as it gets for oil in export markets. The Russians are desperate for wheat and corn and other grains, and there is no place other than the U.S. for them to get it in the magnitude they need. The only way we can get a fair price from the Soviet Union is to let the [U.S.] government handle the sale as an exclusive bargaining agent.
*Interview/U.S. News & World Report, 9-15:17.*

**Murray L. Weidenbaum**
*Director, Center for the Study of American Business, Washington University; Former Assistant Secretary for Economic Policy, Department of the Treasury of the United States* 1

A massive expansion of government controls over private industry is clearly under way. Government officials are playing an ever-larger role in what traditionally has been internal business decision-making ... Because of the very substantial costs and other adverse side-effects that they give rise to, society should take a new and hard look at the existing array of government controls over business. A substantial effort should be made to eliminate those controls that generate excessive costs. Rather than blithely continuing to proliferate government controls over business, alternative means of achieving important national objectives should be explored and developed, solutions that expand rather than reduce the role of the market ...
*At American University, April 12/ The Washington Post, 4-13:(M)1,2.*

2

[On government regulation of business]: Unless you are an anarchist, you must believe that government should set the rules for society. The question is what kind of rules and how many. Economics has an answer for that. It says, carry regulation to the point where the added benefits barely exceed the added costs. That's where you stop. Over-regulation is where the added costs exceed the added benefits.
*Interview, St. Louis/Nation's Business, June:32.*

**Harold M. Williams**
*Dean, graduate school of management, University of California, Los Angeles* 3

American business ... is not perfect; we have false advertising and other unethical business practices. But these are not an inherent part of the system. There is a moral case against monopoly; there is a moral case against shady business practices. But there is no moral case against American business *per se* or against the free-market economy. Yet, that is not the impression in the minds and opinions of many Americans who make up the mood of America. To them, the level of immorality in American business is such that any degree of control or regulation is appropriate, if not required. They do not stop to consider its impact on the institution of American business or the free-market economy.
*At Bank of America meeting/ The National Observer, 6-14:7.*

**Harrison A. Williams, Jr.**
*United States Senator, D—New Jersey* 4

The revelation two weeks ago that Arab banks were using their immense economic power to try to force a boycott of Jewish banking interests was extremely sobering. [The reported boycott should] make us leery of claims that economic power will never be used to win political objectives. The dangers inherent in our traditional open-door policy toward foreign investment [in the U.S.] can no longer be ignored.
*Before National Investor Relations Institute, New York, Feb. 26/ The New York Times, 2-27:54.*

**F. Perry Wilson**
*Chairman, Union Carbide Corporation* 5

... profits are not something "left over" after everything else is taken out. Profits are the lifeblood of growth; without them, business cannot expand, renew or replace the job-creating equipment of our society.

*Interview/The Washington Post, 3-7:(A)9.*

1

The disclosure of bribes and other corrupt activities on the part of some corporations should not inspire efforts to dismantle the economic system in which those few organizations happen to function. From the largest multinational to the smallest retail shop, business men and women make difficult decisions prudently and ethically in the course of running a successful business. Those decisions go unheralded. The issues are not complicated. Essentially, business ethics comes down to a series of do's and don'ts that can be comprehended by anyone over the age of reason. It is wrong to suborn government officials through bribes and other illegal activities. It is doubly wrong when corporate funds are involved. This is so fundamental as to be obvious on the face of it. But it must be said, and said repeatedly, lest our silence be interpreted as tacit affirmation of the unethical and the illegal . . . If, despite management's moral leadership, an employee engages in illegal activity, there must be swift and severe discipline. It is important to demonstrate—both in word and deed—what the consequences will be for such activities. Punitive legislation is not the answer. The motivation to correct corporate abuses is commendable. But this effort should be directed toward the individuals involved and not the institutions to which they happen to belong. Ideally, swift and just corrective action should come from the organization itself.

*Before Commonwealth Club, San Francisco, Sept. 5/Vital Speeches, 10-1:758.*

**Evelle J. Younger**
*Attorney General of California*

2

[Arguing against fair-trade laws] : For years we have been in a schizophrenic position of prosecuting people for violating antitrust laws on the one hand and using the might and majesty of the state of California's government to protect fixed prices on the other. I think we should decide whether we believe in competition or not.

*Los Angeles Times, 4-18:(1)16.*

# Crime • Law Enforcement

**Ralph D. Abernathy**
*President, Southern Christian*
*Leadership Conference*
                                        1

[On revelations of FBI harassment of the late civil-rights leader, Martin Luther King]: I was not shocked. I have known all along the FBI was a powerful force in our government, spying on the personal private lives of individuals and doing everything in its power to destroy the Southern Christian Leadership Conference and to discredit Dr. Martin Luther King and the rest of the leadership . . . The only things I would suggest is for the government getting busy doing things it ought to do. That's eliminating poverty in this country and putting an end to the Mafia, which is at the root of the basis of crime, and go ahead and arrest the real criminals in this country, like [former U.S. President] Richard Milhous Nixon.
*Kansas City, Mo., Nov 19/*
*The Dallas Times Herald, 11-20:(A)10.*

**David Abrahamsen**
*Psychoanalyst*
                                        2

The American dream is, in part, responsible for a great deal of crime and violence. People feel that America owes them not only a living but a good living, and they take short-cuts to get what they feel is owing to them. Frustration is the wet-nurse of violence.
*San Francisco Examiner & Chronicle,*
*5-18:(This World)2.*

**Anthony Amsterdam**
*Professor of law,*
*Stanford University*
                                        3

The ultimate lesson of capital punishment is that human life ceases to be sacred whenever there is some pragmatic reason to take it away. No lesson could be more corrosive, more destructive of the worth of human beings, more likely to treat man as simply an instrument and creature of the state than is the notion that, in order to discourage others, his life may be taken.
*Quote, 3-16:243.*

**Birch Bayh**
*United States Senator,*
*D—Indiana*
                                        4

That part of our population under 22 years old accounts for 61 per cent of the total arrests, while those 25 and under account for a staggering 75 per cent of the total number of people arrested annually for serious offenses . . . The evidence is overwhelming that the system fails at the critical point when a youngster first gets into trouble. The juvenile who takes a car for a joy ride or is consistently truant, or runs away, or views shoplifting as a lark, is confronted by a system of justice often completely incapable of dealing with him in a constructive manner.
*At National Conference of Democratic Mayors,*
*Atlanta, March 1/San Francisco*
*Examiner & Chronicle, 3-2:(A)13.*
                                        5

The rising tide of serious crime inevitably raises the question of whether we are properly allocating our crime-fighting resources by aggressively pursuing the arrest and criminal prosecution of the 13 million American users of marijuana . . . Available studies and research to date have found that the majority of those arrested [for possession] are otherwise law-abiding young people in possession of small amounts of marijuana.
*Washington, May 13/*
*The Dallas Times Herald, 5-14:(A)13.*

**Abraham D. Beame**
*Mayor of New York*
                                        6

The state of the national economy is probably the chief factor in the increase in crime,

58

not only in New York City but throughout the country. The acute inflation-recession resulted in a rise in the cost of living and a decline in employment and production. Unemployment, rising prices and salary lags created needs among those segments of the population most adversely affected by the state of the national economy; and those needs apparently are being satisfied by an increase in such crimes as robberies and larcenies.

*Interview/U.S. News & World Report, 4-7:32.*

**Joseph R. Biden, Jr.**
*United States Senator, D—Delaware*

1

They [liberals] talk about law and order with justice. Now, what the devil does that mean to a man whose wife has been assaulted or his store robbed? It is mindless talk. Crime is crime and punishment follows the crime. But the liberals are afraid of offending the ADA or whatever.

*Addressing Pennsylvania Democrats/
Los Angeles Times, 10-27:(1)18.*

**Jonathan B. Bingham**
*United States Representative,
D—New York*

2

[Saying the manufacture of handguns should be banned]: I think we are literally out of our minds to allow 2.5 million new weapons to be manufactured every year for the sole purpose of killing people.

*Before House Judiciary Subcommittee,
Washington/The New York Times, 2-21:28.*

**Charles L. Black, Jr.**
*Professor of law, Yale University*

3

[Arguing against capital punishment]: I really think that a lot of very sincere people confronted with a breakdown of authority on many levels vainly seek assurance in the retention of this power. Yet most of the people who commit crimes that incite the reaction in favor of capital punishment are crazy. If you can say that a man like [convicted murderer] Charles Manson is sane, then what the hell does sane mean? Furthermore, no one who is affluent gets the chair any more. The reason is not

corruption. It is simply that if you have the resources to get a case looked into, you turn out not to deserve to be put to death. In other words, the affluent person can get proper presentation of his case ... When the state puts a man to death, it signals disrespect for human life that has its effect everywhere. It is a chilling act. No normal person would be capable of holding someone in a cell, filling him with fear, and finally leading him into a room and killing him.

*Interview, Yale University/
Los Angeles Times, 1-16:(2)5.*

**Otis R. Bowen**
*Governor of Indiana (R)*

4

[Supporting capital punishment]: My profession [physician] is dedicated to saving life, and I abhor the thought of taking a life. But I abhor senseless killings by people who have no respect for the lives of others. I have great sympathy for the victims and relatives of victims.

*The Dallas Times Herald, 6-4:(E)7.*

**Tom Bradley**
*Mayor of Los Angeles*

5

I'm convinced that if we are really serious about controlling violent crime, if we are really serious about controlling the destructive delinquency in our schools, then we must insist on controlling firearms. Government already controls such dangerous firearms as machine-guns and flame-throwers, and now we should add handguns to the list ... The political climate, indeed, is warming up for aggressive Federal action to remove the violence of the handgun from society. But I should note that we elected representatives will probably be faced with a backlash from some one-issue gun supporters at the polls. A powerful, well-financed gun lobby has done well in confusing and scaring the public with emotion-packed cries of alarm. As a matter of fact, it's estimated that the gun lobby can generate up to a half-million letters to Congress on nearly a moment's notice.

*At National Conference of Mayors National
Forum on Handgun Control, Los Angeles,
May 28/Los Angeles Times, 5-29:(2)1.*

59

# WHAT THEY SAID IN 1975

**Alvin J. Bronstein**
*Executive director, national prison project,
American Civil Liberties Union*
1

The prime concern of correction officials is control and security, and naturally so. Prisons are dangerous, violent places. Everything the officials do in the way of attempted rehabilitation is matched against the standard of: Will it interfere with control and security? Our prisons are totally unsuited to rehabilitation. With prisoners isolated from families and communities, from the possibility of meaningful work, from normal sexual needs, they are in an environment which is inherently unsuitable. The only way prisons can exist is to coerce order so as to avoid anarchy. It is not possible in that sort of milieu to have a rehabilitative environment . . . Let people who break the law make restitution to society in work that helps the community. John Mitchell, for example. He was convicted in the Watergate trial. It would be ridiculous to send Mitchell to jail. He's a good lawyer. Let him do legal work for the poor. He could help them with their divorce cases, their landlord-tenant disputes, their credit problems, and so on. So that he would not become a public charge himself, he should be paid a minimum wage of $2.50 or $3.50 an hour. That makes much more sense than sending a man to jail.
*Interview, Washington/
Los Angeles Times, 2-4:(2)5.*

**Edmund G. Brown, Jr.**
*Governor of California (D)*
2

I think the people who break the law should be punished. It should be swift and sure . . . The idea that crime is a disease—to be cured by sitting around in groups and talking about your parents—I don't agree with that. I think you have to have rules and apply them, whether it's the President or a pickpocket.
*Before California State Democratic Central
Committee, Sacramento, Jan. 25/
Human Events, 2-8:4.*

**Thomas E. Bryant**
*President, Drug Abuse Council*
3

[Saying he favors decriminalization of marijuana]: Alcohol is by far and away our nation's Number 1 public health drug problem in terms of wrecked lives, violence, traffic fatalities, untold misery to family and friends. Cigarette smoking is injurious to human lungs, hearts, circulatory systems and respiratory systems. But we do not jail those who smoke. Again, we do not associate potential health hazard with criminality.
*Before California State Senate Judiciary
Committee, Sacramento, Feb. 11/
Los Angeles Times, 2-12:(1)25.*
4

All of our law-enforcement efforts are aimed at keeping drugs away from people, and our greatest failing is that we keep ignoring the fact that more and more people want them. We've got to try to better understand why psychoactive drugs are being taken so widely and indiscriminately, and to do something about the underlying social causes: the rejection of traditional values, disillusionment, feelings of alienation, and peer pressure. One thing that's become clear is that even an army of narcotics agents won't prevent the addict from getting his fix.
*The National Observer, 6-21:6.*

**Warren E. Burger**
*Chief Justice of the United States*
5

Speedy trials—and widespread awareness of the certainty of speedy trials with reasonably predictable finality—would be one of the most forceful deterrents to criminal conduct.
*Interview/U.S. News & World Report, 3-31:31.*

**Joseph P. Busch**
*District Attorney,
Los Angeles County, California*
6

Juvenile crime has risen because youthful offenders know they will not be punished. They'll be back on the streets bragging about how nothing is happening to them. We're talking about murder and rape, not hubcap stealing.
*The New York Times, 2-21:37.*

**Don A. Byrd**
*Chief of Police of Dallas*
7

[On who is to blame for the rising crime rate]: The schools, the families, the churches.

Law-enforcement agencies are established to treat only a small segment of the problem. You can't do it with an omnipresence of police. We as parents don't set a very good example in relation to voluntary compliance with the law—driving 70 miles an hour in a 55 zone. We don't set a very good example when a kid steals a car and gets two years probated, but a businessman steals $5-million and doesn't get anything. The kids don't understand; they ask where's the justice? If our society doesn't regroup in that regard, I don't know where we're headed.

*Interview, Dallas/*
*The Dallas Times Herald, 6-8:(A)26.*

**Gerald M. Caplan**
*Director, National Institute for Law*
*Enforcement and Criminal Justice, Law*
*Enforcement Assistance Administration*
*of the United States*

*1*

Today, virtually no one—scholars, practitioners and politicians alike—dares to advance a program which promises to reduce crime substantially in the near future. Although important and tangible progress in improving criminal justice has been made, it has not produced relief from high crime rates. In fact, a more candid assessment is that things are worse than ever . . . First, we have more crime [in the U.S.] than any place in the world; more this year than last, and much, much more than we had in 1964. Last year, reported crimes rose by 18 per cent, the largest increase since the FBI began collecting statistics almost a half-century ago. Second, most of the increase occurred in the midst of high employment and unprecedented affluence and during a period when the Federal government launched a new multi-million-dollar anti-crime program. Third, despite the persistent, often clarion, calls for "law and order," no significant strengthening of the punitive or deterrent features of the criminal-justice system took place during the past decade. And fourth, efforts to understand better the underlying causes of crime have progressed little. Even among serious observers, the attachment to particular explanations has been promiscuous, one theory yielding to another in quick succession.

*At Town House Forum, Los Angeles, Dec. 9/*
*Los Angeles Times, 12-10:(1)3.*

**Hugh L. Carey**
*Governor of New York (D)*

*2*

Crime may once have been far away from many of us. Perhaps some of us once held the desperate delusion that the poison which wastes the children of Harlem would not sooner or later come round into our own. That day is over. We should act against crime if only for the sake of the poor who are its pre-eminent victims. We must act against it for the sake of every man and woman and child among us.

*State of the State address, Albany, Jan. 8/*
*The New York Times, 1-9:30.*

*3*

We can no longer simply say crime is a product of poverty, unemployment, drug addiction, a permissive society or the failure of our system of criminal justice. All this may be true but it does not excuse our responsibility to protect our people from the damage and destruction of violent crime.

*Before Brooklyn Bar Association, New York,*
*Dec. 9/The New York Times, 12-10:31.*

**Norman A. Carlson**
*Director, Federal Bureau of Prisons*

*4*

The plain truth of the matter is we do not know how to treat crime. We can cure tuberculosis; psychiatrists and psychologists can effectively treat paranoia and schizophrenia; but nobody really knows how to treat an offender for assault, robbery and murder. What we call treatment programs for offenders in our institutions today are in reality programs of education, vocational training, counseling and work. There is certainly nothing wrong with these programs. They are in fact programs that are vitally needed; most inmates are poor and lack educational and work skills. But there is no way we can assure that these programs will cure a man or woman of crime. Corrections is an art, not a science. Until the behavioral sciences can give us clues as to what motivates the criminal offender, we cannot assure rehabilitation. All we can do is offer offenders the opportunity to rehabilitate themselves . . . Corrections today is striving for a balanced mission, one that recog-

# WHAT THEY SAID IN 1975

*(NORMAN A. CARLSON)*

nizes that punishment, deterrence and rehabilitation are all valid reasons for incarceration . . .
*The Washington Post, 12-23:(A)10.*

**Harlon B. Carter**
*Director, Institute for Legislative Action;*
*Former president,*
*National Rifle Association*     *1*

[Arguing against gun control]: Gun control imposes restraints and regulations on the ordinary folks along the creeks and hollows of the country . . . These are decent, good people. When Congress talks about gun control, it is stepping on the feet of good, law-abiding citizens, and they're ready to fight about it.
*Interview/The Washington Post, 9-28:(B)2.*

**Frank Church**
*United States Senator, D–Idaho*     *2*

The two [recent] attempts on President Ford's life should remind us once again that violence lurks at every corner, hides in every crowd and haunts every neighborhood. Violence is the most ubiquitous symptom of a disease spreading through our society—an epidemic of lawlessness which, unless checked in time, could prove fatal to democracy itself.
*Before Commonwealth Club, San Francisco/*
*San Francisco Examiner & Chronicle,*
*10-5:(A)17.*

**Harlan Cleveland**
*Director, Program in International*
*Affairs, Aspen Institute; Former*
*president, University of Hawaii*     *3*

There isn't anything we don't know about criminals—their social origins, their economic motives, their techniques, their political affiliations, their mutual education in prison, their very high rates of recidivism. We just don't seem to know how to deter them, rehabilitate them, or prevent their numbers from growing.
*At joint meeting of American Assembly*
*and American Bar Association, Palo Alto,*
*Calif./The National Observer, 8-16:18.*

**John Conyers, Jr.**
*United States Representative, D–Michigan*     *4*

[Saying that public opinion is growing in favor of gun control]: It's coming together. People are going to get angrier and angrier. Every time there's a gun incident or a gun death, more and more people are converting to our side. Owning a gun is no longer good sense.
*The Washington Post, 9-28:(B)2.*

**Edward M. Davis**
*Chief of Police of Los Angeles*     *5*

[Calling for revision of the juvenile-justice system]: . . . the machinery must be changed with the protection of society in mind, and not the protection of a particular juvenile. There are too many people with a Father Flanagan philosophy that there is no such thing as a bad boy. There are plenty of bad boys.
*Los Angeles Herald-Examiner, 2-27:(B)1.*

*6*

I believe that the nature of man is relatively immutable; that from one decade to another, even from one century to another, there's murder and robbery and people who break into homes. What has happened to generate the great increase in crime isn't necessarily a higher percentage of dangerous anti-social people in society; it's a change in the way society has handled those dangerous persons. And so the police, in effect, feel like the little boy trying to empty the ocean with a sand bucket. As we pour the water up on the sand it runs right back into the ocean. We're recycling very dangerous criminals over and over again.
*Interview/Human Events, 3-22:8.*

*7*

I believe in [capital punishment] very firmly, but I don't believe in it for the reasons that a lot of other people do. I don't necessarily stress its value as a deterrent. I don't think you shoot a mad dog to make an example to other dogs. You shoot a mad dog to keep him from biting additional people. And we have in this city records of 13 murders that were committed by paroled murderers. Once a person has purposely killed another human being, I think he has forfeited his own right to live.
*Interview/Human Events, 3-22:10.*

1

[Saying citizens should arm themselves for protection]: At no time in history anywhere has there ever been a police department that has been able to combat crime before it occurs; the cost of it would be prohibitive. And so every person, every family, every home should do an optimum amount of self-protection. And ... we have a right under the Second Amendment ... to keep and bear arms. You have a right to possess in your home and in your business a rifle, a pistol; and King George can't take it away from you, or Uncle Sam either.

*Interview/The Dallas Times Herald, 7-13:(A)15.*

2

"Victimless crime" is generally considered to be narcotics, gambling and prostitution, and I have about 6 per cent of my force assigned to that so-called victimless-crime area. But Number 1, I don't think there is such a thing as a victimless crime. The victim is every user of narcotics. The residue of THC in the human brain from marijuana is an established medical fact. The plight of the young girl who gets taken in by a pimp and made into a whore and is put on dope and put into slavery is well-known to any thinking person. The lifeblood of organized crime is gambling, and although I have no moral scruples about a couple of fellows making a wager, the fact of the matter is that organized crime thrives on illicit income from gambling.

*Interview/The National Observer, 7-19:14.*

3

... swinging mothers who decide to go their sexual way are going to produce a batch of criminals that is going to be unparalleled in the history of this country. I think that the Number 1 emphasis, the Number 1 solution to crime is the proper kind of a home culture. After that, it is the proper kind of a school culture. After that, it gets into the hands of the criminal-justice system. By that time, they are pretty hardened and there is little anyone can do. ... at that point, we are dealing with very hard criminals, and I think that the whole system has to be toughened up appreciably. But

mainly the emphasis has to be on a return to some kind of morality in America.

*TV-radio interview, Washington/*
*"Meet the Press," National*
*Broadcasting Company, 8-10.*

**Robert J. diGrazia**
*Police Commissioner of Boston*

4

We have to face up. The people must understand what we can do as a police department. We deliver a wide range of services which include crime control and attempted crime control, and we are also trying to improve the organization while we are doing it. But I think we suffer because of the vast misconception by the public of what our role really is as police officers and as a police department. . . . it is not just police who are going to eliminate the criminal problem. We have to look at what are the root causes. Is it unemployment? Is it because of a ghetto situation? Is it because of mental-health problems? Whatever. Just don't leave it simply to the police.

*TV-radio interview, Washington/*
*"Meet the Press," National*
*Broadcasting Company, 8-10.*

5

It is my view that [the] law must banish private handguns from this country. I am not asking for registration or licensing or outlawing cheap "Saturday night specials." I am saying that no private citizen, whatever his claim, should possess a handgun. Only police officers and military should.

*Before Senate Committee on Government*
*Operations, Washington, Oct. 8/*
*The New York Times, 10-9:18.*

**Reginald Eaves**
*Public Safety Commissioner of Atlanta*

6

If we caught everybody who committed all today's crime, a new generation of criminals would emerge tomorrow because they are growing up today in the soil of inequity, frustration and despair.

*At Democratic Party meeting on crime,*
*Atlanta/The New York Times, 3-3:18.*

# WHAT THEY SAID IN 1975

**Jiro Enomoto**
*California State Director of Corrections*   1

We shouldn't kid ourselves. Prisons are poor places to put people. I think we lock people up because we don't know what else to do with them.

*San Francisco Examiner & Chronicle, 2-23:(This World)2.*

**Gerald R. Ford**
*President of the United States*   2

Crime in high places—whether in the Federal government, state government, local governments, or in business and organized labor—sets an example that makes it all the more difficult to foster a law-abiding spirit among ordinary citizens... We have seen how law-breaking by [government] officials can be stopped by the proper functioning of our basic institutions—Executive, Legislative and Judicial Branches. But America has been far from successful in dealing with the sort of crime that obsesses America. I mean street crime, crime that invades our neighborhoods and our homes—murders, robberies, rapes, muggings, holdups, break-ins—the kind of brutal violence that makes us fearful of strangers and afraid to go out at night.

*At Yale University Law School convocation dinner, April 25/ Los Angeles Times, 4-26:(1)15.*

**Frederick Hacker**
*Professor of psychiatry and law, University of Southern California*   3

There have been an increasing criminalization of politics and a politization of criminals. It's reached the point where there are no criminals in San Quentin any more. They're all "freedom fighters."

*Time, 6-30:17.*

**Louis Harris**
*Public-opinion analyst*   4

[Saying the majority of Americans favor gun controls]: [Political] candidates will be beaten who will stand up and say that gun-control legislation is wrong... The results [of public-opinion research] are decisive and beyond any question of whether the American people favor gun control. The answer, decisively and firmly, is that they do. They do not see gun control as a cure-all to violence in this country. They do not see violence being stemmed easily or quickly. But what they are saying... is this: "We want Federal control of guns quickly and decisively."

*Before Senate Government Operations Committee, Washington, Oct. 24/ Los Angeles Times, 10-25:(1)1,8.*

**Philip A. Hart**
*United States Senator, D—Michigan*   5

[Calling for a lessening in criminal penalties for marijuana possession]: One of my children is one of these statistics you have here. He's a minor and he's been 20 days in jail for a stub that big; and that's all the education I needed to convince me we are topsy-turvy on this.

*Before Senate Subcommittee, Washington, May 14/The Washington Post, 5-15:(D)14.*

**Clarence M. Kelley**
*Director, Federal Bureau of Investigation*   6

There is growing sentiment among lawmen that the victims of crime are being ignored in the stampede to reinforce [criminals'] civil rights. Shouldn't someone pause to consider the victim of the criminal whose rights we so vigorously exalt? Most certainly. For they are multitudes, these victims—nameless and faceless multitudes. And we can only surmise their grief. Their wounds are too numerous to count, their losses too vast to enumerate... It would be splendid if law enforcement could consist only of honoring and rewarding those who abide by the law, but obviously this is impractical. So we in law enforcement must take the next best approach. In behalf of the victim, in behalf of society, we must seek out and apprehend the criminal violator so that he may be prosecuted, rehabilitated if possible, or separated from society.

*Before Salvation Army Citizens' Advisory Board, Kansas City, Jan. 30/ U.S. News & World Report, 2-24:43.*

1

I am an advocate of the removal of the so-called "Saturday night special" [handgun]. I realize that laws to restrict the use of the "Saturday night special" would be difficult to formulate. Whatever is necessary, however, to stem the tide of these killings of our citizens and our police by these cheap guns should be seriously considered and something done about it . . . It's a community problem and the community should attack it. When you have the great loss of fine officers throughout the country through the handgun predominantly—and the cheap handgun predominantly among them—it's a very fearful situation . . . My answer to you is "Yes," I do support some type of a control and am willing to settle at this point for the banishment from our society of the cheap so-called "Saturday night special."

*News conference, Dallas/*
*The Dallas Times Herald, 2-16:(B)1.*

2

[On Congressional supervision of the FBI] : I would welcome, as a matter of fact, strong oversight. I mentioned this during my confirmation hearings and still feel that it's a good idea to report to Congress from time to time. I just hope that within the process there is not any diminution of our capabilities. I do recognize that you can possibly—by virtue of an absence of oversight—go a little bit beyond what propriety might dictate. I believe that the very strong part of the FBI's work should be the protection of the rights of our citizens and the right to privacy. There's a balance that must be established, just as in the process of making an arrest there is conceivably an invasion of privacy.

*News conference, Dallas/*
*The Dallas Times Herald, 2-16:(B)1.*

3

[Defending FBI surveillance of radical groups] : To ignore the extremists' threats would be to gamble recklessly with the lives and freedoms of the citizens we serve. We will not do that as long as domestic security responsibility is vested in the FBI. It is absolutely imperative that we gather sufficient information and evidence to permit reliable evaluations of these groups' aims

and methods . . . We dare not speculate as to whether they really mean it or whether it is mere rhetoric when militant groups threaten to bomb and destroy public and industrial facilities.

*Before Veterans of Foreign Wars, March 10/*
*The Washington Post, 3-11:(A)7.*

4

You—the American people—must resist deterioration of morals, discipline, family ties and religious conviction—those traditional forces for lawful and honorable behavior. You must remonstrate against lax prosecution of criminals, understaffed prosecutors' offices and sluggish judicial process. [Americans should resist] the poorly trained and ineptly led police agency, if it exists; corruption in law enforcement, in the courts and in political office—corruption that makes a mockery of our heritage of government by laws; judicial and correctional trends that provide more rights and freedoms to criminals than their victims; bail and sentencing policies that have led to a situation in which each year about two-thirds of persons arrested in the United States for criminal acts are repeaters . . . Obviously, something is lacking. And that something, I believe, is a resolute commitment by the American people to resist crime.

*Before Tobacco Institute,*
*White Sulphur Springs, W. Va.,*
*May 20/Los Angeles Times, 5-21:(1)7.*

5

[On criticism of wiretapping, domestic surveillance, etc., by the FBI and other law-enforcement agencies] : We must be willing to surrender a small measure of our liberties to preserve the great bulk of them. If we do not—if investigative agencies charged with national-security responsibilities are so fettered as to be ineffective—then we shall surely finish last in the world arena.

*Before American Judicature Society and*
*National Conference of Bar Presidents,*
*Montreal, Aug. 9/*
*The Dallas Times Herald, 8-10:(A)22.*

6

[Rules governing criminal investigations] cannot be transferred in toto and applied to our

# WHAT THEY SAID IN 1975

*(CLARENCE M. KELLEY)*

national-security efforts. If an individual's rights are violated by a law-enforcement officer, remedies are available. But there is no appeal, there is no such remedy, for a terrorist's bomb . . . They say we [the FBI] should present ourselves as sterling examples of people who know no limits in the recognition of human rights. I agree that this is commendable philosophy, but what if [foreign nations] ignore our noble gesture? What if one of their top priorities is the destruction of our democracy?

*Before American Judicature Society and National Conference of Bar Presidents, Montreal, Aug. 9/ The Washington Post, 8-10:(A)7.*

1

Impartial inquiry and evaluation of national security are considerably different from the relentless bombardment we [the FBI] have been subjected to in the public forum for so many months. The danger is that excessive restraints crippling to our domestic security efforts could be imposed on us . . . We are concerned that the highly publicized scrutiny and criticism of our domestic intelligence operations in recent months will undermine the trust Americans traditionally have placed in the FBI. We must continue to have that trust if we are to function effectively in the future . . . Perhaps our operations will derive benefit from the unprecedented surge of news-media and official interest in the FBI. But we must fervently hope that domestic extremists and foreign agents committed to the destruction of our democracy will not be the ultimate beneficiaries.

*Before Lubbock (Tex.) Chamber of Commerce, Nov. 4/ Los Angeles Times, 11-5:(1)6.*

2

The fanaticism of many . . . urban guerrillas and revolutionaries makes intelligence penetration difficult . . . Many terrorists are expert in the use of false identification and are able to melt into a whole subculture of communes that extends across the nation. [The most difficult part of the problem to understand is] the approbation of terrorist activity by otherwise law-abiding citizens, given apparently because of the so-called idealism of the terrorist. How does today's terrorism differ from the murderous Ku Klux Klan violence of a decade ago? While the motives of the terrorists may differ, motive is of no moment to a murder victim. Decent Americans were outraged over Klan bombings, beatings and killings. Where is that outrage today?

*Before Senate Internal Security Subcommittee, Washington, Nov. 19/ Los Angeles Herald-Examiner, 11-19:(A)1.*

**John Killackey**
*Deputy Police Superintendent of Chicago*

3

The largest group of lawbreakers in Chicago is between the ages of 15 and 20, and the next-largest group is between 10 and 15 . . . If you ask a young person today whether he knows it is a sin to kill somebody, he is likely to ask you, "What is sin?" Boys and girls don't go to church any more, and more and more of them are living in broken homes. Add to this the fact that they are subjected to a steady diet of stabbing, maiming, strangling, shooting, burning and boiling on television and in movies and you can see why young people are not likely to care or know about law and order.

*U.S. News & World Report, 4-7:32.*

**Richard F. Kneip**
*Governor of South Dakota (D)*

4

Through imposition of the mandatory death penalty, we sanction and establish an act as barbaric and oftentimes more premeditated than that which we supposedly refuse to tolerate. I don't believe the death penalty is a deterrent to murder.

*The Dallas Times Herald, 6-4:(E)7.*

**Edward I. Koch**
*United States Representative, D–New York*

5

Corruption appears to be pervasive in our society. I am thinking not simply of the public officeholder who betrays his trust . . . What also troubles me is the corruption of our ordinary citizens. I am thinking of children who learn from their parents to cheat the storekeeper, the telephone company and the government. I am thinking of corporations who in turn cheat the consumer, bribe officials and do not level with their stockholders. We see evidence of this corruption daily in the sale of shoddy merchandise, tax fraud performed openly and without remorse, Medicaid charged for services not rendered, the elderly ripped off by nursing home operators, just to cite a few examples. . . . we ought to consider corruption in the same class as that of a physical assault upon an individual . . . I am equally persuaded that the white-collar criminal, the corruptor, will be deterred and reformed if he or she serves just 30 days behind bars . . .

*Before the House, Washington, July 28/*
*Parade, 9-7:8.*

## Edward H. Levi
*Attorney General of the United States*

1

Many of the objections to gun control . . . simply do not reflect the conditions of modern urban life. They are based on an American style of living that no longer exists in the places where people have congregated to live. And while it is easy to sympathize with those who want handguns to protect themselves from others who have handguns, it is obvious that they contribute to the unacceptable proliferation of handguns in the cities.

*At Law Enforcement Executives Narcotics*
*Conference, Washington, April 6/*
*The Washington Post, 4-7:(A)1.*

2

One of the problems about crime in the United States is that people who commit crime are so seldom caught. But if they are caught, they are so seldom tried. And if they are tried, they are so seldom punished.

*Televised discussion with Georgetown Law*
*Center graduates, Washington/*
*Los Angeles Times, 6-15:(1)1.*

3

If society makes up its mind to have the death penalty and to enforce it with proper speed, it can be effective—and I do favor it for a limited number of crimes. I do not favor it if

our society cannot come to terms with this question. We are so conflicted about it that instead of having a death penalty, we have people sitting in a penitentiary for 10 years while we debate whether or not they should be executed. That's not a death penalty. That's something else. We need to debate the question, and society ought to try to make up its mind on it. We haven't been doing that.

*Interview, Washington/*
*U.S. News & World Report, 6-30:30.*

4

The most frequent phrase I hear when I talk to young lawyers is: "Isn't it true that criminal-law enforcement is very unfair because it's so kind to the rich and so tough to the poor?" In some sense the opposite is true. But we have many communities which feel that crimes of violence are committed by the poor, and therefore it's unfair to stop this kind of thing because Watergate occurred, or some banker only went to the penitentiary for two years and they think he should have gone for five. I find this a fantastic kind of thought, but it's part of the community reaction to our problem. And it is especially thoughtless in regard to the inner city, because the chief victims of violent crime are people in the inner city. It's as though we were depriving them of one of the necessities of life, namely, protection. We're all paying for that now. So the main thing really—it sounds like not much but it's everything—is to change the attitude of the American people, this kind of strange tolerance of crime.

*Interview, Washington/*
*U.S. News & World Report, 6-30:32.*

5

The need for mandatory minimum sentences is based upon the concept of deterrence. If the criminal law is to deter potential criminal offenders from committing crime, there must be some assurance that a meaningful punishment will follow a conviction. The length of the prison sentence need not be great, although undoubtedly in some cases it should be. What is important is that the imposition of prison sentences be quick and certain. This is not true today. A study in Pittsburgh in 1966 indicated that nearly half of all persons convicted of a

# WHAT THEY SAID IN 1975

## (EDWARD H. LEVI)

second offense of aggravated assault and more than one-fourth of all second offenders convicted of robbery were not sent to prison but were rather placed on probation. Research in Wisconsin showed that 63 per cent of all second-time felony offenders and 41 per cent of all persons with two or more felony convictions received no prison term upon the last conviction. James Q. Wilson of Harvard concluded that this evidence "suggests that the judges did not believe jail had a deterrent effect . . ." But at least one reason the judges may not have perceived the deterrent effect of imprisonment is that they have not, as a group, imposed prison sentences with a great enough frequency. Deterrence will not work when the chance of effective punishment is minimal. That is where we are today.

*Before International Association of Chiefs of Police, Denver, Sept. 16/ The National Observer, 10-4:13.*

*1*

[Criticizing the IRS' cutback in cooperation with government crime-fighting agencies]: I understand the argument that you should not misuse IRS tax returns, that you should not misuse the agency to look for crimes that have nothing to do with tax frauds. I don't think that's the problem. I think that in these cases [organized crime, official corruption or narcotics] there's almost always an important ingredient of a tax situation. [In such investigations,] I don't see any reason why the IRS agents shouldn't be used.

*Interview, Washington, Nov. 26/ Los Angeles Times, 11-27:(1)12.*

## Donald T. Lunde
*Psychiatrist, Stanford University*

*2*

In a mere 10 years since 1965 the murder rate has more than doubled and now is the highest in history. Some time this year the murder rate will exceed suicide. That's never happened before in this country . . . People were led to believe the government and society would and could take care of them with jobs, education and a better life. [Now] they're find-ing out the government can't deliver on its promises. The degree of frustration a person feels is far greater when reality is very different from his expectations. All the rhetoric about more police, tougher judges and stiffer penalties is not going to have any effect at all on these people or on the murder rate. Murderers are not a homogeneous group of "bad guys." For the most part, they're husbands, wives, lovers, neighbors, friends and acquaintances. Almost a third of all victims are related to their killers . . . If the economy remains stagnant—and I believe it will for several years—the murder rate will continue to climb.

*Stanford, Calif./ Los Angeles Herald-Examiner, 8-21:(A)6.*

## Henry W. Maier
*Mayor of Milwaukee*

*3*

The one fact that comes through loud and clear is that we will never be able to control crime until we get at its root causes. The incumbent Republican Administration is giving the Joint Chiefs of Staff at the Pentagon all the money they need for the military defense of this nation when what we really need is a joint chiefs of staff and budget for the social defense of America.

*At Democratic Party meeting on crime, Atlanta/The New York Times, 3-3:18.*

## Robert Martinson
*Sociologist; Authority on prisons*

*4*

We have to give up the idea that you can make use of the cage to help the person being punished. What we need is swift, sure, just justice—a system with milder but more certain punishments for more of us.

*Newsweek, 2-10:36.*

## Brooks McClure
*Special Assistant, Directorate of International Security Affairs, Department of Defense of the United States*

*5*

The techniques of police intelligence—penetration of suspicious groups, dossier-keeping, cultivation of informers, undercover activities in general—disturb the average citizen. These are seen as underhanded methods, and there is frequently concern—sometimes justified by events—that they will be misused. The whole **aura** of "secret police" is disagreeable. Yet the problem of terrorism is essentially one of counterintelligence—of frustrating and neutralizing plans and breaking up secret conspiracies by small groups of people seeking to destroy the state. The penalty of failure is death to innocent people, destruction of property and intimidation of the public in a continuous upward spiral. Furthermore, there is a long lead-time in police intelligence before it can work effectively. Waiting until the terrorists are fully organized and trained before taking counter-intelligence measures means sometimes years of suffering before there is any chance of bringing them under control.

*Before Senate Internal Security*
*Subcommittee, Washington, July 25/*
*The New York Times, 11-9:(1)35.*

### Joseph D. McNamara
*Chief of Police of Kansas City, Mo.*

1

I think we need some kind of control over the manufacture and distribution of handguns. I think in addition to that we need to be quite honest with the public and with critics of that approach to admit that it will be a long-range solution. Overnight we will not be able to get out of circulation the alarming number of hand-guns that we have. I would like to see, in addition to some kind of control over the manufacture of handguns, very strong mandatory sentences for those who use handguns or any firearm during the commission of a crime.

*TV-radio interview, Washington/*
*"Meet the Press," National*
*Broadcasting Company, 8-10.*

### Robert M. Morgenthau
*District Attorney,*
*New York County, New York*

2

Abuses of government power in the White House and in other agencies of government, both national and local, in recent times inevitably support a feeling that something must be done to protect the people from uncontrolled police power. There is, however, a danger that such well-justified feelings and frustrations will give rise to over-emotional responses in the

form of harmful legislation which will paralyze the ability of the police to perform their proper functions in protecting citizens against crime.

*Before New York City Council Public*
*Safety Committee, Sept. 29/*
*The New York Times, 9-30:29.*

### Gerhard Mueller
*Director, United Nations Committee on*
*Crime Prevention and Control*

3

Female criminality in all categories is rising between three and five times as fast as male criminality. [In the U.S.,] robberies by females were up 300 per cent in the last five years, compared to a rise of 20 per cent in robberies by males. Homicides by women doubled or tripled compared to those by males . . . Indeed, there is no reason to believe that women are any more honest than men. When they become bank presidents they are just as prone to commit embezzlement as men who have been in those positions . . . I should emphasize that female crime ranks lower by far than male criminality, but the ladies are beginning to catch up . . . As they are immersed into more progressive life-styles, they adopt the same anti-social responses as males.

*News conference, United Nations, New York,*
*May 13/The Dallas Times Herald, 5-16:(F)3.*

### John M. Murphy
*United States Representative, D—New York*

4

[Waving a "Saturday night special" while testifying on the easy availability of these hand-guns]: If I were an advocate of gun possession— say, perhaps, a Sara Moore, Lynette Fromme, a Lee Oswald, Sirhan Sirhan, Jack Ruby or James Earl Ray [all convicted, implicated or involved in assassinations or attempts on public figures] — I might simply take a weapon from my pocket and get rid of the Chairman of this subcommittee . . . Who gave me the gun? A private party who only asked that I pay for it in cash. Am I fit to possess this gun? Have I committed a crime before? Am I mentally competent, an illegal alien or an addict? Nobody asked.

*Before House Judiciary Subcommittee*
*on Crime, Washington, Oct. 9/*
*Los Angeles Times, 10-10:(1)5.*

# WHAT THEY SAID IN 1975

**Patrick V. Murphy**
*President, Police Foundation; Former*
*Police Commissioner of New York City*   1

I guess I have a feeling about unemployment being very closely related to crime because I am well aware that 100 years ago, in New York City, the Irish committed more violent crime than blacks and Puerto Ricans commit in New York today, proportionately; but the Irish were on the bottom of the ladder then. There were signs that said "No Irish" or "No Catholics Need Apply." Really, America is not very much concerned today about crime being committed by Irish-Americans, but the unemployment rate among Irish-Americans is not nearly as worrisome to me as it is among blacks and Puerto Ricans. It may look like a pie-in-the-sky situation, and the politics of it is not yet ripe, in my opinion; but I think America is going to have to face up to the fact that this crime problem will destroy more than just the cities it is now destroying, and we are going to have to face up to a basic cause such as that one.
*TV-radio interview, Washington/*
*"Meet the Press," National*
*Broadcasting Company, 8-10.*

**Joseph Pecoraro**
*President,*
*Chicago Patrolman's Association*   2

[On charges of illegal surveillance by Chicago Police]: You talk about figures and scandals, but it's the quality and dedication of the patrolman on the street that counts in making a department. People always try to run us down like we're the worst department in the country. The spying charges are just another political thing. Hell, our job is to investigate. I'll investigate you; I'll investigate the Pope. We investigate ourselves. We are out to protect the people—that's what investigating is about.
*The Washington Post, 5-18:(F)3.*

**Peter J. Pitchess**
*Sheriff, Los Angeles County, California*   3

[Calling for a national ban on private handgun ownership]: If we don't stop the deadly proliferation, this country will become a jungle, a nation armed to the teeth, where only those with the fastest gun will survive.
*At National Forum for Handgun Control,*
*Los Angeles, May 29/*
*Los Angeles Herald-Examiner, 5-29:(A)2.*

4

[On California's recently passed law reducing marijuana-possession penalties]: Experience has shown that whenever penalties for a particular violation are eliminated or significantly reduced, there is a dramatic increase in the numbers of persons participating in that particular activity. The use of marijuana will proliferate dramatically and will, in a brief period of time, surpass alcohol-related problems. Between the Legislature and the courts we don't have the ability to cope with crime in this country any longer.
*News conference, Los Angeles, July 11/*
*Los Angeles Times, 7-12:(2)12.*

**Wes Pomeroy**
*Chief of Police of Berkeley, California*   5

[On the Federal Law Enforcement Assistance Administration]: I'm very disappointed in it. There is so much bureaucracy and red tape at every level that it's almost impossible to make the system accessible to real needs. I think that if you looked hard at the figures, you'd find that a lot of the money is being eaten up by administration and that damn little is getting put out where the rubber meets the road.
*The Washington Post, 9-21:(A)3.*

**Raymond K. Procunier**
*Former Director, California*
*Department of Corrections*   6

I don't think it's possible to expect a person to get better in prison. I think they ought to be sent there for punishment. I think people can really relate to honest punishment.
*Interview/Los Angeles Times, 5-8:(1)24.*

**Charles B. Rangel**
*United States Representative, D—New York*   7

... a recent article in *The New York Times* reports on the design of a special rifle to commemorate the Bicentennial. The rifle, to be produced in only 200 copies, will be priced at $5,800-$7,250 each. The gunmaker stated: "The gun is not only a weapon, it's a tradition." Tragically, he is right. The new "Spirit of '76" rifle symbolizes the needless deaths of tens of thousands of innocent Americans over the past two centuries from firearms. Accidents and murders from the barrels of guns have cost more American lives than the war in Southeast Asia. Children and teen-agers find guns lying around their homes, play with them, and kill or maim themselves, their friends and their families. One significant factor in the high rate of crime in this country is the presence of literally millions of guns, legal and illegal. When the Colorado designer of the rifle, "Spirit of '76," says, "What we're trying to say is how for 200 years the gun was involved in this country," he has a history of senseless bloodshed to prove it.

*Before the House, Washington, March 26/*
*The New York Times, 4-18:30.*

**Maxwell Rich**
*Executive vice president,*
*National Rifle Association*
                                                    *1*

[Arguing against the banning of handguns]: Mandatory sentences [for people caught using a gun in a criminal manner] —yes, I think we're going that way. If we permit these crimes to occur without proper penalties, if judges are given discretion and people are put out on the street to commit more crimes, and if the chance of putting in a full sentence is virtually nil . . . then we will have more of this . . . [But as far as banning handguns is concerned,] don't forget that we're the greatest country in the world, and that that didn't happen incidentally. It's history—and the Constitution. We [of the NRA] believe in the Second Amendment—that a law-abiding citizen has the right to bear arms, so long as he does not interfere with the rights of others. The Second Amendment is as important to us as the first one, guaranteeing freedom of the press, is to the press.

*Interview, Washington/*
*Los Angeles Times, 10-20:(2)7.*

**James M. Rochford**
*Superintendent of Police of Chicago*
                                                    *2*

Our department answers most calls within three minutes; our men are professionals; they have the best equipment, fairly good pay, good morale, a Mayor [Richard Daley] who supports them as well as any in the country. And yet the criminals we're arresting are back on the streets. Crime is up and the prison population is down. That ought to tell you something.

*The Washington Post, 8-4:(A)2.*

**William B. Saxbe**
*Attorney General of the United States*
                                                    *3*

[On the Federal Law Enforcement Assistance Administration]: I take scant comfort from the estimate that crime might have been even worse without LEAA—since it already is awful beyond description.

*Before Dade County (Fla.) Bar Association,*
*Miami, Jan. 30/Los Angeles Times, 1-31:(1)5.*

**Robert L. F. Sikes**
*United States Representative, D—Florida*
                                                    *4*

[Arguing against gun-control]: Firearms are used by American citizens to protect their lives, families and property. The need to possess them for self-defense today is as great, if not greater, than in earlier periods of our nation's history.

*Before House Judiciary Subcommittee,*
*Washington/The New York Times, 2-21:28.*

**Jay Sourwine**
*Director, Internal Security Subcommittee,*
*United States Senate*
                                                    *5*

[Asking the Senate not to terminate his subcommittee]: I believe the Congress should be kept abreast of subversive activities. I believe the Congress should know about terrorist groups in this country . . . and the subversive influences within such groups, speaking specifically about Communist activity, Maoist activity, Red Chinese. I think the Congress should know about the [Cuban Premier Fidel] Castro network in the United States. Right now, this is the only committee that would be

# WHAT THEY SAID IN 1975

*(JAY SOURWINE)*

expected to do it ... The House Internal Security Committee has been put out of business. The Subversive Activities Control Board has been out of business several years. I'm not arguing ... that *I* should do this, only that the Senate should do this.

*Before Senate Rules Committee,*
*Washington, March 7/*
*The Washington Post, 3-8:(A)3.*

**William A. Stanmeyer**
*Associate professor of law,*
*Georgetown University* 1

A major reason that crime has gone up 11 times faster than population, that shoplifting is destroying retail business, that bus drivers no longer carry change, that drug abuse is leeching away the lives of 10 per cent of our high-school children, that airline passengers face daily risk of hijack, that rape occurs every 15 minutes ... is that, just when we need more-effective law enforcement, the courts have set out, generally, to render it impotent. Just when we most need to strengthen the certainty of sanction, we weaken it! We have seen to it that crime does pay. And the criminal knows it.

*At Hillsdale (Mich.) College/*
*Quote, 5-18:461.*

**Philip G. Tannian**
*Chief of Police of Detroit* 2

We kid ourselves that we cannot have a Hitler here. We can if the [crime] situation gets bad enough, and a majority of citizens want something done about it, and they're willing to pay the price ... If something is not done and done soon, vigilantism may become a battle cry. When you couple that with the tremendous increase in firearms ownership, that gets pretty scary ... The fear level of crime in white suburbs is at least as great as in the inner city. It is out of proportion to what is justified, in my opinion, but it is there.

*At conference on crime, East Lansing,*
*Mich., March 3/*
*The Washington Post, 3-4:(A)2.*

**John V. Tunney**
*United States Senator, D–California* 3

[Supporting gun control]: Guns are certainly part of the traditional frontier spirit. But today we have to make an accommodation to the urban society in which we live. The old six-gun approach is antithetical to today's world. Attitudes are changing gradually because people are increasingly conscious of interdependence. If we don't change, we could go the way of the dead empires of the Tigris and Euphrates.

*Interview, Washington/*
*Los Angeles Times, 10-20:(2)7.*

**Henry Wade**
*District Attorney, Dallas County, Texas* 4

Unfortunately, we have a basic lack of confidence in the criminal-justice system. Good citizens don't report crimes for several reasons. Some carry the negative attitude that it won't do any good—that violators won't be caught and punished. They point to burglaries and thefts, where only about 12 per cent are cleared. And then they say that if they are apprehended and the case gets into the courts, the district attorney and the judges won't try the case. If they do convict and send the guilty to prison, he will get out and come back to commit crime again.

*The Dallas Times Herald, 4-6(B)2.*

**Daniel Walker**
*Governor of Illinois (D)* 5

Soaring crime rates ... throughout the country should be sending public officials a message. It is the people who are afraid—not the muggers, not the robbers, not rapists, not the murderers, not the lawless. That means we have to come up with a system that will make the lawless afraid.

*Human Events, 5-17:19.*

**Joseph Wambaugh**
*Author; Former Los Angeles policeman* 6

The romanticized image of the cop is gone. They don't want to be marshal of Dodge City any more. They don't want to walk through their beat like [TV marshal] Matt Dillon. They have different aspirations today. For one thing, police are younger today. The average age of a street cop is 25—many begin at 21. Basically, they share with their own age group the same hopes, fears and desires. More come from the middle class than before, more go to college and more do things that middle-class people do, like buying boats and taking trips. What is more, they have taken a page from the radicals of the '60s. Often it was the young radicals on one side of the barricades, and young cops on the other. Many of them were Vietnam veterans, too. It had its effect. They saw that protest often worked. One thing police want is more freedom. . . . they demand to be treated in a less authoritarian way. Young policemen don't want to be treated like infantrymen in the Army. They don't want bureaucracy nor do they want to be 24-hour-a-day cops. They want to be total human beings.

*Los Angeles Times, 11-2:(1)10.*

**Lord Widgery**
*Lord Chief Justice of England*

1

. . . I personally think that capital punishment is a very active deterrent in certain carefully defined classes of cases . . . When a gang are going to set out to rob a payroll, they make a plan. And one of the questions which they're bound to ask is: "Are we going to take guns or not?" Without capital punishment, they tend to take guns because there's so little to lose. If they take guns and they kill an innocent bystander, they'll be convicted of murder instead of robbery. But for robbery they would have gotten 12 years, reducible . . . to 8 or 4. For the murder they get life, which in practice is about 12 years concurrent. So the value of the destroyed human life has almost disappeared in the equation. And I'm quite confident that when this question arises of guns or no, that one of the things which affects the decision is the fact that, if you take a gun, it makes so little differ-

ence to your sentence that I'm sure that a deterrent is being removed.

*Interview, Washington/*
*U.S. News & World Report, 1-27:48.*

**Hubert Williams**
*Police Director of Newark, N.J.*

2

The problem with the handgun is that it is dangerous. You can never see it; it can be pulled out from beneath the coat. That is the big problem with it. If someone really wanted to protect their home, they would be better off with a shotgun, if they had to have a gun, than a handgun. So I feel the handguns will not provide Americans any more security. It is only a myth [that] handguns will provide security.

*TV-radio interview, Washington/*
*"Meet the Press," National*
*Broadcasting Company, 8-10.*

**Evelle J. Younger**
*Attorney General of California*

3

[Urging an end to the indeterminate prison sentence] : Our records indicate we're releasing dangerous, violent people. We've reached the point where the law-abiding citizen must be considered. We have to change our whole approach so far as the handling of dangerous criminals is concerned . . . [The sentence] should not be an unreasonable penalty, but it would be a *certain* penalty.

*News conference, San Diego, Nov. 18/*
*The New York Times, 11-20:28.*

4

[Saying there is a level of violent conduct at which there should be no release from prison] : Perhaps a person who has been convicted of several violent felonies has reached that point at which we must simply write him off as a hopeless risk, a habitual offender, and keep him locked up for most of the remainder of his life. This is harsh. Some will call it extreme. But I cannot see any alternative if we are to prevent future tragedies [of violent criminals paroled and committing more violent crimes] . . .

*News conference, San Francisco, Nov. 20/*
*Los Angeles Herald-Examiner, 11-21:(A)3.*

# Education

## Benjamin Alexander
*President, Chicago State University*
1

[On his reintroducing the "D" and "F" grades after two years of CSU having a no-fail grading system]: Any educational institution is cheating its students if it passes those who have not learned, if it graduates those who are inferior in their knowledge and their capacity to compete . . . [High-school] teachers [in low-income and ghetto neighborhoods] felt a collective sense of guilt for the massive under-privilege of their pupils and their families. Teachers were filled with compassion for these youngsters. They hated to give them failing grades . . . The result? We, together with all urban colleges and universities that are serving the kinds of students we are, find ourselves confronted with the problem that many of these students are not adequately prepared to do college-level work.

*At his inauguration/*
*The Washington Post, 5-23:(A)19.*

## Irving Anker
*Chancellor, New York City*
*Public School System*
2

The big-city school is an arena in which many of the crushing social problems of the city itself intrude and are acted out not only by students themselves but more often by forces that invade the schools, generating problems that have their genesis in the surrounding community.

*Before Senate Subcommittee on Juvenile*
*Delinquency, Washington, April 16/*
*The New York Times, 4-17:11.*

3

[On school standards]: There is a lot of debate on what should be minimal objectives. If we make the standards really minimum, then some people will look at them and say, "Is that all you expect? Why don't you insist on more?" Some may even tend to regard the minimum as the maximum. On the other hand, if you establish the minimum closer to what the average or normal youngster should be expected to achieve at the very least, then you are making certain that a lot of youngsters will fall below that level.

*The New York Times, 5-4:(13)5.*

## Lloyd J. Averill
*President, Kansas City Regional*
*Council for Higher Education*
4

The typical private liberal-arts college of the mid-20th century is obsolete. Its sovereign isolation, its protected students, the one-track careers of its faculty, its restrictive curriculum and teaching and its tepid purpose make it unsuited to the needs of the decades ahead.

*At seminar of college presidents,*
*Arlington, Va./*
*The Washington Post, 4-17:(E)3.*

## Jacques Barzun
*Former professor of history,*
*Columbia University*
5

The university has a very clear task and it has no business attempting other tasks, such as carrying out social policies. A man who decides he is going to study certain problems—scientific or philosophical—should do just that. He teaches people who become carriers of this knowlege into action. He has a very important social role to play, but not directly. To get down and dig himself is probably a waste of his talents. If you learn how to milk a cow, the test is immediate and conclusive. But whether social theory is right and will improve a lot of people is an entirely different thing. The World War II emergency turned the university inside out like an umbrella in a high wind. Now every professor has to be in Venezuela or in the neighborhood trying to fix things. It is very shortsighted.

*Interview, New York/*
*The New York Times, 6-17:38.*

**Birch Bayh**
*United States Senator,*
*D—Indiana*
1

[On school violence] : Too often, youngsters arriving at our public schools today are not finding the quiet atmosphere of instruction, enrichment and encouragement, but instead an environment dominated by fear, chaos, destruction and violence.

*Washington, April 9/*
*The Washington Post, 4-10:(A)1.*

**Alice L. Beeman**
*President, Council for Advancement*
*and Support of Education*
2

Why is there a crisis of faith in higher education? I think it is because, in the decades of the 1940s, '50s and '60s—a time of enormous growth and prosperity for higher education—we aroused public expectations that we cannot now fulfill. We were quick to say a few years back, for example, that our universities, with their centers for urban studies and the like, could solve the problems of the cities. We said that our universities, with their sophisticated programs and capabilities for research, could provide the answers to environmental pollution, economic dislocation and various human diseases. And above all, we said that, if you went to college, you would get a good job and a fat paycheck. To some degree, we have produced on all those promises. But we all know, without an item-by-item review, that we promised more than we have achieved. And particularly now, in a time of economic recession and having what may be a long period of low or no growth in the educational-research establishment itself, the promises about good jobs and fat paychecks have a rather hollow ring.

*Before South Dakota College Public*
*Relations Association/*
*The Wall Street Journal, 9-22:10.*

**Terrel H. Bell**
*Commissioner of Education of the*
*United States*
3

To send young men and women into today's world armed only with Aristotle, Freud and Hemingway is like sending a lamb into the lion's den. It is to delude them as well as ourselves. But if we give young men and women a useful skill, we give them not only the means to earn a good living but also the opportunity to do something constructive and useful for society. Moreover, these graduates will experience some of those valuable qualities that come with meaningful work—self respect, self-confidence, independence. . . . in my view, many colleges and universities face declining enrollments today simply because they lack a strong commitment to this first and foremost requisite. Many would argue that a student need merely master the basics in the liberal arts and humanities to be well on the way to becoming educated. As I see it, this is far too narrow a view of education. Education is preparation for life, and living without meaningful work is just not living life to its full meaning and purpose. Certainly, education for employment does not represent a total educational policy. The liberal arts will always have the place as the heart of the curriculum. But we need to liberalize vocational education—and vocationalize liberal education. In the process we will attain the full purpose of education.

*Before Council of Small Private Colleges,*
*Washington, Jan. 14/*
*Vital Speeches, 3-15:351.*

4

An educated person must keep on learning—must renew the basic storehouse of knowledge and keep up with the times. An educated person must be able to gain new knowledge from reading and from life experiences and apply that knowledge to problem-solving. A person must be able to think critically about what he has read, experienced and learned. An educated person must be able to read directions and to teach himself or herself. I have known people with a doctoral degree who could not read the directions for assembling a tricycle. They could not teach themselves how to solve a very simple problem.

*At Edinboro (Pa.) State College*
*commencement, May 24/*
*Vital Speeches, 7-15:607.*

1

A wise man once said to me, "Education is a process, not a destination." Education is the process of moving from cocksure ignorance to thoughtful uncertainty.

*At Edinboro (Pa.) State College*
*commencement, May 24/*
*Los Angeles Times, 8-11:(2)4.*

2

Colleges and universities might ... reconsider the notion that there is something wrong with working with the hands as part of a college course. While appreciating and understanding the *arts* help to shape a broader personality and make a deeper life possible, there is a bit of creativity in each of us, and only a very fine line separates the *arts* from *art* and from *craft*. It has been fashionable in the academic world to downgrade labor produced with one's hands, as if somehow the brain was not involved in making a clay pot. But, especially in this age of sedentary television watching, we need learning experiences that involve physical activity and result in tangible products. I suggest that the dichotomy between so-called academic learning and vocational education is an over-strained distinction. We live in a constantly changing world. Who is to say what is practical and what is pure? Yesterday's esoterics may be tomorrow's essentials. I suspect that opportunities for course offerings exist in fields of learning previously considered by colleges and universities to be outside their province.

*Before Western Association of College and*
*University Business Officers,*
*San Francisco/The National Observer, 6-14:7.*

**Thomas Bonner**
*President, Union College, Schenectady, N.Y.*

3

[Defending liberal-arts education]: Whoever said life was a matter of bread alone? No educated person would argue seriously that the study of history, literature, art or philosophy is irrelevant to a satisfactory life or the enduring values of a citizen. What of the quality of a graduate's life, the realization of one's own goals, success as a parent or marriage partner, or one's contributions as a citizen?

*U.S. News & World Report, 10-13:38.*

**Leon Botstein**
*President, Bard College*

4

[Saying the English language is dying]: The language is languishing because so often it is not used, is not read and is misread. And it is mistaught ... Children growing up today are exposed to a bland reading diet in their first years of school. The pleasures offered to the beginning reader are largely those of the acquisition of a more or less mechanical skill—the ability to recognize, identify and respond to the shapes of letters together and the words they form—rather than the sounds and rhythms of English.

*San Francisco Examiner & Chronicle,*
*10-5:(A)14.*

**Howard Bowen**
*Chancellor, Claremont (Calif.)*
*University Center*

5

In the future we must consider education as something that enriches the personality and improves the life, and not just raise[s] the gross national product. The purpose of education is to change and improve people and not get them better jobs. My feeling has always been that a liberal education produced a liberal kind of person, and that person should make his way into all kinds of jobs, manual and white-collar. What's wrong with having a well-educated electrician?

*San Francisco Examiner & Chronicle,*
*5-11:(A)11.*

**George E. P. Box**
*Professor of statistics,*
*University of Wisconsin, Madison*

6

It has been said that education is what is left after you have forgotten all you learned. If this be true, of what does the precious residue consist? I think it consists of the capacity to learn.

It is an attitude of mind which is never satisfied with its representation of the world; a mind which invites fact to suggest theory, however unwelcome, and requires theory to discover fact which can confirm or discredit opinion. With this you should have no difficulty solving your problems.

*At University of Rochester (N.Y.)*
*commencement/Quote, 7-20:6.*

**John Brademas**
*United States Representative, D—Indiana*
1

I'm always amazed when I go to an education conference and find that many of the participants have never met before. I've suggested there ought to be a series of conferences across the country at which college teachers, student aid officials, researchers, government officials think together systematically and rationally about their objectives and purposes in order to develop common semantics and common statistics.

*The Christian Science Monitor, 1-13:9.*

**Kingman Brewster, Jr.**
*President, Yale University*
2

My fear is that there is a growing tendency for the central government to use the spending power to prescribe educational policies. These are matters which they could not regulate were it not for our dependence on their largesse ... Use of the leverage of the government dollar to accomplish objectives which have nothing to do with the purposes for which the dollar is given has become dangerously fashionable ... Thus if we are to receive support for physics, let's say, we must conform to Federal policies in the admission of women to the Art School, in women's athletic facilities, and in the recruitment of women and minorities, not just in the Federally supported field, but throughout the university.

*Before Fellows of the American Bar*
*Foundation, Chicago/*
*The Wall Street Journal, 3-28:4.*

**Fred Brook, Jr.**
*Director of admissions, University of Chicago*
3

[On the drop in college entrance examination scores]: I'd say students are less anxious

about entering college. With more spaces available in state, private and community colleges, students aren't as worried about finding a space, so they don't prepare as much for the tests. The popular notion is that a student can't study for the SAT, but they can, and did, "gear up" for the tests and prepared themselves psychologically.

*Interview/*
*The Dallas Times Herald, 10-17:(C)4.*

**Edmund G. Brown, Jr.**
*Governor of California (D)*
4

[There is a] fallacy that education is everything, that somehow jobs can be created with a diploma. India has lots of educated people with nothing to do but sit around and play chess.

*Interview, Sacramento/*
*The New York Times, 4-13:(1)57.*

**John H. Bunzel**
*President, California State University,*
*San Jose*
5

It's popularly believed that it is the [college] president's job to provide sex for students, football for alumni and parking for faculty.

*At inauguration of first pub on campus/*
*Los Angeles Times, 9-10:(1)2.*

**R. Freeman Butts**
*Professor in the foundations of education,*
*Teachers College, Columbia University*
6

After all we have passed through in recent years, I should think that we could now face frontally and frankly the proposition that American education does have a positive political role to perform in achieving our historic ideals of political community. Such a proposition will probably be criticized from the right as being an effort to impose a leftist ideology; it will likely be criticized from the left as imposition of middle-class capitalist values or simply wishy-washy liberalism; and it will be criticized by empirical social scientists on the grounds that schools cannot effect social change—they simply follow the dictates of the society. But I argue that if the schools take seriously the authority of the enduring ideals, sentiments and moral commitments of our political community

# WHAT THEY SAID IN 1975

as embodied in the Constitutional regime, and especially in the Bill of Rights, the schools and colleges can help the society to put into practice its democratic ideals. This would indeed be a radical social change. I take hope from the opinion surveys that show that organized education still stands high in public esteem, far above big labor and big business. I certainly believe that we should stress in the schools not only the studies that will stress cultural differences as a basis for ethnic identity and mutual respect, but I deem even more important the studies and activities that will cement civic commonality.

*At National Forum of the College Entrance
Examination Board, New York/
The National Observer, 11-15:13.*

## Raul Castro
*Governor of Arizona (D)* 1

[On cutbacks in education funding]: The universities are not sacred cows. Everyone takes a cut in salary, and here the presidents of [the three state universities] . . . come in with a $2,000 pay raise . . . I mean, that just doesn't make any sense . . . You look in those catalogues at the courses in spring dancing, camp cooking, camp-firing, hiking, guitar-playing . . . To me that is a fringe area; that's a luxury we can ill afford. Well, the answer is, "The quality of education will suffer." Well, so what? Instead of having 10 students in the class, let's put 20; if they have 20, let's put 30 in a class. And instead of having the teachers spending all their life getting Federal funding for graduate students to teach their courses, let's get them back in the classroom and do a day's work.

*Interview/
The Washington Post, 6-1:(A)8.*

## Earl F. Cheit
*Professor of business administration and
education, University of California, Berkeley* 2

There are ways in which institutions of higher education can influence their own future. The problem is to maintain flexibility in a period of declining growth when you have to change by substitution or relocation. It was easier before when you could change by addition.

*The New York Times, 4-18:32.*

## Kenneth B. Clark
*Professor of psychology, City College of
New York; Member, New York State
Board of Regents* 3

[Reflecting on his years as a professor]: I never responded to the "relevance" kick. When students questioned the books I assigned, I'd tell them they didn't have to be in my class if they knew what books to read. I think I was pretty rigid as a teacher. I had the responsibility of determining how we go about understanding this area. It was difficult for me to learn and it would be for my students. I didn't have much tolerance for fads. I didn't believe something was good just because a student said it was good. On the other hand, I have had some students in recent years who are going to think. Last year a student got onto a point and went to the library, studied, and we had knock-down drag-out arguments. It was wonderful. He got an A.

*Interview, New York/
The New York Times, 5-31:40.*

4

If we ran other institutions as inefficiently as we run our schools, we'd be in receivership by now. This is the only developed nation in the world without national organization for public education. There is no magic reason for public education to be a district, city or state problem.

*Newsweek, 9-15:52.*

## Harlan Cleveland
*Former president, University of Hawaii* 5

I have been struck in recent years with the willingness of students and colleagues to sign petitions in defense of teachers who are by common—private—knowledge less than fully competent, just when their contracts are being quietly and compassionately terminated to protect the rights of future students to the best available teaching. The academic executive has two options: to take on the protestors, publicly

78

explain the teacher's weaknesses, and spend a couple of weeks in court as defendant in a defamation suit, or inflict the inferior teacher on the next 30 years of students. In too many cases, the second option looks most inviting— short-term benefits traded for long-run trouble often do. And each such choice brings our society closer to participatory mediocrity.

*Before American Society for Public Administration, Syracuse(N.Y.) University/ The Washington Post, 1-11:(A)12.*

**William Sloane Coffin**
*Chaplain, Yale University*
1

There's too little of real consequence for the future taking place in the academic world. Academics are too academic. They don't have enough of the old scientific spirit; they're not free to use their imaginations, their intuition, their passions. Instead, they want rational control, to impose limits. Very few have the curiosity or determination to find new ways of forming human communities or looking at our global future.

*Interview/People, 5-5:42.*

**Eugene Comey**
*Editor-in-chief, University of Chicago "Law Review"*
2

[Defending grades as a criterion for selection to the staff of his publication]: Grades do mean something. They are almost a certification of intellectual superiority; and the *Law Review* still works on the premise that we want the best students; and if that is elitism, then I'm guilty of the charge.

*Chicago/ The New York Times, 3-3:38.*

**Elizabeth Wooten Cowan**
*Director of English programs, Modern Language Association*
3

[On the drop in scores by high-school students on Scholastic Aptitude Tests]: My basic reaction is to look again at the training we give teachers. Until potential teachers study the intricacies of teaching, reading and writing, and the mechanisms of learning them as thoroughly as they do the literary history of England,

there's not much chance of improvement. I've nothing against literary history, mind you, and I take the standardized-test results with a grain of salt. However, our own research shows that students' basic skills are declining and the deterioration will continue unless teacher training changes.

*The National Observer, 9-20:5.*

**Richard M. Cyert**
*President, Carnegie-Mellon University*
4

Traditionally, universities have not been managed. They have tended to operate as highly decentralized organizations in which deans and department heads operated largely autonomously. This kind of operation was possible and indeed productive because there were plenty of students and adequate resources. Unfortunately, those days are no longer here.

*The New York Times, 6-22:(3)7.*

**Martin Diamond**
*Political scientist; Fellow, Woodrow Wilson International Center for Scholars*
5

[On the skepticism instilled in students by the teaching of the "new history"]: Debunking is a justifiable educational technique when you're dealing with the overly "bunked," when you have youngsters whose heads are filled with innocent daydreams. The trouble today is that everything turns the kids into cynics. The task of education today is to introduce beliefs in heroism and virtue to students who are crudely cynical. The shocking thing today is to tell a high-school student that Lincoln was a man of noble character and monumental intellect.

*San Francisco Examiner & Chronicle, 6-8: (Sunday Punch)5.*

**Glenn S. Dumke**
*Chancellor, California State University and College System*
6

It's very unfair to students to relieve them from the necessity of competing [in school]. They have to face it when they get out. I'm not wedded to ABCDF grades, but academic standards must be maintained. There is beginning to be serious questioning of credit/no-credit and

# WHAT THEY SAID IN 1975

*(GLENN S. DUMKE)*

pass/fail courses. Those trying to get jobs find that a record of such courses works against them.

*U.S. News & World Report, 12-1:29.*

**Thomas F. Eagleton**
*United States Senator,*
*D—Missouri*     *1*

Over the last decade, the Federal government has gone from the role of a benign bystander to that of an active participant in education at the local level. Will the commitment first expressed in 1965, and the programs that gave life to that commitment, be continued and expanded, or will both the commitment and programs dissipate and dwindle away, as has been the case with other well-intended programs of the 1960s? There is some evidence this is happening now . . . The actual reduction which the President [Ford] is proposing for fiscal year 1976 in education is over $1-billion. Cuts in elementary and secondary education programs account for about three-fourths of this decrease.

*Before American Association of School*
*Administrators, Dallas, Feb. 21/*
*The Dallas Times Herald, 2-22:(B)1.*

**Nolan Estes**
*Superintendent, Dallas Public*
*Schools System*     *2*

. . . I think that our society has depended too much, and placed too great a burden, on the public schools to solve many of its problems. When it looked like we had a problem of employment, we looked to the schools for career education. When it looked like we had a drug problem, we turned to the schools. When we were behind Russia in the technological race, we turned to the schools. It just may be that we're expecting too much of our public schools and more than this institution can effectively handle within the present framework.

*Interview/*
*The Dallas Times Herald, 3-9:(A)39.*

**John Kenneth Galbraith**
*Professor of economics,*
*Harvard University*     *3*

. . . student concern with educational reform usually—I would say invariably—ends up with a proposal for the liberalization of standards. Liberalization of standards is a euphemism for lowering of standards. There is much to be said for seeking to liberate as many people as possible from the burdens of physical toil. Liberalization from the burden of mental toil is premature. Any compilation of the 100 best universities in the world would list a vast majority of American and Canadian institutions. It is because, on this continent, we have been much more zealous in protecting our standards, in requiring students to work . . . Student judgment on instruction is valuable, as most will agree, except when it is adverse. Student participation in the selection and promotion of faculty, I believe, is unwise and unuseful. The selection and promotion of faculty is a matter for careful, mature, professional judgment. This is not for students. And it is vital that those making the judgment be required to live with their mistakes. This also excludes student participation, for students are here and soon gone. As Churchill said of democracy, selection of faculty members by their peers is the worst of all systems except for the alternatives.

*At Harvard University class-day exercises/*
*The National Observer, 7-12:15.*

**John Kenneth Galbraith**
*Author; Former professor of economics,*
*Harvard University*     *4*

Complexity and obscurity [in writing technical works for academia] have professional value; they are the academic equivalent of apprenticeship rules in the building trades. They exclude the outsiders, keep down the competition, preserve the image of a privileged or priestly class. The man who makes things clear, depending on the metaphor, is a recusant or a scab. He is criticized not only for his clarity but for his treachery.

*Interview, Cambridge, Mass./*
*The Christian Science Monitor, 12-9:19.*

**David P. Gardner**
*President, University of Utah*
1

Much that passes for education, of course, is not education at all but ritual. The fact is that we are being educated when we know it least. We learn simply by the exposure of living, and what we learn most natively is the tradition in which we live.

*At prayer breakfast, March 7/*
*Vital Speeches, 4-15:414.*

**Melvin D. George**
*Vice president,*
*University of Missouri*
2

... I believe universities are accountable, as institutions of society. We are accountable to our students for the quality of their instruction; we are accountable to our colleagues for the proper functioning of departments and colleges and campuses; we are accountable to funding sources for prudent management of resources; we are accountable to our disciplinary peers for the quality and quantity of our contribution to knowledge. And we have not always been sensitive to this accountability. As a result, things have been imposed on us that seem entirely inappropriate and may well in fact cause unintended perturbations in the system itself. Obviously, we may have to change a number of things within the university. Obviously, we have to be sensitive to expectations that we will be available to students and that we will work hard at teaching and scholarship. But as Max Lerner put it in an article in the *Los Angeles Times* a year or so ago, "The present clamor for accountability is mostly foolishness. The only true accountability is that of teacher and student to each other."

*At University Club, Columbia, Mo., Oct. 7/*
*Vital Speeches, 12-1:114.*

**Alexander Gerschenkron**
*Professor of economics,*
*Harvard University*
3

I have come to have increasing doubts about our education system, particularly about lectures. Class discussions—very good. Office hours—very good. Lectures? They are Middle Ages; they are pre-Gutenberg. It's not an adult way. The adult way is for students to sit down on the appropriate part of their anatomy and study. But lectures? They sit there dreaming and the lecturer has to go into histrionics to wake them up.

*Interview, Cambridge, Mass./*
*The New York Times, 6-19:23.*

**Robert A. Goldwin**
*Special Consultant for Education to President*
*of the United States Gerald R. Ford*
4

[Defending the teaching of liberal arts and humanities]: ... [if students] gained nothing more from their studies than supposedly saleable skills, and can't make the sale because of changes in the job market, they have been cheated. But if those skills were more than saleable, if the study made them better citizens and made them happier to be human beings, they have not been cheated. They will find some kind of job soon enough. It might even turn out that those humanizing and liberating skills are saleable. Flexibility, an ability to change and learn new things, is a valuable skill. People who have learned how to learn can learn outside of school. That's where most of us have learned to do what we do, not in school. Learning to learn is one of the highest liberal skills. There is more to living than earning a living, but many earn good livings by the liberal skills of analyzing, experimenting, discussing, reading and writing. Skills that are always in demand are those of a mind trained to think and imagine and express itself. When the confidence of some in our nation is shaken, and many are confused about the direction we ought to follow in a new world situation, then civic education is more important than ever. And when the foundations of Western civilization are being challenged, and resolution seems to falter because many people are not sure what we are defending and how we ought to defend it, then it seems to me we ought not to abandon liberal studies but rather the reverse; we ought to redouble our commitment to those studies, as if our lives depended on it.

*At New College, University of South*
*Florida, Feb. 2/Vital Speeches, 5-1:445.*

# WHAT THEY SAID IN 1975

**James A. Harris**
*President, National Education Association*    1

Twenty-three per cent of schoolchildren are failing to graduate, and another large segment graduate as functional illiterates. If 23 per cent of anything else failed—23 per cent of the automobiles did not run, 23 per cent of the buildings fell down, 23 per cent of stuffed ham spoiled—we'd look at the producer. The schools, here, are not blameless.
> *Before Senate Subcommittee on Juvenile Delinquency, Washington, April 16/ The New York Times, 4-17:11.*

**Terry Herndon**
*Executive secretary, National Education Association*    2

There is a notion in many communities that the purpose of the school is to perpetuate the culture, to indoctrinate the children in the predominant attitudes of the community. We do not accept that as the role of the schools. In most places, the traditional values have included racism, sexism, white-male dominance, Protestantism and things like that. Some of these values should not be preserved. I think a good school system will expose children to both traditional and alternative values and let the children decide.
> *U.S. News & World Report, 1-27:32.*

3

Inflation has affected teachers as individuals and citizens as taxpayers. The cost of everything is up for the schools, while schools are not able to generate new revenue because citizens are hesitant to increase taxes. This causes school administrators and school boards to cut materials and supplies, to cut preparation periods, to increase the size of classes—and not to increase any salaries. But teachers are not going to accept their situation as victims of a depressed and inflated economy. If necessary, they will strike.
> *Interview/Time, 9-15:51.*

**Charles J. Hitch**
*President, University of California*    4

Of course we [in education] have to be profoundly concerned with how our students fare after they leave us. Of course we have to be responsive to their demands for certain courses and curricula. Of course we must make every effort to be as clear and informative as possible about how many jobs exist ... [But] do we really want jobs *per se* to be our reason for existence? Do we intend vocationalism to supplant the search for truth? All the talk of overspecialization, notwithstanding my own belief, is that our students don't really get into their fields in sufficient depth, and I would like them to be able to without having to worry unduly about relevance to the job market.
> *At Charter Day ceremonies, University of California, Los Angeles, April 3/ Los Angeles Times, 4-4:(2)1.*

**John A. Howard**
*President, Rockford (Ill.) College*    5

College-for-everybody seems to contain the seeds of its own destruction in a democracy; for the democratic concept that every person has a right to his own values and priorities—a concept that is wholesomely applied in the political processes—produces confusion and degeneration in the educational processes. The new egalitarianism has become a cancer which has pervaded almost every aspect of the academic body, eroding the vitality of many a campus with policies that distort and denature the educational process. The proliferation of courses that are virtually non-intellectual and even in some cases ... anti-intellectual, the inflation of grades, the diminution of entrance requirements and the deletion of graduation requirements, the refusal to be concerned with the out-of-class life of the students, the open tolerance of illegal drugs and many other policies widely adopted in recent years, all manifest the same intellectual malady—the divorce of academia from the responsibility to identify valid authority and inculcate in its students a respect for that authority.
> *At Worcester College, Oxford University, England, April 6/ Vital Speeches, 5-15:468.*

6

In higher education today, the reigning philosophy is governed by a value-free concept: How the student, and everyone else, behaves is his own business. Every view of everything is granted equal status and the only offense is to insist that one view is more important than the others. The results of such a philosophy are predictable. Self-discipline lapses if there are no acknowledged evils to avoid. There is no incentive to self-reliance if there is no acknowledged concept of human dignity. If a law is found inconvenient, one simply disregards it, as in the case of using marijuana. Value-free education simply annuls virtue, for virtuous conduct requires a specific understanding of what is right and what is wrong, and behavior consistent with that understanding. Value-free education leaves everyone free to indulge his whims and his passions without regard to the laws or the general welfare. It is a blueprint for anarchy and, to some extent, an unintentional training ground for crime.

*Convocation address, Rockford College,*
*Sept. 10/Vital Speeches, 10-15:24.*

## John R. Howard
*President, Lewis and Clark College*
1

Higher education has always been a vulnerable partner in the alliances within which it operates—never paying its own way by accurately pricing the services it offered, but always relying on the support of government and industry and the philanthropy of thousands of persons—a gift-giving record unparalleled in history. That, translated, says that the good health of higher education, most especially private higher education, depends in the end upon the good health of this nation's economy. If business is bad and profits are down, corporate giving and individual giving both decline ... The colleges and universities, whatever the state of the economy, are now and will always be faced with upward spiralling costs—not because of inflation or poor management, but precisely because they are the institutions man invented to store all that has been learned, to interpret it and synthesize it, to pull it together in some meaningful way so that it can be passed on—"taught"—to some thoroughly confused 18-year-old men and women.

*Before Oregon's Principal Industrial*
*and Labor Leaders, Portland, Sept. 29/*
*Vital Speeches, 11-1:50.*

## Robert M. Hutchins
*Chairman, Center for the Study of*
*Democratic Institutions*
2

The reward system in institutions of higher learning is that you are promoted, your salary is increased, other distinctions are showered upon you in proportion as you do or seem to be doing what is called research. And this emphasis has led to more and more specialization and fragmentation. Even in my time they used to say that one Yale man couldn't talk to another Yale man unless they both happened to remember the score of last Saturday's game. This degree of specialization, even in the best of our institutions—or perhaps especially in the best of our institutions, because they are best because they get more Nobel prizes than the others—has gone to incredible lengths since I was in college and is, I think, getting worse every day.

*Interview/Center Report, June:23.*

## Franklyn A. Johnson
*Professor of administration,*
*Florida Atlantic University*
3

The president of the university is inevitably in the middle of the battles to attain the objectives of the institution, of its various elements, and of its clients. But he must also be *above* the battles in his symbolizing more than any other campus individual or group the integrity, the leadership, the perception to meet any challenge in matters of professional ethics. His faculty and students are watching him! Therefore, in his day-to-day comments, recommendations, decisions and dealings with his associates, he must represent—and be seen to represent—the best in our Judeo-Christian tradition. Always fallible, yes; often mistaken, yes; vicious, venal, vindictive, never!

*At Oglethorpe University, Oct. 18/*
*Vital Speeches, 11-15:90.*

## John G. Kemeny
*President, Dartmouth College*
4

Federal agencies seem to be competing with each other in an effort to enforce a wide variety of regulations, and universities just cannot keep up with them. This red tape makes the administration of educational institutions vastly more

# WHAT THEY SAID IN 1975

## (JOHN G. KEMENY)

complicated. The time may come when an institution will have to place itself deliberately in violation of some of these regulations in order to force a test case in the courts.

*U.S. News & World Report, 6-30:28.*

### Jerome P. Keuper
*President, Florida Institute of Technology*    1

Fund-raising for colleges is getting tough, so we're going the profit-making route. We hope to be able to earn our support instead of asking for gifts. We're going to get into anything that looks profitable, is honest and doesn't compete unfairly with businesses in our community.

*U.S. News & World Report, 1-27:33.*

### John H. Knowles
*President, Rockefeller Foundation*    2

The three major purposes of education—to develop the intellect, to transmit the culture and to acquire marketable skills—have been so heavily weighted toward the pragmatic ideal of "making a good living" that the undergraduate curriculum is a mish-mash of electives and pre-graduate-school requirements. The idea of knowing a little about everything; integrating and synthesizing knowledge in the attempt to gain understanding of both self and life's problems; strengthening the culture and its values; acquiring aesthetic and ethical sense in choice, preference, value and style; and being able to read anything written, understand anything said, and say anything thought—has been lost to the pomposity of idiot savant professionals, technicians and governmental bureaucrats, and to a rigidly compartmentalized faculty which has lost its sense of community and deals with everything but its universal purpose and the issues of teaching, learning and curricular revision.

*At Pine Manor Junior College, Chestnut Hill, Mass., May 19/Vital Speeches, 8-1:640.*

### Kenneth Lansing
*Professor of art education,*
*University of Illinois*    3

Clark Kerr, the former president of the University of California, convinced large numbers of college presidents that the "multiversity" would be good for higher education; and hundreds of other educators convinced the rest of us that big consolidated schools and school systems would improve education in America. But anyone who works in a big institution or anyone who has a child in a large school knows that bigness and betterness are anything but identical twins. Contrary to what some people may think, educational institutions are not like industries. They do not necessarily improve as they grow larger. In fact, they get worse, because the potential leaders lose contact with the teachers and students that they want and need as their followers. This encourages a high degree of internal, competitive, political activity; it increases paperwork; and it makes the activities and accomplishments of the faculty and students impossible to monitor. Problems in management and leadership inevitably develop, and when they do they tend to be large and complicated. This leads to frequent meetings with executives from similar colleges or school systems; and the meetings produce uniformity from top to bottom in the solutions to problems. The end product is a chain of educational discount houses with identical policies, procedures, jargon and merchandise, as well as the same lack of distinction.

*At New England Art Education Mini-Conference, Boston, Feb. 28/ Vital Speeches, 6-1:508.*

### Edward H. Levi
*President,*
*University of Chicago*    4

Academic politics is the lowest form of politics. It's trivial, it can be bitter, it can be enormously personal . . .

*News conference, Chicago/ Los Angeles Times, 2-4:(1)4.*

### William J. McGill
*President, Columbia University*    5

. . . we have achieved no resolution of the deep problems posed by the increasing rigor of education and the prolongation of adolescence that modern forms of higher education seem to require. We have not curtailed the burgeoning competition for academic credentials. If anything, competition for grades and for admission to professional schools is more deeply entrenched now than it was a decade ago . . . It is no credit to American education that so many of our best young people are now forced to take up residence in foreign countries in order to study medicine because no places are available in this country. It is simply scandalous that the United States, with all its resources and all its needs, is unable to find either the energy or the will to provide opportunities for professional training to our best students. We must correct such distortions or face a revival of social unrest from frustrated students who feel that their society actively opposes them in realizing their destinies.

*At Columbia University*
*commencement, May 14/*
*The New York Times, 5-15:34.*

**William F. Miller**
*Provost,*
*Stanford University*
*1*

Higher education, both public and private, is in for very rough sailing in the foreseeable future. If higher education does not experience increases in productivity, then either its workers cannot share in the real growth of salary and wages common to society as a whole or [it] must receive what amounts to a subsidy from the rest of society.

*The New York Times, 4-18:32.*

**Steven Muller**
*President, Johns Hopkins University*
*2*

Of more than 1,500 private institutions of higher education, more than 900—nearly two-thirds—have enrollments of less than 1,000 students. As a class, private colleges and universities tend increasingly to be significantly smaller than their public counterparts. That may make us a sector less cost-effective, but it preserves a crucial quality. It cannot be argued that the faculties of smaller institutions contain individuals who are more-gifted teachers than the members of large faculties. But it can and should be argued that the best teaching may more often occur in very small groups, and that

the intimacy of a small campus may stifle some but bring out the best in others. Public colleges and universities, needing to meet public demands with public dollars, will seldom be allowed to remain small. Cost-effectiveness and mass demand argue for large-scale economies of scale. Independent institutions can elect to control their size, and can, by remaining small, make a crucial contribution to greater freedom of student choice and institutional diversity.

*At Independent Colleges and Universities*
*of Texas Summer Workshop, Houston, Aug. 5/*
*Vital Speeches, 9-15:736.*

**Frederic W. Ness**
*President, Association of American Colleges*
*3*

A good liberal-arts education is, in fact, thoroughly relevant, even though it will not necessarily assure a job immediately on graduation. Nor, indeed, in today's rapidly shifting employment market will many of our widely supported vocational and technical programs. One thing is certain, however: The holder of a baccalaureate from a good liberal-arts institution will have a far wider choice and will be much better able to adjust to changing circumstances.

*The Washington Post, 4-17:(E)3.*

**Barbara Newell**
*President, Wellesley College*
*4*

I'm rather concerned about the narrowing professional training in some educational institutions. It seems to me that the knowledge of the different ways of tackling a problem, exposure to the past, an understanding of the forces of our society and the way we live, an awareness of value systems, are vital ingredients for any profession chosen.

*Dallas, Feb. 19/*
*The Dallas Times Herald, 2-20:(B)2.*

**Ewald B. Nyquist**
*New York State Commissioner of Education*
*5*

[Saying schools should include instruction in morality as an integral part of the curriculum]: The educational system has produced too many people all too willing to put professional success ahead of personal standards, and cleverness ahead of character.

*News conference, Albany, N.Y., Oct. 8/*
*The New York Times, 10-9:50.*

# WHAT THEY SAID IN 1975

**John W. Oswald**
*President,*
*Pennsylvania State University*
1

In these recent days of national anguish [over Watergate], we in education need to re-examine the aloftness we sometimes maintained toward explicit reference to values and morality. We are sorrowfully aware that men of great influence and responsibility have confessed to varying degrees of crimes and misdemeanors, and we are deeply chagrined that each has been trained at an American institution of higher education.

*The New York Times, 1-14:20.*

**Joe Paterno**
*Football coach,*
*Pennsylvania State University*
2

[On criticism that college football costs too much]: I think basically our job is protecting the game for the youngsters who play it. It's got to be a meaningful experience for them, something they enjoy and something they get some good out of, or we can never defend the game no matter how much money we make. We can't have a game that's only purpose is to make money so we can support gymnastics or swimming or keep alumni happy. We've got to have a game that means something to kids who play it.

*Before National Collegiate Athletic*
*Association, Chapel Hill, N.C./*
*The New York Times, 2-21:22.*

**Laurence J. Peter**
*Author, Educator*
3

Education has hoodwinked the public, told them, "We need more this and more that . . ." Well, there are all kinds of problems in education—political, financial, etc. But if you solved all those problems and did not improve the performance of the teacher in the classroom, you wouldn't have achieved very much. Actually, if we give teachers better classrooms, more money, computer-assisted instruction, educational television and everything else they keep screaming for—it would do more havoc

than good if it is in the hands of an incompetent artisan.

*Interview, Los Angeles/*
*Los Angeles Times, 8-11:(4)7.*

**Arthur G. Powell**
*Associate dean for academic affairs,*
*Harvard University Graduate School*
*of Education*
4

Schools are a litmus paper which tells us what the community thinks education should be. The basic concepts of schooling really didn't change much from the 1890s through the 1960s because, for most of that time, there was a consensus on what the public wanted from education. Now educators are not sure what direction to take, and colleges and high schools let students do their own thing from a large array of electives. In other words, the public consensus has broken down.

*U.S. News & World Report, 9-1:43.*

**Diane Ravitch**
*Historian of education, Teachers College,*
*Columbia University*
5

All education implies the transmission of values. How a teacher acts toward children; how he resolves disputes among them; whether or not he requires children to be responsible for themselves and to act responsibly toward others—in short, every lesson he teaches, decision he makes, every expectation he holds, has the potential of influencing his students' ideas about the world . . . By refusing to guide, inspire, prod or challenge his students, by withholding choices and declining to impart skills and attitudes, he may be actively blocking the child's freedom and growth.

*U.S. News & World Report, 9-1:43.*

**Vincent Reed**
*Acting Superintendent of Schools of the*
*District of Columbia*
6

I think that just as you should aid students who have certain deficiencies, so you should aid children whom God has gifted. We can't have our children graduate from high school with no idea of what they can do because they've never been challenged. We've got to motivate all of them to achieve to the best of their abilities.

*Interview, Washington/
The Washington Post, 11-17:(A)1.*

**Wilson Riles**
*California State Superintendent
of Public Instruction*

1

This has become a time of retrenchment and program reductions among school districts . . . Despite current money problems, the vital place that music and the arts occupy in our lives must be recognized in the education of the young. Perhaps never before in our history has it been so important to give our children a sense of beauty and mystery of life and nature . . . Fine-arts programs have been among the first to be cut back in school districts with financial problems. I think we need to look for ways to preserve what remains of this important part of our curriculum.

*March/Los Angeles Times, 5-11:(Calendar)50.*

2

We treat them [high-school students] like children too long. We do not realize they are young adults; they want responsibility. Two generations ago, when society was less complex, they had roles to play. Now we just shunt them off to school. It's bound to lead to boredom.

*The New York Times, 3-2:(1)33.*

**Herbert Salinger**
*Chief placement officer,
University of California, Berkeley*

3

The university is not set up to train young people for jobs. It can take a student for four years and develop his breadth and depth. The university is intended to develop the human being.

*San Francisco Examiner & Chronicle,
10-26:(A)4.*

**John C. Sawhill**
*President, New York University*

4

My principal concern now is of students turning away from the liberal arts toward vocationalism, which is basically nothing but training for your first job out of college. We need to emphasize that the undergraduate experience is

a time when students acquire skills and values, an ability to think through problems, that they need to lead a full and mature and interesting life.

*Interview, New York/
The New York Times, 7-31:45.*

**Eric Sevareid**
*News commentator,
Columbia Broadcasting System*

5

It occurred to me that the current discontent and lack of continuity between the generations in America came about at least in part because of the tremendous increase in school-age children to educate in the 1960s. We hired teachers who weren't much older than their students and had no real understanding of what the country had gone through.

*Interview, Washington/
Los Angeles Times, 7-18:(4)22.*

**Albert Shanker**
*President, United Federation of Teachers*

6

[Criticizing possible class-size increases in New York City resulting from projected teacher layoffs]: Not only will our teachers not accept the increased classes, but many parents will not send their children to school and some district boards will not open the schools for the fall term if the Board of Education goes through with its enlargement plans. For any parent to keep a child in our schools with 40 in a class, while nearby suburbs average 25, would be unthinkable. No education for the children could be expected. And with classes so large, there would be violence and vandalism with which the teachers could not and would not try to cope. We might just as well hold classes on Randalls Island or Lewisohn Stadium.

*Interview, New York, July 20/
The New York Times, 7-21:26.*

**Mina Shaughnessy**
*Dean of academic evaluation,
City University of New York*

7

[On college students who cannot write correctly]: There's no way of learning to write unless you write; and since high schools don't require a good deal of writing, there's no partic-

# WHAT THEY SAID IN 1975

*(MINA SHAUGHNESSY)*

ular reason why we should expect students to be able to write . . . The teaching of writing is a very time-consuming job. You think you can teach subject-verb agreement, but you have to teach what you mean by subject, what you mean by verb, what you mean by agreement. You think as you're walking through a jungle path that you've pulled a leaf, and really it's the tail of an elephant that you're pulling along.

*Interview/*
*The New York Times, 5-4:(13)2.*

## George Steiner
*Literary critic, "The New Yorker"*
*magazine; Extraordinary fellow,*
*Churchill College, Cambridge, England*     1

[On reading and education]: We must keep book prices down, or a generation will grow up that no longer reads, and then we should have to train people to read all over again, as in the Middle Ages. Knowing a work by heart has disappeared; notice the wording, the affection suggested in "by heart." Sometimes it seems to me that contemporary American education is a form of collective amnesia.

*Interview, New York/*
*Publishers Weekly, 4-21:12.*

## Tom Swain
*Assistant director of admissions,*
*University of Michigan*     2

[On the drop in college entrance examination scores]: The test may be at fault on the basis that it is an assumption of what people are supposed to know that may no longer be true. In English classes, for example, the stress on punctuation that was evident a few years ago is no longer around. A lot more is acceptable, and there may even be more-permissive grading at the high-school level. It's quite a contradiction, but over the last few years we've seen an increase in the high-school grade-point averages of new freshmen, while their SAT scores have declined. More-permissive grading may be responsible.

*Interview/*
*The Dallas Times Herald, 10-17:(C)4.*

## Barry Switzer
*Football coach, University of Oklahoma*     3

What concerns me the most today is the campaign against college football by those who think football isn't important . . . The more I'm around colleges and football teams, the more I'm convinced that a good team is a positive influence in a college environment. A good football team implements the academic program. The more interest in football, the more interest in academics . . . College is for people of a young and very impressionable age. They enjoy the feeling of success, and if their football team is successful they have more zest for classes and everything else. I've never known a good football player who didn't enjoy going to class if his team was winning. If you're 0-and-5, it's hard to work up any enthusiasm for anything. But if you're 5-and-0, you enjoy your whole life more—including classes.

*Interview/Los Angeles Times, 10-17:(3)1,8.*

## Willis Tate
*Chancellor and acting president,*
*Southern Methodist University*     4

Under the crunch of inflation, every department in the university, including athletics, is going to have to be very responsible for the money they spend. I'm a very strong supporter of inter-collegiate athletics, not only because of what it meant in my own life but also because it's a very important educational program . . . I defend athletics. I think it's very worthwhile. It also makes it possible for a good many young men to go to college that never would have been able to attend. I think it can be defended. It can also be defended sentimentally. It's a great tradition. Athletics are valuable, but they are not indispensable. Every department is getting a priority. I think athletics have a high priority.

*Interview, Dallas/*
*The Dallas Times Herald, 7-27:(C)1.*

## Clive Warner
*Chairman, department of social studies,*
*Santa Monica (Calif.) College*     5

So much has been handed to [students] and they watch so much TV that many of them can't read or write. And they don't know the joy and the feeling of accomplishment that comes from self-denial and the shouldering of responsibilities. They've really become the victims, a sort of deprived generation of badly informed pseudo sophisticates. They expect, and too often get, inflated grades that don't reflect their real standards of scholarship. That's probably why they don't laugh enough. They're an unhappy bunch, and I'm sorry for them.

*Interview/Los Angeles Times, 7-31:(7)3.*

**George Weber**
*Associate director,*
*Council for Basic Education*
1

Many of the recent innovations in education are healthy and constructive, particularly those designed to give more attention to individual students. But schools are realizing that teaching computational arithmetic instead of the "new" math, teaching reading through phonetic drills, and maintaining better order and discipline are simply the essential foundations a student needs to build on.

*U.S. News & World Report, 9-1:46.*

**Clifton R. Wharton, Jr.**
*President, Michigan State University*
2

General or liberal-arts studies concentrate upon developing broad perspectives, analytic abilities and communication skills, thus not only enriching our personal lives but also enhancing our adaptability to new situations—new job situations included. Thus, general education is as directly relevant to the world of work as any program of vocational training.

*At meeting sponsored by College Placement Council, Washington/*
*The Washington Post, 6-1:(B)7.*

3

The search for ever greater and greater increase in productivity [in higher education] can best be put into proper perspective by contrasting pictures of two extremes. Take first the image of a teacher on one end of a log with a student on the other end, then contrast it with the image of our freshman class of 7,000 sitting in our football stadium while one lonely professor stands at the 50-yard line in front of a microphone. The former represents the ancient notion of teaching; the latter would be a demonstration of extremely high productivity—assuming that it were effective. The choice between these two educational models, as well as among the many idealized models, depends upon a delicate and subjective balancing of educational philosophy and economic efficiency. I often wonder whether as a matter of public policy the ever-growing press for greater productivity is not leading us to the football-stadium classroom. Is this what the students, their parents, or the tax-paying citizens really want? From the criticism I hear, I doubt it. . . . we must keep in mind that realizing productivity gains in higher education is not the same as in business or industrial enterprises. A university is not a factory or an assembly line. Education by its very nature will always heavily depend upon persons. People represent nearly 80 per cent of our academic budget, and we have yet to find adequate substitutes for the human contact in the teaching/learning effort.

*State of the University address/*
*The Washington Post, 7-21:(A)18.*

**James H. Zumberge**
*President,*
*Southern Methodist University*
4

My own history of association with universities leads me to believe that a sound intercollegiate athletic program should be retained. I taught for a year at Duke, which has always been associated with strong intercollegiate athletics. The same is true for Michigan. The same is true for Minnesota where I was a student. And the same is true at Nebraska and at the University of Arizona. In all of these places, the programs of intercollegiate athletics were viewed as part of the traditional scenes on those campuses. The effort has been made to maintain them at a high level of accomplishment. I think that there are a lot of things on university campuses which are not directly related to the classroom experience of our students. We have a band. We offer plays. We offer concerts. We offer lectures. These enterprises are normally thought to be part of the collegiate or univer-

# WHAT THEY SAID IN 1975

*(JAMES H. ZUMBERGE)*

sity scene. I believe they should remain that way, and I hope to see a strong program of intercollegiate athletics continue to be developed at SMU. There are some people who, mistakenly I think, assume that it's impossible to have strong academics and strong intercollegiate athletics side-by-side. I think that argument is fallacious because there are too many examples to the contrary.
*Interview/The Dallas Times Herald, 11-16:(C)4.*

# The Environment

**Keith G. Briscoe**
*President, Buena Vista College*

1

Our civilization was built upon the great wealth of our land and has given us the world's most productive system of agriculture and industry. But history warns us that earlier civilizations had the same opportunities—but lost after the rape of the land had badly depleted their natural resources. New priorities toward our future use of resources will not come from those trained only in one segment of agriculture or technology or industry. Instead, they will come from those who understand that each solution to a problem has psychological, biological, sociological and economic consequences. And that each solution creates a new problem.
*At his inauguration/
The National Observer, 11-15:13.*

**Edmund G. Brown, Jr.**
*Governor of California (D)*

2

You can't keep producing more and more things. I don't think the earth can generate the level of affluence that is enjoyed by a very few number of people and projected on television as the birthright of everybody. The growth that has been the rule in the past—where Los Angeles and the San Fernando Valley were populated with subdivisions, and freeways were built, and cars sold, and an impression was created that we'd never stop expanding the wealth and affluence of our lives—well, I think now we're coming up against some real limits. Oil is not cheap any more. Natural gas is not cheap. The land is not as available. Transportation now is creating a great deal of pollution. People who run these things want more money. People at the lower end demand more. That runs the costs up. We are going to have to run in place just to stay where we are.
*Los Angeles Times, 9-2:(1)25.*

**George E. Brown, Jr.**
*United States Representative,
D—California*

3

Air pollution resembles a social disease—that euphemistic expression for a variety of venereal diseases—because it is generally caused by human beings doing something they really enjoy, without considering all of the consequences. That something that causes air pollution is generally excessive consumption, excessive waste, excessive use of high-powered, highly polluting automobiles, and a variety of other excesses in the use of physical products and energy. Just as careless and irresponsible sexual activity can result in venereal disease, careless and irresponsible attitudes toward the use and consumption of nature's material bounty causes air pollution. There is an analogy also between VD and air pollution in our common attitude of refusing to face up to the two problems publicly, to talk about them rationally, to recognize the difficult steps we must take to eradicate them. With VD, shame and embarrassment inhibit us. With air pollution, conventional attitudes about economic growth, the good life and other valued social goals, inhibit our thoughts and actions.
*Quote, 2-23:171.*

**Earl L. Butz**
*Secretary of Agriculture of the
United States*

4

In U.S. homes, water usage runs about 65 gallons per person per day—and there are 212 million Americans. That's nearly 14 billion gallons a day. Too much of that water is wasted, pumped needlessly from our rivers and wells. Anybody that grew up on a farm with a shallow well and a windmill knows that most of us can get by comfortably on far less water than we now use. I have one member of my staff who

---

*(EARL L. BUTZ)*

grew up on a ranch in the West. He says he was 25 years old before he discovered you could actually run more than a half inch of water into a bathtub without lightning striking you dead. His parents had instilled the idea of water conservation into him very well.

*Before National Conference on Water, Washington/The National Observer, 5-3:13.*

**Fletcher L. Byrom**
*Chairman, Koppers Company; Chairman, The Conference Board* 1

Our friends in Detroit know what happens when the bureaucrats don't get their facts in line. Catalytic converters, which the Environmental Protection Agency foisted on them, are now accused of everything—from starting forest fires to increasing the emissions of sulfuric acid mists, which are more harmful than the hydrocarbon and carbon monoxide emissions they were designed to control. Meanwhile, billions of dollars have gone down the drain and consumers have paid untold fortunes in the costs handed down by the auto industry's need to build new factories, by the petroleum industry's conversion to unleaded gas, and by the need to install separate [unleaded-gas] pumps at about 100,000 service stations.

*At Public Affairs Outlook Conference of The Conference Board/ Nation's Business, May:77.*

**Jacques-Yves Cousteau**
*Explorer* 2

The oceans are very sick from two sicknesses, all man-made. The first is mechanical destruction, the other chemical destruction. Mechanical destruction is due to projects like landfills, coastline developments, dumping, littering, trolling and explosives. Chemical destruction means the liquid wastes of cities, factories, ships. Now, we have all the intentions in our hearts to correct that. But, really, when we think of the human species, it behaves like a stupid animal. When we talk to humans, they can react as intelligent persons. But as a species,

we do exactly the wrong thing all the time. For example, it would be much more economical, instead of fighting pollution, to avoid pollution. But no, that does not come to our mind. We pollute, and after that we try to purify, instead of putting the anti-toxin in to start with. It's just unbelievably stupid. So that's why, if dramatic measures are not taken, one could become very pessimistic. The seas are very sick. The vitality of the sea has drastically been reduced during the past 20 years.

*Interview/The Washington Post, 1-4:(D)3.*

3

What the sea really represents is survival for mankind. Without it, there is no possibility for life on earth. It's that simple. Thanks to pictures taken from outer space, more and more people—especially young people—are aware of how small our planet really is. They look at a picture of the whole earth and see that, in reality, there are no boundaries, no frontiers. A river starts in one country and runs through another country— but it's still the same river.

*Interview, Paris/Parade, 3-16:16.*

**Helen Gahagan Douglas**
*Former United States Representative, D–California* 4

Down through the years, man has disregarded or been unaware that we inhabit a living planet; that the earth, rivers, seas and air have life in them; that they need to be nourished and to breathe, just as we do. We are beginning to suffer the results of this mistreatment. As a consequence, human life is threatened in new and final ways. We see, hear and sense destructive changes in the quality of our environment. We have reached the point where air, water and land must be thought of as an international and national trust. No country, no government, no corporation or enterprise or person has the right to recklessly ignore this fact. The earth in many areas has reached a point of saturation, and the oceans *can* reach a point of saturation. We have to reverse this trend.

*At Marlboro (Vt.) College commencement/ The National Observer, 7-12:15.*

### Gerald R. Ford
*President of the United States*

1

As long as I have anything to say about it, this country's symbol will never be an empty beer can in a river of garbage. [However, as President] I can never lose sight of another insistent aspect of our environment—the economic needs of the American people. I pursue the goal of clean air and pure water, but I must also pursue the objective of maximum jobs and continued economic progress . . . If accomplishing every worthy environmental objective would slow down our effort to regain energy independence and a strong economy, then I must weigh all factors involved . . . We have too long treated the natural world as an adversary rather than as a life-sustaining gift from the Almighty. If man has the genius to build, he must also have the ability and the responsibility to preserve.

*At dedication of National Environmental Research Center, Cincinnati, July 3/ Los Angeles Herald-Examiner, 7-3:(A)2.*

### Henry Ford II
*Chairman, Ford Motor Company*

2

In our own plants, the estimated bill for air- and water-pollution control equipment is $64-million this year. It's $107-million in 1976 and $164-million in 1977. In a sense that's all non-productive money. We don't produce a job by doing that. And despite the cost of money and the unemployment these days, here we are required by the government to spend this ridiculous amount of funds. I think we have to look at both the cost effectiveness and whether the customer is willing to pay. What it boils down to is whether a guy living in Des Moines is supposed to pay to clean up the smog in Los Angeles?

*Interview/Time, 2-10:71.*

### Jay W. Forrester
*Professor of management, Massachusetts Institute of Technology*

3

. . . the most fundamental issue is population versus standard of living. Everything else that is going on, all the other kinds of pressures, are created by rising total demand on the system. We are moving into a situation where the higher the population the lower will be the standard of living, and vice versa. That choice for the most part is not recognized as a choice. But that fundamental underlying choice is being made whether we know we're making it or not. It's being made in terms of rising population if we don't face that issue more squarely than we have.

*Interview, Washington/ The Washington Post, 6-8:(C)1.*

4

Restricting debate [on maximum economic growth] to physical limits invites the rejoinder that technology can circumvent such limits. But any belief that shortages of energy and food can be overcome will be used by people and governments as an excuse to avoid facing the issues posed by the growth of population and consumption. Pushing back the physical limits has taken physical pressures off population growth. But, as a consequence, rising population density and scarcities will shift the pressures to social limits. Social limits are already exerting growing pressures in the form of drug addiction, kidnaping, aircraft hijackings, sabotage, revolution and a returning threat of atomic war. Social limits are not relieved by more emphasis on technology.

*At panel discussion, Woodlands, Tex., Oct. 20/ The New York Times, 10-21:18.*

### Jib Fowles
*Chairman, committee for studies of the future, University of Houston*

5

Mankind is in little danger of going under because of pollution, because the fouling of the environment is a matter much under human control. This species, like any species, is ultimately devoted to its own survival, so there is little chance that it will expire by its own hand. And the earth can support vastly more people without over-taxing them or being over-taxed in return.

*U.S. News & World Report, 6-23:65.*

# WHAT THEY SAID IN 1975

**Thor Heyerdahl**
*Explorer*
1

The ocean is no more than a big salt lake. It can die altogether, the way Lake Erie died. Life on this planet began in the ocean, and it was not possible for any animal species, and of course not for man, to evolve until the plankton had produced enough oxygen to send it out of the ocean into the atmosphere. There was no atmosphere in the sense that we know it today until the marine plankton sent up enough oxygen. And if we take away this botanical plankton we will be where we were in the beginning. It will be impossible to live on land unless we have this source of oxygen coming out of the ocean.

*Interview, Beverly Hills, Calif./*
*Los Angeles Times, 8-31:(1)3.*

**Donald P. Hodel**
*Administrator,*
*Bonneville Power Administration*
2

. . . I've become deeply concerned about the future of the environmental movement. What began as a responsible, needed guardian of our natural resources has become something quite different. It is no longer just a conservation movement, but a crusade to stop all development in this country. As such, this new environmental movement is on a collision course with the growing demand for energy, and there's no doubt in my mind as to which will win. The people of this country will not give up their standard of living because someone tells them that the Spartan life is the good life. They will not forego their own aspirations to pay for someone else's nostalgic quest for Walden Pond. Unless the responsible majority of environmentalists regain control of what used to be their movement, their cause is going to be set back 20 years. When we really feel the energy squeeze—and I think it's almost inevitable—John Q. Public is going to demand somebody's scalp. And the environmental movement will be in for a massive backlash.

*Before City Club,*
*Portland, Ore., July 11/*
*Vital Speeches, 8-1:621.*

**M. King Hubbert**
*Former president,*
*Geological Society of America*
3

Growth, growth, growth—that's all we've known. World automobile production is doubling every 10 years; civilian air travel doubles every 10 years; human population growth is like nothing that has happened in all of geologic history. The world will only tolerate so many doublings of anything, whether it's power plants or grasshoppers. Our culture doesn't know how to deal with a leveling off or a decline, but it will have to. If we do it right, we can stabilize for quite a while. We have to steer ourselves into a stable state with as little catastrophe as possible.

*The National Observer, 5-10:20.*

**Henry A. Kissinger**
*Secretary of State of the United States*
4

The United States is now engaged with some 140 nations in one of the most comprehensive and critical negotiations in history—an international effort to devise rules to govern the domain of the oceans. No current international negotiation is more vital for the long-term stability and prosperity of our globe. One need not be a legal scholar to understand what is at stake. In a world desperate for new sources of energy and minerals, vast and largely untapped reserves exist in the oceans. In a world that faces widespread famine and malnutrition, fish have become an increasingly vital source of protein. In a world clouded by pollution, the environmental integrity of the oceans turns into a critical international problem. In a world where 95 per cent of international trade is carried on the seas, freedom of navigation is essential.

*Before American Bar Association/*
*The New York Times, 10-26:(11)18.*

**David E. Lilienthal**
*Chairman, Development and Resources Corporation; Former Chairman, Atomic Energy Commission of the United States*
5

The extremist proponents of a stop-growth fantasy have spread fear, baseless fear. We have by no means exhausted—hardly touched—the ability of the human mind to devise new answers to old problems. Much of our current economic problems goes back a few years to when we permitted some highly theoretical people to stick figures into computers and make scare headlines about an imaginary limit to growth. These were the people who came forward with the notion that we gain stability and advance humanitarian ends and protect the environment by denying a basic principle of life: growth. When you say, "Stop growth and stop development," you stop human development. Electrical energy is a prime mover for creative and humane forces. Instead of throwing up our hands and saying nay to every prospect of increasing the amount of electrical energy and calling for cutbacks in its utilization, we ought to take an adult view of our capacity to increase its production. Somebody's got to thumb his nose at all this pseudoscientific rubbish and nonsense about the exhaustion of American resources.

*Interview, New York/*
*Los Angeles Times, 5-27:(2)7.*

**Patrick J. Lucey**
*Governor of Wisconsin (D)*
1

The government of America, the politicians of America, the people of America, are hooked. They are hooked on the philosophy of a chicken in every pot, two cars in every garage and the right to claim more chickens, larger pots and bigger, gas-guzzling cars. Few have had the guts to say it is time for "cold turkey." Well, let it be said today: It is time for America to get unhooked, to go the "cold turkey route," to adopt a new Politics of Survival and a new philosophy of governance based upon scarcity.

*Before Tennessee Young Democrats, Nashville/*
*The Wall Street Journal, 7-2:8.*

**James S. Mellet**
*Professor of geology, New York University*
2

We've got to ask ourselves what we can do today to make this country a better place to live 200 years from now, which is what our Founding Fathers did for us 200 years ago. If they were alive today, they would have speci-

fied in black and white the right to clean air and water ... we all have a right to a clean environment because clean air was here long before we were. All environmental impact decisions have been made outside the legislative process by regulatory agencies. If we have concern at all for our posterity, we cannot allow further degradation of our environment. We took enormous risks 200 years ago. Why can't we do that today by guaranteeing a clean environment for Americans 200 years from now?

*New Fairfield, Conn./*
*The Dallas Times Herald, 6-12:(A)33.*

**Edmund S. Muskie**
*United States Senator, D—Maine*
3

[On pollution]: We cannot expect the public to understand when the rhetoric of crisis is accompanied by a program of pablum. If we do not take strong action soon, we may find ourselves too far into the quicksand to struggle out. America has always responded to a crisis with workable solutions. But we must begin now. In the present case, time—like energy, clean air and clean water—is a finite resource.

*Quote, 3-2:193.*

**Jacqueline Onassis**
*Widow of the late President of the*
*United States John F. Kennedy*
4

[Criticizing the tearing down of classic old buildings]: We've all heard that it's too late. [The public has been told] that it has to happen. But we know that it's not so. Even in the 11th hour, it's not too late. Old buildings are important, [and] if we don't care about our past, we cannot hope for our future.

*At rally to save Grand Central Terminal,*
*New York, Jan. 30/*
*The New York Times, 1-31:35.*

**Don Paarlberg**
*Director of Agricultural Economics, Department*
*of Agriculture of the United States*
5

In the long run, looking into the 21st century, unless the rate of population growth is checked, there is no solution to the world food problem. Projected at recent rates, the population chart runs off the page; the numbers be-

# WHAT THEY SAID IN 1975

*(DON PAARLBERG)*

come not only unmanageable, but inconceivable. Indeed, unless there is a reduction in the rate of population growth, we will run into many other problems: over-crowding and the frictions that result therefrom, civil uprisings, depletion of natural resources and degradation of the environment. It may indeed be that these other hazards will become the critical ones, disciplining our numbers, while food supplies are still adequate. It may be that, in specifying the food supply as the factor that ultimately limited population growth, Malthus indentified the wrong factor. What we have done with the Green Revolution and like agricultural advancements is to win a decade, or two, or three, within which to cope with the population problem. If we use this time wisely, our generation will help the world move out from under the Malthusian shadow. If we use it poorly, the bleakest of pessimistic predictions will prove to be right.

*At World Future Society General Assembly,
Washington, June 3/Vital Speeches, 7-15:585.*

## Russell W. Peterson
*Chairman, Federal Council on
Environmental Quality*

1

. . . I favor continued growth—but only after we have sorted out in our minds the difference between "growth" and "consumption." The wonderful American economic machine began by satisfying needs; and it so excelled at this function that before too long it had enough extra capacity to start satisfying appetites—the things that are not absolutely necessary to life, but make it more attractive. Now this extraordinary machine, having satisfied the appetites of the affluent among us, is more and more devoted to *creating* appetites. "Okay," goes the American sales-promotion rationale, "We've sold everybody electric lights, air-conditioning, a refrigerator, a freezer, two TVs, an electric carving knife, and a gadget that turns on a light at dusk. Now . . . what else can we make that uses electricity?" I composed that list carefully: I own every item on it. It is not American industry that is the villain of this homily, but the American consumer—me, and 100 million

well-meaning persons like me. And it is not the American businessman who must be bludgeoned into changing his ways, as if he had deliberately chosen to pollute the water and air, to coat the Mallard with oil, to amplify our wastes with no-return bottles that have to be returned somewhere. All of us have elected environmental damage, albeit unwittingly, by voting for convenience with our dollars, and we will all have to change our ways . . .

*Before American Association for the
Advancement of Science, New York, Jan. 30/
The Washington Post, 2-25:(A)18.*

2

Ecology, I'm afraid, is in danger of becoming synonymous with a soft-headed desire to repeal technology and re-invent the Garden of Eden. When ecological concerns come into conflict with other social needs or appetites, as they increasingly do these days, policy-makers in industry and government tend to regard ecology as a desirable but dispensable extra. On the contrary, our biosphere, the subject which ecology studies, is the meat and potatoes of human life. It is the other things, the supposedly "fundamental" and "practical" concerns of society, which are society's dessert—the extras made possible by man's primeval success at securing, through the good luck of evolution, the most favorable niche in the chain of life.

*Before American Association for the
Advancement of Science, New York, Jan. 30/
The New York Times, 1-31:10.*

3

The trouble with population-control as a national priority is that, while it's all about sex, it has no sex appeal. Americans prefer problems that can be attacked fast, and solved fast. We like to hit problems on the head with our doctorates and our dollars today, and see them crumple tomorrow. And it's awfully hard to keep us interested in a problem which is not only persistent but seemingly far away. We wince in horror and sympathy at the pathetic photos of children with matchstick limbs and swollen bellies—but then we turn the page, or the TV screen erases our horror with a new image, a new sensation . . . and we forget about those kids, those parents, those human beings

dying in distant lands with unfamiliar names . . .
I don't know whether we have already passed the
limits of the earth's human-carrying capacity. I
don't know whether technologies unknown or
already in the works will permit a tripling or
even a quadrupling of human population. I
don't know whether the well-fed peoples of the
earth will stop stuffing cattle with cereals, and
divert them instead to human beings . . . I *do*
know that severe ecological damage often cannot be detected until it is irreversible—until the
long tumble down comes to a sudden stop. And
we *do* know that the ecosystem which supports
man is the one and only life-support system we
have; if we exceed its carrying capacity, we
cannot buy another one.

*At North American Wildlife and*
*Natural Resources Conference,*
*Pittsburgh, March 17/*
*Vital Speeches, 5-1:426.*

1

There is a real struggle today between economics and the environment, a struggle which I
believe is unwarranted . . . Arguments rooted in
[a simple sense of beauty for the environment]
are not strong enough in a time when the
threats against our environment are multiplying
daily, and when each of these threats is supported by powerful economic arguments. We
must be able to demonstrate to our critics that
our concern for the environment is every bit as
practical—even more so, in fact—than their concern for the economy.

*Before National Audubon*
*Society, New Orleans/*
*The Christian Science Monitor, 5-16:10.*

2

We've come a long way [in the environmental movement] in a relatively short interval.
It's only been five years since America decided
that we were going to do this job differently.
There was no one individual responsible for
that major change in direction. It was just an
upswelling from the people. They decided that
we were running roughshod over our environment and heading for disaster. That's why those
in Congress voted almost unanimously for clean
air and water. They got the message from back
home. When the history of this period is written a few decades from now, it will be recog-

nized that we passed a major milestone here in
the early '70s in facing up to the fact that man
must live in harmony with nature.

*Interview/U.S. News & World Report, 8-4:61.*

3

I hope . . . that all nations will learn, in time,
that the resources of the earth are finite, and
that environmental degradation respects no
national boundaries. It is this point of view, this
essential dependence of man on a common
environment, that we must strive to convey.
For the fact is we do have the power to destroy
the earth. However, if man recognizes this dependence, he can arrest his accelerating degradation of the planet and set about restoring its
capacity to support future generations.

*At Field Museum, Chicago/*
*The Washington Post, 11-16:(D)6.*

**John R. Quarles**
*Deputy Administrator, Environmental*
*Protection Agency of the United States*

4

[Americans] have made a fetish of convenience, and we purchase convenience by the
expenditure of materials and energy. In short,
we are simply wasteful . . . using more material,
more land and more energy than is justified
against prospectives of future need. Waste and
pollution are tied together.

*At conference on waste reduction,*
*Washington, April 2/*
*Los Angeles Times, 4-3:(1)4.*

**Ronald Reagan**
*Former Governor of California (R)*

5

Game [wildlife] management contributes
more to ecology than the hand-wringing and
crying of some of the articulate, but impractical, bug-and-bunny folk. A scientific game-
management program was advocated and put
into practice by the sportsmen long before
ecology became a household word. And yet the
myth, largely by urbanites, persists that you are
more interested in destroying wildlife than in
preserving it. There is no question that the past
practices of market hunting and poaching
threatened some species. But you're concerned
about this and the best chance we have of

97

# WHAT THEY SAID IN 1975

*(RONALD REAGAN)*

perpetuating these animals from extinction is through scientific game and wildlife management, not by well-intentioned over-protection that interferes with plans for keeping the herds in balance ... Yet even now there must be controlled hunts on buffalo to keep them in balance with their habitat. However, the effort to maintain wild game at a level where the species can thrive and be healthy is too often described as slaughter and bloodletting promoted by an alleged desire to kill.

*Before Safari Club International,*
*Las Vegas, Nev., Feb. 3/*
*Los Angeles Herald-Examiner, 2-4:(C)4.*

**William D. Ruckelshaus**
*Former Administrator, Environmental*
*Protection Agency of the United States*     *1*

The environment can be saved, but we need to focus less on the inevitable fate of man and more on the quality of his journey, whatever the fate.

*Quote, 2-16:146.*

**Glenn T. Seaborg**
*President-elect, American Chemical Society;*
*Former Chairman, Atomic Energy Commission*
*of the United States*     *2*

[Saying the U.S. in the future will have to be a "recycle society"] : [In a recycle society] the present materials situation is literally reversed; all waste and scrap—what are now called "secondary materials"—become our major resources, and our natural, untapped resources become our back-up supplies. ... products will be built to be more durable, easily repairable with standardized replacement parts; new parts would be easily inserted and goods could be repaired with simple basic tools ... Many items of furniture, housewares, appliances and tools—in addition to low maintenance qualities—will be multi-functional, modular and designed for easy assembly and breakdown to be readily moved and set up in a different location when necessary. When a consumer—or more applicable, a "user"—wishes to replace an item, or

trade for something better or different, he can return the old item for the standard trade-in price.

*Before American Chemical Society,*
*Philadelphia, April 6/*
*Los Angeles Times, 4-7:(1)15.*

**Sam Steiger**
*United States Representative,*
*R–Arizona*     *3*

The optimism of the environmentalists is remarkably well-founded. Congress is still reluctant to take on the environmental lobby. The public is ahead of the Congress in its rejection of environmental extremists. It is a credit to the environmental lobbyists that they can speak louder than the public.

*Interview/*
*The Washington Post, 3-2:(A)1.*

**Eric Stork**
*Deputy Assistant Administrator for Mobile*
*Source Air Pollution Control, Environmental*
*Protection Agency of the United States*     *4*

The EPA is never going to build cars. It's the auto industry that has to build cars. But it's the job of the EPA to make sure the auto industry does in fact build the cleanest cars that are possible to build. In this world, if you want to move a man or an organization, there is no use reaching for his throat, because in our society you are not allowed to shut off his wind. In our society, if you want to move a man or an organization, you have to reach for another part of the anatomy ... The Clean Air Act has given the EPA the best grip on the short hair that any administrative agency has ever had.

*Interview, Washington/*
*The Washington Post, 1-21:(A)2.*

**James Tanner**
*Professor of zoology,*
*University of Tennessee*     *5*

[Calling for the Congaree Swamp in South Carolina to be made into a national preserve]: Somewhere in the country we should save, for eternity if we can choose, a place like the Congaree Swamp is today, as a monument to the past natural wonders of this country and as an example for the future of the interdependence of water, earth and life.

*At rally to save the swamp, Columbia,*
*South Carolina, Sept. 20/*
*The New York Times, 9-22:34.*

**John G. Tower**
*United States Senator,*
*R—Texas*

1

... there are a bunch of Northeasterners who don't understand the economics of the oil business. They won't site refineries in their states; they don't want you to drill off-shore in their states. And yet they want *us* [in Texas] to produce the oil and gas down here at the risk of polluting *our* countryside and then pay us for it what they choose to pay. And I say they can freeze in the dark if that's their attitude.

*News conference, San Antonio, Tex., Aug. 8/*
*The Dallas Times Herald, 8-9:(A)8.*

**Russell E. Train**
*Administrator, Environmental Protection*
*Agency of the United States*

2

We must ask ourselves who are the true conservatives, a term often linked with industry and business. Are they those members of industry who would foul the air so that asthmatics choke and plants wither, or [are they] those business executives who would accept and encourage controls on air pollution? Should those who advocate a "no holds barred" approach to economic progress, who would increase the gross national product regardless of the penalty to public health and welfare, be regarded as conservatives? Is a conservative a corporate manager who would strip the land for coal with such reckless abandon that it is left to posterity as an ugly, useless moonscape? Or would the term apply more fittingly to managers who accept safeguards in strip-mining legislation to restore the land after it has been

overturned? It seems to me that persons who would abuse our land, either through bulldozers or chemicals or sheer bad planning of cities, so that the land is unfit for posterity, really come under the heading of radicals, defined by Webster as those who make "extreme changes in existing views, habits, conditions or institutions."

*At National Wildlife*
*Federation convention, Pittsburgh/*
*The National Observer, 5-24:14.*

3

Compared with [man's] skill and sophistication in *creating* pollution, our ability and instruments for comprehending and controlling it must rank somewhere at the level of the Dark Ages.

*At conference sponsored by World Health*
*Organization, Environmental Protection*
*Agency and University of Nevada,*
*Las Vegas, Sept. 15/*
*The New York Times, 9-16:25.*

**Morris K. Udall**
*United States Representative, D—Arizona*

4

[In speeches around the country,] I tell them that the last three decades were great ones but that the old era has gone; that there is no sense trying to bludgeon our way back to it; that the next 30 years can be great, too, if we're willing to go leaner; that the way to get out of this [environmental] mess is not more of the same ... I hold out a whole laundry list of things we could do to help the economy and the environment at the same time—build small cars instead of the big gas-guzzlers; rebuild the railroad beds of this country; rebuild the inner cities instead of trying to build another ring of suburbs ... I tell them that [San Francisco's] Bay Area Rapid Transit and Washington's subway are the two biggest employers of construction workers in the country, that mass transit can mean jobs.

*The Washington Post, 3-2:(A)18.*

## ENERGY

**Jamshid Amouzegar**
*Minister of Petroleum and the*
*Interior of Iran*                                    *1*

The substantive issue is not whether the oil price has gone up too rapidly. The real issue is whether or not the world is willing to realize that the era of cheap and abundant energy is over. The primary issues are whether past arrangements, policies and practices that were artificially devised and unilaterally imposed on the raw-material-producing countries should be allowed to perpetuate; whether past international injustices and inequalities should be allowed to continue; whether the sovereign rights and interests of developing nations over their national resources and assets should be ignored; and finally, whether a fair and equitable distribution of world economic power and wealth is accepted by all.

*At United Nations, New York, Sept. 2/*
*The New York Times, 9-3:12.*

**Carl E. Bagge**
*President, National Coal Association*        *2*

. . . we as a nation are today immobilized. Despite a clear call from President Ford for a national commitment to coal, Congress has not responded. We have forged no energy policy. We have made no meaningful commitment to domestic resource development. We continue our national self-indulgence in energy extravagance and irrational use of fuels. We continue our inevitable drift still further into the chasm of energy dependence. And while we thrash about, mesmerizing ourselves with the illusion of activity by creating energy slogans, embarking upon innumerable energy studies, constructing even more energy scenarios and

establishing vast new energy bureaucracies, we delude only ourselves in an abortive effort to hide our failure, to conceal our lack of a national will. Many of our political leaders whom we have annointed with the obligation of leadership do not lead; they continue to play their little games precisely as they have in the past. They bicker, they upstage each other. They attack the institutional fabric of our energy industries as though it and not their failure of responsible leadership was the real enemy. And it is this that is the ultimate "cover-up." They continue to exploit the fears of a concerned American public, spewing forth the same old rhetoric which politically polarizes our nation regionally and immobilizes it structurally even further, and which absolutely prevents the formulation of a truly rational national energy policy.

*At National Food and Energy Symposium,*
*Washington, Aug. 20/Vital Speeches, 9-15:725.*

**Benjamin F. Bailar**
*Postmaster General of the United States*        *3*

I am concerned that we in public office have not made it clear that the use of our family cars in the traditional pattern is in basic conflict with energy conservation. . . . our desire for more highways is in basic conflict with our need to reduce air pollution . . . To my mind, all of this raises the question of whether we have accepted the fact that there is a real price to everything of value . . . I sometimes wonder if, as a nation, we are willing to pay the price of things we want, or whether we are trying to cheat ourselves at a grand game of solitaire.

*New York, June 11/*
*The Washington Post, 6-12:(D)13.*

**Dewey F. Bartlett**
*United States Senator, R—Oklahoma*
1

One of the problems in Washington . . . is that there's a dearth rather than an excess of people knowledgeable in energy . . . When I first came to the Senate, we on the Interior Committee were introduced to a man who was to become the adviser to the White House on energy, and who did for a while. He had no background, no connection, no experience, no knowledge of energy, the oil business or oil companies, which was another way of saying he knew absolutely nothing about what he was about to do. I feel very strongly that people should divulge themselves of any apparent conflict of interest. We don't want conflicts of interest, but at the same time we want knowledgeable people. It's the only business I know of in which government is interested wherein real professionals are not very often used—I mean real knowledgeable people—and I think this is one of the reasons we're in the mess we're in.

*The Washington Post, 1-9:(A)8.*

**Charles G. Bluhdorn**
*Chairman, Gulf & Western Industries*
2

When President Ford became President of the United States under the most extraordinary circumstances in our nation's history [the resignation of Richard Nixon], he had a 30-day period during which the entire country rallied behind him after the debacle of Watergate. He had even a greater following and more sympathy than was accorded President Johnson after the tragedy of November, 1963. Timing is everything. Then and there was the one moment when the new President could have called on the American people to make any and all sacrifices. At that moment in time, he could have pushed through a far-reaching [energy] conservation and domestic resource-development program. It would have been a war-time-like plea, and it would have met with a unified and massive response of unconditional grass-roots support by the American people. They were looking for leadership and restoration of confidence. There is no doubt in my mind that the President lost that one golden moment of opportunity. Now I believe it is difficult to get any major [energy] plan moving forward. However, I do agree that it is better to spend $100- or $200-billion on developing our domestic energy reserves than to pump this money into places like Vietnam, as we did readily in the past, or into new military weapons going to the Middle East, as we are doing now. Any price and any program is worth paying for if it avoids the potential of blackmail or ultimate military confrontation and destruction. I think the government should give strong incentives to private enterprise.
*Interview/U.S. News & World Report, 10-13:24.*

**James L. Buckley**
*United States Senator, C—New York*
3

[Arguing against gasoline rationing]: . . . I think few people really appreciate the horror of a rationing program in effect over a three- or four-year period. Memories are awfully short. During World War II, the bureaucracy established was huge. There was black-marketeering, counterfeiting. I'm told there are still 150,000 cases on the books of people who violated the rationing laws. Rationing just isn't going to work, especially if you don't have a war to cause people to be motivated by patriotism. A further point about rationing: Prices would still rise, because if you cut gasoline use by 20 or 30 per cent, service stations will have to increase their margin of profit on each gallon to stay in business at the lower volume of sales.
*Interview/U.S. News & World Report, 2-10:23.*

**Frank Church**
*United States Senator, D—Idaho*
4

I think we could establish a [gasoline] rationing program—when we reach the point where the shortage of gasoline requires it—that would have considerable flexibility. The program I envision would provide a basic weekly entitlement for all drivers, depending upon whether they lived in rural or urban areas. It would feature coupons that could be sold for extra gasoline by those who needed it . . . And it would also establish certain priorities—for farmers, mass transportation and essential public services, for example. But I think a flexible and

# WHAT THEY SAID IN 1975

fair program could be worked out that would have much less adverse effect upon the economy than the President's [Ford] program, though it wouldn't be pleasant. There's no painless way to reduce gasoline consumption.
*Interview/U.S. News & World Report, 2-10:24.*

## Barry Commoner
*Director, Center for the Biology of Natural Systems, Washington University, St. Louis* 1

The lesson of the energy crisis is this: To survive on this earth, which is our habitat, we must live in keeping with its ecological imperatives. And if we are to take this course of ecological wisdom we must accept, at last, the wisdom of placing our faith not in production for private gain, but for public good; not in the exploitation of one people by another, but in the equality of all peoples; not in arms which devastate the land and the people and threaten world catastrophe, but in the desire which is shared everywhere in the world—for harmony with the environment, and for peace among peoples who live in it.
*At Energy Outlook and Global Interdependence conference/ The Center Magazine, March-April:31.*

## John B. Connally, Jr.
*Former Secretary of the Treasury of the United States; Former Governor of Texas (D, now R)* 2

The simple truth is that we still do not have an energy policy worthy of the name. Oil and gas resources are diminishing in the United States. Coal production is rising too slowly. We are approaching 50 per cent dependence on imported oil. Energy conservation measures are weak. We need rapid increases in investment in industrial energy conservation; in insulated housing; in mass transportation. We need smaller and more-efficient automobiles and we need them with the same urgency that we needed bombers in the Second World War. It is only when we have a tough and purposeful program of energy production and energy conservation that we are likely to have the bar-

gaining leverage to bring down the international price of petroleum.
*At World Trade Week convocation, New York/ The Dallas Times Herald, 6-1:(B)3.*

## John H. Dent
*United States Representative, D—Pennsylvania* 3

I defy any mere person in America to write an energy bill at this moment that could get a majority anywhere in this country, because most of us do not know too much about it.
*Before the House, Washington, June 11/ The Washington Post, 6-22:(C)2.*

## B. R. Dorsey
*Chairman, Gulf Oil Corporation* 4

The effectiveness of any energy-independence program revolves around basics. Supply must be increased while waste is eliminated. Capital must be generated without generating additional inflation. The nation can move toward independence by using a practical carrot-and-stick philosophy—such as removing restrictions on autos in return for higher-performance models within a specified time; or it can attempt to reach independence through an inflexible straitjacket philosophy, such as across-the-board rationing of gasoline. The proposed deregulation of new natural gas and decontrol of oil prices are examples of essential steps that must be undertaken if we are to generate the capital that is needed to develop domestic energy resources. But—and here's where I think the Congress will make the decisions that will assure the success or failure of the nation's energy future—industry cannot absorb additional taxes that will rob it of funds, and still get the job done. Energy is a capital-intensive industry, and, without capital, there can be no expansion.
*At Conference for Corporation Executives, Washington, Jan. 28/Vital Speeches, 2-15:281.*

## Bob Eckhardt
*United States Representative, D—Texas* 5

[On the expiration of oil-price controls and the expected higher retail prices]: [The people] don't understand why the price of oil, after it has been doubled, is not sufficient to produce more oil. They don't understand the policy of allowing the price to go up as the sole means of controlling use. The people equate this with what was done with respect to controlling fiscal policy, with increase of interest rates—and the banks draw the interest. Now, why in order to control the use of oil after the price has once doubled do you need to double the doubling again and let the oil companies put the money in their pockets?

*TV-radio interview/*
*"Face the Nation," Columbia Broad-*
*casting System, 8-31.*

## Gerald R. Ford
*President of the United States*
*1*

The economic disruptions we and others are experiencing stems in part from the fact that the world price of petroleum has quadrupled in the last year. But, in all honesty, we cannot put all of the blame on the oil-exporting nations. We, the United States, are not blameless. Our growing dependence upon foreign sources has been adding to our vulnerability for years and years. And we did nothing to prepare ourselves for such an event as the embargo of 1973. During the 1960s, this country had a surplus capacity of crude oil, which we were able to make available to our trading partners whenever there was a disruption of supply. This surplus capacity enabled us to influence both supplies and prices of crude oil throughout the world. Our excess capacity neutralized any effort at establishing an effective cartel, and thus the rest of the world was assured of adequate supplies of oil at reasonable prices. By 1970 our capacity, our surplus capacity, had vanished; and, as a consequence, the latent power of the oil cartel could emerge in full force.

*State of the Union address, Washington,*
*Jan. 15/The New York Times, 1-16:24.*

*2*

[Arguing against gasoline rationing]: I believe that those who propose rationing do not have a clear understanding of what their plan would entail for the American people . . . Rationing provides no stimulus to increase domestic petroleum supply or accelerate alter-

native energy sources. By concentrating exclusively on gas rationing, many other areas for energy conservation are overlooked. In addition to being ineffective, gas rationing is inequitable. Even a rationing system that is designed with the best motives in mind and implemented by the most conscientious administrators would not be fair. If you were to go around the country and ask individuals what they should get under a fair rationing system, you would find that there would be simply not enough gasoline to go around. In fact, to reach our 1975 goal of reducing foreign oil imports by one million barrels per day, a gas rationing system would limit each driver to less than nine gallons a week. Inequities would be everywhere. How would people in remote areas of the country get enough gas to drive into town? How would farmers get enough gas to harvest their crops? What would happen to people who must drive a long way to work each day? And who would make those decisions? It is essential that we recognize the size of the problem which we are attempting to solve. As a consequence, we must evaluate each energy program to see whether, in fact, it actually confronts and solves the problem.

*News conference, Washington, Jan. 21/*
*The New York Times, 1-22:20.*

*3*

[On oil prices and oil embargoes against the U.S.]: In the case of economic strangulation, [the nation has] to be prepared . . . to take the necessary action for our self-preservation. When you are being strangled it is a case of either dying or living. [The] public has to have the reassurance that we are not going to permit America to be strangled to death . . .

*Television interview, Washington, Jan. 23/*
*Los Angeles Herald-Examiner, 1-24:(A)3.*

*4*

The achievement of our independence in energy will be neither quick nor easy. No matter what programs are adopted, perseverence by the American people and a willingness to accept inconvenience will be required in order to reach this important goal. The American economy was built on the basis of low-cost energy. The

# WHAT THEY SAID IN 1975

## (GERALD R. FORD)

design of our industrial plants and production processes reflect this central element in the American experience. Cheap energy freed the architects of our office buildings from the need to plan for energy efficiency. It made private homes cheaper because expensive insulation was not required when energy was more abundant. Cheap energy also made suburban life accessible to more citizens, and it has given the mobility of the automobile to rural and city dwellers alike. The low cost of energy during most of the 20th century was made possible by abundant resources of domestic oil, natural gas and coal. This era has now come to an end. We have held the price of natural gas below the levels required to encourage investment in exploration and development of new supplies, and below the price which would have encouraged more careful use. By taking advantage of relatively inexpensive foreign supplies of oil, we improved the quality of life for Americans and saved our own oil for future use. By neglecting to prepare for the possibility of import disruptions, however, we left ourselves overly dependent upon unreliable foreign supplies.

*Economic report to Congress, Feb. 4\*/*
*The New York Times, 2-5:17.*

*1*

An energy-rationing program might be acceptable for a brief period, but an effective program will require us to hold down consumption for an extended period. A rationing program for a period of five years or more would be both intolerable and ineffective. The costs in slower decision-making alone would be enormous. Rationing would mean that every new company would have to petition the government for a license to purchase or sell fuel. It would mean that any new plant expansion or any new industrial process would require approval. It would mean similar restrictions on home-builders, who already find it impossible in much of the nation to obtain natural-gas hookups. After five or 10 years, such a rigid program would surely sap the vitality of the American economy by substituting bureaucratic decisions for those of the

marketplace. It would be impossible to devise a fair long-term rationing system.

*Economic report to Congress, Feb. 4\*/*
*The New York Times, 2-5:17.*

*2*

... the Congress has done virtually nothing about natural-gas policy for the past two years—much less come up with a plan to meet the expected shortages. This nation cannot remove the insecurity of our dependence on foreign sources of oil while we constantly hold back on assistance to producers right here at home—who can help to make us secure and independent. We simply must have capital investment if we are to discover new sources of oil and new natural gas—and if we are to put people back to work solving our problems. We will not get help from anyone but ourselves. The future of this country is in our own hands ... Instead of betting on what foreign sources may do, we should put our money on what Americans can do and will do. If we offer sufficient incentives, American enterprise here at home will solve our energy problems.

*At Chamber of Commerce's Energy Economic*
*Conference, Houston, Feb. 10/*
*The Washington Post, 2-11:(A)4.*

*3*

We have become increasingly at the mercy of others for the fuel on which our entire economy runs. Here are the facts and figures that will not go away: The United States is dependent on foreign sources for about 37 per cent of its present petroleum needs. In 10 years, if we do nothing, we will be importing more than half our oil, at prices fixed by others—if they choose to sell to us at all. In two and a half years we will be twice as vulnerable to a foreign oil embargo as we were two winters ago. We are now paying out $25-billion a year for foreign oil. Five years ago, we paid out only $3-billion. Five years from now, if we do nothing, who knows how many more billions will be flowing out of the United States? These are not just American dollars, these are American jobs ... Our American economy runs on energy. No energy, no jobs. In the long run it is just that simple. The sudden four-fold increase in foreign oil prices and the 1973 embargo helped throw us into this recession. We are on our way out of the recession. Another oil embargo could throw us back. We cannot continue to depend on the price and supply whims of others. The Congress cannot drift, dawdle and debate forever with America's future.

*Broadcast address to the nation,*
*Washington May 27/*
*The New York Times, 5-28:20.*

1

[Criticizing the House for voting for continued controls on domestic oil prices, a rejection of his contention that decontrol is necessary to stimulate domestic production]: [Americans should not] believe those who tell you they are fighting to hold down your energy costs by postponing the decisions to find and develop more of our own energy ... The truth is that the American consumer can no longer enjoy cheap energy–at least not in the lifetime of most of us. Under the plan I have set forth, we will pay American dollars to American companies to produce American energy for American jobs and American profits and American taxes. This will assure greater American economic stability and American economic and political security. The real danger of an explosion in our economy is not the actions I propose but the inaction that stifles more reproduction here at home and increases our dependence on oil from abroad ... the reckless risk of placing our national livelihood and security in the hands of others. That doesn't represent American independence, self reliance or the pioneering spirit. It is just plain chicken and I don't think Americans admire it.

*At Oklahoma State Fair, Sept. 19/*
*The Washington Post, 9-20:(A)1.*

### John H. Glenn, Jr.
*United States Senator, D–Ohio*

2

We let things like the energy crisis creep up on us, even though the energy experts have been predicting this for a long time. Now much of our national and international relations over the next couple of decades are going to revolve around what we do about food and fuel, particularly fuel. I can't understand why more people don't get disturbed about this energy problem.

If we think we have troubles today, we haven't seen anything yet compared with what is coming if we don't solve our energy problems. Already we have plants shut down because of energy shortages. The cutback in automobile production is due to it in part. Why buy a new car if you are not going to be able to use it? The situation is so cotton-pickin' serious it's frightening, because our position of leadership in the world will turn on what we do about energy.

*Interview, Washington/*
*Los Angeles Times, 1-21:(2)7.*

### Nat Goldfinger
*Research director, American Federation of Labor-Congress of Industrial Organizations*

3

What we need is a comprehensive energy policy. We need quotas on oil imports, with the U.S. government as purchaser of the imports on a closed-bid basis. We need gas rationing of some type, with the ability for people to buy gasoline above the rationed amount with payment of a steep tax above the rationed price. We need an effective government allocation of oil on a regional and industry basis so we don't get concentrations of fuel in some places. We need the development as fast as possible of alternative sources of energy. Finally, we need effective government action on the problem of the major multinational oil companies.

*Interview/The National Observer, 9-20:15.*

### Henry M. Jackson
*United States Senator, D–Washington*

4

[Criticizing President Ford's decision to increase the oil-import tariff in an effort to cut down on imported-oil use]: This one action will cost American consumers $2.5-billion per year, but it is only one step in an Administration program of higher tariffs and higher fuel prices which will take $33.5-billion from consumers and enrich the oil and gas companies and coal producers ... Higher prices for energy and the drain they cause from consumer purchasing power are the chief single cause of the present depression. Further price increases, including the increases that will be generated by the new tariff, threaten to turn the depression

# WHAT THEY SAID IN 1975

*(HENRY M. JACKSON)*

into an economic catastrophe from which this nation may not recover for years.

*May 28/Los Angeles Times, 5-29:(1)12.*

**Neil H. Jacoby**
*Emeritus professor of business and economic policy, University of California, Los Angeles* 1

One of the many adverse consequences of oil-price controls is to favor Arab producers of crude oil over American producers. Presently, the Federal government puts a ceiling of $5.25 per barrel on so-called "old" oil—production from a particular well in the base year 1972. Meanwhile, Americans are paying the Arab and other OPEC producers $11 per barrel for imported oil. The low ceiling price deters U.S. producers from spending money to maintain the output in older wells. If Congress permitted the price of domestic "old" oil to rise to the world level, thousands of owners of oil wells with low production would spend money to increase production, through acidization, fire or water flooding, deeper drilling or other techniques. Why doesn't Congress remove price controls on old oil so that domestic production can expand—or at least not decline any further? Every barrel less produced in the U.S. means one barrel more for the exporting OPEC countries. The only argument advanced for retaining price controls is that American well owners will collect a "windfall" profit by being able to sell their oil at higher prices. But the alternate is to let U.S. production fall, and to buy the oil at $11 per barrel from the Arabs instead. In other words, Congress prefers to pay $11 per barrel from the Arabs rather than to Americans. It appears that the Arabs are more deserving than our fellow Americans. No wonder people are confused.

*Los Angeles Herald-Examiner, 4-2:(A)12.*

**Henry A. Kissinger**
*Secretary of State of the United States* 2

Our objective must be to construct a world energy system capable of providing, on terms fair to all, the fuels needed to continue and extend the progress of our economics and our societies . . . Goethe said that "the web of this world is woven of necessity and change." We stand at a point where those stands intertwine. We must not regard necessity as capricious nor leave change to chance. Necessity impels us to where we are but summons us to choose where we go. Our interdependence will make us thrive together or decline together. We can drift, or we can decide. We have no excuse for failure.

*At International Energy Agency ministerial meeting, Paris, May 27/ The New York Times, 5-29:19.*

**Milton Levenson**
*Director, nuclear power division, Electric Power Research Institute* 3

What people have got to realize is that we don't know of any energy-production system that doesn't insult the environment. They all do, but we can be selective as to what kind of insult and where. If you're in an energy area well supplied with coal, then perhaps that's the best fuel to burn . . . There will be deaths and environmental problems with nuclear power, but they'll be a lot less than from coal. As I said, all energy production will insult the environment, so it's just a matter of selecting the best means under each set of circumstances. We need several energy sources in this country. America is so strong because it has never had to rely on just one kind of fuel.

*Dallas, Feb. 18/ The Dallas Times Herald, 2-19:(E)8.*

**Dennis L. Meadows**
*Associate professor of engineering and business, Dartmouth College* 4

We can't get started on massive coal development given our current air-pollution standards. A rational energy strategy would allow standards to erode between now and 1985, then be tightened again . . . The quality of the environment in the 1990s will be much higher if we start a program of massive coal use now than if we don't. The consequences of energy scarcity are much more environmentally damaging than maximum coal development.

*Interview/Business Week, 5-12:59.*

**Walter F. Mondale**
*United States Senator,*
*D—Minnesota*
1

. . . we are now relying on precisely those energy sources that are in shortest supply over the long term. For every energy unit of oil estimated to remain in the world, there are 200 units of potential energy to be realized from shale. For every unit of natural gas, there are 10 units of coal. And for every unit of oil and natural gas combined, there are 6,500 units of uranium energy available for use in conventional light-water nuclear reactors. We are not using these more abundant sources of energy today primarily for one reason: We simply do not have the technology to exploit them.

*Before Minnesota Joint Council of Engineering Societies, Edina, Minn., Nov. 24/\*\**

**Thomas A. Murphy**
*Chairman,*
*General Motors Corporation*
2

There are a lot of thoughtful, well-meaning people around who, if they had been here when the country was first discovered, would have left us about where we were. A great wilderness, a lot of undeveloped resources—and that would be it. They would have said, "We have to worry about the environment. You can't cut down those trees. You can't break the land to mine coal or iron ore." Further, I venture to say, you probably would not have the automobile today, certainly not powered by gasoline . . . We're seeing the same mentality today. People are saying the same thing about nuclear power. I don't think it is as dangerous [as gasoline]. Given our knowledge, it is probably a lot less dangerous than gas tanks in the early days. In the Model Ts you were sitting on the fuel. In the Model A it was right up in front of you. My point is, there is danger in life. You live with danger. There are some people out there who [say] that if you build nuclear plants to produce the energy we need, you are going to blow yourselves out of existence. Are we going to stop progressing? Reduce our standard of living? I don't think we have to.

*Interview, Washington/*
*Los Angeles Times, 5-14:(2)5.*

**Mohammad Reza Pahlavi**
*Shah of Iran*
3

World petroleum supplies will be finished within 50 years at most. And yet you in America and elsewhere have 400 or 500 years' worth of coal supplies. I keep telling you to use *it*—not *us* [the oil exporters].

*Interview, Teheran/*
*The New York Times, 3-23:(4)15.*

**Gerald L. Parsky**
*Assistant Secretary of the Treasury of the United States*
4

We have been used to an abundance of cheap energy, and the easy availability lulled us into letting our dependence on foreign supplies increase to a point where a group of oil-producing countries can control the price. That is really the crux of our problem: We have lost the ability to allow the market for oil to operate freely. Now we must face the fact that cheap energy is no longer available. $10 or $11 oil is with us, and I believe that if you consider just the economics of the situation, there is no way that the forces of supply and demand will be able to force the price to decline for at least three years. I say this principally because sufficient non-OPEC supply will not be available before then. Further, if we do not take the necessary actions now to insure that supplies of energy will be developed in this country, the price will not have to be reduced after three years—and might go higher.

*Before Investment Association of New York,*
*Jan. 14/Vital Speeches, 2-15:282.*

**Endicott Peabody**
*Acting president, Americans for Energy Independence; Former Governor of Massachusetts (D)*
5

When the OPEC oil prices jumped dramatically in 1973, the air was filled with outcries demanding the establishment of a national oil reserve. Since then, the United States has grown even more dependent on foreign oil sources which now account for some 40 per cent of our oil supply. But the clamor for an oil reserve has died down even though we currently have only a 20-to-30 day oil reserve. Under the best of

# WHAT THEY SAID IN 1975

circumstances, our short-term need for foreign oil will grow. Yet even our best friends and neighbors—Canada and South America—have warned us about expecting too much help from them. No longer are we guaranteed automatic access to their oil and gas resources. Confronted by this sudden turnaround, the United States must establish as a minimum a 6-month oil reserve from its domestic oil sources. Without this reserve our foreign policy, national security and domestic well-being are vulnerable to any action of Middle Eastern potentates—however currently implausible, however potentially outrageous.

*At Western Governors' Conference,*
*Albuquerque, Oct. 30/*
*Vital Speeches, 12-15:139.*

## Dixy Lee Ray
*Former Chairman, Atomic Energy Commission*
*of the United States*                                             *1*

The primary basis we have for judging the safety of nuclear power plants is the 17 years of experience since the first commerical power reactor began operation in 1957. More than 50 nuclear central station plants have been operated since that time, accumulating some 210 reactor years of commercial operation. More than 350 million megawatt hours of electricity have been generated by nuclear means in that period and no member of the public has been injured by the failure of a reactor or by an accidental release of radioactivity. This is a remarkable safety record for any industry and particularly so for a developing technology . . . The combination of research, engineering, technical review and inspection activities, supplementing a careful and safety-conscious design and quality-assurance effort, provides a high degree of assurance that the health and safety of the public will be maintained.

*Interview/Mainliner, May:9.*

## Nelson A. Rockefeller
*Vice President of the United States*                          *2*

It's true that people don't understand [the energy situation]. We don't have an energy *shortage* because we are importing foreign oil.

But we do have an energy *crisis* because we are importing that oil. If imports are cut off, we would have a collapse of our economy. It's the potential crisis that has to be averted by increasing domestic energy supplies.

*At Middle Western Governors Conference,*
*Cincinnati, July 22/*
*The New York Times, 7-23:15.*

                                                                          *3*

Energy is Number 1. Energy is basic to economic vitality, strength, national security and growth. I happen to be a believer in growth. How are you going to have jobs for all these young people coming along unless the economy's growing? And it can't grow without energy—and a secure supply and a steady supply. So energy is the basis for everything.

*Interview/*
*U.S. News & World Report, 10-13:56.*

## Robert W. Scherer
*President,*
*Georgia Power Company*                                          *4*

. . . the American people overwhelmingly support nuclear-power expansion. In a recent nation-wide poll, opinion sampler Louis Harris found that 63 per cent of the American public wants more nuclear-plant construction *now*. Why? Because the public is convinced that our energy problems are real and we must get on with solving them. Supporters of this course of action include voters, neighbors of existing nuclear plants, politicians, businessmen and government regulators . . . nuclear energy can play a major conservational role all its own, by reducing the number of acres to be mined and the energy to be expended to supply an electric-utility industry almost completely dependent upon coal. Simply stated, without more nuclear power, this nation will be crippled by severe electric-energy shortages within the next decade. If this happens, our economy will be a shambles for years to come and our national destiny will hang in a tenuous balance. Either we will have more of it or we truly must suffer incredible economic and technical dislocations in the very near future.

*Before Federal Bar Association, Atlanta,*
*Sept. 10/Vital Speeches, 10-15:28.*

**Hugh Scott**
*United States Senator, R–Pennsylvania*
1

[On increasing foreign oil prices and the possibility of new oil embargoes against the U.S.]: If in this country automobiles ground to a halt and people couldn't get to work, if the temperature in people's homes dropped to 50 degrees, if the wheels of industry ground to a halt, and we couldn't employ people, I can't imagine this country not doing whatever it needed to do, either economic or military, to permit itself to survive, and we wouldn't be worth a damn as a nation if we didn't.

*TV-radio interview/"Issues and Answers,"*
*American Broadcasting Company, 1-5.*

**William E. Simon**
*Secretary of the Treasury of the*
*United States*
2

We must continue to recognize that the chief barriers to all new energy production lie at our doorstep, right here in Washington, D.C., in the problems created by the Clean Air Act, the moratorium on coal leasing, as well as price and supply regulation affecting oil and gas. This Administration is firmly in favor of protecting the public health through balanced clean-air standards and protecting the environment. At the same time, while never losing sight of our environmental and safety concerns, we must strive to insure that our policies are properly balanced to meet our expanding energy needs. We must lift the dead hand of government from any area where it smothers economic incentives and growth. The restraints imposed by the government upon production, sale and use of our energy resources are unnecessarily restrictive and should be swiftly removed.

*Before National Coal Association, Washington,*
*June 17/The New York Times, 6-18:51.*

3

We [the U.S.] were the pioneers in developing nuclear energy, and here we are, 30 years after World War II, and just under 2 per cent of our energy requirements are met by nuclear power. Yet . . . Japan is in the process of finishing its first nuclear park—a group of five or six nuclear plants to take care of a whole region. It takes us 11 years to build a nuclear plant. A plant costs $1-billion and takes five years to prepare for. But it takes you six years to get through the Nuclear Power Commission just for the paperwork that has to be done. Then the environmentalists take you to court and hold you up a little while longer. Then, finally, when you finish up, add another three to four years for actual construction. So you're talking about an additional eight or nine years, at 8 per cent interest. And then you can't write it off, because the regulatory agencies won't let you write off construction costs. So what happens? Some 260 nuclear and coal-powered plants were deferred or cancelled last year and they just sit there . . . That means more Arab oil is guaranteed to flow here every year. And we're paying whatever price the foreign producers want to charge us. I don't understand. . . . it's insane what we're doing.

*Interview/*
*Los Angeles Herald-Examiner, 10-24:(A)8.*

**Maurice F. Strong**
*Executive Director, United Nations*
*Environment Program*
4

Surely one does not have to be opposed to nuclear power *per se* to believe that it is only sensible and rational to assure that the full consequences of our escalating commitment to nuclear energy are evaluated before we drift into over-reliance.

*Nairobi, Kenya, April 17/*
*The New York Times, 4-18:2.*

**Edward Teller**
*Professor of physics, University of*
*California, Berkeley*
5

Certainly, we should look to the future, to nuclear fusion and solar energy; but they should not be over-emphasized now. Things like fusion are very far in the future—we would all be dead by then. This energy crisis, which is exceedingly grave, is solvable, but not in a short time. The only immediate results can be obtained through conservation efforts. My hope is that we all drive small cars and more diesel cars. We should better insulate homes—40 per cent of all new individual homes are mobile units with very little insulation. We should buy from

# WHAT THEY SAID IN 1975

those manufacturers who make things which last longer. These are major tools of energy conservation and are the ones most promptly effective.

*Interview, Berkeley, Calif./*
*"W": a Fairchild publication, 1-24:8.*

**Harold C. Urey**
*Chemist; Assisted in development of*
*atomic bomb*
1

[Urging delay in building atomic power plants]: There is an enormous difference between an accident [at an atomic plant] and, say, the San Francisco earthquake. The latter was exceedingly damaging, destroying some lives and the city, but it was rebuilt pretty much in 10 to 15 years and today is thriving. But with a nuclear plant accident, the problem could last for hundreds of thousands of years. Well, it has been said that all we have to do is dig up the earth [in the exposed area] and take it away. Yes. But where would you move it to? It is this type of thing which worries me about the atomic-energy problem. If we are going to build hundreds of plants in the United States and thousands in the world, then almost certainly there will be the serious accidents of some kind occurring in the next century. And we'll leave to our children, our grandchildren, our great-grandchildren and all our descendants we hope will continue to occupy this planet an enormously serious problem—areas which no one must enter for hundreds, thousands or even hundreds of thousands of years.

*News conference,*
*Los Angeles, Jan. 21/*
*Los Angeles Times, 1-22:(2)3.*

**Leonard Woodcock**
*President,*
*United Automobile Workers*
*of America*
2

[Questioning the need for U.S. cutback of imported oil]: I don't know how many years we have of domestic reserves, known domestic reserves, but let's say 10 or 12. Why should we be deliberately reducing that in a world which

is so dependent upon that commodity? You could make an excellent case for saying, "Let's get all we can from the other parts of the world, and protect our own resources."

*TV-radio interview/*
*U.S. News & World Report, 2-17:18.*

**Frank G. Zarb**
*Administrator,*
*Federal Energy Administration*
3

[On reducing fuel use]: The answer is to increase the value [price] of oil and gasoline in our economy. Then individuals and businesses will make the investment and consumption decisions that will lead to wise conservation of energy. What we have to achieve is a new energy ethic. We need the home-owner to decide to install storm windows, insulate his attic, replace that inefficient old heating or cooling system. We need the motorist to see real savings in a smaller, lighter car. We need the industrialist to think in terms of ordering equipment that is energy-efficient, even though its initial cost may be greater. If we can do that and multiply it time after time, day in and day out, then we will achieve sound energy conservation.
*Interview/U.S. News & World Report, 5-12:57.*

4

Let's conclude once and for all that the [oil-] producing nations are intent on maximizing profits. So long as we [in the U.S.] continue to consume at high rates and don't do anything to reduce imports, they're going to feel free to increase their prices ... All the talk in the world is not going to do us any good. We can stamp our feet, turn blue, pound our fists on the table. But the only answer is to develop our own self-sufficiency in energy. That's the only way to get the attention of the oil producers.
*Interview/Los Angeles Times, 6-15:(1)26.*

5

The debate between advocates and opponents of increased development of nuclear power appears, in some respects, to be even more emotional, even more heated, than debates on other energy resources, such as coal and off-shore oil. Perhaps this is because the potential hazard in the case of nuclear power—

namely, radiation—is newer to us and less tangible than the hazards of air and water pollution from coal and oil. Certainly, it's true that, for more than a quarter of a century, nuclear energy has been most closely associated in the public mind with two devastating bomb blasts that brought World War II to an end and opened the door to the so-called nuclear age. And it's true that, in the years of atmospheric testing and political uncertainty that followed, the nuclear age, for most people, meant, simply, the threat of nuclear war. So, from the outset, nuclear energy has been laden with popular emotion. But we can't base our energy policy on emotion—we must base it on hard facts. And these are the facts: *One*—The risk-to-benefit ratio of nuclear power in regard to public health is favorable, and, like other forms of advanced technology, will be publicly viewed . as such as we go forward with its development. *Two*—There is *no* way we can continue to provide the electricity needed by our nation in the coming years without the responsible expansion of our nuclear resources. And, *Three*—Electricity from nuclear power is a bargain compared to other sources of electricity, even with *all* costs added, such as insurance and safe disposal of radioactive waste. Today—in the second year of the energy crisis, the second year of buying foreign oil at an annual rate of more than $25-billion—it is high time to set aside emotion and examine rationally these and the other facts of energy life. Based on those facts, in regard to nuclear power, we should determine to get on with the job of utilizing this vital, clean and abundant energy resource.

*Before Commonwealth Club, San Francisco,*
*July 11/Vital Speeches, 8-15:669.*

# Foreign Affairs

Sven Andersson
*Foreign Minister of Sweden* 1

. . . we in Sweden find it difficult to side with those who now appear to demand some kind of ideological disarmament in the name of detente, those who seem to want to smooth over and bury fundamental differences in the conception of a society. The ideologies are not dead; they cannot be buried. The fact that we have reached a measure of political and military detente is no reason for such hesitation. We consider that detente and peace even make it possible to carry on a broader debate between nations on fundamental political and ideological issues. We pursue this policy without any desire for confrontation with other countries. I repeat—of course we respect the right of every nation to find its own way to a better society. But an open discussion of the varying concepts of society can in the long run create a firmer foundation for the policy of detente. Increased political suppression in a country can menace detente. Calling attention to this suppression will thus be a way of defending the policy of detente. The friendly and trustful exchange of opinions can also have the same effect, when we tell each other what we really think instead of putting the stopper on all debate.

*The Washington Post, 12-10:(A)18.*

Howard H. Baker, Jr.
*United States Senator,*
*R—Tennessee* 2

[On Congressional investigation of CIA activities]: I disagree with those who say you dare not look into the intelligence field because the Congress shoots its mouth off and can't keep a secret. That's nonsense. We must find out whether the intelligence community perceives it has an obligation to tell us what they're doing. There is no statutory opportunity for an agency of government to lie to Congress, to withhold information.

*News conference, Los Angeles, Feb. 12/*
*Los Angeles Times, 2-13:(1)32.*

George W. Ball
*Former Under Secretary of State of*
*the United States* 3

Today, foreign governments no longer treat our Ambassadors with the respect once accorded representatives of our great country, for the very obvious reason that they [the Ambassadors] are not treated with respect by the Secretary of State [Henry Kissinger]. Whenever a serious problem arises in a particular capital, the Ambassador is normally pushed aside while the Secretary flies out in his airplane or sends one of his personal staff to take charge . . .

*At House Committee hearing, Washington/*
*The Washington Post, 8-19:(A)5.*

Benjamin R. Barber
*Professor of political science,*
*Rutgers University* 4

The United States population is 6 per cent of the world population. Yet we consume something like 30 to 40 per cent of its resources, depending on whether you're talking about food or material. It's a question whether America can preserve its freedom and traditional values without helping less-developed countries. From now on, the pressures on us from the "have nots" will be enormous. The old notion of "lifeboat America" going its way while the rest of the world sinks is not really viable now. Rather, we have to talk about "lifeship earth," on which I think probably the overwhelming reality in the next 25 years will be the reality of interdependence.

*Interview/U.S. News & World Report, 7-7:46.*

**Lloyd M. Bentsen**
*United States Senator, D–Texas*

1

Never before in our history have we seen such a concentration of foreign-policy decision-making in the hands of one person [Henry Kissinger]—one person who wears two official hats [Secretary of State and Presidential national-security adviser], and unofficially wears a third—that of roving ambassador. Running the State Department is a full-time job for any man—even a superman—and it can't be done from a jet plane circling over a Middle East airport.

*At Georgetown University, Feb. 6/*
*The Dallas Times Herald, 2-7:(A)8.*

**Abram Bergson**
*Professor of economics, and former director*
*of the Russian Research Center,*
*Harvard University*

2

...we have got to avoid a drift to isolationism. That would have the most serious consequences. We are in a period where, partly because of Vietnam, isolationist currents are more potent than they have been in the immediate past. The pitfalls include a spirit of anti-Pentagon, anti-CIA carried to the extreme. If the currents go very far, they can be very costly.

*Interview, Cambridge, Mass./*
*Los Angeles Times, 4-22:(2)7.*

**Zbigniew Brzezinski**
*Professor of government and international*
*relations, Columbia University*

3

I think that few people realize the extent to which the success of the Nixon-Kissinger policy depended on the unique combination of [former President Richard] Nixon's and [Secretary of State Henry] Kissinger's special gifts—and what I now have to say may come as a surprise. In my view, the really creative strategic impulses came from Nixon, with Kissinger a brilliant implementer, executor and adapter of the basic strategic concepts initiated by Nixon. With Nixon politically out of the picture for the last two years, the tactician has both been executing tactics and shaping strat-

egy. As a result, we have an extraordinarily covert and fundamentally tactical foreign policy today, a policy lacking in strategic concepts.
*Interview/The Wall Street Journal, 6-24:18.*

**James L. Buckley**
*United States Senator, C–New York*

4

Instead of opening lines of communication, detente has become an end of its own. We are doing all sorts of things to achieve detente, when the Soviets have their own definition of detente. We don't have to curry favors. We are doing all we can to protect the atmosphere of detente. The point of dealing and talking is plausible only if we remain strong.
*News conference, Washington/*
*The Christian Science Monitor, 4-4:4.*

5

[On Communist successes in Indochina, Portugal, the Middle East and the Caribbean]: ... I can't help but believe they now will be encouraged to tighten, to strengthen, the so-called movements of national liberation not only in the Philippines, but also the Caribbean, the Middle East, in Africa—in other words, I think we're going to see a further proving of America's determination everywhere.
*Television broadcast, April 20/*
*The Christian Science Monitor, 4-22:2.*

6

[On lessons the U.S. should learn from the Communist take-over of South Vietnam]: Don't go into actual warfare unless you intend to win and get it over with rapidly. Let's be very careful about making any commitments; and, having made them, let's understand the consequences of breaking those commitments.
*The Dallas Times Herald, 5-1:(B)2.*

**McGeorge Bundy**
*President, Ford Foundation; Former Special*
*Assistant to the President of the United*
*States for National Security Affairs*
*(John F. Kennedy and Lyndon B. Johnson)*

7

Since our [the U.S.'] very size and strength must lead others to tend to rely on us for what they want, it becomes critically important for

# WHAT THEY SAID IN 1975

*(McGEORGE BUNDY)*

us to determine, and for them to understand, just how much of that reliance is justified. We cannot deny our failures, whether in Vietnam or elsewhere, nor is such denial in the national tradition. We cannot deny—indeed we must strongly affirm—our limitations. We cannot and will not do everything everywhere; and we can do nothing, anywhere, that is not matched both to the desires and the efforts of those who turn to us. Nor can we deny—we must loudly proclaim—that we  :  a people of great diversity. Our decisions will never be monolithic, and no one, not even our Presidents, can ever speak for us all. But we are the same people that in a generation have twice helped save the freedom of Europe, that have been first among the nations in the struggle to ward off world-wide nuclear catastrophe, that have shown ourselves ready to respond, time after time, to leadership that appeals to our practical generosity.

*At University of Texas commencement/*
*The New York Times, 6-29:(4)15.*

## Ellsworth Bunker
*United States Ambassador-at-Large* 1

No foreign-policy decision, and particularly no significant change in foreign policy, can take place without the advice and consent of Congress and the informed support of the American people, on the basis of candid and reasonable public discussion.

*Seattle/The Dallas Times Herald, 5-25:(A)31.*

2

[On what makes a good negotiator]: You have to inspire confidence in the people with whom you're negotiating. You have to inspire trust that you are dealing with them fairly and openly. It requires perception, a sensitivity to the other side's problems, or, if you're mediating . . . of both sides' problems. Obviously, it requires patience, perseverance and a sense of humor. You always need that. But it also requires a sense of humility—an awareness that you don't know all the answers and that you have to keep on trying to find them.

*Interview, Washington/Parade, 8-31:5.*

## Fidel Castro
*Premier of Cuba* 3

The United States is no longer in a position to take on warmongering adventures. The world has changed a lot and the United States with it. Only 15 years ago, the United States was very powerful—but no more.

*San Francisco Examiner & Chronicle,*
*1-19:(This World)2.*

## Frank Church
*United States Senator, D–Idaho;*
*Chairman, Senate Select Committee on*
*Intelligence Activities* 4

[On reports that the CIA has been involved in assassination plots against foreign leaders]: Ours is not a wicked country, and we cannot abide a wicked government . . . The U.S. cannot involve itself in any way in murder. The notion that we must mimic the Communists and abandon our principles [is] an abomination.

*Time, 6-16:10.*

5

In the need to develop a capacity to know what potential enemies are doing, the United States government has perfected a technological capability that enables us to monitor the messages that go through the air. These messages are between ships at sea, they could be between . . . military units in the field; we have a very extensive capability of intercepting messages wherever they may be in the airwaves. That is necessary and important to the United States as we look abroad at enemies or potential enemies. We must know. At the same time, that capability at any time could be turned around on the American people and no American would have any privacy left, such as the capability to monitor everything: telephone conversations, telegrams—it doesn't matter. There would be no place to hide. If this government ever became a tyranny, if a dictator ever took charge in this country, the technological capacity that the intelligence community has given the government could enable it to impose total tyranny, and there would be no way to fight back because the most careful effort to combine together in resistance to the government, no matter how privately it was done, is within the reach of the government to know. Such is the capability of this technology.

*TV-radio interview, Washington/"Meet the Press," National Broadcasting Company, 8-17.*

**Dick Clark**
*United States Senator, D—Iowa*
1

In the headlong race for more military power to face the "threat of Communism," we should pause long enough to question whether there may ultimately be a greater threat to world peace, and thereby to our own tranquility, from the developing nations of the world—from that two-thirds of the world that is destitute, increasingly angered, malnourished, illiterate, and multiplying in population at a frightening rate.

*The National Observer, 6-28:15.*

2

If we seize the opportunity, the end of [the] Vietnam [war] could be the beginning of a new era in U.S. foreign policy. The choice is simple: Will we continue the policies of confrontation, which have dominated the last two decades, or will we cultivate new attitudes and relationships that reflect an awareness of the world as it really is—small, perilous and interdependent.

*U.S. News & World Report, 7-7:26.*

**William Sloane Coffin**
*Chaplain, Yale University*
3

. . . Watergate riveted attention on personal immorality, rather than institutional social immorality. People think [former President Richard] Nixon is a crook and [Secretary of State] Henry Kissinger is honest. To me, both of them shared an evil vision whereby the world would be ruled by American power and a few other powerful nations, plus some multinational corporations—none of which are concerned with the suffering of the Third World. To me, that's the immorality that needs to be attacked—an immorality of social vision.

*Interview/People, 5-5:44.*

**Alan Cranston**
*United States Senator, D—California*
4

[The U.S.] should be a peaceful world neighbor instead of a militant world meddler . . . One

of these days our tendency to resort to military forces to resolve our national frustrations will lead to total disaster, for us and all mankind.

*Before the Senate, Washington/ The Washington Post, 5-23:(A)6.*

**Moshe Dayan**
*Former Minister of Defense of Israel*
5

. . . there have emerged just two superpowers in the world—you [the U.S.] and Russia. It isn't just that you have been to the moon and the others haven't. In the military field—in nuclear and conventional weapons, in the manufacturing of airplanes and all sophisticated weapons—there are other countries, but none really count but Russia and America. So the world is divided, dependent for defense on two countries—you and Russia. Can small countries, free countries, democratic countries, count on you? Can we count on you, not when it comes to wars with other small countries, but when it comes to Russia? You are the only country that can stand up to them . . . Now, reading the papers and watching the television here after Vietnam and the collapse there, the feeling among your people is that you don't want to be involved in some foreign war. The question is: If Russia wants to get into one of these local wars, does your generation see itself as responsible, as the leading country of the free world, to stand up against Russia? It will be a very sad day for small free countries if we cannot count on you in such a case. So, in all honesty, what I want to tell you is that we expect you—the young generation of America—to feel yourselves responsible, not only for the security of your own country, but, in extreme cases, for the entire free world.

*At California State University, Northridge/ Los Angeles Times, 4-17:(2)7.*

**Milovan Djilas**
*Author;*
*Former Vice President of Yugoslavia*
6

. . . democratic governments throughout history have been vastly outnumbered by despotic regimes. This is the case today as well. And the United States must create a new sense of unity and community of interests among

# WHAT THEY SAID IN 1975

*(MILOVAN DJILAS)*

democratic countries, and to do that it must seek new departures and new ways.

*Interview, Belgrade/*
*The Washington Post, 5-19:(A)8.*

**Hedley Donovan**
*Editor-in-chief, Time, Inc.* 1

Our failure in Southeast Asia must not be allowed to generate a neo-isolationism. It should help us understand that there are considerable parts of the world where our ability to influence events is modest and where our fundamental interests are slight. We must respect the diversity of the world. We must also renew our faith in the possibility of progress—there are, in fact, plenty of examples of it out there. We must recognize that there are limits on American power without denying or deploring the very great power that we do have. The bedrock of our foreign policy is, in the end, to preserve the independence, freedom and prosperity of the U.S. Everything else is ways and means. Except for one thing: We also expect our foreign policy to enable us to feel good about being Americans, to feel good and be good.

*At Deere & Co., Moline, Ill./Time, 5-19:20.*

**Pierre S. du Pont IV**
*United States Representative, R—Delaware* 2

[On U.S. foreign policy]: In the last Congress, we insisted that a trade agreement with the Soviet Union must include certain promises on Jewish emigration. The result? We were hurt economically because the Russians refused to trade with us on those terms. As for our idealism: Jewish emigration has lessened dramatically. We have boycotted Rhodesian chrome because of the abhorrent racial policies there. But the policies have not changed as a result, and we are buying this scarce resource from the Soviet Union—a nation with even more abhorrent national policies—at a much higher price. In Chile, our CIA helped to subvert a democratically elected government [the government of the late Chilean President Salvador Allende who was overthrown in a coup in 1973] because we

did not agree with the will of its people. Today, Chileans no longer have a democracy. Because of the idealism of the past, we are the only major power that does not formally recognize the People's Republic of [Communist] China. Yet this nation, with almost one-fourth of the world's population, continues to ascend the power ladder. As these examples show, we have neither inspired the world nor helped ourselves. It is as if H. L. Mencken had our foreign policy in mind when he said: "An idealist is one who, on noticing that a rose smells better than a cabbage, concludes that it will also make better soup" . . . I do not mean to imply that idealism is just a by-product of our foreign economic policy and therefore only secondarily important. Idealism should be of primary importance; it should make us generous contributors to the new international economic order, for instance. But it should not lead us to try remaking other nations in our own image. For in doing this, we are bound only to estrange ourselves and our ideals from those we might otherwise help and influence. Developing ties—this is the way to bring the world closer together. And if we do it by being honest and evenhanded, with a careful respect for the integrity of other nations, we are likely to achieve our goals.

*Before the House, Washington/*
*The National Observer, 12-20:11.*

**Thomas F. Eagleton**
*United States Senator, D—Missouri* 3

[Secretary of State Henry] Kissinger's approach to foreign affairs has brought our nation dramatic success. It has brought some failures as well. And for those who have involved themselves in the foreign-policy debate, the Kissinger approach has, in itself, become a central issue. To many his pragmatism has come to mean, rightly or wrongly, a search for solidarity and stability to the exclusion of other important considerations. His preoccupation with the superpowers led many to question whether his success was worth the deterioration of our relations with nations in Africa, South Asia and Latin America. In an effort to highlight the weaknesses rather than the strengths of this record, Dr. Kissinger's critics seem to be offering a totally opposite approach to world affairs.

This approach minimizes the importance of contemporary power relationships. It emphasizes instead the need for social change. Such change is seen as holding the promise of relief for those oppressed peoples who, it is said, are losing ground under the status quo Dr. Kissinger's policies seek to preserve. Advocates of this approach concern themselves with such world-wide problems as human rights, food distribution, ecology and the proliferation of conventional arms. If we are to move toward consensus, we must understand that these divergent views are not irreconcilable. We need not, in my view, abandon the search for balance and stability, especially among the superpowers. Nor can we afford to ignore the needs of the developing world or the plight of those whose inalienable rights are denied by oppressive governments.

> *Before the Senate, Washington, Feb. 20/*
> *The Washington Post, 3-4:(A)14.*

**Amintore Fanfani**
*Secretary, Christian Democratic Party of Italy; Former Premier of Italy*

1

[The current] international situation is a warning to peoples who want to remain free to rely first of all on themselves, and not to tie their salvation exclusively to the help of friends, who are certainly faithful but not always in a position to help half the world simultaneously.

> *Time, 5-19:29.*

**Robert A. Fearey**
*Special Assistant to the Secretary of State and Coordinator for Combatting Terrorism, Department of State of the United States*

2

Terrorists have had some tactical successes, but I don't think they've been successful in achieving their political purposes. Quite the contrary, terrorist organizations are arousing increasing revulsion. If terrorism fails in its basic purposes—which are fundamentally political—in enough instances over a period of time, then it could go out of fashion and become a declining problem. But when you look around the world you see hundreds of millions of deprived and frustrated peoples who are now well aware that there is a better life. They hear and see it

through the media, while their own lot is often getting worse. In these circumstances, terrorism—the resort of the weak—may have increasing appeal. However, we should not give terrorists too much credit for sincere political belief. Many are ordinary criminals using political arguments to rationalize their crimes. And political grievances, no matter how strongly felt, cannot justify the murder of innocent people.

> *Interview/U.S. News & World Report, 9-29:77.*

**Gerald R. Ford**
*President of the United States*

3

I have complete and total confidence that we, representing the major power in Western industrial civilization, can give the leadership to the world ... We have a responsibility. It may mean giving more foreign aid. It may mean giving more leadership in other ways. It may be tightening our belt to be a little stronger militarily, to negotiate diplomatically better. But that's our responsibility, and I happen to think that's our duty.

> *Interview, Washington, Jan. 8/*
> *The Washington Post, 1-12:(A)11.*

4

This nation can be proud of significant achievements in recent years in solving problems and crises. The Berlin agreement, the SALT agreements, our new relationship with [Communist] China, the unprecedented efforts in the Middle East—are immensely encouraging. But the world is not free from crisis. In a world of 150 nations, where nuclear technology is proliferating and regional conflicts continue, international security cannot be taken for granted. So let there be no mistake about it: International cooperation is a vital factor of our lives today. This is not a moment for the American people to turn inward. More than ever before, our own well-being depends on America's determination and America's leadership in the whole wide world. We are a great nation—spiritually, politically, militarily, diplomatically and economically. America's commitment to international security has sustained the safety of allies and friends in many areas—in the Middle East, in Europe, in Asia. Our turning

# WHAT THEY SAID IN 1975

## (GERALD R. FORD)

away would unleash new instabilities, new dangers around the globe, which in turn would threaten our own security.

*State of the Union address, Washington, Jan. 15/The New York Times, 1-16:24.*

1

... if our foreign policy is to be successful, we cannot rigidly restrict in legislation the ability of the President to act. The conduct of negotiations is ill-suited to such limitations. Legislative restrictions intended for the best motives and purposes can have the opposite result, as we have seen most recently in our trade relations with the Soviet Union. For my part, I pledge this Administration will act in the closest consultation with the Congress as we face delicate situations and troubled times throughout the globe.

*State of the Union address, Washington, Jan. 15/The New York Times, 1-16:24.*

2

[Referring to Arthur H. Vandenberg, who headed the Senate Foreign Relations Committee in the 1940s, and who had a nonpartisan relationship on foreign affairs with President Harry Truman]: I do not expect 535 reincarnations of Senator Vandenberg. Yet I do appeal for an open-minded spirit of enlightened national concern to transcend any partisan or internal party politics that threaten to bring our successful foreign policy to a standstill. I challenge the Senate and House to give me the same consideration that Senator Vandenberg sought and got for President Truman. Can't we consult and act rather than pontificate and poke?

*At Republican fund-raising dinner, New York, Feb. 13/The New York Times, 2-14:1.*

3

[Criticizing Congress' insistence on cutting off aid to Turkey because of Turkey's policy toward Cyprus]: The issue is what kind of an ally are we, when we punish our allies more severely than our enemies? What kind of statesmen are we, when we so poorly perceive our own interests? This question is being asked by

nations who look to us for leadership. I can give no answer.

*At Republican fund-raising dinner, New York, Feb. 13/The New York Times, 2-14:12.*

4

The sales of U.S. military equipment to any country is not predicated on trying to help the U.S. economy. We do have a policy of selling arms to other nations if that country feels it has an internal security problem and, Number 2, if it is necessary for one or any of the countries to maintain their national integrity or security. We believe that in many areas of the world a proper military balance is essential for internal as well as external security of the various countries. And where other nations, such as the Soviet Union, [do] sell or give arms to one country or another, if another country feels that for its own security it needs additional military equipment and has the cash, then we feel that it is proper to make a sale from the United States to that country.

*News conference, Hollywood, Fla., Feb. 26/The New York Times, 2-27:20.*

5

I don't think we can conduct American foreign policy on the basis of what other nations think is in our best interest. The United States has to predicate its foreign policy on what it thinks is in America's best interest. Now, we respect the right of other nations to be critical of what we do. But it's my responsibility and, I think, the responsibility of people in authority in the United States to make decisions that are based on what we think is good for America. And that's the way it'll be decided as long as I'm President.

*News conference, Hollywood, Fla., Feb. 26/The New York Times, 2-27:20.*

6

I am convinced that Americans, however tempted to resign from the world, know that it cannot be done. The spirit of learning is far too deeply ingrained. We know that, wherever the bell tolls for freedom, it tolls for us.

*At University of Notre Dame, March 17/The Christian Science Monitor, 3-18:1.*

*1*

In time of recession, inflation and unemployment at home, it is argued that we can no longer afford foreign assistance. There are two basic reasons why Americans cannot adopt this view. First, foreign aid is part of the price we must pay to achieve the kind of world we want to live in. Let's be frank about it: Foreign aid bolsters our diplomatic efforts for peace and security. Second, even with recession we remain the world's most affluent country, and the sharing of our resources is the right, humane and decent thing to do.

*At University of Notre Dame, March 17/*
*The Christian Science Monitor, 3-18:4.*

*2*

It has been said that the United States is over-extended; that we have too many commitments too far from home; that we must re-examine what our truly vital interests are and shape our strategy to conform to them. I find no fault with this as theory; but in the real world such a course must be pursued carefully and in close coordination with solid progress toward over-all reduction in world-wide tensions. We cannot in the meantime abandon our friends while our adversaries support and encourage theirs. We cannot dismantle our defenses, our diplomacy or our intelligence capability while others increase and strengthen theirs ... The security and progress of hundreds of millions of people everywhere depend importantly on us. Let no potential adversary believe that our difficulties or our debates mean a slackening of our national will. We will stand by our friends. We will honor our commitments. We will uphold our country's principles. The American people know that our strength, our authority and our leadership have helped prevent a third world war for more than a generation. We will not shrink from this duty in the decades ahead.

*State of the World Address,*
*Washington, April 10/*
*The New York Times, 4-11:10.*

*3*

[On arguments that Henry Kissinger has too much power, being both Secretary of State and National Security Adviser to the President]: If you were to draw a chart, I think you might make a good argument that that job ought to be divided. On the other hand, sometimes in government you get unique individuals who can very successfully handle a combination of jobs like Secretary Kissinger. If you get this kind of person, you ought to take advantage of that capability. Therefore, under the current circumstances, I would not recommend nor would I want a division of those two responsibilities.

*Television interview, Washington/*
*Columbia Broadcasting System, 4-21.*

*4*

Some seem to feel that if we [the U.S.] do not succeed in everything everywhere, then we have succeeded in nothing anywhere. I reject such polarized thinking. We can and should help others to help themselves. But the fate of responsible men and women everywhere, in the final decision, rests in their own hands.

*At Tulane University, April 23/*
*Los Angeles Times, 4-24:(1)8.*

*5*

On balance, [detente] has been a relationship that has given both sides [the U.S. and the Soviet Union] enough benefits to justify its continuation, whether it was in open communications or agreements in the areas of science, health, environment or otherwise. It has been a good foundation from which to build a broader and more productive relationship ... As long as we are realistic about detente and don't expect it to be the millennium, I think we can build from that relationship and use it for not only the relaxation of tensions between ourselves and the Soviet Union, but as an instrument in calming fears, holding back rash action and keeping the world relatively quiet so we can work for the solution of the problems on a regional basis around the world.

*Interview/Time, 7-28:14.*

*6*

I believe that detente is misunderstood by a number of people. It is being criticized unfairly in many areas. Detente was not supposed to result in achieving 100 per cent of what some people want. Some people want vast internal changes in the Soviet Union. I don't think

# WHAT THEY SAID IN 1975

*(GERALD R. FORD)*

that's something that we can expect from detente. Others feel that in the process of detente we have lost more than we gained. I don't think that's an accurate description. Detente is an effort to get the two major powers to sit down, and where there are problems or where there is a mutual interest, to work together to relieve tensions and to avoid confrontation. There was a benefit from detente in the first Strategic Arms Limitation Treaty, which put limits on the numbers of certain missiles. I think if negotiations proceed in the proper way, even further limitations on strategic weapons can be a benefit from detente. The initiation of negotiations looking to mutual reduction of forces between the two sides in Central Europe, if they're carried out properly, can be a benefit from detente. Detente has helped to cool potential confrontation in the Middle East between the United States and the Soviet Union—and believe me, we need cool heads in trying to resolve the problems between the Israelis and the Arab nations. These are some of the benefits that I see from detente.

*Interview, Washington/*
*U.S. News & World Report, 8-11:20.*

1

A great nation cannot escape its [international] responsibilities. Responsibilities abandoned today will return as more acute crises tomorrow.

*Before White House press corps, Washington,*
*Dec. 19/The New York Times, 12-20:8.*

## Orville Freeman
*Former Secretary of Agriculture of*
*the United States*

2

There are 100 million more illiterate persons in the world today than there were 25 years ago. One out of five human beings in the less-developed world is unemployed or under-employed. In two and a half decades, two thirds of the world's population has increased its per capita income less than one dollar a year. A billion people are hungry. Abject poverty of this kind is not, cannot be permitted to be, an

abstraction. It is a daily pain, a weekly grief, a year-round despair—and a permanent fuse for a world-wide explosion.

*Quote, 6-15:553.*

## John Kenneth Galbraith
*Professor of economics,*
*Harvard University;*
*Former United States Ambassador to India*

3

[The U.S.] did not, after World War II, seek directly to govern people distant from our shores. Like the Soviets, we were too wise for that. Like the Soviets, we proclaimed our aversion to colonial rule. But no less than other powers, we sought to guide the political and economic development of other lands. No less than the colonial powers, we sought to shape these developments to our own preference, which is to say our own image. Our technique, in fact, bore a marked resemblance to that of Britain in the princely states of India—to what, in a less ambiguous age, was called indirect rule.

*At Memphis (Tenn.) State University/*
*The New York Times, 7-12:25.*

## Indira Gandhi
*Prime Minister of India*

4

Is it not a new form of arrogance for affluent nations to regard the poorer nations as an improvident species whose numbers are a threat to their own standard of living? . . . The attitude of most individuals, groups and nations toward right and wrong remains egocentric. Those who have military or economic strength assume the authority to lay down the law for others.

*San Francisco Examiner & Chronicle,*
*1-12:(This World)2.*

## Barry M. Goldwater
*United States Senator,*
*R—Arizona*

5

I've always felt that [Vice President] Nelson Rockefeller would make a fine Secretary of State. I would hate to waste a man's talents on the Vice-Presidency when the Vice-Presidency really, as [Thomas] Jefferson said, is about the worst job in government. I would rather . . . see Vice President Rockefeller finish out his term and then become Secretary of State. He'd make me look like a "dove," to tell you the truth.

*TV-radio interview/"Issues and Answers," American Broadcasting Company, 6-15.*

## Mahbub ul Haq
*Director, Policy Planning and Program Review, International Bank for Reconstruction and Development (World Bank)*
1

[Comparing the Third World with the industrialized world]: Our two worlds, while they touch and meet, rarely communicate. And it is that process of real communication, real dialogue, that we have to encourage today if we are to equip ourselves to deal with problems of this world ... It is rather an unpleasant truth that poor countries ... have often been swindled out of a decent return for their produce in the name of market mechanisms, deprived of their economic independence in the name of world interdependence, seduced by imported life-styles, foreign value systems, irrelevant research designs—all in the name of freedom of choice. When terms of trade turned for once against the industrialized countries last year, it was characterized as the beginning of a world depression and an unmanageable adjustment problem, even though it meant a transfer of merely 2 per cent of the GNP of the developed world. But the industrialized countries conveniently forgot that the developing countries have often lost 10-15 per cent of their GNP through the deterioration in their terms of trade in the 1960s and were forced to make a far more painful adjustment in their consumption levels at a much lower level of income.

*The Christian Science Monitor, 5-5:24.*

## W. Averell Harriman
*Former United States Ambassador-at-Large*
2

[On those who are critical of U.S. detente with countries such as the Soviet Union and Communist China]: Most people think detente is something like rapprochement [reconciliation] or entente [understanding]. Detente means a relaxation of tension between nations, and no one can be against that.

*Moscow/ The New York Times, 5-8:44.*

## Edward Heath
*Former Prime Minister of the United Kingdom*
3

The most common illusion nursed by nations is that they have retained power which in reality they have lost ... But there is a less common illusion harbored by nations in a sudden state of shock—that they have lost power which in fact they still retain.

*At Westminster College commencement, Salt Lake City/The National Observer, 7-19:7.*

## Harold C. Hinton
*Professor of political science and international affairs, Institute for Sino-Soviet Studies, George Washington University*
4

In a world that increasingly resembles a global village, we [the U.S.] can't ignore what goes on in our neighborhood. We don't have to run to the defense of each victim of a mugging, and we can close our doors and forget there is crime on the streets and growing use of drugs. But we do sometimes have to venture out. And the quality of our life is affected by what we find happening when we do.

*Interview/The National Observer, 6-28:15.*

## Stanley Hoffmann
*Director, Center for European Studies, Harvard University*
5

... we are now faced with a whole series of problems for which all of the traditional techniques of management of world affairs are inadequate: the use of force, the balance of power, great-power diplomacy. They still have their uses but very limited ones, and I think we are confronting a world in which we will have to do all of the following: maintain the over-all balance of military might, which we have been, I think, doing pretty well on the whole; maintain something which is completely different and which is what I would call the balance of influence in various parts of the world at a time when we discover that the people who are hostile to us and who may shift this balance against us are very often either not Communists or [are] independent Communists—so that the

# WHAT THEY SAID IN 1975

kind of traditional techniques that we had used in the past, which were essentially military force or the massive injection of economic aid, do not help you very much today.

*Television interview/"The Taking of the Mayaguez," Public Broadcasting Service, 5-15.*

### Hubert H. Humphrey
*United States Senator, D—Minnesota* 1

[On his bill to limit the sales of U.S. arms to foreign countries]: I do not believe that the sale of arms to foreign countries is necessarily evil or wrong. We have important security and foreign-policy interests in the sale of arms to many countries, and this legislation will not halt arms sales. But it will bring rationality to these programs. It will open the policy process to public scrutiny and Congressional oversight, enabling foreign-policy aspects of United States arms to be evaluated in a new fashion.

*Washington, Nov. 13/
The New York Times, 11-14:8.*

### Henry M. Jackson
*United States Senator, D—Washington* 2

While the international position of the United States continues to erode, [President] Ford's repeated celebrations of the successes of detente are an attempt to sell a false sense of security ... He is operating on the premise that Soviet restraint can be purchased by American wheat, by American neglect of traditional allies, by American economic largesse and diplomatic passivity around the globe, and by the abandonment of America's traditional humanitarian and democratic values in issues of foreign policy.

*Before New England Society of Newspaper Editors, Springfield, Mass./
The Wall Street Journal, 12-12:14.*

### Janos Kadar
*First Secretary,
Communist Party of Hungary* 3

There is no peaceful coexistence on the fronts of the ideological struggle. We may be part-

ners in interstate relations. But the ideologies of socialism and capitalism are antagonistic and irreconcilable.

*At Hungarian Communist Party Congress,
Budapest/
The Christian Science Monitor, 3-25:4.*

### Edward M. Kennedy
*United States Senator, D—Massachusetts* 4

To fulfill our vital interests in the health of the global economy, we must not respond with confrontation. The United States is no longer pre-eminent as it was only a few short years ago ... We can no longer control inflation or recession without tackling problems abroad as well.

*San Francisco Examiner & Chronicle,
4-20:(This World)2.*

5

[The lesson of Vietnam was that] we must throw off the cumbersome mantle of world policeman and limit our readiness to areas where our interests are truly endangered. Our European allies have nothing to fear from having learned that lesson; rather, it should be a welcome sight of our having finally begun to recognize the difference between real and illusory interests.

*U.S. News & World Report, 7-7:26.*

### Henry A. Kissinger
*Secretary of State of the United States* 6

The growing tendency of the Congress to legislate in detail the day-to-day or week-to-week conduct of our foreign affairs raises grave issues ... Too often, differences as to tactics [between the Executive and Legislative Branches] have defeated the very purposes that both Branches meant to serve, because the Legislative sanctions were too public or too drastic or too undiscriminating ... The Administration may disagree with a particular decision; we may argue vigorously for a different course ... But we welcome the indispensable contributions of Congress to the general direction of national policy. At the same time, it is important to recognize that the legislative process—deliberation, debate and statutory law—is much less well-suited to the detailed supervision of the day-to-day conduct of diplomacy. Legal prescriptions, by their very nature, lose sight of the sense of nuance and the feeling for the interrelationship of issues on which foreign policy success or failure so often depends.

*Before Los Angeles World Affairs Council,*
*Jan. 24/The New York Times, 1-25:6.*

1

. . . you cannot have a peaceful world without most of the countries, and preferably all of the countries, feeling that they have a share in it. This means that those countries that can have the greatest capacity to . . . determine peace or war that is, the five major centers—be reasonably agreed on the general outlines of what that peace should be like. But, at the same time, one of the central facts of our period is that more than 100 nations have come into being in the last 15 years, and they, too, must be central participants in this process. So that for the first time in history, foreign policy has become truly global, and therefore truly complicated.

*Television interview/*
*Los Angeles Times, 3-16:(9)1.*

2

We must understand that peace is indivisible. The United States cannot pursue a policy of selective reliability. We cannot abandon friends in one part of the world without jeopardizing the security of friends everywhere . . . I'm saying that, as a people, we should not destroy our allies, and that once we start on that course it will have very serious consequences for us in the world.

*News conference, Washington, March 26/*
*The New York Times, 3-27:17.*

3

If there is a decision to resist internal subversion [in a foreign country], I would think that the introduction of American military forces is the worst way of dealing with it because that introduces a foreign element. If we want to be helpful we would be much better off strengthening the government's ability to resist and giving it assistance rather than introducing American military forces.

*Television interview, Washington/*
*"Today," National Broadcasting Company, 5-6.*

4

[On the Communist take-over in South Vietnam]: The fact that we failed in one endeavor does not invalidate all others. If in the aftermath of Vietnam we flee from responsibility as uncritically as we rushed into commitment a decade ago, we will surely find ourselves in a period of chaos and peril that will dwarf all previous experience.

*Before World Affairs Council,*
*St. Louis, May 12/*
*Los Angeles Times, 5-13:(1)1.*

5

[On the U.S. role in the world]: Though we are no longer predominant, we are inescapably a leader. Though we cannot impose our solutions, few solutions are possible without us. There is no other country so endowed to help build a better future. If we sit back, there will be no hope for stability, no resistance to aggression, no effective mediation of disputes, no progress in the world economy. When force becomes the arbiter of conflicts, the standards of restraint in international conduct will erode sooner or later, instability and chaos will become the order of the day.

*Before World Affairs Council,*
*St. Louis, May 12/*
*U.S. News & World Report, 5-26:80.*

6

[On reporters questioning him about whether he or President Ford runs foreign policy and if the President is doing well in that area]: You vultures, you are always asking me that . . . What am I supposed to say? That he's doing a lousy job? He's doing a very good job! It's sort of a stupid debate, don't you think—who's running foreign policy? The President—who else?

*Aboard Air Force One enroute from Brussels*
*to Madrid, May 31/*
*The Dallas Times Herald, 6-1:(A)12.*

7

We have no illusions. We recognize that our values and social systems are not compatible with those of the Communist powers and may never be. But in the thermonuclear age, when the existence of mankind is at stake, there is no decent alternative to the easing of tensions

# WHAT THEY SAID IN 1975

## (HENRY A. KISSINGER)

[other than improved relations with Communist countries]. Should these efforts fail, at least our peoples will know that we had no choice but to resist pressure or blackmail. There can be no conciliation without strength and security, but we would be reckless if we forgot that strength without a spirit of conciliation can invite holocaust.

*Before Japan Society, New York, June 18/*
*The New York Times, 6-19:8.*

1

Detente is not a substitute for American action. Detente is a means of controlling the conflict with the Soviet Union. Detente is not a substitute for American strength. But it can enable us to reduce the risks that we will ever have to make use of that strength.

*Interview/U.S. News & World Report, 6-23:22.*

2

. . . fate has put us in the position where we are the only non-Communist country that is strong enough and domestically cohesive enough to play a world role. Therefore, if certain things are not done by us, they will not be done by anyone. And while it might be fairer if somebody else took some of the responsibility, the fact is that a catastrophe is no less real for having been brought about by attempts to shift responsibility to others.

*Interview/U.S. News & World Report, 6-23:27.*

3

. . . no country should imagine that it is doing us a favor by remaining in an alliance with us. Any ally whose perception of its national interest changes will find us prepared to adapt or end our treaty relationship. No ally can pressure us by a threat of termination. We will not accept that its security is more important to us than it is to itself.

*Before Southern Council on International*
*and Public Affairs and Atlanta Chamber of*
*Commerce, Atlanta, June 23/*
*Los Angeles Times, 6-24:(1)1.*

4

To what extent are we able to affect the internal policies of other governments and to what extent is it desirable? We do not and will not condone repressive practices [in foreign countries] . . . We have used, and we will use, our influence against repressive practices. Our traditions and our interests demand it. But truth compels, also, a recognition of our limits. The question is whether we promote human rights more effectively by counsel and friendly relations . . . or by confrontation propaganda and discriminatory legislation.

*Before Upper Middle West Council,*
*Minneapolis, July 15/*
*Los Angeles Times, 7-16:(1)11.*

5

. . . many of our difficulties abroad are of our own making. If we are to be vigilant against Communist encroachment, we must stop dismantling or demoralizing our intelligence services. If we are to maintain the world balance of power, we cannot assault our defense budget or impose arms embargoes against key allies. If we are to advance our interests in our diplomacy, we cannot deny ourselves flexibility by legislating blanket restrictions on economic relations with other countries. In short, America cannot be strong abroad unless it is strong at home.

*At Southern Commodity Producers Conference,*
*Birmingham, Alabama, Aug. 14/*
*The New York Times, 8-15:2.*

6

If terrorist groups get the impression that they can force a negotiation with the United States and an acquiescence in their demands, then we may save lives in one place at the risk of hundreds of lives somewhere else . . . We are trying to maintain a principle that terrorists cannot negotiate with American officials. And we are doing this in order to protect the thousands of Americans who could become victims all over the world if we once started that process—not only American tourists and students, but also American officials. It is our view that it saves more lives and more jeopardy, and that it will help Ambassadors, who can then hide behind firm rules rather than leave it to the individual decision.

*News conference, Vail, Colo., Aug. 17/*
*The New York Times, 8-18:4.*

*1*

[Saying that Congress may be acquiring too much foreign-policy authority over the Secretary of State and the Executive]: In foreign policy, unless you have an over-all design, your behavior grows random. It is as if, when you are playing chess, a group of kibitzers keeps making moves for you. They may be better chess players than you are, but they cannot possibly get a coherent game developed. Especially if, at the same time, you have to explain each of your moves publicly so that your opponent can hear it. I don't know exactly what the solution is. I know I am spending over half of my time now before Congressional committees. And that, too, is getting to be a problem in policy-making. I spent 42 hours in testimony and in private conversations with Congressmen in a three-week period on the Sinai accord. That is a lot of time, and it is in addition to the normal Congressional contacts.

*Interview, Washington/Time, 10-27:35.*

*2*

The detente debate suffers from a number of misconceptions and oversimplifications. One is that detente is a favor we grant to the Soviet Union, or that we can withhold it as a punishment. The fact is that we are attempting to carry out a foreign policy geared to the realities of the period: One, that the Soviet Union is a nuclear superpower, whose military potential cannot be effectively wiped out in a surprise attack, any more than ours can. This being the case, any war between us will involve colossal, indeed catastrophic, damage. Second, the U.S. is no longer predominant, though it is still probably the strongest nation. Third, the prevention of Soviet expansion, which remains a primary objective of American policy, has to be carried out in a more complicated way than in the 1940s and 1950s. Fourth, the world is no longer monolithic. It is not one in which we can give orders, or in which we can dominate a Western group and the Soviets dominate an Eastern group. And fifth, we have to consider what this country has gone through with Vietnam, Watergate and the attendant Congressional restrictions. For us to run the risks of a confrontation that will be considered by our people as unnecessary is to invite massive

foreign-policy defeats. I believe that the policy we are carrying out with the Soviet Union has put us in the best position to resist Soviet pressures and in the best position to exploit possibilities of positive developments in Soviet policies. Now, however, the debate gets carried on as if we are giving away things to the Soviet Union. Where has the Soviet Union made a unilateral gain?

*Interview, Washington/Time, 10-27:36.*

### Kukrit Pramoj
*Prime Minister of Thailand*

*3*

[On the dependability of U.S. defense agreements]: In all seriousness and with all respect to the United States, with the might of the United States behind you, you tend to lose your will to fight. How can you tie the destiny of a country to the electoral system of the United States? If America had a Napoleon, I'd be at his feet today. But it's not like that. I'm not an America hater, but I must accept a fact about the United States which does not provide constant help, nor a steady policy, in regard to its allies. It depends too much on Congress, and everything depends on the next election. You just don't know what's going to happen next.

*The National Observer, 10-11:6.*

### Melvin R. Laird
*Former Secretary of Defense of the United States*

*4*

[On detente]: My only concern is that in the free world [detente] gives politicians a signal that they can start re-establishing priorities as far as national security is concerned ... Detente must be done with our eyes open and we must not let our guard down ... Detente is not something carried on between friends—because friends don't need to relieve tensions. It is something done between adversaries and antagonists ... I don't have detente with my wife, for example. If word got out in Washington [that] I was having detente with my wife, people would think our marriage was on the rocks.

*At Foreign Correspondents Club, Tokyo, Sept. 3/Los Angeles Times, 9-4:(1)21.*

# WHAT THEY SAID IN 1975

**Russell B. Long**
*United States Senator,*
*D—Louisiana*                                      *1*

A number of Presidents felt they could pursue the high-minded policy of making the United States the policeman for the entire world. But the American people simply are not willing to support that policy any more. This nation is over-extended and over-committed . . . The American people feel over-used.
*Before the Senate, Washington, April 7/*
*Los Angeles Times, 4-8:(1)1.*

**Clare Boothe Luce**
*Former American diplomat and playwright*      *2*

America gives the world the jitters when it doesn't know what it's doing. And that's been the condition of American foreign policy the last 15 years.
*Radio broadcast, Washington/"National Town*
*Meeting," National Public Radio, 4-16.*

**Mike Mansfield**
*United States Senator,*
*D—Montana*                                      *3*

[Saying foreign aid tends to bring troubles for the U.S. abroad]: I believe this thoroughly—because too much of it has been military aid of one sort or another, military assistance, economic assistance tied to military ends. Because of that, I have not voted for foreign aid for a number of years—nor do I intend to until or unless it is changed back to its original concept: and that is on a people-to-people basis so that people in need will be given the sustenance which can be furnished under an aid program. I do not believe in aid to governments, because too much of it stays at the top, too much of it is corrupted, and too little gets down to the people who are in need. And I think that $140-billion in foreign aid since 1946 is too much and the matter should be gone into again thoroughly, completely; and if there is to be a foreign-aid program it ought to be on the old Point 4 basis of people-to-people.
*Interview, Washington/*
*The Christian Science Monitor, 2-28:4.*

*4*

This is not a period for gloom and despair, but rather a time for recognition that we are entering a new era which calls for new policies in a world which is changing rapidly and with which we must co-exist. It is not a question of withdrawing into Fortress America—that is an impossibility in this shrunken world. It is a question of recognizing that World War II was ended 30 years ago. Policies which were good immediately following that are not necessarily good policies today. We are spread too far, too wide, too thin, and we have neither the resources nor the manpower to undertake the kind of foreign policy which has been the hallmark of all Administrations—Democratic and Republican—since the end of World War II.
*Washington/The New York Times, 4-6:(1)29.*

**Charles McC. Mathias, Jr.**
*United States Senator, R—Maryland*            *5*

[On Secretary of State Henry Kissinger's detente policy]: I think Secretary Kissinger is a remarkable public servant. He has begun this process of communication, and he deserves enormous credit for that. We could, I'm sure, disagree on some details. But, on balance, he's made a very great contribution. The alternative to the Kissinger policy of detente is to go back to the cold war; it is to stop the communication between the people in the U.S. and the people in the Soviet Union at the increasing levels which it has now achieved; we would cut ourselves off from the possibility of some relief from the arms race and from the possibility of doing business, which is available at the level of billions of dollars. In short, I see no sensible alternative to detente as I define it: a bridge between two sides. It would be a tragedy to go back to the period of isolation.
*Interview/U.S. News & World Report, 12-8:22.*

**Eugene J. McCarthy**
*Former United States Senator, D—Minnesota*   *6*

Our foreign policy should be a projection of our internal strengths and ideals, rather than something dictated by internal political needs and fears.
*Canton, N.Y./*
*San Francisco Examiner & Chronicle, 4-27:(B)5.*

**John L. McLucas**
*Secretary of the Air Force of the
United States*

1

Apparently for some people, detente and strength are incompatible. Perhaps this view is based on the idea that strength produces tension and conflict. While I would argue that lack of adequate strength can produce just as much, if not more, tension and conflict, I think the real point to be remembered is that detente is a mixture of cooperation and competition, and a very delicate one at that. We need to be acutely aware of detente's limitations as well as its advantages. In 1975, it is not yet based on the complete altruism of man, but rather upon mutual interests—most particularly, avoiding the catastrophe of nuclear war. Political, military and economic developments of the past few years have brought us to this relationship of detente, and we are hopeful for the future. But now is not the time to relax our military posture. If we are no longer in a cold war, we are not yet in a stable peace.

*At Harvard Law School Forum,
Cambridge, Mass., Feb. 13/
Vital Speeches, 4-1:358.*

**Robert S. McNamara**
*President,
International Bank for Reconstruction
and Development (World Bank)*

2

Even the most hardened and unsentimental observer from the developed world is shocked by the squalid slums and ramshackle shanty-towns that ring the periphery of every major city [in the developing world] . The *favelas*, the *bustees*, the *bidonvilles* have become almost the central symbol of the poverty that pervades two-thirds of the globe.

*At meeting of World Bank and International
Monetary Fund, Washington, Sept. 1/
The Washington Post, 9-2:(A)5.*

3

The one billion people of the low-income nations have become the principal victims of the current economic turbulence. They did not cause it. By themselves they cannot change it. And they have little margin to adjust to it. Granted all they can and must do to work out

their own problems, they desperately need additional external assistance. This, then, is the most immediate and pressing problem in the global development scene. What is involved for the developed nations is not the diminution of their already towering standard of life. All that is required in order to assist these peoples so immensely less privileged is a simple willingness to dedicate a tiny percentage of the additional wealth that will accrue to the developed nations over the next five years. Underlying the emergency situation—and partially obscured by it— lies the more fundamental problem of poverty itself, and the need to shape an effective strategy to deal with it.

*Before World Bank Board of Governors/
The New York Times, 10-26:(11)20.*

**George Meany**
*President, American Federation of Labor-
Congress of Industrial Organizations*

4

[On Secretary of State Henry Kissinger]: His policies are giveaway policies. He goes to Egypt and gives [Egyptian President Anwar] Sadat $25-million. He goes to Saudi Arabia and gives them planes, and now we're even going to train the Saudi Arabians. All of these states are our economic enemies. Kissinger even is giving Russia 6 per cent [interest] money. And I say all of these things represent a policy of appeasement . . . a form of blackmail; and blackmail never works.

*News conference, Bal Harbour, Fla., Feb. 18/
Los Angeles Times, 2-19:(1)1.*

5

In the final analysis, the cause of human rights in this world is dependent on the strength—the economic strength, the military strength, the moral strength—of the United States of America. If we falter, freedom is shaken everywhere. And I don't say this because I'm a jingoist or a chauvinist. I say it because I've been around a long time, because I read maps, because I read history, and because I can count.

*At Jewish Labor Committee award dinner/
The Wall Street Journal, 3-14:8.*

*(GEORGE MEANY)*

**1**

Every basic Communist tactic of seizing power is now on display throughout the world: naked aggression in Indochina; political blackmail in the Middle East; . . . an outrageous putsch in Portugal; a heating-up of the cold war in Korea; and a diplomatic and propaganda war in international institutions. The time has come to ask what strings together the multiple disasters that have befallen our foreign policies in recent weeks. To deny that these disasters are interconnected is to take the first step backward—away from serious debate. And nobody, but nobody, with common sense will believe that the Middle East, Vietnam, Portugal, Greece, Turkey, the UN, the ILO—nobody will believe that these are separate, disembodied developments that have no relation to our policies or to the over-all policies of the Communist world . . . The President [Ford] and his Secretary of State [Kissinger] cannot forever sing the soothing lullabies of detente and expect the American people and their representatives in Congress to support a strong national defense coupled with a vigorous defense of freedom in the world. America will be strong only if its people believe there is a *need* to be strong. We will defend ourselves and our allies only so long as we believe we have something worth defending—and only so long as we believe there are real threats, real enemies of what is worth defending. The President cannot—any more than his predecessor [Nixon]—resolve the contradiction of proclaiming detente on the one hand and of demanding of the American people a continuing level of vigilance and sacrifice for the cause of freedom.

*Before AFL-CIO maritime trade department/
Human Events, 4-19:1.*

**2**

If we [the U.S.] have a foreign policy it's being kept secret from the American people. I don't think [Secretary of State] Henry Kissinger knows what it is until he gets up in the morning.

*Before Seafarers International Union,
Sept. 3/The Washington Post, 9-4:(A)13.*

**3**

Wherever there is trouble in the world today, one looks in vain for a shred of hard evidence that the Soviets are following a course of detente. But that's not quite true. They are following detente of a kind—their kind. Their version of detente is very simple: They take, take, take, and give nothing in return.

*Quote, 9-28:242.*

**Hans J. Morgenthau**
*Professor emeritus of political science,
City College of New York*

**4**

United States vital interests are what they have always been: safeguarding its territory and the preservation of its democratic institutions. What has changed is the perception of the role the nation must play to protect those interests. [The defense of those interests] no longer requires us to oppose Communism around the world, especially not in situations where changes come as a result of indigenous forces rather than through outside aggression.

*Interview/The National Observer, 6-28:15.*

**Daniel P. Moynihan**
*Professor of government, Harvard University;
Former United States Ambassador to India*

**5**

[Saying the U.S. should use its food exports as a weapon against Third World countries that support petroleum-exporting nations' use of oil prices as a political tool]: Food growing is the first thing you do when you come down out of the trees. The question is, how come the United States can grow food and you [the Third World] can't? Yes, food is a weapon and we should use it. We would have been shocked to use it a decade ago but now [with the oil situation] we should. We [in the U.S.] were inconvenienced by having to wait 20 minutes last year to fill our tanks. But it has destroyed a generation of economic prosperity for South Asians who now have no prospect of ever getting an automobile to fill up.

*News conference, New York/
Los Angeles Times, 2-27:(1)22.*

**6**

The Third World must feed itself, and this will not be done by suggesting that Americans eat too much. It is one thing to stress what is consumed in the West, another to note what is produced here. In 1973, 17.8 per cent of the world's population produced 64.3 per cent of its product—and not just from taking advantage of cheap raw materials.

*San Francisco Examiner & Chronicle, 3-9:(B)2.*

**Daniel P. Moynihan**
*United States Ambassador/Permanent Representative to the United Nations*
1

[A quarter of a century ago,] the future looked good for the democracies of the world. The colonies of Africa and Asia were becoming independent; the old autocracies, such as Japan, seemed to be following the evolution that had given way to democracy in Western Europe. All of this has changed. One by one, the new democracies have disappeared, and even many of the old ones. Most of the new states and most of the old ones have ended up enemies of freedom as we would know it, as we had inherited it, and as we have tried to preserve it.

*At AFL-CIO convention, San Francisco, Oct. 3/Los Angeles Times, 10-4:(1)18.*

**Edmund S. Muskie**
*United States Senator, D—Maine*
2

Secretary [of State Henry] Kissinger has preferred a personal diplomatic style involving secrecy, surprise and unpredictability as a means of keeping our adversaries off guard. To pursue such a policy, he has sought maximum independence from the Congress and maximum freedom from legislative restraints. This very style has done more to weaken us in the world today than any Congressional action. It has deprived our foreign policy of the consistent, continuous, moral and universal elements which have been the basis of American influence in the world for many years.

*Before Council on Foreign Relations, Chicago, June 2/The Washington Post, 6-3:(A)13.*

3

We cannot achieve our objective in the world through military might alone and we cannot do so even through our enormous economic power. Instead, we must pursue our objectives through a combination of diplomatic skill and interna-

tional political leadership—a leadership position which is enhanced not primarily by the credibility of our military commitments but by the credibility of the political values for which we stand.

*Before Chicago Council on Foreign Relations/ Quote, 7-20:2.*

**Richard M. Nixon**
*Former President of the United States*
4

We, as a country, have to provide strength and leadership. England is at a standstill. France seems in disarray; they really are Latins in temperament, you know, and they seem to be proving it now. Italy has a crisis government. Germany can't rally a world cause. South Africa? Where *do* we expect leadership to emerge?

*Interview, San Clemente, Calif./ Ladies Home Journal, December:54.*

**Don Paarlberg**
*Director of Agricultural Economics, Department of Agriculture of the United States*
5

[Arguing against the U.S. using its food supplies as a weapon in dealing with foreign countries]: If there is one thing more emotionally charged than oil, it is food. It is one thing to tell a person that he is going to have to pay a very high price for the oil to run his car or heat his house. It is quite another to refuse to sell to him—or force him to pay dearly for—the food that he must have to feed his family. We Americans have been moaning and groaning over how the high price of oil has wrenched the economy of the industrialized world. We would look pretty small if we tried to do the same thing with food.

*U.S. News & World Report, 6-2:51.*

**Mohammad Reza Pahlavi**
*Shah of Iran*
6

The United States has to continue to play its role [in the world]. It should not think it has to have a special relationship with every country. It should choose the places where it wants to make a stand, and not disperse its strength so as to be weak everywhere. I do not tell you [the U.S.] where to concentrate. But unless

# WHAT THEY SAID IN 1975

*(MOHAMMAD REZA PAHLAVI)*

you concentrate, the Russians will just sit there, arms folded, and let the system fall apart. What we will have then is not something we can consider to be Western civilization.

*Interview, Teheran/*
*Los Angeles Times, 5-1:(2)5.*

1

[On the decline of the West]: I am worried about so-called liberals who will accept anything that comes from the other side. Anything that is Communistic, that is nihilistic—that is okay [with them]. If a country sinks because of this attitude, then it could become a very dangerous proposition. Because one by one, they [the countries] are going to fall. I am talking about French so-called intellectuals. Maybe they think that the world must change and that before it changes it must break completely. They have nothing to offer. No doubt there is an intellectual international. Evidently they all work for international Marxism. They penetrate everything: people with great fortune and wealth, artists, writers, painters, taxi drivers. They are an army. We can get more trouble from these crazy so-called intellectuals than from the Soviet Union or [Communist] China.

*Interview, Teheran/Time, 6-9:33.*

**Paul VI**
*Pope*

2

We must raise our voice to remind people that it is not upon power that a peaceful and humane international order can be based, but upon the criterion of justice, upon respect and understanding of the rights and need of others, and upon a spirit of generous cooperation of the strongest with the weakest, for their mutual advantage.

*San Francisco Examiner & Chronicle,*
*6-8:(This World)2.*

**Shimon Peres**
*Minister of Defense of Israel*

3

I'm ... not much taken with the present American mood [toward foreign commitments].

I think it is a passing one, and I believe Americans either by nature or inclination cannot limit themselves to the horizons of New York or San Francisco. No danger that faces the U.S. begins on its shores, and in spite of all efforts by various groups in the U.S. to move the country into a policy of isolation, America is basically a universal political creation. If you look at 199 years of American history, I cannot recall an example where the U.S. let down a friend.

*Interview, Jerusalem/*
*U.S. News & World Report, 4-7:16.*

**Carlos Andres Perez**
*President of Venezuela*

4

Venezuela does not speak for the Third World; Venezuela is part of the Third World. What is important and significant is that all the developing nations are speaking the same language. This unity, which has finally become apparent to the world, is what makes the Third World a power. Today, industrialized nations must share decision-making with us. We believe in interdependence, but interdependence among equals rather than an interdependence in which there are subordinates. [U.S.] President Ford and Secretary [of State] Kissinger have made two statements with which we agree. The first is that no country can be subject to decisions that affect it but that are made elsewhere. The second is that it is essential to reach an agreement between producing and consuming countries. We countries of the Third World add one other: We cannot accept the fact that prices of our raw materials are manipulated in the great financial centers of the world. We also believe that an agreement has to be made that will establish an equilibrium in the terms of trade. We are not seeking a confrontation with any country over energy or oil. But, first and foremost, we will not have conditions imposed upon us. Nor are we making efforts to impose our own conditions. We are seeking understanding so that we may create new formulas of trade.

*Interview/Business Week, Oct. 13:56.*

**Ronald Reagan**
*Former Governor of California (R)*

5

Our friends and our adversaries must be convinced that American treaties and other commitments are not only binding but are backed by hardware and hard-nosed determination . . . The free world, indeed the entire non-Communist world, is crying out for strong American leadership, and we are not providing it. Neither are we providing a strong, lasting, consistent foreign policy. Detente works—for now—at the whim of Red Russia and Red China. It will not work as we intended it should unless we maintain our strength.

*Before National Headliners Club,*
*Atlantic City, N.J., May 31/*
*The Washington Post, 6-1:(A)11.*

1

[On the importance of U.S. credibility in the world] : If you will not fight when you can win without bloodshed . . . you may come to the moment when you have to fight with all the odds against you. But there may be a worse case. You may have to fight when there's no chance of victory, because it's better to perish than to live a slave.

*Interview/*
*The Washington Post, 6-3:(A)4.*

2

I'm against detente as a one-way street. It annoys me the way we [the U.S.] tiptoe around. We're so self-conscious about our own strength. I'm for decreasing confrontation but not with us doing all the leaning over backward.

*Interview/*
*Time, 11-17:22.*

**Harry Reasoner**
*News commentator,*
*American Broadcasting Company*

3

I don't think Henry Kissinger [Secretary of State] is God, and most days I don't think he does, either. He can be, to someone watching the movers and shakers from a distance, a large pain in the neck. But at a time when many of our best instincts were submerged by unworthy passions, and much of our strength corrupted and diluted, he, on balance, did much for our reputation and I think saved a lot of lives. A good many of us have done less.

*ABC News commentary/*
*The Christian Science Monitor, 3-31:14.*

**Henry S. Reuss**
*United States Representative, D—Wisconsin*

4

A prosperous economy in the United States and a society with its spirit restored is vastly better for retaining American influence [abroad] than the kind of interventionism and adventurism that have been mistakenly thought of as internationalism in the last few years. Talking to leader after leader all over the world, I'm just convinced that if we move toward full employment without inflation, adopt a free trading position internationally in which we don't, in panic, put artificial restrictions on our exports as we did on soybeans or foreign, job-creating investment here—we will be doing more for world peace and American international well-being than any number of battalions could do. And that idea is not isolationism but a recognition of the fact that military power has been largely—but not of course entirely—superseded by political, social, economic and moral power . . . why don't we try the interesting foreign-policy step of getting our own economy in order at the expense of the military budget and see whether that, in terms of world trade, world investment and world aid, doesn't do great things for our general power and prestige? We don't need to be in Korea or Taiwan or in Vicenza, Italy, and many other places in the numbers we are. If we would send to the Italian people the same amount of wheat for pasta that it now costs to keep the 7,000 American troops in Vicenza, the Communists would be losing elections all over Italy.

*Interview/The Washington Post, 4-21:(A)1,4.*

**Nelson A. Rockefeller**
*Vice President of the United States*

5

[U.S. foreign policy] must be clear and consistent and one on which other nations can count. Maybe this country has got to decide whether, as the nation which has the capacity to stand as the bastion of human freedom, human dignity and respect for equal opportunity throughout the rest of the world, whether we are to continue to accept the responsibility and have burdens, if you want to put it that way, that go with it. Or whether we want to withdraw and say, "Well, we're going

# WHAT THEY SAID IN 1975

## (NELSON A. ROCKEFELLER)

to step aside now and we've carried this lead for a couple of decades and let's let the Soviets accept the responsibilities of world leadership."

*Before American Newspaper Publishers Association, New Orleans, April 9/ The Dallas Times Herald, 4-10:(A)15.*

1

[On whether the U.S. had "learned its lesson" in Vietnam about getting involved in the affairs of other countries]: I think you've got to face the problems before you make these beautiful, broad idealistic statements which are to me somewhat unrelated to the realities of the world in which we live. As to what this country has learned, well, I don't know where you stand on the Middle East [for example]. I don't know what your position is on the support of Israel. I don't know what you'd do in the way of a vote of aid to Israel in the current session of Congress. But it's something we have to face. I think you've got to take the broad realities in addition to the idealism.

*At National Urban Coalition meeting, May 1/ The Washington Post, 5-2:(A)14.*

## Donald H. Rumsfeld
*Secretary of Defense of the United States*

2

Detente must be seen for what it is—a word for the approach we use in relations with nations who are not friends, who do not share our principles, whom we are not sure we can trust, and who have military power and have shown an inclination to use it in the detriment of freedom.

*San Francisco Examiner & Chronicle, 11-30:(This World)2.*

## Dean Rusk
*Professor of international law, University of Georgia; Former Secretary of State of the United States*

3

I can understand why some people want to reject the policy of collective security. The cost of that policy [in Indochina, for example] was grievous—600,000 casualties—and it hasn't been very collective. But what does concern me is

that we're not discussing alternatives. We're moving away from one era, but we're not making up our minds as to what the new era will be . . . It doesn't do much good to reject the mistakes of your fathers, only to embrace the mistakes of your grandfathers. Each generation has to find its own answer—but you better find it!

*Interview, Bethlehem, Pa./ The National Observer, 4-12:4.*

4

Foreign policy is like a cafeteria: so you select the policy you want and you have to pay the cashier at the exit.

*Quote, 4-13:338.*

## Terry Sanford
*President, Duke University; Former Governor of North Carolina (D)*

5

[We should] insist that the military is for defense, and that we can no longer rely confidently on military and economic might to impose our will on the rest of the world. We cannot allow our moral leadership to be mistaken for weakness or lack of resolve, and yet we can better defend our principles and the hopes of civilization by not posing as the biggest bully on the block.

*Announcing his candidacy for the 1976 Democratic Presidential nomination, Washington, May 29/ The New York Times, 5-30:20.*

## John A. Scali
*United States Ambassador/Permanent Representative to the United Nations*

6

The answer to meeting the world's long-term demands for food is not for Americans to eat less, and give more away. The United States already exports 67 per cent of our wheat crop, 22 per cent of our corn, and more than half of our soybeans, or their derivatives. Indeed, the world is already too dependent on America for its food . . . America has no monopoly on fertile land, nor on agricultural skills. The miracle of agricultural production which the American farmer has achieved can be accomplished by others. It is indispensable that many nations increase their crop yields.

*At John Hancock Awards Dinner for Excellence in Business and Financial Journalism, Atlanta/The Wall Street Journal, 2-4:18.*

## James R. Schlesinger
*Secretary of Defense of the United States*

1

Despite detente, the sources of potential differences and conflict among the powers remain numerous . . . With the differences that exist between our own social system and that of the U.S.S.R. and with the differences in political and economic objectives, it would be surprising indeed if there were not an extended period of time between the first steps toward detente and a more deeply cooperative relationship to which we aspire. Meanwhile, we must anticipate that moments of cooperation and agreement will alternate with periods of dispute and competition . . . In such circumstances, the risk of confrontation, crisis and miscalculation will remain present.

*Before Senate Armed Services Committee, Washington, Feb. 5/ Los Angeles Times, 2-6:(1)4.*

2

In these post-Vietnam years with the discontents—one might say the national dyspepsia—induced by the conflict in Southeast Asia, there has developed a revisionist critique of America's historic role. The critique seeks to convey at root that American power and purposes have been a *destabilizing* force in the world, marked by over-weening pride, the imperialist impulse, cold-war passion, and a growing list of alleged blunders. For my part, it is a portrait I do not recognize and cannot accept. Mistakes, undoubtedly. But in the great sweep of history it can, I believe, be said: Never has there been an era of greater security, of such limited conflict, of economic growth, of trade expansion—and, may I add, of civil liberties more generally widespread than ever before. All of this took place under the aegis of American power. No great nation in the history of mankind has used its strength with greater forebearance or its resources with greater generosity . . . *Pax Americana* is the term fre-

quently attached to this historic epoch. I suspect that, if the international structure grows more fragile, its attributes will be regarded with nostalgia even by its present critics. It fostered a unique period of order and stability. Since we are now moving into a period of potential instability, reflected in distortion and disequilibrium of the international payments mechanisms, the tensions in the Middle East and the apparently growing enfeeblement of several European states, we should recognize that in no inconsiderable measure these instabilities are traceable to an erosion of belief in American power and purposes. I trust that we shall also keep in mind that while criticism of America's role has come from idealism, so also the very exercise of American power has reflected the same idealism.

*Before Economic Club, New York/ The Washington Post, 2-6:(A)18.*

3

The Soviets do not use the term "detente." They use the term "peaceful coexistence," which is a phrase coined by Lenin and employed by Stalin. The Soviets see detente as a way to avoid the risk of war and expand their power relative to their former opponents. As long as they believe they can have things both ways, there will be no internal struggle over detente in the Soviet Union. In the long run, the United States cannot accept an interpretation of detente that implies an ever-strengthening of the correlation of forces in favor of the Soviet Union. I think the Soviets will have to come closer to the view of detente as "live and let live."

*Interview, Washington/ U.S. News & World Report, 5-26:27.*

4

The United States does not live in a world where it can wipe the slate clean, clear of obligation, merely as a result of changes in public mood. We live, as all societies have lived, enmeshed in the web of history, and we have taken steps in the past which now bind us in a variety of ways to the well-being of other societies. In the case of Western Europe, when the United States took the lead in establishing the NATO organization, we effectively proposed

# WHAT THEY SAID IN 1975

*(JAMES R. SCHLESINGER)*

that we would provide the nuclear umbrella for our allies in Western Europe. By that action, the United States diminished the incentives, not only in Europe but elsewhere around the world, for the acquisition of nuclear weapons. To this day, a major objective of American foreign policy is to prevent nuclear proliferation—an objective which I believe to be in the interest of all mankind. Similarly in Asia, the United States has assumed obligations that it cannot rapidly shed. It is responsible for the emergence of a democratic Japan subsequent to World War II. It is also bound up inextricably in the affairs of the Republic of [South] Korea—first, by the events of 1945 when we agreed, more or less accidentally, to the division of Korea along the 38th Parallel; second, by our subsequent declaration that Korea would not be a place to station American forces; and third, by their withdrawal and the devastating effects of the Korean War that followed. To repeat, the United States remains bound to these various countries by our prior actions. To reject the accumulated web of obligations means to reject a part of our own history and a part of our own responsibility.

*Before Los Angeles World Affairs Council,*
*Sept. 12/Vital Speeches, 10-15:2.*

1

... unless we are prepared to withdraw into the North American Continent, the contribution of the United States to world-wide military balance remains indispensable to all other foreign policies. Though we should pursue detente vigorously, we should pursue it without illusion. Detente rests upon an underlying equilibrium of force, the maintenance of a military balance. Only the United States can serve as a counterweight to the power of the Soviet Union. There will be no *deus ex machina*; there is no one else waiting in the wings.

*Farewell address, Washington, Nov. 10/*
*The New York Times, 11-11:8.*

**James R. Schlesinger**
*Former Secretary of Defense*
*of the United States*

2

As long as detente is misunderstood by a large segment of the public to imply that the possibility of conflict is over and therefore we can disarm, it has a detrimental effect. In order to achieve detente we must have an underlying equilibrium of force, and that means that we have got to keep our defenses up. Yet the over-all effect of detente—when the public does not see an imminent threat—is to reduce both the interest in and the willingness to support an adequate defense structure. We've heard a good deal of talk about deception in this country in recent years, but the cruelest form of deception is self-deception. We have tended to put the blinders on about what the trends have been. We have tended to avert our gaze from Soviet objectives and tactics because we wanted to believe that the illusory view of detente was true. We should pursue detente, but we should pursue it without illusion—and we must keep our powder dry.

*Interview, Washington/*
*U.S. News & World Report, 12-22:23.*

**Helmut Schmidt**
*Chancellor of West Germany*

3

While we should persist in our efforts toward detente, we cannot afford to delude ourselves about the danger in the continuing Soviet military buildup. As has been said, it is useless for sheep to pass resolutions in favor of vegetarianism while the wolf remains of a different opinion.

*Interview/*
*The Reader's Digest, September:86.*

**Howard K. Smith**
*News commentator,*
*American Broadcasting Company*

4

The votes by House and Senate Democrats for no more aid to Indochina pretty well close an era, the era of United States intervention by force almost anywhere. Today, snide comments on that era fill the air: arrogance of power, delusions of omnipotence, gendarming the world to destruction. Well, there are good things to say about that era. Look back at the Truman Doctrine debates that began it—no arrogance, not even much willingness. We acted because there was nobody else to stop systematic aggression from Greece to Korea. The domino theory we acted against was no myth. After Hitler knocked over the Austrian domino, others follcwed from Holland to the Caucasus. Stalin would have done the same had we not acted. Far from failure, the era of U.S. activism was a success. *The Economist* of London recently compared the three quarters of this century that have now passed. The first and second quarters were failures, with depressions and a world war each. But the final third, when the U.S. acted, it judges the best quarter not only of the century but of history. General prosperity, risen human values from welfarism at home to the liberation of all colonies abroad, and no world war. The current image of the U.S. as foolish meddler will fade with time. Indeed, the era may be looked back on with nostalgia. For with all mistakes reckoned in, humanity made the most gains [and] avoided the worst perils probably ever.

*ABC News commentary/*
*The Christian Science Monitor, 5-20:31.*

**Alexander I. Solzhenitsyn**
*Exiled Soviet author*

1

Soon they [the Soviets] will be twice as powerful as you [the U.S.], and then five times, and 10 times. And some day they will say to you: "We are marching our troops into Western Europe, and if you act, we shall annihilate you." And the troops will move, and you will not act ... The Americans watch the [chess] board very carefully, but [are] so involved with abstract strategies that they do not seem to notice that their pawns have all been taken, their knights are in danger and the game is nearly up ... Is it possible or impossible to transmit the experience of those who have suffered to those who have not suffered? Is it ever possible to warn anyone of oncoming danger? How many witnesses have come to your country, how many waves of immigration, all warning you of the same experiences and the same dangers? Yet those proud skyscrapers still stand, and you go on believing that it will not happen here. Only when it happens to you will you know it is true.

*Before AFL-CIO, New York, July 9/*
*The New York Times, 7-10:27.*

**John J. Sparkman**
*United States Senator, D-Alabama; Chairman,*
*Senate Foreign Relations Committee*

2

The basic purpose of our foreign policy, it seems to me, is to promote conditions by which our relations with other nations will enable this nation to live at peace and freedom. In my opinion, this can best be done by choosing courses of action which will keep open the widest spectrum of options for peaceful change. The world has become a community in its needs, if not yet in its attitudes. Soviet-American detente has profound implications for the security of all nations, not just for the two superpowers. The security and economic stability of Europe and Japan are inseparable from the security and economic stability of the United States. The Arab-Israeli conflict affects and is affected by the energy crisis, and it, in turn, could sow the seeds of a Soviet-American confrontation.

*The Washington Post, 3-20:(A)20.*

3

... the Constitution places in the hands of the President the right to, let me say, originate and execute foreign policy, and he does that through the agency of the Secretary of State. Now, our Committee has the job of deciding just what to do on any of those particulars. You know, there's another provision in our Constitution that says ... the Senate shall advise and consent. Now, I always think of our Committee, the Foreign Relations Committee, as being the body within the Senate to recommend that advising and consenting—in other words, if a problem of foreign policy comes up, it comes to our Committee. [The Committee] does have an impact on foreign policy, but it doesn't make foreign policy, except insofar as the Executive will take our advice and consent.

*Interview, Washington/*
*The New York Times, 3-25:12.*

4

Never before has foreign, economic and domestic policy been so intertwined. Never before, except in times of war, have the people of the U.S.A. been so affected by decisions of a foreign-policy nature, such as those faced in the

# WHAT THEY SAID IN 1975

## (JOHN J. SPARKMAN)

oil crisis or the first great [U.S.-Soviet] wheat sale.

*The Christian Science Monitor, 9-16:7.*

## John C. Stennis
*United States Senator,*
*D–Mississippi*

1

[On U.S. foreign policy]: I don't want to run everywhere where people are in trouble. But as I have seen things develop, you get results when you are armed. It is not the only way to persuade people, but it is a helpful way.

*Washington, May 9/*
*The New York Times, 5-10:1.*

## Adlai E. Stevenson III
*United States Senator,*
*D–Illinois*

2

The Congress is poorly suited for a major role in the formulation and implementation of foreign policy. It is not a role which the Congress seeks. The strong inclination in the Congress is to give the President free rein so long as his power in foreign affairs is not abused and for so long as the judgments are sound. And there lies the rub. The power has been abused, and in the minds of many the judgments have been calamitous. That being so, the Congress is compelled to choose between licensing the continued misconduct of foreign relations or of exercising powers which it is not altogether equipped to exercise. It has no choice except to prevent further miscalculations in the world, as best it can, privately begging for the day when foreign policy is managed by men in whom it can confidently repose authority.

*Before the Senate,*
*Washington, Feb. 7/*
*The Washington Post, 2-18:(A)14.*

3

The Ford Administration has no foreign policy. It has impulses; it has the dreams and odysseys of its Secretary of State [Henry Kissinger]; it has its cliches, slogans. But it has no foreign policy.

*Quote, 8-31:145.*

## Samuel S. Stratton
*United States Representative, D–New York*

4

The Constitution gives the President the primary authority to conduct foreign affairs. Congress will play a greater role because it is clear to the world that, without the support of Congress, neither the President nor the Secretary of State can carry out their plans. But that doesn't make it a good idea for Congress to try to take the upper hand. It's impossible for Congress, for example, to deal with foreign governments. Yet, because of difficulties that occurred during the Nixon Administration and to some extent because of fictional situations, we've been trying these past few months to conduct foreign policy ourselves. And it has not been very helpful. You've got to have cooperation between the White House and the Congress. This is an era in which we in Congress clearly cannot provide the lead, and where we can't even come up with a coherent point of view on many occasions . . . Because we're a body of 535 prima donnas. You simply can't get a single policy with 535 concurrences.

*Interview/*
*U.S. News & World Report, 6-30:39.*

## Maurice F. Strong
*Executive Director, United Nations*
*Environmental Program*

5

Cities like Calcutta, Bombay, Lagos and cities in South America cannot continue the way they are going. The central services, such as sewers and water supply, in such places are just managing to cope and are postponing the day of reckoning by the skin of their teeth. It will take little in the way of a natural disaster, such as a flood or human administrative breakdown, to bring about catastrophe . . . Shantytowns are multiplying three times as fast as socially acceptable suburbs. There are towns without essential services for health, education or employment, towns which deprive inhabitants of even the essentials of a basic standard of life. The situation is fraught with peril for our world.

*News conference, Nairobi, Kenya, June 3/*
*The New York Times, 6-4:8.*

**Stuart Symington**
*United States Senator,*
*D–Missouri*

1

... as Lord Palmerston once observed regarding the behavior of nations: "We have no eternal allies; we have no perpetual enemies. Our interests are eternal and perpetual, and those interests it is our duty to follow." In this connection, consider that 30 years ago our two chief enemies in war were Germany and Japan, and two of our strongest allies were the Soviet Union and China. Therefore, any nation would be foolish to consider present alignments and present appearances of mutual goals to be a permanent state.

*Before the Senate, Washington/*
*The National Observer, 7-26:12.*

**Herman E. Talmadge**
*United States Senator, D–Georgia*

2

No nation ever did more for another than the United States did for South Vietnam. We lost 56,000 Americans. There were more than 300,000 casualties. The war cost us $150-billion. That experience, if it does nothing else, ought to teach us a lesson for all time. The United States government, with all its resources, cannot do for people what they are unwilling to do for themselves. Never again, under any conditions, anywhere in the world, should American troops be committed to a foreign battlefield unless our own national security is directly threatened. And, if that time comes, it should be our unswerving resolve to fight to win.

*Quote, 6-22:578.*

**Margaret Thatcher**
*Member of British Parliament; Leader,*
*British Conservative Party*

3

The cold war is said to be over. The end of the winter's freeze, however, can be the most dangerous time. I am in favor of detente–who isn't? But in a dangerous world I am also in favor of attente, of advancing one step at a time. My experience is that the West did not lose the cold war ... but we are losing the thaw in a subtle and disturbing way. We are losing confidence in ourselves and in our cause. We are losing the thaw politically.

*At National Press Club,*
*Washington, Sept. 19/*
*Los Angeles Herald-Examiner, 9-21:(A)4.*

**George C. Wallace**
*Governor of Alabama (D)*

4

My foreign policy, if I were the President, would be based on the fact that you can't trust a Communist. You never have been able to trust them. I don't believe in confrontation. I believe in negotiation, and I believe in detente. But while I'm detenting, as they say, I wouldn't turn my back on them ... I think the best foreign policy we can have at the present time, with the situation of the Soviets and the Red Chinese, is to be the strongest nation on the face of the earth, because the people we're dealing with don't understand anything but strength.

*Interview, March/*
*Los Angeles Times, 5-8:(1)28.*

**William C. Westmoreland**
*General (Ret.) and former Chief of Staff,*
*United States Army*

5

Since World War II, we have stuck tenaciously to a strategy of containment of expansionism by others that has caused us to over-extend ourselves politically, psychologically and militarily. After Korea, we should have reappraised, figured out some priorities. There should have been some wise men who said, "Stop! We're over-extended." The Kennedy years were the worst.

*Interview, Charleston, S.C., March 28/*
*The New York Times, 3-29:3.*

## INTELLIGENCE

**Frank Church**
*United States Senator, D-Idaho; Chairman,
Senate Select Committee on Intelligence
Activities*

1

As regards covert activities [by the CIA], I think the agency is probably most proud of the support it gave to the constituting of democratic governments in Western Europe in the period following World War II. Now, that kind of covert activity at least conforms to our traditional values. I'm not speaking of the methods that are used. I'm speaking of the objectives. The worst example of covert CIA activity that I can think of was our intervention in Chile where we undertook to depose a government that had been lawfully elected by the Chileans. What we've come to call covert operations has relatively little to do with collecting intelligence. They are clandestine efforts to maneuver things, to control events abroad. If we were to put the CIA back exclusively in the business of operating an intelligence agency and confine it to gathering the information we need for our own defense and to conduct an informed foreign policy, we would find, and the agency itself would today admit, that 95 per cent or 98 per cent of the information that is gathered comes from either overt sources or through the technical facilities that are available to the agency. The old cloak-and-dagger work which is connected romantically with the espionage methods of the past accounts for precious little ... I have no objections whatever to the utilization of whatever means there are at our disposal to collect essential information about foreign governments and their intentions and capabilities. That's intelligence work. I think most of it will come from our technical capabilities. But even if clandestine operations are necessary, I have no objection to them if they are confined to that purpose. But when it comes to manipulating events abroad through covert actions, then the first thing you must realize is that it's not intelligence. That is a method of concealed interference in the affairs of others in order to manipulate them.

*Parade, 9-21:7.*

2

These are the types that you actually would expect to find [on the covert-operations staff of the CIA]: the dare-doer types, the adventuresome types, the people that find their expression in involvement in exciting activities of this kind and sometimes dangerous activities. And what are they doing? They are sitting around thinking up schemes for new interventions all over the world. And why are they doing it? Because they are professional intervenors. Now, this is how they get promoted. This is how they get decorated ... And all kinds of plausible schemes are brought to the President. He is told, "Don't worry about this or that, Mr. President. We can fix it." And it's a very intoxicating thing if you are President of the United States to think you can fix it because you have the wherewithal, the experts who know how to do the job. The trouble with that is that it ultimately reduces the President of the United States to a kind of glorified godfather.

*Before Los Angeles World Affairs Council,
Dec. 8/Los Angeles Times, 12-9:(2)4.*

3

[On what he would do, if he were President, to exert more control over the CIA]: For one thing, I would just take the whole covert-operation wing and cut it out of the CIA entirely and diminish it in size to about one-tenth of its present size and place it in the State Department, where it would be subject to the over-all policy considerations of our government in connection with the conduct of our foreign affairs. As it is [now in the CIA], it's a self-serving apparatus. It's a bureaucracy which feeds on itself, and those involved are constantly sitting around thinking up schemes for [foreign] intervention which will win them promotions and justify further additions to the staff. And thus it has grown and grown in the way that most bureaucracies do. And it self-generates interventions that otherwise never would be thought of, let alone authorized.

*News conference, Los Angeles, Dec. 8/*
*Los Angeles Times, 12-9:(2)4.*

**Clark M. Clifford**
*Former Secretary of Defense*
*of the United States*
*1*

[On the CIA]: Basically, an intelligence operation is an anachronism in a democracy. It is secret. It sometimes uses questionable means. The public can't be informed about it or even told its cost. It is inconsistent with democracy, but it remains a necessity if we are to preserve our form of government. We can't fly blind in the world today.

*Los Angeles Times, 9-28:(1-A)2.*

**William E. Colby**
*Director, Central Intelligence Agency of*
*the United States*
*2*

[On previous alleged misconduct by the CIA]: The things the Agency used to get by with and the stories or non-stories it used to tell the Congress are no longer possible. From now on, we have to operate according to the book; and if the book won't allow us to operate, then the country has to decide either to put us out of business or to change the book.

*The Washington Post, 1-11:(A)13.*

*3*

Any institution in or out of government that has been functioning for over a quarter of a century, as the CIA has, would be hard put to avoid some wrong steps. But any steps over the line in CIA's 27-year history were few and far between and, if wrong, stemmed from a misconception of the extent of CIA's authority to carry out its important and primary mission—the collection and production of intelligence pertaining to foreign areas and developments.

*Before Senate Appropriations Committee,*
*Washington, Jan. 15/*
*The Washington Post, 1-16:(A)1.*

*4*

[On the need for secrecy in the CIA]: There are some "traditional" secrets that don't need to be secret any more ... There are some "bad" secrets—mistakes we've made, things that have gone wrong, sure. But there are some "good" secrets, necessary secrets ... We have people whose lives and reputations depend on our secrecy. We have technical systems whose effectiveness can be annulled if it comes out we are doing a particular thing.

*Interview/*
*Newsweek, 1-20:21.*

*5*

[On recent criticism and investigations of the CIA]: These last two months have placed American intelligence in danger. The almost hysterical excitement that surrounds any news story mentioning CIA, or referring even to a perfectly legitimate activity of CIA, has raised the question whether secret intelligence operations can be conducted by the United States. A number of the intelligence services abroad with which CIA works have expressed concern over its situation and over the fate of the sensitive information they provide to us. A number of our individual agents abroad are deeply worried that their names might be revealed with resultant danger to their lives as well as their livelihoods. A number of Americans who have collaborated with CIA as a patriotic contribution to their country are deeply concerned that their reputations will be besmirched and their businesses ruined by sensational misrepresentation of this association. And our own employees are torn between the sensational allegations of CIA misdeeds and their own knowledge that they

# WHAT THEY SAID IN 1975

*(WILLIAM E. COLBY)*

served their nation during critical times in the best way they knew how.

> *Before House Defense Subcommittee,*
> *Washington, Feb. 20/*
> *The New York Times, 2-21:19.*

1

While I think our country has developed the best intelligence service in the world, I must warn you that it is in danger today. Intelligence by its very nature needs some secrets if its agents are to survive, if its officers are to do their work, and if its technology is not to be turned off by a flick of a switch. We in the American intelligence profession are proud of our open society; this is why we devote our lives to its service. But we also believe that this open society must be protected and that intelligence, and even secret intelligence, must play a part in that protection in the world in which we live. There are secrets in American society. Grand-jury proceedings are secret; Congressional committees meet in secret executive sessions; we have secret military capabilities; and our journalistic profession insists on the right to protect its sources. But, for some reason, secrets of intelligence arouse such public fascination that the letters "CIA" can move a story only tangentially referring to CIA from the bottom of page 7 to the top of page 1.

> *Before Associated Press/*
> *The National Observer, 5-3:3.*

2

[On charges that the CIA has engaged in assassination attempts in the past]: I am opposed to assassinations because I think they're wrong and because I think they frequently bring about absolutely uncontrolled and unforeseeable results—usually worse results than by continuing to suffer the problem that you're facing.

> *Interview, Langley, Va., June 19/*
> *The New York Times, 6-20:10.*

3

...the CIA today is the best intelligence service in the world; it has the most dedicated and talented group of people working for it of any intelligence service in the world. It is the envy of the foreign nations. I think that any attempt to disband it would leave our nation vulnerable in a world in which we now sit 30 minutes away from a nuclear missile aimed and cocked at us, in a world in which our economic resources can be throttled by hostile foreign nations, in a world in which nuclear proliferation can pose a danger to all of us. I think we need good intelligence. I think we have got it, and I think we should continue.

> *TV-radio interview, Washington/*
> *"Meet the Press,"*
> *National Broadcasting Company, 6-29.*

4

[On the critical attacks against the CIA]: Will we destroy [the CIA's] great intelligence capability? Will we have an investigation in 1980 as to why in 1975 we deprived our nation of its technical and foreign sources that provide information about the threats we will face in the years ahead? Will we have publicity or protection? Will we have sensation or safety?

> *San Francisco Examiner & Chronicle,*
> *10-26:(This World)2.*

5

[On the recent criticism of CIA actions and methods]: The members of Congress who said they did not want to know of our activities, the careful circumlocutions used in the directives developed for intelligence—these reflected a consensus that while intelligence was needed to protect America, America was unwilling to admit its use of intelligence. As a result, intelligence made some mistakes and did some misdeeds.

> *At Pacem in Terris Foreign Affairs*
> *Conference, Washington, Dec. 4/*
> *Los Angeles Times, 12-5:(1)13.*

**Robert Conquest**
*British authority on the Soviet Union*

6

[On the U.S. government investigation of alleged misdeeds by the CIA]: The kind of thing that isn't likely to happen to the KGB is that the Supreme Soviet sets up an investigating commission, some of whose members leak information about what the KGB is doing to *Pravda*, which prints it! There are several links in that chain that just wouldn't work in the Soviet Union. A Michael Harrington or a Daniel Ellsberg couldn't exist in Moscow, and if they did, their existence would be rapidly terminated. What the CIA investigation must seem like to the KGB I can't imagine. From its point of view it must be absolute fantasy. It seems rather like that to most Western Europeans, too!

*Interview, London/*
*U.S. News & World Report, 2-24:46.*

**Archibald Cox**
*Professor of law, Harvard University*
1

[Criticizing CIA methods]: . . . surely we cannot plot, lie, cheat and commit murder abroad and remain humane, honorable, trustworthy and trusted at home . . . We cannot create Howard Hunts [former CIA agent and convicted Watergate conspirator] for cloak-and-dagger work overseas, and then bring them home and put them in the White House and expect them to act different than they were trained. A CIA indifferent to human life in other lands will seldom shrink from performing experiments upon unsuspecting Americans, running through drills with lethal gasses and storing them in disregard of even the President's instructions. It is time the nation had a leader who will outspokenly condemn these wrongs, confine such agencies to gathering foreign intelligence, and rid the government of those who tolerated the worst offenses.

*Before Union of American Hebrew*
*Congregations, Dallas/*
*The Dallas Times Herald, 11-16:(B)3.*

**Alan Cranston**
*United States Senator, D—California*
2

The CIA should have adequate protection, but we have to think out very thoroughly precisely what that protection should be. I think the naming of agents is improper. But if an agent acts in violation of the law, that's something else again. In a case of that sort, it's a matter of individual judgment whether or not it should be made public. Basically, it's my view that the CIA has had too much power—and this has led to a lot of abuse. You can't really draw

a distinction between the use of power by the CIA to protect sensitive information and the use of that same power to do almost anything they choose and then cover it up. We certainly need more control over the intelligence agencies—and that control must include a greater ability by Congress to decide what should and should not be classified as secret.

*Interview/U.S. News & World Report, 8-18:38.*

**Gerald R. Ford**
*President of the United States*
3

[On the current investigation of the CIA for alleged illegal activities]: In a world where information is power, a vital element of our national security lies in our intelligence services. They are as essential to our nation's security in peace as in war. Americans can be grateful for the important, but largely unsung, contributions and achievements of the intelligence services of this nation. It is entirely proper that this system be subject to Congressional review. But a sensationalized public debate over legitimate intelligence activities is a disservice to this nation and a threat to our intelligence system. It ties our hands while our potential enemies operate with secrecy, skill and vast resources. Any investigation must be conducted with maximum discretion and dispatch, to avoid crippling a vital national institution.

*State of the World address, Washington,*
*April 10/The New York Times, 4-11:10.*

**Barry M. Goldwater**
*United States Senator, R—Arizona*
4

[On Congressional investigation of the CIA]: The wholesale foraging of the Congress into the details of foreign policy and the intelligence services upon which it depends can only serve to give comfort to our opponents and to embarrass our friends.

*U.S. News & World Report, 12-1:13.*

**W. Averell Harriman**
*Former United States Ambassador-at-Large*
5

The Russians are not nuts; they are not crazy people; they're not Hitler. But they are trying to dominate the world by their ideology and we [by the current critical attacks on our

# WHAT THEY SAID IN 1975

*(W. AVERELL HARRIMAN)*

intelligence community] are killing the one instrument which we have to fight that ideology, the CIA.

*Interview, Washington/*
*"W": a Fairchild publication, 11-28:16.*

**Richard Helms**
*United States Ambassador to Iran; Former Director, Central Intelligence Agency of the United States*     *1*

[On charges that the CIA engaged in assassination of foreign leaders]: I don't know of any foreign leader that was ever assassinated by the CIA. That's my honest belief... There were always discussions of everything. Two men may have sat in the State Department or the Defense Department and discussed things that may not be acceptable to the American people. That happens all the time.

*News conference, Washington, April 28/*
*Los Angeles Times, 4-29:(1)19.*

**Fred C. Ikle**
*Director, Arms Control and Disarmament Agency of the United States*     *2*

At this time, our intelligence services are under severe public scrutiny. Unquestionably, a democratic nation is wise to monitor carefully every facet of its government operations, particularly those that cannot be conducted in full public view. And it goes without saying that all our government agencies—including the intelligence services—must operate within the law. But the current rash of publicity and leaks is something that goes way beyond our tradition of openness and the public's right to know. Of course, we all can delight in a good spy story. And the temptation must be strong today to publish titillating accounts of delicate intelligence operations and to be the first in going public. I believe, however, the American public will not long feel entertained by indiscretions that disable our national intelligence capability. This capability, built up over many years, has permitted our government to assess the military effort of our potential adversaries so that we could meet threats realistically. And it has made it possible for us to move forward with arms-control agreements on which we could rely. Now this capability might be wrecked by irresponsible public disclosure. Whether our adversary receives such information from a paid spy, or reads it in a self-serving book or a well-meaning newspaper—the end result is the same. Our law-makers, I am sure, will have the widest public support in drawing a discriminating line between legitimate secrecy and irresponsible concealment, between mischievous disclosure and the openness democratic societies must have. I am sure the American people will support—indeed, demand—adherence to a code of ethics, or, where needed, a code of law, that protects both the nation's standards of decency and its safety.

*Before World Affairs Council,*
*Pittsburgh, June 10/*
*The Wall Street Journal, 6-12:10.*

**Henry A. Kissinger**
*Secretary of State of the United States*     *3*

[On criticism and Congressional investigations of CIA actions and methods]: We must discover the excesses [in CIA activities] of the past, overcome the abuses that are uncovered... But it should be possible to cleanse our institutions without disrupting the conduct of our nation's business abroad and buffeting all the instruments of our policy... [There should be an end to] the delusion that American intelligence activities are immoral, the suspicion that the confidentiality of diplomacy is a plot to deceive the public, or the illusion that tranquility can be achieved by an abstract purity of motive for which history offers no example.

*Before Economic Club, Detroit, Nov. 24/*
*The Washington Post, 11-25:(A)1.*

**Richard M. Nixon**
*Former President of the United States*     *4*

[On the CIA, in view of recent critical attacks on the Agency and Congressional investigations of its methods]: They are going to be polarized for a while, I'm afraid. I can't see how they can be helpful to our security if stripped of the cloak of secrecy. Sometimes, overt acts by the CIA can save thousands of lives and ease pressure points in world diplomacy. Extreme measures [by the CIA] can become necessary if one is putting down evil consequences. The probe will show we accomplished some courageous acts. It will also show we had nothing to do with [the 1973 revolt in] Chile or [the overthrow of Chilean President Salvador] Allende. That was the Chileans.

*Interview, San Clemente, Calif./*
*Ladies' Home Journal, December:52.*

**Otis G. Pike**
*United States Representative, D–New York*
1

If an attack were to be launched on America in the very near future, it is my belief that America would not know that the attack was about to be launched . . . I think there are thousands of dedicated men risking their lives to get intelligence. I think there are other thousands of brilliant men creating magnificent scientific techniques for getting intelligence. Above the gathering level, however, it just bogs down every single time. It is not absorbed; it is not delivered. As far as our getting our money's worth out of it—no way we are getting our money's worth out of it.

*TV-radio interview/"Face the Nation,"*
*Columbia Broadcasting System, 9-28.*

**Nelson A. Rockefeller**
*Vice President of the United States*
2

[On the commission he heads investigating alleged domestic spying by the CIA]: We are going to conduct this inquiry with determination and with thoroughness, and we are going to get all of the facts. We can have, and we must have, an intelligence capability—which is essential to our security as a nation—without offending our liberties as a people.

*Washington, Jan. 13/*
*The New York Times, 1-14:18.*

3

[On charges that U.S. intelligence monitored foreign travels and conversations of dissident Americans]: It depends on who you're talking to. If you're talking to the head of the KGB [Soviet secret police] and you happen to be overheard, and you're [American dissident actress] Jane Fonda, or somebody else, there's no reason you shouldn't be overheard if somebody has the capability to overhear you . . . If we want to survive, we've got to be realistic about protecting our national security.

*Interview, Washington, Oct. 15/*
*Los Angeles Times, 10-16:(1)6.*

**James R. Schlesinger**
*Secretary of Defense of the United States*
4

[On criticism that the CIA maintained files on 10,000 American citizens]: The question, I think, is directed to whether or not the CIA *inappropriately* maintained files on that number of citizens, because files are generated in a variety of ways. They can be generated by overseas activities. The Agency has a responsibility for the gathering of foreign intelligence, and where there are contacts between Americans and foreigners overseas, that leads quite appropriately to the generation of information. The question, I think, is directed toward massive surveillance activities in the United States, and to the extent that that is tied to 10,000 files, that story is overblown.

*News conference, Jan. 14/*
*The Washington Post, 1-16:(A)22.*

**Howard K. Smith**
*News commentator,*
*American Broadcasting Company*
5

Espionage is eminently successful in all nations. There aren't many secrets that can't be found. But intelligence—interpreting and acting on them—are flawed most everywhere. Because all the books on it are now open, World War II is an encyclopedia of cases. Hitler's planned attacks on the Netherlands and on Russia were known to the date in the victims' capitals, but they wouldn't believe it. Hitler had our detailed plans for D-Day, but we were smart enough to get a lot of phony plans to him too, so he never believed the real ones. Books on cases since are not open. But we know that from Russia putting missiles in Cuba to the Yom Kippur war in the Sinai, we had all the facts we needed, but misinterpreted them. Since CIA reform is now in order, the distinction is important. Leave our spies alone. I am inclined to think the President [Ford] right in denying Congress information

# WHAT THEY SAID IN 1975

(HOWARD K. SMITH)

that would hint at their identities, locations or methods. Go to work on the superstructure of intelligence and dirty tricks. That's where the trouble lies and changes are needed.

*ABC News commentary/*
*The Christian Science Monitor, 10-22:28.*

**John G. Tower**
*United States Senator, R–Texas*
                                                    *1*

[On criticism of the CIA for using wartime methods in peacetime]: I think to make a fine distinction on the matter of war and peace ignores the fact that we are confronted in this world by a very powerful adversary that would not hesitate to resort to military means to achieve its political objectives—[a] powerful adversary that itself through its clandestine activities and overt activities generates military activity all over the world to accomplish political ends . . . So I think that we cannot draw this in strict terms of war and peace, in terms of whether or not the United States is actually at war. We are in effect in a war of sorts. That is a war of preservation of the climate in this world where national integrity will be respected.

*Washington/The New York Times, 11-11:17.*

**Vernon A. Walters**
*Deputy Director, Central Intelligence*
*Agency of the United States*
                                                    *2*

[On investigations and criticism of the CIA for alleged past illegal activities]: We [the CIA] cannot resist the advance of Communism if we are tied hand and foot and our pockets are turned inside out and contents exposed for every foreigner to look at. We cannot operate with all of our secrets being turned out for public view. So here we are, rummaging through the garbage pails of history of events of the '50s and '60s. I just hope that equal time will be given to the late '70s and early '80s, because that's when your freedom and mine is going to be decided. The real issue before the American people today is not the truth or the falsehood of some of these . . . allegations, some of them reaching back a quarter of a century. The real issue facing the American people today is this: Is the United States, as a free and democratic nation, going to have eyes to see and ears to hear, or are we going to stumble into the future, blind and deaf, until the day we have to choose between abject humiliation and nuclear blackmail?

*Before Veterans of Foreign Wars,*
*Los Angeles, Aug. 20/*
*Los Angeles Times, 8-21:(1)3.*

# Government

### George D. Aiken
*United States Senator, R—Vermont*

1

[I wish to urge a Constitutional amendment] that would limit the President to a single six-year term. I would also recommend an amendment that would prohibit any member of Congress from becoming a candidate for President or Vice President until he has been out of the legislative body for at least two years. If we could do this, we would find that both the President and the members of Congress could concentrate on doing the work for which they were elected.

*Time, 1-13:18.*

2

The weakness of the Senate now is that it's got too many ambitious members who think too much about gaining prestige in the future and too little about doing their jobs where they are. There's probably a dozen of them right now who have been bitten—and they find it difficult to settle down.

*Parade, 3-9:15.*

### Stanley Anderson
*Professor of political science,*
*University of California, Santa Barbara*

3

Congress does remain the one great declassifying institution in our system of [government] classification. That is a battle that has not really been fought. Maybe it is a battle that will never be fought with any final clarity. But certainly the Congress, as a whole, is not bound by the Executive's classification of government information. Probably its major committees are bound by it. Of course, an individual member of Congress can be whiplashed on an issue such as this by invoking the "if-you-want-to-get-along, go-along" system in Congress. The point that is so important here is that the majority of legislators—whether in America or Scandi-navia—do not really want to know; they do not want to be given information that is confidential; they do not want to monitor the classification system. They are simply willing to let the Executive do whatever it thinks should be done, but they do not want to participate in it. And so they are abdicating their responsibility.

*Panel discussion/*
*The Center Magazine, Sept.-Oct.:52.*

### Wendell R. Anderson
*Governor of Minnesota (D)*

4

Let us be grateful that we are forced now to re-examine—under the harshest light—every [government] program, every habit, every commitment. We are being forced to do what we should have been doing all along: to completely rethink our values. Through all our history of affluence, the people knew that softness and drift and waste were not the fair expression of our national character ... What we must demonstrate to our people is that our system can do the hard things, that our political process is the link that was intended between them and their destiny. We must reaffirm by what we do that our political system is the avenue, not the enemy, of our better selves. If we can help to make people see that, then we will indeed have inaugurated an age in which our will is equal to our hopes.

*Los Angeles Times, 1-23:(2)7.*

### William L. Armstrong
*United States Representative, R—Colorado*

5

[On a proposed increase in Congressional staffs]: If this increase had been accompanied by a corresponding increase in the ability of Congress to cope with the nation's problems, I would not object. But ... Congress seems gradually less and less able to come to grips with basic issues. What ails Congress, it seems to me, is a lack of stomach for hard decisions, a failure

145

*(WILLIAM L. ARMSTRONG)*

of nerve and judgment, rather than lack of staff and facilities.

*The Washington Post, 6-1:(A)9.*

**L. A. (Skip) Bafalis**
*United States Representative, R—Florida*     1

There is an unwritten rule in the Federal government: You never end the fiscal year with money unspent, regardless of whether there is a logical way to spend it. If you put a bureaucrat in the desert and hand him $1,000 with orders to spend it, he would—even if he had to buy sand.

*Washington/*
*Los Angeles Herald-Examiner, 4-22:(A)7.*

**William J. Baroody, Jr.**
*Assistant to President of the United*
*States Gerald R. Ford for Public Liaison*     2

On the most fundamental level, our belief in open government is based on a clear and compelling need for information on the part of the American people. Madison said that "a popular government, without popular information, or the means of acquiring it, is but a prologue to a farce or a tragedy, or perhaps both." Democracy cannot function unless people are informed about what their government is doing. Obviously, it's clear that openness in government has many positive effects: a well-informed citizenry, exposure of misdeeds or inefficiency, greater possibility for evaluation of various programs by the Congress, the GAO and others, and the continued pressure to keep government honest. All these are positive results of openness. However, as we open up government some significant problems of openness can emerge, which involve not only national security, foreign policy and diplomatic considerations, but also governmental efficiency, frank discussion, confidentiality and privacy. Our problem, of course, is to balance these opposing interests and to provide a just and workable formula which protects them . . . Although the unauthorized release of various policy papers, backgrounders, memos and other materials has at times had some beneficial results in specific

instances, it's clear that if this practice became the rule we would end up with government-by-leak. The purpose of internal memoranda is to think through and analyze a problem. And clearly the thinking-through process is an on-going process. By short-circuiting or aborting such a process through leaks, the public perception of government could be that it is irrational and disorganized. This clearly could lead to a loss of confidence in what would seem to be a government bereft of coherence, theme and credibility.

*Before National Press Club, Washington,*
*July 9/Vital Speeches, 8-1:627.*

**John Brademas**
*United States Representative,*
*D—Indiana*     3

I think we [Congress] have, under the American Constitution, the responsibility to initiate legislation as well as the President has a responsibility to propose legislation. Customarily, members of Congress are criticized for sitting supinely back while the White House comes up with all the ideas. That is not going to happen in 1975 and 1976. [President] Ford is a nice man, but I see no evidence of constructive leadership on his part whatsoever in dealing with these tough problems. We will work with him; we will cooperate with him; but we won't sit back and wait for him.

*TV-radio interview, Washington/*
*"Meet the Press,"*
*National Broadcasting Company, 1-5.*

**Peter J. Brennan**
*Secretary of Labor of the United States*     4

[Saying Federal executives should get pay raises]: [The pay freeze] represents pretty shoddy treatment of the men and women from whom the American public expects so much. It is treatment that no unionized worker in this country would accept for a minute. I would therefore urge that President Ford and the Congress get together and give Federal executives the long-overdue pay raise they deserve. Equity demands that this nation do no less.

*At awards banquet, Feb. 27/*
*The Washington Post, 2-28:(A)8.*

**Bill Brock**
*United States Senator, R—Tennessee*

1

The political process is a process of trade-off; and the longer you're here [in government], the more people there are who owe you things, the more obligations you have for things that have been done for you. And the longer you stay, the more you become obligated to the system. That's the distressing thing.

*The Washington Post, 2-23:(A)12.*

**David S. Brown**
*Professor of management,*
*George Washington University*

2

[Saying the Federal bureaucracy is too independent of Presidential authority]: One of the most frustrating things—and I think it is what started [former President] Nixon into this whole Watergate mess—is to be the most powerful man in the world and not be able to have your own bureaucracy do what you want it to do. He started trying to use outside means to change things, and got into trouble ... The top bureaucrats usually are about third or fourth level down from the President. Most of them never see the President. Yet they and the other "supergrades" are the ones who really make things happen in government. Without a lot of solid effort from the top, it is not very likely that those people will be carrying out the will of the political appointees in office.

*U.S. News & World Report, 11-24:22.*

3

Those who initially go to work for government often do so with a strong feeling of public service. This is later displaced by an even stronger feeling for the military service, the Postal Service, the Foreign Service, or whatever service they are members of. But gradually this, too, gives way to another kind of service—self-service—as the job-holder becomes more and more concerned with ... benefits, rights, prerogatives, seniority and other ... emoluments.

*U.S. News & World Report, 11-24:27.*

**Edmund G. Brown, Jr.**
*Governor of California (D)*

4

After a month in office, I really see what everyone's talking about when they speak of a lack of trust, a lack of credibility in government ... The government doesn't trust the press and the press doesn't really trust the government ... I think we have a big job to do both in government and in the press to speak with greater clarity, greater honesty. And I'd like to see the press write English more understandably, more simply. And I'd like to see politicians and those who work in government say what they mean and mean what they say.

*Before California newspaper publishers,*
*San Francisco/*
*Los Angeles Times, 2-8:(1)16.*

5

The fact that there's a problem doesn't mean that more government will make it better. It might make it worse. The interventionism that we've seen in our society is analogous to Vietnam. With our money, power and genius, we thought that we could make the people over there be like us. Then we did the same thing to our cities. When problems don't go away, we escalate the attack until someone gives up. I'm rethinking some of that escalatory social interventionism. Inaction may be the highest form of action.

*Interview/Time, 4-14:34.*

6

People ask me, "What's your program?" What the hell does that mean? The program is to confront the confusion and hypocrisy of government. That's what's important ... Ultimately, people have to believe in some ideal, and they have to believe you're leveling with them. You can't win hearts and minds through planning and technology. In the final analysis, people will support only what they believe ... You ask me what I want. I want to be the Governor of the 54 per cent of the people who didn't vote at all last year. The largest constituency of all is the constituency of no confidence, and that constituency is important to remember. I don't know if we can satisfy them.

# WHAT THEY SAID IN 1975

*(EDMUND G. BROWN, JR.)*

Probably not. But wouldn't it be something if we could?

*Interview, Sacramento/*
*The Washington Post, 5-31:(A)8.*

1

The Federal government is taking onto itself more and more power for local matters for everything from family-planning to criminal justice to health service. Clearly, national issues are not being addressed in a straightforward way while everyone on the other side of the Potomac starts meddling in local and state affairs because of the lack of faith in the ability of people to govern themselves. Decentralization of power—that is important to me. All those things that can be left at a lower level of political organization ought to be.

*Interview, Sacramento/San Francisco*
*Examiner & Chronicle, 6-15:(A)2.*

2

When we pay high salaries to government officials we are creating a class of mandarins who are out of phase with the declining living standards of most people.

*Before trustees of California State*
*University and Colleges, Los Angeles/*
*Los Angeles Herald-Examiner, 7-14:(A)8.*

## Archie L. Buffkins
*Chancellor, University of Maryland,*
*Eastern Shore*

3

I feel we are quickly reaching a point in our society where those in authority consider comfort and survival of higher priority than living with the dissonance resulting from hard decision-making. It is my sincere belief . . . that we need a new generation of leaders with the ability to make hard decisions and live with the consequences of those decisions.

*U.S. News & World Report, 4-21:34.*

## Warren E. Burger
*Chief Justice of the United States*

4

Increasingly, Congress legislates in broad, general terms. Sometimes because the legislation is not as thoroughly considered as it might

be, or because it goes through natural processes of compromise, with resulting ambiguity, the courts are compelled to do the best they can using the accepted rules and canons of statutory construction to try to discern the intent of the Congress. This frequently puts courts in the appearance of engaging in [social, political and economic reform]. Possibly there are some judges who like that function; but I think most would much prefer to have Congress make the basic social, economic and political decisions. My view is that, under our Constitutional system, the elected representatives should make these basic decisions, not tenured judges who cannot be rejected by the people, as Senators and Congress members can be.

*Interview/U.S. News & World Report, 3-31:32.*

## Earl L. Butz
*Secretary of Agriculture of the*
*United States*

5

Our good intentions seem to be leading us into the same sort of trap that stifles most mature governments. In our will to help people less fortunate than ourselves we set up agencies and programs designed to that end. Soon we get an unwieldy government of too much size and not enough productivity—a government of too much structure and not enough substance; one of too many taxes and not enough return; one of too many wishes and not enough thought.

*At Western Illinois University commencement/*
*The National Observer, 6-14:7.*

## Robert C. Byrd
*United States Senator, D—West Virginia*

6

[Saying national leadership should come from the President, and cannot come from Congress]: Leadership requires one man, one voice—a voice that can point the way and inspire, a voice that can lift up the nation and challenge the best that is in our people.

*Before Women's National Democratic Club,*
*Washington, Jan. 13/*
*The New York Times, 1-14:22.*

7

Big government did not spawn itself. Big government is the result of big demand back home. Every message I get from the people is twofold: "Cut the budget. When am I going to get my check?" They are all for cutting the budget in the abstract, but when it comes to making selective cuts, that is another tune. I hope that the people will see that the Senate is responding to their concerns. I also hope that the message will get back to the grassroots that all of us, everybody—taxpayers, special-interest groups and so on—are going to have to exercise some restraints on their own appetites on the Federal Treasury. When they do that, their representatives will reflect that attitude from back home.

*The Wall Street Journal, 12-30:6.*

**Brendan T. Byrne**
*Governor of New Jersey (D)*

1

I'm not too sure that there's anything that prepares you to be Governor. There are things that help. Having run one of the Cabinet positions helps; having been a prosecutor gives you an insight. But there's nothing that really prepares you totally to meet all the problems and make all the judgments you've got to make in this job ... The hardest thing, personally, has been to get movement in areas where the need for movement is clear and where the silly things that bog down a legislature become obstructions ... I don't know—and I challenge the legislature to show me this—that there are a dozen good pieces of legislation passed every year. A lot of legislation is introduced, thousands of bills, hundreds are passed; but it's difficult to put your finger on more than a dozen pieces that really move us forward.

*Interview/The Washington Post, 5-11:(C)5.*

**Fletcher L. Byrom**
*Chairman, Koppers Company;*
*Chairman, The Conference Board*

2

I wish every piece of legislation that came down from Capitol Hill had built into it an assessment of what that legislation would truly cost in terms of its total economic impact. That may have been the most important proposal in President Ford's economic message of last fall, and I wish the Congress would take it to heart. Planning is more vital than ever, because growth

is more vital than ever. Without constructive planning, we will waste resources to a degree that is intolerable.

*At Public Affairs Outlook Conference of*
*The Conference Board/*
*Nation's Business, May:77.*

**Hugh L. Carey**
*Governor of New York (D)*

3

All around us, in this capital, are symbols of splendor, monuments of glass and marble. They stand as living embodiments of an idea of government as an ever-expanding institution, to be paid for from the ever-expanding riches of tomorrow ... Well, tomorrow is here ... and this government will begin today the painful, difficult, imperative process of learning to live within its means ... We cannot continue to pass our responsibilities to the next generation of taxpayers. Now is the time, when economic hardship dramatizes needless spending, to bring government back into line with reality. A program that cannot be justified in hard times should never have been created in good times, and this is the time to rid ourselves of those drains on the pockets of the people.

*Albany, N.Y./*
*Los Angeles Times, 1-23:(2)7.*

**Frank Church**
*United States Senator, D—Idaho*

4

[On the massive spy technology used in foreign-intelligence and national-security operations]: [That capability] at any time could be turned around on the American people, and no American would have any privacy left, such is the capability to monitor everything—telephone conversations, telegrams—it doesn't matter. There would be no place to hide. If this government ever became a tyranny, if a dictator ever took charge in this country, the technological capacity that the intelligence community has given the government could enable it to impose total tyranny and there would be no way to fight back. The most careful effort to combine together in resistance to the government, no matter how privately it was done, is in the reach of the government to know, such is the capability of this technology. We must see to it that ... all agencies that possess this tech-

*(FRANK CHURCH)*

nology operate within the law and under proper supervision so that we never cross that abyss. That's the abyss from which there is no return.

*TV-radio interview/"Meet the Press,"*
*National Broadcasting Company, 8-17.*

**Henry Cohen**
*Dean, Center for New York City Affairs,*
*New School for Social Research* 1

Where private employers trim costs during a recession by mass layoffs, renegotiating union contracts or even going out of business, government responds only to absolute catastrophe. Standards always become floors, and it takes a tragedy to bring any contractions.

*The New York Times, 5-18:(4)1.*

**William S. Cohen**
*United States Representative, R–Maine* 2

Congress is designed to be slow and inefficient because it represents the total diversity in this country. Yet people are accustomed to instant gratification, and when they don't get it, they have instant disappointment and instant cyncism. I don't know if we [in Congress] will ever be able to measure up to public expectations.

*At conference sponsored by Time, Inc.,*
*Washington/Time, 6-9:22.*

**John B. Connally, Jr.**
*Former Secretary of the Treasury of the*
*United States; Former Governor of Texas*
*(D, now R)* 3

When I first went to Washington [as a Congressional aide] in '39, the White House was respected, had considerable freedom . . . Congress was in session only six months out of the year. You lived in a whole different world. In addition to being able to influence the course of human events and the well-being of this nation, the Presidency was somewhat pleasurable and enjoyable. That's all gone. They now want your wife to pay fare on the airplane if she goes with you. They want to know what you had for breakfast and what it cost. Every little detail of a President's life is so subject to

scrutiny and prone to criticism that no man—I don't see how anybody could enjoy it. All of the fun, all of the enjoyment is gone from that office. They've left it with nothing but the drudgery, the headaches and the heartaches of responsibility, and I think it's a tragedy. Respect is gone. Some of these freshmen Congressmen—some 45 of them went down to the White House and one of them bragged they didn't even stand up [when the President entered]. They wanted to show him what they thought of him. You know, this doesn't demean the Presidency; it demeans them. But that's the attitude that's grown up. They want to tear everything down. They want to tear down the Presidency.

*Interview, Houston/*
*The Dallas Times Herald, 6-18:(A)1.*

4

[On whether he will run for the U.S. Senate]: My thought processes are not those of a legislator. I don't believe in compromising all the time, and that's the heart and essence of a legislator's life . . . compromise every issue. You trade, you swap, you bend, you yield, you gain a little and you give a little. It's that kind of existence. I don't like that kind of existence. That does't mean I have to have my way all the time. It just means I don't want to put myself in that kind of position, because I wouldn't be happy in it and I'm not sure I'd be good at it . . . That's just the way I am. I try to be fair in analyzing my own weaknesses.

*Interview, Houston/*
*The Dallas Times Herald, 6-18:(A)8.*

**Archibald Cox**
*Professor of law, Harvard University* 5

For the adventure in self-government to go forward, we need Presidents and Presidential aides who identify themselves with the people, cherish and consider them as the most honest and safe, and therefore admit them to, and share with them, the making of decisions. For the President to lead in common adventure is one thing; to command is another. To help a people make its own decisions, to persuade yet trust their judgment, is the essence of the self-government bequeathed to us; to say, "leave it to me," even to do for the people what is best for them, is to embrace the form of government rejected in 1776. At worst, the shift leads to secrecy, manipulation, lies and cheating. At best, it erodes the sense of sharing the mutual trust which holds a free society together. Trust in government is not to be had for the asking. It begins with trust which those who govern repose in the people.

*Before Associated Harvard Alumni, June 12/*
*The Christian Science Monitor, 6-17:31.*

**Alan Cranston**
*United States Senator, D—California*
1

I believe that we already have more protection for official secrets than we need. My main concern is that classification of information by the government is out of control. Too many different people have authority to classify—and they often do it with excessive zeal to protect themselves and people higher up. They often seem more interested in job security than in national security. Not long ago someone with direct experience testified that more than 99 per cent of classified material should not be treated that way. We would open up a very dangerous situation if we started to write laws that anybody who transmits or receives any classified information without proper authority is guilty of a crime.

*Interview/*
*U.S. News & World Report, 8-18:37.*

**John C. Culver**
*United States Senator, D—Iowa*
2

[On Congressional inefficiency]: There are currently 33 committees and at least 65 subcommittees that have some jurisdictional claim on the new Energy Research and Development Administration. We find ourselves bogged down in duplication, overlap, inefficiency and, ultimately, paralysis. We are unable to cope with the immediate present, let alone the future.

*Quote, 10-26:340.*

**John Diebold**
*Chairman and president,*
*The Diebold Group, Inc.;*
*Authority on management*
3

Governments suffer from a lot of drawbacks in providing services. They're a monopoly.

There's no competition, insufficient pressure to hold down costs; no desire to try something new. Whenever you inject competition into governmental services, you improve the services and give the citizen a choice.

*Interview/*
*U.S. News & World Report, 11-17:82.*

**Dan Dodson**
*Scholar-in-residence,*
*Southwestern University*
4

The underlying issue in government relates to the legitimacy of its authority. The sacred document says, "just powers are derived from the consent of the governed." A large segment of the society is so alienated from government that there is little element of consent in the power it wields over their lives.

*At symposium, Dallas/*
*The Dallas Times Herald, 6-5:(B)3.*

**Michael S. Dukakis**
*Governor of Massachusetts (D)*
5

. . . if the Federal government would commit itself to guaranteeing the basic precommitments for a decent life, then local government could take responsibility for other things. [The precommitments are:] 1—A guarantee of full employment, or government as the employer of last resort. 2—A comprehensive national health plan for everyone. 3—A national transportation system. And 4—A responsibility to a long-range foreign policy that, for instance, does not include propping up every dictator in sight.

*Interview, Boston/*
*The Dallas Times Herald, 11-24:(E)6.*

**Pierre S. du Pont IV**
*United States Representative, R—Delaware*
6

Back in the 1950s and early 1960s, the American people implicitly trusted their President. They believed what he did was clearly in the best interests of the country. Because of everything that has happened, this trust is gone. It's vanished. Now the people are saying to the Congress, "You get involved, because we'd like a balancing force on these questions."

*The Washington Post, 4-4:(A)26.*

**John A. Durkin**
*United States Senator, D–New Hampshire*  1

People are as mad at Congress as they are at the President. The New Deal is dead, and if FDR were alive I think he would agree. There is a feeling among the people that the Federal government has abandoned them, that it is not responsive, that it is out of control. Let's reorganize it and make it effective, diversify it and send more functions back to the local level. People realize that all problems can't be solved in Washington. The people are ahead of the politicians.
*Interview/Los Angeles Times, 10-27:(1)19.*

**Sam J. Ervin, Jr.**
*Former United States Senator,*
*D–North Carolina*  2

If men and women of capacity refuse to take part in politics and government, they condemn themselves, as well as the people, to the punishment of living under bad government.
*Quote, 8-10:73.*

**Frank E. Evans**
*United States Representative, D–Colorado*  3

[Supporting a proposed increase in Congressional staffs]: When I came here 10 years ago, there was a feeling of utter hopelessness, a feeling that we in Congress, because of a lack of ability to discover and develop facts on our own, could not properly legislate. There has been a strong feeling on the part of many of us that we ought to do something to get Congress back on a more co-equal footing with the Executive Branch. The only way we can do that is to equip ourselves with people with skills and who answer to our requests . . .
*The Washington Post, 6-1:(A)9.*

**Gerald R. Ford**
*President of the United States*  4

[On whether the Presidency is a lonely job, a killing job]: Well . . . killing, no; although you have to work a long, long day. But I always did. But I think they're even longer now. I'm here at quarter of 8 every morning, here in this office, after having read The [Washington] Post, The

[New York] Times and the news summary before I ever get here. And then I seldom leave before 7, and I usually take home a pile of things, much to my wife's regret. And–of course, if we go out some place, but that's only two nights a week, maybe. The rest of the time I take home a pile of an hour's or two hours' work. But I enjoy that; it doesn't bother me a bit. Now . . . loneliness. It's not lonely in that I don't see my wife or I don't see my friends. I do. And the staff I have, that I know personally and that I like . . . they negate any loneliness in the sense of being a lonely person. Now, to more specifically define the word "lonely," I suppose you're saying, when you sit there and you have to decide whether to veto or not veto, you're lonely in that you're only the one person that can make that decision–yes. You do a lot of soul-searching.
*Interview, Washington, Jan. 8/*
*The Washington Post, 1-12:(A)11.*

5

[Saying he likes being President]: Every time I give this answer people look surprised. I do . . . I say it and I mean it, and every time I make that comment everybody looks, "My God, he must be an oddball." I do. And it's not because of, you know, working in a beautiful office or living in the White House. I like decision-making. I like the challenges of having to make choices. I like working with people, and that's what the job is. And I like working for people, and for the solution of things. And this is the unique spot in this country where you have all those opportunities.
*Interview, Washington, Jan. 8/*
*The Washington Post, 1-12:(A)11.*

6

. . . they say, "Why do you veto something if you know it's going to be overriden?" And my answer is, if I predicated my judgment to veto a bill on whether Congress is going to override, I'm losing whatever integrity this office has as to doing what is thought to be right by the Executive Branch. Now, if the Congress wants to override, that's their privilege. Maybe it is a confrontation. Maybe it's healthy we have that confrontation in those areas where you have some politics and some substance.

*Interview, Washington, Jan. 8/*
*The Washington Post, 1-12:(A)11.*

1

Ever since I was a youngster, I have had a special feeling for Kansas—because Kansas is where Dorothy lived before she went to visit the wonderful land of Oz, where all kinds of strange, whimsical and unexpected things happened. But I'm beginning to think that if strange, whimsical and unexpected things were what Dorothy was really interested in, she wouldn't have gone to Oz. She would have come to Washington.

*Before Kansas State Legislature, Topeka,*
*Feb. 11/The New York Times, 2-13:19.*

2

[Comparing being President with being a Congressman]: When you've worked in a place [Congress] 25 years, you can't help missing the people—on both sides. It's different. Up there, you're only one of 435. Even if you're a leader, you have to work with 434 very independent people. They can tell you no, and you can't do anything about it. Down here, the President is the final decision-maker on a few things, but you still have to work with those people—in a different relationship. My only ambition in all those years was to be Speaker of the House. Obviously, that was not going to be. So now I'm here. I liked that, and I like this. I'm adaptable, I guess.

*Interview, Washington/*
*The New York Times Magazine, 4-20:66.*

3

I believe it is time for us to declare our independence from governmental bureaucracies grown too large, too powerful, too costly, too remote, and yet too deeply involved in our day-to-day lives. Even though there are many things government must do for people, there are many more things that people would rather do for themselves.

*At Republican fund-raising dinner,*
*Cleveland, July 3/*
*Los Angeles Times, 7-4:(1)16.*

4

Individualism is a safeguard against the sameness of society. A government too large and bureaucratic can stifle individual initiative by a frustrating statism. Our sovereign is the citizen. Governments exist to serve people. The state is the creature of the populace.

*At Fort McHenry, Baltimore, July 4/*
*The Dallas Times Herald, 7-5:(A)1.*

5

I think that America went through one of the most unbelievable periods in the last two or three years that we'd ever want to. And I found myself in a situation where somebody had to take over—internationally, domestically, governmentally. If I can be remembered for restoring public confidence in the Presidency, for handling all these transitional problems responsibly and effectively, for achieving decent results domestically as well as internationally, regardless of how long I serve, I think that's what I'd like on my tombstone.

*Interview, Washington/*
*The Reader's Digest, August:95.*

6

Don't ever forget that a government big enough to give you everything you want is a government big enough to take from you everything you have.

*San Francisco Examiner & Chronicle,*
*10-5:(A)12.*

7

My vetoes in this year alone will save taxpayers some $6-billion by 1977. I think that is positive action by any standard. The veto is not negative; it is an affirmative way to get better legislation.

*San Francisco Examiner & Chronicle,*
*10-5:(A)12.*

8

One of the reasons for this horrendous [government] spending growth is that much of the increase in each year's budget is required by programs already on the statute books. Many of these programs were first enacted years ago, and while individually they might have appeared manageable then, today, taken together, they are out of control. They are like a freight

# WHAT THEY SAID IN 1975

*(GERALD R. FORD)*

train whose lights were first seen far off in the night. That train has been coming closer and closer, and now it is roaring down upon us. If we don't slow it down, Federal spending next year could easily jump to more than $420-billion—without a single new Federal program. Therefore, I propose that we halt this alarming growth by holding spending in the coming year to $395-billion. That means a cut of $28-billion below what we will spend if we just stand still and let the train run over us. More importantly, it means almost a dollar-for-dollar cut in taxes and spending. For every dollar that we return to the American taxpayer, we must also cut our projected spending by the same amount. If we allow "politics as usual" to prevail in the Congress, there will be a temptation to overwhelmingly approve the tax cuts and do nothing on the spending cuts. That must not happen. I will go forward with the tax cuts that I am proposing only if there is a clear, affirmative decision by your representatives in the House and the Senate that they will hold spending next year to $395-billion. I will not hesitate to veto any legislation passed by the Congress which violates the spirit of that understanding. I want these actions to be a first step—and they are a crucial step—toward balancing the Federal budget within three years . . . Sometimes when fancy new spending programs reach my desk, promising something for almost nothing and carrying appealing labels, I wonder who the supporters think they're kidding. From my visits with the American people, I find many of them believe that what the government put in your front pocket, it slips out your back pocket through taxes and inflation. They are figuring out that they are not getting their money's worth from their taxes. They believe that the politics of Federal spending has become too much of a shell game. And I must say that I agree with them.

*Broadcast address to the nation,*
*Washington, Oct. 6/*
*The New York Times, 10-7:24.*

1

The heart of our financial dilemma today is the endless stream of promises made to the American people in the last generation, and continuing right today—that the government can and will satisfy most of the needs of all of our people, and even their wants. I think the language is one of extremes and excess. It is that the government will make all your dreams come true. All you have to do is file an application.

*Nation's Business, November:19.*

## Jay W. Forrester
*Professor of management, Massachusetts*
*Institute of Technology*

2

We've had a tendency to move the local town problems to state government, the state problems to the national government, and the national problems to the UN. Each of these steps eventually tends to run into difficulty. It is my feeling that the solution to the whole must come out of solving problems at a more local level, but solving them in a way that doesn't shift their burdens to their neighbors or to other people.

*Interview, Washington/*
*The Washington Post, 6-8:(C)5.*

## Donald M. Fraser
*United States Representative, D—Minnesota*

3

Under current law, it is [a] crime for a private citizen to lie to a government official, but not for the government official to lie to the people.

*Quote, 8-31:145.*

## Milton Friedman
*Professor of economics, University of Chicago*

4

The talk of tax cuts sounds fine—but it is double-talk. For with the promise of lower taxes go plans for higher government spending. Can government spend more, yet cost less? The answer is clearly no. The true cost of government to us is what government spends, not what we pay in taxes. If government spends more than it takes in from taxes, there are two ways to finance its deficits. One is to print more money. That way lies inflation—which is a hidden tax that can be imposed without anyone having to vote for it. The other way is to borrow money from us, which reduces funds available to build houses, factories and so on, and leaves us saddled with an obligation to pay it back—a still more indirect form of taxation. What we need is a *real* cut in taxes—which means a cut in government spending. Today, out of every dollar you earn, government [Federal, state, local] spends more than 40 cents for you—more than the total amount you spend for food, clothing and housing. Unfortunately, there is no Federal Trade Commission that can prosecute politicians for promising us a free lunch. It is up to you and me to tell our representatives in Washington that we want them to let *us* spend more of our *own* money.

*CBS News commentary/*
*The Reader's Digest, July:16.*

**John W. Gardner**
*Chairman, Common Cause*

1

... whenever you have government, you have favors to hand out. It's the nature of it. In 17th-century America, maybe it was trapping rights. Now maybe it's the ability of a modern President to emphasize one or another kind of industrial expansion. It's built in. When things are going out, there are bound to be things coming back. In a pure system, the things would be handed out on their merit, and that would be that. But humans being human, the favors get handed out as part of a *transaction.* It's really the most marvelously simple system.
*The National Observer, 8-9:12.*

2

Lobbying is not wrong in itself. In fact, it can serve a useful purpose. It is a Constitutional right. But it is wrong to lobby secretly, wrong to deceive the public, wrong to use money in ways that corrupt the public process.
*The Christian Science Monitor, 10-8:17.*

**William M. Goldsmith**
*Professor of history, Brandeis University*

3

I can't find any sustained period in American history when Congress has really led the nation ... It's very difficult for more than 500 individuals representing diverse groups throughout the nation to initiate, direct and become responsible for all the policy development in

government. On the other hand, we've experienced a long period in the very recent past when Congress has not fulfilled its Constitutional obligation both to confront Executive leadership with a cooperative attitude and also to present to the American people alternative policies when the policies of the President seem, in the eyes of Congress, not to be in the interest of the general public. What is needed is a dialectical tension between an able Congress and the President. Not simply on a partisan basis to oppose it for party's sake. But when Executive policy seems inadequate or wrong, the opposition party in Congress should devise alternative policies and fight for them effectively in the public domain. These are the things Congress has not been doing.
*Interview, Brandeis University/*
*The National Observer, 4-26:21.*

**Mike Gravel**
*United States Senator, D—Alaska*

4

[Supporting a bill to increase the size of Senators' staffs] : In a democratic society, there is only one power at hand. That is the power of knowledge. The staff is the ability to acquire knowledge.
*Before the Senate, Washington/*
*San Francisco Examiner & Chronicle,*
*4-20:(A)10.*

**Lee H. Hamilton**
*United States Representative, D—Indiana*

5

The American people are being asked to endure [economic] hardships and suffer deprivations ... How can we make such demands of the public if the sacrifices stop at the government's own door? Government should be out front, pointing the way—but not in a chauffeured limousine.
*Los Angeles Herald-Examiner, 3-9:(A)9.*

**Michael J. Harrington**
*United States Representative, D-Massachusetts*

6

Being in Washington hardens you. It's the Pullman Car Company of the 20th century, and I want to be able to walk away from it. I don't think Washington is part of reality.
*The Washington Post, 9-7:(G)16.*

# WHAT THEY SAID IN 1975

**Fred R. Harris**
*Former United States Senator, D—Oklahoma*
1

The fundamental issue is privilege; it's whether or not America is going to again have a government that looks after the interests of every citizen or continues to protect the interests of the super-rich and the giant corporations. It's privilege that keeps taxes unfair and keeps prices too high and keeps a misguided economic policy and keeps people out of work. And it's privilege that keeps our foreign policy one which is pleasing to multinational companies and taxes people like you to prop up every dictator in the world, it seems, that can afford a pair of sunglasses.

*Before Texas Democrats, San Antonio/*
*The Dallas Times Herald, 12-15:(A)19.*

**Louis Harris**
*Public-opinion analyst*
2

The people are not always right, but today they are leagues ahead of their leaders. They are fed up with the cant and the rhetoric, yes, and the promises, of politicians . . . Most of all, people are fed up with leadership which assumes that they must be alternatively scared out of their wits or patted on the head and fed a diet of "gimmies." They do not have a 12-year-old mentality; they're willing to make sacrifices if asked; and they yearn, perhaps more than anything, to attack their common problems instead of each other. Sadly, too many of their leaders seem to spend 20 or 30 years clawing their way to the top only to find when they achieve that utmost rung that they're 20 years out of date.

*Before Gannett Publishing shareholders/*
*The National Observer, 7-26:12.*

**S. I. Hayakawa**
*Former president,*
*San Francisco State University*
3

I would like to diminish the enormous role of the Federal government, as it penetrates into all our lives, and restore more responsibility to states, and in turn from states to municipalities and localities. If we have a sense of moralessness, a sense that the individual citizen can't do anything about the world, it's because so much

power is concentrated in Washington. The principal isn't principal in his own school. The teacher isn't master in his own classroom. This destruction of the autonomy of local units is a very dangerous trend in our society, a very tragic thing in our society.

*Sacramento, Nov. 18/*
*Los Angeles Herald-Examiner 11-19:(A)4.*

**Jesse A. Helms**
*United States Senator, R—North Carolina*
4

[Criticizing the amount of time off taken by members of Congress] : I'm just amazed at the delays. I know the leadership has its problems trying to schedule votes and home visits for the convenience of members . . . but I believe the American people are watching this, and they resent it. Until we buckle down, we're not going to eliminate this [public] hostility.

*The Washington Post, 5-23:(A)2.*

**Hubert H. Humphrey**
*United States Senator, D—Minnesota*
5

I think a man, to be a good President, has to recognize that he has to be a leader and an educator. He cannot pander to the worst that is in us; he ought to appeal to the best that is in us. He can hire people to be good administrators; those are his Cabinet officers. But what he needs to be is a man that has a philosophy of life for our country, that has great dreams about what America ought to be like. He ought to be what Teddy Roosevelt said, and what Woodrow Wilson said. He looked at the White House as a "bully pulpit." He ought to have inspiration. Wilson said he looked at the White House as the "nation's classroom" and the man who occupied it as the "nation's teacher." He ought to be an educator. He ought to be able to show a path, a sense of direction and, above all, he needs to be candid with the American people.

*TV-radio interview, Washington/*
*"Meet the Press,"*
*National Broadcasting Company, 11-2.*

**Barbara Jordan**
*United States Representative, D—Texas*
6

[Addressing broadcasters, urging television coverage of Congress] : We need you and you

156

need us. Come into the House of Representatives and show what Congress actually does. The people should see the drudgery of deliberation and whether their representative is on the job—or in the gym. If the cameras were there you would make better legislators of us.

*At TV executives meeting sponsored by Television Information Office of National Association of Broadcasters, Houston/ The Hollywood Reporter, 10-7:3.*

**E. Douglas Kenna**
*President, National Association of Manufacturers* 1

People in this country don't realize the sort of economic disaster that has overtaken New York City would happen to the Federal government if our Federal deficit continues to grow ... By 1980, it is estimated governmental operations will cost 50 per cent of the GNP. The only town that is booming in the country is Washington, D.C. There's been no recession there as governmental agencies continue to expand.

*Before Rotary Club, Los Angeles, Nov. 7/ Los Angeles Herald-Examiner, 11-8:(A)3.*

**Henry A. Kissinger**
*Secretary of State of the United States* 2

Democracy in the 19th century was an essentially aristocratic phenomenon. You had limited ruling groups in most countries. This was not true of the U.S., although we did have restricted franchises. And you had, above all, a doctrine of limited government and relatively simple issues. Now the government is involved in every aspect of life. The issues become unbelievably complex. Another problem is that in almost every democratic country so much energy is absorbed in getting into office that leaders are not always as well prepared as they could be and have to learn their job by doing it. All of this has created a crisis of leadership in many democratic countries. But it is a crisis that we must solve.

*Interview, Washington/Time, 10-27:35.*

3

There is no parliament in the world that has the access to policy-making that the Congress

of the U.S. has—not in Britain, not in France, not in any of the democracies. The key decisions have to be subjected to Congressional approval. The democratic process involves an approval [by Congress] of the general direction in which a country is going, as well as of specific individual steps. But to attempt to subject every single decision to individual approval will lead to the fragmentation of all effort and will finally lead to chaos and no national policy.

*Interview, Washington/ Time, 10-27:35.*

4

We must resist the myth that government is a gigantic conspiracy. The truth is the vast majority of public servants are serious, dedicated and compassionate men and women who seek no other reward than the consciousness of having served their country well.

*Before Economic Club, Detroit, Nov. 24/ Los Angeles Times, 11-25:(1)8.*

**Victor H. Kramer**
*Professor of law, Georgetown University Law Center* 5

With noteworthy exceptions, the appointive process as it now exists has consistently failed to provide Federal regulatory agencies with able, energetic and forceful leadership dedicated to the public interest ... Partisan political considerations dominate the selection of regulators to an alarming extent. Alarming, in that other factors—such as competence, experience and even, on occasion, regulatory philosophy—are only secondary factors ... Federal regulatory-agency appointments are part and parcel of the patronage system in its rawest sense. Powerful connections and political acceptability are the principle elements in the selection and reappointment process.

*At Congressional hearing, Washington, Nov. 6/ The New York Times, 11-7:14.*

**Walter Kravitz**
*Executive Director, United States House of Representatives Budget Committee* 6

[On the Budget Control Act of 1974]: It's becoming a cliche in Congress: Sure, everybody

# WHAT THEY SAID IN 1975

*(WALTER KRAVITZ)*

is a conservative on spending; sure, everybody wants to be fiscally responsible, except when it gets to their program, my program or your program. So when Congress puts its energies and directions to attempting to deal with a budget as a whole, it is taking on a very painful thing to do because, for the first time, members of Congress will have to stand up and vote and be recorded by name on what the size of that deficit shall be. That's very hard. You would be surprised by how many liberals become moderates and how many moderates become conservatives when they take a look at the size of that deficit, and they have to stand up and vote for it.

*At "legislative breakfast" sponsored by Chamber of Commerce of the United States/ The Wall Street Journal, 9-17:18.*

**S. Stanley Kreutzer**
*Counsel,*
*New York City Board of Ethics*　　　　*1*

The Senate and the House have set up committees on ethics—but only comparatively recently—to advise members of Congress and their staffs on matters of possible conflict of interest. I would not seek to change that or to bring them under a national commission unless they specifically requested it in special circumstances. But there are close to 3 million persons on the Federal payroll with no place to go—no place to find out if accepting a gift of a luncheon or a dinner or a $5 bill or an outside job might constitute a conflict of interest. The strange part is that they often do accept something; then three or four years later they are excoriated for it. But at the time they really did not know, really did not believe it to be a conflict of interest. What do you do if you are a member of the Cabinet and find someone died and left you stock? Say you're Secretary of Defense and it's General Motors stock. Defense does a lot of business with GM, but the stock has come to you or your wife from a cousin or a father or a sister-in-law. You have no place to go for an opinion or a ruling.

*Interview, Occidental College/ Los Angeles Times, 5-16:(4)1.*

**Philip B. Kurland**
*Professor of law, University of Chicago*　　*2*

. . . there are at least two cancerous growths on the American body politic. One of these is the burgeoning power of the Executive Branch. The other has occurred within the Executive Branch itself, where power has shifted from the departments and old-line agencies to what is called the "Executive Office of the President." In fact, it is here that all government policy is made and . . . the wielders of that power are all unelected, and with little or no responsibility to Congress . . . They are the overlords of the Executive Branch.

*Before Delaware Bar Association/ The New York Times, 6-17:33.*

**Paul D. Laxalt**
*United States Senator,*
*R—Nevada*　　　　*3*

The American people want a change in the direction of government. They want to be left alone. They want the Federal government off their backs—less government, less spending and less taxes.

*July 15/The Washington Post, 7-16:(A)4.*

**William Leavel**
*Professor of political science,*
*University of Denver*　　　　*4*

I think there's a healthy parochialism returning to American politics. You see it in a great number of community and neighborhood organizations springing up, in block associations, in people fighting city hall. I think there's a realization that local government can affect our daily lives to an extraordinary extent and that the national government really isn't solving many of our problems. People, I think, are starting to say, "Maybe we better solve those problems ourselves."

*Los Angeles Times, 12-2:(1)18.*

**Edward H. Levi**
*Attorney General of the United States*　　*5*

A right to complete confidentiality in government could not only produce a dangerous public ignorance but also destroy the basic representative function of government. But a duty of complete disclosure would render impossible the effective operation of government. Some confidentiality is a matter of practical necessity. Moreover, neither the concept of democracy nor the First Amendment confers on each citizen an unbridled power to demand access to all the information within the government's possession.

*Before Association of the Bar of the City of New York, April 28/ The Washington Post, 4-29:(A)2.*

1

The doctrine of separation of powers was . . . designed to control the power of government by tension among the Branches, with each, at the margin, limiting the other. But there is a misperception about that tension. For example, [historian] Arthur Schlesinger once described the doctrine as creating "permanent guerrilla warfare" between the Executive and Legislative Branches. To be sure, the authors of the Constitution had a realistic view of man and government and power. They assumed that from time to time men in power might grow too bold and engage in overreaching that threatens liberty and the balance of the system. They designed the system in such a way that the overreaching—the threatened tyranny—might be checked. But they did not envision a government in which each Branch seeks out confrontation; they hoped the system of checks and balances would achieve a harmony of purpose differently fulfilled. The Branches of government were not designed to be at war with one another. The relationship was not to be an adversary one, though to think of it that way has become fashionable. Adversaries make out their claims with a bias, and one would not want to suggest that the Supreme Court, for example, ought to view each case before it has a chance to increase or protect its institutional power. Justice [Harlan] Stone and others have written of the importance of the Court's sense of self-restraint. That insight applies as well to the Executive and legislature. If history were to teach, that might be its lesson rather than new cycles of aggression.

*The Washington Post, 12-18:(A)22.*

**Elliott H. Levitas**
*United States Representative, D—Georgia*

2

The Federal bureaucracy has evolved into a fourth non-Constitutional branch of government with a thick tangle of regulations that carry the force of law without the benefit of legislative considerations.

*The Washington Post, 12-27:(A)2.*

**John V. Lindsay**
*Former Mayor of New York*

3

Money is not the most important part of government action, and we cannot allow self-styled conservatives to suggest that the debate is between liberal spenders who waste money and conservatives who understand the limits and value of money. That is not the debate. The real debate is over the vigorous exercise of government's moral and legal powers. The men who were once called the "great spenders" for human needs—the authors of the New Deal and the Great Society—are not remembered today for the money they spent as much as for their vision of a better America and their commitment to the struggle for individual rights and liberties.

*At Bicentennial Forum, Boston/ The Christian Science Monitor, 7-15:27.*

4

I think it is very important to the mentality of politicians that they go back to the private world now and then . . . get rid of the trappings of government . . . and stay there as long as possible, maybe even permanently. I see Cabinet officers wandering through airport terminals, surrounded by automatic men in square suits with wires sticking out of their ears, guarding them, surrounding them with layers of protection. These public men forget there are real people out there. They also begin to think they are supermen after a while. That's why a lot of ex-Ambassadors and ex-Governors and ex-Generals like to be called by their old titles long after they hold the positions. Politicians need to drop all of that. So when people say [to me], "What are we supposed to call you?" . . . I tell them John or Mr. Lindsay.

*Interview, New York/ The Christian Science Monitor, 7-29:13.*

# WHAT THEY SAID IN 1975

**Patrick J. Lucey**
*Governor of Wisconsin (D)*
1

In Wisconsin we will have a leaner state budget in 1975—not necessarily because we have no choice but, more important, because we recognize that government cannot ask of others what it will not do for itself.
*Los Angeles Times,*
*1-23:(2)7.*

**James T. Lynn**
*Director, Federal Office of*
*Management and Budget*
2

If you sent out a poll asking people if they want to cut back on Federal spending, probably 85 per cent would say, "Yes, cut it back." But if you listed 150 programs out of the 1,009 Federal domestic-assistance programs we have today, about 80 per cent of the people you polled would list at least one of them where they think more money should be spent. Therein lies the rub. The American people have not yet put the totals together and realized what it's doing to their jobs, what it's doing to their pocketbooks. There's still the attitude of people who run for office, saying: "Spend, spend, spend. Re-elect, re-elect, re-elect." I detect, however, a growing awareness that people are catching on in this regard. Voters are becoming edgy about whether the old politics makes sense.
*Interview/*
*U.S. News & World Report, 10-6:29.*

**Peter MacDonald**
*Chairman,*
*Navajo (Indian) Tribal Council*
3

To us [Indians], the [Federal] government has always been uncomfortably big. Now the government appears to be too big for everyone's comfort. Outlandish reporting requirements, over-regulation and ever-growing programs have produced an economy where no major project can be commenced without bureaucratic approval or an act of Congress.
*Before Los Angeles World Affairs Council,*
*Dec. 9/Los Angeles Herald-Examiner,*
*12-10:(A)13.*

**Gene A. Maguire**
*United States Representative, D–New Jersey*
4

We [new members of the House] ran against Congress, most of us–against its stodginess, its unresponsiveness, its lack of new ideas, its inability to move. A lot of us had the feeling . . . that our problems have been outrunning the capacity of our institutions to deal with them.
*Interview/The Washington Post, 6-29:(A)1.*

**George H. Mahon**
*United States Representative, D–Texas*
5

The fiscal problems that confront us in full bloom have accumulated over decades. They are difficult to dramatize. But it is clear that there are some alarming danger signals at hand. We have more government at all levels than we as a nation seem to be able or willing to pay for.
*Feb. 3/Los Angeles Times, 2-4:(1)12.*

**Mike Mansfield**
*United States Senator, D–Montana*
6

May I say that it is about time that some changes occurred in this body [the Senate]. I have been much impressed by the younger members of the Senate who have been aware of the need for changes, and who are much depressed with people, like myself, who in all too many instances have become traditionalist-minded and who have continued to look backward rather than to live in the present and look to the future . . . I do not think a little sunshine is going to hurt any of us, but it may make this body a more productive institution, and it may bring some life to this body, which I think has been lacking in recent years . . .
*Before the Senate, Washington/*
*The Washington Post, 6-16:(A)2.*

**John J. Marchi**
*New York State Senator*
7

In Congress, unless you're there a million years, you really don't get government experience. It's basically a public-relations job—interpreting government to the public, handling constituents' contracts, that sort of thing.
*The New York Times, 2-20:31.*

**F. David Mathews**
*Secretary of Health, Education and*
*Welfare of the United States* 1

. . . the people out there are telling us something, I want you to know. We kind of kidded around here about it being George the III week, but the colonists are restless again, and they see the Federal government as removed, insensitive, indiscriminate in dealing with them, unjust in the application of the laws, attempting to force through arbitrary laws and regulations in a way that is breeding an unhealthy resentment and resistance. That's what I mean when I say the most important point in our modern history is where it ceased to be "we the people" and became "they the government."
*Interview, Washington/*
*The Christian Science Monitor, 10-8:30.*

**George Meany**
*President, American Federation of*
*Labor-Congress of Industrial Organizations* 2

It is time the President [Ford] remembered that government by veto means the minority forcing its will on the majority.
*At employment conference,*
*Washington, June 24/*
*The New York Times, 6-25:21.*

**Abner J. Mikva**
*United States Representative,*
*D—Illinois* 3

The House is vastly different from what it was six years ago. The change is almost geometric. At first I thought it was because of all the new members. But that's only part of it. We have a weak Executive Branch for the first time in 40 years. Congress is being thrust into this responsibility to do something.
*The New York Times, 3-2:(4)3.*

**George Miller**
*United States Representative,*
*D—California* 4

If you're honest, serving in Congress is a real loser financially, especially when you come from the West Coast and find yourself having to keep two homes. It's public service at its highest. The recent increases in staff and travel allowances were very important because we campaigned in a different style than has been done in a long time—very activist. I hold office hours in every city in my district, and I fly home every other week. If I had to start picking that cost up out of my pocket, that would be the end of my Congressional career. People want to see their Congressman now; they want to talk to him. I think we're more reflective of the public mood because we're out there every weekend. A lot of people hide in Washington. Those are the people that vehemently fought against increasing the number of paid trips.
*Panel discussion,*
*Washington, June 17/*
*Los Angeles Times, 7-22:(1-A)6.*

**William G. Milliken**
*Governor of Michigan (R)* 5

Let me read a brief excerpt from a letter written by one politician warning that the Federal government was gaining too much power: "I see, as you do, and with the deepest affliction, the rapid strides with which the Federal branch of our government is advancing toward the usurpation of all the rights reserved to the states, and the consolidation in itself of all powers, foreign and domestic . . ." That was not written in 1975. It was written in 1825—by Thomas Jefferson. From the beginning, we have worried about states' rights. I submit that the Federal government has grown in direct proportion to the willingness of the states to turn to Washington for all the answers. We have not given away our rights. Nor must we give our responsibilities. We must now reclaim them if the nation is to survive.
*At Midwestern Governors Conference,*
*Cincinnati/The National Observer, 8-23:13-A.*

**Norman Y. Mineta**
*United States Representative, D—California* 6

We [new members of Congress] don't have the protection of six or eight or ten years of incumbency. People have voted for us as if to say: "Let's vote in this new kid on the block and see what he can do. If we don't like it, we'll get rid of him and get another one." When you think about what makes Johnny run, that's it.

# WHAT THEY SAID IN 1975

*(NORMAN Y. MINETA)*

It's like being chased by a guy with a red-hot poker.

*Interview/The Washington Post, 6-29:(A)12.*

### Clarence M. Mitchell, Jr.
*Director, Washington, D.C., bureau,*
*National Association for the Advancement*
*of Colored People* 1

Revenue-sharing is a serious mistake. The Federal government is like putty in the hands of discriminators; the government just won't stand against these big Mayors. It is much easier to track a wrongdoer when his money is assigned for specific purposes.

*At Congressional hearing, Washington,*
*April 17/The New York Times, 4-18:10.*

### Richard B. Morris
*President-elect, American Historical*
*Association; Professor of history,*
*Columbia University* 2

The challenges of the 20th century, so incredibly complicated and demanding, have spawned a huge Executive bureaucracy. I'm sure that Congress didn't really know what it was doing when it set up administrative agencies like the Interstate Commerce Commission and passed the Sherman antitrust law. Such legislation spawned administrative agencies which were under Presidential control and actually constituted quasi-judicial tribunals. So the President was not only an Executive, but he was also a rate-fixer, a watchdog over trusts, stock trading, labor-management relations, consumer and environmental protection, and much more. Congress invested the President with enormous powers that were never conceived of or even contemplated in an earlier and less complex period of time.

*Interview, Washington/*
*U.S. News & World Report, 8-25:57.*

### Rogers C. B. Morton
*Secretary of Commerce of the United States* 3

The tendency of government is, when you have gotten into a great deal of trouble by over-regulation, to try to regulate your way out of it.

*Quote, 6-1:505.*

### Daniel P. Moynihan
*Professor of government, Harvard University* 4

The forces pushing Federalism toward ever-greater centralism are not likely to be overcome except by a genuine, fundamental decision by the American people that the central government should not get larger.

*At National Governors' Conference,*
*Washington/The Washington Post, 2-26:(A)18.*

### Thomas A. Murphy
*Chairman, General Motors Corporation* 5

A guy in Washington, though dedicated to doing the right thing, sits down to his desk and convinces himself that the American public does not really know what is good for them. He says, "I in my wisdom will tell them where they are going to live and how they are going to live. I don't think they should have the things that they want. There has got to be regulation. I am going to see that they change their minds." Well, we have to have laws and regulation; but when you start telling an individual, directly or indirectly, "I don't think you should be able to buy a car that should be able to carry six or more people," you are just a step away from saying to people, "You shouldn't have a home with five or six rooms." I don't think it's right. I think it is dangerous.

*Interview, Washington/*
*Los Angeles Times, 5-14:(2)5.*

### Edmund S. Muskie
*United States Senator,*
*D—Maine* 6

While the Federal government is trying to prime the pump, state and local governments are trying to cut back. While the Federal government is trying to give consumers a tax break, local governments are often forced to raise taxes to keep going. While the Federal government wants to stimulate the economy by putting more people to work, state and local governments must lay off employees and defer public works projects in order to trim expanses. In short, we are working at cross-purposes, and the cost [is] unnecessarily great.

*Before Senate Subcommittee on Intergovernmental Relations, Washington, Jan. 30/The New York Times, 1-31:36.*

1

Why can't liberals start raising hell about a government so big, so complex, so expensive and so unresponsive that it's dragging down every good program we've worked for? We must recognize that an efficient government—well managed, cost effective, equitable and responsible—is in itself a social good. We know that government can do much to improve the lives of every American. But that conviction has also led us to become the defenders of government, no matter its mistakes. We resist questioning the basic assumptions of the structure and role of government, fearing the unknown, fearing that somehow we have more to lose than gain through change. We must adopt government reform as our first priority, as an end in itself. We must do this secure in the conviction that first priority on efficient government is not a retreat from social goals, but simply a realization that, without it, those goals are meaningless. There is no good reason why liberals can't provide that alternative. I read my mail, I talk with voters in the towns of Maine, and I listen. I find everywhere people who can't cite from the Federal Register but know what's wrong anyway. Do we really expect a majority of Americans to support more government programs—no matter how worthy—at a time when confidence in government is at an all-time low? At this time, none of us could sincerely answer "yes." Why can't liberals start hacking away at the regulatory bureaucracy where it keeps costs up and competition away? Why can't liberals . . . talk about fiscal responsibility and productivity without feeling uncomfortable? Our emotional stake in government is so much that we regard common-sense criticism of government almost as a personal attack. And as long as we shrink from offering an alternative to a system of government people have lost confidence in, we can expect to remain in a minority. Our challenge this decade is to restore the faith of Ameri-

cans in the basic competence and purposes of government. That can only come through the hard process of reform.

*Before New York State Liberal Party, New York, Oct. 9/\*\**

**Ralph Nader**
*Lawyer;*
*Consumer advocate*

2

National news media are traditionally responsive to Senate leaders, Cabinet Secretaries and Presidential hopefuls, but far less to those Federal regulators who determine so directly the quality of the cars we drive, the food we eat, the air we breathe.

*At Public Citizen Forum, Washington, March 3/The New York Times, 3-4:16.*

**Richard P. Nathan**
*Former Assistant Director, Federal Office of Management and Budget*

3

[Revenue-sharing] is sort of like a Social Security Act for local governments. Once you turn it on, it's very difficult not to continue it. If a Congressman votes against its renewal, local politicians will say the Congressman's vote was a vote for higher local taxes. And he may wind up seeing one of those politicians as his opponent in the next election.

*U.S. News & World Report, 4-7:48.*

**Ron Nessen**
*Press Secretary to President of the United States Gerald R. Ford*

4

It is just as bad to disbelieve everything a government official tells you as to believe everything. You just can't go to that [press] briefing and assume, "Here comes Ron with another load of lies for you."

*Interview/The Washington Post, 6-27:(A)4.*

5

The President thinks this is a "can't-do" Congress. It can't figure out how to cut taxes. It can't figure out how to put a lid on spending. It can't figure out how to build up domestic oil production . . . It can't figure out what to do about the natural-gas crisis that is right upon us this winter. It can't figure out what to do about programs that are out of control. The President

# WHAT THEY SAID IN 1975

thinks that what this country needs is a "can-do" Congress.

*U.S. News & World Report, 10-27:13.*

**Robert Nisbet**
*Professor of the humanities,*
*Columbia University*                                            1

There are more Americans who literally hate their government today than anything I have ever known of. I can remember in my own experience other times of disenchantment and criticism, such as we saw against Roosevelt and the New Deal, but I have no recollection of people of all ages being either absolutely indifferent or outright hostile to government as they are today. There is a revolt against power, wealth and privilege and the values of the traditional political community.

*Interview, New York/*
*Los Angeles Times, 10-22:(2)7.*

**Bob Packwood**
*United States Senator,*
*R—Oregon*                                                      2

[Defending the amount of time taken off by members of Congress]: Work isn't just what happens on the Senate floor. Work is also answering letters, meeting constituents, attending committees, studying legislative problems and working with staff. The voters' opinions shift monthly. I would not get a representative viewpoint if I just depended on the mail and the polls. All the mail and polls aren't as good as going out and touching the people.

*The Washington Post,*
*5-23:(A)2.*

**Russell W. Peterson**
*Chairman, Federal Council on*
*Environmental Quality*                                         3

It's difficult for the U.S. today, for Canada today, for Mexico today, to squeeze an extra dollar or peso out of our national budgets. Modern economic, social and political life is so complicated that government officials become understandably numb when presented with conflicting lists of priorities, every one of which has a lobby to assert its urgency.

*At North American Wildlife and Natural*
*Resources Conference, Pittsburgh, March 17/*
*Vital Speeches, 5-1:426.*

**William Proxmire**
*United States Senator, D—Wisconsin*                            4

Public officials should not live in a style which is too far removed from the problems of ordinary citizens. Placing them in the back of a chauffeur-driven limousine with their little reading lamps while other people plow through traffic promotes an elitist group or class.

*Washington, Feb. 6/*
*Los Angeles Herald-Examiner, 2-6:(A)5.*

**Dixy Lee Ray**
*Former Assistant Secretary for Oceans and*
*International Environmental and Scientific*
*Affairs, Department of State of the*
*United States*                                                 5

[The State Department] is an agency that is tuned up never to do anything. A decision that should take 10 minutes takes 10 days. I suppose the essence of diplomacy is to avoid taking a final position. People like me should never get involved in an agency like that.

*Interview/People, 8-18:37.*

**Ronald Reagan**
*Former Governor of California (R)*                             6

I don't believe a President should make appointments on the basis of trying to span a political spectrum. I think the President should make appointments of people who will implement his philosophy.

*Interview/*
*Los Angeles Herald-Examiner, 3-9:(A)15.*

**Henry S. Reuss**
*United States Representative,*
*D—Wisconsin*                                                   7

I am a believer that small is beautiful in economics, social organization, government. In government I believe in the maximum possible decentralization back to the neighborhood . . . I think the average person nowadays is overwhelmed by huge, impersonal government, by big government deficits or surpluses, by huge monetary movements instead of programs beamed at individuals . . .

*The Christian Science Monitor, 4-1:34.*

1

[Saying there should be a two-man Presidency—one the ceremonial chief of state, the other the head of government] : It would significantly lighten the tremendous strain on the time and energy of the President by relieving him of onerous ceremonial duties. President Truman concluded that "the pressures and complexities of the Presidency have grown to a state where they are almost too much for one man to endure." Secondly, it would reduce the tendency to deify Presidents, to make them elected kings immune from criticism or dissent. The recent rise of the "imperial Presidency," culminating in the Nixon Administration, has posed a serious threat to the proper functioning of the checks and balances provided in the Constitution.

*July 20/The Christian Science Monitor, 7-22:26.*

**John J. Rhodes**
*United States Representative  R—Arizona*
2

I've felt that for too long Pennsylvania Avenue has been a one-way street. All of the wisdom in the world comes from the White House to the Congress: The Executive proposes and the Legislative disposes. To me this is a demeaning concept. It means that Congress isn't capable of any new idea of its own. That's wrong. There is great wisdom in Congress.

*Interview/U.S. News & World Report, 7-21:34.*

**David Riesman**
*Sociologist, Harvard University*
3

We have always been a somewhat anarchic society, one reason why we have so greatly sought charismatic leadership to overcome our own anarchism . . . Leaders who campaign "agin the guvmint" win popularity when what they are actually seeking is government office. And this is intensified currently by the near paranoia of Americans about leadership which

is the combined result of the depression-inflation and Watergate and its revelations, as well as the more endemic fear Americans have had about leadership.

*U.S. News & World Report, 4-21:34.*

**Nelson A. Rockefeller**
*Vice President of the United States*
4

I am not in a leadership position; I am supporting the President. He can exert the leadership and I can support him. The President has the responsibility and the power, and it is a very lonely position. The Vice President has no responsibility and no power. [It can be different] only if the President wants to use the Vice President and only if the Vice President is experienced enough to know where the pitfalls are. I am not going to get out in front of the President. I am in a delicate situation. I am going to give him the best judgment that I have in any field that he asks me about. After he has made a decision, I will support it.

*Interview, Washington/Time, 1-20:23.*

5

[Criticizing excessive government spending] : When the country continually spends well beyond its income, the only recourse is to borrow heavily or let the printing presses roll—both of which would ultimately destroy our economic strength.

*Before American Newspaper Publishers Association, New Orleans, April 9/ The Washington Post, 4-10:(A)26.*

6

I've known seven Vice Presidents and all come up against the same problems. Henry Wallace used to play tennis every day on the court to work off his frustrations . . . Any effort by a President to give a Vice President responsibility is not politically acceptable.

*Interview/ "W": a Fairchild publication, 8-22:2.*

7

[On the role of the Vice President] : Now, I happen to be of the school that when the President makes a decision, you either support it, or if you don't agree with it and feel strongly, you resign. And I think that's the way you have a

*(NELSON A. ROCKEFELLER)*

strong, hard-hitting Administration. But to go out and poor-mouth what your boss has decided is not serving him well nor is it serving yourself well—because I don't think anyone's self-respect can be very great [in continuing to criticize] after the President has made the decision. If they don't agree with it and they feel strongly, then they ought to resign or support it . . . You can't have an effective Administration, where the President is able really to lead this country, unless you have got that kind of loyalty in the organization.

*Interview, Washington/*
*The Christian Science Monitor, 10-2:1.*

**Peter W. Rodino, Jr.**
*United States Representative, D—New Jersey*
1

I believe that the Constitution of the United States should be amended only as a matter of last resort, to deal with an issue that cannot be resolved in any other way, on which there is a substantial national consensus.

*The Dallas Times Herald, 11-22:(B)2.*

**Donald H. Rumsfeld**
*Assistant and Chief of Staff to President of the United States Gerald R. Ford*
2

The White House staff, in my judgment, should remember several things. First and foremost, the White House staff is not the President. What's really important is what the President wants done and, hopefully, how he wants it done . . . He wants multiple sources of information. He wants to be reasonably sure there's not a single funnel through which he's getting strained material. He wants to have a sense not only of substantive content but of the intensity of the feeling governing it. He wants to have a sense that there's an orderly decision-making process . . . He doesn't want to be surprised or blindsided.

*The Washington Post, 5-19:(A)4.*

**Henry S. Ruth, Jr.**
*Special government prosecutor for Watergate*
3

[Criticizing public cynicism about government and politicians] : You should be skeptical, but a cynicism that turns people totally away from their government is what creates Watergates. You're not watching your government. It scares me how cynical people are now about their government and their politicians.

*Interview, Washington, Oct. 15/*
*Los Angeles Times, 10-16:(1)11.*

**Francis W. Sargent**
*Governor of Massachusetts (R)*
4

The Federal government, in its incredible anxiety to computerize the lives of everyone, has made some very serious invasions into people's privacy. There has been all too much snooping. We should not get rid of computers, but we should give more thought to what goes into them.

*Time, 1-13:18.*

**William B. Saxbe**
*Attorney General of the United States;*
*Former United States Senator, R—Ohio*
5

Congress has lost its ability to operate independently or with any leadership. Take the energy problem, for instance. Briefings were made available to all of us in Congress four years ago which plotted inevitable disaster. I even went out and made speeches about it. Nobody listened. And then, at the worst possible time, we went on this ecology kick. Delaying the Alaskan pipeline three years because some moose might bump his head on it is ridiculous. Then we went overboard on consumerism, and now everybody wants to get rid of government secrecy.

*Interview, Washington/People, 2-17:58.*

**David Saxon**
*President, University of California*
6

A physician working on an experiment hears a knock at his laboratory door. He finds a man, wounded and bleeding. He puts aside his test tubes and binds the man's wounds. But then he glances down the corridor and there, as far as the eye can see, stretches a line of similarly wounded and bleeding people, thousands upon thousands of them. What should he do? Stop his experiment and treat the wounds or close the door and return to his laboratory bench?

That epitomizes the cruel dilemma faced by the state as it seeks to deal with the most urgent, pressing problems of its citizens and at the same time with the long-range programs which promise to provide ultimate solutions.

*Interview/*
*San Francisco Examiner &*
*Chronicle, 11-16:(A)2.*

**William E. Simon**
*Secretary of the Treasury of the*
*United States*

1

I think the direction our country is heading in is a very dangerous one, as regards our traditional system of government, our economic system. Neither man nor government can continue for a sustained period of time to spend more than he receives.

*Interview/*
*Time, 3-31:70.*

2

We must stop promising more and more services to the public without knowing how we will pay for them. For too many years, like the city of New York, we have been trying to burn the candle at both ends, living off our inheritance and mortgaging our future at the same time. Whether we can prevent the nation from falling into the same [financial] plight as our greatest city is now the central issue before us ... Americans are rightfully concerned about the fiscal plight of the largest and richest city in the land because they know that the philosophy which has prevailed in New York—the philosophy of spend and spend, elect and elect—first took root and flourished here in Washington, D.C. As a nation, we began planting the seeds of fiscal irresponsibility long ago. Forty out of our last 48 [Federal] budgets have been in deficit, and 14 out of the last 15.

*Before House Government Operations*
*Subcommittee on Commerce, Consumer and*
*Monetary Affairs, Washington, June 26/*
*Los Angeles Herald-Examiner, 6-26:(A)2.*

3

We see the threat to free enterprise in the growing domination of government spending within our economy. Why has government

spending exploded? Because, I would suggest, we have been willing to assign to the government the responsibility for solving many of the problems that people should be solving for themselves. We begin with the best of intentions but wind up with social programs that are spinning out of control.

*At Junior Achievement conference,*
*Bloomington, Ind., Aug. 12/*
*Los Angeles Times, 8-13:(1)12.*

4

In the United States today, we already have more government than we need, more government than most people want, and certainly more government than we are willing to pay for.

*At Pepperdine University,*
*Oct. 22/Vital Speeches,*
*11-15:72.*

**Raymond L. Smith**
*President,*
*Michigan Technological University*

5

Since the beginning days of our Constitution, thoughtful people have recognized that ours is a most difficult, perhaps impossible, government to sustain over a long period of time. Perhaps 200 years is the limit. Certainly, oninous signs are present: a flood-swollen central government that now funnels about a third of the nation's wealth through its own omniscience and, as Secretary [of the Treasury] William Simon said recently, 60 per cent by the turn of the century; a population demanding that government not free it but to coddle and control it even more; and, most serious of all, entrenched bureaucrats who fail to understand that the greatest social program is that which will develop in a person self-reliance through a hard day's work.

*At Cleveland Cliffs grand opening of*
*Tilden Mine, Cleveland, Aug. 12/*
*Vital Speeches, 10-15:31.*

**Adlai E. Stevenson III**
*United States Senator,*
*D—Illinois*

6

[A] phenomenon of 1976 which I fear: Some of these [Presidential] candidacies, in-

*(ADLAI E. STEVENSON, III)*

cluding Ronald Reagan's and George Wallace's, are not only negative, they downgrade the very idea of government. For the first time in our history, candidates for the Presidency are downgrading the very government which they seek to head. We've always in the past sought to reform the government, not to destroy the government.

*News conference,*
*Chicago, Nov. 24/*
*Los Angeles Times, 11-25:(1)16.*

**Robert S. Strauss**
*Chairman,*
*Democratic National Committee* 1

[Arguing against the idea of less government as espoused by some political candidates]: ... we are a better America for the legislation of the last 40 years. I say to you tonight that they [the American people] don't want less government; they want *better* government. They don't want social programs dismantled; they do want them improved, better directed, more imaginative and more responsive ... We cannot retreat from necessary government action in the name of a simpler America. In a complex and developing society, the nostalgia as well as the lessons of the old must be merged with the creativity and commitments of the new.

*Interview, Dallas,*
*Nov. 19/The Dallas Times Herald,*
*11-20:(B)8.*

**Herman E. Talmadge**
*United States Senator,*
*D–Georgia* 2

[On Congressional staffs]: One of the frustrations the Senator from Georgia has found in being in the Senate is that virtually every member of this body has some smart people who have some wide-eyed thoughts and dreams. When they get to Washington, they have visions of grandeur and come up here to reform the world. They spend their time thinking up new ideas to create new Federal agencies and to spend more money and do various things to create more grandeur for their Senator in the eyes of the electorate of his state ... I would

suggest ... that we could shorten the sessions of this body if we would fire half the staff members of the House and Senate, not permit staff members to come on the floor of the Senate ... and not permit the reading of a piece of paper on the floor of this body. We could finish our business, adjourn and go home by July 4.

*Before the Senate,*
*Washington/*
*The Washington Post, 6-16:(A)2.*

**Margaret Thatcher**
*Member of British Parliament; Leader,*
*British Conservative Party* 3

Governments can only spend the people's money. There is no such thing as a governmental grant—only a taxpayers' grant. The more you expect from government, the more they'll take from your pocket.

*Los Angeles Herald-Examiner, 10-21:(A)10.*

**Mayo J. Thompson**
*Commissioner,*
*Federal Trade Commission* 4

I would hate to see this agency [the FTC] converted into a mini-legislature, spending its time bringing the heavy, hard hand of government in a bureaucratic way, establishing more and more ... [rules on] all that the American people are to do. I am persuaded that a substantial amount of the wrong in the marketplace today is because of government intervention, and I would hate to see the Commission take a prominent role in that area.

*News conference announcing his*
*departure from the FTC,*
*Washington, April 7/*
*The Washington Post, 4-8:(D)11.*

**John G. Tower**
*United States Senator,*
*R–Texas* 5

I do believe the people's right to know should be subordinated to the people's right to be secure.

*At Senate Select Committee on Intelligence*
*hearing, Washington, Oct. 29/*
*The New York Times, 10-30:1.*

**Morris K. Udall**
*United States Representative,*
*D–Arizona*

1

[On Representative Henry Reuss' elevation to Chairmanship of the House Banking and Currency Committee]: He's 62. He defeated a man who was 81. They say he led a youth rebellion. The House is the only place you can lead a youth rebellion and take your grandchildren with you.

*At Hillcrest Jewish Center,*
*New York/The Wall Street Journal,*
*2-24:10.*

**Jack Valenti**
*President,*
*Motion Picture Association of America; Former Special Assistant to the President of the United States (Lyndon B. Johnson)*

2

It is quite plain that the burdens on public officials grow heavier. It may be that in the future we will be facing a situation where the only candidates will be those who have no families, no wife or husband, no private income, no pleasure in a little human comfort, no desire to mingle with men and women on a personal level, no aberrations of thought or behavior, no inclination toward sin, either venal or mortal, no minor derelictions, no human failings.

*Quote, 4-27:396.*

**John Vorster**
*Prime Minister of South Africa*

3

I have always thought that a leader must walk in front of his people; but he should never go so far as to move out of their sight and hearing.

*Interview, Cape Town/*
*The New York Times,*
*12-24:21.*

**George C. Wallace**
*Governor of Alabama (D)*

4

...this is the insane asylum of the United States right up here in Washington. If I ever go crazy I hope I do it up here because nobody would ever notice it.

*Washington/*
*The Dallas Times Herald,*
*2-22:(A)1.*

**Lowell P. Weicker, Jr.**
*United States Senator,*
*R–Connecticut*

5

If you analyze the votes in Congress, I think you will see that often they break down not so much according to one's party as according to one's generation. I think age is a far greater determinant than party affiliation. People who went through World War II, and the years immediately preceding that war, tend to view things differently than those who are younger.

*Quote, 2-9:125.*

**Caspar W. Weinberger**
*Secretary of Health, Education and Welfare of the United States*

6

Let's be candid. The most fundamental problem we face today is lack of confidence in government. Every public-opinion poll tells us this. There is no need to speculate why. We have all lived through a shattering period in our country's history ... Without [confidence in government], we can do nothing.

*Before HEW employees,*
*Washington/The New York Times,*
*1-26:(1)30.*

7

My single overriding observation after these years in Washington is of the growing danger of an all-pervasive Federal government. Unless checked, that growth may take from us our most precious personal freedoms. It also threatens to shatter the foundations of our economic system.

*Before Commonwealth Club, San Francisco,*
*July 21/The National Observer, 8-2:2.*

**Wes Wise**
*Mayor of Dallas*

8

The continuous adverse publicity is part of the reason people are not interested in seeking [public] office. People say to me, "I don't see

# WHAT THEY SAID IN 1975

*(WES WISE)*

why you do it" . . . The reason people are getting turned off to government is because so much is being associated with what is bad. People want to be associated with what is good.

*Radio broadcast, Dallas, Feb. 20/*
*The Dallas Times Herald, 2-21:(B)1.*

## I. W. Abel
*President, United Steelworkers of America*
1

A strike is an important action and a prerogative of labor; but, like every other right, it's got to be exercised with good judgment. It's an act of last resort, pretty much like getting involved in a war.

*Interview, Pittsburgh/*
*Los Angeles Times, 8-31:(1)10.*

## William M. Allen
*Former chairman, Boeing Company*
2

The Number 1 premise of America is hard work. We seem to have gotten to the point where the object in life is to get away from as much work as possible, and people want more and more leisure. This country can't survive on that philosophy. I think the greatest pleasures you can get out of life are the rewards of hard work. Leisure should be something you get in return for work.

*Interview, Seattle/*
*The New York Times, 8-17:(3)7.*

## Benjamin F. Bailar
*Postmaster General of the United States*
3

Productivity is the secret to a strong economy. We only have to look to Western Europe—to England or Italy or France—to learn a powerful lesson: You can't consume without producing.

*Before New York Customer Council, New York,*
*June 11/Vital Speeches, 7-15:578.*

## Birch Bayh
*United States Senator,*
*D—Indiana*
4

Moral leadership demands not the fears that too many jobs will cause inflation but the conviction that too few jobs will cause human suffering. Moral leadership demands the national commitment that every man and woman who wants to work will have a job.

*Announcing his candidacy for 1976 Democratic*
*Presidential nomination, Indianapolis, Oct. 21/*
*The Christian Science Monitor, 10-22:3.*

## Lloyd M. Bensten
*United States Senator,*
*D—Texas*
5

We can't walk away from recession. I think it is time we started acting like the great and successful nation that we are; time to acknowledge our assets; time, in short, to balance the books and seek a true perspective on who we are. In short, we are the world's most successful nation, but we are acting like a failure.

*At Chamber of Commerce dinner,*
*Newport News, Va., Feb. 26/*
*The Dallas Times Herald, 2-27:(A)17.*

## Christopher S. Bond
*Governor of Missouri (R)*
6

. . . I think we are beginning to realize that the Federal government cannot insure a healthy economy. Public-works projects are merely a short-term, temporary solution. I think part of the problem has been unwise Federal policies which have contributed to the inflation and the economic downturn. I think the economy itself is going to be the thing that creates new jobs, not Federal projects and public-works programs.

*TV-radio interview, New Orleans/*
*"Meet the Press,"*
*National Broadcasting Company, 6-8.*

## Lemuel R. Boulware
*Former vice president and labor*
*negotiator, General Electric Company*
7

The only way on this earth that management can change what happens at the bargaining ta-

*(LEMUEL R. BOULWARE)*

ble is by frankly and honestly working long and hard in advance to present the facts that will change the economic understanding and the expectations of the employees and the public. That communication has got to reach every employee and the public to be fully effective. And it has got to explain clearly what makes jobs, what makes the most jobs for the most people, what makes real job security and the best and steadiest jobs. Moreover, it has got to make clear just what makes pay raises possible and who pays them. I think this is still one of the biggest problems—having people understand that business is an organization of people brought together to do things for each other, that not stockholders but consumers pay wage increases, and that profits are not the source of inflation but of jobs. Because management has neglected its job of correcting the misrepresentations in this area, the public has come to feel exactly the opposite: that profits are the inflationary factor and that wage increases, unmatched by productivity increases, are simply helping the employees "catch up." And these misconceptions have continued so long without a management voice being raised that the public has come to feel not only that the union cause is just but that business is so strong and the union so weak that any means is justified.

*Interview/*
*The Wall Street Journal, 3-24:12.*

**Sam Bowles**
*Economist,*
*University of Massachusetts* 1

Socialism is on people's minds as never before. But it's socialism as a set of economic alternatives, not as an ideal or a philosophical concept. And people aren't going to switch to socialism because it'll give them a higher standard of living. They'll do it for much more humanistic needs—a sense of community responsibility, self-worth, a new importance to their labor, a new pride in what they produce.
*Quote, 6-8:529.*

**Rhodes Boyson**
*Member of British Parliament* 2

Trying to have a free-enterprise system without bankruptcy is like trying to have Christianity without Hell.
*The Wall Street Journal, 9-25:16.*

**Kingman Brewster, Jr.**
*President,*
*Yale University* 3

Any politician whose life is dominated by the prospect of standing for re-election . . . has an inevitable bias in favor of spending and against imposts. The ensuing inflation will, of course, be just as brutal as an equivalent tax would be. However, the inflationary impact cannot be traced to a particular political act; it cannot be tallied in terms of yeas and nays on particular bills. So, too, the beneficiary of a particular expenditure knows who his benefactor is, who voted for the subsidy, the public investment or government purchase. He also knows the particular agency or ministry which declared him eligible for the help he wanted. Thus, he can trace his bounty, quite precisely, to its political source. On the other hand, no one can prove that the higher price of groceries is attributable to any particular public expenditure, to any particular legislative act. The clear political identification of the source of public economic benefits and the obscure source and causes of inflationary burdens is bound to favor excessive public expenditures and irresponsible tax cuts. The inflationary bias of representative government seems to me the greatest threat to the survival of a democratic political economy.
*Before English Speaking Union of the*
*Commonwealth, London/*
*The Washington Post, 11-28:(A)14.*

**Edmund G. Brown, Jr.**
*Governor of California (D)* 4

[Supporting collective bargaining and the right to strike for public employees]: I don't think people who work in state government want more than those who work in private industry, nor do I think they want less. I don't think they want more than the state can afford to pay. It's a question of making the facts known and also a question of understanding their needs ... A strike indicates a failure—a failure to communicate, a failure to lead, a failure to do your job. Certainly I don't want any strikes; but in a free society I don't think you can keep people on the job at the threat of a gun.

*Interview/Los Angeles Times, 3-24:(1)19.*

*1*

I don't believe that janitors should be paid more than judges. But I think the gap between them is too great now. If work is interesting and challenging, people should be paid less. Those are the people who get great psychic rewards: Their lives are better because they have the privilege of interesting work.

*Interview/
The New York Times Magazine, 8-24:30*

*2*

For this country to maintain its leadership, we're going to have to work harder and we're going to have to accept possibly a more austere standard of living. And I'm trying to get that view out so it doesn't surprise people when the economy doesn't quite deliver all the goodies we've been brought up to think it has to deliver. It's just a fact of life. I may be wrong and I hope I am. But I think the standard of living is not going to increase the way it has in the past. A world of limits—that's where we are. That's an important concept. It goes slightly against the grain of "America: bigger, better, we can do anything." I don't think we can do "anything."

*Los Angeles Times, 9-2:(1)3.*

*3*

... it isn't fair that some have more opportunities to work while we leave idle so many others. When we face the prospect of unemployment insurance being paid out for two years, people in the middle stages of their life being set adrift in our uncertain economy, that

is unconscionable. It will destabilize our system and ultimately will be very destructive; so, as a people, we have to make up our minds once and for all that work and doing the business of this country is a prime requisite, more important than efficiency, more important than continued growth; and one way or the other we are going to have to arrive at it.

*TV-radio interview, Burbank, Calif.
"Meet the Press,"
National Broadcasting Company, 10-5.*

**Walter D. Burnham**
*Professor of political science,
Massachusetts Institute of Technology*

*4*

[On the effects of the economic slowdown]: There will be a sense of limit all over the place. The atmosphere will be the opposite of the Eisenhower, Kennedy and Johnson years that anything was possible. We may almost come to the point of saying, "You can't do anything, and in many cases you shouldn't try to do anything." Times of depression or recession are conservatizing. It is in the affluent periods when people can afford to demonstrate and rebel and worry about their identity crises. In times like these, they become more square, less interested in Consciousness III, more worried about three meals a day, more job-oriented and the hell with liberal arts. All sorts of things are going to look old-fashioned by comparison with the '60s.

*Interview, Cambridge, Mass./
Los Angeles Times, 12-26:(2)7.*

**Arthur F. Burns**
*Chairman, Federal Reserve Board*

*5*

In addition to the inflation, we have stagnating productivity. People don't work the way they used to. Just talk to businessmen about absenteeism ... Given the way we want to live and the unwillingness of people to work hard, we can't expect a rising standard of living.

*The New York Times, 1-8:55.*

*6*

Taxes have progressively reduced the rewards for working, while government at the same time

# WHAT THEY SAID IN 1975

has increased the share of the national output going to persons who are not productively employed [in the form of welfare and other public assistance]. Twenty-five years ago, a typical worker with three dependents gave up 1 per cent of his gross weekly earnings in Federal income and Social Security taxes. Since then, that fraction has risen steadily and reached 13 per cent in 1974 ... A society as affluent as ours can ill afford to neglect the poor, the elderly, the unemployed or other disadvantaged persons, but neither can it afford to neglect the fundamental precept that there must be adequate rewards to stimulate individual effort.

*Before Congressional Joint Economic Committee, Washington/ U.S. News & World Report, 2-24:52.*

1

Recession is the Number 1 problem in the short run. Inflation is the Number 1 problem in the longer run. It is because of the past inflation that we now have a recession. If we are to have prosperity in the long run, we must guard very carefully against inflation in the future.

*Interview/The Washington Post, 4-20:(A)6.*

2

... economists have a very poor record in forecasting recoveries, because if they can't see where the recovery will come from they conclude it won't come or will be a mild recovery. It's not given to us to see. We have millions of decision-making units in this country. Let's give these decision-making units an opportunity to do their part. You know, we kind of forget we have a dynamic, private-enterprise system, and so many economists and so many others in the private and political sphere talk as if we have a government which pushes the economy and that the economy is a purely passive thing. The economy generates recovery forces of its own just as it generates recession forces of its own. And now I think within the private economy the recovery forces are under way.

*Before Senate Banking Committee, Washington, May 1/ U.S. News & World Report, 5-19:53.*

3

When we reach these [current] levels of unemployment, I get a little emotional. It's a devastating experience when the head of a household loses the esteem of the members of his family. The worst of unemployment is what it does to family life.

*The New York Times Magazine, 8-10:34.*

**Earl L. Butz**
*Secretary of Agriculture of the United States*

4

Too many of us refuse to give a dollar's work for a dollar's pay—and yet wonder why our employers can no longer afford to hire us. Let's put in a dollar's work for a dollar's pay and quit waiting for the government to solve everything for us ... It is only through our efforts as individuals that we will get back our productivity and our economic vigor that seems to be slipping so badly these days.

*Before Chamber of Commerce, Goshen, Ind., Feb. 17/The Washington Post, 2-18:(A)5.*

5

[Saying some labor leaders have too much power and get into government-policy areas they shouldn't]: Let's not kid ourselves. We had a labor leader [AFL-CIO president George Meany] at that point [during U.S. grain shipments to the Soviet Union] who was in many respects more powerful than the President of the United States. He could shut the nation down [by calling grain-shipment embargoes, for example]; the President can't do that. It's a very dangerous situation. When anybody takes foreign policy into his hands as Mr. Meany did last fall and said, as a matter of foreign policy, "I don't like detente"—he said foreign policy is too important to be left to the Secretary of State. Well, I think it's too important to be left to Mr. Meany, too. It's just as wrong for him to take in his hands as it is for ... the president of the PTA. It's wrong for any person to assume that kind of authority; that's virtually what he did ... We have some labor leaders who can shut the nation down. Take the man who heads the Teamsters Union, for example. If he decides to stop the trucks, we're dead in 24 hours in this country ... We've concentrated that kind of power in the hands of a few individuals.

*News conference, Chicago, Dec. 9/*
*Los Angeles Times, 12-10:(1)4.*

**Leonard F. Chapman, Jr.**
*Commissioner,*
*Immigration and Naturalization*
*Service of the United States*
1

[Illegal aliens are taking jobs,] good jobs that are needed and wanted by unemployed Americans ... This problem is not restricted to any geographic area. It is nation-wide in scope and impact and affects everyone ... One of the myths that surrounds illegal aliens is that they toil all day in the hot sun picking cotton or lettuce. This is no longer the case. The illegal alien now holds jobs in industry, in construction and in service occupations. Less than one-third are employed in agriculture. The number of over-stayed and other illegal aliens who are employed at above-average pay is substantial.

*Before Veterans of Foreign Wars,*
*Washington, March 9/*
*Los Angeles Herald-Examiner, 3-10:(A)3.*

**Richard J. Daley**
*Mayor of Chicago*
2

There is no place for age discrimination in our country ... I believe it is very important that this country have a national policy of encouragement and support for the employment of older workers. Unfortunately, we have established an informal national policy of mandatory retirement based on age. Experience, however, has shown that such a policy is a mistake—a serious mistake in economic terms and, much more importantly, in human terms. Experience has shown that mandatory retirement should never be based on age alone. It should be determined by the ability to do a job ... We know that it often takes quite a bit of time before an employee has mastered the skills and knowledge required for a job. With

this in mind, does it make any sense to view workers 45 and older—who are actually just beginning the prime of their lives—as being in any way unemployable? We should be placing great value on the abilities and talents of men and women in their 50s and 60s and beyond.

*Before Senate Subcommittee on*
*Employment and Retirement Incomes,*
*Washington, Aug. 14/*
*Chicago Daily News, 8-14:2.*

**Thomas C. DeButts**
*Vice president,*
*Burlington Northern, Inc.*
3

Would it surprise you to learn that the worker who has a favorable attitude toward his union likewise has a favorable attitude toward his boss? And that this attitude bears no relationship whatever to the militancy of the union or the generosity of the employer? That compensation and benefits are not decisive to the employee who reacts favorably to the institutions which surround his employment? But that the worker who is extravagantly over-paid, or is under-worked, or is non-productive, harbors strong negative feelings toward both his union and his employer? There is something else I know for sure. We gain little insight of the relationship and interaction between the individual and labor and management by consulting academic authorities. If we read on the subject, as I frequently do, we shall find that writers tend to leap to the most sweeping conclusions from bits of information of doubtful significance.

*Before Public Relations Society of*
*America, University of Iowa, June 18/*
*Vital Speeches, 8-1:617.*

**John T. Dunlop**
*Secretary of Labor*
*of the United States*
4

The main growth of our economy must be by action of the private sector. That is where the jobs are. We need to create in our economy ... three million jobs to get back to a year ago. We need to get 1.6 million jobs a year up until 1980. That can't be done by putting peo-

# WHAT THEY SAID IN 1975

*(JOHN T. DUNLOP)*

ple on the government payroll. It has to be done by stimulating the private economy.

*Broadcast interview/"Issues and Answers,"*
*American Broadcasting Company, 8-31.*

*1*

Penalizing people will not solve the problem of strikes of public employees. There will be stoppages on occasion for a variety of reasons. People miscalculate. Often in government you don't have very good managers. But I don't think you solve industrial-relations problems in either the public or the private sector by concentrating on the question of penalties. That's what history teaches me ... [And] if people are compelled to arbitrate, you don't really get the support on both sides for a settlement. It isn't their settlement; it's the arbitrator's settlement. And they don't have the same interest in carrying it out. They didn't have a part in shaping it. They don't know quite what it means, and they then become more anxious to litigate, to fight in court or otherwise over the fine points instead of trying to work it out. The problem that worries me philosophically is that the government—the management side—is yielding to an arbitrator a very major component in the setting of taxes and charges in the public sector. I think that's the responsibility of the elected representatives rather than of the arbitrator.

*Interview, Washington/*
*U.S. News & World Report, 12-15:78.*

## Edwin W. Edwards
*Governor of Louisiana (D)* *2*

...you can't create permanent wealth by passing laws, no matter how well written they are or how fine the paper on which they are written. Productivity alone will effectively stimulate the economy over the long range. Production of our national resources, farm products, forestry products and products of the sea, putting people to work, making things, doing things, producing things will create some permanent wealth and really stimulate the economy.

*TV-radio interview, New Orleans/*
*"Meet the Press,"*
*National Broadcasting Company, 6-8.*

## Edgar R. Fiedler
*Assistant Secretary for Economic Policy,*
*Department of the Treasury of the United*
*States* *3*

We never quite know what's going on [in the economy] until it's gone on. There's always a lag in the economic indicators we use to predict the future. It takes time to collect the data, time to analyze it, and time to separate the meaningless wiggles from the lines that are telling us something.

*The National Observer, 5-10:3.*

## Janet Flanner
*Writer* *4*

I hear that America is going through a sad period. Rubbish! Such silly rumors disfigure the face of our country. Recession is a temporary thing, like adenoids. It can only lead to recovery.

*Interview, New York/People, 2-24:60.*

## Gerald R. Ford
*President of the United States* *5*

We are in trouble. But we are not on the brink of another Great Depression. Our political and economic system today is many times stronger than it was in the 1930s. We have income safeguards and unemployment cushions built into our economy. I have taken and will continue to take whatever steps are needed to prevent massive dislocations and personal hardships, and, in particular, the tragedy of rising unemployment. But sound solutions to our economic difficulties depend primarily on the strong support of each one of you. Self-restraint must be exercised by big and small business, by organized and unorganized labor, by state and local governments as well as by the Federal government ... To improve the economic outlook, we must rekindle faith in ourselves. Nobody is going to pull us out of our troubles but ourselves, and by our own bootstraps. In 200 years as a nation, we have triumphed over external enemies and internal conflicts—and each time we have emerged stronger than before. This has called for determined leaders and dedicated people, and this call has never gone unheeded.

*Broadcast address to the nation, Washington,*
*Jan. 13/The New York Times, 1-14:20.*

*1*

We need fair tax relief that will help not only the poor, but the middle class, the skilled workers, farmers, teachers, reporters, editors, secretaries, sales people, truck drivers, policemen, firemen and other hard-working, middle-income Americans who have seen their earnings and future eroded by inflation and recession. In short, let us not strip incentives from these upward-bound millions who are struggling to improve their lives and their children's lives by serving notice that America no longer rewards those who make it from low- to middle-income status and beyond.

*Before The Conference Board, Washington, Jan. 22/The New York Times, 1-23:24.*

*2*

... I don't believe any President since the end of World War II has faced any more serious economic problems [than I do]. Certainly, no President held office when we had 12 to 14 per cent inflation in the post-war era, and no President since the end of World War II has had 8 to 9 per cent unemployment. We have gone through a rapidly developing recession. We have kept our cool. We had a steady and I think a constructive course, and the net result is we have ended up with substantial progress on inflation, and from all indications we are slowly starting up in the economic climb that is needed and necessary.

*Interview, Washington, July 23/ The New York Times, 7-25:10.*

*3*

I am proud of a free-enterprise system which corrects its own errors, controlled by the marketplace of free and enlightened consumers.

*San Francisco Examiner & Chronicle, 10-5:(A)12.*

*4*

Today, although we still have a ways to go, the economy is well on the road to recovery ... We are making progress. The signs of this progress are clear for all to see. Our gross national product for the third quarter increased by more than 11 per cent—the biggest quarterly increase in two decades. That's progress. Industrial production rose at an annual rate of 20 per cent during the same period—the biggest quarterly

increase in more than a decade—and productivity among American workers has been steadily improving for months. And that's progress.

*At Republican dinner, Charleston, W. Va., Nov. 11/Los Angeles Times, 11-12:(1)7.*

**Henry Ford II**
*Chairman, Ford Motor Company*

*5*

[Saying more national planning will be needed to match resources with consumption]: I'm thinking about a planning group in Washington with stature [but no actual power] so that it looms important in the total scheme of things. That would plan certain gross national product, certain gross population and the usage required, the amount of food to feed that number of people ... What are those people going to use in the way of consumer goods? Where are we going to get those consumer goods from? And what are we going to make? What kind of materials are going to be required? And where are those materials coming from? We're just living in a fool's paradise in this country. We will just have one hell of a time making ourselves self-sufficient. And you know we just have to rely on the rest of the world. We can't become isolationist and hope that everything is just going to turn out fine for us.

*Interview, Detroit, Feb. 12/ The New York Times, 2-17:34.*

*6*

[On the current state of the economy]: In my 34 years as a businessman, I have never before felt so uncertain and troubled about the future of both my country and my company. It is not too much to say that the very survival of our free society may depend on finding good solutions ... People are rapidly coming to the conclusion that nobody knows what to do, nobody is steering, the problems are running away with us and the country is headed straight for disaster ... If timely action is not taken to stop the recession, it may gather so much momentum that there will be no way to stop it except through actions that are so strong and so long-lasting that they will guarantee more inflation down the road.

*Before Joint Congressional Economic Committee, Washington, Feb. 19/ Los Angeles Times, 2-20:(1)12.*

*177*

# WHAT THEY SAID IN 1975

## Lewis W. Foy
*Chairman, Bethlehem Steel Corporation*

1

About a million-and-a-half people will be entering the private labor force every year between now and 1980, and we want to make sure there are jobs for them, and I mean good jobs. But the average investment to create just a single new job opportunity is rising all the time. It's about $25,000 now, and it'll be close to $35,000 by 1980. You might think about that for a moment: $52½-billion in the year 1980, just to create enough new job opportunities for the people coming into the labor force that year. We won't get the economy back into gear unless and until the private sector can generate the capital funds needed for modernization and growth. In the case of my own industry, that's something in the order of $5-billion a year. Corporate profits can't generate that kind of money, not the way things have been going. The equity route is at a dead end these days, and there are limitations to further borrowings. Even if corporate debt weren't at record heights, there's the crowding-out effect of massive borrowing to cover outsized Federal deficits. Where's that private investment capital coming from? How in the world is our "backward" nation going to get moving forward again? In my opinion there's no way to do it without an enlightened and coherent Federal income-tax program . . . The immediate and long-lasting pay-off from . . . tax-related measures will be nothing less than solid economic growth. And I'm not talking about benefits that, as some people say, would just "trickle down" to all Americans. I'm talking about jobs; I'm talking about food on the table and goods in the stores; I'm talking about a dynamic economy that'll build our strength in world markets and bring a new prosperity to this land and all its people.

*At Downtown Rotary Club, Washington, July 23/Newsweek, 9-29:86.*

## Roger A. Freeman
*Senior fellow emeritus, Hoover Institution, Stanford University; Former Special Assistant to the President of the United States (Richard M. Nixon)*

2

The conspiracy theory of tax law—that loopholes are the result of sinister machinations of lobbyists for moneyed interests who either bribed lawmakers or pulled the wool over the eyes of unsuspecting Congressmen and the public—won't stand up under examination. No public laws are subjected to more painstaking and detailed Congressional study, to more open hearings, to more thorough debates, year after year, than the tax laws. With but few exceptions, remedial tax provisions were put in the law not out of inadvertence, ignorance or, as a rule, a desire to give favored groups improper advantages or privileges. On the contrary, most remedial provisions aim to provide greater equity among various economic groups and individuals or to offer incentives for activities that are held to be desirable as a matter of public policy.

*At Hillsdale (Mich.) College, Sept. 29/ Vital Speeches, 12-1:104.*

## Milton Friedman
*Professor of economics, University of Chicago*

3

Anyone who thinks you are going to eliminate 10 or 15 years of bad economic policy in the course of a single moderate recession ought to have his head examined. There's only one way to stop inflation: for the government to spend less and print less, to keep down the rate of growth of money, and by that I mean money in your pocket and money in your checking account. We have not done that in spite of all the talk about restraint on the part of the Federal Reserve. The actual rate of money growth has spelled inflation. The fundamental, underlying engine of inflation is printing too much money, and the underlying reason for printing too much money is the government is spending too much money.

*Interview/The National Observer, 9-20:15.*

## J. William Fulbright
*United States Senator, D—Arkansas*

4

This inflation is a terrible, terrible burden. It was inflation, primarily, that caused the great mass of people to lose confidence in the Weimar Republic. We keep hearing calls for new leadership, which is what happened in Germany. It begins to sound more and more like what people want is a man on a white horse, a dictator. I'm not saying we're going to have *Seven Days in May*. All I'm saying is that it is possible if we don't act wisely.

*Time, 1-13:18.*

**J. William Fulbright**
*Former United States Senator, D—Arkansas*   1

Now our leaders are asking for sacrifice, but their trumpet blows so feebly as to leave one in doubt that they expect or really want it. Fearing political retaliation if they ask for real austerity, they ask for no more than token self-denial; they are asking the least of people, and that, to their dismay, is what they are getting.

*Quote, 6-8:530.*

**John Kenneth Galbraith**
*Professor of economics,*
*Harvard University*   2

Under the Nixon and Ford economists, who are largely the same, we've come through a period of spectacularly bad management based on the notion that the government should do the least possible. Consequently, we have the worst unemployment rate since the Great Depression, combined with an inflation rate which would have been thought intolerable a few years ago. This is the payoff of the great hope that under the Republicans we could return to the economics of the 18th century . . . The whole evolution of society is toward a more complex and consequently more managed economy. Those who think that there was a Golden Age when government was small and everyone was happy are deficient in their historical knowledge. These changes are not compelled by ideology, but by circumstance. We're either going to be governed by great corporations or by the United States. Of the two, we had better be governed by ourselves.

*Interview/People, 7-7:36,37.*

3

For most of modern history, it has been known that you could have inflation. And, in recent times, it's been known that you could have a great deal of unemployment. But it has never previously been supposed that you could have serious inflation and severe unemployment at the same time. And I suppose that there's no secret as to the circumstances that I hold responsible. In the last 40 or 50 years in the industrial countries we've seen the rise and development of the modern trade-union movement. And the large corporations have increased in size and market power, although they've existed for a long while. From the interrelation between the two comes the wage-price spiral. Unions reach out for gains greater than what can be paid for out of improved productivity. The power of the corporation then allows it to recoup from the consumer, usually with something more. The resulting increase in prices and costs becomes the occasion for the next round.

*Interview/U.S. News & World Report, 11-3:41.*

**Ed Garvey**
*Executive director, National Football*
*League Players' Association*   4

I'm not a table-pounder. Quite the opposite. As a negotiator I want industrial peace, not conflict. I think it's my job to resolve conflicts, not create them. No matter who is involved in labor relations, there's not just the *possibility* of difficulties in bargaining, there's a *certainty* of them. There are always going to be problems, and if we can solve them it's important to find the mechanism so that we can.

*Interview, Washington/*
*The New York Times, 10-26:(5)9.*

**Nat Goldfinger**
*Research director, American Federation*
*of Labor-Congress of*
*Industrial Organizations*   5

To an overwhelming degree, the inflation of the past four years or so, and particularly currently, is not related to employment, to wages, to generally excessive demand in the economy, or the Federal budget deficit. The inflation of the past few years is essentially rooted in food prices and fuel and, earlier, in the prices of raw and crude materials. So the people who look for simplistic answers in the size of the budget deficit and Phillips' Curve nonsense are just chasing will-o'-the-wisps, to the detriment of the economic profession and the detriment of the country. What we need is government policy which we have been advocating since 1972. The policy we have been advocating is effective government control of exports of agricultural products, raw and crude materials, and other goods in which the export sales create shortages and inflationary price increases.

*Interview/The National Observer, 9-20:15.*

**William Philip Gramm**
*Economist,*
*Texas A&M University*

1

The government seems to believe that our economic records go back to last Wednesday. We have data that go back 5,000 years, and every recession in that period was caused by debasement of the currency. When the government stops competing with the private sector for money, the inflation ceases. The Federal government is the only cause of inflation, and government edicts don't change a thing. What must be done is to cut government spending. Wage/price controls from ancient Egypt and Greece to [former] President Nixon's Phase 4 have never worked.

*Before Dallas Chamber of Commerce and*
*business executives/*
*The Dallas Times Herald, 6-1:(C)10.*

**H. R. Gross**
*United States Representative, R—Iowa*

2

No effective measures have been taken to stop inflation. The Number 1 thing is to get the [Federal] budget balanced, do what we ought to have been doing long ago: make expenditures match income. Without that, they can use all the gimmickry known to mankind and it still won't work.

*Time, 1-13:18.*

**Mahbub ul Haq**
*Director, Policy Planning and Program Review,*
*International Bank for Reconstruction and*
*Development (World Bank)*

3

The reason inflation is continuing [in the U.S.] is that even the people who are out of jobs are supported by the Social Security Sys-

tem, unemployment benefits, so the demand pressure doesn't go down. No sector is taking a real cut, they are all reluctant to change lifestyles, so inflation and recession can coexist. The difference between now and the 1930s is that people then did take a real cut, and some people went to the wall. Now the labor unions won't take a cut, the white-collar workers won't take it, even the unemployed get benefits. They pass the ball from one to the other, jostle for a diminishing cake, and the economy gets heated ... So you might as well reflate the cake because consumer demand you cannot curb. Holding down the money supply will be very counter-productive. So my only prescription is to get the production moving. It doesn't matter about money supply. Go after an increased output with a vengeance. That in itself will reduce the inflation. Give incentives to the industrial sector, give incentives to the farmer, give tax breaks and credits and depletion allowances to industry so the gigantic production machinery in the U.S. really churns. Once it begins tossing up output, this U.S. economy has all the ingredients for a quick recovery.

*Interview/*
*The National Observer, 9-20:15.*

**Gabriel Hauge**
*Chairman,*
*Manufacturers Hanover Trust Company,*
*New York*

4

Inflation raises all government costs. Viewed locally, it is a principal cause of fiscal stringency. Viewed nationally, it is a consequence of mismatching expenditures and revenues. Inflation is a tax, not approved by the House Ways and Means Committee or by any local government, nor can it be evaded or avoided. It finances deficits by writing down the real value of all obligations. Walter F. Mondale, a leader of his [Democratic] party's liberal wing in the U.S. Senate, is resoundingly right in branding inflation as the most reactionary force in the world.

*Before Regional Plan Association,*
*New York, April 22/*
*Vital Speeches, 6-1:511.*

**Denis Healey**
*Chancellor of the Exchequer of the*
*United Kingdom*

1

[Arguing against policies of high unemployment to reduce inflation]: There's a theory, which is basically a sort of distorted Friedmanite theory, that you have very strict control of the money supply, and that produces unemployment in the short run. But because the money isn't there, firms go bankrupt, chaps get out of work, and, in the end, wages and prices come down. The plain fact is that in a democracy you can only go so far with that sort of policy, and the question is whether you can get far enough for it to work ... And if I may say so, the risks you run by that type of policy were shown in Italy. Guido Carli [governor of the Bank of Italy] told me he was worried that the policy he was compelled to introduce by foreign opinion would produce a Communist [election] victory, and it has.

*Interview, London/*
*The Dallas Times Herald,*
*6-26:(B)11.*

**Walter E. Hoadley**
*Executive vice president and chief*
*economist, Bank of America*

2

We're not only in a recession economically, we're in a depression as far as human psychology is concerned. There is a tendency to postpone judgment, to liquidate, to write off 1975 as a disaster. We can't afford to write off any year, least of all this year.

*San Francisco Examiner & Chronicle,*
*1-19:(This World)2.*

3

The average American is inexperienced and emotionally unprepared to understand or cope with prolonged recession and is largely unaware of what causes inflation. I find young people everywhere looking for information about what's going on and even more for reassurance that we'll "make it" in 1975—an amazing doubt for many of us who have seen our country weather great storms successfully in the past.

*Quote, 3-23:281.*

**James R. Hoffa**
*Former president, International*
*Brotherhood of Teamsters*

4

A man needs a job for self-respect. If he doesn't have a job, his mind thinks about things it shouldn't be thinking about. The secret to success is an active mind and an active body. We're going to see things in this country that we never [have] seen before because there's so much unemployment. Things are bad now, but they are going to get worse. Something bad happens to me, hell, I shrug it off and roll with the punches; you've got to. But a man has to have a job. My philosophy of life is to live each day, be happy when you can and take care of yourself and your family. But this country—it's a tragic situation with the economy and the unemployment.

*Interview, San Francisco/*
*San Francisco Examiner & Chronicle,*
*7-27:(California Living)7.*

**Hubert H. Humphrey**
*United States Senator,*
*D—Minnesota*

5

The Federal Reserve Board is in effect promoting economic strangulation in this country. We are never going to get out of this recession with just tax cuts and jobs and public-service jobs, which I would also include in my program. You have got to have credit, and you have to have a lower interest rate, and that comes from the Federal Reserve Board. I want to say again that unless the Federal Reserve Board joins the team, unless it gets out of its ivory tower over here in this sanitized institution that it has and joins the team, this country is going to go into a depression. And I call on [Chairman Arthur] Burns and the Federal Reserve Board to join up and to quit playing the bankers' game and start playing the game of helping the American people get some jobs, get some economic recovery. And I say again, they have been tightening the noose around this economy, and they have got to loosen up on it and give us a chance to breathe and to grow.

*TV-radio interview, Washington/*
*"Meet the Press,"*
*National Broadcasting Company, 2-16.*

# WHAT THEY SAID IN 1975

**Maynard H. Jackson, Jr.**
*Mayor of Atlanta*
1

Will the 80-90 per cent of employed Americans have to reduce slightly their personal income to provide work opportunities for the 10-20 per cent unemployed or under-employed? I hold it as a fundamental principle that whatever the total quantity of work may be, we must find ways to assure that all interested persons have access to a fair share of such work. The only real solutions to our employment problems are the creation of more jobs and, if necessary, even the fair sharing of available employment.

*Before National Urban League, Atlanta,*
*July 27/The Washington Post, 7-27:(A)3.*

**Eliot Janeway**
*Economist*
2

There's inflation on two counts, and they are both international: the oil gouge and the food giveaways. It's a [Secretary of State Henry] Kissinger depression. If there's something we have to sell, we *give* it away. If it's something we have to buy, we let the price go up. It's not a recession; it's an international disturbance due to a failure of American bargaining power. Send the price of oil back down where it came from. Ask them [oil-exporting nations] how much they want to pay for American missiles: Will they pay five times more or will they charge 80 per cent less for a barrel of oil? How much do they want to pay for an American grain ship? Five times more, or will they charge us 80 per cent less?

*Interview/The National Observer, 9-20:15.*

**Jacob K. Javits**
*United States Senator, R–New York*
3

[Supporting national economic planning by government]: Opponents do not seem to believe that rational planning can be a means for improving competition or for abolishing outdated governmental regulation. Why not? Why should a government planning agency have a bias against capital formation or economic growth?

*Washington, May 12/*
*The New York Times, 5-13:58.*

**Reginald H. Jones**
*Chairman, General Electric Company*
4

I think we are very fortunate in the United States that we have a different kind of labor leadership here than they have in Europe. A lot of people say, "Your labor leaders are against business." This is not true. Certainly we have our areas of difference, and we are adversaries in many respects, but we also have very substantial areas where we understand each other and we have consensus and agreement. Witness the work of the President's Labor-Management Committee as an example. And they [labor] believe in the system, and they believe that we have got to increase the size of the pie before we can start sharing in the pie.

*TV-radio interview, Washington/*
*"Meet the Press,"*
*National Broadcasting Company, 4-20.*

**Vernon E. Jordan, Jr.**
*Executive director, National Urban League*
5

Just as the [Ford] Administration is engaged in a searching reappraisal of foreign policy, so too should it be engaged in an agonizing reappraisal of our failed domestic policy. Any country that can afford to shovel billions upon billions into the bottomless pit of Southeast Asia can afford to keep its own people at work. Any country that can afford to spend a hundred billion dollars a year on weapons and destructive forces can afford to spend a part of that on jobs and constructive forces. And any country that can subsidize its affluent citizenry to the tune of billions of dollars in tax loopholes can afford to subsidize its working people through mass creation of jobs.

*At Morehouse College, May 18/*
*Vital Speeches, 7-1:562.*

6

The extent of hardship and joblessness in the nation is appalling. Three million blacks and 12 million whites are out of work. While the government and the media talk about nine per cent unemployment, the true rate for white workers is almost 15 per cent, while the rate for blacks is an incredible 26 per cent—or more than one out of four. In many innner-city ghetto areas, half of all workers are unemployed, and at least two-thirds of black teen-agers are jobless. The issue is no longer whether the economic gains of the Second Reconstruction will be preserved; the issue has become whether or not black people will survive the massive assault on their ability to earn their daily bread. Our government has busied itself, not with drastic steps to get the country back to work again, but with soothing predictions that the economy is bottoming out and that later this summer, or by fall, business will improve and prosperity will return. Some of these predictions of an improved economy say that all economic indices will improve except one—unemployment. And this is supposed to be good news. To which I say in the words of Isaiah: "Woe unto them that call evil good and good evil." The Administration may think the economy is beginning to float like a butterfly, but it actually stings like a bee, and black people are the ones being stung.

*At National Urban League conference, Atlanta, July 27/Vital Speeches, 9-15:712.*

**Herman Kahn**
*Director,*
*Hudson Institute*
1

Our disagreement with advocates of the limits-to-growth position is usually not whether the problems they raise are real, but instead about the nature of solutions to these problems. Our assessment indicates that the application of a modicum of intelligence and good management in dealing with current problems can enable economic growth to continue for a considerable period of time. We argue that without such growth the disparities that are so regretted today will probably never be overcome, that no-growth would consign the poor to indefinite poverty and increase the present tensions between have and have-nots. We do not expect economic growth [to] continue indefinitely. Its present exponential rate will instead gradually slow to low or zero rates. Eventually, in the 25th century, we should expect a transition to a truly post-industrial economy.

*At panel discussion, Woodlands, Tex., Oct. 20/ The New York Times, 10-21:18.*

**Carl Kaysen**
*Economist; Director, Institute for*
*Advanced Studies, Princeton University*
2

[Treasury Secretary William Simon's] view seems to be that dangers of inflation are so serious that if, in order to forestall them, we have to have five million or six million unemployment for a very long time—I don't know what figure he has in mind; I am inferring from what he says—we will just have to put up with it. I think our democratic society, with its present sense of what is tolerable, simply will not sustain them. I think a fellow like Simon is a dangerous man in a certain way with all good intentions. Five million unemployed may be barely tolerable, but six million or seven million are not. When lots of heads of households are without jobs, and people who have had jobs all their adult lives find they don't have jobs or job prospects, I would say that is not easy to absorb in our present system.

*Interview, Princeton, N.J./ Los Angeles Times, 5-21:(2)7.*

**Jack Kemp**
*United States Representative,*
*R—New York*
3

The answer to inflation is to control government spending, not to control free enterprise. Price, wage, rent and interest controls distort production, misallocate capital investment, create shortages, and eventually drive up the cost of living. What's worse, controls divert attention from the true cause of inflation: the failure of government to exercise fiscal and monetary responsibility. The root of all inflation in the United States is excessive government spending and deficit financing.

*Interview/The Washington Post, 3-7:(A)9.*

**Edward M. Kennedy**
*United States Senator, D—Massachusetts*
4

If you look at what the [Ford] Administration says, you'll see unquestionably that their [economic] estimates are too hopeful. In order to get down to 8 per cent unemployment, it's going to take a 6.9 expansion of the economy. We haven't had that in 15 years. I don't know what's in their minds. They still talk about

# WHAT THEY SAID IN 1975

## (EDWARD M. KENNEDY)

fighting inflation while the Number 1 problem is the recession . . . Their mentality seems to be that the first concern is inflation. That's not alien to a party [Republican] more concerned with the problems of business than the problems of the people. The point is, that isn't the way. For every point of unemployment you cut, you gain $16-billion in tax revenues. Reduce this unemployment 4 per cent and you're talking about the budget deficit. What does he [President Ford] do about it? Congress passes a bill for housing. The President vetoes it. Congress passes a bill for jobs. The President vetoes it. He compares the situation to Harry Truman fighting Congress.

*Interview, Washington/*
*Los Angeles Times, 7-15:(2)5.*

## Howard E. Kershner
*Visiting professor of current economic problems, Northwood Institute*
1

Let us stop living beyond our means and learn to live within them. Let us stop trying to have more by going into debt, while working less. If everyone worked a full, honest day, as our fathers did subduing the wilderness, the output of goods and services would increase, possibly by a quarter or even a half. That's the way to better living. For too long we have demanded more holidays, shorter hours, more fringe benefits, bigger pensions, a shorter working span, and, in general, seem to believe that we can go on consuming more and more while producing less and less. This is impossible, and raising wage scales and issuing worthless paper money only destroys jobs, increases unemployment and makes depression and inflation permanent. When we try to relieve unemployment by giving away money, we increase taxes, cause further inflation, incur heavier interest charges, dry up jobs in the private sector and constantly move into an ever-worsening situation. This type of program leads us toward the darkness rather than the light.

*Before National Coordinating Committee*
*for Constructive Action, Dallas, Sept. 6/*
*Vital Speeches, 10-15:14.*

## Lane Kirkland
*Secretary-treasurer, American Federation of Labor-Congress of Industrial Organizations*
2

The media tend to cover collective bargaining as if it were a Pier 6 brawl. The intricate moves and trade-offs that really make up bargaining aren't as newsy as impassioned rhetoric or a picket-line confrontation. Reporters are given little training in covering collective bargaining. They are told to look for the "news"—the fist-fight, the walkout, the heated exchange—and, as a result, frequently miss the "story," which is the settlement.

*Before International Labor Press*
*Association, San Francisco/*
*The National Observer, 11-29:15.*

## Andrew Knight
*Editor, "The Economist," London*
3

The weakness of democracy—the reason why Karl Marx and others must be laughing in their graves—is precisely that it's about winning votes. No government can afford to have a survival strategy because that means losing votes. So what do you do? Even though you know you're propelling yourself to the next level of inflation, you wait until things get pretty bad and then you reflate. You have to, otherwise you lose the next election. I'm worried looking at this gap between what needs to be done and what politicians feel they can do. Every democratically elected government tries to save its country from the sort of disaster we are now facing in a way that will destroy it later. And the reason they do this is because they feel compelled to go for short-term policies.

*Panel discussion, Brussels/Newsweek, 1-13:34.*

## Allan Larsson
*Undersecretary of State, Ministry of Labor of Sweden*
4

At the end of the 1960s we found a lot of unrest and uncertainty among workers. People were worried about job security, about risks to their health, about technological changes in the work place. We examined our labor laws and decided to change them. Workers should have more say over how to lead and organize work, how a job should be done, what a company's policy should be. Workers should have more say in fields where employers had the options.

*The New York Times, 10-22:10.*

**Wassily Leontief**
*Professor of economics, Harvard University* 1

I'm no radical, but I'm very much for [economic] planning. Central planning is useful for making decisions—provided these decisions are made by public bodies, after thorough investigation and analysis of the alternatives. But for planning to work, you need very powerful enforcement of the government's decisions. Using taxes to direct planning isn't effective enough. You need capital allocation—the government deciding which industries will expand, which will decline, which will diversify. The capital market doesn't allocate capital now. Wall Street doesn't allocate capital, despite what we believe in theory. In practice it's just not working. Obviously we have planning now, but it's not responsive to most people's needs. I think even the industrialists are becoming sick of the present situation, and would welcome more rational policies. Lack of planning hurts everybody. I favor more orderly decision-making procedures, involving all classes of society.

*The National Observer, 2-8:7.*

**Richard L. Lesher**
*President, Chamber of Commerce of the United States* 2

We seldom think of our economic freedom as one of the fundamental freedoms. But it is! Imagine what life would be like if you could not choose your job; if you could not strike or quit; if you could not decide for yourself where to live, what goods to buy or sell, what clothes to wear. All of these activities comprise our economic freedom; to one degree or another, all of them are restricted in controlled societies and, to one degree or another, we are restricting them [in the U.S.]—slowly, but surely. We all take our commitment to freedom for granted. We shouldn't. For many people—many Americans—freedom is being displaced by security as the Number 1 goal. Freedom is a constant challenge. It requires the making of difficult decisions, the taking of dangerous risks. The

chance to succeed is also the chance to fail . . . Can capitalism survive? It *can!* Whether it *will,* I cannot say. It will last as long as we remain a free people. No longer. It will live if we want it to!

*Before International Platform Association, Washington, Aug. 7/ Vital Speeches, 9-15:734.*

**Hannah Levin**
*Professor of psychology, Richmond College, City University of New York* 3

Physicians prescribe milk and vitamins for children who suffer malnutrition, [so] it is time psychiatrists and psychologists include the prescription of work as a way to a more meaningful and satisfying life. And just as the government has begun to assume some responsibility for feeding the poor with food stamps, it must become national policy to provide full employment for all our citizens who wish to work.

*Before American Psychological Association, Chicago, Sept. 1/ Los Angeles Herald-Examiner, 9-2:(A)3.*

**George Meany**
*President, American Federation of Labor-Congress of Industrial Organizations* 4

The people need to know that the leaders of their government see human beings in the unemployment lines, not statistics. The jobless are not loafers; they are the victims of ill-advised government policies . . . [The people] know in their hearts that this nation can bear any burden, meet any hardship, defeat any foe—if their leaders deal compassionately, sensibly, fairly, with all of its people. Fairness to all and favoritism to none—that should be the policy of the Administration and the Congress. That has been the American concept and, if it is adhered to today, the nation will again weather the storm.

*New York/ The Dallas Times Herald, 2-26:(C)12.*

5

It is clear to us that the economy has reached a point where unemployment is feeding on unemployment and the economy's downward slide is gaining momentum. This is not just another recession, for it has no parallel in

(GEORGE MEANY)

the five recessions in the post-World War II period. America is far beyond the point where the situation can correct itself. Massive government action is needed.

> Before Senate Finance Committee,
> Washington, March 12/
> The New York Times, 3-13:20.

1

Dictatorship is not the only enemy of human dignity. Poverty, hunger, disease, unemployment—these are also things that demean the human personality. These are also the things that make people feel less than whole. That is why a man who is out of work, a man who cannot properly feed or clothe or shelter his family does not feel like a whole man—and the same goes for women who bear like responsibilities.

> Quote, 4-20:362.

2

We need long-range economic planning and priorities to minimize unforeseen major developments and reduce the degree to which American society has stumbled and fumbled along in the past few years. As an example, the United States was not prepared for the urban crisis of the 1960s—which could have been foreseen by sensible long-range economic planning in the 1950s.

> The New York Times, 5-18:(3)11.

3

I certainly am thankful to God that I am not an economist. I look back when I was a highschool drop-out, I had a sort of a flair for mathematics; and I think now that if I had gone on I might have wound up being an economist. And, to me, this is a kind of sad profession, although it is the one profession where you can gain great eminence without ever being right. And I point to [Federal Reserve Board Chairman] Arthur Burns as a prime example of that.

> Before Society of American
> Business Writers/
> The Wall Street Journal, 5-30:8.

4

We have a national Administration that speaks about recovery—recovery is at hand—while at the same time calmly projecting a national unemployment rate of 7.5 per cent for the next four years. This to me is some kind of gobbledygook. Who is going to recover? The bankers? The big corporations? . . . Labor cannot and will not accept recovery without jobs for the jobless.

> Before International Ladies Garment
> Workers Union, New York, June 3/
> The Dallas Times Herald, 6-4:(A)20.

5

We don't look at full employment as one of those philosophically correct things that social workers talk about [but as] an economic necessity . . . From jobs come the wages that generate mass purchasing power. There are some powerful forces that are opposed to full employment. Why? Because they believe high unemployment keeps wages down and keeps workers "in their place."

> At conference sponsored by Full Employment
> Action Council, Washington, June 24/
> The Washington Post, 6-25:(A)3.

6

I think what we need in this country is price controls. I think you don't need wage controls. If you have price controls, the wage problems are going to take care of themselves.

> Interview/The New York Times, 8-31:(1)33.

7

What we need is government expenditure to create jobs. I can't see any way we are going to get out of this present dilemma without that . . . I think my main quarrel with the President [Ford] is this fetish that he has on the budget—that the budget deficit can't go up, can't go beyond a certain level. Now, this isn't the way the American economy works. This is not the way a family lives. If a family lived this way, you wouldn't send your kid to college until he got to be 30, because it would take until he was 30 years old to save the money . . . The big corporations in this country go out and borrow billions of dollars to expand, to move along. This country is a great big corporation.

Why shouldn't we borrow money to expand at times when we need to borrow?

*News conference, Washington/*
*U.S. News & World Report, 9-8:49.*

**Arnold R. Miller**
*President,*
*United Mine Workers of America*

1

There is a common misconception that the more we modernize and automate the workplace, the healthier it becomes. But the opposite is often the case. The high-speed, labor-saving machinery now used in coal mining, for example, produces much greater quantities of coal dust in the air than when mining was done by manual labor alone. The same is true in textile factories, glass manufacturing, stonecutting and many other industries. Every 20 minutes we introduce a new chemical substance into the workplace. We have little idea of its effects as it seeps into the blood streams of thousands of workers and fouls their lungs. We cannot even guess what its genetic effects might be on future generations. We dare not wait to find out. The job of cleaning up the work environment will be costly and difficult. But what it comes down to in the end is not a question of cost, but a question of priorities. If this society can devote millions of dollars and thousands of trained workers to the goal of landing a man on the moon, surely we can devote equal resources to making it safe for a man or woman to earn a living here on earth. What we need is the will to make it happen.

*At National Conference on Social Welfare,*
*San Francisco/*
*The National Observer, 12-13:11.*

**Rogers C. B. Morton**
*Secretary of Commerce of*
*the United States*

2

... everybody is in favor of more and better jobs, higher real incomes and a constantly rising standard of living for all. Unfortunately, all those good things are not to be found under a cabbage leaf, nor are they dropped down the chimney by the stork. They come from business making a sufficient rate of profit to reinvest in plant and equipment and to attract

external capital. Yet these economic facts of life seem to be unknown to a majority of American people.

*Denver/The New York Times, 11-1:37.*

**Thomas A. Murphy**
*Chairman, General Motors Corporation*

3

Sure, these are troubled times, but I don't know of any that weren't. It is a matter of degree, of perspective. People talk today about [how] this is terrible, like it was in the '30s during the Depression. But as it is, it isn't that bad. We are getting through it. I am as positive of that as anything I can have an opinion on. I think we are through it for all practical purposes. I don't like the idea of people being out of work. But on the other hand, prices are coming down, credit is coming down. We still have a great country. We have about as many people employed as we have ever had in our history—and making wages beyond anything they have had before. As inflation comes down, they are getting an increase. Inflation is a tax. As it winds down, people will see their purchasing power come back. But consumer confidence lagging behind is what makes for downturn in business.

*Interview, Washington/*
*Los Angeles Times, 5-14:(2)5.*

4

Freedom is a precious commodity and can be eroded gradually. We have to be concerned about all freedoms. Newspapermen come out fighting mad if anyone threatens freedom of the press. College professors come out fighting mad if anyone threatens academic freedom. But you don't get people quite so worked up when someone impinges on operations of the free-enterprise system. In some cases, the way it is presented to the public by the media and others, it seems like a victory for virtue and a cutting down to size.

*Interview, Washington/*
*Los Angeles Times, 5-14:(2)5.*

5

Fundamentally, there are only two ways to organize economic activity—either through voluntary cooperation or by means of coercion;

# WHAT THEY SAID IN 1975

## (THOMAS A. MURPHY)

that is, by freedom or by force. All societies are mixtures of these two forms. At one end of the scale are the command societies where economic activity is centrally directed by government planners. The world has too many examples of these. At the other extreme are unfettered free-market economies or what is known as capitalism. America, thankfully, remains the best example, having been founded and having prospered into the earth's wealthiest and freest country on the principles of private enterprise which are consistent with our national dedication to other freedoms—of worship, of the press, of thought and of individual economic choice.

*Before Greater Detroit Chamber of Commerce,
June 5/Vital Speeches, 7-15:593.*

1

For years the motto of organized labor was said to be the single word, "more." It has not changed, but now we hear talk of "less"—not less wages, not less benefits, but less work, shorter work days, shorter work weeks. This won't wash. The public will see—must see—that less work, not balanced by increased productivity, really means more cost. And more cost is what America cannot afford.

*Los Angeles Herald-Examiner, 11-24:(A)8.*

## Robert R. Nathan
*Economist*

2

No one wants [wage/price] controls, but in these days of a soft economy we could, through controls, really break this self-generating spiral without building pressures for further inflation and without letting unemployment and production and incomes deteriorate. We probably do not need permanent controls to break the spiral, but the distortion from controls would be far less than the costly distortions associated with inflation and recessions.

*Interview/The Washington Post, 3-7:(A)9.*

## Harold R. Newman
*Chief of Conciliation, New York State
Public Employment Relations Board*

3

In all labor negotiations there's a kind of dance, a ballet, that takes place. The union will come to the bargaining table demanding far more than it will ever get. They cannot begin by being locked into a position because they will have no place left to go. The mediator is not a stage director. There's no script. But in knowing when and where to push, we do attempt to stage-manage. We try to find what is a posture and what is a hard-rock position that they hold like Holy Writ.

*The New York Times, 9-5:20.*

## Arthur M. Okun
*Senior fellow, Brookings Institution;
Former Chairman, Council of Economic
Advisers to the President of the
United States (Lyndon B. Johnson)*

4

The economy has now deteriorated to a point most of us have not seen in our adult lives ... It is incredible. A fire is burning, but most of the country is going on with business as usual. Why is there no public clamor? There is no action by government to express that the seriousness of the situation is recognized. Nobody wants to grab the ball and run with it.

*The New York Times, 3-7:18.*

## David Packard
*Chairman, Hewlett-Packard Company*

5

I don't sense any significant trend toward people wanting to work less. There's been a good deal of talk about that, but the experience of our company is that we have many people who are very enthusiastic about what they're doing. They work hard because they enjoy it, and they feel that they are accomplishing something. The goals for personal satisfaction that come from doing a good job will continue to encourage hard work. I don't think we're going to see a serious deviation from the old Protestant work ethic.

*Interview/U.S. News & World Report, 7-7:50.*

## James Pate
*Assistant Secretary for Economic Affairs,
Department of Commerce of the
United States*

6

[The economy is] about to bottom out. We should begin the turnaround in two or three months. Evidence for this is scattered, I know, but it's there. Look at the moderation in the inflation rate. Why, if you wait for clear evidence that the recession has bottomed out then it's already bottomed out.

*The National Observer, 5-10:3.*

**Sylvia Porter**
*Financial writer*

1

We are a nation of economic illiterates and our illiteracy is a threat to the survival of the system we profess to love so much. In our Congress today, policies vitally affecting the survival of our form of economic system are being made by economic illiterates. In the executive suites of great financial and business concerns, and in union headquarters across the nation, decisions directly involving our paychecks, profits and prosperity are being made by men who have only the vaguest idea of what creates paychecks and profits and furthers prosperity.

*Before Washington Press Club, Oct. 16/*
*The Dallas Times Herald, 10-17:(B)8.*

**William Proxmire**
*United States Senator, D-Wisconsin*

2

[Arguing against wage/price controls]: Inflation was running at a 5 per cent rate when we put them into effect [a few years ago] and now it's running at more than twice that. Anyway, both business and labor are adamantly opposed to controls—and no controls program can work under those circumstances. I'd only give such power to the President under war conditions, and even then Congress should set down some guidelines. The most essential thing in solving inflation is to get a tight Federal budget.

*Interview/The Washington Post, 3-7:(A)9.*

**Ronald Reagan**
*Former Governor of California (R)*

3

Inflation has one cause and one cause only: government spending more than government takes in. And the cure to inflation is a balanced budget. We know, of course, that after 40 years of social tinkering and Keynesian experimentation that we can't do this all at once; but it can be achieved. Balancing the budget is like pro-

tecting your virtue: You have to learn to say "no."

*At Conservative Political Action Conference,*
*Washington, Feb. 15/Human Events, 3-1:6.*

4

With all the [economic] doom and gloom that we read, which creates a fear of the unknown, I think it's time for American business at the very top level to ask for a summit meeting with the heads of the communication industry. I don't suggest that the news should be slanted to play down wrongdoing on the part of anyone in the private sector, but I believe [the media] must have pointed out to it what it is doing with the constant chorus of gloom-and-doom reporting. I think the business community could remind the leaders of the communications media that while we can't have a free country without a free press, they can't have a free press without a free economy.

*At oil marketeers' conference,*
*Las Vegas, Nev., Feb. 20/*
*Los Angeles Herald-Examiner,*
*2-20:(A)12.*

5

[On the fact that Republicans have never had much electoral appeal in times of economic stress]: For 40 years or more this country has been following the lute song of the liberals. Suddenly, when they come undone with their planned economy, their deficit spending and their deliberately planned inflation, which they said would maintain prosperity, how the hell do the conservatives get blamed?

*Interview, Los Angeles/Time, 3-17:11.*

**Albert Rees**
*Director, Federal Council on Wage*
*and Price Stability*

6

Not only are [wage/price] controls not needed, but the mere threat of them is creating widespread fear and counter-productive behavior in business and labor organizations. Unions are afraid to moderate their wage demands, and businesses are afraid to lower their prices for fear they will be frozen into an unfavorable position by new control legislation.

*Los Angeles Times, 1-29:(2)4.*

# WHAT THEY SAID IN 1975

**Paul A. Samuelson**
*Professor of economics,*
*Massachusetts Institute of Technology*     1

If you turn the present recession upside down and read on the bottom, it will say "Made in Washington." The weakness in production has been by design and not by accident. They all desired that the economy be cooled off. But it got out of hand, like an avalanche.

> *San Francisco Examiner & Chronicle,*
> *2-23:(This World)2.*

**Hugh Scott**
*United States Senator, R–Pennsylvania*     2

[Saying he is convinced there will be no return to wage-price controls]: Barring a national disaster or a war, I would give them no more chance than I would give a celluloid dog chasing an asbestos cat through hell.

> *U.S. News & World Report, 9-22:8.*

**L. William Seidman**
*Assistant to President of the United States*
*Gerald R. Ford for Economic Affairs*     3

Inflation can destroy the system. It did in Germany, in China and elsewhere. It can destroy us because it will stop functioning of our economic system. It can make us think that creating money can create savings, can create real products. But the activities of the government can do no such thing. The Federal Reserve neither toils nor spins; it only regulates money supply based on the real activity of people in the country doing real things.

> *At economic conference, San Diego, Calif.,*
> *April 3/Los Angeles Times, 4-4(3)19.*

**Laurence H. Silberman**
*Acting Attorney General of the*
*United States*     4

As long as jobs are available for those who enter this country illegally or those who enter legally as non-immigrants and illegally obtain employment, the influx of unauthorized immigration will continue. If we do not act effectively, the tide of illegal aliens will abate only when we have absorbed so many unauthorized immigrants that the U.S. is no longer perceived as economically more inviting than the countries from which they come.

> *Before House Judiciary Subcommittee,*
> *Washington, Feb. 4/*
> *Los Angeles Herald-Examiner, 2-4:(A)2.*

**William E. Simon**
*Secretary of the Treasury of the*
*United States*     5

We're always doing things that are politically attractive and economically make no sense whatsoever. That's why we're in this mess now. We should not heed people who are calling for quick solutions like price controls which history has proven do not work. Anybody with any knowledge of history, any ability for economic analysis and anybody with a reasonably good memory knows that wage and price controls are not the answer to inflation. We should head for less government instead of more government. We're going down the same road as the United Kingdom. Government is the most inefficient organ man created to solve a problem that government brought about to begin with.

> *San Francisco Examiner & Chronicle,*
> *1-5:(Sunday Scene)2.*

6

Frequently, those who support bigger government spending programs and greater governmental control over the economy are pictured as socially progressive, men and women of compassion who care about the problems of the little people. On the other hand, those who believe that the government does not have the ability to solve every problem and that instead we should be strengthening the free-enterprise system are caricatured as a new generation of economic royalists who are indifferent to human suffering and care only about fattening the golden calf of big business. These characterizations would mean little, except for the fact that they are so blatantly phony. My experience in Washington has convinced me that almost every man and woman in a position of high public trust cares deeply about the welfare of our people, especially those who are impoverished or face disadvantages because of their sex or the color of their skin. The central question is not who cares the most, but how we restore our prosperity and reduce human hardships without sacrificing our freedom or destroying the most successful economic system that man has ever known . . . if America continues down the road toward greater governmental control over our economy—a road that we have been moving steadily down for several decades—then your generation will be robbed of your personal and economic freedoms and you will be condemned to an economy with chronic inflation and unemployment. That is really what's at issue in our economic debates . . .

*At Kansas State University, March 18/*
*Vital Speeches, 4-15:386.*

1

History is littered with the wreckage of governments that could not deal adequately with inflation—and I will also suggest that history is littered with the wreckage of finance ministers who spoke the way I am speaking right now.

*Time, 3-31:70.*

2

Even though the problems of unemployment and inflation are especially painful, evidence is gathering on every side that the economy is shifting gears from recession to recovery. We are confident that the recession will bottom out during the middle months of the year, and by the end of 1975 we will definitely be on the road to recovery . . . But the government is not leaving recovery to chance. It is providing tremendous incentive. What we have to do now is make sure we don't do what we've done so often in the past—overheat the economy just to warm it up . . . That is why it is so vitally important to avoid steps now—an even greater budget deficit, for instance, or excessive monetary policies—that might propel us out of the recession but would only catapult us into a new round of spiraling inflation and still higher unemployment . . . If you will look beneath the surface, you will find that the inflation stemming from our fiscal and monetary excesses has been the single most destructive force within our economy—hurting us far more than the recent quadrupling of oil prices, the explosion of food prices and so on.

*Before American Newspaper Publishers*
*Association, New Orleans, April 7/*
*The Dallas Times Herald, 4-8:(D)6.*

3

Nobody likes the results of inflation, but we love what causes it. We love the spending, the creation of money and purchasing power.

*Interview/The New York Times, 4-10:62.*

4

The American economic system today is under attack as it never has been before. And that attack comes as the country is drifting dangerously down the path toward a centralized economy. Now it is time for leaders of the business community to come to the defense of our economic system. It's time to lay it on the line for the American people. We have reached a watershed. Either we continue down the path of recent years—a path that will inevitably lead to socialism in the United States of America—or we fight now to preserve our economic and political freedoms. Let us make it clear to the American people that the choice is between those who believe that government should make the choices for individuals and those who believe that individuals should choose for themselves. And let us make it equally clear where the so-called liberalism of today really leads: to the destruction of our liberty . . . America is still incredibly strong. Its mainspring is the largest and most dynamic marketplace in the world. We have the resources, and we know how to rebuild our economy. The central question is whether we have the will and the courage to rescue ourselves from the relentless drift we have experienced in recent years. It cannot be said too often that a centralized economy in America—the kind of economy we are now constructing—is the surest means we have of destroying the mainspring of our prosperity and our progress.

*At Pepperdine University, Oct. 22/*
*Vital Speeches, 11-15:71.*

5

Some economists are arguing that the President [Ford] should sign tax-cut legislation re-

# WHAT THEY SAID IN 1975

## (WILLIAM E. SIMON)

gardless of what Congress does about spending. I am not persuaded by their argument. Whether or not we enact another tax cut immediately may not have a significant impact on our immediate economic hopes. However, whether or not we bring spending under control and work our way out of horrendous [Federal] budget deficits will most assuredly have a significant impact upon our hopes for the future.

*New York/*
*The New York Times, 12-4:31.*

## Margaret Thatcher
*Member of British Parliament; Leader,*
*British Conservative Party*

1

I believe that we should judge people on merit and not on background. I believe that the person who is prepared to work the hardest should get the greatest rewards and keep them after tax; that we should back the workers and not the shirkers; that it is not only permissible but praiseworthy to want to benefit your family by your own efforts.

*San Francisco Examiner & Chronicle,*
*2-23:(B)2.*

2

We must build a society in which each citizen can develop his full potential both for his own benefit and for the community as a whole; in which we encourage rather than restrict the variety and richness of human nature. Private enterprise is by far the best method of harnessing the individual to increasing the wealth of the nation; for pioneering new products and technologies; for holding down prices through the mechanism of competition; above all, for widening the range of choice of goods and services and jobs. Government must therefore limit its activities where their scope and scale harm profits, investment, innovation and future growth. It must temper what may be socially desirable with what is economically reasonable.

*At dinner sponsored by Institute for*
*Socioeconomic Studies, New York, Sept. 15/*
*The New York Times, 9-16:14.*

## Mayo J. Thompson
*Commissioner, Federal Trade Commission*

3

We need to increase competition in the labor market and thus encourage those who currently have jobs to work more productively at them. We need to rewrite our welfare laws in such a way as to give more people an incentive to accept a productive job and get off the welfare rolls. And most importantly of all, perhaps, we need to increase the number of jobs in the economy to the point where every single American who is able and willing to work will be able to find a job that will use his productive abilities to the fullest. Long lines of people in front of unemployment offices represent more than just economic hardship for the unemployed themselves. Those lines are an affront to the American dream, a denial that this is still the land of opportunity we have always believed it to be.

*At Executive Development Program,*
*Texas A&M University, Jan. 27/\*\**

## Alvin Toffler
*Author; Former associate editor,*
*"Fortune" magazine*

4

Like Generals, conventional economists are too busy fighting the last war. They are practicing Maginot economics—all their guns are pointing in the wrong direction. While the Keynesian economists have created a powerful set of abstract measures to chart such trends as unemployment and inflation, their measurements do not take into account everyday social and ethnological changes that have a profound economic impact—the oil crisis, for example. The speed at which we experience change today has an inflationary effect. You can't measure this, but it won't go away.

*Interview/People, 4-14:34.*

5

It's a mistake to look at our present situation and see it simply as one more economic recession. Industrial society is going through a profound breakdown and transformation. What's happening now will affect our economy for a generation or more. All industrial societies share certain common characteristics: mass production, mass distribution, mass education, the nuclear family. They all rely on big science and big organizations. They all share a materialist value system. You find these traits in Russia, the U.S., Sweden, Japan. And when you look closely, you find each of these is breaking down or moving into crisis. If our problems were only economic, they would be a lot less dangerous. That's why I use the term "eco-spasm" to describe what's happening today. It's not boom or bust, or recession or "stagflation." It's an economic shake-up in the midst of an ecological crisis, technological and political upsets, and revolutionary changes in family structure, values, sexual attitudes, military and geopolitical power balances.

*Interview/U.S. News & World Report, 5-5:53.*

**Rexford Tugwell**
*Economist; Senior fellow, Center for*
*the Study of Democratic Institutions*

1

If we could get out of the [economic] hole we were in back in 1933, it should be nothing for those fellows in Washington to get out of this one ... The similarities aren't very great. I think our situation at present is not nearly as bad as it's being pictured. I think it has been made more critical by the energy problem, but I don't think that's impossible to solve ... They talk about industrial production being down to 75 per cent of capacity today. It was down to 25 per cent then ... The difference between then and now is that this country was half farmers then and now only 10 per cent of our people are farmers. Mostly they were inefficient small farmers. [In the '30s there was] at least 25 per cent unemployment and maybe a lot more. We had no social insurance, either. The farmers were busted and could not buy anything ... We've got a floor under us that we didn't have in the 1930s: Social Security, unemployment insurance and welfare.

*Interview, Santa Barbara, Calif./*
*Los Angeles Times, 3-5:(1)3.*

---

**Al Ullman**
*United States Representative, D—Oregon*

2

The only way you're going to get a handle on inflation is to make the people of America

and the world know that this nation is dedicated to a sound basis. Once they believe that the nation is dedicated to setting goals for the future and has enough brains and policy implementation to carry them out, then individuals are going to be willing to lay out their personal goals and perhaps even accept less in the future. But until we do that, there's no way you can turn this thing around. We need that kind of dynamic, long-range leadership that we just don't have as of now.

*Interview/*
*U.S. News & World Report, 1-20:34.*

**Jay Van Andel**
*Chairman,*
*Amway Corporation*

3

It is hard to see how anyone could argue that free enterprise is not the most successful economic system ever invented. So successful is our system and so high are the aspirations of the American people that we define poverty at an income level that is higher than the average income level of what is called the world's second most powerful nation—the Soviet Union! ... Freedom and free enterprise does something for a human being that cannot be done in any other way. It gives him hope and the incentive that goes with it, and all the plans of all the governments on earth eventually fail if freedom is not present.

*At Amway convention, Washington, June 23/*
*Vital Speeches, 7-15:587.*

**Friedrich von Hayek**
*Economist*

4

There are many bad effects of inflation, but the worst is that it draws labor into employments where they can be kept employed only by accelerating inflation; and the point inevitably arises when inflation cannot be accelerated sufficiently fast to keep them in that inflation. Inflation is like over-eating and indigestion. Over-eating is very pleasant. So is inflation. Indigestion comes only afterwards, and therefore people do not see the connection.

*TV-radio interview, Washington/*
*"Meet the Press,"*
*National Broadcasting Company, 6-22.*

# WHAT THEY SAID IN 1975

**Charles S. Welsh**
*Deputy Secretary of Commerce*
*of Pennsylvania*

1

We all know that having a craft, a trade, a skill, has not always been given the importance, the status, it deserves. We're finally coming out of that, that pompous *hauteur,* but, still, there are a lot of people brought up to believe that a desk and a white collar are preferable to tools and calluses. And what that has really meant, of course, is an awful lot of people sitting around, bored, unfulfilled, in an awful lot of offices— people who'd rather be working with tin snips or a wood clamp.

*Before Industrial Arts Association*
*of Pennsylvania, Harrisburg/*
*The Wall Street Journal, 11-24:12.*

**F. Perry Wilson**
*Chairman, Union Carbide Corporation*

2

America's experience with wage/price controls in 1971-1974 was not a happy one. During that period we suffered distortions and inefficiencies in production, and shortages of such products as meats, canned foods, paper products, metals, plastics and chemicals. And since profit margins were limited, many capital investments which ought to have been made were not. Thus the foundations were laid for the inflation acceleration of the post-control period. I have heard it said that past wage/price controls didn't work because we didn't "do it completely"; but that is not possible. America depends on raw materials imported from every corner of the world, and their prices are independent of our wishes or control. Government has a role in the functioning of the economy. But another period of wage/price controls would do more harm than good for consumers, labor and business alike.

*Interview/The Washington Post, 3-7:(A)9.*

**Richard C. Wilson**
*Assistant professor of economics,*
*University of Texas, Arlington*

3

Congress and the Executive Branch really push hard for an expansionary money policy when the economy is doing poorly. The Fed[eral Reserve] and Board Chairman Arthur Burns know what's best—that the solution is to follow a policy geared to longer-term growth in the economy. They know that trying to interfere with a recession through fine-tuning just aggravates things; that we have to be willing to accept temporary economic setbacks. You can't go push the panic button . . . Assume for the moment [that] forecasting is no problem, that the precise economic impact of fiscal and monetary policy is known. There still remains the problem of how much time elapses before either fiscal or monetary policy have their main impact. Armed with these facts, it would seem that attempts at fine-tuning the economy could more often than not miss their targets and perhaps even cause some instability as the economy has to keep adjusting back and forth as policies change.

*The Dallas Times Herald, 7-16:(D)11.*

**Leonard Woodcock**
*President, United Automobile*
*Workers of America*

4

[Calling for government economic planning in the U.S.]: We can no longer drift from one disaster to another. Planning is compatible with a democratic society. In fact, if we don't take substantial steps toward planning, the days of democracy are very limited indeed.

*News conference, Feb. 27/*
*The New York Times, 2-28:43.*

**Walter B. Wriston**
*Chairman, Citicorp (First National City Bank,*
*New York)*

5

It ought to be evident that a machine which has rusted over the years cannot be repaired overnight by some dramatic thing like wage, price and profit controls—the economic equivalent of tying down the safety valve. Because the curbing of money supply by the Federal Reserve Board is not dramatic and is done "in secret," it is not perceived as having any real effect. Again and again the media succumbs to the ancient philosophical absurdity: If you cannot kick it, it does not exist. That is why fiscal and monetary restraint is "nothing," while controls, which are "something," seem better than "nothing." They can see it happen; therefore, it is real. If [columnist] Jack Anderson has not alerted us, nothing has happened. But the significant realities are still invisible: They are the distortions and long-range disasters that cannot be instantly observed—and so are neglected.

*Before Commercial Club, Boston/*
*The Wall Street Journal, 2-19:16.*

**Jerry Wurf**
*President, American Federation of State,*
*County and Municipal Employees* 1

Our labor movement in America is different from any other. In the other free societies the labor unions are in opposition to the free-enterprise or capitalistic system. Ours is the only labor movement in the whole world that has a commitment to the free-enterprise system.

*Interview/*
*Nation's Business, March:43.*

**Edwin H. Yeo III**
*Chairman, Pittsburgh National Bank* 2

Reflecting the cumulative impact of the errors of judgment, the lack of leadership, the absence of character, that add up to nine years of economic, financial and political mismanagement, our real economy is evidencing substantial symptoms of distress. It is not simply that we are in a recession; we have had recessions before and will have them in the future. The present recession is unusual in the sense that it is accompanied by widespread manifestations of financial strain and a resultant pervasive fear. These strains are a direct result of a process of inflation, including a low rate of savings and thus capital formation, bloated debt positions of individuals and corporations, and a relentless squeeze on profit margins, the reciprocal of which has been sharply higher break-even points for broad sectors of American industry.

*At International Investor's Conference/*
*The Wall Street Journal, 2-3:10.*

# Law • The Judiciary

**Harry A. Blackmun**
*Associate Justice,*
*Supreme Court of the United States*
1

I think it's so easy, because of the pressures here [on the Court] and the demands on our time, for us [Justices] to stay in our ivory tower and not get out. I think we're too confined at times. It doesn't seem to me that we should hit the political circuit, but it's good to hear the voices of America from a different podium than the rostrum before us.
*Interview/The New York Times, 7-14:13.*

**Virgil C. Blum**
*Professor of political science,*
*Marquette University*
2

The history of the [U.S.] Supreme Court clearly demonstrates that the Justices of the Court invariably decide cases on the basis of their own values—their own prejudices, their own economics, their own sociology, their own morals, their own theology, their own philosophy. The Constitution does not say much about anything; it is an open document, made up of vague, broad, undefined words and phrases. Hence, the Supreme Court can interpret it to mean anything the majority chooses. This was put bluntly by Chief Justice [Charles Evans] Hughes when he said, "The Constitution means what the Justices say it means." In other words, the biases, the prejudices, the economic, social, moral and religious values of the Justices written into the Constitution by the Courts force all of us to conform. When a majority of the Court was pro-business, it struck down laws fixing minimum wages. When a majority of the Court was pro-labor, it struck down laws restricting picketing and boycotting. When a majority of the Court was pro-states' rights, it struck down laws prohibiting child labor. When a majority of the Court was libertarian, it struck down anti-pornography laws.

When a majority of the Court embraced anti-Negro and anti-Japanese prejudices, it ruled against black and yellow people.
*At Diocesan Teachers Institute,*
*Fairfield, Conn., Oct. 30/*
*Vital Speeches, 12-15:150.*

**William F. Buckley, Jr.**
*Political columnist;*
*Editor, "National Review"*
3

Libel suits initiated by public figures are intended to make a public point. In most instances the public figure has not been damaged in the sense that his income has diminished as the direct result of the circulation of the libel. That is why in some of the most conspicuous libel suits of the past season—in some of which I have figured—the plaintiffs have generally stipulated that compensatory damages were not sought. Instead, plaintiffs have asked the court to award damages that speak to the intrinsically defamatory nature of the libel; and to punish the tortfeasor for proceeding to write something he had every reason to believe was both wrong and defamatory.
*July 1/Quote, 11-16:420.*

**Warren E. Burger**
*Chief Justice of the United States*
4

[Saying Federal judicial salaries should be raised] : [With rapid inflation, the 1969-level freeze in salaries violates] the Constitutional prohibition against reduction of salaries of Federal judges during their terms of office. The Judiciary, along with the Congressional and the upper-level members of the Executive Branch, are virtually one of the very few segments of the economy who are being asked to meet 1975 costs of living on 1969 incomes.
*State of the Judiciary address before*
*American Bar Association, Chicago, Feb. 23/*
*Los Angeles Times, 2-24:(1)4.*

*1*

[There is in the legal profession an] absence of adequate education in the standards of professional ethics and professional conduct. It is pervasive throughout our profession, and it is a subject we have treated with a mixture of apathy and inertia.

*State of the Judiciary address before American Bar Association, Chicago, Feb. 23/ The New York Times, 2-24:14.*

*2*

The upper level of trial lawyers in this country is as good as the upper level of the trial lawyers of any country in the world. But we have a relatively thin crust of really competent advocates in this country in relation to the demand, given the number of lawyers we have— 300,000 or more. And I have strongly urged and I intend to continue to urge that, at least as far as the Federal courts are concerned, no lawyer be permitted to come into the Federal court to try a case simply on a diploma from a law school or a certificate of admission to the state courts—that we require something more: a demonstration that he has had a certain minimal experience in the trial courts of his state.

*Interview/ U.S. News & World Report, 3-31:31.*

*3*

. . . action or lack of action not even intended to injure the Judicial Branch can pose great dangers. The injury can come from constantly expanding the burdens and jurisdiction of Federal courts without providing the additional judges and needed staffs and equipment to keep the work up-to-date; and it can come from freezing salaries of judges for more than six years in a period of drastic inflation, thus, in economic effect, reducing their real income in violation of at least the spirit of the Constitution. The danger even more to be feared than direct attack, therefore, is neglect and inertia concerning the needs of the courts.

*Before American Society of Newspaper Editors, Washington/ The Wall Street Journal, 7-11:8.*

**Donald Cressey**
*Professor of sociology, University of California, Santa Barbara*

*4*

There is always a tendency to judicialize everything that goes wrong in our criminal-justice system. The judge has one pill in his little black bag; its called judicialization. Is there something wrong down at the police station? Are the police interrogating suspects unfairly? What's the solution? The solution is to run the lawyers in and make it into a trial, an adversary proceeding. Are the probation departments revoking probation unfairly? What's the solution? A trial, judicialize it. Do the inmates have grievances; do they claim they are being victimized in their own inmate disciplinary court? Send for the lawyers; judicialize it. The trouble with that is that solutions are stuck into these problems, but no one ever examines why the problems arose in the first place. Nobody looks to see why it is that police are misbehaving down at the station, or why the prison disciplinary procedures are not working.

*Panel discussion, Center for the Study of Democratic Institutions, Santa Barbara, Calif./ The Center Magazine, Nov.-Dec.:9.*

**Edward M. Davis**
*Chief of Police of Los Angeles*

*5*

. . . judges should be selected not only for their excellent knowledge of the law, but should learn more about human behavior. I think a judge's education is very imperfect when it comes to the sentencing process. He must make a determination of treatment, and he's ill-equipped to do it by virtue of his training . . . If it's impossible to change a sociopath, and if a person is a sociopath, then the judge must be able to make a hard judgment. He must be able to, if necessary, say, "I am going to sentence this person to life imprisonment." Now, that is a very ulcer-producing tough kind of a judgment for any of us to make, and I think judges have to bring themselves to making these kind of tough decisions. They can't be like the little girl who wanted to wear her mother's girdle but didn't have the guts.

*Interview/Human Events, 3-22:9.*

# WHAT THEY SAID IN 1975

*(EDWARD M. DAVIS)*

1

I think the great problem with the American court system is the excrutiating turtle's pace. In Great Britain, they get everything done in a period of 60 days, and here it takes six years to do the same thing. It's an example of due process in America having become an amorphous mass, a sort of non-ending, constantly expanding monster.

*Interview/The National Observer, 7-19:14.*

**Thomas Ehrlich**
*Dean, Stanford University School of Law*

2

...I do think people are putting too much reliance on courts. I also believe that courts are too prone to take on problems that they have no business getting into. For example: To me, the idea of a court deciding whether or not girls should be permitted to play Little League baseball is ludicrous. Congress, too, contributes to this glut, which I call legal pollution. We see the effects in our university. To prove our compliance with all the Federal rules and regulations requires a huge staff, an enormous amount of paper work, and thousands of hours of expensive lawyer work.

*Interview, Washington/*
*U.S. News & World Report, 7-21:50.*

**James D. Fellers**
*President, American Bar Association*

3

To be blunt, if Federal judicial salaries are not raised, and soon, the quality of justice in our society might well suffer ... A significant number of judges presently on the bench are reported to be considering resigning during 1975 if a salary increase is not forthcoming. A very significant number of lawyers [approached about serving on the Federal bench have declined, largely] because of the financial sacrifices which would be required.

*Los Angeles Times, 2-24:(1)4.*

4

Lawyers spend hours and hours doing nonsubstantive, non-legal work. We proofread; we often do 100 per cent of estate-planning when,

in fact, our special knowledge is really required for no more than 10 per cent of the period. We do all of the interviewing, all of the telephoning, and on and on. For example, in estate-planning—when a lawyer does every stitch of the work—the cost of the plan might well be two times or three times as much as it would be if a lawyer became involved only when his special professional expertise was required ... In my opinion, lawyers do not unfairly charge their clients. Rather, they simply do not dispense legal services efficiently.

*Before lawyers, Washington, May 29/*
*Los Angeles Times, 5-30:(1)20.*

**Gerald R. Ford**
*President of the United States*

5

[On the type of person he would appoint as a U.S. Supreme Court Justice]: My feeling is that first you have to have a person who is very qualified in law as such. On the other hand, I don't think you can exclude certain classes of individuals because they don't happen to be a practicing lawyer. We have some very knowledgeable people in the law who might have other current occupations. So, they have to have competence, a very high competence in the law, but that doesn't mean they have to be restricted within a certain framework.

*Before students,*
*Stanford University, Sept. 21/*
*Los Angeles Times, 9-22:(1)9.*

**Marvin E. Frankel**
*Judge, United States District Court*
*for the Southern District of New York*

6

Employed by interested parties, the [adversary] process often achieves truth only as a convenience, a by-product, or an accidental approximation. The business of the advocate, simply stated, is to win if possible without violating the law ... His is not the search for truth as such [and] truth and victory are mutually incompatible for some considerable percentage of the attorneys trying cases at any given time.

*The National Observer, 11-1:14.*

**Marshall J. Hartman**
*Director of defense services, National*
*Legal Aid and Defender Association*
1

Plea-bargaining situations vary, of course, but the bottom line usually is that a guy pleads guilty because he's been advised he'll get less time than he would if he took a trial. It's a rotten and immoral system that threatens to give a man more jail time for exercising his right to trial.

*Los Angeles Times, 2-25:(1)1.*

**Howell Heflin**
*Chief Justice of Alabama*
2

I think I would be remiss if I did not call to ... attention an almost universal violation of the separation-of-powers concept. I am speaking of the performance of non-judicial functions by members of the judiciary for either the Executive or Legislative Branches. Judges are frequently appointed as the head or members of study commissions and groups. The participation of [U.S.] Chief Justice Earl Warren as a member of the Warren Commission, which made a non-judicial study of the assassination of President Kennedy, in my judgment, was a violation of the concept of separation of powers. Many states require Chief Justices and other judges to serve on selection or nominating panels concerning non-judicial offices. This involvement should be eliminated, not only because it violates the separation-of-powers doctrine, but because it affords the opportunity for political entanglements.

*At National Conference of State Legislatures, Philadelphia, Oct. 8/Vital Speeches, 12-1:115.*

**Roman L. Hruska**
*United States Senator,*
*R—Nebraska*
3

[Advocating a national court of appeals]: We believe that under this plan the national court would be able to decide at least 150 cases on the merits each year, thus doubling the national appellate capacity. The effect would be to bring at an early time greater clarity and stability to the national law ... Far from increasing the cost of litigation, cost measured in

both time and money, it should serve to expedite resolution of national issues, to reduce the incidence of purposeless relitigation and, overall, to effect speed and economies.

*At National Conference on Appellate Justice, Coronado, Calif., Jan. 26/ Los Angeles Times, 1-27:(1)13.*

**Leon Jaworski**
*Lawyer; Former special government*
*prosecutor for Watergate*
4

There will be failures and scandals involving members of the legal profession from time to time, just as there are scandals among the members of other professions, regardless of the action the legal profession takes to discipline itself. What constitutes my overriding concern is the attitude of indifference exhibited to the preservation of the profession as one of trust and honor, not only by lawyers who have practiced at the bar for decades but as well by those who are entering the profession in current times.

*Before American Bar Association, Chicago, Feb. 22/The New York Times, 2-23:(1)39.*

5

[Saying plea-bargaining is not so bad a practice as some claim]: The American public has demanded that the story of Watergate be known and, through the processes of justice under law, they have been made known. And I can assure you that had it not been for perfectly fair and just plea discussions, the full story of the break-in and cover-up would never have been known.

*At John Jay College of Criminal Justice commencement, New York, June 1/ Los Angeles Times, 6-2:(1)2.*

6

In these days, when justice miscarries, we find it paraded in prominent headlines, and reformer-activists as well as those who seek radical changes in our system—for which they offer no substitute—talk ceaselessly about it, often dramatizing their comments so as to distort the facts. [A book sites three cases to] demonstrate that our system is a failure. An errant judge is held up as a typical administra-

*(LEON JAWORSKI)*

tor of our process. These unfair characterizations ignore the innumerable trials daily held in which the cause of justice is served well. They ignore the countless dedicated judges who daily administer the law impartially and honorably.

*Before American Bar Association, Montreal,*
*Aug. 8/The New York Times, 8-9:18.*

**Edward H. Levi**
*Attorney General of the United States*
1

The law is a servant of our society. Its enforcement administration can give more effective meaning to our common goals—among them domestic tranquility, the blessings of liberty, the establishment of justice. These goals do not bring themselves into being. If we are to have a government of laws and not of men, then it particularly takes dedicated men and women to accomplish this through their zeal and determination, and also their concern for fairness and impartiality . . . We have lived in a time of change and corrosive skepticism and cynicism concerning the administration of justice. Nothing can more weaken the quality of life or more imperil the realization of the goals we all hold dear than our failures to make clear by word and deed that our law is not an instrument for partisan purposes and it is not an instrument to be used in ways which are careless of the higher values within all of us.

*At his swearing-in ceremony, Washington,*
*Feb. 7/The Washington Post, 2-11:(A)14.*

2

Law is not everything in society. The law is only one of a number of institutions through which we express ourselves and which in turn influence us, maintain our customs and change our habits. Thus, law takes a place along with family structures, religious beliefs, the expressions of art and the explanations of science . . . The public, the press, the academic community, the artists, all by their assertions and conduct inform and develop the law.

*At dedication of law-school building,*
*University of Nebraska/*
*Los Angeles Times, 5-23:(2)7.*

**Thomas J. Madden**
*General Counsel, Law Enforcement Assistance*
*Administration of the United States*
3

[Criticizing plea-bargaining] : Is this the way our system was intended to work? Comparatively few of the crimes that are committed are reported. Few are arrested, then fewer are charged, and still fewer come to trial, as they enter the plea-bargaining process instead. We really have no way of knowing whether our system of justice works, because the system doesn't have a chance.

*Interview/Los Angeles Times, 2-25:(1)1.*

**Thurgood Marshall**
*Associate Justice, Supreme Court of*
*the United States*
4

[The Federal Judiciary is] a small and rather intimate branch of government that on the whole has done its task well in an era when the other branches are constantly accusing one another of doing their tasks poorly or not at all.

*At Law Day dinner of*
*Federal Bar Council, New York/*
*The Dallas Times Herald, 5-22:(B)10.*

**James F. Neal**
*Former chief prosecutor*
*at the Watergate trial*
5

Many things sound like a lack of equal justice. You prosecute some people, and don't prosecute others, for a multitude of reasons. It must be this way. You use some people for witnesses and prosecute others. That's a necessary part of law enforcement.

*Interview/U.S. News & World Report, 1-13:17.*

**Charles B. Renfrew**
*Judge, United States District Court for*
*the Northern District of California*
6

[On the problem of sentencing] : What the hell do you do? In some cases, particularly the first ones I had, I'd wrestle with them, waking up sometimes in the middle of the night . . . Often you just don't have enough information about the person you're going to sentence. You have someone's life in your hands and you're thinking, do I send him to prison for six years? Four years? Seven years? In a way, it's very presumptuous to be a judge. You feel unequal to it. I suppose the only thing that keeps you going is that the job has to be done and that other human beings are doing the job, too.

*Interview/*
*Los Angeles Times, 10-22:(1)29.*

## David Riesman
*Sociologist,*
*Harvard University*                                            1

I would like to see the time come when the massive hemorrhage of some of our best talents into the [field of] law will cease. I have in mind not so much those who seek what may be an illusory economic security or prosperity, but rather those who seek an imitation of [consumerist] Ralph Nader, a greater social usefulness. Our country is already sufficiently litigation-prone and legalistic. The over-supply of lawyers not only helps create its own demand but can get in the way of solving problems. For what in my judgment the country needs are managers and planners—women and men trained in demography, economics, statistics, history and some knowledge of other cultures. In spite of a few efforts, most do not learn these things in law school but rather a kind of omnipotent belief that there's nothing except perhaps a patent case that they cannot get up in a pre-trial [in] two weeks.

*Before American Sociological Association,*
*Chicago/The New York Times, 8-30:17.*

## Arthur Rosett
*Professor of law, University of*
*California, Los Angeles*                                       2

Plea-bargaining is just the visible tip of the discretionary system—deciding who shall be punished, at what level and with what sentence. The whole criminal-justice system is discretionary—from the police pick-up to the court . . . A major reason for plea-bargaining is the inadequacy of criminal law. The definition of crime is such that much of what is defined as criminal behavior is not. Robbery covers everything from an armed stick-up to two kids fighting over a ball. And the law is often too severe.

Grand theft—which, according to the penal code, could be stealing the carcass of a jackass or $5 worth of avocados—carries the minimum penalty of 10 years imprisonment. We need discretion to make the law meaningful.

*Los Angeles Herald-Examiner,*
*11-30:(A)16.*

## John J. Sirica
*Chief Judge, United States District Court*
*for the District of Columbia*                                 3

In an attempt to arrive at a just and fair sentence, a court of criminal justice usually takes into consideration the purpose or purposes to be served by imposing a particular sentence on a particular individual. There may be said to be, among others, four primary reasons that are normally considered in this respect. These are: First, incarceration for the protection of society; second, the matter of punishment; third, the possibility of rehabilitation and the effect of the sentence on the defendants and their families; and fourth, the deterrent effect that the sentence might have on others who may be tempted to commit the same types of crimes . . .

*At sentencing of Watergate defendants,*
*Washington, Feb. 21/*
*The New York Times, 2-22:10.*

4

When a judge loses control of his courtroom and permits lawyers to run the trial, that judge should hang up his robe permanently, for he is no longer able to perform his judicial duties . . . I don't think there is a judge who has sat on the bench who has not lost his patience or temper as a result of the action of some lawyer. . . . as a trial lawyer, I was hard-pressed to control my own temper due to anxiety or frustration, especially in an emotionally charged case. And a few times I can remember making an in-court statement or addressing a judge in such a way that now, as a judge, I would not tolerate coming from a lawyer.

*Before American Bar Association,*
*Montreal, Aug. 12/*
*Los Angeles Times, 8-3:(1)12.*

# WHAT THEY SAID IN 1975

**Justin A. Stanley**
*President-elect designate,*
*American Bar Association*  1

If we cannot deliver justice, we will have injustice. If we cannot deliver legal services at reasonable costs to those who need them, we fail in an obligation and we undermine our whole system. Therefore, we must be receptive to the notion of group legal services, prepaid legal insurance, legal clinics and the like.

*Before State Bar of Texas, Dallas, July 3/*
*The Dallas Times Herald, 7-4:(C)4.*

**John P. Stevens**
*Associate Justice-designate,*
*Supreme Court of the United States*  2

It is the business of a judge to decide cases on the narrowest grounds possible and not to reach out for Constitutional questions. [As a judge,] you don't have the freedom to substitute your own views for the law.

*At Senate Judiciary Committee hearing*
*on his nomination, Washington/*
*U.S. News & World Report, 12-29:40.*

**Meldrim Thomson, Jr.**
*Governor of New Hampshire (R)*  3

If we're ever going to turn this country around, we'll have to do something about the Federal judiciary ... I'm sick and tired not only of them coming in on this anti-busing thing, but of seeing them delay the construction of roads, pipelines, refineries and all the other things. That power should be taken away from the Federal courts at once if this great nation of ours is to progress ever again.

*At Public Affairs Luncheon Club, Dallas/*
*The Dallas Times Herald, 10-21:(B)4.*

**John K. Van de Kamp**
*District Attorney,*
*Los Angeles County, California*  4

If I accomplish one thing in my term as District Attorney it is to eliminate the use of the expression "plea bargaining" from our vocabulary, and at the same time eliminate those features of case settlement that have jus-

tified the use of the term. Bargaining belongs in the marketplace, not [in] the system of justice.

*At his swearing-in ceremony, Los Angeles,*
*Oct. 14/Los Angeles Times, 10-15:(1)1.*

**Lawrence E. Walsh**
*President, American Bar Association*  5

[Expressing doubts about the advisability of lawyers advertising their services]: [I] have a low view of the merits of advertising, not only in law practice but in the commercial field. It is more designed to sell a service or product rather than help the public make a decision ... I think we should have an open mind on the subject, but a tough mind. I don't think advertising should become a symbol of true progress.

*News conference, Los Angeles, Sept. 24/*
*Los Angeles Times, 9-25:(2)3.*

**Lord Widgery**
*Lord Chief Justice of England*  6

[On court procedure in his country]: We have made a great thing, from the very beginning, of the necessity of disposing of criminal cases quickly. We've regarded delay as being one of the major enemies. And we have tailored all our work with a view to getting the case on, because, for one thing, if you get the case on quickly, you don't have to bother so much about bail, you don't have to bother so much about pre-trial publicity and things like that. And within the last three years, we have had a complete review of our criminal-court procedures from top to bottom and have got a new system which is better than the old. Now we're getting our cases through faster than at any time in my experience.

*Interview, Washington/*
*U.S. News & World Report, 1-27:45.*

**Evelle J. Younger**
*Attorney General of California*  7

[Saying perhaps restrictions on lawyers advertising their services should be liberalized[: I am as cognizant as anyone of the potential dangers in advertising. It's not in anyone's interest to market legal services like underarm deodorants. But that's not the issue. The problem is that ordinary people simply don't know how to find a lawyer. And since they don't know how to look for one, they don't try. Advertising reform can do a lot to solve the access problem, because it will make it easier for people to find the attorney that they need.

*Before State Bar of California, Los Angeles, Sept. 22/Los Angeles Times, 9-23:(2)1.*

# National Defense · The Military

**Robert Anderson**
*President, Rockwell International*
1

A United States Congressman, an opponent of the B-1 [bomber], recently denounced Rockwell International because we had the temerity to point out, in our information material, that the B-1, in addition to being an essential part of national defense, was also aiding the American economy. We don't think it's wrong to say that the greatest pool of scientific, engineering and technical talent in the world is developing that airplane. We don't think it's wrong to point out that over 5,000 subcontractors and supplier companies in 48 states are taking part in the B-1 research-and-development program. Why should we keep from the American people the fact that the B-1 program, through 1985, will add more than $56-billion to the gross national product, that it will provide a potential 192,000 jobs, that it will be responsible for the payment of more than $17-billion in Federal and state taxes? Why should this be kept secret at a time when Congress is spending billions of dollars in trying to find jobs for unemployed Americans.
*At Federal Procurement Conference,*
*Los Angeles, April 4/\*\**

2

Through the years, the weaponry on which the Air Force and its sister services have relied to protect this country and its people has borne one primary hallmark: It has been the best of its day—superior to that hurled against it. It was strong enough to crush the forces of aggression in Europe and Asia in the 1940s. It forestalled the take-over of South Korea in the '50s. It served effectively in Southeast Asia in the '60s. However, I believe the greatest achievement of this powerful force has been as a deterrent to the outbreak of world-wide hostilities by instilling in potential aggressors a fear of overwhelming and devastating response. That these defensive systems have been available when needed is a credit

to our national civilian and military leadership who have worked so diligently to maintain world order and, if I may say so, to our country's aerospace industry, which has responded to the requirements of that leadership. The foundation of our nation's strength has been the combined efforts of a strong and flexible military, equipped by an industry that has specialized in transforming into operational hardware the technological innovations that our military has required. This was true in 1776, when hand-forged muskets *won* our freedom. And it is true as we enter 1976, when complex weapon systems stand guard to *preserve* our freedom.
*Before American Defense Preparedness*
*Association, Los Angeles, Oct. 15/\*\**

**Les Aspin**
*United States Representative,*
*D—Wisconsin*
3

[On Congressional relations with the Defense Department]: The advantages the Pentagon has over the Congressman are obvious. It's got massive amounts of information, and massive counter-attack ability. But think of the advantages the Congressman has got. First of all, his office is small and compact. We all know what each of us is doing. Over there it's so damn big and nobody knows what the hell they're doing. So you call one guy and you call another guy. What you do is call 15 different guys and put things together. Another thing you take advantage of is their turnover.
*The Washington Post, 3-2:(B)3.*

**M. G. Bayne**
*Vice Admiral, United States Navy;*
*Commandant, National War College*
4

[On whether the Joint Chiefs of Staff should question or say "No" to the President if they disagree with him over a military issue]: There is no diminution now in any way among the military in loyalty or support for the country. Men in uniform take an oath to defend the Constitution. I sense no change, whatsoever, among the military of their understanding of the need for an orderly command and control process, responsible to civilian decisions. When an order is given, there is no suggestion of questioning the mission. What is being discussed is the question of loyalty and responsibility within the chain of command. The essence of loyalty is to never allow your superior, through your own lack of effort, to make a mistake. Your position in a questionable situation is to convince your superior that he is wrong. If he persists, you have to disassociate yourself. You have to leave. You have to stand up and be counted.

*U.S. News & World Report, 6-16:46.*

**Carl Bernard**
*Professor of military science,*
*University of California, Berkeley*
1

I've got this thorough conviction after 30 years in the military that stupidity is triumphant.
*San Francisco Examiner & Chronicle,*
*1-26:(This World)2.*

**George S. Brown**
*General, United States Air Force;*
*Chairman, Joint Chiefs of Staff*
2

It is often overlooked that detente—the process of reducing tensions with the Soviet Union—has been possible because of American strength and resolve. It was after a prolonged period of cold-war testing and confrontation, during which the United States and the rest of the free world stood fast, that it became possible to move forward with the Soviet Union in negotiations aimed at reducing the chances for grave miscalculations and reducing the risk of nuclear war. In these negotiations, we must continue to safeguard our vital defense interests. To weaken our defense is to weaken the foundation of detente.
*Before Veterans of Foreign Wars,*
*Los Angeles, Aug. 21/*
*Vital Speeches, 9-15:709.*

**Howard H. Callaway**
*Secretary of the Army of the United States*
3

[On the all-volunteer Army]: The Army is not going soft. If we offer good pay, decent living standards and opportunity, we have the right to expect professional performance. So now when the soldier won't meet our standards . . . we fire him . . . We provide competitive wages and offer some tremendous opportunities, and we expect the soldier to produce. With a draftee, the first thing you had to do with him was let him know he was in the Army. You had to get his attention. So we shaved his head, stacked him up two high, 36 men across on both sides of the aisle in a two-decked wooden barracks. We didn't want him to confuse the Army with home. We gave him the platoon sergeant to keep his metabolism stimulated. Now our all-volunteer Army has just got to be different. And by different I don't mean softer— or less combat-ready. Being combat-ready and trained to fight is our business, and we won't sacrifice professionalism to make life easy.
*Before civic club, Atlanta/*
*The Dallas Times Herald, 5-19:(A)12.*

**William P. Clements, Jr.**
*Deputy Secretary of Defense*
*of the United States*
4

It is becoming fashionable in some quarters of late . . . to charge that military force is outmoded in the modern world. It is argued that modern weaponry, especially nuclear armaments, are too destructive to use, and that therefore they won't be used. Further, it is argued that the military power that we applied did not produce the results we wanted in Southeast Asia, nor did it shield us from an oil-price rise that has caused considerable economic problems for us in the aftermath of the Middle East war of 1973. Finally, the advocates of the idea that military forces are outmoded frequently also assert that the Soviet Union is unlikely to attack in any event. Detente, they maintain, means that future conflicts will be non-violent ones and may be settled by negotiation. It is worth noting that this is far from the first time in history that such arguments have

# WHAT THEY SAID IN 1975

*(WILLIAM P. CLEMENTS, JR.)*

been heard. At one time or another, it has been variously asserted that the advent of the machine gun, lighter-than-air craft, the submarine and the bomber had made warfare so destructive that it could never occur again. Yet we know that nothing of the sort happened. The world has adopted these once-unthinkable weapons and gone on to new ones. Indeed, arguments that military forces have been outmoded ignore a basic fact of international politics—one that has been proven repeatedly throughout history: National interests can be guarded and promoted only by strength, and, in our ever-changing world, strength means military strength.

*Before Council on World Affairs, Dallas, April 10/Vital Speeches, 5-15:458.*

1

Savings is a misnomer when speaking of weapons programs and the Defense Department. We have a mission to perform. I'm not looking for a cheap defense unless it is a better defense.

*U.S. News & World Report, 8-18:28.*

**Paul Doty**
*Professor of biochemistry,*
*Harvard University*

2

We and the Soviet Union will soon face a reckoning. For a dozen years, since the partial [nuclear] test-ban treaty of 1963, treaties have been made, roughly one a year, and now with the conclusion of a treaty based on the Vladivostok agreement [of 1974], we will have come to the end of what can be done without actually limiting strategic weapons. With the exception of the ABM treaty, no serious limitations are yet in view; no new weapons systems have been cut back; no new developments have been stopped. The SALT II treaty we expect will bring us to the brink of really controlling strategic arms; either we will move forward into a new era, or arms-control will have failed.

*Before Senate Foreign Relations Subcommittee on Arms Control, Washington, April 16/ The Washington Post, 4-17:(A)2.*

**Russell E. Dougherty**
*General, United States Air Force;*
*Commander,*
*Strategic Air Command*

3

Our ability [to defend ourselves] is inherent in our strategic systems. We want to be able to do anything, anywhere, any time, and with absolute assurance. But, of course, the strategy this country would take would be up to the President.

*News conference, Los Angeles, July 1/ Los Angeles Herald-Examiner, 7-1:(A)2.*

**Gerald R. Ford**
*President of the United States*

4

There is a fashionable line of thinking in America today—as widespread as it is false—that all we need to do to get Federal spending back in line is to hack away at the defense establishment . . . Unfortunately, it is an error that seems to be endemic to Western democracies in times of peace. Again and again, while totalitarian powers of one kind or another have maintained or expanded their strength in peacetime, the democracies—primarily in the West—have neglected strong national and allied defense. . . . the fashion is to deride excessive defense spending. The fact of the matter is that defense outlays have been a dwindling part of our gross national product, falling from 8.9 per cent in 1969 to less than 6 per cent by 1976. If the current declining defense trend continues, we will soon see the day—and so will others—when our country no longer has the strength necessary to guarantee our freedom, to guarantee our security in an uneasy world. We cannot let this happen.

*Before The Conference Board, Washington, Jan. 22/ U.S. News & World Report, 2-3:71.*

5

There are people in the Congress and people throughout the United States who will want in one way or another—I don't challenge their motives—who seek to undercut and make less effective our military capability. It's my deep conviction that peace depends upon a strong defense—a strong Army, Navy, Air Force,

Marines, Coast Guard. The new defense budget that I submitted is a big budget [but] it is a defense budget that is needed, is required to keep us free. To slash that budget, because of some preconceived ideas or without adequate information, is a gamble with our future, our security, our freedom and . . . the chances for our common goal of peace.

*At Women's Forum on National Security,*
*Washington, Feb. 25/*
*Los Angeles Herald-Examiner, 2-25:(A)2.*

1

A posture of deliberate weakness is most dangerous when the world-wide military balance threatens to deteriorate. But, at any time, weakness would be folly for the United States, a great nation with interests spanning the globe. Like it or not, we are a great power, and our real choice is whether to succeed or fail in a role we cannot shirk. There is no other nation in the free world capable of stepping into our role . . . It is of fundamental importance to both the United States and the world at large that the strategic balance be maintained—and strategic nuclear forces are the foundation of our defense. We will work toward further strategic arms limitations; we will maintain a strategic arms balance.

*Before Daughters of the American*
*Revolution, Washington, April 15/*
*Los Angeles Herald-Examiner, 4-15:(A)2.*

2

Today, our fleet of 501 ships is the smallest since 1939, two years before Pearl Harbor. And it is still shrinking. However good their intentions, those who claim that America is over-armed and over-spending on defense are dead wrong. We cannot afford to cut any further without endangering our national security.

*Before Navy League, New Orleans, April 23/*
*Los Angeles Times, 4-24:(1)9.*

3

Today's Army is not only an Army of volunteers. It is an Army of winners, and it is truly representative of the American people. As a matter of fact, the Army is attracting better-educated, better-qualified and highly skilled young men and women into its ranks than ever

before. And most importantly . . . this new Army has kept intact the *esprit de corps* which 200 years of history and tradition have instilled.

*Fort Benning, Ga., June 14/*
*The New York Times, 6-15:(1)1.*

4

Now that Americans are no longer fighting on any front, there are many sincere, but in my judgment shortsighted, Americans who believe that the billions for defense could be better spent for social programs to help the poor and disadvantaged. But I am convinced that adequate spending for national defense is an insurance policy, an insurance policy for peace we cannot afford to be without. It's most valuable if we never need to use it. But without it we could be wiped out. Certainly, the most important social obligation of government is to guarantee all citizens, including the disadvantaged, sufficient protection of their lives and freedom against outside attack. Today that protection is our principal hope of peace. What expense item in our Federal budget is more essential? This is one place where second best is worth nothing.

*At American Legion convention, Minneapolis,*
*Aug. 19/The New York Times, 8-20:12.*

5

The United States must be constant and credible when we speak of American strength at home and on the seas of the world. My aim is not to train America's youth for war, nor to develop weapons to kill. My aim is to develop the military strength which is our mightiest hope for peace.

*At Marine Corps' 200th birthday ceremony,*
*Arlington, Va., Nov. 10/*
*The New York Times, 11-11:40.*

6

Defense is the only part of the Federal budget the Congress cuts with a vengeance. If this trend continues to the year 2000, according to mathematical projections, the United States defense will be reduced to one soldier carrying one rifle—just like the statue at Concord Bridge.

*San Francisco Examiner & Chronicle,*
*11-15:(This World)2.*

# WHAT THEY SAID IN 1975

**Fred R. Harris**
*Former United States Senator, D—Oklahoma* 1

Cut our obese defense budget ... If the Russians don't have any better sense than to spend themselves into bankruptcy with unnecessary military expenditures, we ought not to follow suit.

*U.S. News & World Report, 12-1:22.*

**James L. Holloway III**
*Admiral, United States Navy;*
*Chief of Naval Operations* 2

Technology has not changed the basic fact that it is more difficult for a hostile nation to cross the water than to cross a land barrier. Therefore, our defenses are drawn on the other side of the water barriers. So we really need allies on the other side of the water barriers to have an effective defense perimeter.

*U.S. News & World Report, 7-7:27.*

3

I have a very simple formula for determining the size of a navy, and it has three factors. The first is: What is the strategy that your navy is obligated to carry out? Second: What is the threat to that navy in carrying out its prescribed strategy? And third: What risk is the country willing to take in seeing that strategy achieved? Now, in our case, our country has a forward strategy. We are overseas-oriented economically, politically. Our military strategy uses the oceans as barriers in our defense and as avenues of extending national influence. And to implement a forward strategy we need a certain kind of navy—a navy that has carriers to provide air power overseas where we don't have bases. We need big ships because we have to operate far away from our own bases. And we need a certain number of ships because we have to have operating fleets that have the ability to conduct offensive operations, to defend themselves, to defend our allies, to defend our own forward-deployed forces. The threat to the Navy's ability to carry out its share of the national strategy is the Soviet Navy and maritime air. When we look into the future—at the capability of our Navy to carry out its missions, and the effectiveness of the Soviet Navy in preventing us from carrying out our missions—

we feel that we ought to have a Navy of about 600 ships. The final element is risk. If we wanted to be able to execute the strategy on a virtual no-risk basis—that is, be almost assured of winning—I personally believe we would need at least 800 ships and probably 18 to 20 carriers in the mid-'80s. But it's not realistic to anticipate that in a five-year building program we're going to be able to expand that fast. We can reach a Navy of about 600 ships, and with a Navy of that size we have an improved ability to maintain our forward strategy in the 1980s.

*Interview, Washington/*
*U.S. News & World Report, 10-20:61.*

**Fred C. Ikle**
*Director, Arms Control and Disarmament*
*Agency of the United States* 4

The truth is that we are basically defenseless in the United States against threats of nuclear attack that could come from a great many different sources rather than from one or two clearly identifiable potential adversaries ... Imagine the morning after a nuclear explosive has destroyed half an American city. How are we going to apply our theories of mutual deterrence, of first strike and second strike, if we cannot tell whose nuclear explosive it was? Or even if we could tell, but it turned out to be an organization such as might exist in the future— an organization with dedicated people but no clearly defined national territory.

*The New York Times, 5-11:(4)19.*

**Edward M. Kennedy**
*United States Senator,*
*D—Massachusetts* 5

Are we going to take seriously our commitment to curtail the conventional arms race? Or are we going to continue to follow a policy of indiscriminately selling as many weapons as a country wants—as long as it has the cash? If we choose the latter course, then we will be lending credence to one of the worst accusations leveled at this country by our critics—that, for its very livelihood, the economy of the United States depends on a military-industrial complex that cannot be stopped, cannot be controlled.

*Before the Senate, Washington, Feb. 22/*
*The New York Times, 2-23:(1)11.*

**Henry A. Kissinger**
*Secretary of State of the United States*

1

Deterrence is greatest when military strength is coupled with the willingness to employ it. It is achieved when one side's readiness to run risks in relation to the other is high; it is least effective when the willingness to run risks is low, however powerful the military capability.

*The New York Times Magazine, 10-26:93.*

**William P. Mack**
*Vice Admiral, United States Navy;*
*Superintendent, U.S. Naval Academy*

2

As I complete 42 years of service, I would like to leave to the brigade of midshipman a legacy of one idea which represents the distillation of that experience . . . There are many other important concepts. But the one concept which dominates my mind is that of the necessity of listening to and protecting the existence of the dissenter—the person who does not necessarily agree with his commander, or with popularly held opinion, or with you. Unfortunately, history is full of examples—then-Commander Mahan, whose novel ideas of sea power fell on barren ground; then-Commander Sims, whose revolutionary—but correct—ideas on naval gunnery ran counter to those of his seniors; then-Commander Rickover, who fought a lone battle for nuclear power. All eventually succeeded—but *not* with the help of patient, understanding naval officers. Regretfully, each needed help from outside . . . I am not advocating the overthrow of the principle of loyalty to command as we know it. Of course you should support the continuation of the idea of carrying out all lawful orders cheerfully and fully once decisions are made. There is no other way. In the future, I hope some of you will be the best and brightest, but by all means listen to the others—they may be *right*.

*Upon his retirement/*
*The Washington Post, 8-16:(A)14.*

**Mike Mansfield**
*United States Senator, D–Montana*

3

[Criticizing military spending]: A massive outpouring of military equipment, year in and

year out, has distorted the domestic situation of the nation. While we are turning out ever-more-refined military equipment, more nations are doing better [by] producing electronic equipment, pollution-free automobiles, and are buying U.S. resources for manufacture and resale to the United States.

*Burlington, Vt., March 2/*
*The Dallas Times Herald, 3-3:(A)2.*

**Eugene J. McCarthy**
*Former United States Senator,*
*D–Minnesota*

4

I don't think [Presidents] ought to open up [inaugural addresses] by declaring war on the whole world . . . Most of them know what our military power is anyway. Our attitude toward the world would, I hope, be closer to the attitude reflected by Thomas Jefferson when he talks about a "decent respect for the opinion of mankind," instead of a rather arrogant assertion of our military power and of our disposition to use it.

*Interview, Washington/*
*The Christian Science Monitor, 7-23:6.*

**George S. McGovern**
*United States Senator, D–South Dakota*

5

With the purveyors and profiteers of militarism, there can be no compromise. We cannot tell the lie that America will be a prosperous and progressive society while we squander our resources on overkill and overruns and for a feast of weapons to nourish dictatorship around the world. Military waste worsens inflation as it worsens the arms race.

*Quote, 6-22:577.*

**J. William Middendorf II**
*Secretary of the Navy of the United States*

6

For the first time in this nation's history, we are challenged by a powerful threat from the sea. For the last 200 years the Atlantic and Pacific Oceans have been a protective cloak for America, protective buffers which enabled our first President, George Washington, to warn against "entangling alliances." Today, this protective cloak is infested with deadly spiders. This very day, stealthy Soviet ballistic-missile

# WHAT THEY SAID IN 1975

submarines—the "jaws" of Soviet seapower—are on patrol off both our coasts. And Soviet surface ships have circumnavigated one of our states—Hawaii. The build-up of the modern Soviet Navy is unprecedented. From a coastal-defense navy in the 1950s, the Soviets have, since 1962, outbuilt us in every category of ship except aircraft carriers. Today, the Soviet Navy has more than two and a half times the number of submarines as your [U.S.] Navy and almost twice the number of major surface combatants as the U.S. Navy. The Soviets have deployed aboard their ships highly sophisticated sensors, electronics and offensive and defensive weapons systems. They have developed an arsenal of some 20 types of anti-ship-capable missiles and their variants. Having ranges from 20 to 400 miles, these missiles can be fired from aircraft, surface ships and submerged submarines ... We therefore face one of the most significant challenges to our maritime superiority since the end of World War II. That challenge is to rebuild the U.S. fleet to such a size and have sufficient ships of various capabilities that it can do the job assigned in support of our national strategy.

*Before National Security Commission and*
*Committee of the American Legion,*
*Minneapolis, Aug. 15/*
*Vital Speeches, 9-15:706,707.*

## Louis Mountbatten
*Admiral, British Navy (Ret.); Former Chief*
*of the British Defense Staff* 1

Up to 1914, we [Britain] had unrivaled naval power in the world; then gradually during that war [World War I] you [the U.S.] saw the point of it. In the Second World War, you grasped it fully—that the way to control the world is through the Navy and not through the Army. The Air Force merely supports the Navy in these things. You learned the lesson. Now the Russians have learned it. They realize you control the world through the navies. As a sailor, I say this is right. It is quite obvious that any sensible person would understand that if you wish to have great influence and power, you do it through the Navy. Then you come

down to intercontinental ballistic missiles. You can't use them because if you use them it will be the end of civilization. So the only way you can influence world affairs and, in effect, control the world, without nuclear war, is through the Navy.

*Interview, London/*
*Los Angeles Herald-Examiner, 7-2:(A)8.*

## Samuel C. Phillips
*General, United States Air Force;*
*Commander, Air Force Systems Command* 2

Despite reductions in manpower and the dollar squeeze ... I am confident that American strength is still sufficient to protect America's liberty. We remain strong because we have very loyal, knowledgeable defense-minded citizens, from the President on down, looking after the defense interests of the United States. Even our critics in Congress, I believe, favor a strong America. Disagreements arise over means, not ends, over how much strength is necessary, not *whether* it is necessary. In the military services, likewise, we have loyal men and women who have put their careers, if not their lives, on the line to keep the United States strong, free and in search of peace. We have done it through peacetime service and wartime sacrifice. We have done it through determined effort to design, develop and deploy weapon systems that military planners and combat veterans consider indispensable. We have done it by accepting restrictions, reductions and realignments without shirking our responsibility to do the best job possible to protect our heritage and insure future survival.

*At Rotary Club luncheon,*
*San Diego, Calif., April 19/*
*Vital Speeches, 5-1:447.*

## William Proxmire
*United States Senator,*
*D—Wisconsin* 3

[Criticizing Generals and Admirals for having enlisted men as servants and demanding home amenities paid for by the government]: It's like a giant balloon: You squeeze one end and the air rushes to the other. When Congress cuts out funds for military servants, the response is to put $1.1-million in the next budget for doing the same things the servants were doing originally. The Generals and Admirals can't seem to find time to keep up these homes for which they pay no rent. So they establish a "pamper fund" to use taxpayers' funds to provide the creature comforts the servants once gave them. But the Generals and Admirals will get very mad if we don't continue to pamper them.

*Interview, Washington/*
*The New York Times, 5-13:9.*

1

Insinuations of a widening gap between Soviet and United States military power, to the advantage of the Soviet Union, are nonsense, unsupported by the facts.

*Washington, Oct. 26/*
*The New York Times, 10-27:1.*

**Harry Reasoner**
*News commentator,*
*American Broadcasting Company*

2

... a society must have the means to enforce order and protect its citizens. In a good society the soldiers are the agents and servants of the citizenry; they are the good guys, the white hats. The greatest danger of the Vietnam era was that this perception of them—by the country and by themselves—would change. In a democracy, an army that feels itself apart from and antagonistic to the population cannot be effective. And while a world without armies is a lovely dream, it is not here yet. We badly need a military that we can be proud of and that is proud of itself.

*ABC News commentary/*
*The Christian Science Monitor, 5-9:31.*

**Nelson A. Rockefeller**
*Vice President of the United States*

3

While we are committed to pursuing the peaceful potentials of detente, we must remain aware that the Soviets are increasing their military presence throughout the world. This is a hard fact that we have to face. From Somalia to Singapore, from Guinea to Cuba, there is evidence of an enlarged Soviet view of its interest.

We are witnessing today a Soviet surge in every component of military power—from strategic through conventional forces and in research and development. And there is no indication at what levels they will be satisfied. The trend for Soviet forces is up. The trend for ours is static, at best. At this rate, if we do not make the necessary investment, we might find ourselves on a path that could lead to unilateral disengagement from the world without compensating safeguards.

*Before graduating class, United States Naval Academy, June 4/*
*U.S. News & World Report, 8-18:26.*

**Terry Sanford**
*President, Duke University;*
*Former Governor of North Carolina (D)*

4

We've built a tremendous potential for overkill. It's senseless to compare warheads when we've got 7,000 ... and they've [the Soviets] got 6,000 ... What difference does it make if we had 4,000? We still have the capacity to wipe out the world ... The purpose of the military is to defend this country. It's not to throw our weight around in the rest of the world. We've gotten in all kinds of trouble by trying to throw our weight around because we had it.

*Interview, New York/*
*The Christian Science Monitor, 5-29:26.*

**James R. Schlesinger**
*Secretary of Defense of the United States*

5

The only reason we talk about GNP is because we listen to this continuous public charade about the growth of the defense budget. In terms of relative resources and power, we are at the lowest since 1949. Now, it may be the decision of the American people and the Congress that we no longer want to be a military power second to none—though very few people are willing to come forward and state this; but if that is the decision, then we are heading in the right direction.

*Before House Armed Services Committee, Washington, Feb. 18/*
*The Washington Post, 2-19:(A)2.*

# WHAT THEY SAID IN 1975

## (JAMES R. SCHLESINGER)

*1*

Every poll of the American public indicates the wish to maintain a military establishment that is second to none. In fact, a very substantial minority wishes the U.S. to remain militarily superior. There is some difference between that underlying public sentiment and the opinions that are frequently expressed. I think that the American public does not recognize the degree to which we have cut away our own military establishment . . . I feel that I have no alternative but to pursue the goal of public enlightenment about the military balance between ourselves and the Soviet Union. If present trends continue, there is likely to be a very serious setback for the U.S. in the years ahead. And then there will be voices demanding: "Why were we not warned?" I want to be able to say quite clearly, "You *were* warned."

*Interview/Newsweek, 3-17:47.*

*2*

[Saying that, in wartime, the U.S. could conceivably use nuclear weapons first against the Soviet Union]: We would prefer that neither side move in the direction of major counterforce capabilities or disarming first strike, if that were attainable; but the United States is not prepared to see the Soviet Union unilaterally attain that option and that capability . . . We will not be second in this regard . . . The notion that a nuclear firebreak, if ever breached, must inevitably lead to escalation to the top has been supported neither in American military planning, nor doctrine, nor policy statements . . . First use could conceivably—let me underscore conceivably—involve what we define as strategic forces and possibly—underscore possibly—involve selective strike at the Soviet Union. We do not necessarily exclude that, but it is indeed a very, very low probability.

*News conference, Washington, July 1/*
*The Washington Post, 7-2:(A)1.*

*3*

Political stability, which provides the basis for all hopes—or, at least, all realistic hopes—for detente depends, like military stability, upon the maintenance of an equilibrium of force, a world-wide military balance, which precludes the opportunities for adventure, particularly in the Eastern Hemisphere. This underlying requirement for the preservation of international political stability eventually determines what role and responsibility the United States will have to undertake. In effect, it dictates that the United States must continue as the mainstay of what we call, somewhat generously on occasion, the free world. United States military power will also remain the fundamental counterweight to the military power enjoyed by the other superpower—namely, the Soviet Union. These are the fundamental realities of world power.

*Before Los Angeles World Affairs*
*Council, Sept. 12/ Vital Speeches, 10-15:2.*

## James R. Schlesinger
### Former Secretary of Defense of the United States

*4*

We as a nation are indulging in an ostrich syndrome, in burying our heads in the sand and not observing what is going on. The Soviets have increased their military establishment to over 4 million men. Today they have twice as many men under arms as we have. They have, in recent years, produced four times as many subs and surface combatants as we have. They are producing 70 per cent more tactical aircraft. In ground forces equipment, it is a seven- and eight-to-one production ratio. As a share of their national effort, they are at about 15 per cent compared to about 5 per cent for the United States. If you convert that into dollar terms, they are outspending us, leaving pensions aside, by some 45 per cent, and the trend is worsening. What we have is a desire for a flight from reality, and I regard that as most unfortunate for the United States. The question about the [Defense] Department's views on these matters is ritualistic. I have said these things in the past, but the press picks up these questions at the time of budget issues and says that we are waving the flag of alarm.

*TV-radio interview, Washington/*
*"Meet the Press," National*
*Broadcasting Company, 11-23.*

*1*

... the military establishment of the United States is designed to deal with certain external forces, external capabilities. And those external capabilities are expanding. If we impose arbitrary constraints because of budgetary or political factors in the United States, then the military establishment is not able to do its job, or is only able to do that job at a higher level or risk. So it does not seem to me to be appropriate to determine what we should have militarily on the basis of debates about the appropriate size of the government budget over-all, and particularly as it applies to our domestic programs.

*Interview, Washington/*
*U.S. News & World Report, 12-22:23.*

**John F. Seiberling**
*United States Representative,*
*D—Ohio*
*2*

The Pentagon has 3,000 people working on arms sales to other countries while the Arms Control and Disarmament Agency has 12 people monitoring foreign arms sales. That gives you an idea of where the Executive Branch priorities are.

*San Francisco Examiner & Chronicle,*
*11-9:(This World)2.*

**George C. Wallace**
*Governor of Alabama (D)*
*3*

When it comes to our national security, there is only one position our nation can take as far as peace is concerned. That's a position of superiority. Not parity, not inferiority, not sufficiency, but superiority. Anything below this level is an area of no security at all. In simple language, that means "close" only counts in horseshoes, and our national defense is no horseshoe match.

*Television interview, Los Angeles, Aug. 18/*
*Los Angeles Times, 8-19:(2)1.*

**M. F. Weisner**
*Admiral, United States Navy*
*4*

We have a number of critics who say that a large, modern Navy is too expensive. Apparently, their point of view is being heard. Of course, to argue this the critics must conclude that we do not need a large, modern Navy. And if you do not need a large, modern Navy it must be because there is no threat to the United States. Anybody who subscribes to the "no threat" theory is looking at the world through "rose-colored blinders." And, I might add, he does not read the daily newspaper. The Soviet Navy is a potential threat to the United States. Of course we have detente with the Russians, but detente has not slowed the rapid buildup of the Russian Navy. Detente has not deterred the boldness of the Soviet seamen, now seen regularly and in sizable numbers in every major ocean of the world.

*Before Joint Navy League, Honolulu, Oct. 14/*
*Vital Speeches, 12-1:99.*

**Louis H. Wilson**
*General and Commandant,*
*United States Marine Corps*
*5*

I suppose we could not have a Marine Corps. But let's look at it like this: I think that we all believe that a great maritime nation such as ours has global responsibilities, that we must maintain an optimum force for our country to be able to project power ashore from the seas. This is an absolute necessity. If we didn't have a Marine Corps we would have to invent one.

*Interview/The Washington Post, 11-9:(D)2.*

**Herbert F. York**
*Director of science, technology and public*
*affairs, University of California, San Diego*
*6*

Why has the United States been responsible for the majority of the actions that have set the rate and scale of the arms race? Why have we led the entire world in this mad rush toward the ultimate absurdity? The reason is not that our leaders have been less sensitive to the dangers of the arms race; it is not that our leaders are less wise; it is not that we are more aggressive or less concerned about the dangers to the rest of mankind. Rather, the reasons are that we are richer and more powerful, that our science and technology are more dynamic, that we generate more ideas of all kinds. For these very reasons, we can and must take the lead in cooling the

# WHAT THEY SAID IN 1975

*(HERBERT F. YORK)*

arms race, in putting the genie back into the bottle, in inducing the rest of the world to move in the direction of arms control, disarmament and sanity. Just as our unilateral actions were in large part responsible for the current dangerous state of affairs, we must expect that unilateral moves on our part will be necessary if we are ever to get the whole process reversed.

*At a dialogue sponsored by the Center for the Study of Democratic Institutions/ Center Report, April: 7.*

**George D. Aiken**
*Former United States Senator, R–Vermont*
1

When the Presidential bug gets into your veins, the only thing that will get it out is embalming fluid.

*New Hampshire/The New York Times, 5-1:47.*

**Herbert E. Alexander**
*Executive director,*
*Citizens' Research Foundation*
2

We seem increasingly to turn political arguments into Constitutional ones and to leave it to the courts to decide. There is no more-political issue than how we regulate the electoral process, and the issues should probably be settled politically. On one level, the problem is how to apply democratic principles to elections in an age of media politics seemingly dominated by an atmosphere of dollar politics. On another level, the problem is how to resolve the conflict between the right of the public to know and the right of privacy—which must be considered to apply even to public persons. The issues are too important to be resolved by the courts alone, for the issues involve relocating the locus of political power and thus are at the very core of our system.

*At University of California, Davis/*
*Los Angeles Times, 8-3:(4)3.*

**Harry S. Ashmore**
*Associate director, Center for the Study of*
*Democratic Institutions*
3

In all the attacks made on the election reform laws, I do not see any defense of the present *laissez-faire*, marketplace system of politics. I don't see how the present system, which amounts to a financial-means test for entry into the electoral process, can be said to be more open than one under new reform laws—with all the bureaucratic regulation the latter may entail—which would make the means for campaigning equally available to all candidates. There just has to be an electoral-campaign system that does not depend upon the solicitation of private funds. I do not see how providing all candidates equally the means by which they can communicate with the public violates any Constitutional principle.

*Panel discussion/*
*The Center Magazine, Nov.-Dec.:30.*

**Reubin Askew**
*Governor of Florida (D)*
4

I think the two-party system . . . has served this country well. I would hope very much that we do not go into any type of a third party. The difference in this country with so many other countries in the Western world has been the fact that we had a two-party system. It has granted stability. We haven't had to have coalitions of minorities to sit as a President, although we have had some minority Presidents, even in the two-party system. But I believe that we should stick to the two-party system . . .

*TV-radio interview, New Orleans/*
*"Meet the Press,"*
*National Broadcasting Company, 6-8.*

**Saul Bellow**
*Author*
5

What man with his eyes open at this hour could not be interested in politics? I only wish people talked about it at a deeper level than Chappaquiddick or Scoop Jackson or who's-gonna-get-the-nomination. I don't think we know where we are or where we're going. I see politics—ultimately—as a buzzing preoccupation that swallows up art and the life of the spirit.

*Newsweek, 9-1:39.*

# WHAT THEY SAID IN 1975

**John Brademas**
*United States Representative, D–Indiana*  1

In my judgment, here is where we are: We have a White House weakened by Watergate, occupied by a President [Ford] who is not elected, who campaigned hard for his party at the polls [in 1974] and was overwhelmingly repudiated. On the other hand, we have substantial increases in Democratic margins in the House and Senate, chiefly as a consequence, I think, of two negative factors: the Republican mismanagement of the economy and the whole series of events we call Watergate. So we [Democrats] have a kind of quasi mandate. In my own view, however, it is not enough for us to operate in Congress in the next two years on those negative bases. We Democrats have the responsibility to develop a positive, constructive program to deal with the toughest problems facing the American people and to help fill the vacuum of leadership that the Ford White House represents.
*TV-radio interview, Washington/*
*"Meet the Press,"*
*National Broadcasting Company, 1-5.*

**Edmund G. Brown, Jr.**
*Governor of California (D)*  2

[Criticizing the Democratic Party for being too concerned with hotel and restaurant facilities in their search for a site for next year's Presidential nominating convention] : We have a million people out of work. We have a country that's looking for leadership and direction. And I'd rather concentrate on the issues and restoring confidence where it doesn't now exist. Certainly, the Party and the government are suffering from a great lack of belief in this country and that's what we ought to be talking about, not whether the Wilshire hotels have enough rooms or not ... We can sleep in church basements.
*News conference, Sacramento, July 24/*
*Los Angeles Times, 7-25:(1)3.*

**George Brown**
*Former Foreign Secretary of the*
*United Kingdom*  3

I don't know how anybody is going to live under the pressure of top jobs in politics and not have some outlet. Most British statesmen, as far back as one likes to go, have either drunk too much or womanized too much or done both or something else.
*San Francisco Examiner & Chronicle,*
*1-5:(This World)2.*

**James L. Buckley**
*United States Senator,*
*C–New York*  4

Republicanism of the kind that accepts, in the name of moderation, half the liberal Democratic program holds no appeal to those conservative-minded independents and Democrats who were essential to the victorious Presidential election coalition of 1972. Liberal Republicans cannot hope to resurrect Republican fortunes.
*At conservative conference, Washington,*
*Feb. 15/The Washington Post, 2-16:(A)1.*

**Brendan T. Byrne**
*Governor of New Jersey (D)*  5

[On politics] : If you lead a charge and you capture the flag, you're a strong leader. If you lead a charge and you don't capture the flag, they find all kinds of reasons why you're not a strong leader. All I say [is that] this is a business which is judged by results.
*Interview/The New York Times, 3-9:(1)44.*

**John B. Connally, Jr.**
*Former Secretary of the Treasury*
*of the United States;*
*Former Governor of Texas (D, now R)*  6

I basically don't believe in third parties ... If you get three, you'll get four, and if you get four, you'll get five and a whole proliferation of parties that, in my judgment, would ultimately make us almost ungovernmentable. The greatest thing that could happen would be that we could maintain two strong viable parties. But neither of them are going to survive with any influence unless they start facing up to the problem and start talking to the American people in terms the American people can understand ... [The] American people are so disgusted with both parties they won't go to the polls ... this is cutting off your nose to spite your face. As bad as both [parties] might be, there's always the lesser of the evils. But [the] truth of the matter is the American people are turned off . . . No one is talking to them, for them or about them.

*Interview, Houston/*
*The Dallas Times Herald, 6-18:(A)8.*

1

One of the great wrongs in America right now, in my opinion, is the partisanship with which most of problems are being approached. . . . politics is an integral part of the American system. I am not condemning politics. I've even been known to enjoy politics from time to time. Politics, after all, is merely the art of debating conflicting views and hammering out policies which balance the equities as much as possible and promote the national interest. But politics is being redefined these days—and the product ill serves the national interest. We are witnessing in our nation today not the politics of compromise, but the compromise of politics. Our political activity has been compromised into partisanship so blind and unthinking that it threatens to paralyze government and disrupt the standard of living of the American people. But too many people in public life who purport to be leaders are doing little to convince us they can truly lead. We have reached a time when the need for action in 1975 has been overwhelmed by the spectre of an election in 1976—when political eyes cannot see beyond the next election. Whether we are Democrats or Republicans, if we cannot learn to look beyond our own survival in public life, then there is little hope for the survival of this nation.

*Before Dallas Citizens Council, Nov. 19/*
*The Dallas Times Herald, 11-20:(A)22.*

**Archibald Cox**
*Professor of law, Harvard University; Former*
*special government prosecutor for Watergate*
2

In my view, Watergate proved the conscience of the nation as well as the ability of a self-governing people to vindicate, by the process of open government, their own moral sense . . . The question is whether the energy . . . can be channeled into constructive uses or the wave

will expand itself, aimlessly dashing upon all politics and politicians, leaving Watergate to mark only a spasm in a long slide into general cynicism, distrust and despair.

*Newsweek, 1-13:23.*

**Alan Cranston**
*United States Senator, D–California*
3

The public is entitled to know everything they wish to know about a politician's private life if it affects his ability to do what he was elected to do.

*Los Angeles Herald-Examiner, 3-10:(A)6.*

**Walter Cronkite**
*News commentator,*
*Columbia Broadcasting System*
4

[On the Watergate affair]: [Former U.S. President Richard] Nixon and his crowd did not reveal a weakness in our fabric, but only a weakness in themselves. The fabric of democracy proved stronger than any gang of conspirators. The other Branches of our government— the Legislative and Judicial—exercised those checks and balances on our Executive Branch devised by our nation's founders, and, aided by the free press, brought the terrible episode to a close before the damage was irreparable. We are more alert today to the internal dangers to democracy than ever before, and the nation is stronger for the experience.

*At student convocation, Charlotte, N.C./*
*The Dallas Times Herald, 12-28:(B)3.*

**Samuel Dash**
*Director, Institute of Criminal Law and*
*Procedure, Georgetown University; Former*
*Chief Council, Senate Watergate Committee*
5

[On President Ford's pardon last year of former President Richard Nixon for any possible Watergate crimes]: It was the worst possible judgment on his part. I don't think he showed any sensitivity to what was happening in this country as a result of Watergate, or to the feelings of the public. I don't think most Americans wanted to see Nixon in a cell, and I think they would have wanted clemency once there was a trial. But President Ford should have waited until the facts were out. In a real

# WHAT THEY SAID IN 1975

sense, Special Prosecutor [Leon] Jaworski was fired by Ford just as [previous Special Prosecutor] Archibald Cox had been fired by Nixon. By pardoning Nixon, Ford took away the prosecutor's power to do his job.

*Interview/
People, 11-24:13.*

**Roger Davidson**
*Professor of political science,
University of California, Santa Barbara*      1

I favor not so much direct subsidies to [political] candidates as efforts to open up channels of resources for the candidates. I like the idea of free candidate pamphlets sent to all voters. On the Federal level, I like the idea of giving non-incumbent candidates access to the franking privilege and perhaps access to the Library of Congress facilities as well as other kinds of informational resources. I like the idea of asking broadcasters to give blocks of television and radio time to individual candidates and, for debate purposes, to groups of candidates. This would give all qualified candidates equal access to the voters. I would much rather see that than a broad national program of subsidized elections.

*Panel discussion/
The Center Magazine, Nov.-Dec.:30.*

**Sam J. Ervin, Jr.**
*Former United States Senator,
D–North Carolina; Former Chairman,
Senate Watergate Committee*      2

Nothing can prevent another Watergate except that the men and women who seek and acquire political power have two characteristics: They must understand our system of government and be dedicated to it, and they must have intellectual integrity. Candidates who conduct themselves as [former President] Nixon did must not get political power. Perhaps now it's up to the media to keep reminding people.

*Newsweek, 1-13:20.*

[On whether President Ford was correct in giving former President Nixon a pre-indictment pardon last year for any possible Watergate crimes]: No! Historically, the pardon powers put into the Constitution according to James Wilson, one of the Founding Fathers, ought not to allow the President to say to one man, "you will be held responsible for your crimes" and to another man, "you won't be held responsible for your crimes." It was given there to enable the President to correct mistakes that the courts couldn't correct themselves. As a matter of fact, as I construe it, the President has a greater power to pardon people than the Almighty has. Because as I understand what I've read in the Bible, it says the Almighty can't pardon a man until he first repents his sins. I thought President Ford made a mistake. It affected his credibility because he had said three times earlier that he would not pardon until the courts had finished acting. And also, the most basic, fundamental principle of good government is the principle that all men stand equal before the law. I think the premature pardon was a grave injury to that principle.

*News conference, San Francisco/
San Francisco Examiner & Chronicle,
3-23:(California Living)11.*

**M. Stanton Evans**
*Chairman, American Conservative Union*      4

People are unhappy with high taxes, inflation, intrusion into their personal lives, welfare and busing. The American people are becoming increasingly conservative.

*Washington, Feb. 14/
Los Angeles Herald-Examiner, 2-16:(A)2.*

**Gerald R. Ford**
*President of the United States*      5

We must discard the attitude of exclusiveness that has kept the Republican Party's door closed too often while we give speeches about keeping it open ... We must erect a tent that is big enough for all who care about this great country and believe in the Republican Party enough to work through it for common goals. This tent must also be kept open to the growing number of independent voters who refuse to wear any party label, but who will support the strong candidates and good programs we present. These voters must be welcomed and won to our cause.

*At Republican party leadership conference, Washington, March 7/ The New York Times, 3-8:1,30.*

1

One thing I learned in more than a quarter-century of political involvement is that the prospects for victory are seldom so bleak or so good as they seem when you're in the thick of a fight. Time after time, a supposedly ruined party has rebuilt and returned—stronger than ever. And repeatedly, candidates once considered unbeatable have been beaten.

*At Republican fund-raising dinner, Washington, April 15/ The New York Times, 4-16:7.*

2

[On his running for re-election in 1976]: It's always been my philosophy in politics: You run your own campaign, you run on your record and you do your best to convince delegates they ought to vote for you and the people that they ought to vote for you. I never really predicate my plans on what somebody else might do.

*News conference, Washington, June 25/ The New York Times, 6-26:26.*

3

[Saying he will continue to go out in public despite two recent alleged assassination attempts against him] :... I don't think any person as President, or any person in any other major political office, ought to cower in the face of a limited number of people, out of 214 million Americans, who want to take the law into their own hands. The American people expect—and I approve of it; in fact, I think it is right—want a dialogue between them and their President and their other public officials. And if we can't have that opportunity of talking with one another, seeing one another, shaking hands with one another, something has gone wrong in our society. I don't think these individuals who

want to destroy our society and tear up our fabric of relationships represent America. The American people are good people—Democrats, independents, Republicans and others. Under no circumstances will I, and I hope no others, capitulate to those that want to undercut what's good in America.

*Washington, Sept. 22/ The National Observer, 10-4:7.*

**Paul A. Freund**
*Professor of law, Harvard University*

4

My own judgment is that the President should be less disposed to engage in a rather meaningless mingling with [public] crowds. The pressing of flesh as a way of gauging public sentiment means nothing. The entering into crowds is meaningless . . . It's better for a President to judge public response by mail, telegrams. Certainly, it has more significance than having someone reach out and touch the hem of his garment.

*The New York Times, 9-24:27.*

**John W. Gardner**
*Chairman, Common Cause*

5

[On ethics in politics] : I don't use that word ["ethics"]. It suggests elements in human behavior that aren't easily legislated, and it suggests, too, that man is perfectible. You really can't legislate morality. I suppose that when Hammurabi set forth that first code of laws, some court cynic muttered, "Why's the old fool chipping away at that stone? Human nature will never change." You can't pass legislation to stop people from undoing other people. You can't stop the banker from stealing the widow's mite. But I'll tell you what you can do: You can make it a hell of a lot tougher.

*The National Observer, 8-9:1.*

**Leonard Garment**
*Former Counsel to the President of the United States (Richard M. Nixon)*

6

[On the Watergate affair] : Woodrow Wilson said that we are a government of men, not laws. He was wrong. But so is the old civics-book saw that we are a government of laws and not men. All of that is a speechwriter's simplification.

219

# WHAT THEY SAID IN 1975

*(LEONARD GARMENT)*

Watergate showed that we are a government of laws *and* men, interacting with each other and with public opinion in a very complex way. So it would be silly to announce a lot of sweeping conclusions and commandments [in the wake of Watergate]. The one thing I'm clear about is that there's nothing in Watergate that would justify any diminution of the powers of the Presidency. A strong Chief Executive is still an essential part of our Constitutional arrangement. Watergate also taught us that the impeachment clause works, and how it works—which is important—and we've shown that we could undergo this incredible political ordeal and come out on our feet. That must be damned impressive to the world, and it is damned important at this time.

*Interview/*
*The Washington Post,*
*8-10:(Potomac)17.*

**John H. Glenn, Jr.**
*United States Senator,*
*D–Ohio*
1

... people are not sure about politics. Washington seems very remote. People don't feel a close association with officials here. They lack confidence. It is not just Watergate—that contributed to it and became the all-too-visible tip of the iceberg, I guess. But the problem goes back farther—maybe to where the cost of campaigning became so expensive and a lot of lobbyists and special interests moved in to fill the financial vacuum. Over the period of the last 10 or 15 years, I think the general feeling has grown that members of Congress represent the special interests rather than the interests of the people. We find people disenchanted. A man feels the 10 bucks he gives to help a candidate who is running is nothing compared with the $200,000—or whatever the figure is—from the milk fund. One of the things we have to do is restore some confidence in public officials.

*Interview, Washington/*
*Los Angeles Times, 1-21:(2)7.*

**Barry M. Goldwater**
*United States Senator, R–Arizona*
2

If the country can survive this [94th] Congress, it can survive anything ... You have the revolution in the House of Representatives by young members who really don't know what they are doing ... When you find five out of six new members of the House opposed to military spending at a time when this country is becoming weaker in the international field, I think that's dangerous. And you find a Congress now dominated by selfish interest groups, such as the labor movement, Common Cause, the League of Women Voters, and so forth and so on. Also, I'm convinced from the attitudes of members of this Congress that they have no concept of what makes the economy run and they have no concept of how money is used to make money. They have the attitude you can spend and spend and elect and elect even though this country is close to national bankruptcy. I think this is probably the most dangerous Congress we've ever had.

*Interview/The Washington Post, 2-2:(A)14.*

3

A third party would only split the Republican ranks further, and we are in such a minority now that it would practically insure the destruction of the Republican Party. If conservative Republicans adopt the rule-or-ruin attitude, then they are taking exactly the attitude that the extreme liberal branch of the Republican Party took in 1964, which, while they didn't cause my defeat, certainly added to it.

*At Young Republican Leadership Conference,*
*Washington, March 1/*
*The Washington Post, 3-2:(A)21.*

**H. R. Haldeman**
*Former Assistant to the President of*
*the United States (Richard M. Nixon)*
4

I readily confess to a serious failure in judgment as regards Watergate and to the woeful lack of perception as the case developed ... I have to say that I—and I think this applies to all the rest of the top people at the White House and to the President himself—totally failed to

perceive Watergate as a matter of bigger potential danger or a major Presidential concern.
*Television interview, Los Angeles, March 23/*
*The Christian Science Monitor, 3-24:2.*

**Erwin Hargrove**
*Political scientist, Brown University*
1

[President] Ford is an authentic conservative, without the expedience of [former President Richard] Nixon or the right-wing zeal of a [former California Governor Ronald] Reagan. Ford's conservatism is rooted in the Midwest, in the Protestant ethic, and it includes an unquestioning belief in the assumptions of American life—growth, abundance, acquisition, private enterprise, individualism. He's the first true legislative conservative since McKinley to make it to the Presidency, and I think we're about to get a real test of whether a conservative candidacy and approach to government can still be successful.
*San Francisco Examiner & Chronicle, 8-3:(A)23.*

**Bryce N. Harlow**
*Former Counsellor to the President of the United States (Richard M. Nixon)*
2

The most important thing in practical politics is the direction in which things are moving, rather than where they are. If they're static and bad, sure, then the guy in the White House is in a hell of a fix. But if the economy is prospering but not yet prosperous, if the trend is good, that's a bit more propitious.
*Feb. 4/The New York Times, 2-5:17.*

**Philip A. Hart**
*United States Senator,*
*D—Michigan*
3

[Saying politicians are on "ego trips"]: It's true. In spite of the press reports, I admit it: I'm vain, too. The whole notion of getting into politics is ego-massaging. It's the only profession I know in which you're *required* to get up and say what a hell of a fellow you are. You start in politics that way. You say, "Elect me, because I'm better than the other fellow." It feeds on the office-holder. The satisfaction that

comes from power too often requires more power.
*The National Observer, 8-9:12.*

**Edward Heath**
*Former Prime Minister of*
*the United Kingdom*
4

In my experience, the greatest folly in politics or in diplomacy is to use old rhetoric to disguise new realities. Too often politicians are guilty of the failing attributed by Bishop Berkeley to philosophers—that having first raised a dust, they then complain that they cannot see through it. The task of the statesman is to clear the dust, dispel the illusions, and face the realities.
*At Westminster College commencement,*
*Salt Lake City/The National Observer, 7-19:7.*

**Ken Hechler**
*United States Representative,*
*D—West Virginia*
5

We're not in politics because we dislike it. Pressing the flesh gets to be part of your psyche. You have to like people and love eating off paper plates and listening to a high-school band play off-key.
*U.S. News & World Report, 8-25:44.*

**Jesse A. Helms**
*United States Senator, R—North Carolina*
6

I joined the Republican Party, after 28 years of being a registered Democrat, because I believed that it stood most clearly for our heritage of individual freedom and national strength. Yet only 12 per cent of the people think the Republican Party is patriotic. I joined the Republican Party because I felt that it stood for free enterprise, competition and hard work. Yet only 17 per cent of the people think the Republican Party stands for hard work. I joined the Republican Party because I believed in fiscal responsibility and honesty. Yet . . . 60 per cent of the people look on the Republican Administrations and see nothing but waste and corruption. Was I wrong in joining the Republican Party? I do not think so, because I look

# WHAT THEY SAID IN 1975

around and I see the rank and file of my fellow Republicans who believe as I do. The vast majority of Republicans are conservative. They are not rich. They are not unpatriotic. They believe in honesty, frugality and hard work. If the Republican Party cannot stand for these principles, then it stands for nothing at all, and cannot long survive. Its members will desert or simply stay home, or they will look for those who do articulate those principles. The party which is based on geographic or social division is dead.

*At Conservative Political Action Conference, Washington/Human Events, 3-1:20.*

1

I hope the conservative structure will manifest itself in the form of the Republican Party. The die is cast if the Republican Party is going to try to be a party of discount Democrats; that is, just being a little less liberal than the Democrats and not offering the conservatives any reason to be excited, enthusiastic and energetic.

*May 4/The Washington Post, 5-5:(A)2.*

## Hubert H. Humphrey
*United States Senator, D–Minnesota*

2

[On protecting political figures from violence against them]: We can accept handgun registration as a reasonable measure to decrease the likelihood of political violence. We can and must improve candidates' protection by better coordination of all law-enforcement agencies. We should refuse to give assassins celebrity status. We must reject political violence, be it outright assassination or more subtle forms of intimidation and coercion, as having no place in our political process. But no person can be made fully secure. Thus, each public official or candidate must cope with those threats of violence based on his best judgment.

*Interview/Newsweek, 10-6:32.*

3

[On his not being a declared candidate for the 1976 Democratic Presidential nomination]: It's my judgment that right now the person that has no ambition, no declared ambitions, is more

credible. He's freer; you don't have to go around weighing every word as you inevitably do when you become a candidate. I feel I have a role to play in the Party of keeping everybody on the beam. Not just a referee or a healer. Someone that's just a little cut above the pack. The minute you get in it, you're just another one of them . . .

*Interview, Washington/ The Washington Post, 11-3:(A)3.*

## William L. Hungate
*United States Representative, D–Missouri*

4

Being in public life is something like being in a hammock: It's hard to get into, and perhaps equally hard to get out of.

*Announcing he will not seek another term in Congress/The National Observer, 7-19:7.*

5

In the last decade, politics has gone from the age of "Camelot" when all things were possible, to the age of "Watergate" when all things are suspect.

*Quote, 10-5:265.*

6

. . . Watergate increased public suspicion of politicians and public cynicism toward the political process. Reporters seeking skeletons in closets ignore the bodies in the hallway. Students who could not hold a job in a Congressional office are employed by public-interest and other special-interest groups to rate Congressmen. The leaders of these groups make self-righteous proclamations of what the public interest is and what office-holders should do. They remind me of a preacher who hasn't been to heaven describing it to people who aren't going there.

*Los Angeles Times, 12-29:(1)20.*

## Henry M. Jackson
*United States Senator, D–Washington*

7

. . . in the context of a decade of confusion about terminology, never in my lifetime have I seen a greater debasement of the political cur-

rency: What is a liberal? What is a conservative? A middle-of-the-roader? It has all been debased.
*TV-radio interview, Washington/*
*"Meet the Press,"*
*National Broadcasting Company, 2-9.*

**Jacob K. Javits**
*United States Senator, R—New York* 1

[Saying the Republican Party should broaden its base and not be just a party of conservatives] : If we permit a Neanderthal wing in our Party to dominate its processes, we can count on only one outcome—defeat, defeat, defeat. [It is] absurd reasoning that the Republican Party suffered a humiliating defeat in 1974 because its candidates failed to communicate conservative thinking. It was the conservatives who were clobbered by the voters and not the moderate and liberal Republicans.
*At Ripon Society conference, New York,*
*April 26/The Washington Post, 4-27:(A)20.*

2

The genius of the American system is that, when the need is there, politicians of disparate views can unite their efforts.
*New York, Sept. 19/*
*The New York Times, 9-20:22.*

**Leon Jaworski**
*Lawyer; Former special government prosecutor for Watergate* 3

[Watergate] has done a tremendous amount of good for better government. Those who seek office know there's a very high standard expected of them . . . There aren't many who now think they can depart from the straight line. There'll be less use of influence. The attention given to this case will give its results a more lasting effect. It has made its impressions deep-rooted. The good that comes out of it won't be a passing fancy.
*Newsweek, 1-13:19.*

4

[On the Watergate affair] : Still fresh on my mind is the sadness of seeing one of the great tragedies of modern history—men who once had fame in their hands sinking to infamy—all

because eventually their goals were of the wrong dreams and aspirations. The teaching of right and wrong had been forgotten and little evils were permitted to grow into great evils—small sins to escalate into big sins. Perhaps the most incredible of all conditions I encountered in Washington during the investigations was not only a flirting with the truth by some high officials but a blatant flouting of the truth—a contemptible course of conduct that breaks down all confidence in integrity, responsibility and leadership.
*Before Society of Former Special Agents of*
*the FBI, Houston, Nov. 7/*
*The Dallas Times Herald, 11-9:(A)43.*

**James P. Johnson**
*United States Representative, R—Colorado* 5

[On the just-occurred alleged attempted assassination of President Ford] : Mr. Chairman, I think the record should show that for the first time since McKinley, we have a Republican President worth shooting, and I think that's a good sign.
*At House Agricultural Committee meeting,*
*Washington, Sept. 5/*
*Los Angeles Times, 9-6:(1)27.*

**Lady Bird (Mrs. Lyndon B.) Johnson**
*Wife of the late President of the*
*United States* 6

[Saying she would hesitate before urging young people to go into politics these days] : I would pause more in asking them to run. I would waiver now. It's getting harder and harder. You're under closer scrutiny . . . Inquisitiveness into personal lives has accelerated a great deal [since Watergate] . There's the feeling that they're up to something wicked.
*Los Angeles Times, 3-19:(1)2.*

**Jack Kemp**
*United States Representative, R—New York* 7

A candidate must stand for a known set of principles. He must know what he believes in—in a structured way—to have credibility with the people. The candidate who for years swayed back and forth from one side of the issue to the other—the candidate who said one

# WHAT THEY SAID IN 1975

*(JACK KEMP)*

thing in his district—usually conservative—and did something else in Washington—usually liberal—is from the past.

*Interview/Human Events, 2-22:5.*

## Henry A. Kissinger
*Secretary of State of the United States* 1

Show-business people and politicians aren't that dissimilar. Except that politicians play only one role and have a shorter life.

*At dinner in his honor, Beverly Hills, Calif., Jan. 23/Los Angeles Times, 1-27:(4)9.*

## Edward I. Koch
*United States Representative, D—New York* 2

I think of myself as a liberal with sanity. I believe in liberalism without dogmatism. I try to understand the problems of others, and find a way to accommodate them without compromising my basic point of view. The liberals are the people you can least count on for personal support when the chips are down. To them, it's "What have you done for me lately?" Conservatives take a longer view.

*The New York Times, 4-18:29.*

## Jerzy Kosinski
*Author* 3

[Commenting on how easy some in the U.S. are taking the Watergate affair]: It is fantastic. Americans can digest anything—bones . . . rocks . . . heavy water. [Watergate conspirator] John Dean talked to me about the subject of his book [on Watergate] as casually as you would talk if you were writing a book about Easthampton. It's as if Eva Braun had lived and was writing about Hitler and saying, "Well, yes, some bad things happened, but you know . . ." I could not imagine this kind of party taking place in Europe. I tell you, the European part of me is traumatized, but the American part calms me down.

*At cocktail party for Maureen (Mrs. John) Dean, New York/ "W": a Fairchild publication, 11-28:11.*

## Philip B. Kurland
*Professor of law, University of Chicago* 4

It is hard for me to accept the fact that it was a bare 10 months ago that a President of the United States [Nixon] was forced to resign his office because of abuse of power by him and his Administration. The successor in office, after pardoning his predecessor, has behaved as if the events of Watergate never occurred. Like Nixon, President Ford has asked us to look forward and not backward, to forget—indeed, to ignore—the evils that occurred, to view the pardon he so generously granted to Nixon as if it wiped out not only the former President's criminal liability but also the deeds that gave rise to that liability. Unlike Nixon, President Ford has been rather successful in his effort. And I expect this success is due to the fact that none of us likes to recall pain and unpleasantness. Moreover, the press, the mother of Watergate, has lost interest in it, for its primary concerns, as always, are not with the principles of government, but with scandal. This leaves a large responsibility with the Bar to attend to the problems of the governance of a nation dedicated to "liberty and justice for all." For nothing is clearer than that the events of Watergate demonstrated real and continuing dangers to American freedom and justice. Watergate revealed more than the weakness of evil men in high places. Watergate revealed basic institutional deficiencies that have not and will not be corrected unless and until an aroused American public or an aroused Congress demands and secures reform.

*Before Delaware Bar Association/ Los Angeles Times, 6-22:(5)3.*

## Paul D. Laxalt
*United States Senator, R—Nevada* 5

Campaigning is like trying a law suit: The jury's a little bigger, but there's a verdict in each case.

*Interview, Washington/ The Christian Science Monitor, 1-22:2.*

**G. Gordon Liddy**
*1972 Presidential campaign finance counsel to former President of the United States Richard M. Nixon; Convicted Watergate conspirator*

1

[Defending the Watergate affair] : . . . if one is engaged in a war, one deploys troops, one seeks to know the capability and intentions of the enemy and things of that sort. If one is engaged in politics, one deploys his political troops, one seeks to learn the capabilities and intentions of the other side, the opposition. It's like brushing your teeth . . . it's basic. Power exists to be used . . . if Watergate is as it's alleged to be, it was an intelligence-gathering operation of one group of persons who were seeking power, or to retain power, against another group of persons who were seeking to acquire power. That's all it was.

*Television interview,*
*Oxon Hill, Md./*
*"60 Minutes,"*
*Columbia Broadcasting System, 1-5.*

**James B. Longley**
*Governor of Maine (I)*

2

I think that the two-party system historically has served this country fairly well, but not recently. I think the choice of [George] McGovern and [Richard] Nixon in 1972 did not really provide this country much of a choice [for the Presidency], and I think the two parties need to ask themselves some hard questions: Are they serving the country well when they give the country that type of a choice? I mean that as a challenge, because hopefully the two parties will listen. I happen to feel that there is an emerging segment of the population and, as I understand it, it could very easily be Number 2 in position from the standpoint of enrollment. I am speaking of the unenrolled or independent voter.

*TV-radio interview,*
*New Orleans/*
*"Meet the Press,"*
*National Broadcasting Company, 6-8.*

**William S. Mailliard**
*United States Ambassador to the Organization of American States; Former United States Representative, R–California*

3

[On his decision in 1974 not to seek re-election to Congress because of his dwindling percentage of the vote over the years]: An incumbent can hang on if he wants to spend enough money on a campaign. I found it distasteful to have a political base that would be so marginal I'd have to look at the political implications of everything I'd do. I could find myself fudging on my own convictions.

*The Washington Post, 6-29:(E)10.*

**Frank Mankiewicz**
*1972 Presidential campaign manager for Senator George S. McGovern*

4

[On the danger of violence against a President who enters public crowd situations]: When a President plunges into a crowd shaking hands, is that a "dialogue with the people"? Its elimination would damage only the network news, which would then have an extra few seconds to fill. If the President wants a dialogue, let him listen to some Congressmen who disagree with him. [President] Gerald Ford's manhood is not at stake, however much he may talk of "standing tall" or not "yielding" to a cowardly minority [of assassins] . He is a trustee, the embodiment of the American nation and its political system; and, like all trustees, he should act prudently to conserve the assets. The risks will increase so long as we continue to encourage the possession and use of handguns. A pistol is being used in the sole manner for which it is designed when it kills a human being. Since we are not yet serious about guns, let us at least withhold the most costly target.

*Interview/Newsweek, 10-6:34.*

**Charles McC. Mathias, Jr.**
*United States Senator, R–Maryland*

5

The political parties today are really operating on the fringes of the American political system. When we see the Republican Party moving in the [Ronald Reagan] direction . . . you have the broad center ground of America,

225

# WHAT THEY SAID IN 1975

*(CHARLES McC. MATHIAS, JR.)*

for almost the first time in history . . . unoccupied, and the central issues in American life are not being attended to because the caretakers are not where they ought to be.

*San Francisco Examiner & Chronicle,*
*11-16:(This World)2.*

**Tom McCall**
*Governor of Oregon (R)*  1

[Saying his call for the two major parties to face issues is not the same as that espoused by Alabama Governor George Wallace]: This is not a George Wallace approach I'm talking about, where you cuss out a lot of Americans and prey on the fears of the people, scolding and threatening in a sea of negative bluster.

*At Western States Republican Conference,*
*Portland, Ore., Oct. 4/*
*San Francisco Examiner & Chronicle,*
*10-5:(A)15.*

**Eugene J. McCarthy**
*Former United States Senator,*
*D—Minnesota*  2

There are three ideas that are bad [about the two-party system]. First is the tradition of loyalty to the President, which we saw in excess in the Democrats supporting the [Vietnam] war when [Lyndon] Johnson was running and opposing the same war after [Richard] Nixon got in. Then we saw the Republicans being loyal to Nixon far beyond the point they should have. Second, in counterpoint, is the concept of the loyal opposition that justifies obstructionism and irresponsibility. It works out so that you've just got to be against things because you're a Democratic Congressman and the President is a Republican. The third bad idea is the concept of the President as leader of the party. It was better when we let the Postmaster General be head of the party. The idea of the President being head of the party would be all right in a parliamentary system, but it isn't all right in ours.

*Interview, Washington/*
*The National Observer, 6-7:5.*

3

Anything that tends to destroy organized political effort is a serious threat to the democratic process. And the effect of the new Federal election law is to make organized political effort difficult. It makes two organizations—the Republican Party and the Democratic Party—the favored instruments of the government. That's like saying you have freedom of religion in this country if you give citizens a choice of two religions, both supported by the state. We say, "You have political freedom in our society; you can vote either Democratic or Republican." If this kind of a proposal had been made at the Constitutional Convention, it would not have lasted two minutes and the person who proposed it would not have been consulted on any subject from that time on. What disturbs me most is that critics and analysts have been so indifferent to this law's potential for warping and making our whole political process undemocratic.

*Panel discussion/*
*The Center Magazine, Nov.-Dec.:26.*

**George S. McGovern**
*United States Senator, D—South Dakota*  4

I'm not a [1976 Presidential] candidate. I told the people of South Dakota when I ran for re-election [to the Senate] last fall that I'm not going to be a candidate. But if I were offered the nomination? Sure, I'd take it. And so would anybody else. No proven politician who had any standing would reject the national convention.

*Interview, Washington/*
*The Washington Post, 3-9:(A)21.*

5

[On President Ford's insistence on appearing in public despite two recent assassination attempts on him]: Plunging into crowds and working up and down the airport fences . . . has to be curtailed and curtailed seriously. In all honesty, there are some very superficial reasons why candidates engage in that kind of . . . handshaking. The first reason they do it is to get some kind of symbolic demonstration that they're close to the people. The second reason is to raise their own spirits. When you're under attack by your opposition or by editors and others [and are] down a little, there's no better time to go out and shake hands with a lot of warm, smiling, potential voters. On top of this, if word gets out that you're in danger or some kind of incident occurs, then you have an additional reason to do it, and that's to demonstrate that you're brave. Now, none of these are very good reasons. None of them have much to do with the national interest.

*Before Senate Appropriations Subcommittee,*
*Washington, Sept. 30/*
*The Washington Post, 10-1:(A)12.*

**Thomas J. McIntyre**
*United States Senator, D—New Hampshire*
1

[On Alabama Governor George Wallace] : If he's for the common man, why does his state have one of the most regressive tax systems in the country? If he is the populist he says he is, why has he so neglected public education—the stepping-stone for common people—that Alabama ranks 50th among all states in per pupil education spending? If he's for law and order, why hasn't he been able to stop the rise in crime in his own state? In 1973 violent crime was up 5 per cent nationally, but it went up 13 per cent in Alabama. If he is, indeed, against government spending and budget deficits, why has Alabama's state debt gone up 180 per cent since he first became Governor?

*Concord, N.H., May 31/*
*San Francisco Examiner & Chronicle, 6-1:(A)11.*

**George Meany**
*President, American Federation of Labor-*
*Congress of Industrial Organizations*
2

[On Alabama Governor George Wallace] : He's the perfect demagogue . . . I mean, the fellow has no political philosophy. He knows absolutely nothing about foreign affairs. He's against the tax collector; and if you read your Bible, the most unpopular person back in the days of the Old Testament was the tax collector. So there's nothing new about that.

*At press luncheon, Washington/*
*The Washington Post, 8-31:(A)6.*

**Takeo Miki**
*Prime Minister of Japan*
3

At the time of the Watergate issue in America, I was deeply moved by the scene in the House Judiciary Committee where each member of the Committee expressed his own or her own heart based upon the spirit of the American Constitution. It was this very attitude, I think, that rescued American democracy.

*Before Japanese Liberal-Democratic Party/*
*The New York Times, 2-11:14.*

**Stewart Mott**
*Associate director, Center for the*
*Study of Democratic Institutions*
4

People say we spend too much money on politics. But the total spent on all political campaigns for all public offices over a four-year span is about one-tenth of one per cent of all the budgets of all local, state and Federal governments. If you were forming a business corporation and selecting your top personnel and directors, you might be willing to spend something more than one-tenth of one per cent of your annual budget to make sure you had the right people running your corporation. We don't spend too much on politics. Perhaps we spend too little, and we do not spend it as wisely and effectively as we might. To take all private money out of politics would professionalize it. But volunteerism has been tremendously important in American life. It is one of the most robust facets of the American political system.

*Panel discussion/*
*The Center Magazine, Nov.-Dec.:26.*

**Edmund S. Muskie**
*United States Senator, D—Maine*
5

I don't close the door [on being a 1976 Presidential candidate], but I don't do anything about keeping it open. My commitments in 1975 in the Senate and in Maine reduce the possibility of being a candidate in 1976. But I don't close the door because it wouldn't be honest . . . I'm not panting at it. I don't need it. I don't have fire in my belly. But if the challenge were there, I could do it with commit-

# WHAT THEY SAID IN 1975

ment and interest. I could even generate quite a bit of interest. It's something I don't need to make my life complete. But it is something that would add a great new dimension to my life. I have a sort of neutrality about it that some theorists can't understand. It's not a take-it-or-leave-it attitude. That's too callous. It's just that in my part of the country, you learn to live with what you get.

*The Washington Post, 3-9:(A)21.*

**Charles H. Percy**
*United States Senator, R–Illinois*

1

[Saying President Ford risks assassination when he wades into public crowds]: You're not really carrying on a discussion with the voters by plunging into crowds. It doesn't make sense to continue that kind of activity. Maybe it's good for the ego, but it does no good for the ego of a dead President.

*At Senate Government Operations Committee hearing, Washington, Oct. 7/*
*The New York Times, 10-8:13.*

**Howard Phillips**
*Former Acting Director, Federal Office of Economic Opportunity*

2

Most Americans are basically conservative in their values, but they have no political structure to exert their impact against the Washington power structure of the liberals . . . Right now, a Congressman more often votes liberal than conservative because he has to answer to liberal media or the big labor unions or the teachers who keep tabs on his voting more than the people back home.

*The Christian Science Monitor, 7-21:19.*

**Kevin Phillips**
*Political columnist*

3

[On violence against politicians]: The 1976 election process could involve Gerald Ford, Edward Kennedy, George Wallace and John Connally—four men threatened by, wounded by or closely involved with assassination. Thus, the memory and specter of political violence will hang over the campaign as never before.

Moreover, thousands of sick minds are reading and watching the never-ending media fascination with [accused or convicted assassins] Fromme, Sirhan, Oswald and Bremer and company. One quick pistol shot can make a lonely psychopath into a household word and historical figure. These thoughts, then, for changing the campaign: First, the media must shift gears, police themselves and stop glamorizing assassins and guerrillas. Second, let our candidates de-emphasize flesh-pressing and whistle-stopping. The real political challenge and crisis is in Washington. Bicentennial-year arrangements should be made for Ford, Rockefeller, Albert, Rhodes, Jackson, Reagan, Humphrey *et al* to meet in frequent policy confrontations and debates of the close, tough, personal nature faced by incumbent and aspiring national leaders everywhere else in the West.

*Interview/Newsweek, 10-6:34.*

**Ronald Reagan**
*Former Governor of California (R)*

4

If, at a time in history, growing numbers of people express belief that a particular person holds the right set of principles to be President, events will find a way of setting themselves in motion which he must accept or pass by.

*Los Angeles Times, 2-24:(2)1.*

5

No one can quarrel with the idea that a political party hopes it can attract a wide following; but does it do this by forsaking its basic beliefs, by blurring its image so as to be indistinguishable from the opposing party? Does any Republican seriously believe that any Democrats that subscribe to the profligacy, the big-government policies of the present Democratic leadership, will be won over to our side if we say these are our policies, too? . . . In the 1972 election we had a new majority—a long-overdue realignment based not on party labels but on basic philosophies. The tragedy of Watergate and the traumatic experiences following it have obscured the meaning of the 1972 election, but the mandate still remains. The people are unchanged philosophically. We must make them see that [what] we [Republicans] stand for is akin to their own hopes and dreams of what this country can and should be. A political party cannot be all things to all people. It cannot compromise its fundamental beliefs for political expediency to swell its numbers.

*At Republican National Committee leadership conference, Washington, March 8/ San Francisco Examiner & Chronicle, 3-9:(A)14.*

*1*

Some people see the term "right" as meaning a Hitler and clicking heels. Myself, I come closer to being a libertarian. What I want is the ultimate individual freedom consistent with an orderly society. My conservatism is because I see government encroaching too much on the people. The plain truth of the matter is that today's liberal is truly the Fascist. I don't mean that in the epithet term that liberals use for anyone to the right of them. But someone very profoundly said years ago that if Fascism ever came to America it would come under the name of liberalism. If you trace liberalism, the liberal is the one who has lost faith in the people, [who believes] that the government must set the rules for us—and this is Fascism.

*Interview, Los Angeles/ Los Angeles Herald-Examiner, 8-10:(California Living)11.*

*2*

I don't have much faith in the third-party movement. I think a third party usually succeeds in electing the people they set out to oppose.

*Broadcast interview, San Francisco, Aug. 29/ Los Angeles Herald-Examiner, 8-29:(A)1.*

**John J. Rhodes**
*United States Representative, R—Arizona*

*3*

Democrats have the image of the party of the people and [Republicans] of the party of big business. We've [Republicans] got to go out on our own and overcome that . . . A Congressional statement of principle and recognition of our identity is an absolute essential, or we're just going to rock along as a permanent minority.

*The Washington Post, 2-23:(A)2.*

**Elliot L. Richardson**
*Former Attorney General of the United States*

*4*

Did Watergate create more cynicism among people, or did it make them more sensitive to standards of political morality? I don't know where you come out in the long run. On the one hand, politicians know that they can't risk cutting corners or hoarding dirty little secrets, if only because they've learned that honesty is the best politics—whether or not there is a real regeneration of morality. On the other hand, there is a serious risk when you investigate corruption. You may do more harm than good if all you do is poke a stick in a muddy pool and stir up the mud without clarifying the water. But politicians govern their conduct in the light of past experience. You can wash the public standard of morality higher and onto the beach if you have a powerful enough wave. The wave then recedes—but the new high-water mark stays there.

*Newsweek, 1-13:24.*

**Nelson A. Rockefeller**
*Vice President of the United States*

*5*

[On whether he plans to run for President in the future] : . . . the American people are worried about *today*. We've got unemployment, we've got inflation, we've got the energy crisis, we've got all sorts of problems. And they want to feel that their government is dedicating itself to the solution of these problems and not worrying about politics and posturing for 1976 or 1980 . . . To discuss politics for 1980 when you've got 8.2 per cent unemployed and inflation and all the other problems I just think is irresponsible. I am not thinking about, concerned about, worried about or interested in 1976 or 1980 . . . [The people are] not interested in speculating about this Senator or that Senator who announces his candidacy, or this Vice President. They could care less. They want these people, including me, to forget politics and they'd like you [the press] to forget politics and say, "What's the government doing to solve their problems."

*Interview, Washington, Feb. 27/ The Washington Post, 2-28:(A)2.*

# WHAT THEY SAID IN 1975

*(NELSON A. ROCKEFELLER)*

1

[On whether he is too old to be considered by Republicans for a possible Presidential nomination]: I have no inhibitions, frankly, as far as my ability to do things is concerned, because of my age. I happen to be enjoying—knock on wood—very good health. I've missed three days of work in 30 years. Two weeks ago we had three parties at the Vice-Presidential mansion. Then I went to the South on a three-day trip. I got back to Washington at 1:30 Saturday morning and left at 11 o'clock Sunday night for London, spent the next day in London opening an exhibition, flew back Monday night from London. I was in the office at 10 o'clock Tuesday morning. And I have no problem with this kind of schedule. Really, I think the age thing is wishful thinking on the part of those—and I don't blame them—who talk about a younger man. Anybody who understands politics knows that, in the case of Vice President, all the younger men don't want a young man there because if a younger man is Vice President in '76 that means he's got the inside track for President in '80.
*Interview/U.S. News & World Report, 10-13:56.*

2

I think the Republican Party only is going to be an effective party if it reflects the best interests of the American people and, traditionally, that is in the center. That is where our country has always been. That is where the Republican Party has won. It is when it reflects the interests of the people and when it solves their problems. That is where I think it is going to be.
*News conference, Washington, Nov. 6/*
*The New York Times, 11-7:16.*

3

[Saying only 18 per cent of the American people are registered Republicans]: You don't win elections with 18 per cent and you don't win it with less than 18 per cent. You win it by majority. I happen to come from a state [New York] where we have one million registered minority for the Republican Party . . . I won [the Governorship] four terms. I didn't win just with the Republicans alone. I won with Democrats and independents. That is the way you win elections if you happen to be a member of the Republican Party.
*Interview/Parade, 12-14:7.*

## Peter W. Rodino, Jr.
*United States Representative, D—New Jersey;*
*Chairman, House Judiciary Committee*

4

[On President Ford's pre-indictment pardon of former President Nixon last year for any possible Watergate crimes]: I'm sure that at the time of the pardon he was impressed with the fact that Richard Nixon was in such a condition of health that God knows what might have happened. But you know, when we get to that position, then we've got to consider the whole country and the country's interest, and you've got to separate your personal feelings from your obligation . . . I'm sure he believes that he's right and that time alone will vindicate him . . . The question that will be asked is why should it have been that, immediately following this impeachment and resignation and while there was yet pending all of these other inquiries and investigations of others who had been involved, did he pardon the one man who was, as he had found, responsible for setting all of this in motion?
*Interview, Washington/*
*Los Angeles Times, 2-20:(1)5.*

5

[On former President Richard Nixon's role in Watergate]: Because of the deceptions he had practiced, and the whole pattern of what was happening, and orders he had issued in conversations with others, I'm sure he had to have general, if not specific, knowledge [of Watergate] . . . [Although his accomplishments in foreign affairs are to be saluted,] when I learned of all these [Watergate] activities, I became disillusioned. While I felt respect for him as the President, I questioned that a man who acted in this manner should lead our country any more. Some may say that the end result sought by Nixon and his subordinates was not to subvert the Constitutional system—

but that was what was happening. That we could not permit.

> *Interview, Washington/*
> *The Dallas Times Herald, 7-31:(A)9.*

**Hughes Rudd**
*News commentator, Columbia Broadcasting System*
1

... I used to be a yellow-dog Democrat, but I hate Democratic malfeasance as much as Republican. I'm not a knee-jerk liberal either—in fact, some liberals would call me reactionary. But that's good because I don't like to be easily categorized. As a matter of fact, I haven't voted for years because all politicians strike me as a bunch of charlatans. I can't think of anybody I'd go out and vote for right now.

> *Interview/*
> *Los Angeles Herald-Examiner, 9-11(B)8.*

**Donald H. Rumsfeld**
*Assistant and Chief of Staff to President of the United States Gerald R. Ford*
2

[Saying the Republican Party must embrace varied political views and people, not just conservatives]: The purpose of a political party is to earn the right to govern and that means you have to get a majority of the votes, and you have to reach out and add. Politics is addition, not subtraction.

> *TV-radio interview, Washington/*
> *"Meet the Press,"*
> *National Broadcasting Company, 3-9.*

**Richard S. Salant**
*President,*
*Columbia Broadcasting System News*
3

[President] Ford is an open man. He runs an open White House; he enjoys the press and the press enjoys him. You don't have to wonder what he means. He is just President, and that's refreshing. He is not playing games. I am convinced that if there were a tape system in the White House today, Ford would emerge exactly as he is in public. That's an enormous difference [between Ford and former President Nixon].

> *Los Angeles/Daily Variety, 5-14:1.*

**William E. Simon**
*Secretary of the Treasury of the United States*
4

[Criticizing the amount of publicity given to assassins and would-be assassins of the President]: All the publicity that's attached to all of these individuals, I believe, tends to exacerbate conditions. I sincerely question the value of all this publicity. It's the responsibility of the press, certainly, to tell the American people indeed what is happening—that is their responsibility in a very straight fashion. But when these people are glamorized on the front pages of our national magazines, I think that this has to be thought of as doing great harm.

> *Before Senate Appropriations Subcommittee,*
> *Washington, Sept. 30/*
> *The Washington Post, 10-1:(A)1.*

**Margaret Chase Smith**
*Former United States Senator, R—Maine*
5

[On Gerald Ford's assumption of the Presidency as a result of Richard Nixon's resignation due to the Watergate affair]: I think Ford was greatly handicapped by being named by a discredited President—and then for him to pardon that man who had not been found guilty of anything. I don't agree with the timing of the pardon. I don't see why Nixon should be pardoned for something he hadn't been convicted of. I was for impeachment. I felt this would give Nixon a chance to come in and give his side of the story. It would clear the record. And nothing is clear yet.

> *Interview, Skowhegan, Maine/*
> *The New York Times, 9-21:(1)56.*

**Lawrence E. Spivak**
*Producer and moderator, "Meet the Press,"*
*National Broadcasting Company*
6

One of the most innovative legislators and best brains I have known is [U.S. Senator] Hubert Humphrey. He doesn't talk off the top of his head. He knows. One of his troubles in the 1968 Presidential campaign was that a lot

# WHAT THEY SAID IN 1975

of people wouldn't believe that one man could know so much.

*Interview, Washington/People, 8-25:54.*

### Robert S. Strauss
*Chairman, Democratic National Committee*   1

[President Ford, personally, is] the same fine, decent man that others characterize him, maybe more so. I have a very high regard for him on that basis. [But] I would also characterize him as totally ill-equipped by background, experience and record to provide the kind of leadership this country needs right now. This country is ready for leadership. We've had six years without leadership—four or five years of corruption [under former President Nixon] and a year now of a bit of incompetence and indifference [under Ford].

*News conference, Washington, May 15/*
*The Dallas Times Herald, 5-16:(A)11.*

### Morris K. Udall
*United States Representative, D—Arizona*   2

Udall's Fourth Law of Politics is that if you can find something everyone agrees on, it's wrong. And the conventional wisdom is just as wrong this year as it was in 1972, when nobody believed George McGovern could be nominated [for the Presidency] and everybody thought Richard Nixon could be beaten.

*Before Prince George's County (Md.)*
*Democratic Women's Club/*
*The New York Times, 5-4:(4)15.*

3

[On Alabama Governor George Wallace and former California Governor Ronald Reagan]: [The Reagan brand is] the old familiar, established brand of traditional right-wing big-business politics. The George Wallace brand [is] a gaudy label promoted by catchy slogans that touch every raw nerve of fear and resentment. And inside this package there is nothing. It is "knownothingism," pure and simple.

*Before Communications Workers of America,*
*San Diego, June 12/*
*The Washington Post, 6-12:(A)4.*

### Jack Valenti
*President, Motion Picture Association of America; Former Special Assistant to the President of the United States (Lyndon B. Johnson)*   4

Both the Democrats and the Republicans have been plagued in this century with purists, do-gooders, fanatics, zealots, stern-eyed gospelers, those with a cause and those with a claim, all of whom are fixed in certitudes about what is plainly right and clearly wrong ... self-righteousness ... it is the blight of our society.

*San Francisco Examiner & Chronicle,*
*4-27:(This World)2.*

### George C. Wallace
*Governor of Alabama (D)*   5

I know the hierarchy of the Democratic Party wishes I would go away to Afghanistan, but unless they come away from what they had in 1972, the people I represent are going to be very much involved ... I was a viable candidate [for President] in 1972—so viable I was leading the popular vote myself. Yes, I'm a viable candidate [for 1976]—if I become a candidate.

*News conference, Washington, Feb. 18/*
*The New York Times, 2-19:18.*

6

I think today that Southerners more than ever feel that their thoughts and attitudes are the mainstream of American political thought because, when I was shot in '72, I had two million votes more than the next man in the primaries in which we contested one another, and that was in Michigan and Maryland and Pennsylvania and Wisconsin ... So the difference in the South now is that we're not going to be excluded, and we believe the nation likes us and we're part of the nation and we just want the liberals and the hierarchy of the [Democratic] Party to understand it.

*Interview, Montgomery, Alabama/*
*The New York Times Magazine, 4-27:46.*

7

[On his running for the 1976 Democratic Presidential nomination]: I'm not running for influence; I'm running for the Presidency. I want to have the influence of people I represent transmitted through me as their spokesman to the Party platform and to the nominees of the Party. Of course, I would like that nominee to be myself. But if not, those delegates and the people that support me would like to have enough influence to make sure that the Party platform would be acceptable to us.

*Interview, Montgomery, Alabama/*
*Newsweek, 11-24:39.*

## Lowell P. Weicker, Jr.
*United States Senator, R—Connecticut*
1

... it has been the custom for both parties [Democratic and Republican] to let their Presidential nominees set up their own campaign organizations. I think we learned two lessons from Watergate. One is that there will never again be a Presidential election committee separate and apart from the national committee. The other is that if we continue to go the convention route for the selection of our Presidential and Vice-Presidential candidates—and I think the convention method is not long for this world—then the convention delegates should involve themselves as much in the selection of the Vice-Presidential candidate as they do in the selection of their Presidential candi-

date. Here again there is an unwritten law that the Presidential candidate must be allowed to select his own running mate for the Vice-Presidency. What we must do is have the Vice-Presidential candidate selected by the 1,500 or so delegates in the convention hall. That is our best guarantee that we will get the finest person for the job.

*Interview/The Center Magazine, Jan.-Feb.:36.*

## Charles E. Wiggins
*United States Representative, R—California*
2

All the time I hear around Congress: "Things have changed so, it's not fun to serve any more." The idea of constantly being "surveilled," subjected to irrational accusations—I think the decision of many who've talked of retiring is due, in part, to this climate. They're saying: "Life is too damned short." I feel that way myself sometimes, especially when I'm subjected to shrill criticism for supporting something in the public interest. There's a hesitancy to do the right thing for people with a legitimate claim. The Congressman asks himself: "But if I do the right thing, how is it going to look on the front page of the newspaper if they write about it?"

*Los Angeles Times, 12-29:(1)20.*

# Social Welfare

**Edmund G. Brown, Jr.**
*Governor of California (D)*
1

[On the maze of Federal and state welfare regulations] : When I tried to look at the system to make some sense out of it, I made the mistake of saying I'd like to see the rules . . . Now I have them here. I thought you might like to see them. That, by my estimate, is about five million words. The Old Testament is about 774,000 words, and I really wonder whether we've made any improvement . . . What troubles me is there is so much human energy that is being squandered because of our present system. We are frustrating those who have to carry it out, we are frustrating those who have to live under it, and we are frustrating those who have to pay for it . . . I have a hunch the reason the system's so complicated is that we don't want to make too clear what's going on.
*Sacramento, March 12/*
*Los Angeles Times, 3-13:(1)1.*

2

The Great Society programs weren't all bad; some were a response to the needs of the people. But some of it was simply creating bureaucratic structures that only claimed to heal the sick and help the poor. Poverty programs, as far as I am concerned, are now the last refuge of scoundrels.
*Interview, Sacramento/*
*The New York Times, 4-13:(1)57.*

**Arthur F. Burns**
*Chairman, Federal Reserve Board*
3

A society as affluent as ours can ill afford to neglect the poor, the elderly, the unemployed or other disadvantaged persons. But neither can it afford to neglect the fundamental precept that there must be adequate rewards to stimulate individual effort.
*Before Congressional Joint Economic*
*Committee, Washington, Feb. 7/*
*Los Angeles Herald-Examiner, 2-7:(C)7.*

**Earl L. Butz**
*Secretary of Agriculture of the United States*
4

Food stamps are available to people on strike and university students. You don't have to be unemployed. It's so easy to get food stamps. That's why you people can't get anyone to work on your farms. This nation wasn't made great by people sitting on their fannies expecting to get paid for it.
*Before farmers, Augusta, Maine, Aug. 14/*
*Los Angeles Herald-Examiner, 8-15:(A)5.*

**Barber B. Conable, Jr.**
*United States Representative, R—New York*
5

Everybody [in Congress] wants to get into the welfare business. The Housing committees are in it through housing aid. The Ways and Means Committee is in it through Social Security; Interstate and Foreign Commerce through health programs. The Agriculture Committee has food stamps. Education and Labor has its programs. Everybody wants a toe-hold.
*U.S. News & World Report, 11-10:40.*

**Carl T. Curtis**
*United States Senator, R—Nebraska*
6

. . . it is totally immoral and dishonest to vote for more welfare-state programs than we are willing to collect the taxes to pay for. Fifteen cents out of every dollar that will be spent by Washington this next year will come from borrowing. These welfare-state programs were not created in the last few months. The welfare state has been built brick-by-brick over several decades. I do not believe that these programs came into existence because of the demands of our citizens. They came into being as promotion schemes by office-seeking politicians.
*Before Nebraska Press Association, Lincoln,*
*April 12/Human Events, 5-10:16.*

**Michael S. Dukakis**
*Governor of Massachusetts (D)*
1

I'm a great believer in hard work, and I expect the people who work for me and work for the government to be the same way. I think if people on welfare in the community have the capacity to work, then we ought to expect them to work, too. You have to confront the reality of the situation and decide how much the state can afford. You just can't walk through a school filled with mentally retarded children, for example, and then return to the office and look at millions of dollars to support the able-bodied. Some hard budget choices have to be made.

*Interview/The Washington Post, 7-5:(A)4.*

**Arthur S. Flemming**
*Commissioner,*
*Federal Administration on Aging*
2

Many older persons live in despair rather than hope. If this situation continues it will, to a considerable degree, be due to sins of ommission on the part of members of the religious community. The church and the synagogue present one of the greatest resources in the area of serving older persons. As a whole, the religious community isn't living up to that potential.

*Quote, 4-27:386.*

**Gerald R. Ford**
*President of the United States*
3

In just seven years, cash benefits under Social Security programs will have risen from $26-billion in 1969 to $70-billion in 1976 . . . By 1976, six Social Security benefit increases will have occurred since 1969. Automatic cost-of-living adjustments to benefits now are provided by law. Allowing the temporary five per cent ceiling I have proposed on benefit increases between now and July, 1976, the increases from 1970 through 1976 in the average recipient's Social Security benefits, taken together, will total 77 per cent. This far exceeds the increases in the cost of living estimated for this period . . . Part of our trouble is that we have been self-indulgent. For decades we have been voting ever-increasing levels of government benefits—and now the bill has come due.

*Fiscal 1976 budget message\*/*
*The Christian Science Monitor, 3-7:5C.*

4

The trouble with a lot of these [welfare, food-stamp] programs, where compassion ought to be the main thrust, is that they get well beyond the properly intended scope. And the net result is that when you try to bring them back to focus on the people who need and deserve help—whether food stamps or welfare generally—when you try to cut out the undeserving so you can give more to the people who are really in need, you can't be compassionate for the ones who get cut out, because they shouldn't have been in the program in the first place. And yet they're the most vocal; they're the ones who feel that because they were on something, they ought to continue. Really, the ones that are deserving of compassion are the ones that complain the least. It's the ones who are sort of the fringe people who cause the most trouble and get the issue confused.

*Interview, Washington/*
*The New York Times Magazine, 4-20:116.*

**John Kenneth Galbraith**
*Former professor of economics,*
*Harvard University*
5

One of the singular features of the modern industrial country and, indeed, one of the causes of inflation is the upgrading of the hitherto dispossessed people. In the past, it was taken for granted that there was a hierarchy of consumption. Recipients of property income, executives got the most. Then came doctors, lawyers, other professional people—including Harvard professors. Then came white-collar workers and then blue-collar workers. At the bottom were the blacks and Puerto Ricans. This structure of consumption is breaking down, and it surely should break down. And it's breaking down not because of the willingness of the people at the top to take less, but because of the insistence of the people at the bottom that they should consume more. It is no longer taken for granted that the children of a blue-collar worker shouldn't have vacations, shouldn't

# WHAT THEY SAID IN 1975

*(JOHN KENNETH GALBRAITH)*

go to college, shouldn't ever go to Europe. I would expect this process to continue and to exert a much stronger pressure on the productive capacity of the industrial countries in the future. It will also affect income distribution. In the past, we have solved the problem of aspirant claims by giving everybody some more—both the rich and the poor. When we can no longer do that, the claims of the affluent will have to give way to those of the poor.

*Interview/U.S. News & World Report, 11-3:44.*

## W. Averell Harriman
*Former United States Ambassador-at-Large* 1

From the long-run standpoint, the Federal government should take responsibility for all welfare. This is an enormous step, it is true, but the government is already paying 50 per cent. It is something you can't do this year, but, as you know, New York's major problem is the large population on relief—something like 1.25 million people. New York has been very generous in its welfare payments. That is one of the reasons why so many people have come to New York from the South and Puerto Rico. But that is a problem everybody should share. You must remember that the problem is not just making payments to persons on welfare but providing housing, education, health and other services that flow from increases in the population for whom there are no jobs. I have always felt we should have a national welfare policy. In many cases it would have encouraged families to have remained in the South in better houses and surroundings than in the slums of New York.

*Interview, Washington/*
*Los Angeles Times, 10-7:(2)5.*

## Vance Hartke
*United States Senator, D—Indiana* 2

It is clear that the entire [veterans'] pension system must be reviewed and overhauled. It is my conviction . . . that any pension system that is developed should meet the following standards: First, every veteran and his dependent should be able to live out their lives in dignity. This means, simply, that no veteran or his widow should be forced to resort to welfare relief, and all should be assured a level of income that clearly places them above the poverty level. Second, veterans with similar needs should receive similar benefits and those with greater needs should be entitled to a greater pension. Third, vets should receive regular increases in their pension that fully account for any increases in the costs of living.

*Before Veterans of Foreign Wars,*
*Washington, March 9/*
*Los Angeles Herald-Examiner, 3-10:(A)3.*

## Leonard Hayflick
*Professor of medical microbiology, Stanford University School of Medicine* 3

There is a whole mythology that goes along with growing old. It is a form of role-playing that has in fact made people feel old and lose interest in life and consequently age more rapidly than they would ordinarily if this whole mythology and bias that society puts on the aged did not exist . . . We have a lot of people who could be very productive but are turned out to pasture at what, as far as productivity is concerned, is a very early age. Society really has to re-evaluate the basic decision that, in the minds of almost all gerontologists, was a bad decision—which is forced retirement at a fixed age.

*Interview, Tulsa, Okla./*
*The Dallas Times Herald, 4-4:(D)3.*

## Lane Kirkland
*Secretary-treasurer, American Federation of Labor-Congress of Industrial Organizations* 4

I would put the problems of the man who does not have a job ahead of the problems of the man who does not like his work. I would put the problems of non-work ahead of the problem of the quality of work. I would put the problem of the aged poor ahead of the problem of the unhappy youth. I would deal with the problems of the unemployed, the sick, the old and the poor, before I would become very obsessed with the problems of the young, the healthy and the affluent. And I suppose that brings us into opposition with the new politics which deals with the problems of the young and the educated middle class.

*Interview, Washington/*
*The New York Times, 9-1:5.*

### John V. Lindsay
*Former Mayor of New York*

1

The welfare system local governments are forced to fund is not the creation of New York or Boston or Philadelphia, but of Washington. And it has been imposed on local people and the local property tax in the most unworkable form possible. It remains America's greatest scandal—not because of its generosity or fraud, but because of its discrimination and bureaucracy and anti-work ethic—a non-productive American system that the American Federal government refuses to reform, and which only it can do.

*At Bicentennial Forum, Boston/*
*The Christian Science Monitor, 7-15:27.*

### William M. Lukash
*Rear Admiral, United States Navy;*
*Physician to President of the*
*United States Gerald R. Ford*

2

Many elderly people don't have to get out of the job market at all. They can maintain their self-esteem by working with young people, working with a new business or by being productive in other ways. Another way to keep older people going is for their families to show some concern. Simply visiting them once or twice a week, talking to them, reading to them or taking them on trips can be an enormous help. It enables retired people to maintain their identity and might save the taxpayers a ton of money by keeping them out of insititutions. We're way behind the times in this area of aiding the elderly, and the funny thing is that most of us are going to be there someday ourselves.

*Interview, Washington/*
*U.S. News & World Report, 11-10:58.*

### William F. May
*Chairman, American Can Company*

3

I am more convinced than ever that we need some kind of livable minimum guaranteed income for every American. I have had a view for the past two years that a negative-income-tax system is the most direct and least bureaucratic way to do it, and I am flattered that both the Democrats and Republicans now seem to agree with that view. If you are below the minimum, the government pays you; if you are above the minimum, you begin to pay your tax, but never at a rate which removes the incentive to earn more. I think this approach is long overdue, as a constructive way to provide for those who cannot provide for themselves, without the contentiousness of our patchwork welfare system.

*At API-FBA Employee Relations Conference,*
*Chicago, Jan. 22/Vital Speeches, 3-1:311.*

### Robert H. Michel
*United States Representative, R–Illinois*

4

We keep pulling more and more Americans under the welfare umbrella, and every time we do we sap that much more energy from the economy, just that much more personal responsibility from individual citizens.

*Before the House, Washington/*
*The New York Times, 10-8:16.*

### Robert Morris
*Gerontologist; Director, Levinson Policy*
*Institute, Brandeis University*

5

There are good nursing homes. There are those that do a fine job and are very responsible. Remember that we have trusted this problem to private business. That is what nursing homes are. Private business has filled a vacuum that no one else wanted to fill, and I think they deserve credit for that . . . Now, having said the good things about nursing homes, let me say the bad things. The way the financing works, the incentives for providing human care are minimal. The nursing home gets paid not according to the goodness of its care but according to the medical and nursing services that are provided. That means the pay favors taking care of the medical treatment side of things as opposed to saying, "Look, there are people to be maintained. They are going to live here the rest of their lives. You have to have decent living arrangements." A doctor will say that a patient needs speech therapy, for example. The nursing home will get extra money for it. The doctor

# WHAT THEY SAID IN 1975

*(ROBERT MORRIS)*

will say a patient needs drugs. The nursing home will get extra money for administering them. But if the doctor says this patient needs to have slow help and retraining to feed himself, or has to be fed so slowly that it may take an hour to get a meal down, then the nursing home won't get the staff to do that. If the patient ought to be gotten out of bed a certain number of times a day, that does not get recognized. The nursing home will only do what it is paid for. It is a business. It has to get its profit. After it has made the profit and paid the doctors and nurses, it doesn't have enough left over for attendants to feed a lot of patients who are sitting around, many of them unable to feed themselves.

*Interview, Waltham, Mass./*
*The Washington Post, 4-29:(2)5.*

**Frank E. Moss**
*United States Senator, D–Utah*    *1*

I'm opposed to mandatory retirement . . . Perhaps they [senior citizens] couldn't work an eight-hour day, perhaps a four-hour day. But older people need something to do and it shouldn't just be self-amusement. They need to do something that their minds tell them is a contribution, of importance. That's one of our greatest sins against the older people, to set them apart in retirement, and contribute to this idea that they're no longer needed. They're just supposed to play shuffleboard or sit on the park bench or something of the sort.

*The Christian Science Monitor, 4-16:21.*

**Vincent Reed**
*Acting Superintendent of Schools*
*of the District of Columbia*    *2*

We [his family] were poor, but we made it. We had to do without some things sometimes, but we made it. That's why I get so upset when we tell our kids they can't learn if they come from meager circumstances. People make the mistake of thinking that if you're poor, you've got all sorts of problems. I know it's easy for somebody who's comfortable to overplay being poor, but I think if you are poor you can make

the best of what you've got and still be proud of what you are.

*Interview, Washington/*
*The Washington Post, 11-17:(A)22.*

**Donald H. Rumsfeld**
*Assistant and Chief of Staff to President of the*
*United States Gerald R. Ford;*
*Former Director,*
*Federal Office of Economic Opportunity*    *3*

One of the very things that was inherent in the design of the OEO programs, namely, the targeting of the poor, tended to harden the crust and separated the poor from the non-poor, rather than making the crust more porous so that there was an opportunity for mobility and inclusion of people who were somewhat separate from society. It's unfortunate that the effort did not produce more good for the country and that it didn't evolve in a way that was more acceptable to enough people that it could be sustained.

*The Washington Post, 5-18:(A)11.*

**Leonor K. Sullivan**
*United States Representative, D–Missouri*    *4*

I believe in equality of opportunity. I voted for a welfare increase to help people. But I cringe as I see us put more and more into the category of "takers" instead of "doers." We're just creating a larger and larger welfare state.

*U.S. News & World Report, 8-4:31.*

**Herman E. Talmadge**
*United States Senator, D–Georgia*    *5*

There are people living in communes, able-bodied but not doing anything to earn their way, who are receiving food stamps. There are people who spend their food stamps on exotic and highly expensive foods. There is a steak supply company here in Washington, D.C., which specializes in the best cuts, which few working people can afford to patronize. Yet, on its window is a sign: "Food Stamps Accepted."

*Quote, 4-20:368.*

**Morris K. Udall**
*United States Representative, D–Arizona*    *6*

Liberals don't have to be wastefuls. We created a lot of programs in the '50s and '60s, the Great Society programs, because we really care about people. We wanted to do something about poverty and health and the problems of old age and so on. But liberals ought to be among the first to say that some of them didn't work. Where I differ with . . . some of the others is that they seem to be putting out a message of a kind of fatalism, of "Sorry, friends, there is not much your government can do for you," whereas my approach would be that if those old programs failed, by God, let's try something else.

*Interview/Los Angeles Times, 10-27:(1)18.*

**George C. Wallace**
*Governor of Alabama (D)*

1

. . . the great mass of middle-class America is probably in the greatest state of anguish and discontent they've ever been in. These people have been the supporters of this system, and they are losing their affluence, and they cannot make ends meet. People on one end are looked after and people on the other end are looked after, but these in the middle have been looking after everybody . . .

*Interview, Montgomery, Alabama/*
*The New York Times Magazine, 4-27:45.*

2

And the welfare programs—theoreticians said, "You can't offend a man's dignity," and billions of dollars have gone to people in California and New York and Ohio and those states— sometimes to the same people under 13 different names. Now, we ought to have had a welfare program that was set up so that if you need it you get it, but if you don't, you don't get it.

*Interview, Montgomery, Alabama/*
*The New York Times Magazine, 4-27:48.*

**Caspar W. Weinberger**
*Secretary of Health, Education and*
*Welfare of the United States*

3

. . . Federal spending has transformed the task of aiding life's victims from a private concern to a public obligation. There are benefits and burdens in this. One benefit is that the care of the less fortunate is guaranteed under law. The sweep of our social-program commitments has brought secure incomes for the elderly, the ill, those who are alone and those who are disabled. They have provided health care for millions and opened the doors of college to young people whose families could not otherwise have given their sons and daughters this opportunity. But, in the process of pouring out all of these compassionate and humanitarian blessings and institutionalizing our social obligations, we have built an edifice of law and regulation that is clumsy, inefficient and inequitable. Worst of all, the unplanned, uncoordinated and spasmodic nature of our resources to these needs—some very real, some only perceived—is quite literally threatening to bring us to national insolvency. We are also creating a massive welfare state that has intruded into the lives and personal affairs of our citizens. This intrusion affects both those it seeks to help and those who do the helping. The entire human-resources field is under the lash of Federal law—doctor, hospital, teacher, college president, student, voluntary agency, city hall and state capitol. All of these are subject to the steadily increasing intrusion of the Congress, which requires that drastic and often unnecessary regulations be adopted by the Executive Branch . . . What we do have to limit is the growth of the welfare state in America. We must summon up a common determination as a people to change drastically our present approach because it is not only not working, but it can ruin all of us. Only a wave of public sentiment in this direction can give Congress the nerve to say "no" to more social programs. As it is, Congress quite evidently believes that the road to popularity and re-election is to say "yes" to every demand for every increase in all existing programs and to agree to most demands for new ones. Above all, we must recognize that personal freedoms diminish as the welfare state grows. The price of more and more public programs is less and less private freedom. It is also the propensity of welfare states to spend beyond their means, leaving the day of fiscal reckoning to another generation. The news today is that we *are* that other generation.

*Before Commonwealth Club, San Francisco,*
*July 21/The National Observer, 8-2:2.*

# Transportation

**Robert Anderson**
*President, Rockwell International* 1

Whenever man has traveled to some distant place, he has always first traveled by dreams and imagination. Transportation is the transformation of those dream voyages into the actual spanning of distances by man. And each time that transportation performs this dream-fulfilling function, civilization follows on the heels of the pathfinders. It has been so on our own American continent—and it will be so as man voyages out into space. For the job of transportation is not just to move people and goods from point to point—it is to also move history forward by enabling the pioneers to explore the new frontiers and by enabling society to capitalize on their discoveries.

*At Canadian National Exhibition,*
*Toronto, Aug. 21/***

**Shizuo Asada**
*President, Japan Airlines* 2

[On "unethical business practices" in the airline industry]: It is not uncommon today for people planning travel to shop around for special under-the-table deals which undercut established fares. True, the beneficiaries enjoy unexpected and undeserved savings. But what happens when the international carriers deal themselves out of business? Who, then, will provide the safe and dependable air transport to which our customers are entitled?

*Before International Aviation Club,*
*Washington, Nov. 18/*
*The New York Times, 11-19:53.*

**Helen Delich Bentley**
*Chairman, Federal Maritime Commission* 3

Our nation's transportation system now faces a crisis of sorts, because the many varied interests that comprise that system are often in conflict—and because it is sometimes impossible to satisfy all these interests simultaneously and still maintain a stable and healthy commerce. The Federal government cannot be all things to all people. Hard decisions must be made and priorities established. When decisions must be made in conflicts between ports, shippers, ship operators and other elements of transportation, those decisions must be fair ones. But, in the final analysis, those decisions must be made for the over-all public interest. Perhaps the only way we can do this is to establish a National Transportation Policy—a policy which clearly spells out our national needs, and gives priority to certain needs. Certainly, such a policy would eliminate much doubt and uncertainty, so that everyone would know exactly where they were going and how they were going to get there.

*Before International Longshoremen's*
*Association, Bal Harbour, Fla., July 23/*
*Vital Speeches, 9-1:682.*

**William T. Coleman, Jr.**
*Secretary of Transportation of the*
*United States* 4

I think it is very important that the Federal government and the people take steps to revitalize the railroads in this country. When you realize in the East, for example, if the Penn Central would shut down for two weeks, that 60 per cent of the manufacturing facilities in the country would have to shut down, when you realize the energy problems, the coal problems, some defense needs, the American people ought to realize there is an immediacy to see that the railroads are completely revised throughout the country. We do have under active consideration programs that will bring about that result.

*TV-radio interview, Washington/*
*"Meet the Press,"*
*National Broadcasting Company, 3-23.*

*1*

We want to make it clear that in any major city or any seaport there would be at least two railroads that would serve that community. But we don't feel that you need six railroads going from Chicago to Omaha. My understanding is that to move freight from California to Boston you may go across 11 different railroads. Now, just the problem of the accounting—because every time you go on someone's railroad you've got to say, "You went 300 miles on my railroad and so, therefore, of the freight bill, I'm entitled to "X" dollars"—that must cost hundreds of millions of dollars each year. Add to that that every time you go on another railroad you usually have to change work crews and the work crew may not have worked the full eight-hour day. And the whole problem of keeping track of the boxcars—my understanding is that almost any day something like 7 to 10 per cent of the boxcars in the country are lost. And you have this whole problem of trying to identify who is responsible for a loss. You ship furniture and it's put on in Chicago in good shape and comes off in Boston damaged and each carrier says, "I didn't do it; the other carrier did it." That's just a tremendous waste of money. There's no sense to it.

*Interview, Washington/*
*Los Angeles Herald-Examiner, 7-28:(A)6.*

*2*

Despite all of the money we've been spending on . . . other methods, the automobile is by far the primary method of transportation, and it will continue to be. We have to recognize that it gave us the great mobility we have in this country. We also have to recognize that it creates about 10 per cent of our job opportunities. Therefore, I think any public policy directed toward eliminating the automobile is a phony, and the politician who suggests it is not acting in good faith. What we have to do is make the automobile a much more efficient vehicle and make its use much more socially responsible. We can make it more efficient by having cars—and driving habits—that cut down on the fatalities on the highways; to have cars that will have gas consumption in keeping with the new petroleum problems . . . In addition,

once you put in a transportation system that makes sense, people will use their cars in a much more socially acceptable fashion. They won't drive into the center of the city and park all day. Instead, they'll drive to a parking lot and then take a high-speed train.

*Interview, Washington/*
*U.S. News & World Report, 11-17:45.*

**Barry Commoner**
*Director, Center for the Biology of Natural*
*Systems, Washington University, St. Louis*

*3*

[Calling for the nationalization of railroads]: . . . if we want to survive the energy crisis, we'll have to expand rail service, not contract it as the government and the railroads seem to believe. In the next 25 years we'll need to be replacing highways with railways. Our rail system will have to become as finely branched as our highway system is today. But in the name of private profit, we are doing this fantastically perverse thing of getting rid of rail lines just when we need them most . . . The pollution effect on small cities would be disastrous. Freight moving through towns by train has little impact on city streets, but the planned rail cuts mean thousands more trucks running through city centers, increasing noise and air pollution, causing more accidents and tearing up streets.

*The National Observer, 8-9:3.*

**J. R. Coupal, Jr.**
*Deputy Administrator, Federal Highway*
*Administration of the United States*

*4*

In an effort to overcome the recognizable problems created by a heavy reliance on the automobile for commuter travel, many opponents of highways have reached the conclusion that the automobile can be replaced by "mass transit." Unfortunately, there is a significant misunderstanding about the definition of mass transit. Most people, when that term is used, conjure up a vision of a shiny aluminum monorail flashing by at 120 miles per hour and replacing all the automobiles. This impression obviously is unrealistic and impractical. Fixed-rail mass transit is a viable solution to the

*(J. R. COUPAL, JR.)*

commuter problem only in a very small number of very large cities with high densities of population. The Urban Mass Transportation Administration has concluded that there are only 10 or a dozen cities in the United States where fixed-guideway transit is a viable solution to the problem. In all the other metropolitan areas of this country, and in all the small cities and rural areas, the transportation of people, whether it be for commuting to work, for shopping, for pleasure, or for use in commerce, can and must be provided by the highway, passenger-car, bus combination.

*Before Western Association of State Highway Officials, Las Vegas, Nev./ The National Observer, 5-17:21.*

## Lewis A. Engman
*Chairman, Federal Trade Commission* 1

[On government regulation of the airline industry]: Our system, which severely inhibits price competition and restricts entry, has led to a fare structure on many routes which economists agree is far higher than that which would prevail if the industry were characterized by price competition and free entry. Several conditions flow from this fact. The absence of any real price competition, coupled with higher-than-competitive rates, leads to large amounts of non-price competition. One important type of non-price competition is in terms of frequency of flights. This in turn leads to large amounts of excess capacity. It is not unusual today for several planes to fly almost identical schedules, each with a small fraction of its seats filled on some flights. In short, there is economic waste—the classic cost-plus syndrome . . . In addition, fixed rates have created a sort of phony war, a war in which airlines compete for business, not on the basis of price, but on the basis of scheduling and comfort. All of us today have standing invitations to fly Cheryl or Karen or Trixie or even Bruce. Those invitations are no more or less than confessions on the part of the airlines that our decision as to which to fly pretty much boils down to whether Cheryl is more attractive than Bruce. This bogus competition, along with creature comforts and the

pressure to up the number of flights, can be explained by the simple economics of the airline industry. We start with an increase in fares. In the absence of price competition each airline tends to compete away the "profits" from the fare increase by engaging in various forms of increased non-price competition. More frills are added. Witness the great free-drink battles of recent times or the lounge wars of some time back. Often, flight frequencies are also increased. Unfortunately, this tends to reduce over-all load factors on all the planes. Rates of return go down, and soon a new fare increase is "required" to maintain the existing rates of return. The whole non-productive cycle starts all over again.

*Before Senate Subcommittee on Administrative Practice and Procedure, Washington, Feb. 6/\*\**

## Henry Ford II
*Chairman, Ford Motor Company* 2

[On mass transit]: No, I don't think it's going to damage our [automobile] business at all. Mass transit is not going to develop to any great extent [in the U.S.]—simply because we can't afford it. There's another thing to consider: This country was built on the basis of the automobile. Go back to the early part of the century when the auto was first introduced. Cities were small. We were an agricultural economy and just starting to become an industrialized country. Distances were great. The suburbs spread out, and everything was built around the automobile. It's different in Europe, where big cities existed long before they heard of an automobile. Transportation systems there were built on mass transit long before the car came. Our development was completely different, and I can't see mass transit replacing the automobile at all. In fact, mass transit might even help the auto business. Look at one of the ideas commonly mentioned: using an auto to get to a fringe parking lot, then switching to some form of mass transit. That would be a great boon to the person who drives a car, not a detriment.

*Interview/U.S. News & World Report, 10-20:28.*

**Lee A. Iacocca**
*President, Ford Motor Company*

1

[On safety and other equipment required by government to be standard on automobiles]: At a time like this, it seems incredible to us that the government of the United States is planning to impose a host of new standards that will give a big push to inflation, depress sales and employment in our industry even further, increase gasoline consumption substantially—and do hardly anything for public health and safety.

*The Christian Science Monitor, 2-11:4.*

**John W. Ingram**
*President, Chicago, Rock Island and Pacific Railroad*

2

While the Interstate Commerce Commission pursues its mandate from Congress to protect the public from the bad monopolists running railroads, the Commission: holds some rates up; holds some rates down; it keeps people from getting *into* transportation; it keeps others from getting *out* of transportation; examines the "public interest" in some questions for several times the length of time usually required for a question to rise in our court system all the way to the Supreme Court. Ultimately, the ICC is destroying the pool of capital used for rail common-carrier service in the U.S. by delays which erode capital, and by failing to recognize that its pursuit of "competition" in transportation has created what the ICC was to control: monopolies—or, more realistically, regulatory cartels.

*At railroad conference, Cornell University/ The Wall Street Journal, 6-26:12.*

**George W. James**
*Economist, Air Transport Association*

3

[Saying CAB regulation of air transport is desirable]: Airline customers have a need for such [small-city] services at times, to places and under circumstances ordinary business would not provide . . . Free-market forces would result in scheduled airlines leaving many less-profitable markets and concentrating only on certain of the major routes—with the consequences that me-

dium and smaller-sized cities of the Northeast, Midwest, South and Far West would suffer.

*Before Senate Subcommittee, Washington/ The New York Times, 2-18:39.*

**Edward M. Kennedy**
*United States Senator, D—Massachusetts*

4

When we have 210 million people and 125 million automobiles and motor trucks, when we use 52 per cent of our petroleum and 24 per cent of our total energy for transportation, when we produce nearly 10 million automobiles and junk another seven million each year, when we find our railroads going bankrupt, and when we carried 19 billion mass-transit fares in 1945 but only 5.5 billion in 1973—when we find out all of these facts—then it is time to redesign our transportation system.

*San Francisco Examiner & Chronicle, 8-31:(B)2.*

**Howard E. Kershner**
*Visiting professor of current economic problems, Northwood Institute*

5

The Interstate Commerce Commission might be said to have destroyed the railroads, and is in the process of destroying our bus lines and the trucking industry. Instead of keeping trucks loaded both ways, it often sends them loaded in one direction, to return empty. It often sends them in circuitous, roundabout ways instead of the shortest distance between the place of origin and the destination of the cargo. This is typical of what regulative agencies are doing.

*Before National Coordinating Committee for Constructive Action, Dallas, Sept. 6/ Vital Speeches, 10-15:14.*

**Harding L. Lawrence**
*Chairman, Braniff International Airways*

6

[Opposing President Ford's proposed deregulation of commercial airlines]: The "free entry and free exit" provisions of this proposed measure could tear down the whole air transportation industry and result in a "blood bath" which would be the end of many carriers. The result could be that one or two monopolistic companies would emerge—with tremendous cash resources but inefficient. Many areas that now have air service would suffer . . . There are

243

# WHAT THEY SAID IN 1975

some who have complained from time to time about the slowness of the Civil Aeronautics Board and other regulatory boards in making their decisions. But we are a nation of laws and it is better to have the careful judgment of many dedicated men who serve on those boards. If we lose that "due process of law," there will be only 19 free countries left in the world, instead of 20. Anyone with a property right is entitled to be heard. No one can take away that "due process of law" right, because the people won't put up with it.

*Interview, Dallas/*
*The Dallas Times Herald, 10-23:(F)11.*

**Marshall McLuhan**
*Professor of English, University of Toronto* 1

Mass transportation is doomed to failure in North America because a person's car is the only place he can be alone and think. He has to be a social animal at home, so he will refuse to give up the privacy of his car, no matter how much it costs or how convenient buses, subways, or car pools could be.

*Newsweek, 9-22:14.*

**Toby Moffett**
*United States Representative, D–Connecticut* 2

[On nationalization of railroads]: People don't react that negatively. As far as many of them are concerned, the important thing is to keep their rail service; who owns it is a secondary matter. Besides, they know that in Europe government-owned rail systems work well. The people are way ahead of the politicians on many issues, and nationalization may very well be one of them.

*The National Observer, 8-9:3.*

**Thomas A. Murphy**
*Chairman, General Motors Corporation* 3

People need automobile transportation in this country. All through the [oil] shortage, they continued to use their cars. That's our living style. Whether the automobile caused it or made it possible, this is what people in this country want. Nearly 80 per cent of people get

to and from work in a car. We are in a period when sales have been running well below the calculated "scrappage" rate, based on an assumption of what the useful life of an automobile is. If the type of transportation which the user has become accustomed to is going to be continued, he has to have a replacement. Scrappage is a function of the economy because people can make the cars last a little bit longer if they want to. And they do in an economic downturn. The one thing that gives me some assurance that auto sales have got to turn around is the way the market for automobiles developed. Everybody, regardless of his income, has the opportunity to have access to an automobile. There are people who never buy a new car. There are also people who always buy a new car. During a period like this, the new-car buyer is just as well off as ever. He makes his car go a year or two longer than he intended. But the used-car buyer's supply is being held up because he is waiting for that used car to come from the new-car buyer.

*Interview/*
*Business Week, 7-28:51.*

**John E. Murray**
*Vice president, Association of American Railroads* 4

Railroad management is among the best this side of Celestial Management. For it is this management . . . that faces and survives the toughest, looniest, most unpredictable business and government conditions in a time not noted for ease, sanity and certitude. The problem isn't railroad management; it's government interference with management. What other management has its competition outrageously subsidized? Its ability to merge and prosper governmentally delayed for over a decade? Its income taxed beyond that of others? Its non-profit lines continued by mandate? And its legitimate pricing of service forbidden by lagging administrators from keeping up with costs? What other industry had almost 1.5 million people 30 years ago and now has only ½-million, while increasing its productivity almost 15 per cent?— in fact, by a whopping 110 billion ton-miles! Instead of being defamed, railroad management should be acclaimed. The real questions for the college professor are not how railroads are doing, but what is government doing to them. And not why are the railroads doing so poorly, but how are they doing so well, while being treated so poorly. And for those who say that government management of railroads will work, they are just like those who say that, after all, earthquakes will work—if you happen to be holding a cocktail shaker, it'll mix things up for you. In World War I the government took over the railroads and it cost the taxpayer $2-million a day to run them. In World War II the government didn't take over the railroads and they pumped $3-million a day into the U.S. Treasury. Which way would you rather have it?

*Before Pacific Coast Shippers Advisory Board, Monterey, Calif., Sept. 25/ Vital Speeches, 11-1:49.*

**Ralph Nader**
*Lawyer; Consumer advocate*
1

[Calling for the dissolution of the CAB]: Instead of efficiency, we have widespread waste and an airline industry that operates at only half its capacity. Instead of low fares, we have rates that are much higher than those of unregulated airlines. Instead of promoting price competition, the Board has actively suppressed it, acting less as a regulator than a cartel manager.

*Before Senate Subcommittee on Administrative Practice and Procedure, Washington, Feb. 25/ The Washington Post, 2-26:(E)14.*

**Robert Oppenlander**
*Treasurer and vice president for finance, Delta Air Lines*
2

[Arguing against deregulation of the airline industry by the CAB]: It is my considered opinion that the probability of degrading and eroding our air-transportation system is much greater than the probability of improving it by deregulation. We are vitally concerned about what happens if these changes to the system are made and they do not work as the critics [of the CAB] expected they would. What happens when instead of many carriers ... providing lower fares to more people, there are fewer carriers than we have now, serving fewer people,

at higher fares? . . . Since 1948, the round-trip air fare from New York to San Francisco has gone up 21 per cent in current dollars . . . In that same period of time the price of automobiles had increased more than 220 per cent; housing more than 110 per cent . . . During that same period, median family income has increased almost 300 per cent. Who would provide airport facilities and guarantee their financing for carriers with freedom of entry but no obligation to remain?

*At Harvard Business School/ The Christian Science Monitor, 3-25:4.*

**David Packard**
*Chairman, Hewlett-Packard Company*
3

[Criticizing government-required equipment and specifications for automobiles]: We have a recession today largely because the public is not willing to buy new automobiles that the Federal government has designed and priced for us. I know I don't want a 1975-model car designed by Congress. I would rather use my 1972 model for a few more years—and I think I have a great deal of company around the country.

*At Joint Financial Management Improvement Program conference, Washington, Jan. 20/ The New York Times, 1-21:47.*

**John B. M. Place**
*Chairman, Anaconda Company*
4

[Over-regulation of business by government has] so interfered with the normal functioning of our economic life that we are in danger of strangling it to death. Some of our airlines are facing bankruptcy because they cannot compete. Raising fares is one thing, but airlines can't even cut fares without Civil Aeronautics Board consent. Railroads and trucking firms are so bedeviled by a myriad of rules and regulations that giving the consumer good service at reasonable prices is becoming increasingly difficult.

*The Christian Science Monitor, 4-22:12.*

**Harry Reasoner**
*News commentator, American Broadcasting Company*
5

[On the recent exchange of routes between Pan American and Trans World Airlines which eliminated wasteful competition between

# WHAT THEY SAID IN 1975

them]: ... the wisdom of the decision doesn't change its effects, which are melancholy. Not only the sometime wastefulness, but the frequent excellence of American industry is based on competition, and the chance to win great reward by competing is the basis for a kind of American effort that has probably produced more good than evil. No matter how good their intentions, neither airline will be quite as much on their toes on a non-competitive route. One man remembers the days when only Pan Am flew the Pacific beyond Honolulu; the filet mignon stopped at Hawaii, and from then on it was cheese sandwiches. Well, maybe a few cheese sandwiches, in a lot of areas, will be good for the country. But it's pardonable to wistfully remember the filet mignon.

*ABC News commentary/*
*The Christian Science Monitor, 2-12:12.*

## Paul Reistrup
*President of Amtrak (American National*
*Railroad Passenger Corporation)*          *1*

[On U.S. travelers who unfavorably compare American railroads with those of Europe]: The trains that these people are talking about are the Trans-Europe Expresses. Most American tourists ride the fancy ones. There's no doubt about it: The TEEs are great—but they are new. There are plenty of older trains over there. When I go to Europe with my family, we ride like regular citizens—we even carry cheese in a bag. We ride second class, sit on hard leather seats, wipe dirt off the window sills. Today, in the U.S., we're largely running a 24-year-old-equipment fleet that hasn't been all that well maintained. I hope that we will do a better job with those older cars—but they're still old. Three years from now, when we have our new trains in this country, I'm going to invite the Europeans over here and we'll show them what's good. It can be done.

*Interview/U.S. News & World Report, 8-25:69.*

## John J. Riccardo
*President, Chrysler Corporation*          *2*

[On government standards and regulations for automobiles]: There are 37 separate motor-vehicle standards related to safety alone. They add enough weight to cause a fuel-economy penalty of between two billion and three billion gallons of gasoline annually. Those standards include head restraints that cost the public $800-million. Now that they are on the cars, the evidence shows that they are only marginally effective. We have bumpers that cost $1.3-billion. The Department of Transportation says it is now inclined to agree with industry studies showing that the initial cost of the system and the cost of the fuel-economy penalty associated with the heavier bumpers exceed all measurable benefits. In this case the consumer comes out with a net loss. By comparison, the two most effective safety devices on cars today—lap and shoulder belts and the energy-absorbing steering column—together cost the customer less than the Federally mandated bumpers, and were developed by the industry independent of any government regulation. I am sure you also remember the ignition interlock system on 1974 models. This government-mandated device forced a driver to buckle-up a bag of groceries on the front seat before the car would start. As we warned, the public rejected this pinball-machine approach to automotive engineering. The price tag for this bureaucratic exercise in social progress was $250-million. And that's peanuts compared with the bill for the air bag—unless we can get the public protectors to listen to the facts and write the air bag out of the regulations. On the positive side, this experience has helped expose the false idea that the public will accept any solutions government might legislate.

*Before Michigan Association of Certified Public*
*Accountants/The New York Times, 7-20:(3)12.*

## Gilbert F. Richards
*Chairman, the Budd Company*          *3*

I strongly believe that the automotive industry will soon begin to recover from the depths of the recession it has been in. The United States has a basic dependence on the automobile. I don't believe that can be changed. The chairman of Ford Motor Company observed recently that "this country developed in a particular way because of the automobile, and you just can't push a button and change it." The private automobile will be the basic means of transit for most Americans for the foreseeable future. I am convinced the demand for automobiles will be there. Older cars are wearing out. Thirty million additional drivers' licenses are expected to be issued in the next 10 years. And, even though the price has gone up, a new car is still a good buy. In spite of inflation, the average American wage-earner works fewer hours to buy a new car today than in 1965. Ten years ago it took 816 hours worth of wages and at the end of 1974 it took only 552 hours worth. The basic strength for recovery of the automotive industry is there.

*Before Western Highway Institute,*
*Kansas City, Mo., Sept. 16/*
*Vital Speeches, 10-15:19.*

**Reuben Robertson III**
*Counsel, consumerist Ralph Nader's Aviation*
*Consumer Action Project*
1

I think what needs to be done now is radical surgery in the air-safety field. I think that really we ought to take this air-traffic function out of the FAA, where it has been subjected to the grossest abuses over the years, and the most gross incompetence, and put it in an agency either of its own or make it a part of NASA for example, which has a system-analysis capability and a demonstrated competence in technical fields.

*San Francisco Examiner &*
*Chronicle, 3-2:(A)16.*

**C. R. Smith**
*Former chairman, American Airlines*
2

The only thing to an airline is its people. Anybody can buy an airplane. But an airline is a service institution; its people make it great.

*At dinner in his honor,*
*Tarrant County, Tex., April 15/*
*The Dallas Times Herald, 4-16:(E)12.*

**Stanley Steingut**
*Speaker of the New York State Assembly*
3

[Saying New York City's new 50-cent transit fare is too high and that the Federal government is not supplying enough subsidy]: The

Federal government has turned its back on the problems of the localities. It's been negligent too long. It's absurd, when they can bail out the bankrupt railroads, Lockheed [Aircraft Corp.] and the oil companies, that they can turn their backs on the straphangers.

*Aug. 12/The New York Times, 8-13:27.*

**Norbert T. Tiemann**
*Administrator,*
*Federal Highway Administration*
4

I personally feel that the time is not far off when we will have to bite the bullet and restrict private automobiles in the central business district, or at least a part of it, in many of our cities. Auto-free or pedestrian-oriented zones would be feasible in a variety of urban settings—commercial, residential, historic and institutional. I know that action in this direction has already been taken in a number of European cities and, on a limited scale, in a few American cities. However, the greatest attention has been focused upon commercial areas with high concentrations of pedestrian activity, involving many short trips between shops, offices and parking facilities. Restricting or excluding cars from certain areas of historic, esthetic or monumental importance can create areas that might be better enjoyed by people walking or riding special forms of conveyances, be these jitneys, minibuses or whatever.

*Before International Bridge, Tunnel and*
*Turnpike Association, Paris/*
*The National Observer, 10-11:13.*

**Charles C. Tillinghast, Jr.**
*Chairman, Trans World Airlines*
5

We feel over-regulated and under-regulated. Now, that may sound like a ridiculous statement, but it's not. In the airline industry you find one of the few government efforts to have at one and the same time strict regulation and fierce competition. By that I mean that we are told what routes we can fly, what fares we can charge, and so on. But at the same time, the CAB is proliferating the number of airlines allowed on many routes—to promote competition. The result is disastrous. Let me give you a classic case: Pittsburgh to Chicago. This run

# WHAT THEY SAID IN 1975

used to be shared by United and TWA. We each averaged load factors of 60 to 65 per cent. That's a profitable operation, because 52 to 53 per cent probably represents the break-even point. Then—in the name of competition—the CAB put Allegheny Airlines on the Pittsburgh-Chicago run, and now the three of us are operating with load factors that, in a good month, may be in the low 40s . . . I think we're bound to have regulation, but the powers that be should recognize that we can't live with both heavy regulation and heavy competition.

*Interview/U.S. News & World Report, 7-28:42.*

**Lynn Townsend**
*Chairman, Chrysler Corporation*   *1*

[On a possible trend toward sub-compact cars]: People have to give up too much in the ride and comfort in the sub-compacts. We think compacts are the ideal size for the average family. That's where the customer gets his biggest bang for the buck . . . You really cannot comfortably package in a sub-compact more than four [persons] and generally, in most of them, the two that are packaged in the rear seat—you just can't ride in that rear seat for very far.

*The Washington Post, 5-26:(A)3.*

**Murray L. Weidenbaum**
*Director, Center for the Study of American Business, Washington University; Former Assistant Secretary for Economic Policy, Department of the Treasury of the United States*   *2*

To me, Congress' decision to reverse the Federal regulators on the interlock, seat-belt system [in automobiles] this year was encouraging. It's an example of what can happen when the public gets aroused. It became obvious to Americans that they were paying through the nose for a complicated system they didn't want. It was extravagant nonsense. Congress got the picture pretty fast. It threw the interlock out the window. But only, of course, after the auto industry had spent millions to perfect and install it.

*Interview, St. Louis/*
*Nation's Business, June:30.*

## James Abourezk
*United States Senator, D–South Dakota*

1

In a free society—and ours is relatively free—the normal assumption would be that people live in metropolitan areas because they want to. But the public-opinion polls do not support that assumption ... If [people] want higher wages and decent social services, they have to take the urban crush, the smog, the ugliness and the depersonalization of life that is characteristic of city life. If they like the friendliness, the greater personal identity, the more human scale of living that goes with smaller towns and rural areas, then they have to give up the expanded economic opportunities, the greater availability of education, health care and other social services that are available only in cities.

*At conference on rural America, Washington, April 14/The Washington Post, 4-15:(A)3.*

## Joseph L. Alioto
*Mayor of San Francisco*

2

Some people think that Mayors are professional moaners. But the fact is, because we walk the edge of the volcano, we have a better understanding of when the next eruption will take place.

*At luncheon, Washington, March 4/ The New York Times, 3-5:19.*

3

Sure there are inconveniences [in city life]. That's what a city is. You look back at what we regard as the great cities of the world—Florence, Rome, Paris, London. They all have these things. You don't expect Walden Pond; if you like that better, you better go to Walden Pond. If you like the city, you have to take what the city has. It involves noise; it involves dirt; it involves some measure of pollution, prostitution and crime.

*Los Angeles Times, 3-30:(1)3.*

## Pearl Bailey
*Entertainer; Member, United States delegation to the United Nations*

4

I ride home from the theatre at night, remembering what New York was when I was a girl, and it makes me cry. The politicians have milked this city dry, and the people have given up. This one's on welfare; that one wants something for nothing. Instead of going to work in the morning, they're hanging around, waiting for the bars to open; and, while they're waiting, they grab some woman or child and either mug them or rape them or beat them. What is it with these people? ... It's not just New York. Look at Philadelphia, Cleveland, Los Angeles—every city in this U.S. is based on the pride of its citizens. And they better wake up to the fact that the government does not run the people; the people run the government. I'm not a worrier; I'm a carer. Now, if we don't all start caring, we are going to destroy the world.

*Interview, New York/ San Francisco Examiner & Chronicle, 12-28:(Datebook)20.*

## Edward C. Banfield
*Professor of public policy and political science, University of Pennsylvania*

5

[On New York City's fiscal crisis]: I don't see what's to stop the [labor] unions from shaking the city down for whatever money it can accumulate. The laws have prohibited striking all along, but it's a practical problem—how do you put 30,000 or 40,000 striking teachers or policemen in jail? Obviously you don't. And if you fine them, you have to put back in their pockets what you take out. If the people of New York will tolerate strikes by public employees, against the law, and not tolerate politicians who crack down on strikes, then I can't see that it will be possible to get New York to live within its budget. It would require a funda-

# WHAT THEY SAID IN 1975

*(EDWARD C. BANFIELD)*

mental change by the unions and on the part of the middle and upper classes toward the "do-good" activity that New York is more generous with than most cities. I'm afraid that the real trouble is that it's run by the upper and middle classes and they're too moral and too "righteous" to do the painful and sometimes wrong things that have to be done to run a big city. You won't find the policemen striking in Chicago.

*The New York Times, 7-30:35.*

### Abraham D. Beame
*Mayor of New York*

1

[On his city's fiscal crisis and the Federal and New York State governments' turn-down of financial aid]: The fact that I must submit to the City Council and Board of Estimate a crisis budget presents a humiliating prospect for this great city. The unwillingness to respond to the city's program is an insult to every person who calls himself a New Yorker . . . I must submit to you a budget that cuts $285-million in tax levy funds out of our education budget . . . In health, hospitals and mental health, we will be required to close still more facilities, discontinue scores of contracts with voluntary agencies and generally lower the health care to the public with a slash of $112.2-million in tax levy funds. In the Fire Department, we are eliminating 2,300 jobs, resulting in an increase in response time to fires and eliminating scores of engine and ladder companies. In sanitation, a $50-million tax levy cut means still further reductions in refuse collections . . . In the cultural and recreational areas, we will be forced to close large numbers of branch libraries or reduce the days that they would be available to the public. Zoos and museums would be open for fewer hours, park maintenance materially reduced and recreation programs severely curtailed. In police, we will have to cut $185-million . . . While I will continue to do whatever is necessary to maintain adequate police protection, the price of achieving this will have to be still further offsetting cuts in other vital areas. I must remind you that these are not threats. What I'm describing is the budget of the city of

New York . . . The challenges to us and to the quality of life we cherish in this city have never been greater. It will require every businessman, every official, every union leader, every New Yorker and every banker to make very real sacrifices. I can pledge to you that I will devote all of my energy and my understanding of this city to keep it functioning as effectively as possible in the face of punishing indifference that reaches from Wall Street to Albany to Washington.

*Budget address, New York, May 29/*
*The New York Times, 5-30:8.*

2

[Calling for fiscal restraint during his city's current financial crisis]: The role of our cities has changed dramatically in response to national trends, heightened aspirations and shifting policy. We've seen the demand for city services soar, outstripping our ability to pay for them with local dollars. The very national and state programs which help defray some of the costs of providing these services also add to their cost because they require matching local contributions . . . To make up the difference between its modestly growing revenues and rapidly escalating demands, the city during this current period of need had resorted increasingly to borrowing for the cash required to stretch the budget. This kind of financing is questionable at best, even when the economy is strong. But the economy didn't remain solid. The city, in effect, gambled against a future which didn't come. Instead of economic expansion, we have deep recession; instead of stability, we have runaway inflation; instead of an enlightened political will to share national obligations more equitably, we've been told to go it alone. That is why we must act today and act decisively. We have exhausted the possibilities for negotiation and discussion. Now our options in time are running out. There must be financial restraint and service cutbacks. There must be fiscal reform and management resolve. Our program of austerity must be accelerated. There must be immediate steps to restore our credit. These steps are necessary, painful and not easily taken. But there is no choice. We must restore the city's fiscal integrity. We must demonstrate that despite unrelenting economic pressures and punitive isolation, the city can and will meet its greatest challenge. I know this will impose an added burden upon us. I know it means great sacrifices. But I also know that we have the inherent strength and unflagging determination to do what must be done.

*New York, July 31/*
*The New York Times, 8-1:18.*

1

[Asking Federal aid for New York City during its current fiscal crisis]: The 8 million Americans who live in New York merely ask of the Congress and the President [Ford] ... the simple act of guarantee to permit us to continue the reforms and the economies now under way in the city. Now, there are ample precedents. The Federal budget this year reflects more than $200-billion in guarantees covering everything from the Washington Metro to the construction of a chemical plant in Yugoslavia. We seek the time that a guarantee offers, so that we can complete the program for recovery that has already been launched ... Whatever fate awaits New York, our country's tragedy would be greatly compounded if our national leadership deludes itself into thinking that sacrificing our city will somehow exorcize the demons plaguing all of urban America. The real problems and economic pressures affecting New York should be the subject of constructive concern—and not derision. Subjecting America's largest city to humiliation and impoverishment does not enhance either the economy or the moral fiber of our nation. It is unimaginable to me that any other head of state in this world would abandon the premier city of his nation or punish its people as an object lesson.

*Before National Press Club, Washington,*
*Nov. 5/The New York Times, 11-6:46.*

2

[On President Ford's decision to provide Federal financial assistance to New York City during its current fiscal crisis]: I want to stress that the President's action—crucial as it may be—does not bring our serious difficulties to an end. The coming months and years will mean new sacrifices for all New Yorkers and new demands upon every segment of the city's population.

*News conference, New York, Nov. 26/*
*Los Angeles Times, 11-27:(1)22.*

**Lloyd M. Bentsen**
*United States Senator, D—Texas*

3

[On New York City's current fiscal crisis]: I am personally opposed to providing any [Federal] assistance to New York City unless it puts its financial house in order, as I have consistently said. [New York] has obviously lived beyond its means for years [and must] now balance its budget and live within its income. And if they do these things, and under these conditions only, the Federal financing bank could buy some of their short-term securities to restore confidence to the municipal-bond market ... [President Ford] apparently feels this city should go through the bankruptcy route; but it would be my hope that this could be avoided. It doesn't do any of us any good to have a major U.S. city default on its debts.

*Before Texas Association of*
*Broadcasters, Houston, Oct. 29/*
*The Dallas Times Herald, 10-30:(A)10.*

**Joseph R. Biden, Jr.**
*United States Senator, D—Delaware*

4

[On the reluctance of Congress to give financial aid to New York City]: Cities are viewed as the seed of corruption and duplicity, and New York is the biggest city. [I do not share that view, but] there is a general negative feeling toward New York City, a feeling that "who can do anything?" and "what difference will it make?"

*The New York Times, 5-25:(1)1.*

**Tom Bradley**
*Mayor of Los Angeles*

5

That is the major problem [of American cities]—the money. We simply are too reliant on the property tax as a source of revenue. It goes up about 5 per cent per year while our cost of living and expenses go up about 11 per cent. We are falling more deeply into the bot-

*(TOM BRADLEY)*

tomless hole each year. So we've got to find alternate ways of getting revenue.

*Interview, Los Angeles/*
*Los Angeles Herald-Examiner 6-22:(A)3.*

1

If the Federal government can maintain the U.S. commitments to foreign defense budgets, then it can maintain a national commitment to social progress in our cities ... Just as billions of dollars in post-war economic aid for Europe were spent following World War II, the same sort of investment should be made at home. The goal of such an ambitious program should be to recapture the attractive, healthy life-style which made this country thrive. To this end, urban recovery should become a high national priority.

*At convocation sponsored by Fund for*
*Peace and Center for the Study of*
*Democratic Institutions, Washington, Dec. 2/*
*Los Angeles Herald-Examiner, 12-2:(A)3.*

**Hugh L. Carey**
*Governor of New York (D)*

2

[Criticizing Federal Reserve Board Chairman Arthur Burns' proposal that New York State institute a short-term tax to ease New York City's current fiscal crisis as a sign of good faith before Federal aid is considered]: We welcome the Spartan approach, but we're not prepared to sack Athens. The suggestion that New York redeem its honor by imposing new taxes fails to recognize that New York is the highest-taxed state in the nation, and New York City the highest-taxed locality in the world. We tax everything that moves and breathes. The very notion that we should tax our way out of this problem while the [Federal] Administration talks about a [Federal] tax reduction indicates that the advice is coming from the wrong source.

*Before Senate Banking Committee, Washington,*
*Oct. 10/The New York Times, 10-11:39.*

3

[Criticizing President Ford's plan for Federal-court supervision of a New York City bank-

ruptcy as the way to handle the city's current fiscal crisis]: The Ford formula would make New York City a ward of a Federal court—with an appointed judge acting as Federal marshal, instead of Washington acting as a guarantor while the city and state repair its fiscal integrity. This is not a defense of the Federal system—it is a wholesale assault on it. And with only life and property protected, with Mr. Ford deliberately omitting any reference to schools, sanitation and other basic services, the Ford formula is a plan for Federally supervised martial law. We want time to tighten our belts. Mr. Ford proposes to put that belt around our necks.

*News conference, Oct. 29/*
*Los Angeles Times, 10-30:(1)1.*

4

[On a loan-guarantee program now before Congress to help New York City during its current fiscal crisis and which President Ford says he will veto]: This is the single most important fact that the White House chooses to ignore: The loan-guarantee plan now before Congress does not give New York City one red cent. It gives the city time to pay its debts and reform its practices. Our case rests on one simple idea: We don't think it's right for the people of Iowa or California or Michigan to pay for the mistakes of New York City. The problem is that Mr. Ford has attacked New York for something we do not want or seek—a Federal bailout from the Treasury. Some of what Mr. Ford said was exactly right. There is a sorry history of reckless fiscal policy in New York City going back years—perhaps decades. And there is blame enough for everyone: city officials and interest groups; banks that did not ask the hard questions; a state legislature and hand-picked Vice President [former New York Governor Nelson Rockefeller] that specifically authorized every fringe and pension benefit and every unwise borrowing Mr. Ford now attacks so righteously; and Presidents who diverted tens of billions of dollars to foreign dictatorships and senseless war, and who plunged our economy into its worst crisis in 40 years. We all share the responsibility. And the city record, particularly in caring for those driven from other states and other lands by poverty and oppression, is far more honorable than that of most. But it is not our job to point fingers of blame. It is our job to face what has happened, and to set it right with the least damage possible. What Mr. Ford says he's for is what we're for—we don't want to fling open the doors of the Treasury to New York City or anybody else. We don't want to be bailed out. We don't want any city to be a ward of the Federal government. What do we want? We want Washington, in effect, to stand behind us—to give investors the confidence they now lack to invest in New York City. That money will enable us to pay our debts and to keep public services alive, while we work our way back to a balanced budget.

*State-wide broadcast, Albany, Nov. 1/*
*The New York Times, 11-2:(1)61.*

1

The President's [Ford] decision to recommend Federal loan assistance to the city of New York [during the city's current fiscal crisis], coming as it does on the eve of Thanksgiving Day, gives all New Yorkers a special occasion to rejoice and express our sense of relief. I am pleased by the President's decision. It represents a vindication of New York's case and the merits of our position. . . . bankruptcy for New York City is now behind us. Talk of collapse and chaos should now disappear. In its place, we should talk of the work of rebuilding confidence in New York City, and insuring that New York's place in the nation is maintained. That work is well under way and will continue. [But] this does not mark the end of our difficulties. Painful burdens remain ahead of all of us.

*Nov. 26/Los Angeles Times, 11-27:(1)22.*

**Frank Church**
*United States Senator, D—Idaho*
2

[Urging Federal aid for New York during that city's current fiscal crisis]: If during the past demented decade the Federal government had spent a tenth as much salvaging our own biggest city as we squandered on Saigon [South Vietnam], New York City would not now be teetering on the brink of bankruptcy. [New York] needs some time and it needs some help,

and don't tell me that the Federal government has no responsibility. Don't tell me that an Administration which asks to put $250-million to prevent [Lockheed Aircraft Corp.] from going bankrupt can be indifferent to the needs of New York City. We must bring the Federal focus home again. If it is our peculiar passion to make everything right in the world, where better to begin than in our own disordered house? And if the President [Ford] must counsel with important leaders, let him start with the Mayors. Who else lives closer to the heartbeat of the people?

*Before League of California Cities,*
*San Francisco, Oct. 20/*
*Los Angeles Times, 10-21:(1)20.*

**A. W. Clausen**
*President, Bankamerica Corporation*
3

[On New York City's current fiscal crisis]: Similar to other progressive cities in recent years, New York City has oriented its revenue structure more toward business-sensitive taxes than to its realty base, such that economic gains in the form of increased sales, income and the like could be more readily translated into the city's revenue stream. This process, in boom economic periods like the '60s, is insidiously self-feeding. Revenues rise sharply and consistently. In New York, the increase in revenue availability stimulated corresponding demands to spend, for better facilities, higher salaries and larger subsidies for social-service programs. This spending surge was nurtured as well by the Federal government, whose matching support funds for water, sewer, highway and numerous other construction projects and programs lured cities into the grantsmanship trap . . . The turn of the '70s marked a change for the worse in the economic fortunes of our nation and no less for the city of New York. Revenue projections went sharply awry, as the unexpected slackening in income and sales growth rates impacted heavily on city tax returns. Instead of reducing services or cutting expenditures, the city elected to borrow to cover its revenue shortfall . . . Major urban centers outside of New York resemble the city in a number of important respects. Their revenue structures, for example, are remarkably

# WHAT THEY SAID IN 1975

similar. Does any city dare to laugh? On what basis? There are differences, certainly, of degree and magnitude, but the substance of the explosive is remarkably like New York's in large cities across the nation. The fuse in some cities is already alight.

*Before Senate Banking, Housing and Urban Affairs Committee, Oct. 18/ The Washington Post, 11-2:(F)4.*

**Harlan Cleveland**
*Director, Program in International Affairs, Aspen Institute; Former president, University of Hawaii*  1

There isn't anything we don't know about the modern city—its demography, its water table, its engineering design, its art, its slums, its economics, its politics. We just don't seem to know how to make it beautiful, accessible, solvent, safe and clean.

*At joint meeting of American Assembly and American Bar Association, Palo Alto, Calif./ The National Observer, 8-16:18.*

**John B. Connally, Jr.**
*Former Secretary of the Treasury of the United States; Former Governor of Texas (D, now R)*  2

[Calling for Federal aid to New York during the city's current fiscal crisis]: No useful purpose can be served by permitting a great national city, a great international city, to go down the drain. We can't let New York go under without it having an almost disastrous impact on all the countries of the world. Trying to hurt New York, you only hurt the nation ... The United States would go through a traumatic shock if the city of New York should default.

*New York, Oct. 10/ Los Angeles Herald-Examiner, 10-11:(A)2.*

3

[On New York City's current fiscal crisis]: The Congressional investigators who love to investigate the CIA and the FBI and other exotic subjects should have the courage to investigate New York City to determine what happened

and how other cities can avoid the pitfalls. New York is a great institution and I don't want to see it collapse, but neither do I believe we should miss this opportunity to curb the power of one of the most insidious influences in America today: the unlimited political and monetary power of the public-employee unions which are beginning to hold our cities hostage. One way we can recapture managerial control of our cities is to insist upon strong laws against strikes by municipal employees.

*Before Dallas Citizens Council, Nov. 19/ The Dallas Times Herald, 11-20:(A)22.*

**Jacques-Yves Cousteau**
*Explorer*  4

Psychologists today believe that people in cities behave like captives. The pattern of frustration, desperation, suicides now observed with captive animals is observed in city life.

*Interview/The Washington Post, 1-4:(D)3.*

**Clelio Darida**
*Mayor of Rome (Italy)*  5

[On the U.S. Federal government's refusal to aid New York City in its current fiscal crisis]: The basic difference between New York City and Rome is that the Italian state gives us credit and Washington doesn't give New York City credit. If I had one message for [New York's] Mayor [Abraham] Beame, it would be to get all American cities to put pressure on your central government. Cities can't survive by themselves.

*Interview, Rome/ The Christian Science Monitor, 11-26:14.*

**John Diebold**
*Chairman and president, The Diebold Group, Inc.; Authority on management*  6

The real problem with most city services is they're labor-intensive at a moment in history when that's a suicidal approach. It can only mean traumatic increases in costs as people are less and less inclined to do dirty work or menial jobs. The reason most city jobs stay so labor-intensive is they're bound up in politics and there's no motivation to apply science and technology.

*Interview/*
*U.S. News & World Report, 11-17:82.*

**Gerald R. Ford**
*President of the United States*

*1*

[On New York City's current fiscal crisis] : During the last decade, the officials of New York City have allowed its budget to triple. No city can expect to remain solvent if it allows its expenses to increase by an average of 12 per cent every year, while its tax revenues are increasing by only 4 to 5 per cent per year . . . The record shows that New York City's municipal wages and salaries are the highest in the United States. A sanitation worker with three years' experience now receives a base salary of nearly $15,000 a year. Fringe benefits and retirement costs average more than 50 per cent of base pay. There are four-week paid vacations and unlimited sick leave after only one year on the job. The record shows that, in most cities, municipal employees have to pay 50 per cent or more of the cost of their pensions. New York City is the only major city in the country that picks up the entire burden. The record shows that when New York's municipal employees retire they often retire much earlier than in most cities and at pensions considerably higher than sound retirement plans permit. The record shows New York City has 18 municipal hospitals; yet, on an average day, 25 per cent of the hospital beds are empty. Meanwhile, the city spends millions more to pay the hospital expenses of those who use private hospitals. The record shows New York City operates one of the largest universities in the world, free of tuition for any high-school graduate, rich or poor, who wants to attend. As for New York's much-discussed welfare burden, the record shows more than one current welfare recipient in 10 may be legally ineligible for welfare assistance. Certainly, I do not blame all the good people of New York City for their generous instincts or for their present plight. I do blame those who have misled the people of New York about the inevitable consequences of what they are doing or were doing over the last 10 years.

The consequences have been: a steady stream of unbalanced budgets; massive growth in the city's debt; extraordinary increases in public-employee contracts; and total disregard of independent experts who warned again and again that the city was courting disaster. There can be no doubt where the real responsibility lies. And when New York City now asks the rest of the country to guarantee its bills, it can be no surprise that many other Americans ask why.

*At National Press Club,*
*Washington, Oct. 29/*
*The New York Times, 10-30:46.*

*2*

[Saying he is against a Federal guarantee for New York City's debts during its current fiscal crisis] : By giving a Federal guarantee we would be reducing rather than increasing the prospect that the city's budget will ever be balanced. New York City's officials have proved in the past that they will not face up to the city's massive network of pressure groups as long as any other alternative is available. If they can scare the whole country into providing that alternative now, why shouldn't they be confident they can scare us again into providing it three years from now? In short, it encourages the continuation of "politics as usual" in New York—which is precisely not the way to solve the problem. Such a step would set a terrible precedent for the rest of the nation. It would promise immediate rewards and eventual rescue to every other city that follows the tragic example of our largest city. What restraint would be left on the spending of other local and state governments once it becomes clear that there is a Federal rescue squad that will always arrive in the nick of time? Finally, we must all recognize who the primary beneficiaries of a Federal guarantee program would be. The beneficiaries would not be those who live and work in New York City because the really essential public services must and will continue. The primary beneficiary would be the New York officials who would escape responsibility for their past folly and be further excused from making the hard decisions required now to restore the city's fiscal integrity. The second beneficiary

*(GERALD R. FORD)*

would be the large investors and financial institutions who purchased these securities anticipating a high rate of tax-free return.

*At National Press Club, Washington, Oct. 29/The New York Times, 10-30:46.*

### Jay W. Forrester
*Professor of management, Massachusetts Institute of Technology*

1

I see no solution for urban problems until cities develop the courage to plan in terms of maximum population, a maximum number of housing units, a maximum permissible building height and a maximum number of jobs. A city must also choose the type of city it wants to be. To become and remain a city that is all things to all people is impossible.

*The Washington Post, 6-8:(C)4.*

### Milton Friedman
*Professor of economics, University of Chicago*

2

[On New York City's fiscal crisis] : Go bankrupt. That will make it impossible for New York City in future to borrow any money and force New York to live within its budget. The only other alternative is the obvious one—tighten its belt, pay off its debt, live within its means and become an honest city again. That's a much better solution from the longrun point of view, but whether it's a politically feasible solution I don't know, whereas the first one is.

*The New York Times, 7-30:35.*

### John Kenneth Galbraith
*Former professor of economics, Harvard University*

3

[On New York City's fiscal crisis] : The remarkable thing is not that this city's government costs so much, but that so many people of wealth have left. It's outrageous that the development of the metropolitan community has been organized with escape hatches that allow people to enjoy the proximity of the city while not paying their share of taxes. It's outrageous that a person can avoid income tax by

moving to New Jersey or Connecticut. Fiscal funkholes are what the suburbs are.

*The New York Times, 7-30:35.*

### Bernard Gifford
*Deputy Chancellor, New York City Public School System*

4

A city's greatness cannot be measured by the height of its tallest buildings; the length and breadth of its public transportation system; the number of nightclubs, sports stadiums or convention centers; or the presence of great museums of art and archeology beckoning us to peer into the past. All of these things are wonderful and their existence is a sign of a city's vitality and vibrancy. But they don't add up to greatness. A city's greatness is measured by its collective compassion toward its poor, its aged, its sick—the very people who are so often consigned to the junk heap of history by cynics and purveyors of benign neglect—those who inform us that the urban crisis is no more; that the problems of our major urban areas would disappear if we would only stop talking about them.

*At United Federation of Teachers College Scholarship Fund awards, Hunter College, New York, May 20/ The New York Times, 5-25:(4)7.*

### Luther H. Gulick
*Former City Administrator of New York; Former president, Institute of Public Administration*

5

The great tragedy is that out of our advanced social consciousness we [in New York] have gone so far in doing things for people through city government that we're now way beyond our means. In our eagerness to ameliorate the lot of the poorest 20 per cent of our people, we have tried to use the city as an instrument for redistributing the wealth [through welfare and other social services]. What we forget is that no city can do that to a greater extent than other cities without putting such a heavy tax burden on its productive enterprise that it handicaps them and eventually drives them out.

*The New York Times, 5-18:(4)1.*

**John Gunther**
*Executive director, United States*
*Conference of Mayors*
1

While the Federal government is trying to stimulate the economy by cutting taxes, cities have to do just the opposite by raising theirs. And, already, real-estate taxes are so high that, in Hoboken, New Jersey, for example, a home-owner pays an amount equal to the total value of his house every eight years.

*U.S. News & World Report, 4-7:30.*

**Richard G. Hatcher**
*Mayor of Gary, Indiana*
2

The President [Ford] does not have to worry about other cities' asking for the same kinds of loans that New York is seeking. I know of no Mayor who wants that to happen—to have to give up control over his own city. What President Ford ought to know, however, is that almost every city in this country is operating with a services deficit—a default on its obligations to provide services for its citizens. This is true even in the most solvent cities. Frills have gone long ago in most cities. We are cutting back now on basic services—hospitals, sanitation, fire and police protection.

*At National League of Cities convention,*
*Miami Beach/*
*U.S. News & World Report, 12-15:26.*

**Roy Hattersley**
*Minister of State*
*of the United Kingdom*
3

[On U.S. President Ford's refusal to give Federal assistance to New York City during its current fiscal crisis]: What is happening in New York City could not happen to a British city because of the acceptance of the government of its responsibilities to its cities. More than 50 per cent of the services, such as police, are entirely the responsibility of the central government. So we cannot conceive of a local entity being allowed to founder.

*Los Angeles, Nov. 11/*
*Los Angeles Herald-Examiner, 11-12:(A)7.*

**Gabriel Hauge**
*Chairman, Manufacturers Hanover*
*Trust Company, New York*
4

For all the difficulties of life in metropolitan areas, the important thing to note is that people appear to prefer them to the places from which they came. They have been voting with their feet for a long time and the verdict is clear. As a migrant from a small rural Minnesota town myself, I can attest to the fact that cities are exciting, rewarding places to be. It was, I believe, the American writer, O. Henry, who exclaimed, "The wonderful, cruel, enchanting, bewildering, fatal great city." Urban centers have been places of opportunity—where the jobs are, the varied jobs, the bigger and better jobs, the prospect of changing jobs and moving up . . . Large metropolitan regions are, of course, more than producers of goods and jobs and careers. They are a vast, complex apparatus for living. Their range of recreation, education, health, cultural services, their choice of goods and shops, is much larger than the bill-of-fare offered elsewhere. This engine of production, source of amenities and center of consumption is, indeed, a society in itself.

*Before Regional Plan Association, New York,*
*April 22/Vital Speeches, 6-1:509.*

**Walter W. Heller**
*Professor of economics, University of*
*Minnesota; Former Chairman, Council of*
*Economic Advisers to the President of*
*the United States (John F. Kennedy)*
5

[On the fiscal problems of cities]: The low-income people are becoming stranded in the city while those who make up the tax base are moving out. Apart from that, there's the problem of the growing strength of civil-service unions—no one knows where that will end. The civil-service unions have almost taken control of New York and San Francisco, which have increased civil salaries and pensions beyond what is reasonable. In the case of New York, you're reaching a point where you have to have Federal intervention. There's the billion-dollar welfare bill, and the problem of 200,000 illegal aliens flocking around the city. All of this serves to sabotage the community spirit within

# WHAT THEY SAID IN 1975

*(WALTER W. HELLER)*

the city . . . At the present there are four or five cities in bad shape, but you don't see cities falling like dominoes. In many ways, the greatest damage being done to cities is linked to the monetary policy by [Federal Reserve Chairman] Arthur Burns and the restricted fiscal policies of [President] Ford, [Presidential Economic Advisers Chairman Alan] Greenspan and [Treasury Secretary William] Simon. It's a bad time to restrict the movement of money. What is needed is an increase of incomes and profits. The solution lies in Washington.

*Interview/*
*"W": a Fairchild publication, 11-14:22.*

**Carla A. Hills**
*Secretary of Housing and Urban*
*Development of the United States*    1

The crisis of the cities will not be solved by making *their* deficits part of a rapidly growing *Federal* budget deficit.

*At United States Conference of Mayors,*
*Boston/Time, 7-21:13.*

2

An abandoned house isn't just an old derelict down by the railroad in an Edward Hopper landscape. Abandoned with that house are a part of all of the things that made it live. Mundane things—like water and sewage lines, roads and transportation systems, and utilities. Vital things—like theatres, schools and churches. And precious pieces of the history and culture that give the city majesty. A tighter economy, a scarcity of energy, and changing demographic trends now demand us to use all the ingenuity we can summon to preserve and recycle these assets. Our studies conclude statistically what we should have concluded intelligently more than a decade ago: that it is far less costly to recycle a city than to build a suburb.

*At Washington Press Club/*
*The National Observer, 10-18:13.*

**Hubert H. Humphrey**
*United States Senator, D—Minnesota*    3

[On New York City's current fiscal crisis and President Ford's refusal to give Federal aid]:

The city of New York will be helped if it needs help. The only question is when. What the President is saying is, let the city go down the drain first, run the risk of the cutoff of vital municipal services and then possibly the Federal government will come in and have to bail it out. What we propose in Congress is that there be a Federal guarantee under strict circumstances where the city will have to put its budget in balance, where the state will take over the fiscal responsibility of the city and where there will be severe penalties for any failure to produce on the plan that is adopted. President Ford is attempting to punish New York. What New York needs is a friendly doctor with a prescription, not a mortician that tells New York that it ought to die and then hope for a resurrection.

*TV-radio interview, Washington/*
*"Meet the Press,"*
*National Broadcasting Company, 11-2.*

**Herman Kahn**
*Director, Hudson Institute*    4

[Saying he hopes the Federal government will not be too helpful to New York during the city's current fiscal crisis]: If New York is helped without going through some *mea culpa,* but is just helped casually, pumping in all this money might cause a wild inflation. But if New York goes through some drastic unpleasant experience, maybe even being deprived of home rule, there'll be a reform in city behavior. For instance, if you cancel rent-control, you'll likely find an upsurge in creative activity. People don't realize how destructive rent-control is. Other problems in the cities will get better because they can't possibly get much worse. In the area of education there's been a deterioration in achievement-test scores. So parents are beginning to get up in arms, and they're forcing schools to go back to basic drills. A lot of what happens around the country depends on what happens in New York. It becomes an example of what happens with bad management, or how you get away with things. The crisis could really lead to a positive result. The bankruptcy of New York City will make people realize there's no such thing as a free lunch. They'll react against handouts. There'll be cutbacks and stiffer requirements for welfare. But at the same time the so-called "deserving poor" will get their relief allowances as a matter of right.

*Interview/*
*"W": a Fairchild publication, 11-14:23.*

**Edward I. Koch**
*United States Representative,*
*D–New York*
1

[Requesting Federal financial aid for New York City]: [I told Federal Reserve Board Chairman Arthur Burns,] "You bailed out the Franklin National Bank. It took a billion dollars in Federal funds and you took the position that if the Franklin National went under there would be a rippling effect that would harm other banks. Why in the world would you not do that for New York City, any city?" . . . We did not expect him to say "sure," but we wanted him to see our concern and advise the President [Ford] that our request is reasonable.

*May 13/The New York Times, 5-14:38.*

**Irving Kristol**
*Professor of urban values,*
*New York University*
2

Urban problems are real, but the conglomeration of urban problems into something called an urban crisis is largely the function of . . . television, which has to make a national issue out of every event . . . Cities have always had problems. When you call it a crisis, it's a matter of labeling.

*Interview, Los Angeles, April 7/*
*Los Angeles Times, 4-8:(3)8.*

**Moon Landrieu**
*Mayor of New Orleans*
3

This city has over the past 10 or 15 years grown poorer and older and smaller—or perhaps I should say the population has—while the suburbs have grown larger, younger and more wealthy. Yet the center city is still required to furnish the basic services for the entire metropolitan area without any significant contribution from the suburban areas.

*New Orleans/The New York Times, 3-24:24.*

**Samuel J. Lefrak**
*President, the Lefrak Organization,*
*real estate*
4

In the cities we centralize goods, services and people. You can take a short stroll, buy a newspaper, a painting, consult your lawyer, visit a museum, go to a show or library, and enjoy a good meal. Suburbia is filled with thousands of individual homes, each with an inefficient heating and cooling system, and dependent on the automobile and roads. Tons of steel and petroleum have to be mobilized to buy even a bottle of milk. The suburbs, too, can be crippled by increased taxes, crime, narcotics, restrictive zoning and over-burdened delivery systems. The suburbanite may claim that his castle is sacrosanct, but the high costs and inadequate transportation will hasten a return to the cities. We have to begin rebuilding our cities now in order to meet demands of the future. And we must rebuild our slums. This reconstruction must be primarily on remaining recycled land within the city rather than in the suburbs where no basic facilities exist and would have to be installed. We shall require a vast infusion of Federal money to rebuild our cities. We need an overhaul of the urban educational system and urban transportation system. We need an urban Marshall Plan.

*Before Annual Real Estate Conference*
*sponsored by Institutional Investor magazine/*
*San Francisco Examiner & Chronicle,*
*7-6:(Sunday Homes)A.*

**C. Eric Lincoln**
*Chairman, department of religious and*
*philosophical studies, Fisk University*
5

Anyone who expected the election of a black Mayor to end the problems of crime, poverty, housing, unemployment and the countless other frustrations of the cities is both politically and intellectually naive. There is no magic in being black.

*U.S. News & World Report, 4-7:34.*

**John V. Lindsay**
*Former Mayor of New York*
6

. . . our cities didn't inflict these monumental American problems on themselves. They

# WHAT THEY SAID IN 1975

*(JOHN V. LINDSAY)*

have borne the impact of strong American national policies and priorities—one after another, with devastatingly destructive effect. For 20 years, Washington sponsored and underwrote the flight of the middle class to the suburbs with massive subsidies for highways and FHA housing, and nothing was given for urban mass transit and urban housing for the middle groups who stayed.

*At Bicentennial Forum, Boston/*
*The Christian Science Monitor, 7-15:27.*

**Henry W. Maier**
*Mayor of Milwaukee*

1

[Milwaukee's city budget] tells us what we must do just to survive; but it doesn't spell out what must be done—and for which we do not have the resources—to adequately improve the quality of life in housing, health, pollution, recreation, jobs, public safety and the vast array of postponed capital improvements. Our city is afflicted by a deprivation rate, which, even before the recession, showed that 45 per cent of our citizens live below the levels set by the U.S. Labor Department for an adequate standard of living. We are afflicted by the fact that our nation is not meeting the need to reorder national priorities to help the central cities.

*Before Milwaukee Common Council/*
*The New York Times, 9-29:27.*

2

We, along with other cities, are part of a deepening trend. That trend is toward an ever-growing concentration of the poor, and the relatively poor, in the central cities of America. New York just got hit first [with its current fiscal crisis]. It's time to factor out the real causes of the dilemma. All large cities are in the trend New York is in. It's a matter of time.

*Interview/The New York Times, 9-29:27.*

**Robert Moses**
*Government planner and builder; Former*
*New York City Parks Commissioner*

3

[On New York's current financial crisis]: All hands are swapping opinions about the troubles which afflict our metropolis, how they came

about so suddenly and what to do to regain our reputation. We face bankruptcy and receivership. We are in what Sean O'Casey called a state of chassis. Only a genius like O'Casey would invent such a word to describe the collapse of a pathetic old wagon falling apart in the middle of the marketplace. The nation echoes with the moans of dismayed Mayors rending their garments, lifting their trembling mendicant hands for Federal handouts and offering few alternatives but staggering new taxes and mortgaging the future with long-term debt to meet current expenses.

*Before New York Chamber of*
*Commerce and Industry/*
*The Wall Street Journal, 9-30:22.*

**Arthur H. Motley**
*Chairman, "Parade" magazine*

4

[On New York City's current fiscal crisis]: New York's financial result has taught a lot of people what businessmen have known: If the books aren't balanced, some day you'll go broke. That's considered a conservative policy—but more than that, it's a fact of life . . .

*Interview, Dallas/*
*The Dallas Times Herald, 10-18:(B)1.*

**Nelson A. Rockefeller**
*Vice President of the United States;*
*Former Governor of New York (R)*

5

[On whether there should be Federal aid to help New York City during its current fiscal crisis]: I don't think the Federal government can stand back of a history of over-spending and over-commitment [by New York] with a blank-check operation and still preserve the solvency of our nation. Every level of government —like every family—has got to bring its expenditures in line with its revenues . . . Year in, year out, city leaders overestimated their revenues and underestimated their expenditures, and ended up with a deficit. Each year they met that deficit by floating short-term notes. Those have accumulated now to a point where the city has an accumulated deficit of 3.2 billion in short-term notes. In addition, it turned out, the city was using capital bonds to meet current operating expenditures. Now the city leaders find themselves in a very, very difficult situation. If they continue on that course and the Federal government simply picks up the check, this would be the beginning of the end of the solvency of the United States. Cities are creatures of the state. The states have the responsibility under the Constitution and under the legal structure of our country.

*Interview, September/*
*U.S. News & World Report, 10-13:55.*

1

[Saying that, once New York City enacts a plan to eliminate its budget deficit by 1978, there should be Federal aid to help the city in its current fiscal crisis]: When the necessary actions are taken and a solid base is established for restoration of budgetary and fiscal integrity for the city, it is my belief that at this point a basis will have been established for help to bridge that difficult period—between the adoption of the necessary measures required by the State Emergency Financial Control Board this October and the restoration of investor confidence in the city's full financial viability by June 30, 1978. It is therefore essential that the Congress as a whole focus on the problem now and enact appropriate legislation. Helping [to] bridge this gap—to give opportunities for these economies and improved management measures to take root and produce results—is certainly in the interest of all of us.

*At Columbus Day dinner,*
*New York, Oct. 11/*
*The New York Times, 10-12:(1)58.*

**George G. Seibels, Jr.**
*Mayor of Birmingham, Ala.*

2

[Criticizing the high pay demands and strikes by city employees]: We have reached the end of the line, and other cities have reached the end of the line. And the person causing this ... is your civil-service worker. When a high-school girl who can hardly find the bathroom ... starts to work at $450 a month and is close to $600 in three years, that's not modest pay.

Don't shed any crocodile tears for public employees.

*Nation's Business, October:25.*

**William E. Simon**
*Secretary of the Treasury*
*of the United States*

3

[Arguing against Federal guarantees for New York City debt during the city's current fiscal crisis]: It [would create] a new series of debt because equity demands that if we do it for New York City, we have to make it available to all other states and local governments, in excess of $20-billion of borrowing each year ... It puts the Federal government directly involved in the fiscal and financial affairs of state and local governments in the United States, and this in my judgment contravenes the Constitutional principle of Federalism. I would think Thomas Jefferson and others would be twirling in their graves, because if we have to involve ourselves in the financial affairs and give guarantees, then we have to protect the Federal interest and, as a result, we would have to say, "Well, we will tell you when to borrow, how much you can borrow and what your priorities are." That is not what this country is all about ... I believe in states' rights, and I think this would be an intolerable precedent.

*TV-radio interview, Washington/*
*"Meet the Press,"*
*National Broadcasting Company, 9-7.*

4

[On what is most needed to save New York City during its current fiscal crisis]: We're not just talking about money but about solving basic long-term problems, because in the absence of strong actions, like ending rent-control and strengthening the pension system and dealing forcefully with extravagant labor demands, New York City is not going to get back to a sound budget basis and regain access to the capital markets. What is needed is for people, instead of shrieking and pointing fingers, to sit down like rational human beings and talk about what the solutions are and stop frightening the American people with demagoguery.

*Interview/*
*U.S. News & World Report, 11-10:34.*

# WHAT THEY SAID IN 1975

## George Sternlieb
*Director, Center for Urban Policy*
*Research, Rutgers University*

1

The mood in the cities has changed from resentment to sullen resignation. Five or six years ago, we thought aging cities could survive if they came to political and economic terms with the suburbs. But now the decline has gone too far. Jobs, housing, even restaurants and cultural institutions increasingly are in the suburbs. Our society has decided it's cheaper to turn our old cities over to the poor and buy them off with welfare.

*U.S. News & World Report, 4-7:29.*

2

We are at the end of 35 years of housing subsidies. Society just is not interested any more—there is no political clout to the cities and the best we can do is optimize a wasting asset.

*At Conference on Neighborhood Conservation, New York/The New York Times, 9-27:19.*

## Daniel Walker
*Governor of Illinois (D)*

3

Unless we ensure a free and constant flow of funds into the neighborhoods of our great urban centers, we can write off those areas. Our cities are a composition of smaller communities. They preserve the cultural heritage of our people. If these component parts are allowed to deteriorate because of inadequate mortgage money, the cities as a whole are sure to crumble.

*Before Senate Banking Committee, Washington, May 5/Los Angeles Times, 5-6:(3)17.*

## Barbara Ward
*British economist*

4

[On the Federal government's refusal to aid New York City in its current fiscal crisis]: . . . how tragicomic it surely is to devote over $90-billion to an arms budget and then hang the title "bankrupt" round the neck of the Statue of Liberty. The poor, the homeless, the huddled masses, the wretched refuse of the teeming shores, for whom it was once a beacon of hope, will see instead the image of a system indifferent to their problems and incapable of

solving them. "I lift my lamp beside the bankrupt door." With that perception, the battle of ideas and hence of effective defense may already be halfway to defeat.

*The Washington Post, 11-19:(A)14.*

## Harry H. Wellington
*Dean, Yale University Law School*

5

. . . Mayors are soft bargainers for a number of reasons. By settling with the public employees' unions Mayors win the support of labor generally, and labor is a very strong pressure group. The settlements often do not become a burden until after a particular Mayor has left office. The pay increases get lost in the maze of the budgetary process and are hard to trace. Finally, the people want labor peace; they don't want the disruption of vital municipal services. Hence, there is no great pressure on Mayors to be tough bargainers until a city gets into a crisis like New York . . . What is needed is to bring the message home to the population that the cost of labor peace may be very dear indeed in the long run—that the Mayor who gives in too easily is not a good Mayor and politician. Let the Mayor hear that and know that the people will be behind him if he is tough. Then you can transform him from a weak to a hard bargainer. Then the unions would have to react to that, and their reaction would be to modify their demands.

*Interview, New Haven, Conn./ Los Angeles Times, 8-28:(2)5.*

## Kevin H. White
*Mayor of Boston*

6

[On the financial plight of many large cities]: The real solution will only come when this country makes up its national mind what it wants to do about the cities—whether it wants to abandon them or whether it wants to tolerate them, which I think they do today, or whether they want to treat them as they are, real centers of our civilization. If we reach that point, the money isn't the question. Money is never the question in national defense, except in terms of need, and I think domestically there should be no limitation on money or response to American cities. It is whether or not we care about them and want to preserve them. That is the ultimate question, and then money follows from that.

*TV-radio interview, Boston/*
*"Meet the Press,"*
*National Broadcasting Company, 7-6.*

1

[On the controversy over the busing of schoolchildren for racial balance in his city]: If it wasn't for this busing problem I think we'd have every reason to be festive [about Boston]. But even that controversy has some encouraging side effects, because if the people had given up on the city and their neighborhoods they wouldn't care less what happened. As it is, they're fighting for their turf. Provided one side doesn't drive the other out, the strength of our city is in the neighborhoods, the cohesiveness and deep-rooted stability they offer. They hold the city together, and what I'm trying to do is prevent the two sides from destroying each other, physically or emotionally. But when you have an emotional split like this, it's like a break in the family. It never really mends.

*Interview, Boston/*
*Los Angeles Times, 8-29:(1)14.*

**Pete Wilson**
*Mayor of San Diego*

2

Many of us who felt that President Ford was right in requiring New York City to make major fiscal reforms before providing Federal aid still would warn that all cities need more of the total tax dollars. Too much of the tax dollar is spent at the state and the Federal level—especially Federal—and not enough at the local level . . . In California we now have a law that says if the [state] legislature mandates something to a locality, then the state must fund it.

We need something like that for the Federal government.

*At National League of Cities convention,*
*Miami Beach/*
*U.S. News & World Report, 12-15:26.*

**Robert C. Wood**
*President, University of Massachusetts; Former director, Joint Center for Urban Studies*

3

[On New York City's fiscal crisis]: There have to be massive infusions of national and state money because cities happen to be national and state assets, and the commercial centers that New York supports between 42nd and 59th Streets and on Wall Street are things important for the nation as a whole. The second thing is probably more theoretical or egghead. We have to seriously go back to Henry George and consider that the city take over ownership of city land. If, in urban renewal, we had leased land instead of selling it to private developers, most of the cities, including New York, would be better off. The third thing is that we have to come to grips with the existence of about 2,100 governments . . . in the metropolitan area. You can't simply put burdens on the central city and let the suburbs take the cream.

*The New York Times, 7-30:35.*

**Coleman A. Young**
*Mayor of Detroit*

4

[On his city's dependence on the automobile industry, which is currently in a slump]: Detroit must diversify its industrial and commercial base if it is to escape the situation in which we now find ourselves. Every time—as the saying goes—the automobile industry catches a cold, Detroit catches pneumonia.

*U.S. News & World Report, 4-7:36.*

# PART TWO

# International Affairs

### Idi Amin
*President of Uganda*

1

We are preparing for [the invasion of] South Africa and Rhodesia. We are already raising an army. It will be truly voluntary and include Ugandan soldiers and airmen and those from other countries. I can tell you that we already have one division—nine battalions—in training for this campaign. They have been training overseas in socialist countries. When they start fighting, you are going to see a fire bigger than in Northern Ireland. This force is capable of living off the land. They will operate guerrilla-style within the borders of South Africa—educating people against the regime, making sabotage, blowing up bridges and hijacking planes. By next year—no, by the end of this year—you will see them going in. Some are there already. The only answer is for Rhodesia and South Africa to give up. If they don't, they are going to have a big problem.

*Interview/Newsweek, 8-4:41.*

2

[On Soviet involvement in the civil war in Angola]: We should not let ourselves be brainwashed by the Western powers that the presence of Soviet technicians in Angola is an indication that the Soviet Union wants to colonize Africa. When Africa is in trouble, it is the [Communist] Chinese, the Soviet Union and other socialist countries which come to our rescue, and not the Americans or the British. Africa must therefore support the Soviet Union and not be discouraged.

*Kampala, Uganda, Dec. 25/*
*The Washington Post, 12-26:(A)1.*

### Houari Boumedienne
*President of Algeria*

3

Geography and history condemn France and Algeria to cooperate ... Relations between France and Algeria can be good, or they can be bad. They can never be ordinary.

*The Christian Science Monitor, 4-24:16.*

### Leonel Cardoso
*Former Portuguese High Commissioner for Angola*

4

[On the independence of the former Portuguese colony of Angola]: Portugal leaves without sentiments of guilt and without having to be ashamed. I sincerely regret that it is not possible for me to take part in any commemorative ceremony at the greatest hour in the life of the Angolan people. But, given the actual circumstances, that would mean an interference by Portugal in the sacred rights of that people to decide its own future.

*Luanda, Angola/*
*San Francisco Examiner & Chronicle,*
*11-16:(This World)13.*

### Alan Cranston
*United States Senator, D—California*

5

[On the U.S. Senate's vote to cut off American military aid to Angola during that country's current civil war]: In refusing to vote more money for the covert funding of paramilitary activities in Angola and environs, we have rejected the road to another Vietnam. We have only to listen to the global-confrontation terms used to describe what is at stake there. This is the rhetoric that led us into Vietnam.

*The Washington Post, 12-25:(A)18.*

### Gerald R. Ford
*President of the United States*

6

[On the U.S. Senate's vote to stop further military aid to Angola during that country's current civil war]: The Senate decision to cut off additional funds for Angola is a deep tragedy for all countries whose security depends on the United States. Ultimately, it will pro-

# WHAT THEY SAID IN 1975

foundly affect the security of our country as well. How can the United States, the greatest power in the world, take the position that the Soviet Union can operate with impunity [in Angola] many thousands of miles away [by aiding one faction in the Angolan civil war] with Cuban troops and massive amounts of military equipment, while we refuse any assistance to the majority of the local people who ask only for military equipment to defend themselves? The issue in Angola is not, never has been and never will be a question of the use of U.S. forces. The sole issue is the provision of modest amounts of assistance to oppose military intervention by two extracontinental powers, namely the Soviet Union and Cuba. This abdication of responsibility by a majority of the Senate will have the gravest consequences for the long-term position of the United States and for international order in general.

*Before White House press corps, Washington, Dec. 19/The New York Times, 12-20:8.*

## Henry M. Jackson
*United States Senator, D—Washington*    1

Too often, American policy toward Africa has been not to lend a hand in assistance . . . All too often it has been to show the back of the hand in pushing aside African affairs. In South Africa the United States cannot be neutral in a struggle for racial justice and political liberty. We must give full support to the efforts now under way to bring about real changes in South African racial policies. These efforts have shown a sensible and moderate attitude toward the South African problem. But Africans will not—and America must not—accept words instead of deeds.

*At Pan-African Business Center dinner, New York, May 28/ The Washington Post, 5-29:(A)12.*

## Kenneth Kaunda
*President of Zambia*    2

What gives Zambia and Africa great cause for concern is . . . America's policy toward Africa— or it is the lack of it, which of course can mean

the same thing. A no-policy position may not be a neutral position indicative of a passive posture, but a deliberate act of policy to support the status quo or to influence events in one direction or another at a particular time. [Ten years ago] America did not wait for and march in step with colonial powers, but rather boldly marched ahead with the colonial peoples in their struggles to fulfill their aspirations. Have the principles changed? Southern Africa is poised for a dangerous armed conflict. If we want peace, we must . . . vigorously work for ending apartheid. America must now be in the vanguard of democratic revolution in southern Africa.

*At White House state dinner, Washington, April 19/The Dallas Times Herald, 4-21:(A)3.*

3

[On Soviet involvement on the side of the Communist MPLA faction in the Angolan civil war]: I feel we must speak plainly on Angola. We are a non-aligned nation and we spoke out plainly against the United States on Vietnam. Now we must be morally and politically courageous and tell the Soviets: "You are wrong." As for U.S. arms help for other Angolans, that is an effect of the situation, not the cause. A truly non-aligned country must condemn Soviet influence in Angola. It is not just a political issue; it is a moral issue . . . I must stress that MPLA, UNITA and FNLA are no longer liberation movements. They are just political parties. Angola was liberated when the Portuguese left [earlier in the year]. Outsiders have no right to select Angola's political leaders. The UNITA-FNLA coalition has every right to request arms from the U.S.A. when the MPLA receives such arms from the Soviet Union. We cannot complain about this—until reason at last prevails in Angola. The Soviet Union has supplied arms to MPLA all along. If the United States is asked by the others to help them accordingly, who am I to stand in their way? We in Africa must look at Angola in a sober, cool way, not emotionally. Much as we condemn South African presence in Angola, we cheat ourselves if we think that by condemning South Africa we are settling things. The South African presence, too, is an effect of the problem, not a cause. The only possible meaningful solution is to have a political compromise among the disputants. If African leadership is to be meaningful, such a political solution must be found. What is going on right now—Angolans killing each other—is tragic.

*Interview, Chinsali, Zambia/*
*The New York Times, 12-31:21.*

**Kim Il Sung**
*President of North Korea*
*1*

We were very happy to see the African continent struggling with all energies to build a new life since it was liberated from the yoke of the colonialists. What impressed me most was that all the African peoples are dynamically fighting to build new societies, prospering, sovereign and independent states. The African peoples, united firmly around their parties, governments and leaders, are vigorously turning out to the building of new societies and exerting especially great efforts to defend political independence and achieve economic self-support. We saw in this a bright future of Africa.

*Interview, Nouakchott, North Korea, May 31/*
*The New York Times, 8-1:5.*

**Henry A. Kissinger**
*Secretary of State of the United States*
*2*

In underlining our goal of peaceful change for southern Africa, I want to emphasize the importance of an early settlement in Namibia. My government's opposition to South Africa's continuing occupation of Namibia and our rejection of South Africa's apartheid system are well known. The United States has consistently conveyed our position on this subject to South Africa. We will continue to do so.

*At United Nations, New York, Sept. 22/*
*The New York Times, 9-23:16.*

*3*

[Criticizing Soviet and Cuban involvement in the Angolan civil war]: We are not opposed to the MPLA [the Soviet-backed faction in Angola] as such. We make a distinction between the factions of Angola and the outside intervention. We can live with any of the factions in Angola, and we would never have given assistance to

any of the other factions if other powers had stayed out of it. Unless the Soviet Union shows restraint in its foreign-policy actions, the situation in our relationship is bound to become more tense. And there is no question the United States will not accept Soviet military expansion of any kind . . . The question is not whether the country of Angola represents a vital interest to the United States. The issue is whether the Soviet Union, backed by a Cuban expeditionary force, can impose on two-thirds of the population its own brand of government. And the issue is not whether the United States should resist it with its own military forces. Nobody ever suggested the introduction of American military forces. [If the U.S. adopts a national policy opposing military and economic assistance] to people who are trying to defend themselves without American military forces, then we are practically inviting outside forces to participate in every situation in which there is a possibility for foreign intervention.

*News conference, Washington, Dec. 23/*
*Los Angeles Times, 12-24:(1)1,6.*

**Joseph R. L. Kotsokoane**
*Foreign Minister of Lesotho*
*4*

Change is inevitable but not accurately predictable in southern Africa. But we Africans know that if peaceful methods fail, then the alternative is an armed struggle which could lead to a racial conflagration involving all of southern Africa . . . We Africans are reasonable people who would rather talk than fight. But the Africans will not hesitate to fight if that is the only way to bring about majority rule in Zimbabwe [Rhodesia], or Namibia, or until there is meaningful change in South Africa so the blacks are accorded equality and human dignity.

*Interview, Los Angeles, Oct. 10/*
*Los Angeles Times, 10-11:(1)23.*

**Samora M. Machel**
*President of Frelimo (Mozambique*
*independence movement)*
*5*

[On Frelimo's struggle for the independence of Mozambique]: After 500 years of colonialization and 10 years of war, the situation which

# WHAT THEY SAID IN 1975

*(SAMORA M. MACHEL)*

exists in Mozambique is not alarming; on the contrary, it is very normal. It is a situation which permits us to start and advance more rapidly to develop Mozambique. When we started the war we had absolutely nothing, but in 10 years we have deeply transformed our country. We have uprooted colonialism, transformed men, made Mozambique known to the world. And that was in wartime.

*Interview/The New York Times, 6-25:3.*

## Clarence M. Mitchell, Jr.
*Civil-rights leader; Member, United States delegation to the United Nations*
1

[Criticizing the apartheid system in South Africa]: There is a system of political laws, which are designed to stifle and intimidate political opposition, laws which make criminal acts which are not criminal in any free society. Indeed, certain acts which form the rough give-and-take that is the lifeblood of democracy are considered criminal in South Africa ... Moreover, although its supporters say it enjoys a fine old tradition of independence and integrity, the judiciary has been repeatedly frustrated in the exercise of that tradition. Judgments giving the benefit of the doubt to liberty and freedom have been overruled by express legislative amendment.

*At United Nations, New York, Nov. 28/*
*Los Angeles Times, 11-29:(1)3.*

## Mobutu Sese Seko
*President of Zaire*
2

In Angola, during 14 years of struggle against Portuguese colonialism, the assistance of powers outside Africa to the Angolan liberation movements was ludicrous, at best symbolic. But when those who overthrew the Caetano dictatorship [in Portugal] on April 24, 1974, included in their program the accession to independence of the Portuguese colonies, the same powers which divided us and spilled blood in our country hurried to give arms to the Angolan liberation movements in order to cause the same horrors that we lived through after our independence. Each time that Africans try

to settle their own affairs, these same powers intervene in the name of some particular ideology and furnish arms to provoke disorder. The same quantity of arms could have been given to assist the nationalist movements in Namibia [South-West Africa], Zimbabwe [Rhodesia] and South Africa to liberate themselves from the colonial yoke in a few weeks. But nothing has been done, for the moment, to help them. The attitude of these foreign powers proves to us that when Africans struggle against imperialistic or white racist regimes, some of the so-called progressive ones do nothing but cross their arms and remain impassive spectators, thus abetting the shameless exploitation of the black man. But when Africans succeed in obtaining their independence and the former colonizer leaves, that is the moment those foreign powers choose to furnish armored cars, missiles, warplanes and all kinds of sophisticated arms in order to transform internal African quarrels into civil wars and thereby have the Africans annihilate themselves.

*The Washington Post, 12-21:(E)6.*

## Daniel P. Moynihan
*United States Ambassador/Permanent Representative to the United Nations*
3

[Criticizing Soviet intervention in Angola]: The European colonizers, which had come to conquer every square foot of Africa, save only Ethiopia, have now left Africa. Most have left in good repute and with good and strong and friendly feelings and ties that endure with the areas, not nations, which they had come to occupy. But at just the moment when the European colonizers of the 17th and 18th and 19th centuries have departed, at just that moment a new European colonizing, colonial imperial nation appears on the continent of Africa, armed, aggressive, involved in the direct assault upon the lands and the people of Africa. The European colonial power is back, a new colonial power, more mighty than any that ever preceded it. It has come with its arms, with its armies, with its technology, with its ideology; and recolonization commences, or, more accurately, the effort now to recolonize Africa commences. The question is whether it will succeed.

The enormous and critically important question is whether African nations themselves will allow themselves to be parties to a new European conquest. Now, it is well known to the members of this [UN General] Assembly that the Organization of African Unity has condemned all intervention in Angola—all intervention. The OAU has done this and was right to have done it. The United States of America, for one, has condemned all intervention in Angola and we are happy to join the OAU in that matter. Which of the great powers, as they are called, of the world has *not* condemned all intervention in Angola? You know very well which has not. It is the Soviet Union which has not—the European power now engaged in colonial expansion in the continent of Africa.

*At United Nations, New York, Dec. 8/*
*The Christian Science Monitor, 12-16:35.*

**Cornelius P. Mulder**
*Minister of Information and the*
*Interior of South Africa*
1

We [in South Africa] have rejected the word apartheid [but] we believe in the policy of separate development. We believe there is unity in diversity, because to force the different races to live together and act alike could lead to bloodshed.

*News conference, Los Angeles, June 6/*
*Los Angeles Times, 6-7:(1)24.*

**Abel Tendekai Muzorewa**
*Methodist bishop; Leader, Rhodesian*
*black nationalist movement*
2

Today, we in Zimbabwe [Rhodesia] working through the ANC are pursuing a double strategy. We will pursue an internal strategy of negotiations, because I as a Christian believe in non-violence. The people in Zimbabwe are also a peace-loving people; they would prefer that, if it is possible, we should get our independence through peaceful actions. But we must also be prepared for other possibilities. If in our negotiations we come to the point where we are absolutely convinced that the [Prime Minister Ian] Smith regime and its imperialist allies do not want to talk, or if they continue to attack

our people, then our external policy is to protect our people and fight for our independence, as other groups around the world have done.

*At University of California, Los Angeles,*
*May 18/Los Angeles Times, 5-19:(1)3.*

**Julius K. Nyerere**
*President of Tanzania*
3

[Saying that guerrilla war may be the only means of establishing black-majority rule in Rhodesia]: We very much regret the need for war. It can only bring dreadful suffering to the people of Rhodesia, both black and white. It will therefore leave a heritage of bitterness which will make the eventual development of a non-racial, democratic society in that country very much more difficult.

*Oxford, England/*
*The Christian Science Monitor, 11-24:3.*

**Alan Paton**
*South African author*
4

[South African] relations with black countries is no good unless there is also change within [South Africa]. This will be difficult in a country where the majority of those in power truly believe in their own [white] superiority and fear the consequences of giving power to the black man. More and more people are trying to hide these feelings today, but they still exist and remain the concealed root of our problems. Fear is the great operator here—and it is the government's hard task to accommodate this fear while still easing discrimination.

*Interview, Kloof, South Africa/*
*The Christian Science Monitor, 10-31:12.*

**Holden Roberto**
*Leader of FNLA, anti-Communist faction*
*in Angolan civil war*
5

[Asking the West to aid his cause against the Soviet-backed Communist MPLA]: I am calling on the West to save Africa from Communism. Can they not see what is happening? In an age of diminishing mineral and food resources, the Soviet Union is making a bid for control of southern Africa, the world's richest source of

# WHAT THEY SAID IN 1975

*(HOLDEN ROBERTO)*

gold, diamonds, uranium and other strategic minerals, as well as the area of greatest agricultural potential. And what of the strategic naval threat that a Soviet presence in Angola poses to the West's sea routes? I am asking for help to save my country from a new and ruthless imperialism. But I can also say, in all sincerity, that I am asking the West to save itself. I am astonished that I have to shout this to deaf ears.

*Interview, Ambriz, Angola/*
*Newsweek, 12-29:28.*

**Mohammed Siad Barre**
*President of Somalia*  1

There is no Soviet military equipment in my country under Russian control ... We believe the Indian Ocean must become a zone of peace, with no bases for foreign powers anywhere. Foreign bases are provocative, and we condemn them. We believe that sovereignty is sacrificed when rights to a base are given. If there were no foreign bases in the world, there would be peace ... Of course, the Soviets have given us much help, and we are grateful for that. They have been teaching us and giving us arms and technicians. During the drought, and when we were resettling refugees, they came to our assistance with planes and trucks manned by Russians. Does this mean we are in their pocket? No. If the U.S.A. sent me 10 planes, the pilots could be American. Would this suggest I am in the American pocket? Have we sold our freedom or sovereignty? No, sir. I am poor but I am free. A Soviet socialist cannot tell me about Somalian problems, which must be put in an African context. I know and have suffered under colonialism, and I don't want to go back to it. Freedom is my dearest value. My country is neutral and will do everything possible to maintain an equal distance between the two blocs.

*Interview/U.S. News & World Report, 7-21:32.*

**Ian Smith**
*Prime Minister of Rhodesia*  2

I think it is important to bring the [black] African in [to the government], to encourage him to play a bigger part. This is common sense—logical ... I think that if a person is a Rhodesian he has as much right to any position in Rhodesia as any other Rhodesian, whatever his color. I don't like talking about governments or people in office by color. I think if we get to this stage we will have failed in the deal we are pursuing in Rhodesia. We believe in quality as opposed to quantity, if I may put it to you that way. We think that the ideal is to be governed by the best people who are available in Rhodesia, irrespective of their color, and I think we must continue in this line of thinking ... I don't believe we can prejudge [when a multiracial government might come about]. It depends on the right people coming forward, and then one could go into the timing. For a while now, we have been going through a period in Rhodesia where most of the black leaders have been sitting, sulking in their corner, if I may use that expression; and under those circumstances it is very difficult to make an assessment of them and decide whether it is possible to use them or not.

*Interview, Salisbury, Sept. 19/*
*The New York Times, 9-20:6.*

**John V. Tunney**
*United States Senator, D–California*  3

[Saying the U.S. should not give military aid to counter Soviet intervention in the civil war in Angola]: Why does a country like Nigeria, whose pro-Western and pro-American sentiments have been voiced again and again, fail to perceive the threat to its security posed by Cuban and Russian advisers? The reason is that the Africans don't perceive this as the grand checkmate move in Soviet world strategy that [U.S.] Secretary [of State Henry] Kissinger does. They see it for what it is—an internal conflict growing more out of tribal animosities than from any real difference in ideology.

*Before the Senate, Washington, Dec. 15/*
*Los Angeles Times, 12-16:(1)18.*

**John Vorster**
*Prime Minister of South Africa*  4

[Addressing his country's black leaders]: If there are people who are raising your hopes that there will one day be one-man, one-vote in the white Parliament for you, then they are misleading you, for that will never happen . . . Whites will continue to govern South Africa.

*January/*
*U.S. News & World Report, 3-31:64.*

1

I don't see any reason why an independent white country and an independent black country can't both find a place in the sun in the continent of Africa, because we are as much of Africa and we have as much right to claim our portion of Africa as any other African country has to claim its portion of Africa.

*Interview, Cape Town, Feb. 10/*
*Los Angeles Herald-Examiner, 2-11:(A)4.*

[On the civil war in Angola]: I know of no Chinese involvement in Angola. But there are substantial numbers of Russians—maybe 500—plus maybe 5,000 Cubans. There is an extensive Soviet air-and-sea lift of arms [to the Communist Angolan faction] . . . If it was just a question of the Angolans themselves, the war would be over already. The [Communist] MPLA has inferior forces and controls only one-fourth of Angola's territory and population. But the Russians send sophisticated weapons—tanks, 122-millimeter rockets mounted in clusters of 50 on lorries, infantry-borne SAMs. Only big powers can offset this arsenal, above all the 122-millimeter rockets. It is certainly beyond our [South Africa's] limits.

*Interview, Cape Town/*
*The New York Times, 12-24:21.*

# The Americas

**Joaquin Balaguer**
*President of the Dominican Republic*

1

We are living in a world wracked by violence; and in most of Latin America, even where under-development has for some time been partially resolved, the outlook for public order and stability is not very heartening. Most of our peoples, hungry and under-nourished, are clamoring for a more equitable distribution of national wealth. The air resounds with the desperate cry of the masses demanding radical social reforms as our only possible instrument for achieving the peace for which we all yearn.

*Before Inter-American Development Bank Assembly of Governors, Santo Domingo, May 19/The New York Times, 6-6:36.*

**Hugo Banzer (Suarez)**
*President of Bolivia*

2

Bolivia is not a military dictatorship but a democratic, Christian, nationalist and popular regime, because it has the support of the people.

*The Washington Post, 3-17:(A)14.*

**Ellsworth Bunker**
*United States Ambassador-at-Large;*
*Chief U.S. negotiator at*
*Panama Canal Treaty talks*

3

[On whether the U.S. should relinquish sovsovereignty over the Panama Canal to Panama]: While it is true . . . that we could attempt to maintain our present position with regard to the Panama Canal, we would have to do so in an increasingly hostile atmosphere. In these circumstances we would likely find ourselves engaged in hostilities with an otherwise friendly country—a conflict that, in my view, the American people would not long accept. At the same time, we should bear in mind that the Canal is vulnerable to sabotage and terrorist acts. We would find it difficult, if not impossible, to keep the Canal running against an all-out Panamanian opposition.

*At Ranier Club, Seattle, May 22/ The Washington Post, 6-27:(A)3.*

4

Putting it simply, I believe our [U.S.] interest in keeping the [Panama] Canal open and operating for our own strategic and economic purposes is best served by a partnership agreement [with Panama] for a reasonably additional period of time. The plain fact of the matter is that geography, history, and the economic and political imperatives of our time compel the United States and Panama to a joint venture in the Panama Canal. We must learn to comport ourselves as partners and friends—preserving what is essential to each, protecting and making more efficient an important international line of communication, and, I suggest, creating an example for the world of a small nation and a large one working peacefully and profitably together.

*At Ranier Club, Seattle, May 22/ Vital Speeches, 7-1:548.*

5

The United States does not own the Panama Canal Zone. Contrary to the belief of many Americans, the United States did not purchase the Canal Zone for $10-million in 1903. Rather, the money we gave Panama then was in return for the rights which Panama granted us by treaty. We bought Louisiana; we bought Alaska. In Panama we bought not territory, but rights.

*Before Los Angeles World Affairs Council, Dec. 2/The New York Times, 12-3:20.*

**Harry F. Byrd, Jr.**
*United States Senator, I– Virginia*

6

[Saying the U.S. should not give up sovereignty over the Panama Canal]: The Canal is of great economic, political and military importance. From an economic point of view, were the Canal to fall into hostile hands or were it to be closed, a ship traveling from New York to Los Angeles, for example, would have to travel 8,000 additional miles—increasing fuel consumption by over 70 per cent, and the time of travel by more than a month. That would increase the cost of exports and imports to the United States, and it would greatly increase the cost to the consumer. From a military point of view, the Canal has been a mainstay in our defense posture for the Atlantic-Pacific, and for our role in the Western Hemisphere. The Canal enables the rapid deployment of our fleets, and, with the exception of our large carriers, virtually all major military ships, including nuclear submarines, can go through the Canal, and do ... Now, I don't oppose a new treaty [with Panama]. Certain aspects of the old [Canal] treaty could very well be changed. It could be updated and modernized. There's only one aspect that I feel is not negotiable, namely, the elimination of sovereignty As to the rest of it, I have no objection to the negotiations.

*Interview/*
*U.S. News & World Report,*
*10-6:37.*

**Howard H. Callaway**
*Secretary of the Army*
*of the United States*

1

[On whether the U.S. should relinquish sovereignty over the Panama Canal to Panama]: There's a feeling in this country [the U.S.], and it's not just the right wing, that Teddy Roosevelt helped the Panamanians get their independence ... negotiated the [Canal] treaty, paid for it, paid France [for the Canal rights], conquered yellow fever, brought [the Panamanians] their sole economic enterprise ... There's the feeling that the Canal is enormously valuable, that we paid for it and it's ours. I can promise you, if you start calling moderates around the country and Congress, you'd find support for this position.

*Interview, June 26/*
*The Washington Post, 6-27:(A)3.*

**Fidel Castro**
*Premier of Cuba*

2

[Denying that Cuba had in any way been involved with the 1963 assassination of U.S. President John Kennedy]: It is not within the tradition of the socialist revolution to physically eliminate its enemies. We have another concept of things. As a matter of principle, we are against this tactic and it would have been stupid to be responsible for such a serious act. It would be absurd, stupid, irresponsible, crazy and, besides, very dangerous for Cuba. And besides, Kennedy was an adversary we knew. We did not think anyone else would have been better and they might have been worse. He was very intelligent and he was beginning to understand the error of U.S. policy against Cuba when he was killed. Perhaps Kennedy himself would have taken steps toward changing that policy.

*News conference, Havana, May 7/*
*The Dallas Times Herald, 5-8:(A)3.*

3

I do not think we should talk about exporting revolutions because they cannot be exported. What we should talk about is the attempt by the United States to export counter-revolution [to Latin America] ... We are willing to negotiate with the United States with absolute seriousness, frankness and responsibility. But we would not like to do so with a dagger at our throat. This is not a condition; I would call it the essential requisite for equality to exist, to discuss with dignity ... This does not mean that we object to establishing contact nor does it mean that we object to holding talks. But we maintain the principle that in order to engage in deep negotiations it is necessary that the economic embargo imposed against Cuba by the United States be lifted.

*News conference, Havana, Aug. 21/*
*The Washington Post, 8-23:(A)1,13.*

4

[On alleged U.S. CIA plots against Cuban leaders over a period of time]: [The plots involved] poisons capable of killing entire cities, pistols with silencers, and microscopic poisoned

# WHAT THEY SAID IN 1975

*(FIDEL CASTRO)*

bullets that practically leave no wound on the skin; pens with small holes, usable without the victim knowing about it to innoculate toxic products of delayed effect, that kill and are untraceable after death. Never in the history of international relations have such practices been systematized ... against the lives of leaders of another country. Nevertheless, not one voice in the concert of the Organization of American States was raised to denounce such criminal practices; and this was the infamous institution that, for finding Marxism-Leninism incompatible with the system, expelled us from its rolls and, invoking subversion, subjected us to the brutal measures of an economic blockade and political isolation.

*At Cuban Communist Party Congress, Havana/*
*The Washington Post, 12-20:(A)11.*

*1*

[On U.S. President Ford's criticism of Cuban involvement in the civil war in Angola]: What can they [the U.S.] threaten us with; what can they take away from us that they haven't taken already? This we can call absolute impotence. Nothing remains to be cancelled. We do not depend on them for anything ... The Yankee imperialists were the owners of Latin America and Latin America does not want an owner any more.

*At rally, Havana, Dec. 22/*
*The Washington Post, 12-23:(A)3.*

**Ray S. Cline**
*Former Director of Intelligence and Research,*
*Department of State of the United States*
*2*

[Saying then-President of the U.S. Richard Nixon and then-Presidential Assistant, now Secretary of State, Henry Kissinger were personally responsible for CIA activities in Chile in the early 1970s]: [They] were very impatient with the CIA and State Department, who were resisting their efforts [to instigate a coup against then-President of Chile Salvador Allende]. As a result, the operations were handled personally by Kissinger and Nixon. They didn't intend to stage an assassination, but did evi-

dently temporarily order cooperation with the [Chilean] group attempting to kidnap General Rene Schneider [Chilean Army Chief of Staff]. Another group, in fact, attempted the kidnaping and stupidly murdered him [in 1970] ... [CIA involvement in Chilean affairs was carried out] exclusively and directly by order of the President [Nixon] and his Assistant for National Security Affairs [Kissinger] [because] I was in the State Department at the time and the matter was not considered by other senior members of government, because they were not in favor of it.

*News conference, Dallas, Dec. 1/*
*The Dallas Times Herald, 12-2:(A)6.*

**John B. Connally, Jr.**
*Former Secretary of the Treasury of the*
*United States; Former Governor of*
*Texas (D, now R)*
*3*

I believe we should place new emphasis on our relations with Latin America—but not as some outdated Latin American policy that treats every nation south of us as if it were cut from the same pattern. We should quit speaking of a "Latin American policy." We should begin treating each of these nations as a sovereign state with its own particular problems and opportunities for friendly relations and trade with the United States.

*Before Dallas Citizens Council, Nov. 19/*
*The Dallas Times Herald, 11-20:(A)22.*

**Miguel Angel de la Flor**
*Foreign Minister of Peru*
*4*

[On U.S.-Latin American relations]: We are conscious of the presence of the United States, of a lack of equilibrium. There is the industrialized U.S.A.; then, various stages of developing lands in Latin America. We want good relations with you [the U.S.], legitimate equality, mutual respect and non-intervention in internal affairs. We had to nationalize and expropriate foreign enterprises. When your government sought to protect your companies, that produced trouble. But, since 1973, relations have begun to improve, although we still favor ideological pluralism and East-West cooperation.

*The New York Times, 12-10:43.*

## Luis Echeverria (Alvarez)
*President of Mexico*

1

I think you [the U.S.] should re-establish balanced relations [with Cuba], as should all American countries. The Cubans have done very positive things, in spite of the economic blockade, in an effort full of imagination. It would be preferable to have friendly diplomatic relations without a spirit of revenge.

*Interview, Mexico City, Jan. 2/*
*The New York Times, 1-8:2.*

2

...in reality, there is a Latin American blockade on the United States. It is a blockade in the minds of the peasants, the workers, the university students and the new generation. It is a psychological blockade, a moral blockade that the United States is not going to erode until it radically changes its policy vis-a-vis all Latin America.

*Cuba/*
*The New York Times, 8-27:33.*

3

[On charges that his speeches have aroused antagonism toward the U.S.]: ... my speeches have emerged from a general feeling from which I take my thoughts. We [Mexico] belong to the Third World. We are defending our economy. We are struggling to survive. We would like to be friends, not servants. We have to be nationalistic or we shall perish.

*Interview, Mexico City/*
*The New York Times, 11-20:18.*

## Gerald R. Ford
*President of the United States*

4

Very frequently in my daily meetings with Secretary of State [Henry] Kissinger, we discuss Latin American policy, including our policy toward Cuba. The policy today is the same as it has been; which is that if Cuba will re-evaluate and give us some indication of a change of its policy toward the United States, then we certainly would take another look. But thus far there's no sign of [Cuban Premier Fidel] Castro's change of heart, and so we

think it's in our best interest to continue the policies that are in effect at the present time.

*News conference, Hollywood, Fla., Feb. 26/*
*The New York Times, 2-27:20.*

5

[On Cuban involvement in the Angolan civil war]: There are between 4,000 and 6,000 Cuban combat military personnel in Angola. The action by the Cuban government in sending combat forces to Angola destroys any opportunity for improvement in relations with the United States. They've made a choice which, in effect, and I mean it very literally, has precluded any improvement in relations with Cuba.

*News conference, Washington, Dec. 20/*
*San Francisco Examiner & Chronicle,*
*12-21:(A)10.*

## Indira Gandhi
*Prime Minister of India*

6

[Criticizing the U.S. for its alleged involvement in the overthrow of Chilean President Salvador Allende in 1973]: Some powers which had tasted success in their destabilization game in Chile nurtured similar designs against India. The defense made by American politicians that they had not toppled the Allende government in Chile, but had only financed some parties whose policies were akin to theirs, is strange indeed. This only meant that they brought about the toppling, through local agents, while they poured in money and material. These local people were just dummies. In fact, it was a kind of direct intervention.

*At Congress Party convention, New Delhi,*
*Dec. 31/Los Angeles Times, 1-1('76):(1)4.*

## E. J. (Jake) Garn
*United States Senator, R–Utah*

7

... there is no significant economic advantage to the United States in a resumption of full trade relations with Cuba. Nor is it a persuasive argument that if we treat them like one of us they will become like one of us. In fact, most Western European nations have had full relations with Cuba for more than 15 years. There is little evidence that Cuba's anti-Western line has softened. In fact, while the open rhetoric

# WHAT THEY SAID IN 1975

## (E. J. (JAKE) GARN)

has been toned down somewhat, there is ample evidence that revolutionary activities in other countries continue to be instigated and abetted by [Cuban Premier Fidel] Castro. For instance, this last September Castro hosted in Havana an international conference designed to show Communist solidarity with the revolutionary Puerto Ricans trying to separate that island from its U.S. ties. . . . we have no real incentive to resume diplomatic and trade relations with the Cuban Communists, and every reason to continue a diplomatic quarantine of this carrier of the revolutionary virus. Cuba is now firmly within the Soviet orbit and shows every indication that it will remain so. Resumption of diplomatic and trade relations would simply legitimate a cruel, repressive regime, which shows little tendency to reason in its own foreign policy.

*Before the Senate, Washington, Nov. 13/\*\**

## Edward M. Kennedy
*United States Senator, D—Massachusetts*      1

I believe the idea of isolating Cuba was a mistake. It was a reversion to the cold war of confrontation with the regimes that were opposed to the United States and other democratic societies. Frankly, it has been ineffective. Whatever the reasons and justifications may have been at the time, now they are invalid. I believe the United States, in association with the inter-American community, should respect the experiment that has taken place in Cuba and normalize relations with it . . . [The late U.S. President John Kennedy had his difficulties with Cuba], but one of the things in which he firmly believed—and he said so—was making a world safe for diversification, which is important in hemispherical relations . . .

*Television interview, Mexico City, Feb. 9/*
*Los Angeles Times, 2-10:(1)13.*

## Henry A. Kissinger
*Secretary of State of the United States*      2

The United States is concerned by the growing tendency of some Latin American countries to participate in tactics of confrontation be-

tween the developing and developed worlds. We accept non-alignment as a necessary, largely positive, force. We believe that the developed nations—and particularly the United States as the most powerful industrial country—have a special obligation to be sensitive both to the legacy of history and to the imperatives of change. It is therefore ironic that some nations seek to exact by confrontation what can only be gained through cooperation, and that countries which once chose non-alignment to protect themselves from blocs are now tending to form a rigid bloc of their own. In doing so, they obstruct the association with the industrialized nations on which their own economic and social progress ultimately depends. Such tactics are particularly inappropriate for the Western Hemisphere where they threaten to repudiate a long tradition of cooperative relations with the United States at the very moment when the United States has dedicated itself to common progress.

*Before Combined Service Club, Houston,*
*March 1/Vital Speeches, 4-1:356.*
3

If the OAS sanctions [against Cuba] are eventually repealed, the United States will consider changes in its bilateral relations with Cuba . . . We see no virtue in perpetual antagonism between the United States and Cuba. We have taken some symbolic steps to indicate that we are prepared to move in a new direction if Cuba will. [But] fundamental change cannot come unless Cuba demonstrates a readiness to assume the mutuality of obligation and regard upon which a new relationship must be founded.

*Before Combined Service Club, Houston,*
*March 1/The New York Times, 3-2(1)4.*

4

[The U.S. has] cooperated with steps to ease the inter-American boycott against Cuba, and to restore a more normal relationship between the nations of the Americas and Cuba. But let there be no illusions: A policy of conciliation will not survive Cuban meddling in Puerto Rico or Cuban armed intervention in the affairs of other nations struggling to decide their own fate.

*Before Economic Club, Detroit, Nov. 24/*
*The Washington Post, 11-25:(A)11.*

**Alfonso Lopez (Michelsen)**
*President of Colombia*

1

The governments of the United States in their dealings with Latin America [over the years] are wont to adopt slogans and policies of uneven content, such as the "Big Stick" and the "Alliance for Progress," through the "Good Neighbor" until arriving at the "New Dialogue." I believe the moment has arrived for the formulation of a policy to govern our relations between the neighbor to the North and Latin America. . . . we have entered the era of joint responsibilities—responsibilities of the United States toward Latin America but also responsibilities of Latin America toward the United States.

*Panama City, Panama/*
*The New York Times, 4-10:31.*

2

[On his country's decision to forego further U.S. aid]: We have concluded that foreign aid breeds an unhealthy economic dependency and delays or undermines measures that should be taken for development. Certainly, there are no points of conflict with Washington that would prompt us to decline further financial aid. Personally, it has always struck me as strange that nations of the Third World having disputes with the United States nevertheless accept foreign aid from Washington . . . Fortunately, we have relatively little foreign investment in our country, and that may be why relations between our countries are free of conflict.

*News conference, New York/*
*The New York Times, 10-4:40.*

**Allan J. MacEachen**
*Secretary of State for External*
*Affairs of Canada*

3

[On his country's economic relations with the U.S.]: We considered three options: 1) maintenance of the status quo; 2) closer integration with the United States; and 3) strengthening of the economy and other aspects of national life in order to secure our independence. The decision was taken to adopt the third option. With it we have chosen to develop

a comprehensive, long-term strategy intended to give direction to specific(s) and programs which will reduce Canadian vulnerability to the magnetic pole of the United States.

*Before Winnipeg chapter, Canadian*
*Institute of International Affairs,*
*Jan. 23/The New York Times, 1-25:5.*

**Michael Manley**
*Prime Minister of Jamaica*

4

A developing country . . . first of all has got to try to create the kind of popular expectations that are not related to the millionaire's dream. The millionaire's dream is a fantastic thing, if you're America with all your economic and physical frontiers to conquer; there is the space to accommodate them. In Jamaica, there isn't the space to make it work through that dream. What that dream does is to create a few millionaires and a hell of a lot of paupers . . . I think that Jamaica's critical task now is to cut itself free from the tremendous influence that the American economic dream has had on Jamaica, because Jamaica hasn't the resources or the situation within which that dream can happen. Some other dream may be able to happen. That's not the dream that can happen here.

*Interview, Jamaica/*
*Los Angeles Times, 4-23:(1-A)2.*

**Gale W. McGee**
*United States Senator, D—Wyoming*

5

[On whether the U.S. should give up sovereignty over the Panama Canal]: The real question is whether we can protect the Canal and keep access to it without a new agreement with Panama. The Canal is probably the single most explosive, emotional factor in our Hemisphere affairs today. In these times of briefcase bombs, it's almost indefensible in a hostile situation. In addition, our dependence on the Canal has changed considerably in the last few decades. It's no longer as important to our national security as it seemed in the earlier days of this century. Today, the Canal is a relatively small item in all of our calculations. Nonetheless, it is a very large item in the calculations of our

# WHAT THEY SAID IN 1975

neighbors in the Hemisphere. Our access to the Canal can be assured only by stability in the Hemisphere. And that just isn't going to happen unless we can make some new accommodation with Panama.

*Interview/*
*U.S. News & World Report, 10-6:37.*

**Marcos G. McGrath**
*Roman Catholic Archbishop of Panama*
1

[Saying there should be a new U.S.-Panamanian treaty giving Panama more control over the Canal]: As the U.S. proclaimed almost 200 years ago the principle of national dignity and independence; as it fought two world wars to free other nations from political servitude and without any territorial aims nor gains for itself; as it declared the Philippines independent and after World War II led the cause of independence of old European colonies—so it can now recognize Panama's claim to genuine and complete national independence. [The U.S.] will find its interests in the Canal sufficiently guaranteed, and its respect in the world—especially in this new world of the Americas—newly refurbished.

*Washington/*
*Los Angeles Herald-Examiner, 6-5:(A)7.*

**Peter C. Newman**
*Editor,*
*"Maclean's" magazine (Canada)*
2

[Canada's] quarter-century-old admiration of all things American exhausted itself in the blazing villages of Vietnam, the dark labyrinth of Watergate, and the long-overdue realization that the United States was crowding out not just our industries but our way of life. By the very act of confronting our problems of domination from without, Canadians may be able to re-work the miracle of their existence. In any case, we have now joined the mainstream of history at last.

*The New York Times, 1-11:2.*

**Alejandro Orfila**
*Secretary General, Organization*
*of American States*
3

This historical moment has presented us with problems of hemispheric political importance. An adequate solution to them is imperative. Among these issues looms the question of the Panama Canal and that of the politico-juridical situation deriving from the separation from the OAS of the present government of Cuba and the sanctions adopted against it . . . [Also,] Latin America and the United States need each other. The United States cannot ignore Latin America, nor can Latin America ignore the United States. The extreme positions which proclaim the damage to this relationship go against history.

*On assuming his post,*
*Washington, July 7/*
*The Washington Post, 7-8:(A)2.*

**Carlos Andres Perez**
*President of Venezuela*
4

It is necessary that the U.S. stop managing our [Latin America's] interests at its will. The stage when the U.S. could reach agreements with each Latin American state individually is over. If the United States does not understand that a sentiment of Latin American community has arisen, and does not . . . negotiate on terms of equality with this community, then we will not be able to seal a new friendship between North and South America.

*Interview/*
*Newsweek, 1-27:43.*

5

[Saying the U.S. should relinquish its sovereignty over the Panama Canal to Panama]: The Panama Canal, in the name of justice, in the name of mankind, cannot continue to be alien and someone else's. The Panama Canal belongs to Panama, and belongs to the world, but does not belong to a foreign power . . . we have addressed the President of the United States of America, explaining to him the reasons moving us to request the earliest return of the Panama Canal to its legitimate owner: the Republic

of Panama. It is a propitious and happy circumstance, undoubtedly, that next year, 1976, with the difference of hardly a month, there will be celebrated the 150th anniversary of the Amphictyonic Congress of Panama, on June 22, and the Bicentennial of the Independence of the United States, on July 4. In the name of Washington and Bolivar, we ask that the Panama Canal be restored to the Panamanians . . . I would like all our countries to celebrate the memory of Washington in an act of justice which gallantly, and living up to its credos of freedom, the Great Republic of the North could perform by telling the world: "What we have demanded for other peoples, what we have demanded for other worlds, that which has cost American blood, freedom and dignity, we also know how to express with our example, giving unto Panama its Canal." Saying in this fashion, with the entire planet as its witness, that democracy is authentic and alive, and is practiced for the benefit of international justice, of integral universal justice.
*Panama City, Panama/*
*The New York Times, 4-10:31.*

1

In the past, many [Latin American] military dictatorships were very repressive, but now several of them are making an effort in the opposite direction. In any event, they represent a failure of democracy. Part of the responsibility for this situation can be attributed to the U.S. and to the countries of Western Europe. We have been subjected to exploitation, which has prevented us from developing our economies. We have been manipulated by the great powers and the multinational corporations. Whether a government is democratic or dictatorial is not a legitimate matter of concern for them. They only care about how the government behaves toward them and their interests. Of course, we must also assume our share of the responsibility for the present situation, but we believe that there has been a lack of effort on the part of developed nations to foster the economic conditions for democracy in Latin America.
*Interview, Caracas/Time, 11-3:42.*

**Augusto Pinochet (Ugarte)**
*President of Chile*
2

Every Chilean must clearly understand that our sacrifices will have to be redoubled and that surely we will have to bear even greater hardships than at present. To the total ruin that Marxism bequeathed us at home, its low aggression from abroad has been added.
*U.S. News & World Report, 1-13:56.*

3

There will be no elections in Chile during my lifetime nor in the lifetime of my successor.
*Concepcion, Chile, June 17/*
*The Washington Post, 6-21:(A)10.*

4

[On how long the military expects to be in power in his country]: I never said how long it would last. Nobody said "two or three years." Those who set deadlines were the politicians, who always spoke of four, six, seven, or 10 years. For what was it they wanted? They wanted us to clean up the house, to spruce it up like dumb servants so they could occupy it once again. And we'd go back to the old days . . . What would politicians do? They would go back to dividing the people. We are trying to unite Chileans and to introduce a sense of order to the nation. All the politicians would do is to produce polarization anew. All the work we're doing would be wiped out in one strike.
*Interview/*
*The Christian Science Monitor, 9-11:6.*

5

[On criticism that his regime is repressive]: The immense majority of our compatriots accept and support restrictions, because they understand that they are the necessary price for tranquility, order and social peace that have made us an island within a world invaded by violence, terrorism and generalized disorder.
*At celebration of his junta's second anniversary/The New York Times, 9-21:(1)30.*

6

[On the coup in 1973 in his country through which he came to power]: I can swear to you

# WHAT THEY SAID IN 1975

*(AUGUSTO PINOCHET [UGARTE])*

as a Christian that I never had any kind of contact with anyone from the [U.S.] CIA or with any ambassador, U.S. or otherwise. I wanted to be free of any obligation to anybody. And, of course, I wanted to protect my intentions by total discretion. Why, afterward, even my family asked what kind of help I received from the United States. I told them: "Not even good-will." In that I am very much disappointed.

*Interview, Antofagasta, Chile/*
*The New York Times, 11-30:(4)13.*

*1*

I am an enemy—a true enemy—of Communists. I attack them, and where I can, I destroy them.

*The Washington Post, 12-1:(A)1.*

**Matthew J. Rinaldo**
*United States Representative, R—New Jersey*
*2*

[Saying the U.S. should not give up control of the Panama Canal to Panama]: The United States made the Panama Canal a symbol of our vision and genius. It was the U.S. that put together the diplomatic, engineering, financial and organizational resources needed to overcome the failures of others to build a waterway. It is imperative that we continue to maintain sovereignty over the Canal, and not relinquish it to another nation for purely political reasons.

*Human Events, 5-3:7.*

**William D. Rogers**
*Assistant Secretary for Inter-American Affairs,*
*Department of State of the United States*
*3*

[On U.S.-Cuban relations]: As to our policy, when and if the multilateral measures against Cuba are repealed by the OAS, there are a considerable number of issues on both sides. Trade is one. We are also concerned with the question of family visits in both directions; we are concerned with prisoners now in Cuban jails; we are concerned with the return of aircraft-hijack ransom money which found its way to Cuba and which Cuba has retained; we are concerned with the question of compensa-

tion for expropriated U.S. property; we are concerned with Cuba's attitude about Puerto Rico; and we are concerned whether Cuba is prepared to follow a clear practice of nonintervention everywhere in the hemisphere.

*Before House Subcommittee, Washington,*
*June 11/Los Angeles Times, 6-12:(1)5.*

**Dudley Thompson**
*Foreign Minister of Jamaica*
*4*

[On his country's new socialism]: The doctrine we hold is based on a firm moral conception that all men not only are created equal but are entitled to equality of opportunity in every phase of their lives. It is not a materialist doctrine, neither Fascism nor Communism. Religion is a strong part of our lives; Jamaicans are a very religious people. We believe that considerations of human dignity, personality and preservation of a free press and the right to participate in the decision-making process must be guaranteed.

*Interview, Kingston/*
*Los Angeles Herald-Examiner, 7-20:(A)16.*

**Omar Torrijos (Herrera)**
*Head of Government of Panama*
*5*

[Saying the U.S. is stalling negotiations for a new Panama Canal treaty]: I am the man in the middle, caught between the students who want action and the oligarchs who would like to get rid of me. For almost seven years I have been careful to promote peaceful relations all around the Canal Zone. That the students haven't broken anything over there yet is possible only because they have faith in the people leading the negotiations. I haven't lost hope, but I cannot live just on hope . . . I am not very impatient, but we have 70 years of history of trying to negotiate a fair deal with the United States. I thought this time was different. But it seems it is the same all over again. We feel you [the U.S.] have not been truthful with us, that things are being done to turn us from a friendly nation into an unfriendly nation. When you come to the crucial moment you don't face up to the problem. In the crucial moment your negotiators start mentioning the Pentagon and the Congress. This is not an anti-Yankee people. We get along well with Americans in general. With those outside the Canal Zone we get along fine, but we are often enemies with the Canal Zonists.

*Interview, Panama City, July 24/*
*The New York Times, 7-28:3.*

**Pierre Elliott Trudeau**
*Prime Minister of Canada*

1

[Announcing economic controls to try to stem inflation in his country]: In the scramble for security [against future inflation], it is the big and powerful who are winning at the expense of those who are unable to protect themselves. That is why there is an urgent need to cool the fires of inflation now. And that is why, in the enforcement of these guidelines, we will be concentrating on those who until today have had the power to get what they want . . . although the guidelines will be enforced against relatively few groups, they can only work if everyone is willing to accept these new limits and considers himself bound by them. This battle must be fought by all . . . The basic cause of inflation in Canada is the attempt by too many people and too many groups to increase their money incomes at rates faster than the increase in the nation's wealth. If I could persuade you of nothing else tonight, I would want to persuade you that no amount of government control, not even a vast army of bureaucrats operating the most massive restraining machinery, not even a total freeze on all prices and incomes of all Canadians, could permanently cure the disease of inflation.

*Broadcast address to the nation, Ottawa,*
*Oct. 13/Los Angeles Times, 10-14:(1)14.*

**Juan Velasco (Alvarado)**
*President of Peru*

2

From now on, the new dialogue should be among Latin-American countries only—without the United States. [The U.S. should be excluded from high-level policy conferences] until it adopts a new attitude, a more honest and just behavior toward smaller countries.

*News conference, Lima, Jan. 30/*
*The New York Times, 1-31:8.*

# Asia and the Pacific

**Zulfikar Ali Bhutto**
*Prime Minister of Pakistan*      *1*

[Tensions would ease on the Asian subcontinent] if India were to play a modest role and not aspire to control the destiny of this region and dearly pretend to be Mother India feeding her children. There is this worry, this anxiety; people feel this. If India did not have an expansionist outlook, what would be the need for India to have exploded the atomic device [last year], because India does not need to divert her resources for this kind of weapon. Otherwise, her defense budget is staggering. There is an objective, a purpose to this . . . When [U.S.] Secretary of State [Henry] Kissinger went to India [last October], why did Indian leaders press him to accept India as a major power, as a quasi-power, and try to get the United States to agree to India having a kind of Monroe Doctrine role in this region. It would not be necessary if India did not hold to a kind of hegemonic concept.

*Interview, Rawalpindi, Jan. 21/*
*The New York Times, 1-22:2.*

*2*

[On democracy for his country]: We've had years of military rule and all sorts of ideas what a democracy means and doesn't mean. We are in the process of finding our feet. We've had a hoary history as far as constitution-making is concerned. In martial law everyone is silent and there is the silence of the grave. In a democracy it means volcanoes and earthquakes all the time. Otherwise it wouldn't be a democracy. A democracy has to function according to our condition, our values, our outlook. If sometimes we have been undemocratic, it might be so. We have a tradition and temper to control.

*Interview, Rawalpindi/*
*The New York Times, 2-2:(1)14.*

*3*

[On the lifting of the U.S. arms embargo on his country]: I have observed that the lifting of this embargo is being strangely interpreted in India. Actually, India has nothing to fear from this development . . . Pakistan has neither the resources nor the wish to enter into an arms race which reverses its entire economic progress.

*Los Angeles Times, 2-26:(1)5.*

*4*

[On relations with India]: Our quarrel—whether you call it an Indo-Pakistani dispute or a Hindu-Moslem one—is by far the oldest in the world. It goes back for centuries, and was further fanned by 150 years of British imperialism and its policy of divide-and-rule. Ancient feelings don't disappear all at once. But the Simla conference in June, 1972 [at which India and Pakistan agreed to work toward better relations] was a good one. It is pure conjecture [that India might start a war]; but a man of prudence would not rule it out—and you have to be a man of prudence if you are running a country.

*Interview, Larkana, Pakistan/Time, 12-29:26.*

*5*

[On relations with Bangladesh]: If the people of the two countries want good relations, neither India nor any other country can prevent those good relations from taking shape. Bangladesh was once part of Pakistan, so there will be considerable warmth in that relationship; no nation should misunderstand that. However, to what extent the relationship is to develop is really for the people of Bangladesh to determine. It was they who wanted the separation. It is now up to them to tell us how close they want to come to us. We don't want to kill Bangladesh with kindness.

*Interview, Larkana, Pakistan/Time, 12-29:26.*

### Birendra (Bir Bikram Shah Deva)
*King of Nepal*

1

[Calling for a close bond between the monarchy and the people]: Only a dedication of this breadth and magnitude will enhance the dignity and honor of this Himalayan kingdom, enabling us to hold our heads like the towering peak of the Everest itself . . . The throne embodies this country's sovereignty, integrity and national dignity together with our independence.
*At his coronation, Katmandu, Feb. 24/
The New York Times, 2-25:2.*

### Mervyn Brogan
*Lieutenant General and former Chief of the
General Staff, Australian armed forces*

2

[On the current Communist military successes in South Vietnam and U.S. reluctance to send further military aid to the Saigon government]: . . . the situation gives greater scope for subversion in contiguous Southeast Asian countries. In the long run, it could pose a similar threat to Indonesia and ourselves. The domino theory has got to be given a certain amount of credence. If the dominoes don't fall down right before your eyes, a situation can nevertheless arise in which there will be a creeping paralysis throughout the whole area.
*Interview/The New York Times, 4-8:13.*

### Zbigniew Brzezinski
*Director, Research Institute on International
Change, Columbia University*

3

It seems to me that our [U.S.] presence in South Korea is directly related to our relationship with Japan. I think we ought to be cognizant of the fact that if we now, under domestic pressure, were to disengage precipitously from South Korea, that this would have demonstrable effects on Japan. It would be unsettling in the first instance for the Japanese, and in the longer run it would precipitate domestic reactions in Japan and the adoption of foreign policy stances by Japan, particularly in regard to nuclear weapons, which would not be welcome from the standpoint of American-Japanese relationships, nor would they be conducive to greater international stability. Thus I would

argue that the lessons of Vietnam are not applicable to South Korea, that the maintenance of American presence is necessary to the preservation of stability in that part of the world.
*TV-radio interview, Washington/
"Meet the Press,"
National Broadcasting Company, 5-11.*

### Alastair Buchan
*Former director, International
Institute for Strategic Studies, London*

4

I am certain that the triangular U.S.-Soviet-Chinese relationship is the cornerstone of American foreign policy, and clearly that relationship depends on continuation of the Sino-Soviet conflict. On the other hand, it is not in America's interest to see the level of Sino-Soviet tension increase. That would simply intensify the Russians' hidden phobias about China. The result would be bigger Soviet spending on arms and a more suspicious Soviet attitude toward the world in general.
*Interview/U.S. News & World Report, 6-30:62.*

### Robert C. Byrd
*United States Senator, D–West Virginia*

5

The People's Republic of [Communist] China is a highly regimented, controlled, collectivist state—determined to be self-reliant, self-contained and independent of foreign domination, interference and influence. However much one may disagree with a system that takes away personal freedom, such a system is working—or appears to the visitor to be working—in mainland China a quarter of a century after the upheaval of World War II and its aftermath in that vast Asian land. How long it may continue to work—how long the Chinese people may continue to accept the complete control of their lives—remains to be seen.
*Before the Senate, Washington, Sept. 4/
Vital Speeches, 10-1:742.*

### Yeshwantrao B. Chavan
*Foreign Minister of India*

6

[Expressing misgivings about possible resumption of U.S. arms supplies to Pakistan]: I conveyed to him [U.S. Secretary of State

# WHAT THEY SAID IN 1975

*(YESHWANTRAO B. CHAVAN)*

Henry Kissinger] our deep concern about the harmful effects of arms supplies to Pakistan on the peace of this region as well as on Indo-American relations . . . If at all I happen to go to the United States . . . and if by that time a decision is not taken, I will try to strongly express the views of this country and see that some wisdom prevails there . . . [Resumed arms to Pakistan] will not only create new tensions between India and Pakistan but also revive old misgivings about the United States' role in the region.

*Before Parliament, New Delhi, Feb. 18/*
*The New York Times, 2-19:3.*

*1*

[Indian Prime Minister Indira] Gandhi's role in the past four years has become inseparable from the life of the people of India. What happens to her happens to India; what happens to India happens to her. Her person, her thinking, her life have completely become identified with the people.

*At Congress Party rally, Parliament House,*
*New Delhi, June 18/*
*The Dallas Times Herald, 7-19:(A)2.*

**Chiang Kai-shek**
*President of Nationalist China*

*2*

We have reached the starting point of a new era—the beginning of our successful suppression of Chinese Communist wickedness and the establishment of a new China through construction in our bastion of freedom and the enforcement of our strength . . . If we look only at the road beneath our feet, we shall find that it is rough and tortuous; we shall feel as though we may stumble at any time. However, if we take every step with firm stride and look forward, we shall be happy to see that new roads are opening up at every turn and that the sky is bright.

*New Year's message, Taipei, Jan. 1/*
*Los Angeles Times, 1-2:(1)7.*

**Alan Cranston**
*United States Senator, D—California*

*3*

In Korea, as in Vietnam, there is no evidence that the Communist dictatorship of the North

is part of any monolithic world-wide Communist conspiracy, while there is considerable evidence that, as in Vietnam, it is an independent Communist force, more like Yugoslavia than Poland or East Germany.

*The Washington Post, 6-4:(A)7.*

**Richard A. Falk**
*Professor of international law,*
*Princeton University*

*4*

What we are seeing in Asia is a coming to terms with [Communist] China on the part of nations such as the Philippines and Thailand with which we [the U.S.] have long had formal military alliances. We can wring our hands over it and worry about Communist influence. But actually it's a case of others following up the detente we've begun with China by forging their own detentes. And it probably contributes to regional stability in a way our presence in Asia never could.

*Interview/The National Observer, 6-28:15.*

**Hiram L. Fong**
*United States Senator, R—Hawaii*

*5*

One of the most important steps the Congress of the United States could take to help avert the outbreak of war in South Korea would be to provide funds to expedite modernization of Republic of Korea forces. [A sizeable U.S. withdrawal] could well lead North Korea's [President] Kim Il Sung to miscalculate our resolve and our intentions, just as he miscalculated our resolve and our intentions in 1950, after our Secretary of State excluded South Korea from our Pacific defense perimeter. Should South Korea fall under the domination of Communist North Korea, Japan would be in dire jeopardy, for the Korean peninsula is like a pistol aimed at Japan.

*Before the Senate, Washington, June 25/*
*The Washington Post, 6-26:(A)4.*

**Gerald R. Ford**
*President of the United States*

*6*

I believe it's highly desirable under our mutual defense treaty with South Korea to maintain a U.S. military contingent in South Korea.

We have now roughly 38,000 U.S. military personnel in South Korea. I think it's keeping the peace in Korea, and I think it's important for the maintenance of peace in the Korean peninsula that that force stay in South Korea.

*News conference, Washington, June 9/*
*The New York Times, 6-10:20.*

1

[On his just-completed trip to Communist China]: I visited China to build on the dialogue started nearly four years ago. My wide-ranging exchanges with the leaders of the People's Republic of China ... enhanced our understanding of each other's views and policies. There were, as expected, differences of perspective. Our societies, philosophies and varying positions in the world give us differing perceptions of our respective national interests. But we did find common ground. We reaffirmed that we share very important areas of concern and agreement. They say and we say that the countries of Asia should be free to develop in a world where there is mutual respect for the sovereignty and territorial integrity of all states; where people are free from the threat of foreign aggression; where there is non-interference in the internal affairs of others; and where the principles of equality, mutual benefit and coexistence share the development of a peaceful international order. We share opposition to any form of hegemony in Asia or in any other part of the world ... Our relationship is becoming a permanent feature of the international political landscape. It benefits not only our two people but all peoples of the region and the entire world.

*At University of Hawaii, Dec. 7/*
*The New York Times, 12-8:14.*

2

... American strength is basic to any stable balance of power in the Pacific. We must reach beyond our concern for security. But without security, there can be neither peace nor progress. The preservation of the sovereignty and independence of our Asian friends and allies remains a paramount objective of American policy. We recognize that force alone is insufficient to assure security. Popular legitimacy and social justice are vital prerequisites of resistance against subversion and aggression. Nevertheless, we owe it to ourselves, and to those [whose] independence depends upon our continued support, to preserve a flexible and balanced position of strength throughout the Pacific.

*At University of Hawaii, Dec. 7/*
*The New York Times, 12-8:14.*

3

[U.S.] partnership with Japan is a pillar of our strategy. There is no relationship to which I have devoted more attention. Nor is there any greater success story in the history of America's efforts to relate to distant cultures and people. The Japanese-American relationship can be a source of pride to every American and to every Japanese.

*At University of Hawaii, Dec. 7/*
*The New York Times, 12-8:14.*

**Indira Gandhi**
*Prime Minister of India*

4

[On India's good relations with the Soviet Union]: Haven't they stood by us whenever we have needed any help? When we wanted to first industrialize, they were the first people to help us with heavy industry. Whenever there was any war, we have not asked for their military help, but they have stood by us.

*Interview, New Delhi/*
*The New York Times, 2-13:12.*

5

The decision of the United States to resume arming Pakistan shows that the policy-makers of that great country continue to subscribe to the fallacy of equating Pakistan and India. It is a policy which has caused tension in the subcontinent. The United States decision amounts to reopening of the old wounds and it hinders the process of healing and normalization ... It is totally specious to argue that arms should be supplied to Pakistan because we in India are developing a self-sufficient defense industry. It is even more dishonest to argue that our nuclear research poses a danger to Pakistan.

*Before upper house of Parliament, New Delhi,*
*Feb. 26/The New York Times, 2-27:2.*

# WHAT THEY SAID IN 1975

*(INDIRA GANDHI)*

*1*

[On the declaration of a state of emergency in her country]: The President has proclaimed an emergency. This is nothing to panic about. I am sure you are all conscious of the deep and widespread conspiracy which has been brewing ever since I began introducing certain progressive measure[s] of benefit to the common man and woman of India in the name of democracy ... All manner of false allegations have been hurled at me. The Indian people have known me since my childhood. All my life has been in the service of our people. This is not a personal matter. It is not important whether I remain Prime Minister or not. However, the institution of the Prime Minister is important, and the potential attempt to denigrate it is not in the interest of democracy or of the nation. We have watched these developments with utmost patience for long. Now we learn of new programs challenging law and order throughout the country with a view to disrupt normal functioning. How can any government worth the name stand by and allow the country's stability to be imperiled? The actions of a few are endangering the rights of the vast majority. Any situation which weakens the capacity of the national government to act decisively inside the country is bound to encourage dangers from outside. It is our paramount duty to safeguard unity and stability. The nation's integrity demands firm action.

*Broadcast address, New Delhi, June 26/*
*The New York Times, 6-27:12.*

*2*

[On when civil liberties will be restored in her country]: It is very difficult to give a date. Naturally, this is not a permanent situation. There are many different types of people involved. There are the recognized political parties. There were certain groups with whom they had combined, which said they were not political, which didn't believe in democracy, never said they believed in democracy. This was the major danger. If those who genuinely believe in democracy are willing to observe the rules of democracy, then this whole process could be expedited. As you know, although we have censorship of the press and some people are under detention, the whole opposition is not under detention. In fact, most of them are out. Most of those who are in prison are not political people. Some of them are what you call bad elements, which the police have on their list, and others are of these parties which we have banned; and, as I said, the parties banned are not political parties but are those which had plans for violence and had committed violence in the past ... I am deeply committed to democracy, not merely because it is a good idea, but because, for a country of India's vast size and great diversity, I think democracy—that is, the people's participation—is the only way to make it function ... A Prime Minister's primary duty is really to keep the country's unity and integrity. If you lose that, then how do you keep democracy or anything else?

*American TV-radio interview, New Delhi/*
*"Meet the Press,"*
*National Broadcasting Company, 8-24.*

## Andrei A. Grechko
*Minister of Defense of the Soviet Union*

*3*

While building up its military potential in Europe, imperialism at the same time seeks to avoid easing tensions in Southeast Asia, the Middle East and the Eastern Mediterranean. Imperialists allot a special place in their plans to establishing a united anti-Soviet front with the participation of [Communist] China. In this they find understanding on the part of the Peking leadership that has openly embarked on the path of struggle against the Soviet Union and against the world socialist system.

*May 29/Los Angeles Times, 5-30:(1)24.*

## Hirohito
*Emperor of Japan*

*4*

Needless to say, Japan is not free from the effects of world-wide trends and events. But I hope Japan will continue to keep the good parts of our ancient traditions and help to build the basis of a lasting peace throughout the world in cooperation with other countries. The world is changing, but I hope Japan will be a peaceful country at home, endeavoring to build good international relationships and developing into a country worthy of respect around the world.

*Interview, Tokyo/Time, 10-6:42.*

### Kim Dong Jo
*Foreign Minister of South Korea*

1

[Addressing UN delegates on tunnels allegedly constructed by North Korea in the demilitarized zone to facilitate invasion of his country]: I wish to take this opportunity to extend an invitation to all of you gathered here to visit my country and see these tunnels for yourselves. You would then be in a position to judge whether they have been built for any purpose other than military—to facilitate a southward invasion. These tunnels provide the most compelling recent evidence of North Korean intentions. They are the latest—but not, I fear, the last—in an infamous record of deliberate armistice violations by the North . . .

*At United Nations, New York, Oct. 21/*
*Los Angeles Times, 10-22:(1)34.*

### Kim Il Sung
*President of North Korea*

2

In an endeavor to save themselves from crisis, U.S. imperialism and South Korea's ruling clique are intensifying their Fascist repression of the South Korean people and further stepping up their preparation of war against the northern half of the republic. However, history is not moving as the imperalists and their lackeys expect, but advancing steadily as the people, makers of history, wish and act. If the South Korean rulers continue to suppress at the point of the bayonet the people's discontent and wrath that is underlying South Korean society, it will result in a greater revolutionary explosion. If revolution takes place in South Korea, we, as one and the same nation, will not just look at it with folded arms but will strongly support the South Korean people. If the enemy ignites war recklessly, we shall resolutely answer it with war and completely destroy the aggressors. In this war,

we will only lose the Military Demarcation Line and will gain the country's reunification.

*Peking, April 18/The New York Times, 5-31:7.*

3

. . . the reunification of our divided homeland is our supreme national task and, at present, it is the highest goal our people must attain. Three decades have gone since our country was liberated from Japanese imperialist colonial rule. But it still remains divided into North and South. The territorial division and national partition caused by the U.S. imperialist occupation of South Korea has brought tremendous national calamities and sufferings to the Korean people and laid a serious obstacle to the coordinated development of our people. In the first days of the country's division by foreign forces, our Party and the government of the republic advanced the most reasonable policy of national reunification and have since made untiring efforts to put it into effect. The basic policy consistently followed by our Party in the struggle to reunify the country is to reunify the country independently on democratic principles and by peaceful means.

*Interview, Algiers, Algeria, May 29/*
*The Washington Post, 9-7:(A)32.*

4

The U.S. imperialists and their lackeys are raising a hue and cry over the "threat of southward invasion" [by North Korea], though they know full well that we have no intention to "invade the South" . . . Revolution is not exported. This is the principle of us revolutionaries. It is the South Korean people themselves who launch revolution in South Korea; we cannot do it for them.

*Interview, Nouakchott, North Korea, May 31/*
*The New York Times, 8-1:5.*

### Kim Jong Pil
*Premier of South Korea*

5

[Criticizing "irresponsible" demands for the restoration of democracy in his country]: It is to be worried that some quarters among our people, failing to properly recognize reality, are

*(KIM JONG PIL)*

staging open attempts to create social confusion and divide national opinions by engaging in impatient, irresponsible and academic controversies. The government would try to persuade them to understand, but it cannot and would not indefinitely let go things that will shatter the country's stability. The government cannot but take a serious view of the possibility that the so-called demands for the restoration of democracy could lead to what [North Korean President] Kim Il Sung desires to see.

*At ceremony opening government offices for new year, Seoul, Jan. 4/ San Francisco Examiner & Chronicle, 1-5:(A)14.*

## Kim Young Sam
*Leader, New Democratic Party of South Korea*     *1*

There are many Koreans who are now doubting [as a result of the Communist takeover in South Vietnam] whether the United States would help us; but the situation here is quite different. Even in just geographical terms, Korea's location puts it in a direct relationship to the interests of [Communist] China, the Soviet Union, Japan and the United States . . . I think [the U.S.] Congress can make that distinction [from Vietnam].

*Interview, Seoul/ Los Angeles Times, 5-9:(1)19.*

## Henry A. Kissinger
*Secretary of State of the United States*   *2*

[On the resumption of U.S. arms supplies to Pakistan]: To maintain an embargo against a friendly country with which we have an allied relationship, while its neighbor [India] was producing and acquiring nearly a billion dollars worth of arms a year, was morally, politically and symbolically improper.

*News conference, Feb. 25/ The New York Times, 2-27:2.*

*3*

Asia's share of the world's population and resources is immense. In the last two decades, the Asian-Pacific economy has experienced more rapid growth than any other region. It is here that the United States has its largest and fastest-growing overseas commerce. We have as vital an interest in access to Asia's raw materials as Asia has to our markets and technology. The ties between Asia and America have a deeper philosophical and human dimension. The influence of America and the West stimulated the transformation of much of Asia during the past 100 years. From the days of the New England transcendentalists to the modern period, Asian culture and ideas have significantly touched American intellectual life, thereby reflecting the universality of human aspirations. The role of Asia, then, is potentially decisive for the solution of the contemporary agenda of peace and progress and the quality of life. This is why, in spite of recent events, the United States will not turn away from Asia, or focus our attention on Europe to the detriment of Asia.

*Before Japan Society, New York, June 18/ The New York Times, 6-19:8.*

*4*

We are not opposed to North Korea as such. What we don't want to do is have bilateral talks with North Korea to the exclusion of South Korea. We don't want to have South Korea maneuvered into the position of an international pariah while we settle the future of North Korea in negotiations with other countries. We would be prepared to participate in any negotiations or in any conference whose composition was reasonably balanced that included South Korea. Similarly, if the Soviet Union or the People's Republic [of Communist China] were prepared to recognize South Korea, we would be prepared to recognize North Korea.

*Interview, Washington/Time, 10-27:37.*

## Lee Kuan Yew
*Prime Minister of Singapore*     *5*

An era has come to an end. America was the dominant power in Southeast Asia for 30 years since the end of World War II. Once America acknowledged that she could no longer intervene in Southeast Asia, it is fair to assume that the contest for influence over the peoples in the region will be mainly between the People's Republic of [Communist] China and the Soviet Union, both of whom openly avow their duty to help Communists everywhere and to promote revolution. The fate of Southeast Asian countries is to be caught in a competitive clash between these two. China has the advantage of historic associations with the region. Memories of past tributes paid and an awareness of geographical proximity make all in Southeast Asia anxious not to take sides with the Soviet Union against the Chinese, even though the Soviet Union is ahead on military technology. Most hope to maintain equal relations with both China and the Soviet Union. But this may not be possible unless these two Communist centers cease to compete for ideological and nationalist supremacy—a prospect which appears remote. Meanwhile, a continuing American naval presence and increased economic relations will help the rest of Southeast Asia to adjust less abruptly and to make the task of learning to live with a Communist Indochina less painful.

*Before New Zealand National Press Club, April 7/ The Washington Post, 4-13:(C)6.*

**Etienne M. Manac'h**
*Former French Ambassador to the People's Republic of (Communist) China*

*1*

China expects to play a major role by the end of the century that will accord with their strategic position, their massive population and their wealth of natural resources. China is like the U.S.—an immense geographical area with a relatively homogeneous people and possessing almost everything it needs for economic development. China will doubtlessly find short cuts leading to rapid economic development, and its military strength will run parallel with economic progress. Moreover, China has some atomic arms. But the Chinese won't imitate Russia and the U.S. and engage in an absurd nuclear-arms race at the sacrifice of a healthy economy.

*Interview, Pont-Aven, France/ U.S. News & World Report, 7-7:64.*

**Mike Mansfield**
*United States Senator, D–Montana*

*2*

What we are witnessing, in my opinion, is the beginning of an end of an era, which will make a [U.S.] shift away from the Asian mainland and a concentration of sorts in islands of the Pacific. The shift will reflect what I believe is a geopolitical truism, namely, that the United States is not an Asian power but a Pacific power.

*Interview, Washington, March 14/ The New York Times, 3-17:3.*

**Ferdinand E. Marcos**
*President of the Philippines*

*3*

There is no certainty that in case of external aggression the United States would come to the rescue of the Philippines. Commitments of American Presidents [now that the U.S. has backed away from Indochina, leaving Cambodia and most of South Vietnam in Communist hands] would appear to have little value except as forms of psychological reassurance, since it is clear that they cannot, by Presidential fiat, diminish or expand the contents of the [mutual defense] treaty without Congressional consent . . . The United States is in the midst of a profound reassessment of its foreign policies and their priorities in the light of its national objectives. The refusal of the United States Congress to extend further assistance to Indochina suggests strongly that in its new assessment Indochina, and by extension Southeast Asia, is no longer an area of vital concern to the United States . . . It would seem that some American leaders feel that the broad and complex problem of security in Asia—which includes economic development—may be better left in the hands of a surrogate power, which in the present case is Japan. This gives us food for serious thought.

*Policy address, Manila, April 16/ The Washington Post, 4-17:(A)16.*

*4*

[On the Communist take-over in South Vietnam]: It is not my intention to wave a placard saying Americans go home. Our people are far

# WHAT THEY SAID IN 1975

(FERDINAND E. MARCOS)

too deeply attached to reach this point of bitterness . . . [But] the U.S., we hope, will understand, must understand, that we in the Philippines face something of greater magnitude than indignity or shock [over the Vietnam situation], and this is sheer physical survival. The U.S. must understand that we cannot wait until events overtake us and our country. We reserve the right to make our own accommodation with the new realities of Asia . . . I do ask, with all the sincerity of trusted friends, whether the [U.S. bases in the Philippines] have not outlived their usefulness, whether they have not lived beyond their appointed task. I do ask whether our mutual defense treaty in the light of Indochina has not become a dead letter.

*Address to the nation, Manila, May 23/*
*Los Angeles Times, 5-24:(1)10.*

1

The old modes of thought can no longer sustain us or any other nation in Asia. We must review our alliances, reappraise our destiny, and, in a word, go out into the world . . . It may be pointed out that as a people we are good and dependable friends and fearlessly loyal allies. [But] when our friendship is repeatedly depreciated or taken for granted [we must act in our national interests]. I believe a new age dawns upon Asia and the whole world. It is an age where the most subtle forms of foreign domination or intervention must disappear. We are Asians. We live in Asia. Our future is in Asia. And we should remodel our thoughts and our policies in accordance with that . . . fact.

*At banquet, Peking, June 7/*
*San Francisco Examiner & Chronicle,*
*6-8:(A)1,27.*

2

I would like to see if we can conduct some form of elections without the evils of the elections conducted under the old society—the corruption, the coercion, the cheating, the use of government funds, and the hoopla and everything else. It is my feeling that where there is any lack of consensus or there is controversy as

to who should be the leader in any locality, we should throw this to the people and experiment as to whether we now have the capability to conduct a good, clean election, at least locally.

*Interview, Manila/*
*The Christian Science Monitor, 10-24:6.*

3

If by virtue of any arrangements or treaties there should be deliveries to our country of foreign equipment and technology, we seek arrangements and understandings wherein we shall also build our capability so that in the future this will render obsolete and unnecessary further and future deliveries of military aid to our people. It is our dream to establish a country that is self-reliant . . . so we can with this same self-reliance say that our strongest and most dependable ally is still the United States.

*Welcoming U.S. President Gerald Ford, Manila,*
*Dec. 6/The Dallas Times Herald, 12-7:(A)29.*

## Takeo Miki
### Prime Minister of Japan

4

Japan is a major economic power in terms of GNP, but Japan has no intention of becoming a great power in military terms. Japan has no intention of developing nuclear weapons. We will [continue to] have a relatively light defense capability.

*Interview, Tokyo, July 23/*
*The Washington Post, 7-24:(A)34.*

5

[Saying his handling of Japan's affairs has been inadequate]: I was very much impressed with the serious attitude those leaders [at the recent summit conference in Rambouillet, France] showed. I learned that the European politicians were dealing with the issues of politics, diplomacy, economics and military seriously, as though those were matters of life and death of a nation or a culture. Till then, I had been thinking that I had been doing my best ever since the beginning of the Miki Administration. But compared with the difficulties those European politicians have, I felt strongly that my efforts have been far from adequate.

*News conference, Tokyo, Nov. 19/*
*Los Angeles Herald-Examiner, 11-20:(A)19.*

1

Japan cannot survive without international cooperation. To Japan, isolation is the way to ruin. I would like the Japanese people really to understand the position of . . . Japan in the world. Japan's politics should not look inward too much. Though domestic issues are important, we are in an era now where foreign and domestic issues are inseparable. So Japanese politics should look more outward.

*News conference, Tokyo, Nov. 19/*
*The New York Times, 11-20:9.*

**Park Chung Hee**
*President of South Korea*

2

[On criticism of repression of dissent in his country]: Illegal acts that foment social disorder and confusion in the face of threats of aggression from the North must be controlled to safeguard the basic rights of the majority. People [who] criticize what we do in [South] Korea measure the situation with the same yardstick that they use in the U.S. Here the situation is much more desperate. Only 25 miles from Seoul, an enemy is bent on destroying us. We cannot allow disorder. If we liberalize internally, if we let the students riot and the workers go on strike, the resulting confusion will be utilized by the North. [The late French President Charles] de Gaulle wielded extraordinary power when he took over at the time of Algeria, but there was no criticism . . . I am at a loss to understand criticism of us when we are faced with questions of survival.

*Interview, Seoul/Time, 6-30:39.*

3

As the North Koreans have not renounced their scheme to communize the South by force, I see slim prospects for unification in the near future. When a foundation of peace has been secured by accelerating dialogue and cooperation between the South and North, we can proceed to unification through free elections conducted in proportion to the population. But judging from their actions, the North Koreans are not interested in dialogue. [North Korean President] Kim Il Sung has publicly asserted that he will not continue the dialogue unless

the present government [in the South] resigns and the U.S. withdraws its forces. They are employing the same tactics that the Viet Cong used in Vietnam when they said they would negotiate only if [then-South Vietnamese President Nguyen Van] Thieu stepped down. When Thieu stepped down, they said [Tran Van] Huong was not eligible; and then when [Duong Van] "Big" Minh came, there was nothing left to negotiate.

*Interview, Seoul/Time, 6-30:39.*

4

The leaders of Japan state often that the peace and security of Korea—these days they say the Korean Peninsula—are very important and essential to their own security and stability. If this is the true intent of the people of Japan, if they truly wish for the stability of Korea, if they truly wish for the prevention of war on this peninsula and if they truly wish for the prevention of the communization of this country [South Korea], then they must try to find out what they should do to contribute to the realization of such wishes. I firmly believe that the Japanese at least should not do things that are harmful to this republic and that are helpful to the North Koreans [such as trade with North Korea]. But unfortunately the truth is that, whether intentionally or not, the Japanese at some times have done things which were detrimental to the security of this republic.

*Interview/The New York Times, 9-16:9.*

**Andrew Peacock**
*Foreign Minister of Australia*

5

We make no apologies for regarding the ANZUS pact—the central plank of the American alliance—as of the greatest importance to Australia. Despite its recent setbacks, the United States is still the most powerful democracy in the world and still by far the greatest economic force. Its presence in the Asian and Pacific areas is essential.

*The New York Times, 12-21:(4)5.*

**Charles H. Percy**
*United States Senator, R—Illinois*

6

[On his recent trip to Communist China]: Mao [Tse-tung] is the George Washington of his

# WHAT THEY SAID IN 1975

*(CHARLES H. PERCY)*

country. It's incredible—the signs and sayings of Mao are everywhere. Example: "We shall harness the Yellow River"—that's all he says and suddenly millions of people are volunteering to work on it. That's how they've eliminated corruption and dope. It's a Mao philosophy and principle, carried out through peer-group pressure. If somebody steals a bicycle, 100 people in the streets chase down the thief. In Chicago, most of them would turn their backs. I told one man that I'd heard dope pushers were taken into the streets and shot. "No," he told me, "we reason with them." I didn't ask what he meant by "reason."

*Interview, Laguna Beach, Calif./*
*"W": a Fairchild publication, 9-5:13.*

## Mujibur Rahman
*Prime Minister of Bangladesh*                     1

All the Western press does is to criticize my Administration and give me sermons [such as on his country's current food-supply problem]. They did that in 1971; they are doing it today. They have their motives for doing so—you know and I know it. You can hear all that kind of rubbish in the Hotel Intercontinental [in Dacca]. You can take it from me there will be no famine because I have started doing something about it now. For the first time I have launched on a compulsory procurement; I am buying food wherever I can. We shall organize distribution through fair-price shops . . . Ask them [Western observers] to go to hell! You will see that it is not my Administration that will collapse but their mental faculties which will collapse. They have ulterior motives. They failed in the past; they will fail now. Wait and see!

*Interview/*
*The New York Times Magazine, 1-26:9.*

## Donald L. Ranard
*Former Director, Office of Korean Affairs,*
*Department of State of the United States*     2

I am in essential agreement with the [U.S.] Administration as concerns the security of [South] Korea, and as concerns the importance

of the American commitment to that country. Where I differ, and have differed throughout my four-year tour as country director for Korea, is in our government's reaction to human-rights issues abroad and their role in foreign policy. Respect for human rights was incorporated in all of the documents and laws which framed our government and which eventually made our country the leader of what we once were prone to call the free world. I find it unbecoming to our heritage and to our role in world affairs that the United States should be tongue-tied in expressing its revulsion and disdain for the violations of basic human rights that are taking place currently in [South] Korea . . . If there is one lesson we should have learned from Korea, it is that its people will not endure forever a government which denies them a right to participate. Unless the present course of events is arrested or reversed, there will be trouble in Korea. And, should that occur, how much better for the United States that our role has been honorable and consistent with our ideals. Our conduct to date on human-rights issues has not been so.

*Before House Subcommittee on International*
*Organizations, Washington/*
*The Christian Science Monitor, 7-21:31.*

## William B. Saxbe
*United States Ambassador to India*               3

We've learned in the last 27 years that India is not close to us [the U.S.], and perhaps it never can be. The most that can develop is grudging respect, which these days would be a major accomplishment . . . I don't see improving relations between our two governments as my basic role. I'm here to represent the government of the United States. I believe in our culture and policies, and if the Indians find them acceptable, that's fine. But I'm still here, whether they accept them or not.

*Interview, New Delhi, March 18/*
*The Washington Post, 3-19:(A)1.*

## James R. Schlesinger
*Secretary of Defense of the United States*       4

South Korea guards the approaches to Japan. It lies in a confluence of four great powers—the U.S., the U.S.S.R., [Communist] China and Japan. Also, it represents a historic involvement and commitment by the United States. Any sudden weakening of that commitment—particularly after Vietnam—would be of such major significance that it could unravel the situation in Asia and possibly elsewhere.

*Interview, Washington/*
*U.S. News & World Report, 5-26:25.*

**Tan Sri Ghazali Shafie**
*Minister of Home Affairs of Malaysia*
*1*

The theoretical validity of the domino theory itself is highly suspect. The nations of Eastern Europe went Communist, but Finland to this day has not, nor have the other Western European states contiguous to them. Each of the Southeast Asian countries is a unique entity with its own history, culture, values and institutions that respond differently to challenges, however similar, that they face. To postulate that Malaysia will succumb to Communism simply because Vietnam became Communist is to ignore the vast differences between the Vietnamese and Malaysian circumstances . . . The threat to security for most Southeast Asian nations now comes from anti-national subversion. But the efficacy of subversion is minimal if a state pursues just and enlightened policies that bring, and are seen to bring, tangible benefits to its people. Whether or not a country goes Communist depends on the success of the internal and external policies of that country itself. The fall of the American military dominoes [in Indochina] need not presage the fall of political dominos.

*Los Angeles Times, 5-15:(1)6.*

**Joseph J. Sisco**
*Under Secretary of State*
*of the United States*
*2*

[Saying the U.S. arms embargo to Pakistan will be lifted soon]: We have felt a rather anomalous situation has existed in the area where one side [India] has been getting arms from the Soviets and has its own production capacity, whereas the other side, an ally I might add, with whom we have a formal relationship, has been denied this insofar as the United States is concerned.

*TV-radio interview, Washington/*
*"Meet the Press,"*
*National Broadcasting Company, 2-23.*

**Richard L. Walker**
*Director, Institute of International Studies,*
*University of South Carolina*
*3*

Before the United States expands contacts with the People's Republic of [Communist] China further, it is important that we let Peking know that we will insist on mutuality. We will not accept a neo-imperialist imposition of others' standards on us. In imperial times, those who came to the court of Peking as petitioners and supinely accepted the dictates of the Chinese emperor were treated with contempt. Those who insisted on some reciprocity eventually won respect.

*At Sino-U.S. relations forum sponsored by*
*Institute of Chinese Culture, New York/*
*The Wall Street Journal, 10-24:14.*

## INDOCHINA

**Leonid I. Brezhnev**
*General Secretary, Communist Party*
*of the Soviet Union* 1

The lessons of the epic of Vietnam attest to the all-conquering force of Marxist-Leninist ideas ... The epic of Vietnam furnishes live evidence of the effectiveness of the actions of solidarity of the fraternal socialist states. In this sense, it serves as important and impressive proof that in the present-day world an end can be put to the imperialist policy of aggression and arbitrariness.

*Moscow, Oct. 28/*
*Los Angeles Times, 10-29:(1)4.*

**Dale Bumpers**
*United States Senator, D–Arkansas* 2

[Saying the U.S. should not continue aid to Cambodia]: One, obviously Cambodia I don't think by anybody's definition has any strategic value to the United States. Two, they are very helpless and unfortunate victims of the Vietnam war. They just happen to be unfortunate in having borders that join South Vietnam. They never should have been a part of the war, and I think we are to blame for them being ... It isn't a democracy, and the government of [President] Lon Nol was not duly elected by the people, so we are not really trying to save a duly elected government. Finally, of course, the question comes, do the people of Cambodia really want us to sustain the Lon Nol government? The answer is obviously no, because less than 30 per cent of the males eligible for military service are serving in the Cambodian army. So for those reasons, completely aside from the moralistic reasons which I think are compelling, I think we ought to discontinue our aid to Cambodia.

*TV-radio interview, Washington/*
*"Meet the Press,"*
*National Broadcasting Company, 3-16.*

**Bob Carr**
*United States Representative, D–Michigan* 3

[Arguing against further U.S. military aid to Indochina]: With the signing of the Paris peace accords two years ago, the American people were led to believe U.S. involvement in Indochina had finally come to an end. If the Democratic members of this Congress are to live up to that agreement, they should go on record and demonstrate to the American people that the shaping of U.S. foreign policy does not belong solely to President Ford and [Secretary of State] Henry Kissinger. The bloodbath has been going on for years with the help of American money, and I think it's time we said, "Enough."

*Washington, March 12/*
*Los Angeles Times, 3-13:(1)22.*

**Chatichai Choonhavan**
*Foreign Minister of Thailand* 4

[On whether the U.S. has a moral obligation to defend Thailand]: Moral? The United States does not have any morals at this point. They have already pulled out from Cambodia and South Vietnam. So we are going to have to depend on ourselves.

*News conference, May 2/*
*The Washington Post, 5-3:(A)1.*

**Yeshwantrao B. Chavan**
*Foreign Minister of India* 5

[On the current Communist military successes in Cambodia and South Vietnam]: These developments in Indochina are the culmination of a heroic struggle waged by the people of Indochina to assert their independence and sovereignty and their determination to shape their destiny without external interference. They represent the inevitable victory of forces of nationalism over attempts to undermine such forces through outside intervention, and constitute a gratifying vindication of the consistent policy maintained by us on this question over the years.

*At seminar, New Delhi, April 23/*
*Los Angeles Times, 4-24:(1)15.*

**Frank Church**
*United States Senator, D—Idaho*
1

For more than 20 years, a succession of American Presidents has committed this country to an impossible dream in Indochina: the maintenance of our chosen house-of-cards governments against an indigenous hurricane. These Presidents, including Mr. Ford, have been the prisoners of delusion, beguiled by the belief that they could impose governments of their choice upon the people of Indochina . . . The Presidents' advisers have been wrong at every turn. They mistook [the late North Vietnamese President] Ho Chi Minh's war for independence as a mask for Russian or Chinese aggression; they acted on the famous assumption that, while French intervention had proved intolerable, American intervention would be welcome . . . The incompetence of the State Department has been exceeded only by its intransigence. As reversals swelled from a trickle to a tide, each President was fastened to the weightstone of the same failing policy . . . A strong President would admit the failure and move at once to replace our mistaken policy with a new and different one. It is in Southeast Asia that the reappraisal of American foreign policy should begin.

*Interview/The National Observer, 4-12:14.*

**Clark M. Clifford**
*Former Secretary of Defense of the*
*United States*
2

[On the current Communist military successes in South Vietnam and Cambodia]: . . . not one more cent should be used to send additional military supplies either to Vietnam or Cambodia. The die has already been cast. The basic difficulty with the South Vietnamese forces is that they had everything with which to fight but really nothing to fight for. The Thieu

government has been a dictatorial and repressive government. It is clear that the North Vietnamese have violated the peace accord of 1973, but the South Vietnamese government has also violated it. [South Vietnamese President Nguyen Van] Thieu has refused to go through with the negotiations provided for, so there really has been no alternative but continued war. Today the United States should inform the parties that it will send no more materials of war to Vietnam or Cambodia, because to do so merely means that Vietnamese and Cambodian people will go on dying.

*Interview, Washington/*
*Los Angeles Times, 4-9:(2)5.*

**Alan Cranston**
*United States Senator, D—California*
3

[Opposing further U.S. military aid for South Vietnam]: Probably no amount that we gave would change the situation there [the increasing North Vietnamese military victories]. Plainly, we have done enough. Congress, I think, will see that we do not keep this going everlastingly, because all we are doing now is paying for a war that will go on as long as we are willing to pay for it with American taxpayer dollars. I think we went wrong by intervening in the civil war in the first place and by involving ourselves so deeply on behalf not of a democracy but on behalf of a corrupt dictatorship that could not win the allegiance of its own people, which is a basic reason for their failure. [Had the U.S. not intervened], the situation might have had the same general outcome, but hundreds of thousands, if not millions of people who have died, been wounded or uprooted from destroyed homes and villages, would not have suffered that fate. I think we have greatly heightened the misery and prolonged the agony by our intervention . . . On the bloodbath matter, I want to make it plain that there's now a bloodbath, we are helping to pay for that bloodbath, and it's speculation about whether there will be a bloodbath after the fighting is over. Right now we know there's one and we know that we're prolonging it by our prolonged involvement.

*News conference, Los Angeles, March 31/*
*Los Angeles Times, 4-1:(1)5.*

# WHAT THEY SAID IN 1975

**Walter Cronkite**
*News commentator,*
*Columbia Broadcasting System*
1

Our [the U.S.'] troubles at home and overseas really began with Vietnam, a matter in which we became embroiled out of pure if misguided motives. And we went astray. The world saw us, I'm afraid, as simultaneously arrogant in making it our war, and then weak and vascillating when quick victory did not ensue. The opposite is nearer the truth. Our leaders did not share with the American people the decision to get into Vietnam, nor at any time did they level with the people on the depth of the commitment. And it was this that brought them down. The popular reaction showed not weakness but the strength of our democratic system. And we are now even stronger—because it is unlikely that any Administration in the foreseeable future will try to commit the nation to overt adventures without popular support . . . without the united support that will assure that we are prepared to carry out our commitments.

*At student convocation, Charlotte, N.C./*
*The Dallas Times Herald, 12-28:(B)3.*

**John Gunther Dean**
*United States Ambassador to Cambodia*
2

[Calling for additional U.S. military aid for Cambodia]: Let there be no doubt in anybody's mind that if these funds are not forthcoming, the Cambodians here would not be able to continue their struggle [against Communist insurgents]. Not because they despair, not because they lack the will—because we Americans will deprive them of the means to continue.

*Before foreign press corps, Phnom Penh,*
*Feb. 26/The New York Times, 2-27:3.*

**Pham Van Dong**
*Premier of North Vietnam*
3

The support and precious assistance of the Soviet Union, the other socialist countries and the world people in general have played an important part in our winning repeated successes and in our scoring the great victory recently [the take-over of South Vietnam] . I wish the Soviet people many more and yet greater successes in building the technical and material foundation of Communism.

*May 9/The Washington Post, 5-10:(A)10.*

4

[In the aftermath of the recent Communist take-over of South Vietnam] : We demand that the U.S. government strictly observe the spirit of Article 21 [of the 1973 Paris peace agreement] concerning the U.S. obligation to contribute to healing the wounds of the criminal war of aggression the U.S. has waged against North and South Vietnam. On this basis and on the principle of equality and mutual benefit, the Democratic Republic of [North] Vietnam government will normalize its relations with the United States in the spirit . . . of the Paris agreement of Vietnam and will settle the remaining problems with the United States.

*Before National Assembly, Hanoi, June 3/*
*Los Angeles Times, 6-4:(1)9.*

5

In the new situation [the Communist take-over of South Vietnam] , everyone has longed for the reunification of the country [North and South] . In reality, the country has already been reunited because all problems have been settled in the name of a single country, a single people and a single economy. The fact that there still exist two countries, and that both countries have applied for membership in the United Nations, is a natural process, as South Vietnam has been recognized by most nations in the world. However, reunification has progressed favorably and it can be achieved quickly. We must carry it out quickly, but logically.

*October/The New York Times, 11-9:(1)23.*

**Hedley Donovan**
*Editor-in-chief, Time, Inc.*
6

The fall of Southeast Asia [to Communism] is unquestionably a defeat for the U.S.—not so much because of its intrinsic importance as because of the importance we insisted on giving it, and not because it creates doubt so much about our faithfulness as about our judgment and our competence. In this sense, there really is such a thing as world-wide "credibility," not to be exaggerated, not to be dismissed. The leading exaggerators, shockingly enough, were the President of the U.S. [Ford] and the Secretary of State [Kissinger]. For a fortnight or more, they kept applying to the events in Cambodia and Vietnam a kind of twilight-of-civilization rhetoric and even urged the world to believe that if these regimes fell it would be because the U.S. had betrayed them. They have since toned down that line of talk, and doubtless we shall recover from those self-inflicted wounds. But Vietnam will haunt us for a long time to come.

*At Deere & Co., Moline, Ill./Time, 5-19:20.*

### Daniel Ellsberg
*Former U.S. government consultant,*
*Rand Corporation*

1

[On the Communist take-over in South Vietnam]: This is a success for the American people who Constitutionally forced an end to the war on an unwilling [Ford] Administration. It's a success of democratic process against the policies of six successive Administrations. The American Administration has been defeated. When people say Congress and the public defeated it, it's true. And that's the success . . . It took the American public to get Congress to use the blunt instrument of cutting of funds. That was the only way to deflect the policy. If it had been left to the Administration, the war would still be going on. It would be incomparably worse.

*Interview/*
*San Francisco Examiner & Chronicle,*
*5-4:(A)28.*

### Gerald R. Ford
*President of the United States*

2

We cannot turn our backs on these embittered countries [Cambodia and South Vietnam]. U.S. unwillingness to provide adequate assistance to allies fighting for their lives would seriously affect our credibility throughout the world as an ally. Last year, some believed that cutting back our military assistance to the South Vietnamese government would induce negotiations for a political settlement. Instead, the opposite has happened. North Vietnam is refusing negotiations and is increasing its military pressure. I am gravely concerned about this situation . . . [The U.S. cannot] look the other way when agreements that have been painstakingly negotiated are contemptuously violated.

*Message to Congress, Jan. 28\*/*
*The Washington Post, 1-29:(A)12.*

3

We seek to stop the bloodshed and end the horror and the tragedy that we see on television as [Communist rebel] rockets are fired wantonly into Phnom Penh [Cambodia]. I would like to be able to say that the killing would cease if we [the U.S.] were to stop our aid [to the Cambodian government], but that is not the case. The record shows, in both Vietnam and Cambodia, that Communist take-over of an area does not bring an end to violence, but on the contrary subjects the innocents to new horrors. We cannot meet humanitarian needs unless we provide some military assistance. Only through a combination of humanitarian endeavors and military aid do we have a chance to stop the fighting in that country in such a way as to end the bloodshed.

*News conference, Washington, March 6/*
*The New York Times, 3-7:16.*

4

Peace in Cambodia has not been prevented by our failure to offer reasonable solutions. The aggressor believes that it can win its objectives on the battlefield. This belief will be encouraged if we cut off assistance to our friends. We want an end to the killing and a negotiated settlement. But there is no hope of success unless the [U.S.] Congress act[s] quickly to provide the necessary means for Cambodia to survive. If we abandon our allies, we will be saying to all the world that war pays. Aggression will not stop; rather, it will increase. In Cambodia the aggressors will have shown that if negotiations are resisted, the United States will weary, abandon its friends and force will prevail . . . If we cease to help our friends in Indochina, we will have violated their trust that we would help them with arms, with food and with

*(GERALD R. FORD)*

supplies so long as they remain determined to fight for their own freedom. We will have been false to ourselves, to our word and to our friends. No one should think for a moment that we can walk away from that without a deep sense of shame. This is not a question of involvement or re-involvement in Indochina; we have ended our involvement. All American forces have come home. They will not go back. Time is short. There are two things the United States can do to affect the outcome. For my part, I will continue to seek a negotiated settlement. I ask that Congress do its part by providing the assistance required to make such a settlement possible. Time is running out.

*News conference, Washington, March 6/*
*The New York Times, 3-7:16.*

*1*

...I cannot help but notice that since the military situation in Cambodia has become very serious, and since the North Vietnamese have launched a very substantial additional military effort against South Vietnam, against the Paris peace accords, there has been, as I understand it ... a potential request from Thailand that we withdraw our forces from that country. And I noticed ... that the President of the Philippines, Mr. [Ferdinand] Marcos, is reviewing the Philippine relationship with the United States. I think these potential developments to some extent tend to validate the so-called domino theory, and if we have one country after another—allies of the United States—losing faith in our word, losing faith in our agreements with them, yes, I think the first one to go could vitally affect the national security of the United States.

*At University of Notre Dame, March 17/*
*U.S. News & World Report, 3-31:12.*

*2*

I must say that I am frustrated by the action of the Congress in not responding to some of the requests both for economic and humanitarian and military assistance in South Vietnam [during the current Communist offensive], and I'm frustrated by the limitations that were placed on the Chief Executive over the last two years. But, let me add very strongly, I am convinced that this country is going to continue its leadership. We will stand by our allies, and I specifically warn any adversary they should not under any circumstances feel that the tragedy of Vietnam is an indication that the American people have lost their will or their desire to stand up for freedom any place in the world . . . I believe that there is a great deal of credibility to the domino theory. I hope it doesn't happen. I hope that other countries in Southeast Asia— Thailand, the Philippines—don't misread the will of the American people and the leadership of this country into believing that we're going to abandon our position in Southeast Asia. We are not. But I do know from the things I read and the messages that I hear that some of them do get uneasy. I hope and trust they believe me when I say we're going to stand by our allies.

*News conference, San Diego, Calif.,*
*April 3/The New York Times, 4-4:12.*

*3*

The North Vietnamese, from the moment they signed the Paris accords, systematically violated the cease-fire and other provisions of the agreement. Flagrantly disregarding the ban on infiltration of troops into the South, they increased Communist forces to the unprecedented level of 350,000. In direct violation of the agreement, they sent in the most modern equipment in massive amounts. Meanwhile, they continued to receive large quantities of supplies and arms from their friends. In the face of this situation, the United States—torn as it was by the emotions of a decade of war—was unable to respond. We deprived ourselves by law of the ability to enforce the agreement— thus giving North Vietnam assurance that it could violate that agreement with impunity. Next, we reduced our economic and arms aid to South Vietnam. Finally, we signaled our increasing reluctance to give any support to that nation struggling for its survival. Encouraged by these developments, the North Vietnamese in recent months began sending even their reserve divisions into South Vietnam. Eighteen divisions, virtually their entire army, are now in South Vietnam. The government of South Vietnam, uncertain of further American assistance, hastily ordered a strategic withdrawal to more defensible positions. This extremely difficult maneuver, decided upon without consultations, was poorly executed, hampered by floods of refugees, and thus led to panic. The results are painfully obvious and profoundly moving.

*State of the World Address, Washington, April 10/The New York Times, 4-11:10.*

1

[On the aftermath of Communist military success in South Vietnam]: Today, America can regain the sense of pride that existed before Vietnam. But it cannot be achieved by refighting a war that is finished—as far as America is concerned. The time has come to look forward to an agenda for the future, to unity, to binding up the nation's wounds and restoring it to health and optimistic self-confidence. We are saddened, indeed, by the events in Indochina. But these events, tragic as they are, portend neither the end of the world nor of America's leadership in the world.

*At Tulane University, April 23/ Los Angeles Times, 4-24:(1)8.*

2

[On Americans who oppose allowing refugees from Communist-conquered South Vietnam to immigrate to the U.S.]: It just burns me up, these great humanitarians. They just want to turn their backs. We didn't do it with the Hungarians; we didn't do it with the Cubans; and, damn it, we're not going to do it now.

*At Republican leadership meeting, Washington, May 6/Los Angeles Herald-Examiner, 5-6:(A)1.*

3

. . . there are a number of lessons that we can learn from Vietnam. One, that we have to work with other governments that feel as we do that freedom is vitally important. We cannot, however, fight their battles for them. Those countries who believe in freedom, as we do, must carry the burden. We can help them, not with U.S. military personnel but with arms and economic aid so that they can protect their own national interests and protect the freedom of their citizens. I think we also may have learned some lessons concerning how we would

conduct a military operation. There was, of course, from the period of 1961-or-2 to the end of our military involvement in Vietnam, a great deal of controversy whether the military operations in Vietnam were carried out in the proper way—some dispute between civilian and military leaders as to the proper prosecution of a military engagement. I think we can learn something from those differences, and if we ever become engaged in any military operation in the future—and I hope we don't—I trust we've learned something about how we should handle such an operation.

*News conference, Washington, June 9/ The New York Times, 6-10:20.*

4

[On whether the U.S. should have a "presence" in Vietnam now that the South as well as the North is Communist-controlled]: In the light of the attitude of the North Vietnamese vis-a-vis the Paris accords of January, 1973, with their repeated violations and no disposition on their part to have any regrets or make any changes, I see no possibility under current circumstances for us to establish any presence there. In South Vietnam, which I think we have to recognize is dominated by the North Vietnamese, I can see no "give" on their part. One question, for example—and it is a terribly frustrating one—is the fact that, despite the Paris accords, we have not been given any access to information concerning MIAs, in total violation of the Paris accords. Well, if they can't give something they have agreed to, which would be the best example of humaneness, I just don't see any possibility for an American presence in North or South Vietnam under current circumstances.

*Interview, Washington, July 23/ The New York Times, 7-25:10.*

5

In Indochina, the healing effects of time are required. Our policies toward the new regimes of the peninsula will be determined by their conduct toward us. We are prepared to reciprocate gestures of good-will—particularly the return of the remains of Americans killed or missing in action, or information about them. If

# WHAT THEY SAID IN 1975

*(GERALD R. FORD)*

they exhibit restraint toward their neighbors and constructive approaches to international problems, we will look to the future rather than to the past.

*At University of Hawaii, Dec. 7/*
*The New York Times, 12-8:14.*

## J. William Fulbright
*Former United States Senator, D–Arkansas*
1

[On the current Communist military successes in South Vietnam]: The whole thing is a tragic mistake in judgment on our part; and what's going on there now is the normal, almost inevitable, outcome of the tragic intervention on our part in a civil war. It was simply a question of time: This civil war would have ended in 1954 if we hadn't intervened militarily. Of course, we could have behaved like the British, taken over the place as a colony, opened our schools, provided public services, just like a colony. But that sort of behavior is unfashionable. And the way we intervened, with the best of motives but a lack of understanding of their cultural situation, put us in a *Mission: Impossible* situation—but this was *truly* impossible, not like on TV. We have nothing to be ashamed of. Everybody makes mistakes . . . But this line that [President] Ford and [Secretary of State] Kissinger are taking—that we're now discredited around the world—is absolute nonsense. The worst thing we can do now is pretend we did not make a mistake in Vietnam. How else can you explain what's happened there if it wasn't a mistake?

*Interview/The National Observer, 4-12:4.*

2

[On the Communist take-over of South Vietnam]: I'm not depressed by the loss of the war. I'm no more depressed than I would be about Arkansas losing a football game to Texas. I see nothing wrong at all about saying we lost. I'm unable to understand the reluctance of our government to admit we made a mistake in going into the war in Southeast Asia.

*Little Rock, Ark., May 21/*
*The Washington Post, 5-23:(A)7.*

## John Kenneth Galbraith
*Professor of economics, Harvard University; Former United States Ambassador to India*
3

[On the U.S. pull-out from the Indochina war]: When before has a great country stopped in the middle of a war, assessed the wisdom of its participation, decided it was wrong, asserted the judgment against all of the chauvinist tendencies aroused by armed conflict, dismissed from power those responsible and brought its participation to an end? The answer is never, for unlike the French before us, we had a choice. The country corrected the error of its leaders on Vietnam. It was not a defeat but a triumph of good sense. Surely our critics abroad might take more notes of this achievement. Does it not say something for democracy?

*At Memphis (Tenn.) State University/*
*The New York Times, 7-12:25.*

4

You will ask why, in relation to Hanoi, the [Communist] Chinese and Russians did better [than the U.S. in Vietnam]. One answer is that they were wiser: No Chinese or Russian troops were sent; no great body of advisers debouched; there was a Pentagon East but no Kremlin East. To this day we do not know which country, China or the Soviet Union, was more influential in North Vietnam. They weren't thrown out because they weren't there.

*At Memphis (Tenn.) State University/*
*The New York Times, 7-12:25.*

## James M. Gavin
*Lieutenant General, United States Army (Ret.)*
5

[On the current Communist military successes in South Vietnam]: I think what is happening was inevitable. Either it had to come out this way or we had to continue to the occupation of Hanoi and certain war with [Communist] China . . . At this moment I'd like to get it all behind us. There is no one to be blamed. The people I'm sorry for now are the poor civilians, thousands of women, children and non-combatants, that suffered so in the dying hours of this thing... Somehow my mind today was going back to the closing days of World War II when we found thousands and thousands of people dying in concentration camps... It's so sad; this is what troubles me about it now.

*Interview/*
*The Washington Post, 4-13:(K)1.*

**Barry M. Goldwater**
*United States Senator,*
*R—Arizona*

1

[Commending President Ford's use of the Marines to effect rescue of the U.S. merchant ship *Mayaguez* and her crew after it was seized by the new Communist government of Cambodia]: This country needs an indication of strength and leadership in the President's office and he's finally come through with it... Had he not done what he did, every little half-assed nation in the world would be taking shots at us, and I think now they're going to think twice before they try it.

*May 15/*
*Los Angeles Herald-Examiner, 5-15:(A)2.*

**Robert P. Griffin**
*United States Senator, R—Michigan*

2

[On the current Communist military successes in South Vietnam and Cambodia, and the reluctance of the U.S. to provide military aid to the besieged governments]: By default and through caucus decisions of the majority party, it has become painfully obvious to all who watch in the United States and around the world that Congress is turning its back on allies in Indochina who are struggling to defend themselves... Such an abandonment by Congress not only of allies but of a huge investment that includes 50,000 American lives should at least be a conscious and deliberate decision made by the Senate as a whole—for it is a decision that carries with it into history consequences and responsibility of enormous proportions.

*Before the Senate, Washington, March 26/*
*Los Angeles Herald-Examiner, 3-26:(A)4.*

**Philip C. Habib**
*Assistant Secretary for East Asia and*
*Pacific Affairs, Department of State*
*of the United States*

3

The nub of the case for [U.S.] aid to Cambodia is simple. It comes down to a decision as to whether or not the United States is prepared to supply the ammunition, food and materials that are necessary for a people who want to defend themselves. There is no doubt that the Cambodian population living within the areas of the country controlled by the Cambodian government wish to resist the effort being made by the Khmer Communists to overrun their forces. But neither is there any doubt that without the adequate supply of arms and food the government will not be able to stand... A great nation has priorities. We have priorities in foreign policy as well as in domestic policy. Cambodia is not an isolated affair of little significance to the United States. It has to be viewed in the larger framework of Indochina, and that affects Southeast Asia and Asia as a whole. The amount being asked does not constitute a substantial drain on the American economy. Furthermore, all of this money will be spent in the United States for ammunition, medicines and materials. So it is not as if you were subtracting something from the economy. As I say, this is related to Southeast Asia in general. There is no question but that the Cambodian situation is a derivative of the larger conflict in Vietnam, which in turn is caused by the ambitions of Hanoi.

*Interview, Washington/*
*Los Angeles Times, 3-9:(6)5.*

**Tom Harkin**
*United States Representative, D—Iowa*

4

[On the current Communist military successes in South Vietnam]: I think what has happened just sort of gives lie to the whole Vietnamization program. And I think it points up once again the truth of what President John Kennedy said 12 years ago, that in the end it was their [South Vietnam's] war—they were going to have to win it or lose it... If they won't fight for themselves then I sure don't think we ought to do their fighting for them, or

# WHAT THEY SAID IN 1975

*(TOM HARKIN)*

even give them more aid that they're just going to turn over to the Communists.

*Interview/The Washington Post, 4-13:(K)3.*

**W. Averell Harriman**
*Former United States Ambassador-at-Large* 1

The most ghastly blunder we made was getting into Vietnam. We should have never let France go back into Indochina. I have a telegram on file in which I objected to our aid to France in Indochina in *1949.* If it hadn't been for Vietnam, [Senator Hubert] Humphrey would have been President [of the U.S.], we never would have had Watergate and Nixon, and we would not have had the recession . . . As I look back, what I regret most was that I wasn't able to influence [then-President Lyndon] Johnson to abandon the war in Vietnam. To see that war go on, to find him listening to people with such a completely wrong point of view. Every day there were those whispering in his ear, "No President ever lost a war." That was red meat for a Texan.

*Interview/*
*The Washington Post, 12-7:(Potomac)75.*

**Michael J. Harrington**
*United States Representative,*
*D–Massachusetts* 2

[Criticizing President Ford's use of the Marines to rescue the U.S. merchant ship *Mayaguez* and her crew after it was seized by the new Communist government of Cambodia]: They contemplated from the start a military response to convey to the world that we are still a tough guy . . . Our response was inappropriate; it was an exercise in petty *machismo.*

*Washington/The National Observer, 5-24:5.*

**Hubert H. Humphrey**
*United States Senator, D–Minnesota* 3

[On the Communist take-over of South Vietnam]: There's great sadness when you see the collapse of part of a country, when you see the incredible suffering, turmoil and panic which gripped so many. We shouldn't feel, though, that we've [the U.S.] let anyone down. No outside force can save a country that lacks the will or political leadership. What we've learned is that there aren't American answers for every problem in the world. We made judgments about that part of the world based on our experience in Europe. We were a world power with a half-world knowledge. It's clear that there's blame enough for all of us. I include myself.

*Interview/Time, 5-12:20.*

**In Tam**
*Exiled former Premier of Cambodia* 4

[On the Communist take-over of Cambodia]: Above all, I blame [former] President Lon Nol. Lon Nol knew he couldn't do anything to help the country, but he wanted to keep all the power to himself. The Americans gave enough money, but we failed to help ourselves, and the funds flowed into the hands of the corrupt.

*Interview, Bangkok/*
*The Washington Post, 4-27:(A)15.*

**Henry M. Jackson**
*United States Senator, D–Washington* 5

[On the revelation of secret written promises by then U.S. President Richard Nixon to then South Vietnamese President Nguyen Van Thieu to use force, if necessary, to enforce North Vietnamese compliance with the 1973 Paris peace accords]: There is a fateful difference between the Administration's publicly expressing a desire to retain certain options in the event of North Vietnamese violations of the Paris accords and the President's secretly committing the United States to exercise one or more of these options. By failing to disclose the precise nature and texts of secret understandings reached with South Vietnam, the Administration misled a foreign government and the [U.S.] Congress as to the nature and extent of the U.S. commitment to that government. The [Ford] Administration has been accusing Congress of violating commitments and obligation[s] to South Vietnam the Congress never heard of, let alone endorsed.

*May 1/The Washington Post, 5-2:(A)12.*

**Vernon E. Jordan, Jr.**
*Executive director, National Urban League*
1

We cannot absorb the true lessons and meaning of the Vietnam experience into our history while continuing to punish the innocent victims of America's war policy. To finally heal the wounds of war, we must take positive steps toward a national reconciliation that does right by those who fought and those who didn't; by those who felt their overriding duty was to their government, and those whose first call was to conscience. That is why I call for complete, immediate, universal and unconditional amnesty [for U.S. Vietnam draft-dodgers and deserters]. The legal and economic burdens placed on the backs of millions of young men must be lifted—now. Those who resisted the war should be welcomed back without penalty. Those with less-than-honorable discharges should be restored to their full rights and privileges. And those who enlisted or were drafted into that bitter war and came back only to find unemployment and discrimination should get the hero's welcome of jobs and equal opportunity to go along with their medals and memories. I did not come lightly to this position in favor of total amnesty. Rather, it is the result of my experience on the Presidential Clemency Board—an experience that brought home to me the full unfairness of the treatment accorded the different categories of people caught up in the snares of our system of military justice . . . It is time to wipe the slate clean. It is time to finally end the war by ending the punishment inflicted upon those who refused to take part in it.

*At Urban League conference, Atlanta/*
*The National Observer, 9-13:14.*

**Robert W. Kastenmeier**
*United States Representative, D—Wisconsin*
2

[Criticizing President Ford's use of the Marines to rescue the U.S. merchant ship *Mayaguez* and her crew after it was seized by the new Communist government of Cambodia]: There seems to be a temptation to resort to military action to demonstrate American military might following the debacle in Vietnam. A great and powerful nation presumably has options other than acting so precipitously, and

it appears that such options were not exhausted. This action could set a dangerous precedent in resolving relatively minor international incidents in years to come.

*The National Observer, 5-24:5.*

**Edward M. Kennedy**
*United States Senator, D—Massachusetts*
3

[Calling for an end to U.S. military aid to South Vietnam, where there is a current wave of Communist military victories]: Congress must finally put an end to this senseless spending for a war most Americans no longer support. What we need today is an immediate truce in South Vietnam. We need a return to the conference table and a renewal of diplomatic efforts to accomplish the political goals of the cease-fire agreements. I think the American taxpayer would be shocked to learn that the cease-fire war has already cost the United States some $8-billion. And no matter how often Congress acts to limit Federal spending in Indochina, the Administration always finds ways to spend more by backdoor financing or supplemental appropriations. There apparently remains a determination within the Administration to impose its views on the countries of the area. And in the absence of any change in Vietnam, on American terms, we shall continue to fuel a senseless war.

*Jan. 25/*
*San Francisco Examiner & Chronicle,*
*1-26:(A)15.*

**Khieu Samphan**
*Deputy Premier and Minister of*
*Defense of Cambodia*
4

[On the Communist take-over of Cambodia]: This is the greatest historic victory our nation and people have ever experienced. This army was created, trained and has grown up in the hot fire of a difficult, complex people's war against U.S. imperialism, the largest, most ferocious imperialist force in the world. This army began fighting empty-handed and fought until it created an excellent path for the struggle, successfully attacking the enemy everywhere—in the mountains and in the plains—continuously attacking in the dry and rainy seasons, and

*(KHIEU SAMPHAN)*

successfully crushing all forms of the war of aggression of the U.S. imperialists.

*Radio broadcast, Phnom Penh, April 22/*
*The New York Times, 4-23:17.*

## Kim Young Sam
*Leader, New Democratic Party of*
*South Korea*                                                    1

The reason South Vietnam fell [to the Communists] was because the people there didn't have faith in their government. That situation was caused by the long-term, one-man rule by [President Nguyen Van] Thieu and his dictatorial politics which indulged corruption, outlawed freedom of speech, controlled religious groups and oppressed opposition parties. A country was destroyed for the sake of keeping one man in power.

*Interview, Seoul, May 8/*
*Los Angeles Times, 5-9:(1)19.*

## Henry A. Kissinger
*Secretary of State of the United States*              2

[Calling for continued U.S. aid to Cambodia]: If a supplemental is not voted within the next few weeks, it is certain that Cambodia must fall [to Communist insurgents] because it will run out of ammunition. Therefore, the decision before us is whether the United States will withhold ammunition from a country which has been associated with us and which, clearly, wishes to defend itself. This is a serious responsibility to take ... I know it is fashionable to sneer at the words "domino theory." I think this is a very grave matter on which serious people have had a divided opinion. And we've been torn apart by the Vietnam war long enough. But I do not believe we can escape this problem by assuming the responsibility of condemning those who have dealt with us to a certain destruction.

*News conference, Washington, Feb. 25/*
*The New York Times, 2-26:1.*

3

[Calling for continued U.S. military aid for South Vietnam]: We are not saying that every part of the world is strategically as important to

the United States as any other part of the world. The problem in Indochina today is an elementary question of what kind of people we are. For 15 years we have been involved in encouraging the people of [South] Vietnam to defend themselves against what we conceived as external danger. [In the 1973 peace agreements] there was never any question that the United States would continue to give economic and military aid to [South] Vietnam. What we face now is whether the United States not just will "withdraw its forces"—which we achieved—and not just "will end the loss of American lives," but whether it will deliberately destroy an ally by withholding aid from it in its moment of extremity.

*News conference, March 26/*
*The Dallas Times Herald, 3-27:(A)21.*

4

[On the current Communist military successes in South Vietnam and the U.S. Congress' reluctance to allocate more military aid]: I, for one, do not believe that it was ignoble to have sought to preserve the independence of a small and brave people ... But where so many think that the war was a dreadful mistake, where thousands grieve for those they loved and others sorrow over their country's setback—there has been sufficient heartache for all to share. The Vietnam debate has now run its course. The time has come for restraint and compassion. The Administration has made its case. Let all now abide by the verdict of the Congress—without recrimination or vindictiveness.

*Before American Society of Newspaper*
*Editors, Washington, April 17/*
*Los Angeles Times, 4-18:(1)14.*

5

[We cannot] overlook the melancholy fact that not one of the other signatories of the Paris [peace] accords has responded to our repeated requests that they at least point out North Vietnam's flagrant violations of these agreements. Such silence can only undermine any meaningful standards of international responsibility.

*Before American Society of Newspaper*
*Editors, Washington, April 17/*
*Los Angeles Times, 4-18:(1)14.*

*1*

Over the years of the Vietnam debate, rational dialogue has yielded to emotion, sweeping far beyond the issues involved. Not only judgments but motives have been called into question. Not only policy but character has been attacked. What began as consensus progressively deteriorated into poisonous contention.

*Before American Society of Newspaper*
*Editors, Washington, April 17/*
*The New York Times, 4-18:15.*

*2*

[On the Vietnam war, which ended recently in a Communist take-over]: I think it will be a long time before Americans will be able to talk or write about the war with some dispassion. It is clear that the war did not achieve the objectives of those who started the original [U.S.] involvement, nor the objectives of those who sought to end that involvement, which they found on terms which seemed to them compatible with the sacrifices that had been made. What lesson we should draw from it, I think we should reserve for another occasion. But I don't think that we can solve the problem of having entered the conflict too lightly by leaving it too lightly, either.

*News conference, Washington, April 29/*
*The National Observer, 5-10:7.*

*3*

[On the use of the Marines to effect rescue of the U.S. merchant ship *Mayaguez* and her crew after it was seized by the new Communist government of Cambodia]: [It] ought to be made clear that there are limits beyond which the United States cannot be pushed, and that the United States is prepared to defend those interests, and that it can get public support and Congressional support for those actions. But we are not going around looking for opportunities to prove our manhood. We would far have preferred it [that] this [seizure] had not happened . . . We were forced into this.

*News conference, Washington, May 16/*
*The Washington Post, 5-17:(A)10.*

*4*

The lesson of Indochina is that military support is not enough. There must be a local will to resist. There is no question but what popular and social justice are, in the last analysis, the essential underpinning of resistance to subversion and external challenge.

*Before Japan Society,*
*New York, June 18/*
*The Washington Post, 7-8:(A)17.*

*5*

I have always considered Indochina a disaster [for U.S. policy]—partly because we did not think through the implications of what we were doing at the beginning . . . We let ourselves down by entering too lightly on an enterprise whose magnitude was not understood, by methods which were the . . . problem, and then were caught by what I would think was a minority, but nevertheless a very determined minority, in a situation in which the effective public support disintegrated . . . I think probably the Congress came to reflect public sentiment so that finally, in the ultimate collapse [of South Vietnam] last spring, there was clearly no public support for any continuation of the American effort. All the public-opinion polls seemed to show this . . . It is one thing to have a crisis that lasts a day or two such as the Cambodia incident or the *Mayaguez* [ship seizure] incident—but the real test is to sustain a crisis over an extended period of time. And there I would think that anything that looks to the public like a massive foreign involvement would require the most meticulous justification before it could be supported. This is our difficulty in the Congress.

*Television interview, Sept. 10/*
*"Firing Line," Public Broadcasting Service.*

*6*

[On U.S. involvement during the war in Indochina]: That chapter in our history, which occasioned so much anguish, is now closed. As for our relations with the new governments in that region, these will not be determined by the past; we are prepared to look to a more hopeful future. The United States will respond to gestures of good-will.

*Before Economic Club, Detroit, Nov. 24/*
*The Washington Post, 11-25:(A)11.*

**Kukrit Pramoj**
*Prime Minister of Thailand*                                    1

Some have voiced their concern that in the face of recent events in Indochina [Communist take-overs in South Vietnam, Cambodia and much of Laos], Thailand too will change, but in a way that would confirm their worst suspicions about the strength of Thailand's conviction ... If our seeking to overcome old obstacles and to renew dormant ties with our neighbors is perceived as a "change" on our part, then change we must. This change is not founded on fear or weakness, but on courage and strength with dignity. It does not dictate that we discard the old and rush in blindly to embrace the new, where friendship is concerned. However, it does dictate that we must not keep alive old fears at the expense of new realities.

*At dinner in his honor, Kuala Lumpur,*
*Malaysia, June 9/*
*The Washington Post, 6-10:(A)14.*

**Nguyen Cao Ky**
*Former Premier,*
*and former Vice President,*
*of South Vietnam*                                              2

What has happened in the past two weeks [increasing North Vietnamese military victories in South Vietnam] is not because we didn't have $300-million in military aid from the U.S. The armament and equipment were still there and the manpower resources were still there. The problem is purely one of leadership. It's not been the business of the Americans. It's our own responsibility and we have only ourselves to blame. Everything [military supplies] we've left behind now in Pleiku, in the highlands, in Da Nang and Hue, I'm sure it cost more than $300-million. The problem for South Vietnam is here [in the head]. When the people and soldiers have no more will to stay and fight, what can you do? What has brought on this mentality? It's because of very poor leadership, because of corruption when the commander of a battalion, regiment or division has to buy his position—then it's finished for the army.

*Interview, Saigon, March 31/*
*Los Angeles Times, 4-1:(1)5.*

[On South Vietnamese refugees who came to the U.S. after the Communist take-over in their country]: We Vietnamese are the newest refugees in your history. We know your country is a land of immigrants. Your sons and daughters fought to keep Vietnam free, and we Vietnamese wish to earn your respect and friendship. We wish not to be hawks or doves, but eagles.

*Los Angeles Times, 11-9:(6)9.*

**Georg Leber**
*Minister of Defense of West Germany*                           4

[On the current Communist military successes in Cambodia and South Vietnam]: I think that our most important ally [the U.S.] should feel that we did not regard him in Asia as an imperialist aggressor—to use Communist terminology—but that, on the contrary, we knew very well what was at stake there [in Indochina] ... Even a nation as great as the United States cannot prevent a country from losing its freedom if that country itself is not prepared to provide the minimum essential prerequisites for preserving this freedom ... [The events in Indochina are] another lesson teaching us to be on our guard when concluding agreements [with Communist nations].

*Interview, Bonn/*
*The Christian Science Monitor, 4-24:6.*

**Lee Kuan Yew**
*Prime Minister of Singapore*                                   5

The Thais know that the patience and perseverance of the Americans have not matched that of the Communists—not simply the Communists in Vietnam, but their suppliers, the People's Republic of China and the Soviet Union ... Rather than go through the mincing machine, it makes more sense [for the Thais] to seek diplomatic and political solutions.

*Los Angeles Times, 4-10:(1)7.*

**Robert L. Leggett**
*United States Representative, D–California*                    6

[Arguing against continued U.S. military aid to Indochina]: Everybody around the world thinks the U.S. is nuts. We're going bankrupt and the Ford Administration wants to send more millions to Southeast Asia. It's crazy. Turning down aid would be a reflection of economic responsibility.

*U.S. News & World Report, 3-17:17.*

**Lon Nol**
*President of Cambodia*
1

Our people are endowed with a Constitution and many institutions, democratic institutions. We are just defending the Constitution and the institutions. I was brought to this high office by the institutionalized organization. But for the peace of my country and the welfare of my country I would do whatever is possible and necessary so that peace and the welfare of my people can be achieved.

*Phnom Penh/The Washington Post, 3-2:(A)1.*

**Mike Mansfield**
*United States Senator, D—Montana*
2

[Criticizing U.S. military aid to Cambodia and South Vietnam]: We've been going through too many tunnels and have never really seen the light ... Our policy there indicates to me that we don't know how to break clearly when the time comes to do so. [The Ford Administration is asking for] enough funds to carry on through the end of the dry season; and when that is done they will come back and ask for more.

*Washington, March 8/*
*San Francisco Examiner & Chronicle,*
*3-9:(A)25.*
3

This is not the time for either the Executive or the Legislative Branch to begin pointing the finger [of blame for the current Communist military successes in South Vietnam and Cambodia] ... Let us recognize that there is enough blame to go around and that it affects all of us. So, let us start afresh ... Let us do what we can, together, to bring this country out of the economic morass and out of the quagmire which we helped to create in Indochina.

*Before the Senate, Washington, April 7/*
*Los Angeles Times, 4-8:(1)8.*

**Graham A. Martin**
*United States Ambassador to South Vietnam*
4

... it is my objective, dispassionate analysis that if we give the aid that we had promised on the military side, there is no way that South Vietnamese military forces can be defeated by the North. If we give enough economic aid over the next two or three years, the progress could be very dramatic and I would think that in the case of both military and economic aid, if we have the wit and the intelligence to give the proper amounts now for the next three years, we could look forward to a diminution and perhaps total elimination of that aid. That, I think, is the reason for the violence of the opposition within the U.S. to the continuance of proper amounts of aid at this moment. The violence of the opposition—of those who have been committed to a North Vietnamese victory— of those who because of their own previous estimates or their own self-serving prophecies do not now want to be proved wrong—this violence arises largely from their realization that we Americans are now at this final stage where we can complete the American involvement in Vietnam, leaving it as I believe most Americans want to leave it—economically viable, militarily capable of defending itself with its own manpower and free to choose its own government as its own people may themselves freely determine. It is within our grasp within the next three years. Of this I am certain.

*Interview, Washington/*
*Human Events, 2-22:15.*
5

[On the current Communist military successes in South Vietnam and U.S. Congressional reluctance to supply military aid to the besieged government]: You have a nation here that we encouraged to resist, gave assurances to, not in treaty form, but quite precisely. There was no question that we would replace arms one for one. For all sorts of specious reasons we have reneged on every one of these agreements. My only regret is that I did not speak out more openly, to the distaste of the Department of State. The Executive Branch has fallen flat on its face presenting the truth.

*Interview/Time, 4-21:19.*

**Paul N. McCloskey, Jr.**
*United States Representative, R–California*     1

[On U.S. aid to Cambodia]: It's just a question of how do we get the fewest Cambodians killed, and get out of there as quickly as we can . . . I'm not prepared to just abandon that perimeter around Phnom Penh and those people without food or ammunition or medicine. I think we owe them that much as a result of what we've done to them.
*San Francisco Examiner & Chronicle,*
*3-9:(This World)12.*


**George S. McGovern**
*United States Senator, D–South Dakota*     2

[Saying the U.S. should return most South Vietnamese refugees who were brought to America in the wake of the Communist take-over of their country]: America will not turn away those few who might be endangered by a return to their homeland. [But] 90 per cent of the Vietnamese refugees who left would be better off going back to their own land now that the initial panic has subsided. The final blunder of Vietnam may be that the [U.S.] Administration has chosen evacuation of nearly 100,000 Vietnamese as a substitute for accommodation in their own country. That policy should be reversed. I have never thought that more than a handful of government leaders were in any real danger of reprisals. The great majority of Vietnamese refugees do not fall into that category. Most of them left in panic out of fear of a bloody final battle for Saigon that did not materialize.
*Lecture, Eastern Illinois University, May 4/*
*The Washington Post, 5-4:(A)19.*


**Thomas J. McIntyre**
*United States Senator, D–New Hampshire*     3

[On the Communist take-over in South Vietnam and Cambodia]: The final, ultimate and most reprehensible betrayal of truth in this endless travesty is the misbegotten effort—already under way—to dump a load of guilt and anguish upon the American people for the fall of South Vietnam and Cambodia in order to save face for the establishment and soothe the tender egos of those whose prophecies self-destructed before they self-fulfilled.
*San Francisco Examiner & Chronicle,*
*5-4:(This World)2.*


**Walter F. Mondale**
*United States Senator, D–Minnesota*     4

[On President Ford's request for $300-million in military aid for South Vietnam]: The Administration knows that the $300-million won't really do anything to prevent ultimate collapse in Vietnam, and it is just trying to shift responsibility for the bankruptcy of its policy to Congress and the Democrats. The Administration can't ask Congress for more Vietnam aid and say no to food stamps and Social Security adjustments for senior citizens [in the U.S.].
*The New York Times, 1-24:3.*


**Norodom Sihanouk**
*Exiled former Chief of State of Cambodia*     5

[The U.S. would have] no reason to be ashamed if she now decides that she will no longer be concerned with Cambodia but that she will leave it to the Cambodians to settle this matter [of rebel insurgency] themselves. If, however, the United States continues to ultimately destroy and debase the small Cambodian nation, she will hardly have a chance to prevent history from condemning her for all times. [The Cambodian insurgents] are not Communists and they do not have the intention of making the future Cambodia a socialist or people's republic. [But] even if we were Communists, neither the U.S. Constitution, international law or the UN Charter contains provisions that would give the United States or any other power the right or oblige them to intervene . . . [The insurgents] sincerely wish to be your good friends, but the U.S. government has turned down all our proposals for peace, reconciliation and resumption of diplomatic relations . . .
*Telegram to key members of U.S. Congress,*
*Feb. 7\*/Los Angeles Times, 2-28:(1)13.*


6

After [the Khmer Rouge Communist] victory [in Cambodia], I seriously believe I will retire. I was placed on the Cambodian throne at the age of 18½ and I am now 52½. I think I have amply served my country. I am not a Khmer Rouge, I am not a Communist and I do not understand Communism; but the Khmer Rouge have always recognized me as Cambodian Chief of State. They have made me president of the Cambodian popular resistance, but that does not mean that I can see any role for myself after victory. Even if one thinks of a sharing of power, there will be a clash. I am a very independent man. After victory, I will be Chief of State and there will be an entirely Communist government and administration. So either I am a puppet of the Khmer Rouge or I remain independent and there will be trouble.

*Interview, Peking, April 14/*
*The New York Times, 4-15:16.*

1

[On the Communist take-over of Cambodia] : We did what they said we could never do. We defeated the Americans. What little Cambodia was able to do any other country ought to be able to try . . . We will soon have a reunited Vietnam . . . The United States won't be able to hold onto Taiwan forever. The same goes for South Korea. Perhaps the United States will have to abandon its outer defense perimeter and fall back to Japan, the Philippines, Indonesia. Then we will constitute a formidable body—from Cambodia to Korea— because in Laos, too, the reactionaries will have to get out. In Thailand, the people will also rise. How long will it take? Not very long.

*At Friends of Badminton meeting, Peking/*
*The New York Times, 4-25:12.*

2

[On what he will do as a result of the Communist take-over in his country, which he supported] : I will accept accreditation letters and sign decisions from the Khmer Rouge. I'll sign them with my eyes closed, without getting too deeply into what they say—at the rate of 100 documents in five minutes. I'll come back to Peking [where he has been living] to give receptions, and then I'll go and harass the U.S. at international conferences.

*News conference/*
*San Francisco Examiner & Chronicle,*
*5-4:(This World)13.*

**Norodom Sihanouk**
*Chief of State of Cambodia*

3

[On his new position since his return to Cambodia after the Communist take-over] : The government is controlled by the people. They deserve to lead the government, so I do not assume the responsibility of government. But I am not an ambassador; I am Chief of State. You have many countries, like Great Britain and Italy, where the heads of state do not rule the state; they are symbols of government. So you must not be surprised that I am President of Cambodia, that I am the head of state, but that Cambodia is ruled by the people and not by the head of state.

*News conference, New York, Oct. 3/*
*The New York Times, 10-4:3.*

**Tran Kim Phuong**
*South Vietnamese Ambassador to the*
*United States*

4

[On the current Communist military successes in his country and the reluctance of the U.S. to furnish military aid to South Vietnam] : The United States does not respect the Paris [Vietnam peace agreement] . . . I think that the people around the world would draw only one possible conclusion: that it is probably safer to be an ally of the Communists, and it looks like it is fatal to be an ally of the United States.

*Television interview, Washington/*
*San Francisco Examiner & Chronicle,*
*4-6:(This World)11.*

**Douglas Pike**
*American authority on Southeast Asia*

5

[On Vietnamese Communism] : Communists consider themselves very moral. When they eliminate "social negatives," it's not done with glee or pleasure. They are not a bunch of bloody-handed monsters with fangs. Those who so characterize them do truth a disservice. The Vietnamese Communists are determined, sometimes fanatical, persons dedicated to creating in Vietnam an entirely new social order. They see what they have to offer as a total system. It cannot be bought piecemeal, because it won't

# WHAT THEY SAID IN 1975

work except as a complete package. Part of the system is what they call revolutionary violence—in plain terms, killing persons who cannot fit into the new social system being created; if they remain, they become a cancer in the body politic. Hence, one way or the other they must be eliminated.

*Interview/U.S. News & World Report, 4-21:20.*

**Ronald Reagan**
*Former Governor of California (R)* 1

I realize that millions of Americans are sick of hearing about Indochina, and perhaps it is politically unwise to talk of our obligation to Cambodia and South Vietnam. But we pledged—in an agreement that brought our young men home and freed our prisoners—to give our allies arms and ammunition to replace on a one-for-one basis what they expend in resisting the aggression of the Communists who are violating the cease-fire and are fully aided by their Soviet and Red Chinese allies. Congress has already reduced the appropriation to half of what they need and threatens to reduce it even more. Can we live with ourselves if we, as a nation, betray our friends and ignore our pledged word? And if we do, who would ever trust us again? To consider committing such an act so contrary to our deepest ideals is symptomatic of the erosion of standards and values.

*At Conservative Political Action Conference, Washington, Feb. 15/Human Events, 3-1:6.*

**Dean Rusk**
*Professor of international law, University of Georgia; Former Secretary of State of the United States* 2

The domino theory is actually a euphemism for something else—the doctrine of world revolution—and I don't know why we want to conceal that . . . When I left office [in 1969], there were tens of thousands of North Vietnamese soldiers in Laos, Cambodia and South Vietnam. These weren't dominoes. They were armed men.

*At Lehigh University/ The National Observer, 4-12:4.*

**Raoul Salan**
*General, French Army (Ret.); Former Commander-in-Chief, French forces in Indochina* 3

[On the current Communist military successes in South Vietnam]: It's lost. . . . this is the brutal end, a tragedy for Vietnam and a defeat for the United States. But there is no reason to be surprised. [The late North Vietnamese President] Ho Chi Minh told me himself in 1946 that he dreamed of a great Indochina stretching from the Chinese border to Camau Point and from the Mekong River to the South China Sea . . . Well, it is nearly done. All of those who know the Vietnamese Communists knew this would be the ultimate end when the peace agreements were signed in Paris [in 1973]. The North Vietnamese Army—today perhaps the best in the world—used the time since then to set up a fantastic logistics system. Times have changed, they have modern equipment and know how to use it. I can't see how they can be stopped . . . The United States should take note and awaken to the lessons of war, for militarily it is the victory of Soviet methods over those of the Americans.

*Interview, Paris/ The Washington Post, 4-24:(A)6.*

**Arthur M. Schlesinger, Jr.**
*Historian; Professor of Humanities, City University of New York* 4

[On the Communist take-over of South Vietnam]: The people [in the U.S.] are taking it in their stride. People recognize it's a final liberation from the damaging obsession that America's vital interests are at stake in a civil war . . . Future historians will be hard put to explain what happened. Defeat signifies our accepting realities. I think it's healthy, altogether healthy and liberating. People realize we're not omnipotent.

*Interview/ San Francisco Examiner & Chronicle, 5-4:(A)30.*

**James R. Schlesinger**
*Secretary of Defense of the United States* 5

I think that the impact of the outcome in Southeast Asia is primarily psychological—what it does for perceptions of American will and determination, American steadfastness, rather than the underlying structure of international health.

*Interview/The Washington Post, 3-24:(A)5.*

1

[On the reluctance of the U.S. Congress to appropriate more military aid to South Vietnam during the current successful Communist offensive]: If we are to refrain from giving aid in those cases in which we do not know the outcome, then we will, through a self-fulfilling prophecy, create the fall of many countries. I think in this case it's a question more of the national honor, the perception of American commitments. No one can say at this stage that provision of military equipment represents the equivalent of a gilt-edged investment. What one can say is it represents a continuation of the American commitment so that all parties will see that the United States was the nation that gave a reasonable chance for the South Vietnamese.

*TV-radio interview, Washington/*
*"Face the Nation,"*
*Columbia Broadcasting System, 4-6.*

2

[Addressing the U.S. armed forces on the Communist take-over of South Vietnam]: In this hour of pain and reflection, you may feel that your efforts and sacrifices have gone for naught. That is not the case. When the passions have muted and the history is written, Americans will recall that their armed forces served them well. Under circumstances more difficult than ever before faced by our military services, you accomplished the mission assigned to you by higher authority. In combat, you were victorious and you left the field with honor. Though you have done all that was asked of you, it will be stated that the war itself was futile. In some sense, such may be said of any national effort that ultimately fails. Yet our involvement was not purposeless. It was intended to assist a small nation to preserve its independence in the face of external attack and to provide at least a reasonable chance to survive. That Vietnam succumbed to powerful external forces vitiates neither the explicit purpose behind our involve-

ment, nor the impulse of generosity toward those under attack that has long infused American policy.

*Message to the armed forces, April 29*/*
*Los Angeles Times, 4-30:(1)16.*

**Souvanna Phouma**
*Premier of Laos*

3

[Saying the Communist Pathet Lao may soon take control of the country]: We must stop the fighting. The war has reached an end. Important changes have taken place which some had not expected so suddenly, but they are here. It is our great chance to preserve our country from further bloodshed which surely would take place if one continued to ignore the march of historical events.

*Constitution Day address, Vientiane, May 11/*
*Los Angeles Times, 5-12:(1)1.*

**John J. Sparkman**
*United States Senator, D—Alabama*

4

Now more than ever, the Vietnamese and Cambodian governments will have to make their own way. [Southeast Asia] is belatedly recognized as an area of limited American security interests. It would be futile to raise again the question of American involvement . . . The Administration should be prepared to explain in what exact ways the national interest of the United States will be served by military assistance to enable the Saigon and Phnom Penh governments to continue fighting in their respective countries . . . Even with vast amounts of aid at their disposal, they have steadily lost the confidence of their people and proved unable to cope with their adversaries. It is evident now, even if it was not evident before, that the Paris [peace] accords were essentially a basis for American withdrawal and the return of our prisoners, an arrangement for that "decent interval" beyond which the struggle for Indochina would go on among the indigenous parties.

*Jan. 29/*
*Los Angeles Times, 1-30:(1)4.*

# WHAT THEY SAID IN 1975

## Stuart Symington
*United States Senator,*
*D—Missouri*

1

[Arguing against $300-million in additional U.S. military aid for South Vietnam]: Specifically re Vietnam, I just can't see how and why the fighting there is vital to the security of the United States. For years we were told we were going to get out of Indochina. I would be willing to see some money spent there, such as technical aid—possibly some money to improve the land. But heavy military aid—how long can we go on with it? I became convinced back in 1967 that we ought to get out, because the [South Vietnamese] government didn't represent a majority of the people, and [I] felt in 1972 those governments [in Indochina] were going to fall regardless of what we gave them. Now we need the money right here [in the U.S.]. We've a lot of hungry people in this country. Some of the letters I get make one very sad. Based on my mail, the overwhelming mood in Missouri and the nation is against further military aid to South Vietnam. People say, "What difference does $300-million make?" Actually 522 million, counting Cambodia. But one can say that about every program. The President's [Ford] budget proposes a $52-billion deficit for next year. The capitalistic system cannot live indefinitely with a $52-billion negative account. Under these circumstances, I oppose continuing the Vietnam and Cambodian aid.
*Interview/U.S. News & World Report, 2-24:22.*

## Nguyen Van Thieu
*President of South Vietnam*

2

...you must remember that as long as this leadership remains in power in Hanoi, they will continue to pursue the goal of domination of the whole of Indochina by force. They are all there in Hanoi, the old doctrinaires, the old revolutionary men, that never abandon their goal of 50 years ago or 30 years ago. They are not politicians. Sometimes I say that they are more Communist than [those in] Moscow and Peking ...
*Interview, Saigon/*
*The Washington Post, 1-29:(A)18.*

3

[Asking for continued U.S. military aid]: Do the American people like the sacrifice of 50,000 American boys to be in vain? How can you imagine coming here just to run and abandon the men who continue your ideals? [If the U.S. abandons South Vietnam,] all Vietnam will be a Communist country. All Indochina. All Southeast Asia. The whole world.
*Interview, Saigon/*
*Time, 2-10:14.*

4

Decreased United States aid during the past two years has seriously affected the morale of our troops as well as the faith of Vietnamese people in American promises. I have told the Americans that we need at least $1.5-billion per year to defend the entire territory of South Vietnam. If we get only $700-million then we will be able to defend only one-half of our territory ... $300-million [as suggested by some U.S. officials as sufficient to South Vietnam] would be enough for only 30 days of fighting. It is especially absurd considering the Americans, who fought the Communists for six years with billions and billions of dollars, have withdrawn, leaving us behind to continue fighting without money and without B-52s.
*Broadcast address, Saigon, April 4/*
*Los Angeles Herald-Examiner, 4-5:(A)2.*

5

[On the current Communist military successes in his country]: The United States assured us of piece-for-piece arms replacement. But there was no piece-for-piece replacement ... Meanwhile, South Vietnam stands in a defensive position, could not do much, could not bomb North Vietnam because of the lack of military aid. We could not back up our defense lines because we did not have enough helicopters, ammunition, weapons, and had to retreat, and we were blamed for not being capable of defending the land. Step by step, more lands were lost to Communist control. While the North Vietnamese received sufficient aid from the Soviet Union and Red China, South Vietnam could not even hit a single hair of North Vietnam's leg. Every time we have one division, they come up with two divisions. If we have five tanks, they come up with 20 tanks ... I have told the Americans that if the Vietnamese people of both South and North are to fight against each other without aid from anyone, and if we are defeated, then they may say that we failed because we are so weak. But one should realize the fact that the North Vietnamese Communists aren't better than us, because, like us, they did not even manufacture one single round of ammunition, rocket, one single tank. So we fight here not only for our own defense, but also for resisting the Soviet Union and Red China.

*Resignation address, Saigon, April 12/*
*Los Angeles Times, 4-22:(1)10.*

**Robert Thompson**
*British authority on Southeast Asia*
1

We are about to see strategic surrender of the United States ... The American withdrawal from Indochina is the greatest retreat the world has seen since Napoleon himself retreated from Moscow.

*San Francisco Examiner & Chronicle,*
*3-23:(A)20.*

**Morris K. Udall**
*United States Representative, D—Arizona*
2

[Saying South Vietnamese refugees, in the wake of the Communist take-over in that country, should be granted admission to the U.S.]: We're talking about one-tenth of one per cent of our work force, and half of them are kids. It isn't a horde. It can be assimilated. This country took in 800,000 Cubans, 35,000 Hungarians. We're a humanitarian country. We got in the war in Vietnam trying to do the right thing, but it was a mistake. We defoliated, bombed, made refugees—700,000 orphaned and abandoned kids. We caused great misery and dislocation, and now we have to take these people in. I may have a minority view but that's my view.

*At Prince George's County (Md.) Democratic*
*Women's Club/The New York Times, 5-4:(4)15.*

**Um Sim**
*Cambodian Ambassador to the United States*
3

[On the current Communist military successes in his country and the reluctance of the

U.S. to send military aid to his besieged government]: We are the patient and the United States is the doctor. You have found our case is hopeless, but we have to cling to life until we die ... The fact is there is not a commitment in writing [for the U.S. to defend Cambodia] but you induced us into this fighting. The United States has taken advantage of our innocence and lack of experience ... From now on, I think the Cambodian people would feel satisfied if the United States solemnly swears after the abandonment of Cambodia that the United States will no longer be involved in our region. If it is sure that the United States will wash its hands completely of us, then the Cambodian people will know where they stand. You Americans should make up your minds that if you abandon Cambodia and Vietnam you should not be involved there ever again.

*Before Washington Press Club, April 11/*
*Los Angeles Herald-Examiner, 4-13:(A)2.*

**James Wagonseller**
*National commander, American Legion*
4

[Arguing against extension of President Ford's clemency program for U.S. Vietnam draft-dodgers and deserters]: The American Legion is disappointed and dismayed by President Ford's decision to extend the provisions of his clemency plan for an additional month ... At a time when honorably discharged veterans are having a difficult time in finding employment, we believe the efforts of the government should be directed toward helping those who served their country in its time of need rather than those who chose to abrogate their responsibilities as citizens.

*Jan. 30/Los Angeles Times, 1-31:(1)6.*

**George C. Wallace**
*Governor of Alabama (D)*
5

[Reflecting on the current wave of Communist military successes in South Vietnam]: There is going to be a great revulsion in this country [the U.S.] against our going in there and not winning that war. The people of this country are going to remember the politicians who were intimidated by the loud noisemakers in the streets. This is an emotional thing. The people can't stomach a government that wasted all that money and all those lives for no purpose. They supported their government because they're patriotic Americans, but if we weren't going to win it, we should never have gone in. We ought to have bombed them out of existence up in North Vietnam. People say that would be barbaric; but if we had done it when some of us first said it, it wouldn't have cost one-tenth or one-fifteenth the lives that have been lost—and we would have won. We should have bombed them into submission, or we shouldn't have gone in there in the first place ... The real warmongers are those who cut the heart out of our defense for all these social-welfare programs; and those who said, "oh, no, you mustn't carry the war to [North Vietnam]"—they're the ones who are going to have to answer for this.

*Interview, Montgomery, Alabama/*
*Los Angeles Times, 4-7:(2)7.*

**William C. Westmoreland**
*General (Ret.) and former Chief of Staff,*
*United States Army; Former Allied*
*Commander in Vietnam*                                    1

[On the current North Vietnamese offensive in South Vietnam and the U.S. Congress' reluctance to continue military aid to the South]: It's moot to talk about [U.S.] recommitment now that Congress has swung the pendulum back too far and hamstrung White House initiative. But we never have committed enough force in this war, and that's the only thing those people [Communists] understand. I never recommended it when I was involved, but, who knows, when the total history is written it might show that the use of several small-yield nuclear weapons at some early point conceivably could have put an end to the whole thing and caused less suffering in the short run than subsequently was caused in the long run.

*Interview, Charleston, S.C., March 28/*
*The New York Times, 3-29:3.*

2

[On the Communist take-over of South Vietnam]: It was heartbreaking, but it was not surprising. I've gone through the anguish of seeing Vietnam deteriorate bit by bit. I must say the process has been more rapid than I thought would be the case. It was a sad day in the glorious history of our country. But elements in this country [the U.S.] have been working for this end. We failed. We let an ally down. But it was inevitable after Congress pulled the rug out from under the President with the War Powers Act. Hanoi was home free at that moment, for our only trump was gone. Other countries in Southeast Asia must be lonely and frightened. People who dismiss the domino theory are all wet.

*Interview/Time, 5-12:20.*

**Elmo R. Zumwalt, Jr.**
*Admiral, United States Navy (Ret.); Former*
*Chief of Naval Operations*                               3

[On the revelation of secret written promises by then U.S. President Richard Nixon to then South Vietnamese President Nguyen Van Thieu to use force if necessary to enforce North Vietnamese compliance with the 1973 Paris peace accords]: [The pledge] demanded by Thieu was his price for going along with a very unfavorable truce ... a bad truce for the South Vietnamese because it left the enemy intact in their country, in the South. The Nixon-Kissinger Administration must bear a large share of the blame for the fact that [the U.S.] Congress failed to honor those commitments that had been made in the name of the country. The view that I had was that apparently Congressional leaders weren't informed in any formal way that these agreements were made. And if that was the case, in my view, the error clearly lies with the Administration, for both making [the agreement] and not communicating it [to Congress].

*Interview/The Washington Post, 5-2:(A)12.*

**Lindsay Anderson**
*British motion picture director*
1

One of the things I like about America is the lack of class consciousness. If there is one, it's based on money, not an accident of birth. The reason that England is in such a bad way is that everyone hugs the past. Their infatuation with old motor cars, old trains, old ways of behavior and *Upstairs, Downstairs* [a period TV series] doesn't exactly equip them for survival in the latter half of the 20th century. I have a clear conscience. I have tried to warn them in my films, but they haven't listened.

*Interview, New York/*
*San Francisco Examiner & Chronicle,*
*2-16:(Datebook)15.*

**Sven Andersson**
*Foreign Minister of Sweden*
2

There are many reasons why Sweden has chosen a policy of neutrality. First of all, we consider it the best means of safeguarding our independence and the democratic structure of our society. Another reason is our geographical position. If you look at a map you will see that Northern Europe covers half of the European border between East and West. We have not wished to be the last outpost of either of the blocs. Another reason is that we believe that Swedish policy promotes favorable conditions for detente in Europe. The security pattern in the northern European area has been one of remarkable stability. The Swedish policy of neutrality is part of this pattern. If it is shaken, stability is also shaken ... What we do *not* consider neutrality demands is that we should be required to be neutral in our opinions.

*At Institute of Foreign Affairs, Washington/*
*The Christian Science Monitor, 10-7:35.*

**Yuri V. Andropov**
*Director of KGB (Soviet secret police)*
3

The ill-wishers of socialism, who are annoyed over the Soviet Union's growing prestige, are trying to sow doubts regarding the real democracy of the Soviet system. Unscrupulously distorting facts, they think up all kinds of questions about some "infringement" of civil rights in the U.S.S.R. [as well as] seek out occasional shortcomings in our life and blow them up out of all proportion. How can one speak of real civil rights for the broad popular masses in the capitalist countries where people are living in constant fear of losing their jobs? . . . It is poor consolation to these millions of deprived people and their families that they are permitted to go to the gates of the White House or to a Hyde Park lawn and air their different views, for this will not improve their life one iota. Socialism's adversaries are now concentrating on ideological sabotage. Realizing the futility of approaching Soviet people with the idea of a capitalist comeback, they seek to strike a pose of democratizing socialism, improving it. [This] boils down to the aim of undermining Soviet power from within. Soviet people see through all this very well.

*Novo-Moskovsk, U.S.S.R., June 9/*
*The New York Times, 6-10:11.*

**Carlos Arias (Navarro)**
*Premier of Spain*
4

[Saying his government is committed to political reform, albeit cautiously]: The first step always shows the direction in which one wants to move. If this step means the beginning of a long journey, I would like to say that we want to go very far and very high. There is no end to the long journey of a nation on the march. [The government is trying] as hard as it can and as well as it can to create the necessary bases so the journey undertaken by the Spanish people leads the country, in order and progress, toward the participation of all in the building of peace and justice.

*Interview, Madrid\*/*
*The New York Times, 2-20:5.*

# WHAT THEY SAID IN 1975

## Raymond Aron
*French political analyst* 1

. . . I have been struck by how we [Europeans] put ourselves in the balcony of history. If a Communist party seems on the verge of coming to power, we call it an American defeat. If the U.S. intervenes through the CIA, we then denounce American imperialism. If, for example, Portugal goes Communist, it becomes an American defeat rather than a European defeat. Obviously, Portugal is closer to Paris than New York. The consequences of a Communist government [in Lisbon] will be felt more in Madrid and Paris than in New York. But we are acting like voyeurs, counting the blows to see who is winning and losing and never asking ourselves what [our] responsibilities are.

*Interview/Time, 5-19:29.*

## Jose Pinheiro de Azevedo
*Premier of Portugal* 2

Without the armed forces there is no authority, and without authority there is no government.

*Broadcast address to the nation, Lisbon, Oct. 13/Los Angeles Times, 10-14:(1)5.*

3

It is too early to say how long my government will last. In my opinion, it is not now going in a good direction. The left in Portugal is unhappy. They believe the government is too far to the right. And it is necessary to do something about this because the government is not of the right . . . I talk often with the leaders of the Communist Party. I am not quite sure that they support me very strongly. But they like me. I explain to them everything I think. That is why they like to hear me. I am quite certain that they support me sufficiently; not very strongly but strongly enough so that I can work with them. The Communist Party is not yet dangerous. All Communist parties can become dangerous, but it is not now. The Italian, French and Spanish Communist parties are now mild. But in the future? We don't know. Portugal has the same problem.

*Interview, Lisbon/Time, 10-20:38.*

## Anthony Wedgwood Benn
*Minister of Industries of the United Kingdom* 4

[Arguing against Britain's continuance in the Common Market]: The European dream has become a nightmare. The Common Market has proved a ghastly failure that already has cost many British workers their jobs and industrialists their factories, while the Germans and French have been reaping the benefits.

*Los Angeles Times, 6-5:(1)14.*

## Abram Bergson
*Professor of economics, and former director of the Russian Research Center, Harvard University* 5

There is a significant difference between a dictatorship of the right, under which Portugal has lived, and a dictatorship of the left, in the direction of which Portugal now appears to be moving. It does seem with right-wing dictatorships that occasions arise when it is possible for the rascals in power to be thrown out. When you look at the left, it seems to be terribly difficult to throw the rascals out. Once you get the party or the group in power in Communist societies, once the party has nationalized property on a wholesale scale and seized the lever of powers, including radio, press, TV and the arts, there is no record that gives hope that that party can be thrown out and its political and economic structure abandoned . . . I don't want to make too much of Portugal. But, on the other hand, here we have a country that is part of NATO that has been non-Communist and that is moving rapidly in the direction of public ownership, toward a cessation of democracy as we know it in the West. This is not only a substantive defection from NATO, but a rather novel development. I don't recall any case previously where a country in Western Europe has moved in the direction of authoritarianism, socialism or Communism.

*Interview, Cambridge, Mass./
Los Angeles Times, 4-22:(2)7.*

## Enrico Berlinguer
*Leader, Communist Party of Italy* 6

International Communism presents a varied panorama. Within this panorama is the Italian

Communist Party with its particular traditions and its original traits. We have always assumed the best democratic and patriotic traditions of the country, going back to the *Risorgimento*. Our Party has fought to guarantee all fundamental freedoms, including freedom of assembly and speech, within a more progressive social and economic framework. We have never believed, even in 1945, that one single party—single class—can solve the problems of our country. The Italian Communist Party is a mass party, as distinguished from some Communist parties based on cadres or militants. We have a membership of nearly 1.7 million. More than half are workers from industry and agriculture. But we also have white-collar members, artisans, intellectuals, doctors, teachers, working women and housewives—the working people in the broadest sense.

*Interview/Time, 6-30:31.*

## Kurt H. Biedenkopf
*General secretary, West German*
*Christian Democratic Union*

1

[On his country's economic recession]: We have sort of lost perspective on the economic possibilities of our system. We now face the need to adjust to realistic expectations of how much wealth our economy can supply and what people have a right to expect of it ... [The current recession is like] being taken off dope. We weren't really like drunkards; we were really doing quite well [before the 1973 oil crisis]. But we have reached the limits of our expansion. We've got to readjust our priorities and that means a debate about what comes first. Our system of social welfare itself—the pensions, health care, rent, education and income subsidies, civil-service benefits—is under test. We are beginning to find out that the system is so expensive it is doubtful whether we can finance it. We didn't really feel it for the last 10 years because there was such a high economic growth rate. We traditionally have had good labor relations and a rather well-structured social system, so we were able to appease social conflict by this distribution of income. But it was a substitute [for good management] ... Growth does not necessarily have to come from

bigger gross national product. It can also come from more efficiency, and that's exactly what we have got to get used to. We must go through the whole social system and analyze and reduce spending in areas where it serves social comfort rather than social need.

*The Washington Post, 9-28:(B)3.*

## Willy Brandt
*Former Chancellor of West Germany*

2

I think detente as a process is not just opening a new chapter in a book. The process has ups and downs. I think the main thing is whether or not the two big powers, the U.S. and the Soviet Union, will go on being interested in taking measures which would avoid nuclear confrontation. I think this is the main thing. Then in addition to it, if we look at the European scene, there is much more exchange than there has been for many years; and even East and West Germany ... are in a better, not in a worse, situation in relation to each other than only a few years ago. We could also look at this Geneva conference on security and cooperation in Europe, which I think will be brought to a conclusion this summer—the largest East/West conference ever held in history—which will bring some progress. So I think as far as Europe is concerned, detente, well it does not lead automatically to better and better conditions, but there is no alternative to it to begin with, and I think it will bring further results.

*TV-radio interview, Washington/*
*"Meet the Press,"*
*National Broadcasting Company, 3-30.*

## Leonid I. Brezhnev
*General Secretary, Communist Party of*
*the Soviet Union*

3

It is difficult to imagine [a lasting peace in Europe while] hotbeds of conflict and potential war [exist] in the Middle East, Southeast Asia and other areas. That is why, simultaneously with the struggle for a lasting peace in Europe, we pay the most serious attention to the strengthening of relations between the Soviet Union and the United States—relations which are so important from the viewpoint of peaceful coexistence and are based on mutually

# WHAT THEY SAID IN 1975

advantageous cooperation. [These relations] are more or less taking a favorable course.

*At Hungarian Communist Party Congress, Budapest, March 18/ The Washington Post, 3-19:(A)26.*

## Seyom Brown
*Senior fellow in political science, Brookings Institution* 1

West Berlin is a classic case in which the language depicting it as vital departs from the reality. In strategic terms, there's nothing vital about possession of West Berlin; we [the U.S.] and the Germans and everyone else could survive without the enclave. But because of the symbol we've made it, if it went, the erosion of morale in Germany and throughout the Western Alliance would be enormous.

*Interview/The National Observer, 6-28:15.*

## Zbigniew Brzezinski
*Director, Research Institute on International Change, Columbia University* 2

I think [U.S.] detente with the Soviet Union is at a plateau, but there have been changes in the nature of that detente. I would say that in terms of the last six years initially in the detente relationship, the United States exercised initiative. I believe that lately, for a variety of reasons, the Soviet Union has been exercising initiative. In fact, the Soviet Union now firmly believes that the detente relationship provides an umbrella under which qualitative, politically qualitative, changes can take place in the West. The Soviets have lately developed a very interesting theory that the center of revolution has returned from the LDCs, from the developing countries, to the West, and the detente provides an umbrella for significant political change as the Soviets have said expressly, in Portugal, in Spain, in Italy, in France. In that sense I believe the detente relationship today is one in which the initiative rests with the Soviets.

*TV-radio interview, Washington/ "Meet the Press," National Broadcasting Company, 5-11.*

## Alastair Buchan
*Former director, International Institute for Strategic Studies, London* 3

I think NATO still is an American vital interest. I say that not simply because I come from a NATO country but because it's one aspect of a complicated economic, financial, energy, cultural and strategic relationship. If the formal political-alliance mechanism was dissolved, then I think it would be extremely difficult for either Europe or the United States to continue to work toward coherent policies on money, energy and world order in general.

*Interview/U.S. News & World Report, 6-30:62.*

## James L. Buckley
*United States Senator, C–New York* 4

The revolutionary campaign of the Portuguese Communist Party has been planned, supported, armed and guided by the Kremlin. If this Communist drive to power should succeed and be consolidated, the strategic implications for the West will be these: The Soviet Navy will acquire basing rights that will render the Mediterranean untenable to the U.S. 6th Fleet. Communist—and by extension, Soviet—control of the Azores will deny the United States basing facilities essential to the airlifting of military supplies to the Middle East, while dramatically restricting existing surveillance of the deployment of Soviet submarines in the Atlantic. Soviet submarines based in Portugal will threaten the sea lanes connecting the United States and its West European NATO allies, who will in effect find themselves squeezed into a strategic vise between Communist East Europe and a Communist Portugal.

*News conference, Washington, March 21/ Los Angeles Times, 3-22:(1)23.*

## Santiago Carrillo
*Secretary general, Communist Party of Spain* 5

We are at the end of the dictatorial regime of [Spanish chief of state Francisco] Franco, but what is not clear is what will come immediately after. Different forces are in motion. On one side are those people who talk of democracy without the participation of the Communists.

On the other side there is the *junta democratica*, which includes Communists, socialists, monarchists, liberals and representatives of all economic and social classes. We want a democratic regime as one understands it in the West, with universal suffrage. You cannot end Fascism with a center-left policy that excludes the Communists. The *junta democratica* is the best solution. If the democratic forces do not come to power in Spain, the country could go the way of Portugal. By that I mean there could be a serious radicalization that could include the young officers of the Spanish Army. That is a great danger because the way to socialism in Western Europe must be democratic.

*Interview, Paris/Time, 7-28:22.*

### Otelo Saraiva de Carvalho
*General, Portuguese Army; Chief of military security*

1

It is becoming impossible to make a socialist revolution [in Portugal] by peaceful means. The armed forces are disposed to enter a harsh road of repression, which until now we have avoided . . . I have just come back from a socialist country [Cuba] and I can tell it is worth the sacrifice.

*Lisbon, July 30/Los Angeles Times, 7-31:(1)12.*

### Frederick Donald Coggan
*Archbishop of Canterbury, England*

2

[Britain] is drifting into chaos. The truth is, we . . . are without anchors. A common enemy in two world wars drew us together in united action—and we defeated him. Another enemy [economic—inflation, unemployment, balance of payments] is at the gates today—and we keep silent.

*News conference/Newsweek, 10-27:89.*

### William Cardinal Conway
*Roman Catholic Primate of All Ireland*

3

I happen to believe in a united Ireland—eventually. But it can only come when the majority of Irish, on both sides of the border, want it . . . [The IRA] campaign of terror can't bomb a million Protestants into a united Ireland.

*People, 10-20:23.*

### Francisco da Costa Gomes
*President of Portugal*

4

I realize that the American people do not take the same view as Europeans on the presence of a Communist party in a coalition government. But I cannot see why it is thought that a party such as the Portuguese Communist Party, which is definitely committed to the [Armed Forces Movement] program, should not form part of the government—all the more so because it represents an important sector, not very extensive but important, of the population of Portugal.

*Interview, Lisbon/
Time, 5-5:41.*

5

Leaving ideologies aside, we must humbly recognize that almost all the people were with our [1974] revolution and that today we have to admit that this is no longer the case. The march of the revolution has accelerated faster than the people have had the capacity to absorb it. It sincerely seems to me that national independence cannot be achieved in the near future by any way that involves antagonizing the West. The freedom, independence and happiness of the Portuguese people require more good sense than idealism, more intelligence than pride, more moderation than brave words.

*Before Armed Forces Movement general
assembly, Lisbon, July 25/
Los Angeles Times, 7-26:(1)9.*

### Alan Cranston
*United States Senator,
D—California*

6

[On Turkey's take-over of U.S. bases in retaliation for the U.S. Congress' embargo of arms as a consequence of Turkey's invasion of Cyprus last year] : Congress is not going to back down because of this. If we can't control how our allies use our arms we shouldn't arm them, particularly when there is a violation of the law and of treaties.

*July 25/
Los Angeles Times, 7-26:(1)8.*

# WHAT THEY SAID IN 1975

### Alvaro Cunhal
*Secretary general,*
*Communist Party of Portugal* 1

There will not be a Communist Portugal in the proximate future. The question could be phrased like this: In the same way that the Soviets did not accept a Czechoslovakia that was escaping from their orbit, how could the U.S. accept that Portugal escapes from its orbit? There is no problem here of a Portugal that escapes from one orbit to go into another orbit. There is no question of a Portugal that makes a move to enter into the Warsaw Pact to be a strategic zone of the Soviet Union against any country. But we are not going to tell our people, "Don't try socialism even if you want it, because those outside will not permit it."

*Interview/Time, 5-5:42.*

2

We Portuguese Communists need the military. A popular front with the Socialists . . . is of no use to us. We have already signed such a pact with the Armed Forces Movement [who run the country]. A popular front is not possible here without the military. The Socialists' mistake was . . . to isolate themselves from the military despite all the votes they received [in the recent election]. We Communists do not accept the game of elections. No, no, no! I could not care less. If you think that the Socialist Party, with its 40 per cent and the Popular Democratic Party with its 27 per cent, constitute a majority, you are mistaken! . . . For me, democracy means getting rid of capitalism, the monopolies. In Portugal there is now no possibility of a democracy like the one you have in West Europe . . . Portugal will not be a country with democratic freedoms and monopolies; it will not be a fellow traveler of your bourgeois democracies, because we will not allow it. Perhaps we will again have a Fascist Portugal. That is a risk which must be run, even though I do not believe it, because I do not believe in a Fascist coup. We Communists can prevent it, thanks to our alliance with the military. We will certainly not have a social democratic Portugal. Never. Make that quite clear, won't you?

*Interview/*
*The Washington Post, 6-27:(A)30.*

### Bulent Ecevit
*Former Premier of Turkey* 3

Our army is politically conscious, but it knows it will lose its military strength and the support of the people if it interferes excessively [in government]. I think the army will refrain from intervention in the future. It found when it intervened in 1971 that it couldn't influence this society any more because it had become too complex. And during our recent six-and-a-half-months' crisis [when Parliament couldn't agree on any government] there were no hints of military intervention.

*The New York Times, 5-3:33.*

### Melih Esenbel
*Foreign Minister of Turkey* 4

[Saying his country is planning to close some or all U.S. bases in Turkey following the U.S. Congress' cutoff of Turkish military aid because of his country's Cyprus policy]: First let me say that your aid is no favor to Turkey. For $90-million—a paltry sum by present-day standards—the U.S. and NATO are getting one of the best security bargains in the world . . . Turkey controls the vital Dardanelles exit from the Black Sea and has permitted the installation of 20 American early-warning, listening and tracking stations. Either some of your [U.S.] Congressmen were not properly briefed, or they have done something irresponsible that has jeopardized the defense posture of the entire Western Alliance . . . We are not interested in aid programs that have expiration deadlines and which say, "If you do not do thus-and-so at the end of a certain time, you will be cut off without military aid" . . . If you want a relationship based on [these] new rules, we would rather end the relationship.

*Interview/Newsweek, 2-24:36.*

### Amintore Fanfani
*Secretary, Christian Democratic Party of*
*Italy; Former Premier of Italy* 5

The U.S. has a natural role as leader of our [Atlantic] Alliance. It has the right to ask its allies to think a bit more about their own situation. It is admirable that the U.S. came forward and on two occasions intervened in defense of the liberty of the world, in World War I and World War II. But can a country carry this burden for its whole history?

*Interview, Rome/Time, 6-2:29.*

1

[On compromise with the increasingly strong Italian Communist Party]: The day that the Christian Democrats accept the historic compromise, they are finished. It would also be the end of free Italy. Even in the case [of a real economic disaster], I would not advise it, because we are always at the central point: Either Communism changes, really changes, and it is no longer Communism; or Communism remains Communism and leads inevitably to a totalitarian regime.

*Interview, Rome/Time, 6-2:29.*

**Garret Fitzgerald**
*Foreign Minister of Ireland*

2

Always in the Protestant community [in Northern Ireland] there was an underlying recognition that ultimately Ireland would be united—and a desire to put it off for as long as possible for a variety of reasons. In the '60s, the belief that this would happen became increasingly acceptable to a minority of Protestants, especially perhaps in the middle classes rather than in the working classes. But then, of course, the events of the last few years and the murderous campaign of the IRA, which has cost 1,100 lives, 300 members of the security forces, several hundred members of the IRA themselves and many hundreds of civilians murdered, either by their activities or by Protestant paramilitary gangs reacting against their activities—this has had a profound effect in Northern Ireland; and certainly the date at which any kind of reunion would be possible has been postponed.

*Interview/*
*The Dallas Times Herald, 2-21:(A)3.*

3

[Arguing in favor of a united Europe]: In the modern world, even the largest European economies are small. Therefore, national objectives and even national sovereignty are best protected by merging interests in a larger unit.

*The Christian Science Monitor, 2-24:(B)12.*

4

[On Ireland's joining the Common Market three years ago]: Relations with Britain have altered considerably. For the first time in our history we're in a position of sufficient equality with Britain and the rest of Europe. The vote to join was the completion of our becoming independent. Our national inferiority complex has lifted. The psychological effect has been quite great.

*The New York Times, 8-3:(1)3.*

**Gerald R. Ford**
*President of the United States*

5

[Criticizing the U.S. Congress' decision to cut off military assistance to Turkey because of its Cyprus policy]: [That action] will seriously impair our relations with a valued ally, and achieve no benefit whatever. It will adversely affect Western security generally, and with serious consequences to the strategic situation in the Middle East. And, most tragically of all, it does nothing to improve the lot of those Cypriots in whose name this Congressional action was supposedly taken.

*At Republican fund-raising dinner, New York,*
*Feb. 13/The Washington Post, 2-14:(A)4.*

6

The United States and the Soviet Union share an interest in lessening tensions and building a more stable relationship. During this process we have never had any illusions. We know that we are dealing with a nation that reflects different principles and is our competitor in many parts of the globe. Through a combination of firmness and flexibility, the United States has in recent years laid the basis of a more reliable relationship founded on mutual interest and mutual restraint. But we cannot expect the Soviet Union to show restraint in the face of the United States weakness or irresolution. As long as I am President, America will maintain its strength, its alliances and its princi-

# WHAT THEY SAID IN 1975

*(GERALD R. FORD)*

ples—as a prerequisite to a more peaceful planet. As long as I am President, we will not permit detente to become a license to fish in troubled waters. Detente must be a two-way street.

*State of the World address, Washington,*
*April 10/The New York Times, 4-11:10.*

1

United States military assistance to an old and faithful ally—Turkey—has been cut off by action of the Congress [as a result of the Cyprus crisis]. This has imposed an embargo on military purchases by Turkey, extending even to items already paid for—an unprecedented act against a friend . . . Our long-standing relationship with Turkey is not simply a favor to Turkey; it is clear and essential mutual interest. Turkey lies on the rim of the Soviet Union and at the gates to the Middle East. It is vital to the security of the eastern Mediterranean, the southern flank of Western Europe and the collective security of the Western Alliance. Our U.S. military bases in Turkey are as critical to our own security as they are to the defense of NATO.

*State of the World address, Washington,*
*April 10/The New York Times, 4-11:10.*

2

Our relations with Western Europe have never been stronger. There are no peoples with whom America's destiny has been more closely linked. There are no peoples whose friendship and cooperation are more needed for the future. For none of the members of the Atlantic Community can be secure, none can prosper, none can advance unless all do so together.

*State of the World address, Washington,*
*April 10/The New York Times, 4-11:10.*

3

Our [U.S.] troops in Europe . . . are a key element in shielding Europe from military attacks or pressures. Present force levels are necessary to maintain a satisfactory conventional military balance between the [Western] Alliance and the Warsaw Pact nations. Unilateral U.S. reductions would upset that balance and

constitute a major political change. The United States has agreed with our allies that there will be no unilateral troop reductions except through mutual negotiations.

*Before Daughters of the American*
*Revolution, Washington, April 15/*
*U.S. News & World Report, 4-28:16.*

4

I am concerned about the Communist element and its influence in Portugal and therefore Portugal's relationship with NATO . . . I don't see how you can have a Communist element significant in an organization . . . formed for the purpose of meeting a challenge by Communist elements from the East.

*Interview, Washington, May 23/*
*U.S. News & World Report, 6-2:18.*

5

[On the North Atlantic Treaty Organization]: We must preserve the quality and integrity of the alliance on the basis of unqualified participation, not on the basis of partial membership or special arrangements. The commitment to collective defense must be complete if it is to be credible. It must be unqualified if it is to be reliable.

*At NATO summit meeting, Brussels, May 29/*
*Los Angeles Times, 5-30:(1)1.*

6

[On the East-West European security agreement which he will soon sign in Helsinki]: The fact that these very different governments can agree, even on paper, to such principles as greater human contacts and exchanges, improved conditions for journalists, reunification of families and international marriages, a freer flow of information and publications, and increased tourism and travel, seems to me a development well worthy of positive and public encouragement by the United States. If it all fails, Europe will be no worse off than it is now. If even a part of it succeeds, the lot of the people in Eastern Europe will be that much better, and the case of freedom will advance at least that far.

*Before European ethnic organization leaders,*
*Washington, July 25/*
*Los Angeles Times, 7-26:(1)7.*

*1*

I am here [at the European Security Conference] because I believe, and my countrymen believe, in the interdependence of Europe and North America—indeed, in the interdependence of the entire family of man . . . And I can say without fear of contradiction that there is not a single people represented here whose blood does not flow in the veins of Americans and whose culture and traditions have not enriched the heritage which we Americans prize so highly . . . To our fellow participants in this conference: My presence here symbolizes my country's vital interest in Europe's future. Our future is bound with yours. Our economic well-being, as well as our security, is linked increasingly with yours. The distance of geography is bridged by our common heritage and our common destiny. The United States therefore intends to participate fully in the affairs of Europe and in turning the results of this conference into a living reality.

*At East-West European Security Conference,*
*Helsinki, Aug. 1/*
*The Washington Post, 8-2:(A)9.*

**Valery Giscard d'Estaing**
*President of France*

*2*

[Saying his country must have its own military force equipped with nuclear weapons]: [France] must be capable of insuring her defense herself, independently, and it must be ourselves who decide in which circumstances to use our arms. . . . to imagine that France could assure her defense independently without nuclear arms is a stupid proposition . . . Up until now—and this was doubtless [an] inheritance from the cold war—the French military concept was one of deployment toward the East. I believe that, in the present hour, the dangers in the world are dangers that can come from all sorts of areas in the world.

*Television address, Paris, March 25/*
*The New York Times, 3-26:5.*

*3*

[Saying the Common Market needs a push toward political unity]: I think we have exhausted the possibility of purely technical and economic steps . . . What we need is some political coordination, and with political coordination we will give a new push to political unity . . . My predecessors were very reserved and doubtful about the possibility of a political role for the EC. But I think times are changing. Now there is a strong desire on the French side to have some kind of political unity or union. Also, the extreme discussions of the past between the integrationists and the supranationalists have diminished. Now there is a more practical approach. And again the challenge we face now is of a political nature.

*Interview, Paris, May 23/Business Week, 6-9:78.*

*4*

We are a very traditionalist country. I belong by education and belief to the French tradition. I am a Catholic. But for a long time I have thought we are backed into a dead-end because we did not accept the necessary evolutions for some basic facts of life—we were not adapting ourselves to social and economic changes. Now, in one year, we have liberalized the divorce and abortion laws. What has pleased me is not so much the fact that we changed the laws and that we now have good legislation, but that what we did was so well accepted by Parliament and public opinion.

*Interview, Paris/*
*San Francisco Examiner & Chronicle, 7-6:(A)30.*

**Barry M. Goldwater**
*United States Senator, R—Arizona*

*5*

[It is] possible to perceive of Western Europe as a hostage to be held against us by the Soviet Union because, relatively speaking, Europe is growing militarily and politically weaker and therefore more militarily dependent upon the United States, and because we at the same time have bound ourselves to Europe by such a tight alliance as the [North Atlantic] pact. We of the United States may have a liability on our hands more than we have an asset . . . It may become more in our interests to deal with each European country on its merit rather than pretending Europe is a united whole. This would give us flexibility. One example of the use of such flexibility might be that of deploying

# WHAT THEY SAID IN 1975

forces, say, to aid our friends and our own interests in the Persian Gulf. The time may be at hand when this is a more important venture for us than protecting a Europe reluctant to protect itself.

*Before the Senate, Washington, June 3/*
*The New York Times, 6-4:12.*

## Vasco dos Santos Goncalves
*Premier of Portugal*

1

The Portuguese revolution is a long-range final goal: the construction of a socialist society. First we have to consolidate democracy with measures in the economic field to combat the power of the monopolies and *latifundiarios* [large land-owners]. Portuguese Fascism and monopolistic capitalism left the country in a state of extreme deterioration. This is the reason for the nationalizations [of banks and insurance companies]. We are aware that we have grave problems to solve along the road we have chosen. We are trying out a new kind of economy in Portugal, even though we still live in a capitalistic system. This creates serious problems for us because we have to manage these new state companies with the human resources we possess.

*Interview/Time, 5-5:40.*

2

[On opposition to his Communist-leaning government]: We are like Germany when there was anti-Semitism. Now it is anti-Communism. Portugal is again facing the danger of Fascism . . . We have never had a better government since the 25th of April [of last year, when the current Administration overthrew the Marcelo Caetano regime].

*At rally, Almada, Portugal, Aug. 18/*
*Los Angeles Times, 8-20:(1)8.*

## W. Averell Harriman
*Former United States Ambassador-at-Large*

3

Our objectives and the Kremlin's are not possible of reconciliation. They want to see the world dominated by dictatorships of the proletariat, a totalitarian system, and we want to see a world controlled by governments that are responsive to the will of their peoples. I felt in 1945 as I feel today—that we ought to do our best to come to agreements in specific situations so as to avoid confrontation as much as we can. That's one of the troubles we have with the talk of detente today. Some people think that suddenly the Russians have become nice people. They aren't nice people, in our sense.

*Interview, Washington/*
*The National Observer, 12-13:12.*

## Enver Hoxha
*First Secretary, Communist Party of Albania*

4

The policy of our country is not the policy of those states with a hundred flags in their pockets. Our People's Republic does not lower its flag either before blackmail and terror, before the ruble or the dollar. Should we follow this just, principled and bold policy or go down on our knees, lick the boots of the American[s] and the Soviets, and become a prostitute state?

*The New York Times, 5-18:(4)3.*

## Jorge Jesuino
*Minister of Information of Portugal*

5

It may have been an error to let the political parties be formed after last April 25 when the army toppled the old dictatorship in the name of democracy. We are not very satisfied with the political parties—any of them, especially the extreme left. They are aggressive; they fight the movement. [The exception is the Communist Party, which] works with diligence and competence.

*News conference, Lisbon, April 10/*
*The Washington Post, 4-11:(A)10.*

## Means Johnston, Jr.
*Admiral, United States Navy;*
*Commander-in-Chief, Allied Forces/*
*Southern Europe*

6

. . . thus far, Turkish military forces are maintaining their normal NATO commitments. However, the recent action taken by the U.S. Congress to terminate military aid to Turkey [because of Turkish policy toward Cyprus] has not only strained U.S.-Turkish relations but also has possible implications for NATO-Turkish ties, and it certainly has contributed significantly to the loss of solidarity in the Southern Region [of Europe]. The termination of U.S. aid and sales to Turkey is bound to degrade the readiness of Turkish forces and therefore NATO as a whole. I sincerely hope the U.S. aid program can be restored as rapidly as possible and that Turkey will remain dedicated to the wisdom of peace and security through our collective Alliance strength.

*Interview, Naples, Italy/*
*U.S. News & World Report, 6-2:22.*

## Juan Carlos I
*King of Spain*

1

[On his assumption of the throne]: Today a new stage starts in the history of Spain. This stage along which we shall advance together has its starting point in peace, in work and in prosperity, the fruit of a common and collective will and strength. The monarchy will be the faithful guardian of this inheritance and will attempt in all moments to maintain the closest relationship with the people. Let us understand with generosity and nobility of spirit that our future will be based on a true consensus of national concord. Let no one believe that his cause will be forgotten; let no one expect an advantage or a privilege. Together we can do everything if to all we give a fair opportunity. I will preserve the laws and see that they are preserved, taking justice as my guiding light and knowing that the service of the people is the end that justifies all my functions. Justice is necessary for liberty with dignity, prosperity and greatness. A just order, equal for all, permits the recognition, within the unity of the kingdom and of the state, of the regional characteristics, as the expression of the diversity of the peoples that constitute the sacred reality of Spain ... A free and modern society requires the participation of all in the decision-making process, in the media, in the different levels of education and in the control of the national wealth. It is a communal enterprise and a government task to make this participation every day truer and more efficient.

*At his investiture, Madrid, Nov. 22/*
*The New York Times, 11-23:(1)2.*

## Janos Kadar
*First Secretary, Communist Party of Hungary*

2

No sort of new dictatorship is about to come [in Hungary]. The old one, the proletarian dictatorship, will persist. People have come to see and know that this is not a bad kind of dictatorship. In it you can live in freedom, bring works about and can earn esteem, if you are an honest person.

*At Hungarian Communist Party Congress,*
*Budapest, March 21/*
*The New York Times, 3-23:(1)19.*

## Eamonn Kennedy
*Irish Ambassador to the United States*

3

What you see in [Northern Ireland] is a social conflict between the descendants of Protestant settlers of the 17th century and the Catholic dispossessed. They may seem to be wearing the badges of religion, but they are actually the badges of caste ... If we were really arguing about religion, it wouldn't be much hope; but if we are arguing about social and economic conditions, we can do something about it.

*Before Overseas Press Club, New York,*
*March 19/Los Angeles Times, 3-20:(1)9.*

## Henry A. Kissinger
*Secretary of State of the United States*

4

There can be no peaceful international order without a constructive relationship between the United States and the Soviet Union—the two nations with the power to destroy mankind. The moral antagonism between our two systems cannot be ignored; it is at the heart of the problem. Nevertheless, we have succeeded in reducing tensions and in beginning to lay the basis for a more cooperative future. The agreements limiting strategic arms, the Berlin agreement, the significant easing of tensions across the heart of Europe, the growing network of cooperative bilateral relations with the Soviet Union—these mark an undeniable improvement over the situation just a few years ago ... The course of improving U.S.-Soviet relations will not always be easy, as the recent Soviet rejection of our trade legislation has

# WHAT THEY SAID IN 1975

demonstrated. It must, nevertheless, be pursued with conviction despite disappointments and obstacles. In the nuclear age there is no alternative to peaceful coexistence.

*Before Los Angeles World Affairs Council,*
*Jan. 24/Vital Speeches, 2-15:259.*

1

The expansion of Soviet military power and its extension around the world is a serious concern to us. The willingness of the Soviet Union to exploit strategic opportunities ... constitutes a heavy mortgage on detente. If detente turns into a formula for more selective exploitation of opportunities, the new trends in U.S.-Soviet relations will be in jeopardy. If our contention in peripheral areas persists—even more, if it becomes exacerbated—the progress achieved in other areas of detente will ultimately be undermined.

*Before World Affairs Council, St. Louis,*
*May 12/Los Angeles Times, 5-13:(1)16.*

2

In a new era of eased confrontation in Europe, the fate of Berlin will determine the future of the efforts to insure security through negotiations and cooperation. As Berlin was the greatest symbol of heroism of the immediate post-war period, it is also the acid test of the period we now hope to enter. Only if Berlin flourishes will detente flourish. Only if you [in Berlin] are secure will Europe be secure. This has been America's attitude for 30 years; it has not changed. On behalf of [U.S.] President Ford and the American people, I reaffirm our historic relationship today.

*West Berlin, May 21/*
*Los Angeles Times, 5-22:(1)15.*

3

[On the minority Communist-leaning government in Portugal]: [The United States] will oppose and speak out against the efforts of a minority that appears to be subverting [last year's] revolution for its own purpose. The Portuguese people should know that we and all the democratic countries of the West are deeply concerned about their future and stand ready

to help a democratic Portugal. [The Soviet Union] should not assume that it has the option, either directly or indirectly, to influence events contrary to the right of the Portuguese people to determine their own future. The involvement of external powers for this purpose in a country which is an old friend and ally of ours, is inconsistent with any principle of European security.

*At Southern Commodity*
*Producers Conference,*
*Birmingham, Alabama, Aug. 14/*
*Los Angeles Herald-Examiner, 8-14:(A)1.*

4

The details of a Cyprus settlement are for the two communities [Greek and Turkish] themselves to decide. However, in keeping with United Nations resolutions which the United States has fully supported, the following principles are believed by my government to be essential: A settlement must preserve the independence, sovereignty and territorial integrity of Cyprus. It must insure that both the Greek Cypriot and the Turkish Cypriot communities can live in freedom and have a large voice in their own affairs. The present dividing lines cannot be permanent; there must be agreed territorial arrangements which reflect the economic requirements of the Greek Cypriot community and take account of its self-respect. There must be provision for the withdrawal of foreign military forces other than those present under the authority of international agreements. And there must be security for all Cypriots; the needs and wishes of the refugees who have been the principal victims and whose tragic plight touches us all must be dealt with speedily and with compassion.

*At United Nations, New York, Sept. 22/*
*The New York Times, 9-23:16.*

5

We are disturbed by the dramatic gains by the [Italian] Communist Party in [local elections in] June. Basically, the United States cannot determine the domestic structure of Italy by its own initiative; basically, the future of Italy is not an American foreign-policy problem. But having said that, the United States hopes very much the Christian Democratic Party, which has been the governing party, revitalizes itself so that it can gain the necessary public support and a coalition can be put together by the democratic parties to prevent the entry into the government of the Communist Party of Italy. Since the impact on NATO [of] having one of the major countries with a major Communist Party participation would be very serious, we're giving Italy as much advice and as much encouragement as we can.

*Before House International Relations
Committee, Washington, Nov. 6/
The New York Times, 11-9:(1)15.*

**Andrew Knight**
*Editor, "The Economist," London*

1

We [the British] are a government of opposition, no matter who is in power.

*Interview/
"W": a Fairchild publication, 9-19:2.*

**Joseph Luns**
*Secretary General, North Atlantic
Treaty Organization*

2

We [in NATO] are following events in Portugal [last year's coup and the current leftist government] with understandable interest, and I must confess a certain preoccupation. Democracy has not been as strong as we would want to see it, but progress has not yet been abandoned. If we are faced with an eventuality of a situation of Communists in domination, then we will have to consult on a course of action; and I am sure it will be clear enough if we do reach such a situation. In the meantime, it is business as usual and Portugal is participating fully and normally in the work of NATO.

*News conference, Brussels, May 28/
Los Angeles Times, 5-29:(1)14.*

3

[Calling for an end to the U.S. arms embargo against Turkey]: I have not come to pressure the American government, which is master of its own house. I have come to express the NATO point of view, which is that the arms ban has become a festering sore on the political

and military body of the alliance. NATO has been badly weakened by it.

*News conference, Washington/
Los Angeles Herald-Examiner, 9-14:(A)12.*

4

[NATO foreign] ministers cannot afford, I believe, to overlook what is happening away from the conference table—how the arsenal of the Soviets is constantly being strengthened across the board and particularly at sea, and how they choose to behave in the world at large.

*News conference, Brussels/
Los Angeles Herald-Examiner, 12-11:(A)2.*

**Makarios III**
*President of Cyprus*

5

[Saying Greek Crypriots will not accept the establishment of a separate autonomous Turkish Cypriot state]: We shall resist, we shall struggle, we shall sacrifice ourselves if necessary, but we shall not yield. We will on no account recognize *faits accomplis* ... Your demonstrations are an expression of the determination of the Greeks of Cyprus not to succumb to the force of Turkish arms.

*At rally, Nicosia, Feb. 14/
The Washington Post, 2-15:(A)1.*

6

Turkey is trying to create the impression [that] the substance of the [Cyprus] problem is confined to differences between Greek and Turkish Cypriots over the constitutional structure of their state. The real problem is the Turkish aggression, the seizure [in 1974] and continued occupation of a large part of Cyprus territory, the displacement and transformation of 200,000 Greek Cypriots into refugees, the appropriation of Greek properties, brutalities and other similar acts.

*On first anniversary of Turkish invasion
of Cyprus, Nicosia, July 20/
Los Angeles Times, 7-21:(1)6.*

**Sam Nunn**
*United States Senator, D–Georgia*

7

Other than the defense of North America, no security interest is more important to the

329

# WHAT THEY SAID IN 1975

*(SAM NUNN)*

United States than the defense of Europe. Europe is the ancestral home for most Americans, and we remain tied together by history. We share the same sources of civilization, spiritual commitments and views about democracy and the preservation of free society. Beyond these strong historical and cultural ties lie some equally important economic realities... For these reasons, few would argue with me when I say that a major U.S. interest is to help preserve a strong and free Europe. However, some have suggested that detente with the Soviet Union has reduced the importance of NATO. I don't agree with this assessment. While detente is a desirable goal and while we want to ease tensions with the Russians and other potential adversaries throughout the world, we cannot forget that the Soviet goal of defeating Western democracy has never been renounced. Detente should be pursued by the West, but it should be defined as an easing of tensions, not as the arrival of the millenium.

*Before NATO chiefs of staff/*
*The Washington Post, 5-29:(A)18.*

## Conor Cruise O'Brien
*Irish diplomat; Minister for Posts and*
*Telegraphs of the Republic of Ireland*     *1*

If Britain withdrew [its troops] from Northern Ireland now, the result would be a shattering civil war bringing disastrous consequences on all parts of the country and on all sections of the population... This is a small country, much afflicted by ballads and by persons shooting and bombing their way to a place in the ballads-to-be. I have developed a resistance to romanticism, an aversion to the ballad form, a horror of the manic passages in the poetry of Yeats, and a tendency to see the influence of literature over politics as a contagion to be eradicated where possible.

*The New York Times, 6-22:(4)15.*

## Shimon Peres
*Minister of Defense of Israel*     *2*

When the Soviets play in any part of the world, it is part of their play for the rest of the world. I don't think the Soviets ever gave up their ambition to run the world—to bless it with Communist perfume and organize it with Soviet discipline.

*Interview, Jerusalem/*
*U.S. News & World Report, 4-7:17.*

## Nikolai V. Podgorny
*President of the Soviet Union*     *3*

[The Soviet Union] is prepared to take new political steps to further improve our relations with the United States, France, the Federal Republic of [West] Germany and other capitalist states, to consolidate the achievements made and to make the process of detente irreversible and to insure that it spreads not only to all zones of the world and not only to the main spheres of world politics and economics, but also to the military field. The post-war years have shown clearly that the best battlefield is the conference table. The meetings of Leonid Brezhnev and other Soviet leaders with the statesmen of the United States, France, the Federal Republic of Germany and other capitalist countries and the constructive agreements reached as a result of them, confirmed in practice the feasibility of detente and the possibility of businesslike cooperations despite differences in ideological concepts and political views.

*Izvestia newspaper article*/*
*The New York Times, 2-13:9.*

## Peter Ramsbotham
*British Ambassador to the United States*     *4*

What is Britain like as a country to live in? Well, it is still a humane and civilized country. We are not a violent society. Our police are unarmed. People can walk the streets at night. Our physical environment remains largely unspoilt. Our rivers and air are certainly cleaner than for centuries because of our stringent controls. The British cultural scene is as lively as it ever was. And underpinning the whole structure is our democratic system. Parliamentary democracy is so deep-rooted, so flexible in its operation and so firm in its purpose that it would need a cataclysm far greater than our present economic difficulties to shake it. Curiously enough, despite our economic problems, despite inflation and unemployment, the British are not unhappy. A few months ago, the European Community in Brussels, of which Britain is a member . . . carried out a study to find out which nation in the Community was happiest, less discontented. And who headed the poll? The British. I think this may partly be because we have a strong sense of history—and in a paradoxical way, because of that historical sense, we are not over-nostalgic. We knew that the past—however glorious, however exciting— was not necessarily better than today. Indeed, for most people it was a good deal worse.

*Before Economic Club, Detroit,*
*April 21/Vital Speeches, 6-1:498.*

**Ronald Reagan**
*Former Governor of California (R)*
                                                    *1*

[On the sale of U.S. wheat to the Soviet Union]: We and our free-world allies should face the question whether we are not contributing to the slavery of their [the Soviets'] own people as well as a danger to ourselves by bailing out their creaking, incompetent system when it finds itself in trouble. Would they without our help have to abandon arms-building in order to feed their people or face the possibility of an uprising and revolution by a desperate and hungry populace? If the answer is "yes," then we are faced with a question of national security and pure moral principle.

*At Republican fund-raising dinner,*
*Anaheim, Calif., Dec. 11/*
*Los Angeles Times, 12-12:(2)1.*

**Merlyn Rees**
*British Secretary of State for*
*Northern Ireland*

I will not be influenced by any views which are backed with threats of the bomb and the bullet. I share the feeling of outrage and disappointment of the people of Northern Ireland that the Provisional IRA have . . . shown a total lack of concern for the people's clear call for an end to violence.

*San Francisco Examiner & Chronicle,*
*1-26:(This World)15.*

**Elliot L. Richardson**
*United States Ambassador to*
*the United Kingdom*
                                                    *3*

Eccentricity tends to be prized in Britain rather than being a source for derision. The British pomp and circumstance combine in a unique way the attributes of dignity and informality which in itself is indicative of a highly evolved civilization.

*Interview/*
*"W": a Fairchild publication, 9-5:4.*

**Nelson A. Rockefeller**
*Vice President of the United States*
                                                    *4*

[Criticizing the Congressionally voted U.S. cut-off of military aid to Turkey because of Turkey's policy in last year's Cyprus crisis]: Now, if I were a Turk and had built my army totally on American weapons and spare parts and was dependent on them and had paid cash for delivery of weapons, and then got cut off when I was trying to defend a minority of mine who had really been having a rough time on an island, I'd have to think twice [about U.S. relations and commitments].

*Interview, en route to Taipei, Taiwan,*
*April 15/The Washington Post, 4-16:(A)10.*

**Joao Tomaz Rosa**
*Member, ruling Armed Forces Movement, and*
*head of the Ministry of Labor, of Portugal*
                                                    *5*

There is absolutely no possibility of Portugal becoming a Soviet base. Foreigners say the Armed Forces Movement is led by Communists. It is just not true. We are not ideologists, but idealists. I don't think there is one member of the Revolutionary Council who sympathizes with the Communist Party—farther down, yes . . . The primary reason for our movement was Portugal's colonial war, and the concrete life of Portugal. We were saturated with war, with death, and we saw a great country like the United States could end its colonial war in Vietnam. Why should we, a small country, continue such a war? We saw Portugal was isolated because of the war, because of Fascism, and that the West only wanted a calm Portugal. For them we were like a farm—interesting only for

# WHAT THEY SAID IN 1975

*(JOAO TOMAZ ROSA)*

strategic value and vacations. At home we had too many poor, and an impoverished middle class, four hundred rich families and much misery. Those are the reasons for the movement . . . We are not a regime that will import political systems. We want neither a socialism of the East nor a socialism of the West. We have an idea of a *via socializante* [socialistic path], not socialism as such. We are not Eastern and not Western, but a Euro-African people with a universal vocation—our overseas traditions, our geographic location on the Atlantic shore. I think Portugal will stay in the North Atlantic Treaty Organization and participate in the defenses of the Atlantic. Not even responsible people of the Communist Party want to quit NATO.

*Interview, Washington, March 24/*
*The New York Times, 5-25:3.*

## Pierre Salinger
*Journalist, "L'Express," Paris; Former*
*Press Secretary to the President of the*
*United States (John F. Kennedy)*　　　1

. . . despite the talk of our [the U.S.'] diminished credibility, the Europeans tend to think of the United States as a more reliable ally, with Vietnam over, than we were before. There's always a hard core of anti-U.S. feeling over here, on the left and on the far right. But there is a great middle section of the spectrum that is very sympathetically disposed. I lecture a lot, at youth groups, on campuses, at Rotary Clubs, and I don't feel that hostility that you might once have expected.

*Interview, Cannes, France/*
*Los Angeles Times, 5-27:(4)1.*

2

. . . in the eyes of Europeans, [U.S. President] Ford appears to be a nice, weak President. There's no great regard for him here. By contrast, [former U.S. President Richard] Nixon was considered a hero . . . Europeans liked Nixon because of the force with which he exerted his foreign policy, even though this was sometimes at their expense. Europe is schizophrenic vis-a-vis the United States. They're

unhappy when a strong United States intrudes in their affairs, and they are unhappy if the U.S. is too weak to assert its real role in the world.

*Interview, Paris/*
*San Francisco Examiner & Chronicle,*
*6-8:(This World)20.*

## Erwin Schech
*Professor of sociology and economics,*
*University of Cologne (West Germany)*　　3

[On why the hopes of a united Europe are fading]: It is because we ask so much more of government now. We ask it to provide not only peace and prosperity but social justice, welfare, good-quality environment, happiness. There aren't any international organs for that. They do not exist. So we turn back to the only effective governments we have—national government.

*The New York Times, 3-23:(1)20.*

## James R. Schlesinger
*Secretary of Defense of the United States*　　4

In the case of Western Europe, a number of the nations over there have enjoyed American protection and have felt they have had virtually a free ride with regard to their own defenses. It's less of an issue of whether the United States is inclined to abandon Europe than whether the Europeans are inclined to abandon themselves . . . The propensity has existed in Western Europe to base their defense budgets on hope, on illusion, on the prospects of arms reductions by the East. Many of them have wanted to cut their defense expenditures to respond to various naive impulses within their electorates. That trend will have to be curbed. The assumption that U.S. protection in and of itself relieves some European states of building forces in their own behalf is something that disappeared with the growth of Soviet military capability in recent years. At this stage of the game, the European nations must take defense very seriously. They cannot be driven primarily by domestic political or budgetary considerations.

*Interview, Washington/*
*U.S. News & World Report, 5-26:26.*

**James R. Schlesinger**
*Former Secretary of Defense of the
United States*
1

[On Soviet policy in Europe]: I think if you look at the situation in Portugal, if you look at the attitude toward the Communist parties in France and Italy, if you look at the pressures that are being applied to Norway, if you look at what has been happening in Berlin—in which the Soviets clearly are whittling away the obligations into which they entered in the Four Power Agreement—that, in Europe, you have serious causes for concern. And one might add to that, that over the last decade the Soviets have dramatically improved their conventional-force posture in Eastern Europe, adding 140,000 men, roughly, to their deployments in Europe . . . All of these, I think, are indications of a nation that is not as yet willing to live and let live.

*TV-radio interview, Washington/
"Meet the Press,"
National Broadcasting Company, 11-23.*

**Helmut Schmidt**
*Chancellor of West Germany*
2

Thirty years after the end of the Second World War, and 25 years after the establishment of the two German states, no one can any longer ignore the reality of their existence. The fact that they exist simultaneously governs to a large extent the state of the German nation. There are many questions over which the two German states are at odds. But they also have many things in common. They both call themselves German—no other state in the world calls itself German. The Germans do not want to—and if anyone wanted to they could—deny that they belong to the German nation . . . That is why the relationship between the two German states has, in our view, a special character indeed. We stick to this view even if the leadership of the GDR mistakenly regard this as an attempt by the Federal Republic to impose an inferior status on the GDR. The Federal government is of the opinion that recognizing the special nature of the relationship with the GDR does not constitute an attempt to meddle with

the latter's sovereignty but merely underlines the fact that Germans live in both states and that we Germans are entitled to determine our national destiny according to our own free will. This is the conviction by which the Federal government will continue to operate.

*Before Bundestag, Bonn, Jan. 30/
Vital Speeches, 3-15:322.*

3

One thing stands out vis-a-vis the rest of Europe [and West Germany]. That is the role of the German trade union movement. There is only one labor federation here, as compared with two or three rival associations in some countries. And in this single federation there are only about 16 large unions as compared with up to a hundred, often competing, elsewhere. And our unions have a much greater and more useful influence than in most nations. They have gained experience over the years and they have behaved well. Also, governments have been granting an ever-greater role to the unions. This is beneficial to workers, to enterprises and to the national economy as a whole . . . In Italy, Belgium and Britain—to name but a few—the number of strike days lost to production is far higher than in Germany. Strikes are rare here. Our unions prefer to negotiate and compromise. And, as a consequence, they have gained higher real wages than in any other European country. Restrained functioning of our unions has paid off in wages for workers and in calm for our society. This is very different from the behavior of many unions in Europe or in the U.S.A.

*Interview, Bonn/
The New York Times, 5-28:37.*

4

[On the current East-West European security conference]: Progress in reducing tensions depends far more on how far we can use this common base for practical steps which will justify the hopes of peoples. This conference could soon be forgotten if all of us fail to work hard to ensure that these hopes are in fact fulfilled. This conference has not created any new international law for Europe. But we have created common rules for the way we in Europe want to associate and live together with one another.

*At Conference of Security and Cooperation in Europe, Helsinki, July 30/ Los Angeles Times, 7-31:(1)1.*

### Eric Sevareid
*News commentator, Columbia Broadcasting System (United States)* 1

[Britain is America's] closest ally, always regarded as the strongest and most reliable. But it's a serious question whether it can be so regarded any longer. It is not merely that her military strength is ebbing and her economic strength weakening, but that Britain is drifting slowly toward a condition of ungovernability. It is now a debatable question whether Parliament, or the great trade unions, are calling the political tune. The country, as one English writer puts it, is sleepwalking into a social revolution, one its majority clearly does not want but does not know how to stop ... In the last year, the cost of living rose some 21 per cent, but average wages by 32 per cent, and worker productivity steadily falls, as does business investment. The city of London is financially broke. Property taxes rose by 75 per cent in two years. Thousands of middle-class people move out of the city every year, like New York. Unemployment, Britain's special nightmare, rises steadily, and great corporations are insolvent, one after another ... The powerful Communist influence in trade-union leadership is no longer disputed. What do they want? Not a Communist Britain in the foreseeable future; much more likely a chronically weak, dispirited Britain, able to play no effective role in the world or the [Atlantic] Alliance. That would suit very nicely the long-range strategies of the Soviet Union.

*CBS News commentary/ The National Observer, 5-17:21.*

### Mario Soares
*Leader, Socialist Party of Portugal* 2

[On his country's Communist-leaning government]: ... we are a European country and we can never forget this circumstance. We are integrated in the European labor market by a million emigrants who are in Europe and who have links with Portugal; they send funds home which represent half our budget. We are also linked through trade, 80 per cent of which is with Western Europe. If we severed relations with Europe, Portugal could not survive. Portugal is not Cuba. Our geographical position puts us at the crossroads of the Mediterranean and the Atlantic. I do not think that the European countries could bear the idea that Portugal might fall into a Communist dictatorship. This would change the geostrategic stance of Europe and the world and would damage the policy of European security.

*Interview/ Time, 5-5:41.*

3

What divides millions of Portuguese is not the building of socialism, not the construction of a society which does away with exploiters and the exploited. What divides us is the building of the state: whether it is constructed from a single party and in an authoritarian way—that is, Stalinist—or whether it is constructed from a new pluralistic and democratic experience which also calls for a real direct democracy and solutions pointing to self-sufficiency ... One conception takes into account the Portuguese geopolitical conditioning leading toward national independence and a democratic organization of the state, with a large social base made up of the petite bourgeoisie and the middle classes. The other [the Stalinist] conception leads inexorably to a totalitarian state and to Portugal's abrogating her system of current alliances and falling into the orbit of the Eastern bloc through a necessarily repressive route. Such a course has very limited popular support ... The Socialists obviously adhere to the first solution. It is tragic that the Communists do not. They remain dependent, at least for now, on groups allied with the far left, which accentuates their anarco-populism and would destroy the apparatus of the state—with terrible consequences for the Portuguese economy.

*Interview/ Los Angeles Times, 8-14:(2)7.*

**Alexander I. Solzhenitsyn**
*Exiled Soviet author*

*1*

Something which is almost incomprehensible to the human mind is the West's fantastic greed for profit and gain, which goes beyond all reason, all limitations, all conscience. I have to admit that Lenin foretold this whole process. Lenin, who spent most of his life in the West and knew it much better than Russia, always said that the Western capitalists would do anything to supply the Soviet economy—"They will fight with each other to sell us goods cheaper and sell them quicker so that we'll buy from one rather than from the other." And in the difficult moments of a Party meeting in Moscow, he said: "Comrades, don't worry when things are hard with us. When things are difficult, we will give a rope to the *bourgeoisie* and the *bourgeoisie* will hang itself with this rope." Then, Karl Radek, a witty fellow you may have heard of, said: "Vladimir Ilyich, where are we going to get enough rope to hang the whole *bourgeoisie?*" Lenin said immediately: "They'll supply us with it." Nikita Khrushchev came here and said: "We're going to bury you [the West]." People didn't believe that—they took it as a joke. Now, of course, the Communists have become more clever in my country. They do not say, "We're going to bury you" any more. Now they say, "Detente." Nothing has changed in Communist ideology. The goals are the same as they were.

*Before AFL-CIO, Washington, June 30/*
*U.S. News & World Report, 7-14:44.*

**Antonio de Spinola**
*Former President of Portugal*

*2*

[On the current Portuguese political situation]: I cannot envision democracy unless it be parliamentary and multi-party, although it must be essentially Portuguese in its implementation and objectives, and exceedingly just in its economic and social development. Any other way will only continue to deceive us into seeing as democratic what, at the end of the day, is a badly disguised neo-Fascism.

*Interview, Lisbon, January/*
*The Washington Post, 3-14:(A)18.*

**Margaret Thatcher**
*Member of British Parliament;*
*Leader, British Conservative Party*

*3*

If a Tory [Conservative] does not believe that private property is one of the main bulwarks of individual freedom, then he had better become a socialist and have done with it. Indeed, one of the reasons for our electoral failure is that people believe that too many Conservatives have become socialists already. Britain's progress toward socialism has been an alternation of two steps forward with half a step back.

*Time, 2-24:30.*

*4*

[On the just-announced Labor-government budget which provides for higher income taxes]: In my experience, I have never listened to a budget which put so much extra tax on the British people at one go. It is a typical socialist budget—equal shares of misery for all.

*April 15/Los Angeles Times, 4-16:(1)4.*

*5*

Look back to that very creative age, the Victorian. It was an age when people built; it was a very constructive age. What did it have that we didn't? First, stability in the value of money. Second, a tremendous faith in a free society. Third, faith in the future of Britain. That's the kind of thing we've got to restore. The British people haven't changed. All the qualities that made us great are still there. All the potentialities, too. It is our task to restore those potentialities. We can do it. We shall do it.

*Sheffield, England/*
*The Christian Science Monitor, 4-17:16.*

*6*

[Criticizing Prime Minister Harold Wilson's social and economic policies]: We are witnessing a deliberate attack on our values, a deliberate attack on those who wish to promote merit and excellence, a deliberate attack on our heritage and our great past. We must not be bullied and brainwashed out of our beliefs. No wonder so many of our people—some of our best and brightest—are depressed and talk of emigrating . . . [Many Labor Party M.P.s] seem

# WHAT THEY SAID IN 1975

anxious not to overcome our economic difficulties, but to exploit them, to destroy the free-enterprise society and put a Marxist system in its place ... We are all *un*equal. No one, thank heavens, is like anyone else, however much the socialists may pretend otherwise. If the adventurers who strike out in new directions in science, technology, medicine, commerce and industry are hobbled, there can be no advance. Everyone must be allowed to develop the abilities he knows he has within him in the way he chooses.

*At Conservative Party conference,*
*Blackpool, England, Oct. 10/*
*The New York Times, 10-11:5.*

## Stansfield Turner
*Admiral, United States Navy;*
*Commander-in-Chief, Southern Europe,*
*North Atlantic Treaty Organization*                    1

NATO has been in business since 1949, and for 26 years we have successfully withstood the military challenge of the Soviet Union and the Warsaw Pact countries in this area. These successes, in fact, have been responsible for detente itself. I don't think an American President would be going to Russia or [Communist] China were it not for allied strength. The cornerstone of detente is an adequate military defense ... Allied interests and American interests are closely bound to Mediterranean countries. We must not slip behind the power curve—or let our strength atrophy. And we must renew our sense of urgency in order to maintain the strength that preserves our freedom.

*Interview, Naples, Italy/*
*Los Angeles Times, 10-25:(1)18.*

## George C. Wallace
*Governor of Alabama (D)*                    2

Frankly, I think [U.S.] detente [with the Soviet Union] has been a failure. While we're detenting with them, the Soviets are still arming groups all over the world. On the other hand, they get our latest computer techniques. The best way to have good relations with Russia is to be so strong militarily that they will want to

talk with you. The best way to get along with them is, when you sit down at the table, they know they're looking at a nation that's strong.

*Interview, Montgomery, Alabama/*
*U.S. News & World Report, 5-26:49.*

## Harold Wilson
*Prime Minister of the United Kingdom*                    3

[On the just-concluded national vote in which, by a margin of 67 per cent to 33 per cent, the British people elected to remain in the Common Market]: Their verdict has been given by a majority bigger than that achieved by any government in any general election in the history of our democracy. No one in Britain, in Europe, or the wider world should have any doubts about its meaning. It meant that 14 years of national argument are over.

*London, June 6/*
*Los Angeles Times, 6-7:(1)6.*

4

[On the East-West European security agreement]: The documents we are about to approve cannot in themselves diminish the tension and insecurity which have affected the peoples as well as the governments of Europe since the end of the war [World War II]. But they do represent more than good intentions, more than a desire to set our relations on a new course. They are a moral commitment to be ignored at our mutual peril, and the start of a new chapter in the history of Europe.

*At Conference of Security and Cooperation*
*in Europe, Helsinki, July 30/*
*Los Angeles Times, 7-31:(1)1.*

5

We [Britain] haven't got vast military forces, though we make a bigger contribution to NATO than anyone of our size and spend more of our GNP on defense than any other European country. Our contribution is now experience. [Former U.S. President] Nixon used to say to me ... "If it's an African question, we'll ask you because you have so much more experience than we have." Modestly, I'm not speaking for myself or even my Cabinet, but certainly our parliamentarians and administrators are trained to deal with these problems. We can do more in that way, perhaps, than we were doing with defense.

*Interview/Time, 8-4:35.*

1

[On his country's current economic difficulties]: Everyone on both sides of industry must recognize that you can't take out of industry more than you put in. That means that restraint on incomes is not of itself enough. With it must go harder work, work better organized, and, through more and better-directed investment, more machine-power at the worker's elbow. This year justice will be rough, but justice will be there nonetheless. It is the government's duty to ensure that however rough the going—there will be justice. If we failed now, the going would become increasingly rough, with precious little justice left to share out. We now have a better chance to conquer the evil of recurrent inflation than at any time in the last 30 years. The country is alerted and determined. There is a consensus in industry, and between industry and government. And, since we know that by the end of the '70s our national economic position can be transformed by our North Sea oil assets, the sacrifices we make now can lead to a new era for our people. The prospects for our country if we were to fail would be grim indeed. But I do not believe we will fail. Inflation may well take years to eliminate, but by working together I believe that by this time next year a crucial advance will be seen to have been made. That is why I ask that the next year be a year for Britain—for Britain, by all of us, the people of Britain.

*Broadcast address to the nation, Aug. 20/*
*Vital Speeches, 10-1:746.*

2

[Saying American supporters of the IRA are responsible for the terrorism in Northern Ireland]: The fact is that most of the modern weapons now reaching the terrorists in Northern Ireland are of American origin—possibly as much as 85 per cent of them. They are bought in the United States, and they are bought with American-donated money ... Those who subscribe to the Irish Northern Aid Committee are not financing the welfare of the Irish people, as they might delude themselves. They are financing murder. When they contribute their dollars for the old country, they are not helping their much-loved shamrock to flower. They are splashing blood on it. Nor are they helping the minority Catholic population.

*Before Association of American*
*Correspondents in London, Dec. 17/*
*The New York Times, 12-18:16.*

# The Middle East

**Yigal Allon**
*Foreign Minister of Israel*                                    1

I don't think there is a crisis between [the U.S. and Israel], but I begin to feel some indication about the possibility of pressure on Israel. I think it would be good to tell our friends in the United States that any compromise which Israel is ready to make within the context of a political agreement will be done without any pressure. And any compromise which Israel cannot afford, from a security point of view, will not be conceded even under pressure.

*News conference, Tel Aviv, April 13/*
*The Washington Post, 4-14:(A)11.*

2

[On the new Sinai accord between his country and Egypt, and the U.S. role in that agreement]: . . . I don't see why Americans should be concerned about the growing role of the United States in the Middle East. On the contrary, I think they should be pleased with the fact that, after many years of Soviet progress in the area, the U.S. is again becoming the major power in the Mediterranean and the Middle East. Now, in the Sinai, the U.S. was not invited to send troops, nor was she asked to undertake any military role in separating the forces between Israel and Egypt. If Congress approves, America will play a very important role in a mission of peace within the framework of the early-warning systems. In the passes, American civilians will serve, jointly, Israel as well as Egypt. They are not expected to interfere or get involved in any possible conflict. The American President has the full right to remove the American personnel whenever he thinks they are somehow in danger, their lives in jeopardy, or if it serves American interests. I would say that Americans can be proud of the fact that two conflicting countries, at war for 28 years, found it possible to invite one power to station between them, even in a civilian manner.

*Interview, Jerusalem/*
*U.S. News & World Report, 9-15:34.*

**Idi Amin**
*President of Uganda*                                           3

Without the United States of America there would be no Israel. The United States' persistent support for Israel stems from this sad history of colonization. The United States of America has been colonized by the Zionists, who hold all the tools of development and power. They own virtually all the banking institutions, the major manufacturing and processing industries, the major means of communications, and have so much infiltrated the CIA that it has become a murder squad.

*At United Nations, New York, Oct. 1/*
*Los Angeles Times, 10-2:(1)16.*

**Yasir Arafat**
*Chairman, Palestine Liberation Organization*      4

Why do you ask me about recognizing Israel? Why do you ask me about guarantees for Israel? Why don't you ask Israel about guarantees for Palestinians? We Palestinians have lost our home and our lands. We are refugees without rights in our own land. I don't even have a passport. The question is whether Israel recognizes *us*. The question is whether the United States cares about fundamental human liberties.

*Interview, Beirut/*
*The Washington Post, 4-1:(A)15.*

5

[Criticizing the new Sinai accord between Egypt and Israel]: This plot shall collapse under the unshaken will of the Palestinian people. Wrong are the United States and Israel if they believe the Egyptian Army would stand idly by should the Palestinian revolution be struck down. No Arab ruler is capable of conceding one inch of Arab land to Israel. We shall continue to fight and fight and fight until we bring off the miracle and win back our land. There will never be an American peace in the Middle East. Peace can only be made by the Palestinians. Let us all unite and stand one rank and one gun against the United States and against the U.S. presence in the area.

*On being presented with medal by World Peace Council, Beirut, Sept. 1/*
*Los Angeles Herald-Examiner, 9-2:(A)2.*

1

Criticizing the new Sinai agreement between Egypt and Israel and the U.S. role in the agreement] : . . . the so-called price the U.S. is paying for a minimal Israel withdrawal from a few miles of desert is the most modern arsenal supplied to any foreign country since you [the U.S.] flooded South Vietnam with weapons at the end of 1972 . . . It is too much for too little . . . At this rate it will take 50 years and several more wars before we [Arabs] recover the [Israeli-occupied] territories, and America will be bankrupt long before . . . the Arab people will not be able to accept, even less digest, an agreement that ignores completely and does not even take into consideration the rights of the Palestinian people, now recognized by 105 nations. In fact, it goes out of its way to avoid the heart of the whole Middle East conflict . . . you Americans seem to have forgotten how your whole involvement began in Vietnam after the French defeat at Dienbienphu in 1954—just a handful of "experts and advisers." Objectively speaking, the circumstances are admittedly different. Yet the pattern has many similarities. You will now be involved inside an Arab country as part of a partial settlement, not on the frontiers between two states as part of a final settlement.

*Interview, Beirut/Newsweek, 9-15:35.*

**Hafez al-Assad**
*President of Syria*

2

[On Israeli demands for secure borders]: With modern weapons, there are no secure borders. The Israelis are not serious. In 1967 they occupied the Golan Heights. They said it was to protect their settlements. In 1973 they pushed the Syrian Army about 17 kilometers in the

north and 25 in the south. The range of our artillery is 30 kilometers, so the Syrian Army can still shell their settlements. And now they have built new settlements. If we are to pursue their logic, after a while they will ask for new secure borders to protect their new settlements. That is why I believe they are interested in expansion.

*Interview, Damascus/*
*Time, 2-3:39.*

3

If the Israelis return to the 1967 frontier—*and* the West Bank and Gaza become a Palestinian state—the last obstacle to a final settlement will have been removed . . . When everything is settled, it will have to be formalized with a formal peace treaty. This is not propaganda. We mean it—seriously and explicitly . . . This is not a new logic in Syria's policy; it is our fundamental position, decided by party leaders . . . If [however] American guarantees [for Israeli security] should be made before complete withdrawal and the recognition of Palestinian rights, the only result would be deep and lasting hostility between the Arabs and America. And in my assessment, these sorts of guarantees, short of a final settlement, would make the U.S., in effect, a co-occupier of Arab land. Under these conditions, you [the U.S.] would never be able to have friends in the Arab world.

*Interview/Newsweek, 3-3:34.*

4

[On whether the U.S. must have contacts with the PLO]: If we all agree that peace cannot be established without a just solution of the Palestine question, and taking into consideration that the Arabs are unanimous in regarding the PLO as the sole legitimate representative of the people of Palestine, and if the United States wants to push forward the process of peace, it is obvious in these circumstances that a contact with the PLO is inevitable. This is only logical.

*Interview/The Washington Post, 3-5:(A)10.*

5

[The new Sinai agreement between Egypt and Israel] is a step backward from peace, and it will precipitate the next crisis . . . It ignores the nature of the conflict by attempting to divide the problem into separate compart-

*(HAFEZ al-ASSAD)*

ments ... Egypt's agreement to end the state of belligerency and allow Israeli goods through the [Suez] Canal should have been conceded only in return for a complete withdrawal [by Israel] from the occupied [Arab] territories and the achievement of Palestinian rights ... The billions you [the U.S.] are giving Israel for a few miles of Arab land will only encourage Israeli arrogance and intransigence ... The U.S. has become a direct party in the Arab-Israel conflict. This is not in the Arab interest and certainly not in the U.S. interest.

*Interview, Damascus/Newsweek, 9-22:39.*

1

It seems to us now that the policy of the United States has three goals: to strengthen Israel, to weaken the Arab nation and to divide it, and to weaken or eliminate Soviet influence in the Middle East. The pursuit of these goals makes it difficult, if not impossible, to accomplish a just and lasting peace in this area, and the goals explain why so little has been achieved since the [Arab-Israeli] war of October, 1973.

*Interview, Damascus, Sept. 27/*
*The New York Times, 9-28:(1)17.*

2

[On the U.S.' cool attitude toward the PLO]: My first reaction is sorrow that a superpower with special responsibility for world peace and immense interests in this region ties its decisions to those of Israel. Particularly because the PLO is recognized by the great majority of world countries as the sole legitimate representative of the Palestinian people, who are at the core of the Middle East problem. Israeli propaganda tries to make people believe Israel should not negotiate with the PLO because the PLO does not recognize Israel and intends to destroy it. How can we ask a displaced people to take the initiative in recognizing those who displace them?

*Interview, Damascus/Time, 12-8:27.*

**Shlomo Avineri**
*Dean, social sciences faculty,*
*Hebrew University, Jerusalem*

3

There is a growing body of opinion in intellectual circles here that Israel would be better off trying to negotiate directly with the Arabs rather than rely on [U.S. Secretary of State Henry] Kissinger as an intermediary. This opinion holds that there is a fundamental clash between Israel's regional interests and America's global interests, and that the price of Kissinger's intermediary services is that Israel must subjugate too many of its own basic interests out of deference to Washington.

*The Washington Post, 3-13:(A)32.*

**Charles G. Bluhdorn**
*Chairman, Gulf & Western Industries*

4

We are today confronted with a very critical situation. The Shah [of Iran] and the sheiks are playing a very shrewd, successful game. On the one hand, they raise oil prices by 400 per cent, and on the other, when they have debilitated the economies of the Western world, they proceed to pick the depressed pieces at a fraction of their value. In other words, they are using our money, which they accumulated at blackmail levels, to buy our own country's assets at 10 cents on the dollar.

*San Francisco Examiner & Chronicle, 6-8:(B)2.*

5

The Shah of Iran sits on his throne and pontificates about how we can't control inflation here in the U.S. [and so therefore the OPEC nations must keep up the price of their oil exports]. The fact of the matter is that the prices of most commodities have been coming down very rapidly during the past year, including even the price of the so-called mythical gold. At the cost of a tremendous recession, we have succeeded in bringing down the inflationary spiral which is now being reactivated by its OPEC originators. Not long ago, OPEC didn't want to take U.S. dollars any more because they felt our currency had gone to pot. Now that the dollar has strengthened, they shifted gears quickly and, momentarily at least, are willing to give the U.S. another chance. When has such hypocrisy ever been seen in our lifetime? Obviously, this whole operation is assured of success as long as we're willing to underwrite it ... I mean that the U.S. and its allies are undercutting each other in their eagerness to deal with the Shah and the sheiks. We have given up any effort to escape this black-mail. Does the Shah want atomic power plants? We race to fill the order. Does he want F-15s or F-16s or F-17s? We are here to serve. We can't wait to sell all these fellows our latest technology and equipment, even if it hasn't been supplied to our own armed forces. It looks as though we have decided to make the Middle East a testing ground for our weaponry. And we're in competition with our Western allies on this score. Adolf Hitler would turn in his grave—with envy—if he knew about the weaponry and nuclear plants that we are building up over there. What we're saying to the blackmailers is this: "Go ahead, rob our bank. Then we'll give you the weapons so that you can rob us a little more." This is really infamous!

*Interview/*
*U.S. News & World Report, 10-13:21.*

### Houari Boumedienne
*President of Algeria*
1

Does Israel have such strength that it can forbid Americans to ask Israel to withdraw from occupied Arab territory? We do not understand this policy. The problems of the U.S., the problems of [the U.S.] Congress, are complex and intricate, but they are not the problems of the Arabs. We have an Israeli occupation. Is it legal or illegal? We should be talking the same language . . . It would be pointless to ask the U.S. to be hostile to Israel. But if you can reconcile your interests with those of the Arabs as well as Israel—a difficult equation—then peace will extend to the whole region. We ask you only to treat the Arabs as friends and put aside your big-stick policy.

*Interview, Algiers/Time, 2-10:31*

2

It is imperative to link the price of oil to that of other raw materials . . . Is it conceivable to ask us to produce more than market demands at the very moment when the United States is taking measures to limit that market? This is a contradiction, and we cannot explain satisfactorily the fact that Americans, Europeans, Australians and Canadians refuse to produce enough food. Should we turn the tables and insist that they keep a very high level of

production so as to bring about a rapid drop in the price of these commodities?

*Interview/*
*The Christian Science Monitor, 3-3:1,4.*

### Leonid I. Brezhnev
*General Secretary, Communist Party*
*of the Soviet Union*
3

Sometimes deliberations are made that full [Arab-Israeli] settlement in the Middle East is hard to achieve, and that instead of this, partial agreements are what one should be contented with in the years to come. Partial bilateral measures, as is known, have already been implemented in the Middle East. Have they eased the tension in the area? Unfortunately not. Have they offered tranquility to peoples of the Middle East? No, they have not. Certain persons apparently would like to offer to the Arab peoples something of a soporific, hoping that they will be lulled and will forget their demands for restoration of justice and full liquidation of the consequences of aggression. But a soporific dulls one only for a short while, after which a man wakes up to face the same real life with its problems.

*At luncheon honoring visiting British Prime*
*Minister Harold Wilson, Moscow, Feb. 14/*
*Los Angeles Times, 2-15:(1)16.*

### Alastair Buchan
*Former director,*
*International Institute for Strategic Studies*
4

I think the region of primary concern is the Middle east. For one thing, events there involve the central balance of power between the United States and the Soviet Union. Also, it is complicated by the interrelationship between the Arab-Israeli conflict on one hand and oil on the other. There is clearly a great deal of concern in this country that failure to solve the Arab-Israeli conflict will lead to a gradual alienation of the Arab world and that this in turn will damage the material interests of the United States, Western Europe and Japan.

*Interview/*
*U.S. News & World Report, 6-30:62.*

**Mosbah Budeiry**
*Commander, Palestine Liberation Army*
                                                    1

I don't approve of these left-wing [Arab guerrilla] groups. I'm here to liberate my land—as soldier, not politician. What's the use of being socialist or Communist when you have no land where you can put your ideals into practice? The PLA is totally non-political. We're friend to all Arabs—even King Hussein [of Jordan].

*Interview, Damascus, Syria, Jan. 31/*
*The Washington Post, 2-1:(A)12.*

**Frank Church**
*United States Senator,*
*D–Idaho*
                                                    2

The [arms sales] competition is out of control. We and the Europeans are in an unprincipled race to arm to the teeth the newly rich nations of the Persian Gulf . . . We are on a treadmill with no end in sight.

*At Senate Subcommittee on Multinational*
*Corporations hearing, Washington, June 9/*
*Los Angeles Times, 6-10:(1)5.*

                                                    3

There is so little comparison [between U.S. involvement in Indochina and the current Middle East situation] ! In Indochina, we blundered into a civil war among the people of a region of no strategic importance to the United States. The leaders we supported lacked the capacity to enlist the support of their people. Contrast this debacle with the Israeli experience—a democracy that has asked for the means to defend itself against outside forces and has never called on American troops to fight for it. That's the biggest contrast. It is inconceivable to abandon Israel. If the Russian-equipped Syrian and Egyptian armies should ever overrun Israel, the Soviet Union would be placed in a position of pre-eminent influence in this strategic part of the world. Obviously, this would be a severe setback to the United States and such principal allies as Western Europe and Japan who depend so totally on the Middle East for fuel supplies.

*The Washington Post, 6-15:(Potomac)20.*

**Etienne Davignon**
*Director, International Energy Agency;*
*Coordinator of foreign policy for the*
*European Common Market*
                                                    4

. . . the imperative necessity of a solution in the Mideast has now appeared as an element of our domestic policies in Europe. Since the 1967 war, the majority of people in government came to the conclusion that the Israeli position was excessive, and that is why European opinion shifted from normal sympathy for Israel's extraordinary achievements in making the deserts bloom toward distaste for what seemed to be arrogance of power. Today the majority feels a fair solution should be on the 1967 frontiers and that the Palestinians should have a homeland. What remains totally unacceptable is any proposition which could lead to the disappearance of Israel.

*Panel discussion, Brussels/*
*Newsweek, 1-13:35.*

**Moshe Dayan**
*Former Minister of Defense of Israel*
                                                    5

I don't think [U.S. Secretary of State Henry] Kissinger had—or ever could have had—any real ideas about possible Middle East solutions. How can even the most brilliant man have ideas about the Middle East and Vietnam and China, Russia and the Syrian hills of Quneitra? He never heard of the Mitla Pass before; there is no reason why he should have. I don't support Kissinger's idea of step-by-step diplomacy for settlements with the Arabs . . . Look what we have with Jordan now—open bridges with free traffic between Israel and Jordan. If Kissinger had to achieve this, he would have shuttled between here and Jordan for the rest of his life, and he still wouldn't have done it. We were lucky Kissinger didn't touch it.

*Interview/*
*Newsweek, 3-3:35.*

                                                    6

I am not afraid of Geneva [as a site for Arab-Israeli peace negotiations]. I don't believe it will become a forum for Arab extremism. We are strong and mature enough to run it our way. It doesn't matter where we negotiate: at the Waldorf-Astoria, Kilometer 101 or a nice hotel in Geneva. Even though Geneva would not be the disaster some people think it would be, I would not prefer Geneva because we could get bogged down there for six months . . . The best thing is separate negotiations with Egypt and then, if the Arabs insist, the finalization of the arrangement at Geneva.

*Interview/*
*Newsweek, 3-3:35.*

1

Next to our own problems in Israel, the most important thing is that there will be a strong United States of America. You must be strong militarily so that you will be able to stand up against Russia. But if you are not strong, then [the Russians] will be able to do whatever they please. You must be strong enough economically and morally so that you won't be subject to pressure from the Arabs when they want to sell you their oil. And when you negotiate for us with the Arabs—and we realize that you want to improve your relationship with the Arabs—I wish you well and I hope you will be able to do it. But don't try to pay for your oil with Israeli soil. I know the Arabs and they will promise you oil, provided you put pressure on us. We hope that you are strong enough, not only economically, but morally, not to do it. We rely on you. We count on you and we want you to mediate between us and the Arabs—but only as a strong country, independent and the leader of the free world.

*At California State University, Northridge/*
*Los Angeles Times, 4-17:(2)7.*

**Simcha Dinitz**
*Israeli Ambassador to the United States*

2

There is no contradiction between the independent existence of Israel within secure borders and the expression of a Palestinian identity in a neighboring, independent Jordanian-Palestinian state. The only obstacle that prevents this progress is the continued resistance in the Arab world to the very existence of Israel as an independent Jewish state.

*Before National Press Club, Washington/*
*The Christian Science Monitor, 12-5:3.*

**Abba Eban**
*Former Foreign Minister of Israel*

3

We can press our demand for an over-all peace agreement with the Arabs at Geneva rather than quibble over small territorial concessions that get us little in return. This has always been Israel's strongest argument—its demand to live in peace. Its weakest has been the insistence on holding Arab territory. We could go to Geneva prepared to make massive withdrawals to achieve peace. In any event, we should avoid the apocalyptic vision we have had of Geneva. It could hold out more hope of peace in the long run than parceling out bits of territory step-by-step.

*Interview/*
*The New York Times, 1-16:2.*

4

Our central truth is there will never be a Middle East without a sovereign state of Israel at the very heart and center of its life. But in the Arab-Israeli conflict, one side totally denies the very existence of the other . . . If the world can get used to the existence of 20 Arab states and not get used to the existence of one Jewish state, the situation is nothing but a modern version of anti-Semitism.

*Before Women's Division, United Jewish*
*Welfare Fund-Israel Emergency Fund,*
*Los Angeles/*
*Los Angeles Herald-Examiner, 2-28:(B)2.*

5

My basic feeling is that insofar as [Egyptian President Anwar] Sadat and [Jordanian] King Hussein talk about peace, they don't mean what we mean. By peace we mean that relations between Egypt and Israel have to be like the relations of Egypt with Italy or France. They have to behave toward Israelis as they behave toward Italians and French. The essence of peace is non-discrimination. Every peace agreement signed in the last 50 years between countries who were previously at war consists not only of acts of abstention—from war, from sabotage, from boycott and hostile propaganda. Peace goes beyond the range of mere abstention into the sphere of affirmative relationships—of

*(ABBA EBAN)*

trade, tourism, diplomatic relations and regional cooperation. That is what we mean by peace.

*Interview/*
*San Francisco Examiner & Chronicle, 7-20:(B)2.*

1

[On the new Sinai accord between Egypt and Israel]: Acceptance of the settlement is better than rejection of it. Its shortcomings are very tangible and concrete, and its gains are very speculative. But if the alternative to acceptance is deadlock or war, it must be accepted.

*Time, 8-25:23.*

**Ismail Fahmy**
*Foreign Minister of Egypt*

2

I look at the Middle East as a human body in which some country—history tells us it was Britain—tried to transplant a foreign organ. The body tried to resist, and this process of rejection has been taking place against Israel for the last 28 years. For years the U.S.A. and some other countries supported the transplant and prevented the rejection of the organ. Now we are told that Israel is there, it is a fact and we have to live with it. After October 6 [the start of the 1973 Arab-Israeli war], we are ready to live with Israel if she is willing to live with us. This means she must give up her ambition to dominate the Arab countries, whether by expansion or other means. We may sign a peace treaty with Israel provided—and this is a big proviso—that Israel is ready to live in peace with its neighbors as a Middle Eastern country, not a European country or an additional state of the U.S.A. Israel cannot live in peace until it leaves its neighbors in peace; and the fact is that on the map, on the ground, the Israelis occupy by force Egyptian land, Syrian land, the West Bank of Jordan and the Gaza Strip, and are trying to attack Lebanon every minute. Israel is looking to implement its dream of swallowing part of southern Lebanon and realize a larger Israel—reaching to Iraq, with borders deep in the heart of the Arab countries. If Israel is willing to relinquish its expansionist policies, I believe we can live in peace. Now over 80 countries recognize Israel, and this hasn't helped it reach peace; but if it is

recognized by five or even four of its neighbors, there can be peace. Israel must respect the boundaries of the Arab countries and accept a Palestinian state next to it.

*Interview, Cairo/*
*U.S. News & World Report, 4-21:24.*

3

[Accusing the Israelis of bad faith in seeking a new Sinai agreement with Egypt through the U.S.]: They want to bargain—on every level and in every direction. They link everything to what they can get from the U.S., and this is blackmail. They know they must be out of the passes, but they want a price. They are trying to gain time. They are looking at the internal situation in the U.S., trying to figure out if [President] Ford is the strong man, if [Secretary of State] Kissinger can last, if the Congress will respond to their tactics, and how many million dollars they can squeeze out of you [the U.S.]. The ultimate objective is to hold on to as much land as possible.

*Interview, Cairo/*
*Time, 8-4:27.*

**Faisal (ibn Abdel Aziz)**
*King of Saudi Arabia*

4

It remains our policy, our genuine concern, to strengthen Saudi-American relations. It would pain us deeply to see the interests of the U.S. in this area, and certainly in our country, go down the drain. Don't be surprised by our tenacious pinning of our hopes on the U.S., because historically America has stood for freedom and liberty and the championship of just causes. Even in Vietnam, the U.S. went across thousands of miles and committed its own forces in defense of South Vietnam, which was threatened by aggression from North Vietnam. We read the message. The U.S. should take a similar stand against aggression, against a continuous Israeli expansionist movement.

*Interview, Riyadh/*
*Time, 2-10:26.*

5

An intransigent attitude on the part of the Israeli government in the long run will prove not to have been in the interest of Israel and certainly not in the interest of Jews as a people. Because the longer Israel maintains this obstinate attitude, the more likely it is to evoke the ire, the dissatisfaction, the resentment of the people of the world. That in itself will rub off on the Jewish people, which is something we deplore. The more Zionism resorts to intrigue, whipping up animosity, the more the world by innuendo will blame not just Israel but the Jewish people, some of whom are completely innocent. We consider it logical to expect the good Jews, who are not interested in this kind of expansionist glory, to stand up to Zionism.

*Interview, Riyadh/Time, 2-10:26.*

**Salah Farid**
*Chairman, League of Arab States Permanent Delegation to the United Nations*
1

We have nothing against the Jews. The Arabs and Islam have never persecuted them. But we are opposed to the Zionists. Israel's enemies come from within, not without.

*The Dallas Times Herald, 2-26:(B)8.*

**Gerald R. Ford**
*President of the United States*
2

The interests of America as well as our allies are vitally affected by what happens in the Middle East. So long as the state of tension continues, it threatens military crisis, the weakening of our alliances, the stability of the world economy, and confrontation among the nuclear superpowers. These are intolerable risks . . . I pledge the United States to a major effort for peace in the Middle East—an effort which I know has the solid support of the American people and their Congress. We are now examining how best to proceed. We have agreed in principle to reconvene the Geneva conference. We are prepared as well to explore other forums. The United States will move ahead on whatever course looks most promising either toward an over-all settlement or interim agreements. should the parties desire them. We will not accept stagnation or a stalemate, with all its attendant risks to peace and prosperity and to our relations in and outside of the region.

*State of the World address, Washington, April 10/The New York Times, 4-11:10.*

**Donald M. Fraser**
*United States Representative, D–Minnesota*
3

Israel, as an arms beneficiary of the United States, is not in danger now, but I wouldn't want to say what lies down the road. A change in attitude will not come about because of high [Arab] oil prices. Israel is not blamed for that. But appearances are changing: President [Anwar] Sadat of Egypt is viewed as a moderate, the Palestine Liberation Organization has gained legitimacy and Israel is increasingly seen as intransigent.

*Interview/ The New York Times, 2-14:2.*

**Indira Gandhi**
*Prime Minister of India*
4

[On the creation of Israel after World War II]: Suddenly a problem, which was a European problem, was lifted from Europe and put there [in the Middle East] without any regard, without any preparation as to what the repercussions would be. Now, our [India's] leaders . . . had the greatest of sympathy with what the Jews had to go through, for instance, during the Hitler period and of course before. But we felt it was not a solution—the manner in which Israel was created. However, we accepted Israel. We have never said it should not exist. But it has to come to terms with its neighbors.

*Interview, New Delhi/ The New York Times, 2-13:12.*

**Nahum Goldmann**
*President, World Jewish Congress*
5

The honeymoon between Israel and the non-Jewish world has come to an end . . . In the past, when we Jews supported Israel to the full, we did so in an atmosphere of world sympathy for Israel, of respect and admiration for it, and in conformity with the policies of most of the democratic countries. With the fortunate exception for the time being of the United States, all this has changed radically. We may have to face open conflicts with the Middle East policies of many countries in the near future, and we must be prepared for it. The real test of solidarity

# WHAT THEY SAID IN 1975

*(NAHUM GOLDMANN)*

with Israel will come when we support it against the views of the states in which we live.

*Before World Jewish Congress, Jerusalem, Feb. 3/The New York Times, 2-4:2.*

**Andrei A. Gromyko**
*Foreign Minister of the Soviet Union* 1

Israel may get, if it so wishes, the strictest [security] guarantees with the participation—under an appropriate agreement—of the Soviet Union. These guarantees would insure peaceful conditions for the existence and development of all states of the Middle East . . . At the heart of the [forthcoming Middle East Geneva] conference program, in our opinion, should be: first, agreement on the liberation of all Arab lands from foreign occupation; second, agreement to insure the legitimate rights of the Arab people of Palestine up to the establishment of their own state; third, agreement to insure and guarantee the rights of all states of the Middle East, including the state of Israel, to independent existence and development.

*At dinner honoring Syrian Foreign Minister Ismail Fahmy, Moscow, April 23/ The New York Times, 4-24:5.*

**George Habash**
*Leader, Popular Front for the Liberation of Palestine* 2

We want and look forward anxiously to a new [Arab-Israeli] war. Israel may win a quick war, but the result of a long war will definitely be in our favor. A new war is no danger to the Palestinian people. They can't suffer any worse than they have since the 1948 creation of Israel on their homeland. But it will be a grave threat to Israel's existence and U.S. imperialist interests.

*The New York Times, 2-12:3.*

**Mohammed Hassanein Heikal**
*Former editor, "Al Ahram," Cairo* 3

[On talk of U.S. military intervention in the Middle East in the event of Arab oil embargoes, too high oil export prices, etc.]: I find it difficult to take seriously. The

Israeli lobby is pushing it, but cooler heads surely realize that the U.S. would then lose the area completely. Moderates would be swept out of power—or become anti-American radicals, which is the same thing. It would backfire and make the Bay of Pigs and Vietnam seem like picnics.

*Interview/ Newsweek, 1-27:41.*

**Eric Hoffer**
*American philosopher* 4

It's the cowardice of the free world that lets a bunch of grubby Arab sheiks . . . push us [the U.S.] around. Every free country is falling over each other to sell out Israel for a barrel of Arab oil. The Jews are alone in the world. If Israel should perish, the holocaust will be upon us. Israel must live.

*San Francisco Examiner & Chronicle, 4-20:(This World)2.*

**Hussein I**
*King of Jordan* 5

If, in the immediate future, Israel changes its basic line, there is ultimately great hope. But it now looks as if they are working above all to create a military machine the like of which has never before existed in this part of the world. And they are doing this at the expense of their economic development, their social welfare, their progress. This makes me feel they may again stress the military approach. And that must lead again to war. If Israel continues along such lines it must obviously lose world support . . . We must have progress toward peace—or we will have a more serious war than ever before. You can't have a no-war-no-peace situation that doesn't eventually wind up in war.

*Interview, Amman/ The New York Times, 3-5:35.*

**Rashid Karami**
*Premier of Lebanon* 6

[On the civil war in his country between Moslems and Christians]: If Islam allows murder, then I don't want to be a Moslem. If Christianity allows killing, then I am against

Christianity. We have reached zero-level and even slipped below it in every aspect of life.

*Before cease-fire committee/ San Francisco Examiner & Chronicle, 11-30:(This World)17.*

### Edward M. Kennedy
*United States Senator, D—Massachusetts*

1

[Arguing against U.S. arms sales to Persian Gulf nations]: It was little more than a decade ago that we watched a parade of United States military advisers streaming to another volatile part of the world—Indochina—to assist "internal security forces" to operate the massive quantities of tanks, aircraft and other military equipment that we were sending them. Sending large numbers of Americans to the Persian Gulf to engage in military training will compromise our independence from what happens there. It is only a short step from there to Americans serving as mercenaries in foreign wars.

*Before the Senate, Washington, Feb. 22/ The Washington Post, 2-23:(1)1.*

### Abdel Halim Khaddam
*Foreign Minister of Syria*

2

[Criticizing the new Sinai accord between Egypt and Israel]: We [Syria] shall not fall into the trap of the recently concluded Sinai agreement. That agreement is merely one of those misleading attempts. It is a step for dragging our people to surrender to the will of the aggressor. The world will . . . realize that such an agreement was not a step toward peace, but was rather a temporary truce that threatened the whole region with explosion . . . How can our people believe that that agreement will bring peace close, while part of its cost is [for the U.S.] to supply Israel with missiles which have a range that can reach the capitals and towns of the Arab countries surrounding the center of aggression? How can we consider that agreement a step toward peace, that has paved the way for a U.S. presence in the area and when it has rendered the United States a main party to the conflict, with all the dangers underlying such presence—dangers that threaten the future

of our people? Who can rightly recall how the United States got involved in Vietnam?

*At United Nations, New York, Sept. 30/ The Washington Post, 10-1:(A)4.*

### Mohammed Ali Aba al-Khail
*Minister of Finance of Saudi Arabia*

3

[On his country's oil exports]: We feel our responsibility to the whole world. We also know we cannot attain our own development goals without a stable international economic system. We favor lowering the price of oil; but the industrial countries must help by checking their inflation. We must get a fair price so that we can build an alternate source of income that will continue after our oil is depleted.

*Interview, Riyadh/ The New York Times, 1-26:(3)58.*

### Khalid (ibn Abdel Aziz)
*King of Saudi Arabia*

4

We are doing our duties vis-a-vis Arab brothers and will also fulfill our obligations toward the Palestinian state once it is established. At such time when these things have been accomplished and Israel has withdrawn from all the occupied territories, including Jerusalem, she can live within her 1967 borders.

*Interview, Riyadh, May 24/ The Washington Post, 5-25:(A)1.*

### Henry A. Kissinger
*Secretary of State of the United States*

5

As we make peace [in the Arab-Israeli conflict], we must balance the requirements of physical security against the needs of good faith and good will and recognition. And we have to relate the tangible possession of territory to the intangible necessities of legitimacy, acceptance and a desire for peace. That is a very difficult process.

*At dinner in his honor, Jerusalem, Feb. 11/ The Dallas Times Herald, 2-12:(A)3.*

6

An active American role [in the Arab-Israeli issue] is imperative—because of our historical and moral commitment to the survival and well-being of Israel; because of our important interests in the Arab world, an area of more

# WHAT THEY SAID IN 1975

*(HENRY A. KISSINGER)*

than 150 million people sitting astride the world's largest oil reserves; because the eruption of crisis in the Middle East would severely strain our relations with our allies in Europe and Japan; because continuing instability risks a new international crisis over oil and a new setback to the world's hopes for economic recovery threatening the well-being not only of the industrial world, but of most nations of the globe; because a crisis in the Middle East poses an inevitable risk of direct U.S.-Soviet confrontation and has done so with increasing danger in every crisis since the beginning. We can never lose sight of the fact that U.S. foreign policy must do its utmost to protect *all* its interests in the Middle East.

*Before Southern Council on International and Public Affairs, Atlanta, June 23/ The Washington Post, 6-24:(A)1.*

1

The Middle East will continue to be an area of anguish, turmoil and peril until a just and durable peace is achieved. Such a peace must meet the principal concerns and interests of all in the area; among these are territorial integrity, the right to live in peace and security, and the legitimate interests of the Palestinians. In the Middle East today there is a yearning for peace surpassing any known for three decades. Let us not doom the region to another generation of futile struggle. Instead, let the world community seize the historic opportunity before it. The suffering and bravery of all the peoples of the Middle East cry out for it; the hopes and interests of all the world's peoples demand it.

*At United Nations, New York, Sept. 22/ The New York Times, 9-23:16.*

## Mike Mansfield
*United States Senator, D—Montana*

2

As far as I am concerned, I don't want to become involved in the Mideast any more than I want to become involved in Vietnam, because one Vietnam is one Vietnam too many . . . I don't think the Congress would approve a preemptive war on the part of any country, including Israel and the Arab nations, because this

Congress is becoming more peace-minded, becoming more practical, and becoming more aware of the tinder boxes which are located here and there throughout the world. And they do not want to see them ignited and blown up.

*Interview, Washington/ The Christian Science Monitor, 2-28:1.*

## George S. McGovern
*United States Senator, D—South Dakota*

3

American policy should take into serious consideration the question of recognizing the Palestine Liberation Organization. [It is] imperative for some kind of Palestinian national entity to emerge, because it is difficult to achieve stability in the area unless the Palestinians exercise an efficient political existence.

*Beirut, March 29/ The Washington Post, 3-30:(A)22.*

4

[On the new Sinai agreement between Egypt and Israel] : Pending the submission to Congress of related aid agreements [by the U.S.] , I announce my provisional support of the new Egyptian-Israeli interim agreement, [but] with certain reservations. [If the agreement] provides an occasion for complacency, it will prove to have been a misstep and a misfortune. The ultimate merit of the present agreement will become clear only when we know whether it has in fact led toward a general settlement. The agreement is a pause, not a peace. It is a precious gift of time to negotiate that peace.

*Sept. 3/The New York Times, 9-4:8.*

## George Meany
*President, American Federation of Labor-Congress of Industrial Organizations*

5

[On the Arabs' use of their oil exports as a weapon against the U.S.] : Every American schoolchild could have told the government how to handle the blackmail demands of the Arab oil sheiks. The response should have been, "Not one cent for tribute." Instead, [U.S. Secretary of State] Henry Kissinger had a new quotation for the history books: "Pay." And pay we did. And we will continue to pay until the United States deals with the blackmailers in the manner that they deserve. No tribute, no foreign aid, no trade, no jet fighters to these people—nothing until the blackmail stops.

*At AFL-CIO board meeting, Washington, Jan. 23/The New York Times, 1-24:11.*

## Daniel P. Moynihan
*United States Ambassador/Permanent Representative to the United Nations*

1

[On recent Israeli air raids on Palestinian camps in Lebanon]: The United States deeply deplores these attacks just as we have consistently deplored those despicable terror incidents which have caused the loss of life in Israel. We are prepared to support an appropriate resolution which registers the strong disapproval of this [UN Security] Council of *all* acts of violence in the Middle East, particularly those which result in the deaths of innocent civilians, and calls on all parties to refrain from any action which might endanger peace negotiations.

*At United Nations, New York, Dec. 5/ Los Angeles Herald-Examiner, 12-5:(A)1.*

## Farah Pahlavi
*Empress of Iran*

2

Iran has finally found its place on the map of the world. I think the present image of Iran is that of an ancient, traditional country that is also rich, progressive and dynamic. And I hope that image will not change because of the oil problem—that if people in Europe or America are paying more for gasoline, shoes, groceries, that they don't feel it's our fault. People should understand that we are an old country that suffered for years because we lacked material facilities. Now we are using our wealth to solve our problems. How else could we do it? Basically, I hope that our country will progress and that our people will have a decent standard of living—but without losing the human, spiritual side of life. That is really the big challenge facing Iran.

*Interview, Teheran/Parade, 1-12:10.*

3

Everybody knows [Iran] is a dynamic country making progress, but people don't under-

stand the system of government. We had a very weak leadership and the country was coming apart. There were so many parties, so many politicians. It was really a mess. Now, after 30 years, we have strong leadership. The policy of the King and the government is to educate politically the people so they can more and more participate in the planning. That's why it's so interesting. We have a challenge from the world to see if a monarchy of this kind works— a monarchy that makes a revolution from the top and introduces social laws that don't exist in other countries—land reform, laws for women's rights, laws for factory workers.

*Interview, Teheran/San Francisco Examiner & Chronicle, 10-26:(Sunday Scene)2.*

## Mohammad Reza Pahlavi
*Shah of Iran*

4

[On Arab oil-export boycotts]: Once the tankers are loaded, we [Iran] don't mind where the oil goes. It is a purely commercial transaction for us. We have never really boycotted any country. We think that politics and commerce are separate. We have not taken part in the first oil embargo, and we will not take part in any other.

*News conference, Zurich, Switzerland, Feb. 18/ Los Angeles Herald-Examiner, 2-18:(A)1.*

5

[On his decision to allow only one political party in his country, the National Resurgence Party]: Parliamentary government will continue. What we have here is what our people want. Now our new party has been joined by the whole country. It represents the fundamental aims of our nation. Everybody, every Iranian, is in our party. It is far different from Russia where only 10 to 15 million, out of a population of 250 million, are members of their single party. And we are working continually to increase participation of all the people in our political and economic life ... in 13 years we will be where West Europe is today. Within 25 years, all told, we will catch up with Europe as it then is. Economically. We may be more advanced socially. After all, our program of reform and participation covers all facets of the nation. But funda-

(MOHAMMAD REZA PAHLAVI)

mentally our society, to achieve its goals, must remain based on discipline.

*Interview, Teheran/
The New York Times, 3-22:31.*

1

The idea of Iran having nuclear weapons is ridiculous. Only a few silly fools believe it. The best guarantee that I do not want nuclear weapons is the program I have launched in conventional weapons. I want to be able to take care of anything by non-nuclear means. As to nuclear weapons, Iran could never have enough. How many do you think it would take to count against the Russians? Or the United States? How much would they cost? Then we would have to buy all the equipment for launching missiles. It's ridiculous.

*Interview, Teheran/
Los Angeles Times, 5-1:(2)5.*

2

The [Arab-Israeli] situation is very delicate and might be explosive because one party [Israel] does not apply and implement the resolutions of the UN Security Council. When one does not obey the resolutions of the Security Council, then you have the law of the jungle. Anything might happen. I see the security of Israel in international guarantees. A few more kilometers eastward or westward will not add to its security. Even the Soviet Union is saying that if Israel goes back to the pre-1967 borders, it is ready to guarantee the borders of Israel. Morally, we [in Iran] have got to support our Arab friends, not only because of religion but really because of international right and law. We don't see any wisdom in Israel's policies. We have always recognized the existence of Israel, but we have got to say that the Israelis are becoming impossible. If *you* [the U.S.] cannot, we cannot exert additional pressure on Israel.

*Interview, Teheran/Time, 6-9:33.*

3

Everybody must know that if this country is attacked, we are going to resist. And if it is not an atomic attack, they will have to concentrate a lot of troops to be able to overcome us. And everybody would weigh this before they do anything. Atomic—that's beyond us; but don't think the world could afford to lose Iran. There is such an interdependence between Iran and Europe because we can supply so much of their energy, and also close relations with the Americans. The balance of the world will be completely unbalanced if anything happened to us. This is corresponding to your nuclear deterrent; this is *our* nuclear deterrent.

*Interview, Teheran, Sept. 23/
The New York Times, 9-24:8.*

**Charles H. Percy**
*United States Senator, R—Illinois*

4

... until [Israel] is willing to take some risks for a peace which is clearly in her self-interest, peace will continue to elude her. Some Israeli leaders appear to believe the current state of no-war, no-peace can continue indefinitely. If they do, I think it is a dangerous misconception. The Arab confrontation states believe that while they might lose a next war, or even another after that, time in the long run is on their side. And I tend to agree with them.

*Before Senate Foreign Relations
Committee, Washington, April 20/
The Dallas Times Herald, 4-21:(A)8.*

**Shimon Peres**
*Minister of Defense of Israel*

5

I do not believe that [big-power security] guarantees are either practical, or real or stimulating. In a way, guarantees are like bank loans: They are given once you convince the bank that you do not need them. If you really need them, everybody is embarrassed to take the risk.

*Interview, Tel Aviv/
The Christian Science Monitor, 1-27:1.*

6

[Saying that an agreement of non-belligerence between Egypt and Israel must be made directly and not through a go-between]: ... it must be an agreement done at noon, in broad light, and between the two parties concerned ... We are not going to marry the father-in-law or someone like that; we are going to marry the girl. I mean, let *her* agree, somewhere, somehow.

*Tel Aviv, March 2/*
*Los Angeles Herald-Examiner, 3-3:(A)4.*

1

We don't refuse to sit with the Palestine Liberation Organization because they are demanding the West Bank. Let's not forget that Israel is willing to sit with [Jordan's] King Hussein, who is demanding exactly the same thing. The difference is that while Hussein is demanding the West Bank, [PLO leader] Yasir Arafat is demanding the whole of Israel as a starting point. He wants the destruction of Israel.

*Interview/*
*Time, 3-3:33.*

2

The Arab military structure is built like a four-story house. First there are the neighboring countries: Egypt, Syria, Jordan and Lebanon. Then there are the Arab countries that sent expeditionary forces during the Yom Kippur war; this is the second story. The third story is the rest of the Arab countries; out of 19 countries, 11 participated in the last war, which leaves eight countries that are purchasing arms and are an emergency source of supply. And then comes Soviet Russia which can act quicker because she has more arms in her stores, and because the process of decision-making is far quicker in Russia than the one that is used in the West and the United States.

*Interview, Tel Aviv/*
*The Washington Post, 3-14:(A)26.*

3

. . . when I think about Israel and compare it to other nations, I would say that Israel is militarily like a Sparta, nationally like an Athens and spiritually like a Jerusalem. All the three phenomena are here and highly active. In all those 27 years [of Israel's existence], in four wars, the democratic process never stopped. It is a fiercely democratic country . . . And in spite of all the modern language many people use, I believe it is very much a Jewish state.

*Interview, Tel Aviv/*
*The Washington Post, 3-14:(A)26.*

4

The Russians have invested much here [in the Middle East], and I am sure they will now try to introduce some additional initiatives in order to deepen their roots in the Arab world. However, I doubt they will succeed, because history shows that the more Russians you have, the less pro-Russian is the mood.

*Interview, Jerusalem/*
*U.S. News & World Report, 4-7:17.*

5

The social changes in the Middle East are basically toward urbanization. The population centers are growing. People's expectations are forcing Arab governments to shift their orientation from war to the pressing issues of domestic improvement. Economically, the price of arms is becoming prohibitive. A military aircraft that cost $1-million ten years ago costs $20-million today. Even if you produce oil, there is a limit to what you can spend for weapons. Militarily, the destructive power of modern weapons is so great that even the winner will have to pay so heavily for a war that no triumph will ever justify the cost in human terms.

*Interview/*
*Time, 10-6:38.*

**Muammar el-Qaddafi**
*Chief of State of Libya*

6

[On U.S. Secretary of State Henry Kissinger's diplomatic efforts at solving the Arab-Israeli conflict]: I never pay attention to news of Henry Kissinger's movements. I don't even know when he comes and goes. The real aim of the American policy is to raise the Arabs against each other. It aims at creating a gap between Egypt and Syria . . . In my opinion, the Palestinian question can only be settled through the contribution of the struggle—and the struggle between the Palestinians and the Israelis will continue.

*Interview/*
*The Washington Post, 2-25:(A)14.*

**Yitzhak Rabin**
*Prime Minister of Israel*

7

We must clearly distinguish when we discuss Israeli policy. With respect to our neighbors, we

351

# WHAT THEY SAID IN 1975

want to be able to defend ourselves with our own force, and therefore we want defensible borders and a strengthening of our military forces, which, together with such borders, will enable us to stand alone. But if it comes to the threat of intervention by another power, we expect, like the rest of the free world, that the United States will fulfill its duty and prevent military intervention by that power.

*At Bar-Ilan University, Tel Aviv, Feb. 20/*
*The New York Times, 2-21:4.*

1

If [Egyptian] President [Anwar] Sadat really wants peace or to move significantly toward peace, he will find Israel a ready partner. But we are not talking in a vacuum. We are talking after 26 years of experience of efforts to bring about peace, after armistice agreements that were violated. We are talking after the war of 1956, in which Israel withdrew to the pre-1956 war lines without achievement of peace, on the assumption that the mere withdrawal to the pre-war lines, the establishment of the United Nations Emergency Forces, would lead in the long run toward peace. Then we had the Six-Day War, and again we were ready to negotiate peace on the basis of a territorial compromise. Then came the Yom Kippur war. Now, therefore, let's be more specific. The mere statement that might be for public relations consumption, that a certain Arab leader desires peace, doesn't mean very much to me.

*Interview, Jerusalem/*
*The Washington Post, 3-1:(A)2.*

2

...in the long run, close cooperation between an Arab country and the Soviet Union has brought an addition to the Arab countries' desire and capability to go to war. In all cases, the outcome was more shipment of arms, more extreme positions, more demands in the political area, and normally, as a result of it, bringing the area closer to war. Therefore, wherever and whenever I see relations between an Arab country and the Soviet Union growing looser, I consider it to be a contribution toward peace.

*Interview, Jerusalem/*
*The Washington Post, 3-1:(A)12.*

3

I hope there will be no erosion of the U.S.' understanding of Israel's position. Israel is a real democracy that shares the basic principles, morality and free way of life of the U.S. I believe that a strong Israel is an asset to the U.S. in the Middle East. If I look backward, I see that the support of the various Administrations has not harmed the U.S. in this region. I'd say the opposite. Despite the U.S. supply of arms to Israel during the Yom Kippur war, the gates of Cairo and Damascus later were opened to an American President. The Arabs realize that the U.S. is a factor in any effort to bring about a real political settlement of the Arab-Israeli conflict.

*Interview, Jerusalem/Time, 4-7:13.*

4

Israel's position is we want peace, a real one. We want boundaries of peace that will make Israel capable of defending itself by itself. We have never asked guarantees of other countries, including the United States, because we believe that a peace agreement must stand on the merits of the agreement itself, and not be dependent on somebody outside coming to defend it. I would say more than that. I think an agreement based on the possibility of dragging major powers into local conflicts is a wrong concept. That doesn't help to keep peace; in fact, it endangers world peace. What we want is to be capable of defending ourselves, even after a peace agreement is reached. We do not want a peace agreement that ends up as a peace on a piece of paper. We want peace based on the realities of relations between peoples of all the countries involved in the area.

*Interview, Washington/*
*U.S. News & World Report, 6-23:30.*

5

[On the new Sinai accord between Egypt and Israel]: There will be in this agreement a change in the relationship between Egypt and Israel. This will not be hidden, but open, contractual and public. And the change will be that the two countries will undertake not to employ or threaten to employ force in the relations between them. And now, of course, you will ask: Are you sure that Egypt will keep her word, will be faithful to her obligations? It is difficult for me to answer that. I hope and trust that she will. But the same question can be asked of any treaty.

*Television interview, Jerusalem, Aug. 22/*
*The New York Times, 8-23:9.*

1

It is imperative that the whole solution of the Palestinian issue should be tied to Jordan. Israel should vehemently oppose any tendency to establish a third state in the area between it and Jordan. Any Israeli agreement for political negotiations with a Palestinian faction necessarily lays the groundwork for such a possibility ... The establishment of such a state would lead to an "Arafatist" [PLO] state whose whole purpose is the destruction of Israel.

*Interview/The Washington Post, 12-6:(A)12.*

2

... when you agree to political negotiations with a Palestinian element, it means you begin to accept a third state between Israel and Jordan. Such a state would be a cancer in the heart of the Mideast. It would be a weak state, run by extremists whose dream would remain the annihilation of Israel. And the first foreigners to come there would be the Soviets. Such a state would also be 10 miles from Tel Aviv. Even their short-range rockets could reach all our populated centers. And if the Soviets put SAM missiles there, they could interdict all our civilian and military flights. Terrorism would spread all over Israel. This is something no Israeli could tolerate. And no doubt the whole Arab world would be dragged into a struggle for the fulfillment of [PLO leader Yasir] Arafat's dream. Therefore, Israel cannot accept as a matter of principle—unless Israel decides to commit suicide—the creation of an independent Palestinian state between us and Jordan.

*Interview/Newsweek, 12-15:57.*

**Zaid al-Rifai**
*Prime Minister of Jordan*

3

It is easier for them [Israel] to continue to live in a state of war. It keeps the country

united. It enables them to get support from the United States and from Jews and Zionists all over the world. They like to maintain the idea they are the underdog—a small country besieged by hostile neighbors. That is the Israeli point of view. What concerns us is the American position. We don't expect the United States to stop supporting Israel. We recognize that it may be in your national or domestic interests to continue supporting Israel. But what we would like to know is where the American commitment ends. Is Israel right or wrong in holding on to the occupied [Arab] territories? We believe that when [U.S. Secretary of State Henry] Kissinger failed in his last shuttle-diplomacy efforts, it wasn't really a failure of Kissinger, but a failure of American policy in the area. You [the U.S.] have not made it clear that you think Israel must give up the occupied territories, and that encourages the Israelis to think they can hold on to them ... how much more pressure will you have to apply to get Israel to withdraw from all the occupied territories? We believe the United States should present a plan of its own. What is the American position about a final peace settlement? How does the United States view the future map of the Middle East? The important thing is to maintain the momentum of the peace efforts. This situation is like a man on a bicycle: If he is traveling at a certain speed, he is fine. If he slows down, he starts to wobble. If he stops, he falls off. If the momentum of the peace efforts stops, there is bound to be war.

*Interview, Amman/*
*Los Angeles Herald-Examiner, 7-30:(A)6.*

**Anwar el-Sadat**
*President of Egypt*

4

In the last 20 years we were in constant confrontation with the Americans. We started a new era in relations one year ago, when [U.S. Secretary of State] Henry Kissinger visited me here. What am I asking from the U.S.? Look, I am not asking the U.S. to break its special relations with Israel. But I am now your friend, and I have the right to ask you as a friend to be logical with me. Keep your special relations with Israel, but treat me as a friend also.

*Interview, Aswan, Egypt/Time, 2-3:39.*

# WHAT THEY SAID IN 1975

*(ANWAR el-SADAT)*

**1**

... in my generation let us try and end this state of belligerency that has already taken more than 26 years now between the Arabs and the Israelis. Let it be our job in our generation to end this state of belligerency officially and in Geneva ... We are ready. But Israel must also be ready. I think time is on our side. I am sure of it. Time is on our side. But in spite of that we are saying that we are ready to end this state of belligerency. Peace is very essential to rebuild my country here. We have suffered a lot during the last seven years. The infrastructure of the country itself has been damaged to an extent you can't imagine. For seven years we were spending, and we have already spent more than $10-billion on our armed forces which should have been used for our domestic needs.

*Interview, Cairo/*
*The Washington Post, 2-17:(A)10.*

**2**

We do not ask America to be on our side, nor do we ask America to drop Israel. We know that in the U.S. you have certain special relations with Israel. But one question that must be clarified, to us, to Israel and to the whole world: Is the U.S. protecting Israel within its borders or is it also protecting Israel in its gains of others' lands? From our side, we have no objection at all that America protect Israel within its borders, even to the extent of providing every Israeli with a tank and an airplane. But I think the time has come that the U.S. should understand its interest and its friendships in the area and should take an objective look.

*Interview, Cairo/Time, 4-14:37.*

**3**

[On the re-opening of the Suez Canal]: While making this initiative as a contribution to peace, Egypt reminds friendly nations that parts of its dear soil are still under foreign occupation [by Israel] and that an entire people [Palestinians] are still suffering the consequences of suppression and homelessness. Egypt reiterates its determination to do its holy duty toward its own and other Arab lands—in the Golan Heights, Sinai and Palestine—and toward usurped Arab rights.

*At re-opening of the Canal, June 5/*
*Los Angeles Times, 6-6:(1)10.*

**4**

... the Israelis are not only not capable of working out a peace settlement [with the Arabs] but they fear peace, politically and otherwise. They have a very weak government. A very weak leadership. They fear they may lose the aid they receive from America and from Jewish communities all over Europe. They fear peace because they do not know what it will mean for them. But I say this: Let us try to end this situation that has lasted for 27 years. Let us end it officially and with guarantees from both of us. Then we can start a new era in a new atmosphere.

*Interview, Alexandria, Egypt, July 9/*
*Los Angeles Herald-Examiner, 7-9:(A)8.*

**5**

When the day comes for me to reveal the documents exchanged between us and the Russians, you will see that no person with dignity can accept the method of Russian dealing ... They have a way of dealing, namely, that when you send them an urgent request, which may be one of destiny, they do not answer you, and say that the Soviet leaders are in the Crimea where the Soviet leaders spend four months from May to October. Of course, you have to wait for their return to Moscow, and, of course, they need a month and a half to rest a bit in Moscow. They will then answer you, if they ever do. With the Americans it is different. They answer all my requests, whether positively or negatively, within 48 hours. They put my mind at ease when they answer ...

*Interview/*
*The Washington Post, 9-10:(A)17.*

**6**

Israel is an established fact ... [It] is a reality. And if some want to bury their head in the sand, I am not one of those people ... Beating around the bush, throwing Israel into the sea and the destruction of Israel is mere talk that does not represent the truth.

*Interview/The Washington Post, 9-10:(A)17.*

*1*

The United States has to be counted among the supporters of any revolution that seeks the freedom and dignity of man. Consequently, is there any logical reason why the United States should treat the Palestinian problem differently? You are well aware that the Palestinians have suffered occasionally from excesses, lack of discipline and abuse. They feel, not without justification, to be sure, that the Palestinian people have long been neglected by the international community. It was only a few years ago that their legitimate struggle caught the imagination, and hence gained the sympathy, of the world. Nations began, after being aware of the plight of the Palestinians, to recognize their right to self-determination and statehood. Even when nations had their reservations as to certain aspects of the Palestinian resistance, that did not hinder them from lending it their understanding and support. Of almost all nations, the United States remains as the sole dissenter in the long-overdue trend of establishing contacts with the Palestinians. Contacts bring understanding. Understanding helps develop solutions.

*Before joint session of Congress, Washington/*
*The National Observer, i 1-15:7.*

**James R. Schlesinger**
*Secretary of Defense of the United States*

*2*

I think that the United States has got to hold the ring in the Middle East. There's just nobody else who can stand up to the Soviet Union. Some Americans want to go off in a sulk for five years. But if we do, we'll wake up some bright day and discover that the Soviets have achieved paramount power in the Eastern Hemisphere. We just are not in a position to indulge in that luxury.

*Interview, Washington/*
*U.S. News & World Report, 5-26:27.*

**Howard K. Smith**
*News commentator, American*
*Broadcasting Company*

*3*

The assassination of [Saudi Arabian] King Faisal may, as reporters say, be the work of one psychotic individual. But it is a warning that

Saudi Arabia and its equally feudal neighbors in the Persian Gulf are in for volatile years and challenged control. The wealth pouring in brings change with it. An educated middle class and a working class are being created for the first time. With ability they shall, as all rising classes have ever done, claim power too. The feudal structure and the leaders they deal with are destined to go. The development carries warnings above all to the United States and Israel. The image of the backward, inefficient Arab is going—a modern, skilled one is in its birth throes. It is not a matter of courting Arabs for wealth or oil; it is a national interest for us to strengthen links to Arabs to exercise what influence we can to keep the coming rulers from going the anti-American, possibly the Russian, way. Pro-Soviet dominance in the Persian Gulf would be geopolitically as upsetting as the loss of Czechoslovakia to Hitler. For Israel, it means it can still win wars, but at successively higher cost against an ever more modernized, better armed and ruled Arab world.

*ABC News commentary/*
*The Christian Science Monitor, 4-9:31.*

**Ahmed Zaki al-Yamani**
*Minister of Petroleum of Saudi Arabia*

*4*

[On whether Arab oil exports will decrease in price]: Decrease, no. Oh, no. Why should we? To sell more? The OPEC countries don't need to sell any more. It is more reasonable to wonder whether the price will increase. Within the OPEC, as everyone knows, we don't share all the same opinions. Some insist on raising the price by 35 per cent; some, $4 a barrel. Others are in favor of a smaller increase . . . We're [Saudi Arabia] waiting to see how the industrialized countries behave, whether they really intend to meet the oil-producer countries half way. In other words, lower the prices of the goods you sell us, which you can since you have a monopoly in the field, and we'll behave accordingly. Do you know how much we pay for a barrel of mineral water? Double what you [in the industrialized world] pay for a barrel of excellent crude oil. Our attitude, therefore, seems justified to me. In any case, it's our last

# WHAT THEY SAID IN 1975

*(AHMED ZAKI el-YAMANI)*

word. If you really intend to lower prices, we'll do our best to freeze the present price of oil. Otherwise, we, too, will vote in favor of an increase, even though we won't demand a drastic one ... We know that if your economy collapses, we'll collapse with you. Money in itself counts for nothing. It only counts if it is put back into circulation and transformed into industry, technology. In other words, unless the countries of the West are prosperous, we can't import your industry and your technology. We're not all interested in seeing you collapse, neither for political reasons, since we're fighting Communism, nor for economic ones. I'll go further: I don't believe the other OPEC countries are either, be they pro-Western like Kuwait, Abu Dhabi or Iran, pro-Eastern like Iraq or neutral like Algeria. But there's a problem: Not all of them believe that a new increase in oil prices will lead to disaster.

*Interview/*
*The New York Times Magazine, 9-14:19,28.*

*1*

If Israel recognizes the rights of the Palestinians, I believe the Palestinians will recognize the rights of Israel. To throw Israel into the sea is no longer the attitude of those who care for peace ... If Israel returns the occupied [Arab] territories, the problem [of expelling Israel from the UN] will not rise at all. The expulsion of Israel from the United Nations isn't one of our aims. Our aim is to retrieve the occupied territories, obtain peace in the Middle East and establish a state for the Palestinians. If Israel accepts, we won't resort to extremes. If Israel doesn't accept, we'll resort to everything: Israel's expulsion from the United Nations, an embargo on our oil, the use of our monetary power.

*Interview/*
*The New York Times Magazine,*
*9-14:35.*

## Zaid bin Sultan
*President, United Arab Emirates*

*2*

The price of [Arab] oil [exports], like the price of any other commodity, must be determined by the free play of market forces. The trouble with oil is that, while all other commodities went up time and again in the 30 years since the Second World War, oil remained more or less constant. It has now caught up with the parade. Next, we must sit down with consumers and Third World partners to discuss the price of all commodities and goods affected by inflation. If the other commodities come down, say, 10 per cent, our oil may come down more than that. But first we must remove the element of confrontation.

*Interview/*
*Newsweek, 3-10:35.*

## Lincoln P. Bloomfield
*Professor of political science,*
*Massachusetts Institute of Technology*
1

The problem is not to save the General Assembly, which seems to me to have virtually destroyed its usefulness [through such actions as the recent vote condemning Zionism] , but to make very sure that all the important programs that reflect basic United States interests in interdependence in peace don't get sacrificed. There has got to be a fundamental reappraisal of the structures for carrying out international business in such a way that the important action programs in peace-keeping, arms control, food, energy, trade, resources, population get decoupled from what has become a meaningless propaganda forum.

*Interview, Nov. 11/*
*The New York Times, 11-12:17.*

## William F. Buckley, Jr.
*Political columnist; Editor,*
*"National Review"*
2

[On the General Assembly vote condemning Zionism]: The General Assembly long ago abdicated the authority to cause uproar. Do you get mad at the Bronx Zoo? We [the U.S.] shouldn't pull out of the United Nations. We shouldn't stop debating in the General Assembly. But we should stop voting in it—permanently. See what effect their resolutions would have then.

*Interview, Nov. 11/*
*The New York Times, 11-12:17.*

## Alexander Dallin
*Professor of history and political*
*science, Stanford University*
3

Moscow has evidently learned what may not be fully understood in this country [the U.S.]: To turn one's back on the UN is precisely what one's worst enemies would wish. If the U.S.

cannot control the UN, it cannot afford to ignore it either, in a world in which interdependence has become proverbial.

*At Senate review of the UN, Washington/*
*The Christian Science Monitor, 5-29:6.*

## J. William Fulbright
*Former United States Senator, D–Arkansas*
4

The best hope for peace is through an international organization, through negotiations, not balance of power. We ought to use the UN not only to control armaments but pollution and the equitable participation of all countries in the products of the seas. The concept of the UN is the only alternative to using force. We and the Russians ought to make up our minds to use the Security Council, to take our problems there and discuss them . . . We won't always get what we want. We have got to be reconciled to action by a collective body. In any really important, vital thing we still have the veto. But the point is we ought to use the UN, to gradually establish its credibility. I think we ought to be talking about gradually developing a permanent UN force to be used in places like the Middle East and Cyprus. All I can say in a word is that we ought to use the UN and accept it as an important instrumentality of world peace. The best psychology going in the world is to engage in common enterprise, and the UN is a good place to do it.

*Interview, Washington/*
*Los Angeles Times, 3-3:(2)7.*

## Leonard Garment
*Member, United States delegation to*
*United Nations Social Committee*
5

[Calling for world-wide amnesty for political prisoners]: There are people who will continue to suffer because the United States has not proved capable of demanding their release in words that command universal respect . . . It is

# WHAT THEY SAID IN 1975

*(LEONARD GARMENT)*

a shame, but there is a shame which is perhaps even worse. It is that this body [the UN] at this time seems not to care. It cares to condemn violations of human rights in those countries it chooses to make pariahs, but it will not permit a universal, precise, consistent and clear appeal to free political prisoners everywhere.

*At United Nations, New York, Nov. 21/*
*The New York Times, 11-22:7.*

### Ernest A. Gross
*Former Deputy United States Delegate*
*to the United Nations* 1

Largely due to our fault in the cold-war period, the General Assembly came to be in the public mind identified with the United Nations instead of what it actually is—a show window. We have attributed too much weight to United Nations resolutions and encouraged the box-score-mentality approach to resolutions which of themselves have no practical legal consequence. Disgusting and discouraging action like this [the Assembly vote condemning Zionism] confounds the friends of the United Nations and confirms its enemies.

*Interview, Nov. 11/*
*The New York Times, 11-12:17.*

### Chaim Herzog
*Israeli Ambassador/Permanent*
*Representative to the United Nations* 2

The move to oust us [Israel, from the UN] is only a symptom of what I see as the [Ugandan President] Idi Amin-ization of the UN. To see 70-odd nations voting the same way on any given issue is ridiculous, a travesty of democracy. How can they agree? Each country has its interests and independence. Yet they raise their hands together. Accepting the PLO's [Yasir] Arafat last fall is a precedent for UN entry of the IRA, the Basque movement and all other groups aspiring to statehood. Soon, somebody will be voted out of the UN by the color of his eyes or hair or the kind of policy or regime in his country.

*Interview, Israel/Newsweek, 8-4:44.*

### Henry A. Kissinger
*Secretary of State of the United States* 3

[The late UN Secretary General] Dag Hammarskjold once predicted that the day would come when people would see the United Nations for what it really is: not the abstract painting of some artist, but a drawing done by the peoples of the world. And so it is—not the perfect institution of the dreamers who saw it as the only true road to world harmony; and not the evil instrument of world domination that the isolationists once made it out to be. Rather, it is, like so many human institutions before it, an imperfect instrument—but one of great hope, nonetheless . . . It is there that each nation, large or small, rich or poor, can—if it will—make its contribution to the betterment of all. It is there that nations must realize that restraint is the only principle that can save the world from chaos, and that our destinies are truly intertwined on this small planet. It is there that we will see whether men and nations have the wisdom and courage to make a reality of the ideals of the Charter and, in the end, to turn the parliament of man into a true expression of the conscience of humanity.

*Before University of Wisconsin Institute*
*of World Affairs, Milwaukee, July 14/*
*Vital Speeches, 8-15:647.*

4

Ideological confrontation, bloc-voting and new attempts to manipulate the Charter to achieve unilateral ends threaten to turn the UN into a weapon of political warfare rather than a healer of political conflict and a promoter of human welfare. The process is self-defeating . . . The United States has been by far the largest financial supporter of the United Nations. But the support of the American people, which has been the lifeblood of the organization, will be profoundly alienated unless fair play predominates and the numerical majority respects the views of the minority. The American people are understandably tired of the inflammatory rhetoric against us, the all-or-nothing stance accompanied by demands for our sacrifice which too frequently dominate the meeting halls of the UN.

*Before University of Wisconsin Institute*
*of World Affairs, Milwaukee, July 14/*
*Los Angeles Times, 7-15:(1)1,20.*

**Hans J. Morgenthau**
*Professor emeritus of political science,*
*City College of New York*
*1*

The national composition of the Secretariat of the United Nations shows a disproportion in favor of the Arab bloc of nations which cannot be considered to be accidental. That is particularly true of Egypt, Syria, Sudan, Tunisia, Iraq and Lebanon. The representation of Egypt is 238 per cent above what it ought to be in view of objective criteria. The excess for Syria is 66 per cent, for Sudan 83 per cent, for Tunisia 66 per cent, for Iraq 71 per cent, and for Lebanon 50 per cent. The Division of Personnel of the Secretariat is dominated by representatives of the same bloc: The Director of Personnel, with the rank of Under Secretary General, the Deputy Director of Personnel, and the Special Assistant to the Director of Personnel, are Arabs. If one combines this extreme disequilibrium in the composition of the Secretariat with the moral perversion which has come to the fore in the General Assembly of 1974, one realizes to what extent the United Nations has not only become the political instrument of certain blocs of nations but has for all practical purposes ceased to represent the collective will of its membership according to the provisions of the Charter.

*Before House Foreign Affairs Committee,*
*Washington, Feb. 4/*
*The Washington Post, 2-20:(A)22.*

*2*

Today, the core of a typical voting majority of the General Assembly is composed of ministates . . . lacking in all or most attributes of nationhood, who enjoy the semblance of sovereignty only by courtesy of the world community, and who could not exist . . . without foreign subsidies.

*The Washington Post, 11-20:(A)19.*

**Daniel P. Moynihan**
*United States Ambassador/Permanent*
*Representative to the United Nations*
*3*

The United Nations should be as near as possible to universal in membership. As new nations are formed, they should be seen as having a presumed right to membership, given their fealty to the [UN] Charter. It is just that principle that has brought us from an original membership of 51 to the present membership of 138. It is just that principle which will take us still higher, for there are more than half a dozen new nations waiting in the wings. But we must not apply partisan political tests to membership. The United Nations cannot work if we do.

*At United Nations, New York, Aug. 11/*
*The National Observer, 8-23:3.*

*4*

Every day at the UN, on every side, we [the U.S.] are assailed because we are a democracy. In the UN today there are in the range of two dozen democracies left; totalitarian Communist regimes and assorted ancient and modern despotisms make up all the rest. Nothing so unites these nations as the conviction that their success ultimately depends on our failure. Most of the new states have ended up as enemies of freedom.

*At AFL-CIO convention, San Francisco/*
*Time, 10-20:49.*

*5*

[On a UN committee's endorsement of a draft resolution condemning Zionism as a form of racism]: This obscene resolution must not pass the General Assembly. It is an attack not on Zionism but on Israel. As such, it is a general assault by the majority of nations on the principles of liberal democracy which now are found only in a dwindling number of nations. If it succeeds, the inevitable consequence will be that the United Nations cannot survive, cannot function. You can have one-party states. You cannot have a one-party United Nations.

*Oct. 21/*
*Los Angeles Herald-Examiner, 10-26:(A)16.*

*6*

While we [the U.S.] have done our diplomacy elsewhere, we have settled into a pattern of accepting enormous, although nominal, defeats and insults at the UN. I think we were insufficiently aware of the impression that we made by submitting to a kind of treatment no

# WHAT THEY SAID IN 1975

## (DANIEL P. MOYNIHAN)

other great power would dream of accepting. It arose from indifference on our side but it was seen as appeasement by others. I'll give you an example. Last Friday, by a vote of 108-to-1, the Fourth Committee condemned the American naval base on Guam. *Nobody* in my mission even bothered to tell me. And do you know, the State Department did not want us to issue even a simple statement saying, "We wish you weren't doing this." The old view was that, if we don't pay any attention to it, then the other countries won't. On the contrary, they say, "You see, you can do something to the U.S. you wouldn't *dare* do to the Soviet Union or the [Communist] Chinese." Do you think the Russians would forgive you for voting for them to get the hell out of their naval base in Somalia!

*Interview/*
*The New York Times Magazine, 12-7:117.*

1

[On his dramatic and enthusiastic style at the UN]: [I have been] careful, lawyer-like and perhaps on occasion a trifle too intellectual. If it is threatening behavior to come into the UN with facts, with arguments, with carefully prepared ideas, to that extent we were threatening and to that extent we would propose to go on being so.

*News conference, United Nations, New York/*
*Los Angeles Times, 12-19:(1)2.*

## Charles H. Percy
*United States Senator, R–Illinois*
2

[On whether the U.S. should continue to play a major role in the UN in view of recent UN actions such as the General Assembly's vote to condemn Zionism]: As we consider the future U.S. role in the UN General Assembly, we should bear in mind that a U.S. withdrawal from Assembly deliberations would only leave the Assembly in more complete control of those nations which have chosen to politicize that body. It is my profound belief that the United States should stay in the United Nations and in every element of it, including the General Assembly and the specialized agencies. We

should stay and fight for our views, for our interests, for our position, for our principles. I can think of no greater folly than to abandon any element of the United Nations to those whose purposes are antithetical to our own.

*The Christian Science Monitor, 11-26:16.*

## Radha Krishna Ramphul
*Ambassador/Permanent Representative*
*to the United Nations from Mauritius*
3

[Saying U.S. Ambassador to the UN Daniel Moynihan's manners and language are abusive]: ... Mr. Moynihan made an interesting confession: He is having difficulties carrying on his diplomatic assignment on behalf of his government. He confessed, in so many words, [that] delegations were shy of contacting him in the formulation of resolutions. Of course they are. They live in positive dread of his manners, his language and his abuse. Indeed, they treat him like a pariah ... We do not think a member state should permit its representatives to use the United Nations as a forum for developing their personality cult for publicity— and for dramatic performances. Just as it is said of an officer of the American Army that he is an officer and a gentleman, so should it be said, "at the United Nations, one must be a diplomat and a gentleman."

*At United Nations, New York, Dec. 15/*
*The Dallas Times Herald, 12-16:(A)4.*

## John A. Scali
*United States Ambassador/Permanent*
*Representative to the United Nations*
4

The time has come to create a new spirit of constructive compromise in the United Nations. To do so, there will need to be less emphasis on rounding up bloc votes and more on accommodation and conciliation ... Reversing the current trend toward division and confrontation in the United Nations does not depend on our [the U.S.'] efforts alone. I am convinced, however, that we must walk the extra mile to overcome suspicion. We are not the guardians of the status quo.

*Before Massachusetts State Federation*
*of Women's Clubs, Boston, Jan. 28/*
*The New York Times, 1-30:8.*

1

If, because of choice or neglect, the world community fails to make the United Nations work, the alternative is not cooperation elsewhere in some other more promising forum, but inevitably a fundamental breakdown of the main path to international cooperation . . . I see a different future, however. I see a United Nations capable at last of fulfilling the mandate of its founders. I see a United Nations serving as the international community's principal forum for peace-making and peace-keeping. I see the United Nations being used by its members as the court of first resort to settle differences, rather than as the court of last resort for their conflicts. I see a world in which 150 nations live at harmony and in peace—their security preserved collectively and their prosperity pursued cooperatively. I see a world in which nations frankly recognize that there may be deep differences on fundamental issues but continue to work at narrowing these differences and at the same time move ahead in areas where they are able to agree. And there are such areas where patient diplomacy can make the difference. This is no dream. It is a realistic alternative. It requires only that we and other nations begin to use the United Nations to its capacity to help it fulfill its potential.

*Before Senate Foreign Relations*
*Committee, Washington/*
*The Christian Science Monitor, 6-4:40.*

**Charles H. Smith, Jr.**
*Chairman, Chamber of Commerce of*
*the United States*

2

This world body, for which so many of us held high hope and esteem in its early years, has proven to be quite incapable of resolving major world problems or disputes, whether they be political, economic or military. To a major degree, this impotence is a result of a constitution that provides equal voting power for all nations regardless of geographic size, population, economic or military strength, except for the U.S.S.R. For reasons that apparently satisfied those who originally led the effort to organize the UN, the nation that is identified on every map and geography text as the U.S.S.R. is divided, for voting purposes in the UN and each

of its specialized agencies, into three states. Consequently, the U.S.S.R. has three times as many votes as any other state. In any event, the constitution that creates a world fantasy by giving equal voting power to tiny island states—Malta, Trinidad and Singapore, for instance—and giant land masses—Australia, Canada and Brazil, for instance; or equal voting power between nations with gigantic populations—China, India and Indonesia, for instance—with those of tiny populations—the Chad or Kuwait, for instance; or equal voting power between nations whose economics have a tremendous impact on the world scene—like the United States, Japan and the German Federal Republic—with nations with little or no positive impact on the world economy—and there are many—results in the Disney World approach to solving world problems . . .

*Before Chamber of Commerce,*
*Berea, Ohio, Jan. 28/*
*Vital Speeches, 3-1:299.*

**John G. Stoessinger**
*Professor of political science,*
*Hunter College*

3

[On the General Assembly vote condemning Zionism]: It would be a mistake for Americans to turn their backs on the United Nations. Israel, the nation most directly affected, remains a member and continues to present her case before the world forum. The United Nations is still a valuable instrument for peace, as attested by the peace-keeping forces in the Middle East and in Cyprus. Americans would not decide to tear up their Constitution because some of their leaders may at times act irrationally or outrageously.

*Interview, Nov. 11/*
*The New York Times, 11-12:17.*

**Kurt Waldheim**
*Secretary General of the United Nations*

4

The Secretary General cannot function like a Prime Minister, because he has no power to do so. The power of the Secretary General is more of a moral power. I have to try to persuade governments to do—or not to do—this or that. But I am my own personality. I have my own approach. One is quiet preventive diplomacy;

# WHAT THEY SAID IN 1975

*(KURT WALDHEIM)*

the second is the public statement. In more than two-thirds of the cases I prefer quiet diplomacy. But if I think speaking out will produce results, I don't hesitate.

*Interview/People, 2-3:60.*
*1*

The world *is* divided, and here in the UN, at least, there is a chance for all the factions to talk to—and yes, even shout at—each other. Without this organization, there is no other place, nothing. So, even though we now face criticism . . . I am confident that people will be wise enough to not say, "Let's give up the ship." Yes, I am confident that we will be able to ride out the storm.

*Interview,*
*United Nations, New York/*
*Parade, 2-9:6.*

# War and Peace

**Leonid I. Brezhnev**
*General Secretary,*
*Communist Party of the Soviet Union*
1

. . . I should like to stress the significance of one major question. It has not yet been reflected in agreements between states, but it is assuming, in our opinion, ever greater urgency with each passing day. What I have in mind is that the states, above all the big powers, should conclude an agreement banning the development of new weapons of mass destruction, new systems of such weapons. The level of present-day science and technology is such that there arises a serious danger of development of still more frightful weapons than even the nuclear ones. The reason and conscience of mankind dictate the need for raising an insurmountable barrier to the development of such weapons.

*Election speech, Moscow, June 13/*
*Los Angeles Times, 6-14:(1)18.*

**Howard H. Callaway**
*Secretary of the Army of the United States*
2

I believe that if the others clearly realize that we are prepared to counter the threat of war, then we shall not have to live through the horror of war.

*At North Atlantic Treaty Organization*
*conference, Munich, Feb. 2/*
*The New York Times, 2-3:3.*

**Chou En-lai**
*Premier of the People's Republic of*
*(Communist) China*
3

The two superpowers [the U.S. and the Soviet Union] are the biggest international oppressors and exploiters today, and they are the source of a new world war. Their fierce contention is bound to lead to world war some day. The people of all countries must be prepared. Detente and peace are being talked about every-

where in the world; it is precisely this that shows there is no detente, let alone lasting peace, in this world.

*Before National People's Congress, Peking,*
*Jan. 13/The New York Times, 1-21:12.*

**Luis Echeverria (Alvarez)**
*President of Mexico*
4

The world is preparing for war—both the United States and the Soviet Union. There is an opposition of interests, a desire for universal predominance. Nuclear weapons are a preparation for war, and I do [not] believe that anyone, speaking objectively, can believe that atomic equilibrium is going to insure peace indefinitely. Only a new general consciousness can do that.

*Interview, Mexico City, Jan. 2/*
*The New York Times, 1-8:2.*

**Fred C. Ikle**
*Director, Arms Control and Disarmament*
*Agency of the United States*
5

[What is to be feared] is the use of a bomb. It's now 29 years since a nuclear weapon has been used. And we forget. Ten to 15 years down the road, it could happen. We do not have defenses. We've been lulled. We no longer have the deterrence of direct emotional contact with the fearsomeness of a nuclear weapon. We've been focused on the Russian and Chinese threat. But deterrence between matched big powers won't work with a group that has nothing to lose, a group that is not deterrable or perhaps even identifiable . . . The Indian [test] explosion on May 18, 1974, was the watershed event, like *Sputnik*. Now we know it can be done . . . It may be that no real action will occur until there's . . . a dramatic event. The world will be a very different place on the morning after a nuclear explosion.

*Interview/*
*The Washington Post, 2-23:(Potomac)11.*

363

# WHAT THEY SAID IN 1975

*(FRED C. IKLE)*

1

[Saying the U.S. should renounce the first use of nuclear weapons against cities]: To have effective deterrence, we need not guarantee to kill millions of innocent people—people who could never influence the decision we wish to deter . . . Too many people have lost the sense of proportion as to what is needed—and what is morally justified—to deter nuclear aggression. For fundamental morality, we should not rig our forces in such a way as to cause mass killing—totally unnecessary killing—in any nuclear war.

*Before Milwaukee Institute of World Affairs,*
*Nov. 24/The New York Times, 11-25:7.*

**Herman Kahn**
*Director, Hudson Institute*

2

*Somebody's* going to use nuclear weapons. One can easily imagine an uprising in East Germany or Poland or Czechoslovakia, say, leading to a major confrontation, and one side or the other using a small number of nuclear weapons for demonstration purposes, and the other side sort of retaliating, tit for tat. Then both sides will stop, because they're scared. You see, the first side will use nuclear weapons to show it's not scared, then the second retaliates to prove *it's* not scared either—and then they stop. Because they're scared.

*Interview, Boston/*
*"W": a Fairchild publication, 5-30:17.*

**Henry A. Kissinger**
*Secretary of State of the United States*

3

In a world of nuclear weapons capable of destroying mankind; in a century which has seen resort to brutal force on an unprecedented scale and intensity; in an age of ideology which turns the domestic policies of nations into issues of international contention—the problem of peace takes on a profound moral and practical difficulty.

*Before Upper Midwest Council,*
*Minneapolis, July 15/*
*The New York Times, 7-16:3.*

**Li Chiang**
*Minister for Foreign Trade of the People's*
*Republic of (Communist) China*

4

The current international situation is characterized by great disorder under heaven, and the situation is excellent. The factors for both revolution and war are increasinng. . . . the intensifying contention between the superpowers is bound to lead to war some day. . . . in any case, the future of the world is bright.

*At United Nations, New York, Sept. 2/*
*The Washington Post, 9-3:(A)12.*

**J. William Middendorf II**
*Secretary of the Navy of the United States*

5

When a war comes, it costs a great deal more to correct a miscalculation than it costs to maintain mutual-security pacts.

*U.S. News & World Report, 7-7:27.*

**Drew Middleton**
*Chief military correspondent,*
*"The New York Times"*

6

There are three types of conflicts in which the U.S. and U.S.S.R. are likely to become involved, either as acknowledged enemies or as supporters of client states. Two types we [the U.S.] could win; the third—probably not . . . The Class A war is the "unthinkable," a high-intensity war that would start in Europe and almost certainly involve the early use of tactical nuclear weapons. It carries the strong possibility of escalating into an all-out nuclear conflict. The Class B, or medium-intensity, war would most likely break out over the control or survival of a country which is important to one of the powers. The independence of Israel is crucial to us, for example, just as the survival of [Cuban Premier Fidel] Castro is important to the Russians. The Class C conflict is the low-intensity "brushfire" war of the sort we started out fighting in Vietnam. We can win a Class B or Class C war with the total commitment of the American people, something we didn't see in Vietnam. But the outlook for an American victory in a major war in Europe is dim indeed. And that is the war for which a generation of American and Russian Generals have been preparing.

*Interview/People, 9-29:36.*

**Samuel C. Phillips**
*General, United States Air Force;*
*Commander, Air Force Systems Command*

1

Just as disease or crime or natural disaster will occur despite our best preventive efforts, so war is also an ever-present possibility. Through human effort, it can be delayed, diverted, limited; but no one can safely assume at this point in time that it has ceased to be a threat to our society. No vaccine can innoculate the human race against armed attack. No agreement that outlaws war can prevent a party to that agreement from violating it if he so desires. For that reason, it is prudent to be prepared.

*At Rotary Club luncheon, San Diego,*
*Calif., April 19/Vital Speeches, 5-1:446.*

**Hugh Sidey**
*Washington bureau chief, "Time" magazine*

2

Any war—every war—is a huge human error composed of smaller mistakes. Nobody wins. One simply makes fewer blunders than the other side.

*TV commentary/*
*The National Observer, 5-24:14.*

**Stuart Symington**
*United States Senator, D—Missouri*

3

A great scientist once characterized the nuclear picture of the 1950s as "two scorpions in a bottle." Today there are six scorpions in that bottle, and we now know that soon there will be many more. So it is becoming increasingly apparent that what any two countries may decide will not necessarily be decisive, no matter how many nuclear weapons they may possess. Any country which possesses nuclear weapons could provide a grave threat to virtually any other country, a condition which implies future danger to all nations. In this nuclear age, while the spread of atomic weapons continues unchecked, the assurance of any nation that it would not seek nuclear weapons—or would only seek nuclear explosive devices for "peaceful

purposes"—may only reflect its current public attitude ... In any case, the nuclear genie is now out of control, and the number of scorpions continues to grow.

*Before the Senate, Washington/*
*The National Observer, 7-26:12.*

**Teng Hsiao-ping**
*Vice Premier of the People's Republic*
*of (Communist) China*

4

So long as imperialism exists in the world, its existence engenders war ... What prevails is not a so-called irreversible process of detente but the increasing danger of a new world war.

*Los Angeles Times, 5-25:(1)28.*

**Kurt Waldheim**
*Secretary General of the United Nations*

5

... to build world peace involves more than the efforts of a few men, and more than preventing wars. We must get at the causes of unrest in the world—the misery and starvation that is the lot of two-thirds of the world's population. The poorer countries are demanding that something be done, demanding that the wealthier countries listen to them. And more than anything else, perhaps, that is why we have had some of the recent confrontations in the UN General Assembly. I do not like these confrontations, but they do have real roots, and they do indicate that some changes must take place. And besides ... we must always remember that a war of words is better than a war with guns.

*Interview, United Nations, New York/*
*Parade, 2-9:6.*

6

Never before in peacetime has the world witnessed such a great flow of weapons of war. The world cannot be safe, secure or economically sound when global military expenditures are nearing $300-billion a year, and when some $20-billion of weapons are sold annually in the international arms trade. On this anniversary [of the signing of the UN Charter 30 years ago], I address a most urgent appeal to all nations, great and small, nuclear and non-nuclear, to exercise unilateral restraint, to slow

# WHAT THEY SAID IN 1975

*(KURT WALDHEIM)*

down their arms races and to limit the traffic in arms . . . The United Nations and the nuclear age were both born in 1945. It is a matter of profound concern that in these 30 years, despite the achievement of a number of important agreements for the limitation and control of armaments, no way has been found to halt or effectively limit the arms race in either nuclear or conventional weapons. The dangers of the proliferation of nuclear weapons not only remain but have actually increased.

*The New York Times, 6-27:2.*

**William C. Westmoreland**
*General (Ret.) and former Chief of Staff, United States Army* 1

Maybe in our open society we can't fight limited wars, but God help us if we can't; because small wars are fought to prevent large wars.

*Quote, 7-20:2.*

PART THREE

*General*

# The Arts

**Ansel Adams**
*Photographer*
1

I don't worry about [the future of photography]. There's always going to be a lot of bad stuff that reflects the trend. There is a cynicism rampant, and people have become extremely private and centripetal. There isn't an outgoing expression. But I'd be the last one to restrict anybody from saying things because you never know [if] what they're going to say will be fundamentally important. All art is advanced because of people who have something new to say. All this erotic business, however, is being done by people who consider themselves artists by virtue of their self-imposed isolation from society. It's very childish. In photography, being that it draws its image from reality, you have to be very careful how you go. I think the majority of pictures that people make are healthy, though. There's always some work being done that is very powerful and that is going to last.

*Interview, Boston/*
*The Christian Science Monitor, 1-17:5.*

**Amyas Ames**
*Chairman, Lincoln Center*
*for the Performing Arts,*
*New York; Chairman, National*
*Committee for Cultural Resources*
2

To understand what is happening to the arts [in the U.S.] today, you have to remember generations ago to the time when education was going through a similar [funding] crisis. Everyone wanted universal education, and government funds at all levels were provided to meet the needs. The same thing has happened with medical research. Now the time of the arts has come.

*Interview, New York/*
*The New York Times, 5-20:48.*

**Lindsay Anderson**
*Motion picture and stage director*
3

[It is out of] tensions that art is born . . . Life is composed of tensions. The tension between traditionalism and anarchy, or the respect for tradition and the feeling for individual liberty, is a profound tension to which there is probably no single answer. And we work out our answers, or our ways of dealing with these problems, in terms of art. And then everybody has to draw their own conclusions from the work.

*Interview, New York/*
*The Christian Science Monitor, 8-29:23.*

**Al Capp**
*Cartoonist*
4

[On the art of the late Pablo Picasso]: What a lot of garbage. I once told a group of art-lovers that abstract art is the product of the untalented, sold by the unprincipled to the undiscriminating.

*Interview, New York/*
*The Dallas Times Herald, 4-19:(A)4.*

**Henri Cartier-Bresson**
*Photographer*
5

Photography, for me—it's a way of understanding what I see. I see the various elements. And the pleasure is when I shoot; beyond that, I haven't any . . . And I'm never thinking of photography. Never, never! I forget the camera. It's just to be present. The camera has really no importance. None. It's just a way of communicating; that's why we should have film in the camera . . . And I don't even look at the photographs. If I see too many pictures, I don't feel like going and taking pictures. I'm interested in what I see, and not in photography . . .

*From television program, "Cartier-Bresson's*
*New Jersey: A Shortcut Through America"/*
*The New York Times, 7-8:31.*

369

# WHAT THEY SAID IN 1975

**Gardner Cox**
*Portrait painter*

1

[On how he paints portraits]: I struggle till I get the feeling—till it feels like them to me. I do a bale of sketches, one eye, a piece of hair. A pound of observation, then an ounce of painting.
*Interview/The Washington Post, 5-31:(C)7.*

**Elmyr de Hory**
*Painter*

2

You will always find a trace of someone else in [a painting], but that is inevitable. There is no artist who can stand alone. If you look for it, there is always a trace of someone else. Only once in 500 years will you find a titanic talent like Leonardo da Vinci.
*Interview, Ibiza/
San Francisco Examiner & Chronicle,
3-9:(Sunday Punch)5.*

**Will Durant**
*Author, Historian*

3

In morality, art, music, we're floundering around. I used to say art was the transformation of chaos into order. Now it seems to be the transformation of order into chaos. I have it in for chaos. I don't like chaos.
*Interview, New York/
The National Observer, 8-2:20.*

**Federico Fellini**
*Motion picture director*

4

[People] are always seeing things in a very conventional way. We are afraid of news. We don't want to be open. We want to hear what we know, to see what we have seen, to read what we have read, to know what we know. We defend ourselves about new things; we don't accept. That is why real art is always revolutionary. It is against the old conventional laws. Real art is always very offensive because it offends our stupidity, our nearsightedness, our fear. We want to live in safety; we don't want to be disturbed. In many ways—in a political sense, a religious sense, an art sense. We don't want to know; we don't want to be free.
*Interview, New York/
The Christian Science Monitor, 1-29:5.*

**Robert G. Goelet**
*President, American Museum of Natural
History, New York*

5

[On his assuming the presidency of the museum]: I feel like the little boy who's been given the key to the candy store . . . I can't think of anything I'd rather be doing. I have a personal weakness for fish and birds; I'm nuts for fossils; and I have a healthy respect for poisonous snakes.
*The New York Times, 12-1:15.*

**Nancy Hanks**
*Chairman, National Endowment for the
Arts of the United States*

6

In a time of stress, in a time of despair, people do turn to the arts and to culture far more. The most dramatic example is the British government, which began their Federally sponsored program for the arts during the darkest days of the war [World War II] to keep in people's minds the fact that there are beautiful things as well as terrible things.
*Before Senate Interior
Subcommittee, Washington/
The Christian Science Monitor, 4-22:15.*

7

There is no crisis in the arts; the only crisis is our failure to view them as a resource to improve our cities . . . a tremendous resource for stimulating the vitality, humaneness and the economy of our cities and towns . . . Cities . . . throughout history have been concerned with their cultural life, particularly their museums. Too often they have left the performing arts, the neighborhood arts and certainly the individual artists to fend for themselves. But their primary failure is to consider the arts as a resource. Why else would some cities be taking action that will force their museums to close— just when they are needed most by their citizens? When the doors close, the paintings are not going to rot, the plants will be watered, hopefully the animals will be fed, the history of science will be preserved. In the performing arts, dance will be created, new music composed, plays written, neighborhood arts will struggle, folk arts will survive. We won't be hurting the cultural resource—for the short term—but we will be depriving people when they have too much deprivation in their lives anyway. I say we will not be hurting the cultural resources for the short term—we will, of course, in the long haul. We will be creating a "cultural deficit." We will be diluting a resource.

*At United States Conference*
*of Mayors, Boston/*
*The Christian Science Monitor, 7-16:31.*

1

Music festivals were sold out last summer. Folk festivals were mobbed. Broadway had its best season in years and is counting on a better one in 1975-76. Attendance is high in theatres all over the country. Movie houses are full. But while the [arts] market is healthy, its cornerstones—the non-profit cultural institutions and creative artists—require assistance from a variety of sources . . . The financial problems of some cities have caused severe cutbacks in maintenance funds for museums. The Detroit Institute, for example, had to close for a month.

*At House-Senate hearing on the*
*future of her agency, Washington/*
*Los Angeles Times, 11-25:(4)18.*

**Louis Harris**
*Public-opinion analyst; Chairman, Board*
*of Associated Councils of the Arts*

2

It is . . . significant that Americans not only see the arts as vital to the quality of life, but also as an integral component of a healthy economic environment. Some 80 per cent of the public in 1973 felt that it was important to the business and economy of the community to have available facilities like museums, theatres and concert halls; and that proportion rose even higher to 85 per cent in the survey just completed . . . The American people are no longer content with dreams measured by ownership of objects or units of consumption. Of this change, which is reflected not just in arts surveys but in almost every kind of testing of public opinion our firm has undertaken recently, the arts are the beneficiary.

*Before House Education Subcommittee,*
*Washington/Variety, 10-1:119.*

**Katharine Hepburn**
*Actress*

3

I think there is a magic in man. His spirit, his attitudes toward his fellow man. his capacity for love and for infinite service, is, for me, a thrilling thing. But it is seldom depicted any more. And I grieve about that . . . We need to laugh. And our entertainment should reflect that need. But instead, freakdom has taken over. All the media are the same. The movies, the theatre, even books and paintings, are full of all kinds of junk that is just not true—at least for me. The assumption is that the audience is totally uninspired, and that pornography and depravity is what we all want to see. I find it offensive . . . and very sad . . . I love to make an audience laugh because I think laughter is very healthy. But I think any form of total concentration is healthy which relieves you of thinking about yourself. Too much concentration on yourself is totally demoralizing. And in most of what masquerades as entertainment today I find a general concentration on ugliness, and hopelessness. This is not the normal human condition . . . My reaction to pornography is this: I've had all of it. It's a bore. There is hope in human beings, not hopelessness. There is wonder and darlingness. And there is love. Why must they take repulsive, degraded people and impose their stories upon us?

*Interview, Los Angeles/*
*The Christian Science Monitor, 3-6:5.*

**Norris Houghton**
*President, American Council for the Arts*
*in Education; Dean of theatre arts,*
*State University of New York, Purchase*

4

If the arts are as important to the quality of life as we think they are, why do we not start that education right at the beginning? It is time to add to the cognitive skills. There are areas of the imagination that can be opened up, not through reading books, but through looking and listening. We want to take the arts out of the educational periphery and make them more central, more important. It is just as important to know about Beethoven as about Copernicus.

*Interview/*
*The Christian Science Monitor, 7-3:31.*

# WHAT THEY SAID IN 1975

**Jenkin Lloyd Jones**
*Editor and publisher, "The Tulsa Tribune"*

1

Some art grad could do a fascinating Ph.D. thesis if he researched the going prices for some of the carbuncles and boils that museums were snapping up only yesterday. How much that was heralded with canapes and champagne is now in the basement? Whatever happened to most of those annual nominees for "painter of the century" who had the esthetes yoicking this way and that like ill-trained coon-dogs? Callou-callay! Art that communicates is coming back. And beauty is being let out of the ghetto.

*April 26/Quote, 6-1:507.*

**Ellsworth Kelly**
*Painter*

2

Painting is a source; it teaches people how to live right. It's not just decoration. We will know in the next few years whether or not modern painting is going to have an effect. For me, it means right living, right looking, doing things the right way.

*Interview, Chatham, N.Y./*
*"W": a Fairchild publication, 9-19:17.*

**John H. Knowles**
*President, Rockefeller Foundation*

3

The arts and humanities tell us who we are, who we have been, where we are disjointed, and what we might become.

*News conference, New York/*
*The Christian Science Monitor, 4-23:10.*

**Reuben Mamoulian**
*Former motion picture director*

4

Until I was 17 I believed passionately in art for art's sake. Then when I was 18 I began to believe in art for life's sake—that the real value of art is what it does for people—and that is what I have believed in ever since.

*Interview/Los Angeles Times, 7-25:(4)1.*

**Henry Moore**
*Sculptor*

5

There is a book ... called *The Archetypal World of Henry Moore.* The author sent me a copy, but I didn't get through the first chapter because he was explaining the motives behind my work and what makes me tick. It's like telling the punch line before the joke. Perhaps there's a reason behind what I do, but I don't want to know it. There must be a mystery.

*Interview, England/People, 9-1:28.*

**John Portman**
*Architect*

6

It doesn't give me any satisfaction to draw up a visionary concept unless I can build it and, to build it, I realized quite early that somehow I would have to learn something about controlling the flow of decisions and dollars which determine how well that concept is implemented and, as important, taken care of over the long haul. So I have made it my business, and my art, to know about the life-cycle of buildings—the birth of them, the management of them through infancy to intensive use, the maintenance of them and what maintenance costs, the real-estate mechanisms, the financing mechanisms. If the architect doesn't understand these things at least well enough to talk sensibly with those who do, those who do will understand these things for him. This is not the way for architects to have a stronger influence on the environment of our society; and if I have primary passion, it is seeing to the establishment of that influence, as a matter of course, in the building process ... The completeness of a building is not just that you design it, leaving the thing to whatever happens. A building, or a group of buildings, must have a certain staying power; and this staying power is not so much a matter of architectural style as it is a matter of architectural scale—the relationship of a building, and what goes on in it, to everyday people.

*Interview, Atlanta/*
*The Christian Science Monitor, 5-19:17.*

**Robert W. Sarnoff**
*Chairman, RCA Corporation*

7

At one time there might have been grounds for predicting that the arts would be among the first to suffer a severe drop at the earliest signs of economic dislocation. The expectation would have been based on a widespread popular conviction that the arts were luxuries and therefore expendable in hard times. [That view failed to take into consideration] the strength of the cultural renaissance that had overtaken the country and the sophistication of corporate interest in the arts . . . A flourishing artistic and cultural environment inevitably stimulates the economic life of a community and enhances its attractiveness as a place to live and work . . .

*At dedication of Center for*
*Creative Studies College of*
*Art & Design, Detroit/*
*Daily Variety, 2-20:3.*

1

. . . the arts serve the world of business in a highly specialized way—as an incubator of ideas, techniques and skills that are indispensable in the design and marketing of products. When a corporation engages talent for product design, advertising and promotion, it profits substantially from art and design for which it does not pay—the insights and concepts that are borrowed freely from a living artistic heritage. There are no artisans without artists; there is no commercial art without art pursued and created for its own sake. All of the economic reasons that justify support of the arts apply as much in adversity as in prosperity. It is worth recalling that perhaps the heaviest single financial commitment to the arts in America's history occurred at the depth of the great Depression of the 1930s.

*At Conference on Business*
*and the Arts, Boston, Sept. 23/*
*Vital Speeches, 11-1:60.*

**Egon Seefehlner**
*Director, Berlin Opera*

2

In Berlin, not enough people in government speak for art. They speak for money. In Vienna, they don't ask how much but who . . . The big difference between Vienna and Berlin is that in Vienna if the government resigns it's page-two news; if the director of the opera resigns it's on page one.

*Newsweek, 12-1:96A.*

**Peter Shaffer**
*Playwright*

3

I do not believe that art and insanity have anything to say to each other. The greatest art—the symphonies of Haydn or the paintings of Bellini—virtually defines sanity for me.

*New York/*
*The New York Times Magazine, 4-13:38.*

**Beverly Sills**
*Opera singer*

4

As recently as 25 years ago, if the name was unpronounceable, the artist was automatically considered great [in the U.S.]. Today, plenty of us with very pronounceable names are doing just fine, and the snobbish stupidity that "if it comes from Europe of course it's better" is a dead issue. We can, should and must take pride in what we have given birth to, raised and cultivated [in this country]. Our artists, our museums, our singers, our dancers are among the best in the world today, and they are our greatest strength. They can give us the world of peace and beauty we dream of, because art is the signature of a civilization.

*At art symposium, Austin, Tex./*
*The New York Times, 10-6:29.*

**Lord Snowdon**
*Photographer*

5

[On his photography]: If somebody said they could recognize a style of mine, that would be my failure. My job is to report in a totally chameleon-like way, to dissolve into a wall, to record, and that's all. I'm not an artist . . . What I will never do is I will never explain a picture. I will never try to say why it's there or why I've taken something, because it's up to the viewer to work something out himself.

*Interview, New York/*
*The Christian Science Monitor, 6-6:18.*

6

It's nonsense to call photography "art." Photography is only a way of informing people about life. Pictures are to look at in papers and magazines, and then the newsprint should be used to wrap up fish.

*New York/Family Weekly, 6-22:18.*

# WHAT THEY SAID IN 1975

## Raphael Soyer
*Painter*

1

The big quality [in my work] is human. I paint people in the context of their daily lives. That's why Degas is my favorite—he was a very profound painter. He painted dancers, but not in the usual pretty way. He caught their charm, but he also drew them scratching themselves, yawning. He drew them in the context of their own lives. He painted nudes in a new way—he didn't paint idealized women, idealized figures. He painted realistic, truthful women—woman the way she is.

*Interview/*
*"W": a Fairchild publication, 11-28:11.*

## Tom Stoppard
*Playwright*

2

[On politics in art]: I'm not impressed by art *because* it's political. I believe in art being good art or bad art, not relevant art or irrelevant art. The plain truth is that if you are angered or disgusted by a particular injustice or immorality, and you want to do something about it *now, at once,* then you can hardly do worse than write a play about it. That's what art is bad at.

*Interview, London/*
*The New York Times, 10-19:(2)5.*

## Michael Tilson Thomas
*Orchestra conductor*

3

[A main reason for America's recent cultural blossoming is the result of] the very thing we used to be condemned for: "Americans have no roots, no culture, they're just a jumble of people from all over the place." Well, exactly so. We have absorbed all those cultures, and created a magnificent new one of our own. There has never been a country before that has been in such a position.

*Interview/U.S. News & World Report, 5-19:57.*

## George C. Wallace
*Governor of Alabama (D)*

4

The great middle class is a mass of good people, and they're getting tired of the proliferation of filth in textbooks and on the screen, and especially on television. It's just downright indecent—*sickening*—and it contributes to the breakdown in law and order . . . They make fun of religion, talk about sex acts, even describe some of them, and they make fun of patriotism . . . Nobody's trying to be a goody-goody, but you don't have to be a goody-goody to be offended. The Supreme Court has to write a hundred pages on what pornography is. The average man who works in a steel mill can tell you right off whether that's filth or not.

*Interview/Newsweek, 4-21:44.*

# Fashion

## Bill Blass
*Fashion designer*

1

Men in America tend to be overweight and make matters worse by wearing clothes that are too big for them—the Zero Mostel look—or too small—the Oliver Hardy look. Ill-fitting clothes are one of the biggest problems. [Also bad is] dressing youthfully when you're past the first flush of youth and being sheepish by dressing like everyone else. The problem is, only a handful of men have the security to care what they look like.

*Interview, New York/*
*"W": a Fairchild publication, 3-7:17.*

2

Women have been wearing men's clothes forever. I've always thought that there isn't anything sexier than a gal in a man's trench coat—if she's sexy and pretty. As a man, I react favorably to women borrowing my clothes. It's always flattering to be copied.

*The New York Times Magazine, 4-27:(2)38.*

## Marc Bohan
*Fashion designer*

3

Ready-to-wear is part of a general democratization that is taking place everywhere. It's part of a bigger revolution. Couture remains the work of artisans. The big jewelry houses sell luxury for luxury's sake. Couture clothing is, after all, at least useful even if it is not an investment.

*Interview, Paris/*
*"W": a Fairchild publication, 2-7:14.*

## Donald Brooks
*Fashion designer*

4

Clothes are only a supplement. It may sound a bit funny coming from a designer, but I don't think clothes are madly important. The complete woman starts with her own brain. It is flighty, silly and very lightweight for any woman to think otherwise.

*Dallas, April 15/*
*The Dallas Times Herald, 4-16:(G)1.*

## Roberto Capucci
*Fashion designer*

5

High fashion is finished. Today women have become objects; they put on the fad of the moment. . . . they are afraid to look old so they camouflage themselves like girls covering themselves with rags. Our clients used to come from show business and the aristocracy, but today they are rich bourgeoisie and an aristocracy that is rapidly thinning out. Those clients are finished; they were part of a world that is disappearing. Once women came to us for an entire wardrobe; now they come for a special occasion, a marriage, a birthday, or a very private party in some princess' house. Once we could choose: I'll dress this one, I won't dress that one. Now we can't choose anything. It is sad, after having spent so much time and energy, to see what happens to our collection. It's not fun any more. There's no excitement. Young ones aren't interested in high fashion any more . . . The happiest moment is the moment of creation. I like to get up at dawn, when my ideas are freshest. But a creator isn't free to design what he likes any more. It is very sad.

*Interview, Rome/*
*The Christian Science Monitor, 9-15:(B)12.*

## Pierre Cardin
*Fashion designer*

6

I'm tired of simple clothes that could be made by anybody. We couturiers have almost killed Paris as a center of creativity. Poiret—everyone said he was grotesque. Chanel—her contemporaries called her vulgar. Fifty years from now, which one of us will be numbered among the real creators? The couture should

# WHAT THEY SAID IN 1975

take risks. I see my role to provoke. To shock. With ready-to-wear getting better all the time, unless the couture offers something different, why should it expect to attract and keep a clientele?

*Interview, Paris/*
*"W": a Fairchild publication, 2-7:2.*

**Hubert de Givenchy**
*Fashion designer*
1

I am crazy about this profession. I have wanted to have my own couture house since I was a child. The biggest happiness I know is to arrive here early in the morning. To listen to the Portuguese cleaning women sing. To be alone in my studio with my beautiful fabrics. To hear the workers arriving, the phone starting to ring. For me, it is like a heart beating. My day always ends too soon. I'd never change my profession for anything in the world.

*Interview, Paris/*
*"W": a Fairchild publication, 2-7:8.*

2

The couture customer doesn't want to pay all that money for a dress everyone else is going to be wearing. And she wants to be first with something entirely new. For her, fashion's like bread that's good when it's hot from the oven, not when it's stale.

*"W": a Fairchild publication, 2-7:7.*

**Oscar de la Renta**
*Fashion designer*
3

In times of stress, inventiveness is needed and competition is strong. But pure fantasy is not the story [in fashion] now. Money is not exactly abundant. Women are much more choosy. They must be stimulated to buy, yes. But they're only buying those things that serve their needs. No woman who buys clothes in my price range buys out of real need. But she can be tempted. She can use clothes to cheer herself up. Fashion is the only frivolity we indulge ourselves on a daily basis.

*Beverly Hills, Calif./*
*Los Angeles Times, 2-13:(4)1.*

**Erte**
*Fashion designer*
4

. . . the American press has always considered me—what you call it—a freak. They do not understand that what I have always stood for in design for women and men is harmony. I firmly believe that every human being has a duty to make himself as attractive as possible. Not many of us are born beautiful. That is why I have always attached so much importance to clothes. Clothes are a kind of alchemy: They can transform human beings into things of beauty or ugliness.

*Los Angeles/Los Angeles Times, 11-5:(4)6.*

**John Fairchild**
*Publisher, "Women's Wear Daily" and*
*"W" magazine*
5

"Style" is an expression of individualism mixed with charisma. Fashion is something that comes after style.

*The Dallas Times Herald, 7-16:(G)1.*

**Rhonda Fleming**
*Actress*
6

I've never gone along with way-out [fashion] trends. I like to adapt and choose what is right for me. Every chic woman knows the value of personal compromise.

*Interview, Los Angeles/*
*Los Angeles Times, 6-29:(5)4.*

**Ted Lapidus**
*Fashion designer*
7

There is no greater happiness for a designer than to have many, many women all over the world wear his clothes. The real creator is happy and proud for a wider audience. The film director is not really satisfied if his movies win the acclaim of critics but play to an empty theatre. Neither is the fashion designer who dresses a few old ladies in the name of haute couture.

*Los Angeles/Los Angeles Times, 9-17:(4)4.*

8

It is most difficult to create simplicity. I find that too many designers try to add on when they should be thinking of taking off. [Fashion] needs simplicity to make it work.

*Los Angeles Herald-Examiner, 11-10:(B)1.*

**Yves Saint Laurent**
*Fashion designer*

1

What I hate are the eternal "shows"—to present fashion four times a year as a sort of spectacle in 1975 seems to me ridiculous. This idea of a "show" is what kills fashion and gives a false impression to the general public, whether it's couture or ready-to-wear. I feel there should be a continuous creation of clothes. If I continue the haute couture, it is to give the equivalent of the principle of my ready-to-wear clothes that don't date, that aren't "fashion."

*Interview, Paris/*
*"W": a Fairchild publication, 2-7:12.*

**Vidal Sassoon**
*Hair stylist*

2

Long hair for men fortunately doesn't mean anything any more. Hair is making a social statement, but from a point of fashion. We have come a long way from the youths who wore so much long hair it became a uniform—its own form of uniformity.

*Quote, 4-13:348.*

**Emanuel Ungaro**
*Fashion designer*

3

Clothes, apart from cars, are the only things that move in the street. They have a determining influence. A social function. A dynamism. I am not ashamed to be creating clothes in the world today. Why should I have any more shame than a painter? More and more I am convinced of the value of the couture. We are the professionals in this business of clothes.

*Interview, Paris/*
*"W": a Fairchild publication, 2-7:11.*

**John Weitz**
*Fashion designer*

4

Today, accountants look like Shakespearean actors, space salesmen look like art directors, hairdressers wear short hair, clothes designers dress totally conservatively, the computer programmer wears six-inch heels, an orthodontist comes on like a cowboy and a rancher like a college student. I watch people going into Hunting World and coming out in their safari suits and I wonder who are the real hunters and what have they been hunting lately. Everybody's into reverse role-playing.

*The New York Times Magazine, 9-21:(2)75.*

# Journalism

## Jack Anderson
*Political columnist* 1

Since Watergate, the [newspaper] editors are going along with the establishment. The establishment, the Cabinet, have been shaken with what happened, that the press can topple [a] President. The press itself is shaken by it. A lot of editors and reporters are wearing a hair shirt—sackcloth and ashes and lace; and they're over-doing it a little bit, trying to prove too hard how patriotic and responsible we are, that we're not against the establishment, the government, that we're not all gadflys. The country was better served by a watchful press.

*Radio broadcast/*
*The Washington Post, 3-20:(A)15.*

## James Bellows
*Editor, "Washington Star"* 2

We [of the press] are so well educated, so well paid, I'm not sure we know what's important to the people in the country. [There are too many] green-eyeshade editors who believe the latest little tidbit has to be jammed into the papers, when all the public wants is a little understanding. The public likes to know more how their dollars are spent rather than high-flown policy.

*At Town Meeting, Kennedy Center,*
*Washington, Sept. 17/*
*The Washington Post, 9-18:(B)4.*

## Benjamin C. Bradlee
*Executive editor, "The Washington Post"* 3

[On whether his paper should have printed a story about a secret CIA mission to raise a sunken Soviet submarine]: On the one side, there's a claim by a government official of some standing that what you're about to print will harm the country's national security. But on the other side, you have the conviction that you're being conned, that what is at stake is not any national security, but just plain embarrassment. You're forced to make these decisions with incomplete information and with speed. This decision was made, and so be it. I do not today have information to know whether it's true or false that the national interest was harmed with the publication this morning. The only place where you could get that information is the CIA itself, and I'm not sure I'd believe them, anyway.

*March 19/The Washington Post, 3-20:(A)15.*

## David Brinkley
*News commentator,*
*National Broadcasting Company* 4

I think you guys [in print journalism] owe us [in broadcast journalism] a vote of thanks. We're driving people back to reading newspapers. We titillate you with little hints about what's happening. We give you so little information that you have to get a newspaper to find out what the hell we're talking about. The one function that TV news performs very well is that when there is no news we give it to you with the same emphasis as if there was news. We're very good at no news.

*Interview, Washington/*
*Los Angeles Times, 10-28:(4)13.*

## Warren E. Burger
*Chief Justice of the United States* 5

When the media make attacks on judges—I'm speaking now not of criticism necessarily of the opinions, but criticism in the broad sense—by a long-standing tradition in this country, judges never respond. Therefore, there is at least some obligation on the media to act with the same kind of restraint with which the media expects judges to act. For example, the powers of the Supreme Court are sometimes said to be virtually unreviewable. The same thing can be said

378

for the power of the media. The media is indeed becoming almost a fourth branch of government, in an informal sense, a de facto sense. Its powers should be exercised with restraint, just as the powers of the Supreme Court of the United States should be exercised with restraint . . . That does not mean it is the duty of the free press to defend the judiciary. I think it is the obligation of the free press to see that all the facts are exposed to the public so that the people, the readers and the listeners can make a fair judgment on criticism of the Judicial Branch.

*Interview, July/*
*Los Angeles Times, 9-24:(1)4.*

**Al Capp**
*Cartoonist*

1

[On his painting full-sized canvases of his comic strips] : It occurred to me that my work is being destroyed almost as soon as it is printed. One day it is being read; the next day someone's wrapping fish in it. The American comic strip is as unique and as precious an art as jazz. I think it should be preserved.

*New York/*
*People, 5-5:11.*

**Prince Charles**
*Prince of Wales*

2

[Scolding the British press for sensationalism] : I have read so many reports recently telling everyone who I am about to marry that, when last year a certain young lady was staying at Sandringham, a crowd of about 10,000 appeared when we went to church. Such was the obvious conviction that what they had read was true that I almost felt I had better espouse myself at once so as not to disappoint too many people . . . I often wonder as I read my newspapers—I shan't say which—and glance at the TV, whether those in the journalistic professions really appreciate the immense responsibility they have when reporting facts or commenting upon events and ideas.

*At Parliamentary press corps*
*luncheon, London, March 3/*
*Los Angeles Times, 3-4:(1)15.*

**Harlan Cleveland**
*Director, Program in International Affairs,*
*Aspen Institute; Former president,*
*University of Hawaii*

3

The passion for public hearings, too much of the time, serves only the purpose of having held a public hearing so that it cannot be later said a public hearing was not held. Occasionally, the public hearing actually attracts an audience; on these occasions, the news reports feature the most extreme and partisan statements heard, and ignore as unnewsworthy the voices of reason and counsels of compromise. The provoking and advertising of controversy is not the same as "openness," but it is a hallowed tradition of journalism that if there is no controversy, if there is merely cooperation and compromise and consensus, the process must not be open enough.

*Before American Society for Public*
*Administration, Syracuse (N.Y.) University/*
*The Washington Post, 1-11:(A)12.*

**John B. Connally, Jr.**
*Former Secretary of the Treasury of the*
*United States; Former Governor of Texas*
*(D, now R)*

4

Since World War II, our society has changed in startling and fundamental ways. No change has been more significant than the burgeoning of the television industry with its ability to put the world with living color and seeming reality into our nation's homes. It is not an over-statement to say that television today wields power and influence in this country second only to that of the President. A John Chancellor, a Walter Cronkite, a Harry Reasoner, a Howard K. Smith [all news commentators] are regularly heard—and heard with the great advantage of being presumed objective—by millions of people. Any one of them has more direct impact and potential influence on the public than the Speaker of the House, the majority leaders and the minority leaders of both houses of Congress combined.

*At Associated Press Broadcasters*
*convention, San Antonio, Tex.,*
*May 30/Variety, 6-4:34.*

# WHAT THEY SAID IN 1975

## Alan Cranston
*United States Senator, D–California*
1

The First Amendment is not a piece of special-interest legislation for the newspapers, radio and television. It is a governmental guarantee to a free people without which they could not remain free for long. One of the fundamental services that a free press renders to a free people is to watchdog the various levels of government—the officials, the bureaucrats who handle the people's money and who wield awesome power over the people's lives and freedoms.

*At American Civil Liberties Union Southern California chapter conference, Los Angeles, May 31/Los Angeles Times, 6-1:(3)13.*

2

I'm more concerned about the need for protecting reporters and the free flow of information to the public than I am about the need for protecting government agencies. I think that we need a shield law to exempt reporters from prosecution for refusing to reveal their sources. A great deal of the information that the American public gets about what its government is up to does not come out in formal press releases. It comes from digging by the press and from leaks by officials who think the government is doing improper things. If you close that off, you would threaten the free press and the ability of the people in this democracy to know what is going on . . . A free press is an essential restraint on government; it is basic to our Constitutional concept of a government of limited powers. I think the Founding Fathers had a very acute understanding of that when they wrote the First Amendment. They were more concerned about protecting people against the abuses of government than enabling the government to do things for people—or to people.

*Interview/U.S. News & World Report, 8-18:37.*

## Walter Cronkite
*News commentator,*
*Columbia Broadcasting System*
3

[On his TV news program] : I never go home without feeling we've done an inadequate job. I guess we can't do everything; but the things that get left on the cutting-room floor, on my desk—that ought to have been broadcast that day—appall me.

*Interview, New York/*
*San Francisco Examiner & Chronicle,*
*1-26:(A)19.*

4

There *is* a lot of bad news published and broadcast today, because there are a lot of problems; and we'll never solve them if we don't expose them to the light of day. As one of the messengers who brings you the daily diet of bad tidings, let me pass on just a word of advice: Listen and read the news reports carefully, for they are the fire alarms of our civilization—identifying the areas for concern, alerting us to dangers that need alleviation.

*At student convocation, Charlotte, N.C./*
*The Dallas Times Herald, 12-28:(B)3.*

## Lewis A. Engman
*Chairman, Federal Trade Commission*
5

. . . the Fairness Doctrine represents an unfortunate step away from freedom of speech, an unfortunate intrusion into the marketplace of speech. In an unrestricted media market, the incentives are all in the direction of airing diverse views. In diversity there is controversy, and in controversy the networks know very well that there are dollars. The Fairness Doctrine turns those incentives upside down. Its penalties act as an inhibition. With it we get less diversity, not more. As broadcasters shy away from controversy and pull punches, we get even greater homogeniety in programming. In the pursuit of fairness we get only blandness. . . . the actual requirements of the Fairness Doctrine . . . were . . . to devote a reasonable amount of time to the discussion of controversial issues, and to afford reasonable opportunities for opposing viewpoints. I put it to you that by enforcing the second requirement, we make impossible the fulfillment of the first. We are stifling debate. I cannot see how that can ever lead us to a nation free from bias, dishonesty and injustice. The Fairness Doctrine, like our fair-trade laws, is an instance in which benevolent-sounding words have masked a miscarriage of our free-market system. It is high time for Congress to abolish it.

*At communications law program, University of California, Los Angeles, Oct. 29/\*\**

**Oriana Fallaci**
*Journalist, Interviewer*

1

[When conducting an interview,] I'm never insulting, no, but I can be brutal. When I have a brutal question to put, I always say: "Now I'm going to put [to] you a brutal question." I don't write that because it would be monotonous to read that each time. The questions are brutal because research of truth is a kind of surgery. Surgery hurts.

*Interview, Rome/Time, 10-20:69.*

**John Kenneth Galbraith**
*Former professor of economics,*
*Harvard University*

2

The moods of America, as written by the columnists, come from [journalists] Evans and Novak talking to Joe Kraft, who then talks to Tom Wicker, who then asks Scotty Reston, who gets back to Evans. The closed-circuit recycling of information in Washington has little to do with what's going on in America.

*Interview, Cambridge, Mass./*
*The Christian Science Monitor, 12-9:19.*

**Julian Goodman**
*Chairman, National Broadcasting Company*

3

Through the Fairness Doctrine it has become easy for special-interest groups to challenge many television programs and to put forward their version of "fairness" under the camouflage of objectivity ... The fact that relatively few of these complaints are pursued by FCC inquiry—and fewer still upheld by the FCC or the courts—is good indication that broadcasters are meeting their obligations to the public. Yet the possibility of drawing fairness challenges that can result in lengthy and expensive court battles has the effect of stifling aggressive journalism in broadcasting. Many broadcasters are made to steer clear of controversial issues because of the high price tag that could be placed on freedom of expression. Where legitimate self-interest stops and the dictatorship of special interest begins can only be determined by giving a fair hearing to the many representative groups who seek us out. But willingness to listen should not carry with it the condition that broadcasters must bow down to every group or individual that has an ax to grind.

*At National Conference of Christians and*
*Jews, Memphis, April 28/*
*Daily Variety, 4-29:8.*

**Harvey Jacobs**
*Editor, "Indianapolis News"*

4

Reporters are a brash lot, most of them; some of them downright rude. But probably they have heard every kind of story, faced every dodge and bluff, and have dealt with too many stuffed shirts. They work under very great time stresses, particularly the TV reporter whose deadlines and time frames are almost unbearable. The TV reporter or interviewer might have to say, "Senator Jones, give us your impression of the President's new energy plan. We have 30 seconds." The newspaper reporter has a little more time, and he or she generally goes after the background of the story rather than just a 30-second quote. But because of their manners and techniques, all reporters become slightly suspect. By the very nature of his business, the good reporter is an invader of privacy; he disturbs the peace; he is looking for the story behind the facade. Andre Malraux said it well: "The truth about a man lies first and foremost in what he hides."

*Before Rotary Club, Indianapolis, Sept. 29/*
*Vital Speeches, 11-15:87.*

**Hobart D. Lewis**
*Chairman and editor-in-chief,*
*"The Reader's Digest"*

5

We are still essentially a family magazine, and the new areas remain within the scope of our original diversification, which was into family help and entertainment ... Our basic philosophy is in helping the reader and his family and contributing to their improving themselves. It's a basic ingredient and it hasn't diminished. We should have more of it. Tastes change and so does our content. I know that when [the *Digest*'s founder], DeWitt Wallace, brought out an article on syphillis, it was among the first. When we published *Love Story*

# WHAT THEY SAID IN 1975

*(HOBART D. LEWIS)*

we used six four-letter words which would have been unheard of in the old days.

*Interview, Pleasantville, N.Y./*
*The New York Times, 3-28:54.*

**L. D. McAlister**
*Managing editor, "The Atlanta Journal"*     1

Too many people feel they are getting enough news from TV. They're not, but they feel they are. We must find more ways to involve the public in the feeling that reading newspapers should be part of their life.

*San Francisco Examiner & Chronicle,*
*10-26:(This World)2.*

**Harold Mendelsohn**
*Chairman, department of mass*
*communications, University of Denver*     2

[On the popularity of all-news radio stations]: It's part of a general social-psychological phenomenon. Americans are now very anxious about knowing what happens the instant it happens. Deep in the recesses of their consciousness is the damn thermonuclear thing and the related fear that we must all be ready at an instant's notice for some tragic catastrophe. People constantly feel in imminent danger. Subconsciously, they're terrified that if they don't keep up, they'll be caught short.

*Los Angeles Times, 9-2:(1)20.*

**Ralph Nader**
*Lawyer; Consumer advocate*     3

[American journalism is] one of the few institutions that has remained all but immune from consumer comment. The mass media has grown aloof to their audience because there is so little organized criticism from without.

*At University of Wisconsin, Madison/*
*The Christian Science Monitor, 4-11:2.*

**Ron Nessen**
*Press Secretary to President of the*
*United States Gerald R. Ford*     4

The most difficult part of my job these past six months has been to overcome a mood of hostility and suspicion and distrust that was built up between the press corps and the White House during the Watergate years and the Vietnam years. And I have only been partly successful in this... One of the terrible legacies of Vietnam and Watergate is that many [reporters], and many of their readers and viewers and listeners, simply do not believe what government officials tell them. [Since President Ford took over,] the clouds of suspicion and mistrust have begun to lift. But we have a distance to go. I'm going to work like hell as Press Secretary to see that we get there. The best remedy for the hangover of suspicion is honesty.

*Before Sigma Delta Chi,*
*Washington, March 18/*
*The Dallas Times Herald, 3-19:(A)24.*

5

[On his job as Press Secretary]: When you're trying to live down [former Press Secretary to President Nixon, Ronald L.] Ziegler and those who came before Ziegler during the Vietnam war and the disbelief and cynicism that has grown up, you only have so much good-will and believability left. And if you burn it all up and you've got none left, then I think maybe you should step aside and let them get someone new in here who could then burn up his own credibility. I frankly think that any Press Secretary is going to use it up pretty fast.

*Interview/*
*The Washington Post, 6-27:(A)1.*

6

My experience as a news reporter for 20 years convinces me that sometimes the American people miss the full complexities and background of important issues in their newspapers, television, radio and magazines. This happens once in a while because of the pressures under which reporters, editors and producers must work: the deadlines, the competition, the lack of air time or newspaper space, the need to find something catchy for the headline.

*Before National Association*
*of Realtors, San Francisco/*
*The Christian Science Monitor, 11-21:17.*

**John B. Oakes**
*Editorial-page editor, "The New York Times"* [1]

If we of the press do not in fact have the freedom guaranteed us by the First Amendment, we cannot in any meaningful way be responsible, either to our readership or to ourselves. And conversely, if we of the American press do not hold ourselves responsible, we are not likely to hang on very much longer to our freedom ... [This can be accomplished] by acting with a sense of humility, by remembering that we may not always be right in every case, by insisting on the highest standards of probity and of fairness, by consciously striving to increase our credibility, improve our accessibility, to [emphasize] our accountability to the public.

*At Dickinson College, Carlisle, Pa., Feb. 23/*
*The New York Times, 2-25:38.*

[2]

[On why his newspaper does not carry political cartoons]: A political cartoon, to be any good, has to be so striking and so dramatic as to be, in its very nature, unfair ... A good strong cartoon is very likely to distort an editorial position that can be made more clearly, more fairly and more accurately through the use of words.

*The New York Times Magazine, 11-9:50.*

**German Ornes**
*Chairman, committee on freedom of the press, Inter-American Press Association; Editor, "El Caribe," Santo Domingo* [3]

[On press freedom in the Western Hemisphere]: Since the majority of the nations of our continent won their independence, the American press has never gone through such a deep crisis as that which it now faces. As for liberty—and, very particularly, freedom of the press—the American continent is, today, a cluster of islands of liberty encircled by an angry sea of oppression and dictatorships ... U.S. newsmen now live under a threat of harsh legal sanctions if they refuse to reveal their sources of information. The right of journalists to protect their sources is recognized in the legislation of many states, but it is not recognized by U.S.

Federal law and a majority of the courts. [Newspapers] have suffered serious difficulties due to extreme labor demands. Either for ideological or practical reasons, an increasing number of unions are going beyond reasonable limits in their dealings with publishers.

*Before Inter-American Press Association,*
*Sao Paulo, Brazil, Oct. 20/*
*The New York Times, 10-21:40.*

**Everett C. Parker**
*Director, office of communication, United Church of Christ* [4]

[Arguing against a bill to abolish the Fairness Doctrine]: Broadcast licenses have monopoly values running into hundreds of millions of dollars. They were granted in return for promises of public service. To waive these promises gratuitously would amount to a gift of public property so enormous as to make it the biggest giveaway to special interests in the history of the United States. [The bill] is being ballyhooed as a great forward stride to preserve the First Amendment, [but would in fact] not only strip the people of the United States of their freedom of speech and of access to the information we must have to make decisions in a democracy, it would steal from us our very birthright. [Supporters of the bill are] so solicitous of fancied restrictions on the free speech of gigantic networks and other media conglomerates that they want to see ordinary citizens silenced completely for fear they will inhibit broadcasters.

*Before Senate Communications Subcommittee,*
*Washington, April 30/*
*The Hollywood Reporter, 5-1:2.*

**Norman Vincent Peale**
*Pastor, Marble Collegiate Church, New York* [5]

It may seem like we're in a negative trough these days, but that's *your* fault—the media's. It's all this television and radio they throw at you. It's not politics. It's not Watergate—it's the fact newspapers decided to cover Watergate. It's not inflation—it's all the bleak economic commentary that's forced upon us. Now, the public can take just so much of a cycle. And I can tell

*(NORMAN VINCENT PEALE)*

you positively that the public has had it with the negative cycle.

*Interview, Pawling, N.Y./*
*San Francisco Examiner &*
*Chronicle, 5-25:(C)3.*

**William Proxmire**
*United States Senator, D—Wisconsin*
1

[Arguing against the Fairness Doctrine] : [It violates the Constitution] because it's the equal-time rule and other props put in the hands of government powers that permit the government to control communication through the electronic media. There is no question that radio and television broadcasters communicate exactly that which is communicated by printed publications. Broadcasting is no more and no less than electronic publication. And publication is the act of bringing something to public notice. There also is no question in my mind, and in the minds of many others, that the Fairness Doctrine and the equal-time rule clearly abridge the freedoms guaranteed the people under the First Amendment.

*Before Senate Communications Subcommittee,*
*Washington/The Hollywood Reporter, 4-29:1.*

**Sally Quinn**
*Journalist, "The Washington Post"*
2

[Saying that Washington dinner parties are part of the job of a journalist] : When you sit at dinner and talk gardening with a Senator who loves gardening, that's work—because the next day, when you call him for some information on a story, you can probably get it. When you see someone like [columnist] Joe Kraft talking in a corner with [Secretary of State] Henry [Kissinger], Joe's going to get a story and Henry's going to get a point across. A lot gets accomplished.

*Newsweek, 12-1:89.*

**Dan Rather**
*News correspondent, Columbia*
*Broadcasting System*
3

TV news tends to be a headline service, not an in-depth service. Anybody who just watches

TV news cannot be well-informed. You have to read.

*San Francisco Examiner &*
*Chronicle, 1-5:(This World)2.*

**George E. Reedy**
*Dean, College of Journalism, Marquette*
*University; Former Press Secretary to*
*the President of the United States*
*(Lyndon B. Johnson)*
4

For a while, every reporter was out to be Woodward and Bernstein [reporters who broke the Watergate story]. Ten years ago, it was Tom Wolfe and participatory journalism. Fifteen or 20 years ago, it was James Reston. The fads come and go.

*Time, 11-24:78.*

**A. M. Rosenthal**
*Managing editor, "The New York Times"*
5

The question that must be posed to themselves by [newspaper] publishers and broadcasters is whether, given the need to produce a profit margin large enough to keep them viable, they are spending enough money to do their jobs right. And I think most of them are not ... The consumer who would raise hell if he were shortchanged at the supermarket or who found himself buying watered milk says nothing and does nothing to persuade the local editor or publisher or broadcaster that he does want to know what is going on in the world even when there is not a disaster or crisis taking place.

*Lecture, Johns Hopkins University,*
*April 7/The New York Times, 4-9:30.*

6

The public often sees the press as the interrogator and investigator of the government and of politicians, the eternal gadfly. To the extent that this is true, it is a happy and healthy thing. But the public is not often enough reminded that most of the time most of the press functions as the conveyor of the opinions, attitudes and statements of officialdom. This is a legitimate function of the press. But it becomes a danger when the press sees it as its only major function. The very first thing an authoritarian government does is to reduce the press to the function of conveying officially approved information. This can happen in our own society without a take-over of authoritarian society. It can happen if the public sees the government as "we" and the press as "they." It can happen if the courts intervene between information and its publication. And it can happen if the press allows the profit motive to reduce its ability to report news firsthand [and] search out information instead of waiting for it to be given to it, to cut back on the amount of information it distributes.

*Lecture, Johns Hopkins University, April 7/*
*The National Observer, 4-26:13.*

**Hughes Rudd**
*News commentator, Columbia*
*Broadcasting System*
1

On film you can hide things—but the live [TV] camera has [the] superb quality of naked honesty. You come across as what you are—if not immediately, eventually. That's why news commentators are so vivid to viewers ... The public gets more annoyed at TV than it ever does at newspapers because on TV the commentator is actually talking to you, and a lot of people resent being told about things they don't want to hear. The bad mail I get usually concerns us smart alecks in New York telling the rest of the country what to believe.

*Interview/*
*Los Angeles Herald-Examiner, 9-11:(B)8.*

**Richard S. Salant**
*President, Columbia Broadcasting*
*System News*
2

If one believes in a free democratic society, there must be freedom of the press, which is really why the free-press issue is unresolved after 30 years of consideration by the United Nations. It is a choice between freedom, including freedom to be absurd, wrong, bullheaded and exasperating on the one hand, and on the other hand, to be "responsible" but only as defined by the state ... There is no democratic society in which the people are the source of ultimate power through free elections of their governors, without freedom of speech and of

the press ... Press freedom is societal—flowing not only to, but from, the people—and written documents are not the final word. Rather, what provides the ultimate base for true press freedom is the presence of a tradition, a compact, a national convention, a delicate gentleman's agreement. And it may be all too precarious a base. Freedom of the press must altogether depend on public opinion and on the general spirit of the people and of the government. It is at our peril if we fail to persuade the people.

*Australia/Variety, 12-9:54.*

**Eric Sevareid**
*News commentator, Columbia*
*Broadcasting System*
3

American journalists today ... have been forced and lured out of their normal and proper role in our society. They are becoming not just the critics in the aisle but actors in the play. Journalists furiously write about other journalists, and an unhealthy self-consciousness is infecting their ranks. We are important; but we are not *that* important.

*Before International Platform Association/*
*Quote, 9-28:249.*

**William Shawn**
*Editor, "The New Yorker" magazine*
4

[On the occasion of his magazine's 50th anniversary]: I don't understand anniversaries and birthdays. I don't even understand them journalistically. But I have to give in to your interest. It is an occasion to say, perhaps, that *The New Yorker* is here. Naturally, I'm happy, and I can't quite believe it. The odds were against it. We went on our own way, and by going our own course we were in greater jeopardy than we might have been. I hope it continues to work out. We're not certain about the future. It's surprising and pleasing that the magazine is still going. Each issue has to be as good as we can make it. We can't depend on what we did 20 or 30 years ago. I worry about each issue, to make it as good as we can. I read every word in the magazine, at least twice. We're trying to put out a work of art.

*Interview, New York/*
*The Washington Post, 2-16:(F)1.*

# WHAT THEY SAID IN 1975

**Howard K. Smith**
*News commentator, American
Broadcasting Company*
1

What worries me is that difficult times intensify frictions and the friction I fear most is the friction between us, government and press, or the media. We in the press emphasize the negative—what went wrong—rarely what went right in a nation whose history indicates most things went right. We often tend to demoralize rather than inform, and some of you [in government] tend to impatience at the ever-nagging, nosy media, and to consider restrictions upon us. Well, we must fend off these tendencies to a hostile and destructive collision at any cost.
*Before the House, Washington, June 14/
The Christian Science Monitor, 6-23:31.*

**Lawrence E. Spivak**
*Producer and moderator, "Meet the Press,"
National Broadcasting Company*
2

Television has made it much harder to build god-like creatures [in politics], because you see and hear them instantly; and if they falter, or if they don't answer as carefully as they ought to answer, then they have feet of clay.
*Interview, Washington/People, 8-25:54.*

**Arthur Ochs Sulzberger**
*Publisher, "The New York Times"*
3

Unhappily, across the country we are witnessing the dangerous rise of the publisher-judge. [These judges,] undoubtedly out of the best of motives, have taken it on themselves to decide what must not be printed . . . It is not the job of the press, nor of the judicial system, to help a government keep its secrets. On the whole, the government has done a pretty effective job of withholding information. A vigorous adversary relationship between government and press is much healthier than the alternative, where one single unchecked force decides what the public is not to know. Lord knows we have enough of the "official version" of what is going on in the United States. In light of that, we [the press] have a responsibility to provide dissidents with an outlet.
*At meeting of Second Judicial Circuit of
the United States, Buck Hills, Pa., Sept. 12/
The New York Times, 9-13:41.*

**Davis Taylor**
*Publisher, "Boston Globe"*
4

There are the three commandments of the newspaper profession. I am speaking of *accountability*, *credibility* and *respectability*. Now, more than ever, do we owe it to ourselves—and to our readers—to be *accountable* for what we do. It's been said that the pen is mightier than the sword, and it's true—truer today, perhaps, than ever before. And, as this power increases, so does our obligation to be accountable to the people we serve. We should listen more carefully to our readers and those who complain about what we print. They are often more right than some of us edgy journalists—I include myself. We must say what we mean and mean what we say—and welcome all opposing points of view . . . *Credibility* can't be imposed by edict, or cajoled by contest prizes . . . If you have to ask how to go about it, you're unlikely to find out. But one thing is certain: If your readers don't think you have it, you're not going to succeed as a newspaper. That audience will decide whether what we have to say is to be delivered. And they're not going to be hoodwinked . . . In the face of an increasingly complex society, newspapers must be compassionate—as well as concerned. And, if they are, then *respectability* will follow as night does day. A newspaper that is not respected in the end will not be read either.
*Upon receiving Elijah Parish Lovejoy Award
for journalism, Colby College/
The Christian Science Monitor, 11-25:47.*

**Ronald L. Ziegler**
*Former Press Secretary to the President
of the United States (Richard M. Nixon)*
5

Of course I made mistakes [as Press Secretary]. But a Press Secretary is only as good as his source of information. A Press Secretary can make a misleading statement or make a statement that turns out to be untrue later on and still believe deeply in what he said when he made the statement.
*Television interview/"Today" show,
National Broadcasting Company, 2-13.*

## Richard Adams
*Author*

1

I laugh all the way to the bank [about reviews of his books]. I'm afraid I'm not very idealistic about writing. The test of a writer is that people buy the book. It's proof against the adverse reviews. The essence of fiction is that the reader should want to turn the page and go on and on.

*Interview, Washington/*
*The Washington Post, 5-27:(B)1.*

## Richard Armour
*Author; Professor emeritus of English,*
*Scripps College*

2

There are very few humorists who have written first-rate humor after they've become elderly, unlike some of the great musicians and artists. Except, that is, for P. G. Wodehouse, who died recently at 93. I think he was an exceptional case. He was a novelist with a kind of formula of dialogue and characters. But if you write humor of a varied sort, you may have problems. The requirement of humor is a kind of alertness of mind, the ability to see small flaws and foibles; and, as you grow older, that becomes more difficult.

*Interview, Claremont, Calif./*
*Los Angeles Times, 5-8:(4)16.*

## Saul Bellow
*Author*

3

The history of literature in America is the history of certain demonic solitaries who somehow brought it off in a society that felt no need for them.

*Newsweek, 9-1:33.*

4

Many American writers cross the bar in their 60s and 70s and become Grand Old Men, gurus or bonzes of the Robert Frost variety. This is how society eases us out—sees us off on the immortal train, with waving and cheering and nobody listening. Just as well, because there's nothing but bombast coming from the rear platform. If I last long enough, I assume this will happen to me, too. And then there are two possibilities: Either you've run out of imagination, in which case you're ready to be puffed up, held down like a barrage balloon by the cables before you float off into eternity. Or your imagination keeps cooking, in which case you're lucky. You're among the blessed. No man knows which way he's going to go. He can only hope.

*Newsweek, 9-1:40.*

5

Once we had Carl Sandburg, Sherwood Anderson, Theodore Dreiser and Upton Sinclair. Now we have no one. They were our great public writers. Their novels were addressed to a mass audience, and they thought of themselves as spokesmen for a national conscience. They addressed grand issues of social justice and political concern. They were regarded as oracles. Abroad, there were similar writers like Dickens, Shaw, Zola, H. G. Wells, who also wrote well and as populist critics of the social system. Many of them were simplistic, and writers nowadays are, I think, put off by the complexity of social issues . . . It is very regrettable that many writers no longer take an interest in social questions.

*Interview, New York/*
*Los Angeles Herald-Examiner, 12-2:(B)4.*

6

People tend to review a reputation rather than a book. Also, the critics seem to be reviewing one's last book, not the new one in front of their noses—the way someone once said that the Generals are fighting the last war, not the one at hand. The critics have had five years to

(SAUL BELLOW)

think over one's last book and haven't had an occasion to say anything about it in print. So it's a case of waste not, want not. I say this without rancor—merely as an old-timer who's seen this over and over again.

*Interview, Chicago/*
*The Dallas Times Herald, 12-7:(D)9.*

**Nathaniel Benchley**
*Author*                                                                    1'

Those really-young-kids' books are tough. There are a lot of very strict rules—vocabulary; only two sentences to a page; humor, the more the better. Kids love humor. But you should remember never to talk down to them. Actually, writing kids' books is good exercise in basics. They are the essence of story-telling. Of course, every kind of book is different. Nonfiction is nice because the subject is already there; but you are bugged by the fact that you have to stick to the facts. In writing a novel you worry about whether you can interest people in it. And, subconsciously, I suppose you're always thinking "maybe it will sell well." Whatever you do, you have to acquire enough experience at whatever it is to know what you're talking about.

*Interview, Los Angeles/*
*Los Angeles Times, 7-4:(4)9.*

**Richard Condon**
*Author*                                                                    2

I read about a dozen books a week. And I read with one of those yellow marking pencils that you can see through. I read for esoterica, for oddball facts, like who invented the roller skate, or what was the origin of the three balls over the pawnbroker's shop. When I find a fact like that, I mark it with my yellow pencil. Then when I'm writing my novel, I just leaf through my books and pick up the passages I've marked. You see, I'm a great *pre*-editor! I seldom read fiction. I read all kinds of factual books, and I remember the esoterica. They stick in my mind like glue. I own about 90 dictionaries, on everything from falconry to cigars. The only thing I

must know for sure before I start writing on a novel is how it's going to end.

*Interview, New York/*
*The National Observer, 8-16:17.*

**E. L. Doctorow**
*Author*                                                                    3

A novelist is a person who lives in other people's skins, who moves in and out of other personalities for the purposes of his work. It's a kind of madness, I suppose. I think of a writer as being basically a person who does his work for two or three years and then comes up for air. Most of the time I live more quietly while I'm writing than is considered conducive to sanity.

*Interview, New York/*
*Los Angeles Times, 10-12:(Calendar)76.*

**Harlan Ellison**
*Author*                                                                    4

Part of the problem is the Eastern literary establishment feeling that anyone who works west of the Rockies is suffering from oxygen starvation. Brilliant writers who live in the West are almost totally ignored. Bernard Wolfe, Ishmael Reed. And, until he was suddenly discovered by an Eastern establishment figure, Ross MacDonald was totally ignored, though he's been writing for 35 years. The whole long incestuous daisy-chain of people who review each other, and all the academics who take a simple entertaining book and begin slicing it up to find the eternal Appolonian-Dionysian conflict, all of them are an enormous pain in the rear. Point out to me one person who really loved *The Eye of the Storm*.

*Interview, New York/*
*Publishers Weekly, 2-10:9.*

**John Fowles**
*Author*                                                                    5

That's one of my worst faults: hanging on to the thing. I tend to sit on manuscripts. Then it's like constipation; there comes a time when you've just got to purge yourself. But it's very difficult, sending something you've cared about into the world to be exposed to the cold blast of the review columns. I let my manuscript go as if I were sending it off in a coffin; it's just as if there's been a death in the family. There's another thing: Sometimes a line you've written on the typewriter may look absolutely right—but the moment you see it set up in type in proof, you know it isn't. At that stage, the cost of changing it is prohibitive. That's when you envy someone like Dickens, who almost re-wrote his stories on the first proof. Anyway, all these factors combine to make me want to hang on to a manuscript as long as possible. They are a private world and these worlds are very much more warm and satisfactory than any personal relationship.

*Interview/*
*Los Angeles Times, 7-13:(Calendar)30.*

**John Kenneth Galbraith**
*Author; Former professor of economics,*
*Harvard University*

1

All writers know that on some golden morn-ings they are touched by the wand and are on intimate terms with poetry and cosmic truth. I have experienced those moments myself. Their lesson is simple: They are a lovely but total illusion. And the danger in the illusion is that you will wait for these moments. I am per-suaded that most writers, like most shoemakers, are about as good one day as the next . . . The difference is the product of vanity and imagina-tion. The meaning is that one had better go to his or her typewriter every morning and stay there regardless of the result.

*Interview, Cambridge, Mass/*
*The Christian Science Monitor, 12-9:19.*

2

Every publisher seeks to establish relations of warmth, affection and confidence with his authors. He hopes that this will be a substitute, in some small way, for compensation.

*Interview, Cambridge, Mass./*
*The Christian Science Monitor, 12-9:19.*

**Theodor Geisel (Dr. Seuss)**
*Author*

3

I go through one suspense thriller a night to drive the day out of my head. But universally

there's a lack of interest in fiction because non-fiction is more fiction than fiction these days. The complexities of the world are far more intriguing than what a writer can dream up.

*Interview, La Jolla, Calif./*
*"W": a Fairchild publication, 7-25:13.*

**Arthur Hailey**
*Author*

4

I usually have several ideas when I start thinking of the next novel. When I made the decision to write *[The] Money-Changers* it was under the shower at home. In fact, many of my ideas come to me under the shower. Sometimes I'm in there so long that my wife knocks on the door and asks, "Do you know you're in there?"

*Interview, Los Angeles/*
*Los Angeles Herald-Examiner, 4-8:(B)1.*

5

. . . writers develop and change. What it comes down to is, you do the best you can. I think of myself as a story-teller. I've said many times that if I have a tombstone, which one doesn't have nowadays, I'd want on it, "He was a story-teller." But even story-tellers, court jes-ters, adapt themselves to changing times, chang-ing mores. They grow, they grow older, they grow with their audiences and what develop-ments occur in terms of tendencies, freedoms, nuances, all those things. And so, I suppose my stories have changed and probably will continue to do so. If I hadn't changed, I think it would be deleterious and a bad thing.

*Interview, Lyford Cay, Bahamas/*
*American Way (American Airlines) magazine,*
*July:22.*

**Joseph Heller**
*Author*

6

I don't do non-fiction well, and, since I work so hard at writing, I might as well concentrate on what I know I can do. I'm too conscious of myself as a writer to be a journalist. I'm a show-off. When I write I want people to notice me and that I'm doing something different from other people. A journalist—at least the ones I admire—is a writer who can make me

# WHAT THEY SAID IN 1975

forget his involvement so that I can concentrate on the subject of the piece, not the personality of the author. The journalist and the novelist have two completely different intelligences. Journalists almost always compose on typewriters. They rarely do more than one draft. Somehow they think in terms of openings, development, conclusion—all in almost automatic sequences. I envy that gift. But if I had it, I'd be a journalist. You can't have it both ways.

*Interview/Los Angeles Times, 2-20:(2)7.*

1

I don't think it's good to achieve too much at too early an age. What else can the future give you if you've already got all that your imagination had dreamt up for you? A writer is only discovered once in a lifetime, and, if it happens very early, the impossibility of matching that moment again can have a somewhat corrosive effect on his personality and indeed on the work itself.

*Interview/Los Angeles Times, 2-20:(2)7.*

2

. . . one of the advantages of a novel over other literary forms—a play, for example—is that you've got plenty of room for error. You take the masters: Proust is too slow, Melville spends too many chapters in *Moby Dick* on whaling; Faulkner sometimes suffers in clarity; Dostoevski has his digressions, Dickens his sentimentality. There's just no such thing as a perfect novel.

*Interview, New York/*
*The National Observer, 4-19:25.*

**James Jones**
*American Author*

3

In America, a writer will take physical, current things and use them as a setting for his ideas, his people. But the European mind is more abstract. I'd have an idea for a novel and people would shrug their shoulders and say, "Ahh, Balzac already did it. Hugo already did it." So they'd write 35 pages describing curtains in a living room.

*Interview, Sagaponack, N.Y./*
*The New York Times, 8-1:23.*

4

Nothing creates enemies like success. And that I seriously do believe. There's a strange feeling in America that art shouldn't make money. You should suffer in a garret all your life and die like Modigliani did, painting for a bottle of wine. Also, as it was for [F. Scott] Fitzgerald, early success can be very tough. I went through a long period when *From Here to Eternity* was really the bane of my life. I've written seven novels, three of which—*Some Came Running, Go to the Widow-Maker* and *The Thin Red Line*—are better literary efforts than *Eternity* for my taste. But people still come up to me and say, "Oh, Mr. Jones, I just love your book." I know which one they mean.

*Los Angeles/*
*Los Angeles Times, 11-23:(Book Review)3.*

**Elia Kazan**
*Author*

5

[On critics]: For many of them it's just a subtle ego trip! There should always be respect for accomplishment, for a man's achievement; but too often there's just meanness and spitefulness. I think of Bill Inge, a suicide; of Hemingway—a great writer in his early work, even though he became pathetic; of John Steinbeck—and *The [New York] Times* sniping at him when he won the Nobel; Tennessee Williams, who can't do anything right any more; Arthur Miller . . . You can't just sneer at such men; they deserve better.

*Interview, New York/*
*Publishers Weekly, 1-13:19.*

**Louis L'Amour**
*Author*

6

When I was a youngster knocking around the world, writing but unable to sell anything I'd written, I knew something was wrong and I worried about that. I studied the successful writers and discovered what was wrong. The amateur writes *about* his story before he begins to tell it. He takes paragraphs or pages to waltz slowly up to it, before something happens. But the professional begins his story in the middle or close to the end, always with something happening. He reaches out and grabs the reader by the throat, not letting go until the story ends. Now that I've learned that technique, I fuss about other phases of writing. With every new book, I am concerned about being good enough or knowledgeable enough to satisfy all my readers. Probably I can never attain that state of grace, but I try hard. I write for the expert. If a story deals with a geological aspect of the mountains, I write for the geologist. If a story deals with guns, I write for the gun specialist. That takes an enormous amount of research. I don't want to be clobbered by being too lazy to get the facts. I respect my audience and they respect me. I owe it to them to be authentic.

*Interview, Los Angeles/*
*Los Angeles Times, 4-6:(Home)44.*

*1*

[On what he calls the literary world's snobbishness toward his Western frontier-type novels]: If you write a book about a bygone period that lies east of the Mississippi River, then it's a "historical" novel. If it's west of the Mississippi, it's a "Western," a different category. There's no sense to it. We live in a world where a man doesn't like his wife and is carrying on with some other woman, and this story is done over and over again and that is supposed to be important writing. Whereas the opening up of half of our whole United States is not supposed to be important. It's absurd.

*Interview, New York/*
*The New York Times, 5-28:35.*

**Ross Macdonald (Ken Millar)**
*Author*

*2*

...it's extremely difficult for a writer to stay abreast of society, the economy, politics. A writer has to understand, or *imagine* that he understands, the basic forces operating in the world. A writer's challenge is to detect the signs of change, to identify important rumbles and developments a long way off.... a writer's responsibility is to point the way for others, to help them adapt to change. Measured against that responsibility, writing detective stories doesn't seem of historic significance. But life is

a series of detective stories, a succession of baffling characters caught up in puzzling circumstances. With that in mind, I consider myself lucky, even privileged, to be practicing my craft.

*Interview, Santa Barbara, Calif./*
*Los Angeles Times, 6-29:(Home)27.*

**Shirley MacLaine**
*Actress, Author*

*3*

[On how she became involved in writing books]: My whole professional life has been dedicated to making things increasingly specific. I started as a dancer, expressing myself through movement; but that was too abstract. Then I went into musical comedy, which gave me a chance to dance more loosely, and to sing and to use my sense of humor. Then I began to act in more serious roles, and that was the first time I began to think about words. Then, with movies, expressing everything through my face became all-important, and I got deeply interested in the lighting and the cameras. But it all meant nothing if you didn't have any words. So finally I realized the written word was all-important.

*Interview, New York/*
*Publishers Weekly, 3-31:6.*

**Allie Beth Martin**
*Director, Tulsa City-County Library*
*System; President-elect, American*
*Library Association*

*4*

The issue of censorship is as old as libraries. Today there is a great deal more citizen awareness and participation. There is a lot more concern with materials, particularly in school libraries and in the classroom. The Supreme Court has said that the problem of censorship should be dealt with at a local level. That worries me. I agree with the rights of citizens to voice their feelings, but it is a fallacy to believe that one standard can be set for all who patronize a library. There should be a full range in any community, and there must be freedom to choose. The choice should not be limited by either the majority or the minority.

*San Francisco Examiner & Chronicle,*
*2-23:(Sunday Scene)2.*

# WHAT THEY SAID IN 1975

*(ALLIE BETH MARTIN)*

1

[On whether books will go out of style]: No! They are marvelous mechanisms, so portable. You can shift back and forth; and if you want to read the last page first, you can. You can go at your own pace. You have control and accessibility. It's a neat way of communicating.

*San Francisco Examiner & Chronicle,*
*2-23:(Sunday Scene)2.*

**Harry Reasoner**
*News commentator, American*
*Broadcasting Company*

2

I still write from time to time; I have a box full of papers marked Chapter One and Chapter Two. But I can't forget what a mentor of mine in college once said: "It's all right to be a hack fiction writer and it's all right to be an artist. The trouble starts when you start to confuse the two." Personally, I'd rather be a good journalist than a self-conscious novelist.

*Interview, New York/*
*Los Angeles Times, 7-28:(4)13.*

**Barbara A. Ringer**
*Register of Copyrights, Library of*
*Congress of the United States*

3

[On the controversy over libraries photocopying copyrighted material—books, magazines, etc.—for use in classrooms and elsewhere in the library system without paying royalties]: I don't regard authors and publishers and teachers and librarians as natural enemies. It is extremely painful to see them at each other's throats. It's very destructive . . . I think libraries are the first to realize they can't take over the publisher's function. They can't go too far without wiping out the publishers' market . . . And publishers have to realize the world is changing too. They can't just keep raising prices forever. You can't stop progress. What you have to do is preserve the values and rights of authorship in dealing with change.

*The Christian Science Monitor, 6-17:12.*

**Adela Rogers St. Johns**
*Author, Journalist*

4

It's usually painful for me to read something of mine in print. I find countless things I could have done better. Sometimes I'm so lousy I could get sick of what I've done . . . But there is considerable merit in dissatisfaction. If you are dissatisfied with something, you think about it, you analyze what went wrong, and chances are next time you do better.

*Interview, Los Angeles/*
*Los Angeles Times, 2-16:(Home)23.*

**William Saroyan**
*Author*

5

. . . I've been a published writer for 40 years. That's longer than Dickens, de Maupassant or Chekhov. I thought that books were from nature originally. When I discovered that they were not creations of God, like animals, I said, "Hell, I can do that." And I've been doing it ever since.

*Interview, New York/*
*Los Angeles Herald-Examiner, 7-16:(B)4.*

**Sidney Sheldon**
*Writer*

6

For years I watched people go up to such stars as Cary Grant and say, "I loved your movie." I was happy for Cary but I must confess I winced, because it was also *my* movie in the sense that I was the writer and director. Again, I watched people congratulate Barbara Eden on *I Dream of Jeannie,* and rightly so; but nobody seemed to care that it was I who wrote and produced the show. Then I wrote a couple of novels and suddenly my life changed! I had acquired identity. People don't congratulate the publisher, the editor, the printer, the bookseller. The *author* is the star. He goes to a party and he's surrounded by admirers. It becomes a wonderful kind of ego massage.

*Interview, Los Angeles/*
*Los Angeles Times, 10-26:(Home)19.*

**Isaac Bashevis Singer**
*Author*

7

I think the moment you have published a book, it's not any more your private property.

It belongs already, in a way, to humanity. If it has value, everybody can find in it what he finds, and I cannot tell the man I did not intend it to be so. It's like you have a son, and this son marries a girl whom you don't like. You can say to your son, "I did not intend that you should marry this girl." But your intention is not important to him. He is doing what he wants. The same thing is true about whatever we create. Once we have created them, they get an independent kind of life. And everyone can find in them something which he, the writer who writes a story, does not see. I may think that the critics distort, but from their point of view they are not distorting. I just don't criticize. I just let it go. I say to myself, "I have done mine; let them do what they want."

*Interview, New York/*
*The New York Times Magazine, 3-23:24.*

1

The main rule of a writer is never to pity your manuscript. If you see something is no good, throw it away and begin again. A lot of writers have failed because they have too much pity. They have already worked so much, they cannot just throw it away. But I say that the wastepaper basket is a writer's best friend. My wastepaper basket is on a steady diet.

*Interview, New York/*
*The New York Times Magazine, 3-23:33.*

### Mickey Spillane
*Author*

2

My [writing] speed depends on the state of my bank account. When it's necessary, I can write 5,000 words a day and finish a book in a few weeks. I don't go deeply into research. There is much more fun, for me as a writer, in playing fast and loose with the people I create, and in twisting reality to suit my needs. I don't believe that truth is stranger than fiction. I think it's the other way around. Best of all, there are no limits to it. Fiction is where the sidewalk of truth ends, and the wide-open road of the imagination begins.

*Interview, Los Angeles/*
*Los Angeles Times, 5-11:(Home)33.*

### George Steiner
*Literary critic, "The New Yorker"*
*magazine; Extraordinary fellow,*
*Churchill College, Cambridge, England*

3

Why do so few novels today make me want to spend time in the company of adults? I'm not sure that the straightforward narrative mode is suitable for grown-up fiction today. Being grown-up seems to be too difficult, and England is being swept by fantasies written for pre-puberty: Tolkien, I'm afraid, and *Watership Down* ... Most of the most interesting and provoking work in fiction today is being done in films. Bright students used to have first novels always—now they have scenarios.

*Interview, New York/*
*Publishers Weekly, 4-21:11.*

### William Targ
*Senior editor, G. P. Putnam's Sons,*
*publishers*

4

Of course there are too many books—you've only got to walk among the remainder tables to see that ... So many books are really just articles. I can think of plenty of books that could have said all they had to say in a few hundred words. And as for cookbooks—to think of all those trees ...

*Interview, New York/*
*Publishers Weekly, 11-10:12.*

### Louis Untermeyer
*Poet, Editor*

5

[His advice for young writers and poets]: Write out of love; write out of instinct; write out of reason. But always for money.

*Interview, Newtown, Conn./*
*The New York Times, 9-30:32.*

### Kurt Vonnegut, Jr.
*Author*

6

Talent is extremely common. What is rare is the willingness to endure the life of the writer. Writers have no one to talk shop to. It is like making wallpaper by hand for the Sistine Chapel.

*At symposium on copyright law,*
*Washington, June 18/*
*The Washington Post, 6-19:(C)10.*

# WHAT THEY SAID IN 1975

**Irving Wallace**
*Author*

1

I go right through [when writing a book]. Some of my books have dozens of characters and run over 1,200 manuscript pages. If I tried to get away in the middle, I couldn't enjoy myself. And I'd start losing threads from getting distracted by other things. I find it's best to work from Page One to the end. Once it's committed to paper, I'll do five or six complete rewrites. I try to take six months off between books, but I don't think a writer can stop working. There's no faucet you can turn off. It's going drip, drip, drip all the time.

*Holiday Inn Companion, Aug.-Sept.:14.*

**Robert Penn Warren**
*Author*

2

I cling to the notion that some significant number of Americans will, in spite of TV and other forces, cling to reading--because only in language can one dimension of the human imagination and self-understanding come into play. What I mean is something like this: At one end of the scale of literature—reading—we have the muscular and neural experience of utterance, actual or suggested. Beyond this there is the whole complex of associations and specificities in language, and the complex interrelated play of image and idea with all other factors. All of this amounts to a special kind of intensification, enactment and fulfillment of the human being--the human self. What really seems at stake is the death of the human pleasure—and fulfillment—in activity. Reading means activity. Watching TV, in general, does not; it is, by and large, passivity.

*Interview/U.S. News & World Report, 7-7:49.*

**Richard Wilbur**
*Poet*

3

There are certain things in writing from which you either shy away or don't shy away. If you don't shy away you can't tell for sure what's going to become of the poem. I think that's very exciting and also a little scary. I always think of poetry . . . in Aristotelian terms as an art of inclusion, as an art in which the maximum inclusion is desirable. So in theory, at any rate, there's nothing one can't or shouldn't say or try to say.

*Interview/*
*The Christian Science Monitor, 4-9:28.*

**P. G. Wodehouse**
*British author*

4

I've always thought there were two things that establish an author: getting a knighthood and being put in Madame Tussaud's [wax museum].

*People, 1-20:19.*

**Herman Wouk**
*Author*

5

[Supporting copyright protection for authors' works]: The erosion of literary property is the erosion of the only support that the life of the spirit has in this country. It is as disorderly to invade the only property a writer has--the fruit of his brain—as it is his castle.

*At symposium on copyright law,*
*Washington, June 18/*
*The Washington Post, 6-19:(C)1.*

**Francis X. Bellotti**
*Attorney General of Massachusetts*
1

Advertising of over-the-counter drugs [glorifies] the ability of various pills to improve the quality of one's life. Madison Avenue over the air waves encourages everyone—including children—to take drugs to get up, to stay awake, to stay slim, healthy and attractive, to eliminate minor pain and discomfort and to go to sleep . . . There is a very direct relationship between drug ads on TV and the addiction young people have to pills of all kinds.

*Before House Communications Subcommittee,*
*Washington/*
*The Christian Science Monitor, 7-21:3.*

**John Cameron**
*Professor of radiological physics,*
*University of Wisconsin Medical School*
2

More than 90 percent of the man-made radiation which Americans are exposed to comes from medical X-rays. Not all of this is unnecessary, obviously, but the overwhelming amount of unnecessary radiation comes from medical X-rays . . . I'm not a [consumerist] Ralph Nader on this whole business. I don't think that stopping excessive radiation is going to save the world. It's not as important as curing alcoholism or smoking or a lot of other things. But it's something we know how to correct, and it's something that should be done.

*Interview, Chicago/*
*Los Angeles Times, 12-8:(1)14.*

**William R. Cast**
*Chairman, committee on malpractice,*
*Indiana State Medical Association*
3

[On malpractice suits] : Physicians are practicing defensive medicine in case they have to justify themselves to a jury. They hospitalize patients who could be home. They keep patients in hospitals longer than is necessary. They order tests and X-rays that are not needed, and they order second tests and X-rays when the first ones have already shown adequate results. These costs are a thousand times greater for patients than what is added to their bills because of premium increases for malpractice insurance.

*U.S. News & World Report, 1-20:54.*

**Morris E. Chafetz**
*Director, National Institute on Alcohol*
*Abuse and Alcoholism, Department of*
*Health, Education and Welfare of the*
*United States*
4

All of the signs and statistics over the past couple of years have pointed to the fact that the switch is on among young people—from a wide range of other drugs to alcohol . . . Parents think it is cute or funny when their son returns home from a party drunk and assume that he is just learning to hold his liquor. A call from the local police station asking a parent to pick up a drunk youngster is likely to evoke a sigh of relief that he is not off somewhere using "drugs."

*U.S. News & World Report, 4-14:40.*

**C. S. Cook**
*Professor of physics, University of*
*Texas, El Paso*
5

As it is now, nobody in the United States has any idea of how large a dose of radiation he has accumulated in his life. Part of the reason for this is apathy, but a more important factor is that no regulations require that records be kept of medical and dental X-ray exposures . . . If we are going to worry about radiation—and some people are greatly worried and appear at every public hearing about nuclear power plants—then we ought to go about it right and

# WHAT THEY SAID IN 1975

*(C. S. COOK)*

worry about all the medical diagnostic radiation we are getting that nobody is keeping track of.
*Interview/Los Angeles Times, 2-3:(1)14.*

**Robert L. DuPont**
*Director, National Institute on Drug Abuse of the United States*                                   *1*

Pre-schoolers and early-graders don't need to know the pharmacology of drugs. But they do need to know the value of self-esteem. The proof is quite simple. There are many addicts who know everything there is to know about drugs, but there are few addicts who shoot heroin or smoke marijuana every day who really feel good about themselves.
*The New York Times, 11-9:(1)62.*

**Roger O. Egeberg**
*Special Assistant for Health Policy to the Secretary of Health, Education and Welfare of the United States*                        *2*

[There] are doctors who don't see [in a patient] what the other 99 per cent of doctors see—a human being. They do things they are not trained to do, performing operations they have no business doing. The careless physician is almost like an accident-prone person. He just can't do the thing right, and he shouldn't be doing it at all.
*Interview/People, 5-12:32.*

**Lewis A. Engman**
*Chairman, Federal Trade Commission*          *3*

[Arguing against the ban on prescription-drug price advertising in the U.S.]: It is a curious set of values which says that the consumer may be given full information about discretionary purchases such as deodorant and mouthwash but cannot be given information that will help him save money on non-discretionary purchases such as drugs which a doctor has prescribed as essential to his good health.
*Washington, June 2/*
*Los Angeles Times, 6-3:(1)22.*

**Rashi Fein**
*Professor of the economics of medicine, Harvard University*                                      *4*

[On the shortage of doctors in rural areas of the U.S.]: There are real forces at work that influence physician distribution, and if we would have the figures changed, we will have to reckon with these forces. Some of the forces have nothing to do with medicine and cannot be controlled by the medical-care system: ... to the extent that the rural area is in relative difficulty in [cultural, social and educational opportunities], physicians will find that area less attractive; ... the heavy emphasis in medical education on hospital training, rather than ambulatory care; ... the pressures toward specialization and sub-specialization; ... the failure of government to feel any obligation to make certain care is available to all the people ... It is not that physicians are not humane. Rather, it is that they are human, and in an entrepreneurial society in which the profits and income maximization motive are driving forces, physician supply in rural areas is likely to grow worse rather than better.
*At workshop sponsored by National*
*Conference on Rural America,*
*Washington, April 15/*
*The Washington Post, 4-16:(A)2.*

**Judah Folkman**
*Professor of surgery, Harvard University Medical School; Surgeon-in-chief, Children's Hospital Medical Center, Boston*      *5*

[The medical profession] is perhaps the only human activity where every attempt to *relieve* suffering is accompanied by the risk that we may *cause* suffering. Sometimes the risk is small, sometimes great, but it is always there. Now, I am not talking about injections which hurt, or medicines that taste bitter. What I am talking about is what you and I know deep down, but what I think we have never dared explain to the public: that good clinical judgment is learned from making bad judgments. Yes, a little clinical judgment can be learned from one's teachers and some from reading the experience of others. But the vast majority of good clinical judgment and clinical skill is learned the hard way—from practice! . . . That this is not understood can be seen in the increasing inability of juries to distinguish between human error and outright negligence. Every simple honest mistake becomes potential malpractice liability. It is also evident in the tendency of our elected representatives to see hospitals only as public utilities with patients labeled customers. The terms "consumer" and "provider" assume that medical practice can be completely standardized.

*Class Day address, Harvard University Medical School/The New York Times, 6-6:31.*

**Donald S. Fredrickson**
*Director, National Institutes of Health of the United States* 1

I don't think the general public fully appreciates how difficult and slow the discovery of basic knowledge may be. For instance, I don't think that arthritis is incurable. But I don't know how to cure it today. I think that premature occurrence of most of the major chronic diseases that afflict us today will be largely preventable. And many of them may be curable. But it will be mainly an act of prevention in the years to come. We'll have to be patient. We'll have to collect information effectively. But the public must realize that they themselves are frequently going to have to be involved in helping determine whether the answer has really been found. By that I mean we're going to see in the future a lot more large-scale clinical trials of discoveries from bio-medical research. That's because often it's not possible to prove that one has really found a cause, a cure, a treatment or a prevention of a disease unless very large numbers of people are observed over long periods of time on a controlled and randomized basis.

*Interview, Washington/ U.S. News & World Report, 6-16:67.*

**George E. Godber**
*Chairman, committee on smoking and health, World Health Association* 2

It seems fair to conclude that most countries have pursued their action [against cigarette smoking] in desultory fashion, have achieved only limited progress, particularly over the short term, but have lost in some other directions. There has been some reduction in the number of boys and young men starting to smoke, but unhappily there has been an increase in the number of girls and young women starting to smoke . . . We may not have eliminated cigarette smoking completely by the end of this century, but we ought to have reached a position where a relatively few addicts still use cigarettes, but only in private, at most in the company of consenting adults . . . The fact that smoking by the mother during pregnancy is a material danger to the fetus is far less well-known than it should be. The knowledge that exposure to involuntary secondary smoking may cause an increase in carbon monoxide and even nicotine content of the blood of non-smokers or that the incidence of respiratory infection to the first year of life is increased in the infants whose parents smoke is probably not understood. The message that the penalty for cigarette smoking begins to be paid from the very earliest stage in life and is not something postponed until old age is certainly not well appreciated.

*At World Conference on Smoking and Health, New York, June 2/ Los Angeles Times, 6-3:(1)10.*

**Carl Goetsch**
*President, California Medical Association* 3

[On malpractice insurance]: The situation is so critical in terms of the very high cost of malpractice coverage that if the [California] Legislature fails to achieve significant reform, we [doctors] as individuals will have no choice but to cease practice.

*News conference, Beverly Hills, Calif., June 1/Los Angeles Times, 6-2:(1)1.*

**Robert A. Good**
*President and director, Sloan-Kettering Institute for Cancer Research; Director of research, Memorial Sloan-Kettering Cancer Center, New York* 4

If we could get the body to recognize cancer cells as soon as they start to grow, then we

# WHAT THEY SAID IN 1975

## (ROBERT A. GOOD)

could destroy or prevent further growth of those cells. What we're after is control of cancer—the prevention of the advancement of cancer. Nobody would worry about cancer if it wouldn't grow. Cancer is dangerous because it is progressive . . . Right now, cancer therapy depends upon a combination of the best surgical skills, radiation treatment and chemotherapy. Some of the cancer drugs had a profound effect, and we have been able to make cancer knuckle. Tomorrow our treatment will be a little bit better, coupled with newer drugs and the increasing use of immunotherapy as we know more about it. The day after tomorrow we will probably know enough about immunotherapy to use it to get rid of large masses of cancer. And then, the day after the day after, we should be learning the language of the cancer cell, why and how it grows, and then we can control its growth after learning its signals. That's the payoff. Right now we're taking the very first steps.

*Interview, New York/*
*"W": a Fairchild publication, 9-19:5.*

## Milton D. Heifetz
*Chief, department of neurosurgery,*
*Cedars-Sinai Medical Center, Los Angeles*   *1*

. . . our attitudes, our values concerning the dying and those living a sub-human existence are distorted and produce devastating cruelties. I treasure life but I do not believe life is warranted if it cannot be lived with some measure of grace and dignity. The human who cannot speak, who cannot think, who would live as a vegetating mass of protoplasm without any hope of recovery, should not be forced to live . . . Those who would aggressively treat or demand treatment for a dying sub-human patient with no hope of recovery [and] contrary to the patient's request—even though they would not wish to be treated if they, themselves, were in that condition—act hypocritically. They masquerade under a facade of morality. The doctor who believes that his function is to preserve life as long as he has the ability to do so in spite of his patient's desires is, unless adhering to a religious precept,

psychologically weak. His safety lies in the fact that doctors are rarely blamed by society for prolonging life. These doctors are secure in the knowledge that when the patient dies, the family can say everything had been done to keep the patient alive, even if the patient lived as a vegetable. Many physicians accept this approach. It helps them medically. It helps them legally. It helps them psychologically. But many of us condemn it.

*Interview, Beverly Hills, Calif./*
*Los Angeles Times, 8-17:(5)1.*

## Franz J. Ingelfinger
*Editor, New England Journal of Medicine*   *2*

In the name of ethics, anti-intellectualism and anti-science are encouraged, hostility to medicine is nourished, clinical investigation is compromised if not castrated, and the cause of probity itself is harmed . . . The public, instead of being induced to participate in medical experimentation—to join the investigator in a common search for increased knowledge—is frightened off, convinced that guinea-pigism will be its lot. Serious and human concerns as to the allocation of scarce medical resources, the considered management of those with hopeless disease and the pros and cons of abortion for individual and societal purposes deteriorate into quarrels by activist groups ever ready to label the opposition as Nazi experimenters or fanatic inquisitors. Whenever medical ethics is used to promote an atmosphere so charged, then its use is unethical. Public fears of medical research are readily translated into legislation that is designed to alleviate those fears but that—incidentally or purposefully—hamstrings the search for new knowledge.

*News conference, San Francisco, April 8/*
*Los Angeles Times, 4-9:(1)3.*

## Jan Koch-Weser
*Associate professor of pharmacology,*
*Harvard University Medical School*   *3*

Drugs with definitely toxic potential . . . were thought to have contributed to the death of some patients; but who would argue that these agents are too dangerous to use against lymphoblastic and myeloblastic leukemia, Hodgkin's Disease and metatistic bronchial carcinoma? Fatalities during the use of such drugs must be accepted as the price for the hundreds of thousands of lives they save each year . . . Few drugs that help anybody will not hurt somebody . . . There are very few, if any, drugs presently marketed in this country whose benefits do not outweigh their risks.

*U.S. News & World Report, 6-16:62.*

**Lester B. Lave**
*Professor of economics, Carnegie-Mellon University*                          *1*

Current medical care comes from the interaction of many health professionals in many settings. Medical care is too complex to be left to the doctors. An individual working with only his tools and personal knowledge is as out of date as the horse and buggy.

*Pittsburgh/*
*The New York Times, 1-15:46.*

**A. W. Liley**
*Obstetrician; Professor,*
*University of Auckland*
*(New Zealand)*                          *2*

[Criticizing the liberalization of abortion laws]: The medical indications [reasons] for abortion these days are very small. The only thing "medical" about abortion is the technique—certainly not the indications. Doctors have become hatchet men for social indications. Nowhere else in the field of social legislation is there such a vast discrepancy between intentions [of liberalized abortion laws] and the sordid realities of what has gotten into practice . . . When people talk of freeing society of the burdens of unwanted or defective babies, I say that the morally handicapped cause more misery and suffering in the world than the physically or mentally handicapped ever do. Who is more responsible for pollution—a university graduate or a child in an institution for the mentally retarded? I'm sure there were more Ph.D.s than mongoloids among the architects of the Vietnamese war. "Every child a wanted child" is a great motto; but it would be just as comforting to say, "Every grandmother a wanted grandmother."

*Interview, Los Angeles/*
*Los Angeles Times, 6-9:(1)3.*

**Walter J. McNerney**
*President, National Blue Cross Association*          *3*

[On the effect of malpractice suits on hospital costs]: First of all, there are the skyrocketing insurance premiums, and then there are the tremendous awards. But what people may not realize is that doctors are practicing defensive medicine and ordering all sorts of tests to ward off malpractice suits. This raises hospital costs . . . We cannot have the tremendous awards juries are giving for pain and suffering. Medical expenses and rehabilitation should be covered, but where the money is excessive it is for "pain and suffering" which are hard to determine.

*Interview/*
*San Francisco Examiner & Chronicle,*
*4-13:(Sunday Scene)4.*

**C. Arden Miller**
*President, American Public Health Association*          *4*

[Arguing against the thesis that major life-and-death medical decisions, such as prolonging life in apparently hopeless cases, should lie largely with the doctor]: If uncertainties over moral and ethical issues cause us to always answer, "Let the doctor decide," then we are surrendering humankind to the dominance of rampant medical technology. Society through all its institutions—including schools, churches, legislatures—must search for an ethical basis to problems that need enlightenment from many perspectives.

*U.S. News & World Report, 11-24:31.*

**Daniel G. Miller**
*Medical director, Preventive Medicine Institute, Strang Clinic, New York*          *5*

Clinics have been established as paragons of technical achievement with little consideration given to who is being examined or what happened to them after they were examined. In-

# WHAT THEY SAID IN 1975

*(DANIEL G. MILLER)*

stead of talking to engineers and technicians, preventive oncologists [cancer specialists] should have been talking to health educators and behavioral scientists. We should have been learning what it takes to get people into early-detection facilities and what it takes to get them to comply with preventive-medicine recommendations . . . For motor vehicles we now have simple testing procedures carried out in many community garages. If something is out of line, a recommendation is made on the spot. The same thing can be done for cancer and certain other preventable diseases. Simple premedical tests could be carried out at community hospitals by paramedical personnel for very nominal fees. Instead of getting a stamp for a windshield, I would suggest a stamp for the income-tax form allowing a rebate.

*At conference sponsored by American Cancer Society and National Cancer Institute/ The Dallas Times Herald, 5-5:(A)4.*

**Walter F. Mondale**
*United States Senator, D—Minnesota*     *1*

What we need is to get free enterprise and competition working to encourage more-efficient and more-effective health-care delivery. And that's where the HMO comes in . . . The HMO is an encouraging sign. And a number of us in Congress believed that if we could encourage establishment of more HMOs, then perhaps competition would force a reduction in cost increases through our diverse medical system . . . HMOs are not a panacea for all our health-care problems. But I believe that the HMO is a crucial spearhead in our effort to develop a health system with its own inbuilt incentives for effective and affordable health-care delivery.

*Before Midwest Conference on the HMO, Minneapolis, Nov. 25/\*\**

**William Nolen**
*Physician, Author*     *2*

It's a wonderful feeling to see someone come in with a perforated ulcer, say, really suffering,

and to be able to operate and help him. When you're a surgeon, you have to surge.

*People, 5-5:31.*

**Max H. Parrott**
*President-elect,*
*American Medical Association*     *3*

As a compassionate humanist, I believe in national health insurance. But I . . . and the American Medical Association . . . favor a form of it that would be voluntary, as far as the individual subscriber is concerned . . . a form of it that would ensure a maximum of financial coverage with a minimum of Federal involvement. As a humanist, I believe that the delivery of health care can be broadened in ways that respect the integrity of both its giver and its receiver . . . Utilitarianism and humanism cannot coexist equally . . . as the people served by the planned health-care systems of Britain, Sweden and other European lands have learned. Yes, the health services in America are pretty much a non-system . . . and may seem an anomaly in a land as businesslike as ours. But look at what this non-system has accomplished. Look at what it signifies in terms of flexibility and creativity. Look at our decline last year in the five diseases that are the principle killers—heart disease, cancer, strokes, influenza and pneumonia, and ills of early pregnancy. Certainly, much of the credit must go to the free-spirited way in which our physicians act . . . interact . . . and vie with one another. So, finally, I ask: Could the pace of America's medical advances be maintained in a cramped and rigid system? Could a utilitarian system outdo the good it would undo? Should the health care of tomorrow be an economic commodity . . . rather than an act of humanistic faith? And to ask the penultimate question: Would the individual patient . . . under such a system . . . fare better . . . or worse?

*Before Society for the Advancement of Humanistic Studies in Gynecology, Snowmass Mountain, Colo., March 12/ Vital Speeches, 4-15:416.*

**Lord Ritchie-Calder**
*Senior fellow, Center for the Study of
Democratic Institutions*

1

Today, the doctor's abilities far exceed his judgment because medical science and technology have given him means to treat or operate on conditions which would have been intractable a few years ago. Indeed, he could construe his Hippocratic oath as making it incumbent upon him to apply any knowledge he has, down to the most recent discovery reported in the latest medical journal, or the newest drug offered him by a pharmaceutical firm. In present circumstances, it is possible that he might be sued for professional incompetence or malpractice for withholding an up-to-date form of treatment. In the United States, a medical practitioner was successfully sued for damages for not prescribing a new drug of which he had never heard. The judgment which innovation imposes on a doctor exceeds the professional common sense on which the "good doctor" would rely in good conscience. In the words of the biophysicist, Leroy Augenstein, "The doctor is being asked to play God."

*Before World Health Organization
Medical Society, Geneva/
The Center Magazine, March-April:59.*

**Milton Roemer**
*Professor of health services administration,
University of California, Los Angeles*

2

[On the rise in malpractice claims]: I believe malpractice continues because quality-control measures have not been sufficiently implemented. The principal rational response to the crisis should be to improve the quality of medical and surgical care through more vigorous professional surveillance. It's ironic that while the medical profession has become very agitated by the malpractice problem, it has opposed Professional Standards Review Organizations, which would be a kind of corrective ... Malpractice claims are probably overdone because there are patients who are angry at the high cost of medical care. This makes for a poor doctor-patient relationship.

Then the anger is exploited by attorneys who stand to earn large contingency fees.

*Interview/Los Angeles Times, 6-4:(1)28.*

**Jonas Salk**
*Director, Salk Institute for Biological
Studies, San Diego*

3

... polio became an epidemic disease as a result of an improvement in hygienic conditions. In earlier times, natural immunity developed during the course of the first six months of life. In those days there was a very high infant mortality associated with intestinal infections. Those diarrheal diseases would bring about a high mortality, and the survivors would very likely have acquired a polio virus infection which would immunize them for life. So polio is, in effect, a disease of civilization ... Diseases associated with pollution from auto and industrial emissions are similar to the problem of polio. They are diseases of civilization.

*Television interview/Center Report, April:23.*

**James H. Sammons**
*Executive vice president, American
Medical Association*

4

HEW may be conscientious in wanting to save millions of dollars—the difference between costs of brand-name drugs and their so-called generic equivalents. It may be sincere in thinking the elderly and the poor would be just as well-served by the substitution. But what does professional judgment say? It says that, while two [ducks] may swim, waddle and quack alike, they may not be the same duck once they are ingested by the patient. Identical twins have been known to emit different scent with the same cologne. So think of the complications that can occur when two not-so-equivalent drugs go inside the complex systems of widely differing people. Even if the generic drug is chemically pure and quality-controlled, it may not be the practical equivalent of the brand-name product. Other criteria are to be considered. What about bioavailability, for example? In other words, is the drug absorbed in a manner that allows a consistent blood level? To illustrate, let me refer to digoxin ... which is

# WHAT THEY SAID IN 1975

*(JAMES H. SAMMONS)*

used for cardiac disorders. Even small differences in the bioavailability of various makes of that drug can mean the difference between lack of any discernible effect . . . a satisfactory therapeutic response . . . and dangerous toxicity. In addition, a so-called equivalent drug may deteriorate "on the shelf" at a faster rate. And it may encounter greater resistance from the patient . . . because of its dosage form, taste or what have you. HEW assumes too much equivalence not only between drugs . . . but between its MAC regulations and the intent of Congress.

*Before American Bar Association,*
*Montreal, Aug. 11/*
*Vital Speeches, 9-1:696.*

### Ed W. Schmidt
*President, Texas Medical Association*
1

Most of the problems encountered by medicine originate with the Federal government . . . If history projects itself into the future, by 1985 HEW will be spending more than $500-billion per year. The pattern of this growth is built in by law, and Congress gives no inclination to alter the inexorable trend toward a welfare state.

*Before Texas Medical Association,*
*San Antonio, May 1/*
*The Dallas Times Herald, 5-2:(D)1.*

### Peter Shaffer
*British playwright*
2

I've always wondered, because of my frequent sojourns in America, how much good psychiatry and all the rest of it was doing those of my acquaintances who were in treatment. I know a couple who appear to have benefited from it; but most, whatever they may think, haven't changed at all. I began to wonder some time ago whether it might not be a false religion with a lot of worshipers. If you were at a party in England and said, "My analyst told me . . ." which, God knows, is common enough here [in the U.S.], everyone would stop talking. There would be a slight sense of being in the same room with someone who was clinically insane, or close to it. Not very many other people in

England consult them. Americans may think it square and backward of us, but I'm not so sure. I think a great deal more self-reliance and tolerance of personal eccentricity would do the American character a great deal of good.

*Interview, New York/*
*The New York Times Magazine, 4-13:30.*

### Rodney Smith
*President, British Royal College*
*of Surgeons*
3

[On Britain's socialized medical system, citing inefficiency and an exodus of doctors seeking better pay in foreign countries]: You can't accept this without a progressive slide in standards, and that means, quite simply, that more patients will die or have an unsuccessful operation. We are not running out of time in this respect. We *have* run out of time.

*London, Oct. 8/*
*Los Angeles Times, 10-9:(1)1.*

### Thomas Szasz
*Professor of psychiatry, State University*
*of New York, Syracuse*
4

[Arguing against forced treatment of people whom society classifies as mentally ill]: Involuntary psychiatric treatment is a Communist kind of social control. To me, it's like slavery. The problem is not how to improve it, but how to abolish it . . . A person with a problem should be able to go to a priest, a rabbi, an astrologer, the Salvation Army or a rescue mission—any place he feels he can find help. We don't use the law to get people to go to a dentist; we should apply that same principle to psychiatry.

*Dallas/The Dallas Times Herald, 4-7:(A)5.*

### Albert Szent-Gyorgyi
*Biologist; Scientific director, National*
*Foundation for Cancer Research,*
*Woods Hole, Mass.*
5

The essential point is that every cell has an explosive ability to grow and to multiply. So the main problem about cancer is not what makes its cells grow, but what is it that keeps them from growing if they are not damaged by some outside factor. What is the brake? . . . It is hoped that more detailed knowledge will allow one to pinpoint more sharply the primary disturbance in cancer and will help to find means to correct it, leading to both the understanding and control of this disease. We can only control what we understand.

*At meeting of Nobel laureates,*
*Lindau, West Germany/*
*The National Observer, 7-5:3.*

**Malcolm C. Todd**
*President,*
*American Medical Association*
1

[On malpractice suits and malpractice insurance costs]: Malpractice is the Number 1 problem that faces the American medical profession ... The malpractice problem is so critical that if the legislatures do not respond to remedial legislation we are absolutely going to have utter chaos in this country, because for the first time in history you are going to see massive walkouts and withholding of services by American doctors.

*Interview, Atlantic City, N.J./*
*The New York Times, 6-15:(1)44.*

**James D. Watson**
*Professor of molecular biology,*
*Harvard University; Director, Cold*
*Spring Harbor (N.Y.) Laboratory*
2

The American public is being sold a nasty bill of goods about cancer. While they're being told about cancer cures, the cure rate has improved only about 1 per cent. The grim cancer statistics are about as bad as ever. Today, the press releases coming out of the National Cancer Institute have all the honesty of the Pentagon's.

*At cancer symposium, Massachusetts*
*Institute of Technology, March 6/*
*Los Angeles Herald-Examiner, 3-7:(A)3.*

3

[On cancer research]: Naturally, as human beings, we all hope for striking clinical advances in the near future. But as scientists *per se,* all that we can truthfully say is that at long last cancer research can be very good

science indeed, and we are now moving much faster than we could have anticipated only several years ago ... There will be a need for long and firm financial and moral support by Congress and the American public if we are to reach our goal of understanding what cancer is at the molecular level. But we must also realize that thoughtlessly dispensing very large sums may be totally without any positive effect. For unless we are careful, the current war on cancer will increasingly resemble our Vietnam debacle: "Just a few hundred million more into this year's budget, and the tables will finally turn."

*Interview, Cold Spring Harbor, N.Y./*
*The New York Times, 5-6:10.*

**Caspar W. Weinberger**
*Secretary of Health,*
*Education and Welfare*
*of the United States*
4

The increasing difficulty physicians have in obtaining malpractice insurance—at any price—has reached crisis proportions in the United States ... The loss of insurance coverage for physicians would have an immediate impact on the public's access to quality health care. It would most certainly drive up the cost of medical care even further and it would increase the number of tests and procedures ordered by physicians solely to protect themselves ... High malpractice insurance premiums and the defensive medicine that results cost the public between 3 billion and 7 billion dollars a year.

*U.S. News & World Report, 1-20:53.*

**Jack E. Zimmerman**
*Director, intensive care unit,*
*George Washington University*
*Medical Center*
5

[On major life-and-death medical situations, such as prolonging life in apparently hopeless cases]: I don't think the courts can decide these kinds of things. I think it's up to families

# WHAT THEY SAID IN 1975

*(JACK E. ZIMMERMAN)*

and doctors largely working together and, finally, more up to doctors, advising the family. I would like to see the courts out of it entirely and this really be judged a matter that can't be left up to the law. There's just no way you can legislate a series of signs or symptoms that will indicate the plug should be pulled [at a certain point] . . . Until we learn considerably more in medicine, that things become black and white, I don't see how law can make these things any more clear.

*The Washington Post, 11-24:(B)6.*

# The Performing Arts

## MOTION PICTURES

**Jack Albertson**
*Actor*

1

[On the Academy Awards]: It isn't fair to make people compete when each role is so different. They ought to pick the five top actors of the year, give them each a gold watch and send everybody home.

*Interview, Los Angeles/*
*Los Angeles Herald-Examiner, 2-3:(A)12*

2

A "star" is someone who brings in millions of dollars at the box office. We don't have too many of them laying around. The truth is that you can become a nonentity overnight, as well as a star. Show business is a weird racket. Great talent waits around for a break, while people with less than a modicum of talent make it.

*Interview, Beverly Hills, Calif./*
*Los Angeles Times, 10-12:(Calendar)25.*

**Woody Allen**
*Actor, Director, Writer*

3

Writing the script is the only part [of film-making] I enjoy, because you do that quietly at home. There's no pressure, and I like writing anyway. I've always been most pleased with the things I've written, and I can get right down to work. I don't have problems with dawdling or forcing myself to sit down at the typewriter. So the writing is fun; but that's where the fun ends. Once you're into production of a film script, the work becomes incredibly arduous and tedious. It's a thoroughly unpleasant experience. There's no breaking-up on the set. You don't hear a laugh out of anyone for months at a time. I'm grumpy and preoccupied . . . Everybody's grumpy. And cold and sleepy . . . Believe me, it's a miserable group of people in a miserable set of circumstances. I can safely say

there's not a light moment on the set of my films from the first shot to the last.

*News conference, New York/*
*The Washington Post, 6-9:(B)5.*

4

I know I can make a picture that people will laugh at, and that's the primary thing to do. To make a comedy that has a message but isn't funny enough, that's a big mistake. Better if it's very funny and doesn't say anything. The ideal thing is to be funny and also say something significant. That's hard to achieve. As a rule, the comedies of the Marx brothers, which are among my favorites, and W. C. Fields, usually don't explore things with any depth.

*Interview, New York/*
*Seventeen, November:123.*

**Robert Altman**
*Director*

5

Actors are magnificent—I respect their work very much. Their whole body is their art. They deserve credit for that. Sure, they're often children, too, but I understand that. When I first started watching movies, I never knew there were directors. I saw actors up there on the screen. *They're* all out there, while you and I can hide behind something.

*Interview, Los Angeles/*
*"W": a Fairchild publication, 5-30:20.*

6

[On film critics]: They've kept me alive. They're the only voice, the only reporting done other than advertising. Even if they were all dumb and wrong and full of it, they'd still be necessary. Otherwise, there'd be no forum—it would depend on who had the most money to buy the biggest ad.

*Interview, New York/*
*Los Angeles Times, 7-6:(Calendar)30.*

405

**Lindsay Anderson**
*Director*
1

I've made a number of documentary films that are just as personal [as my features], if not more so. In a certain way, documentary film is capable of being more subjective and more poetic than is the feature film. The difficulty in a feature film is that you have the demands of the narrative ... to assimilate into the poetic expression. Whereas a documentary film can be more purely lyrical, more purely poetic.

*Interview, New York/*
*The Christian Science Monitor, 8-29:23.*

**Michelangelo Antonioni**
*Italian director*
2

I find that you Americans take my films too literally—you are forever trying to puzzle out "the story" and to find hidden meanings where there are perhaps none. For you, a film must be entirely rational, without unexplained mysteries. But Europeans, on the other hand, look upon my films as I intend them to be looked upon, as works of visual art, to be reacted to as one reacts to a painting, subjectively rather than objectively. For Europeans, "the story" is of secondary importance, and they are not bothered by what you call "ambiguity."

*Interview, New York/*
*The New York Times, 5-4:(2)15.*

**Alan Arkin**
*Actor*
3

I guess people are returning to films; that's what the statistics show. But what else have they got in entertainment? No choice, except the crap on television. But pictures today are all wrong. Very seldom do I go to the movies. They're too damn depressing. One disaster picture after another. That stinks.

*Interview, Los Angeles/*
*San Francisco Examiner & Chronicle,*
*9-7:(Datebook)19.*

**Samuel Z. Arkoff**
*Chairman and president, American*
*International Pictures*
4

The motion picture business is like the fashion business: Cuffs go and then they come

back. Nothing stays the same, but no idea is ever dead. Some of the younger executives in the business have computer systems to work it all out. Well, God bless them. But the only computer system I have is experience and flying by the seat of my pants.

*Interview, Los Angeles/*
*Daily Variety, 6-19:26.*

**Rona Barrett**
*Entertainment columnist*
5

I'm not friends with the stars because if I were I couldn't tell the truth about them. We are all neurotic, but their neuroses are constantly fluctuating, which makes it very difficult to be intimate with them.

*Interview, Los Angeles/*
*People, 12-15:34.*

**David Begelman**
*President, Columbia Pictures Corporation*
6

You might compare the creation of [movie] stars with the production of automobiles. We're bound to come out with new stars just as General Motors is bound to come up with cars. The creation comes out of the public demand.

*Interview/*
*"W": a Fairchild publication, 6-13:8.*

**Ingmar Bergman**
*Director*
7

I have a ridiculous passion for clarity—not to be understood but to be felt. If you can't feel, you won't understand. Stravinsky said that he hadn't understood a bar of music in his life, but he'd felt it.

*Interview, Los Angeles/*
*Los Angeles Times, 11-9:(Calendar)36.*

**Ingrid Bergman**
*Actress*
8

When I was in Hollywood, there were stables full of actresses. Of course, there are some strong women stars today, too, like Barbra Streisand, Faye Dunaway, Elizabeth Taylor and, in England, Glenda Jackson. But it certainly isn't the way it used to be. I can't figure out what has gone wrong—why, over the past

10 years, so many have disappeared. Maybe it's that television took so many. Or maybe it's because of pornography which, by showing everything, robbed women of their dignity as human beings, and made them seem so ugly that people lost interest in them. But I do know this: With everyone being naked, I wouldn't want to act if I had to start now. I think instead of being an actress I'd be an assistant director or something and keep my clothes on.

*Interview, New York/*
*Los Angeles Times, 1-12:(Calendar)16.*

1

Acting is the best medicine in the world—no matter what is the matter with you. If you are not feeling well, it goes away because you are busy thinking about something that isn't yourself. We actors are very fortunate people.

*Interview, New York/*
*The New York Times, 4-20:(2)6.*

**Tony Bill**
*Producer*

2

One of these days I'd like to direct—not to keep control of the material, which is what everybody always says, but to narrow the gap between me and the material. Now it's like giving up your child to be raised by someone else. I don't want to control; I want to enforce the collaboration. Too often the director, for reasons involving his own ego, discourages the collaboration. They don't listen to the prop men or anyone else who's got a suggestion. The decisions are finally your own, but you've got to listen.

*Interview, Beverly Hills, Calif./*
*Los Angeles Times, 10-24:(4)1.*

**Charles Bronson**
*Actor*

3

Once upon a time, I would have worried what the critics might say, but I found out that's the way to become a loser in this business. Worrying about the critics will keep you on the bottom rung of the ladder of world box-office receipts the rest of your life. Critics are different in every city in the world and will never agree. It is not their nature to agree. Even

when they print glowing reports about you, the only thing to do is ignore them. You can be Judith Anderson and get all the beautiful reviews in the world and it doesn't get you a dollar in the bank.

*Interview, New Orleans/*
*Cosmopolitan, July:141.*

4

I know I've been criticized for the violence in my pictures. Particularly in something like *Death Wish*. But I don't think any of it was gratuitous. If there's physical contact between people they call it violence. But if you take a close look at nature you'll find just as much so-called violence goes on there as creatures struggle to survive. But I don't make any secret about it: I'm not in movies for social reform. I'm in it for the box office, and I'm in it for the money.

*Interview, Los Angeles/*
*San Francisco Examiner & Chronicle,*
*8-31:(Datebook)16.*

**Mel Brooks**
*Writer, Director*

5

The script is the most important element in film-making; and besides, it's the part I like best. Your vision is still intact. That's why I direct, to protect that vision. And even then, I lose some control. After all, movies are essentially collaborative. They're the most expensive art form ever invented. Leonardo didn't need a studio chief for the money to draw a lower jaw. All he needed was a nickel for a pencil. Goya could paint you a national tragedy for $1.69. But to make a movie you need $1-million.

*Newsweek, 2-17:58.*

**George Burns**
*Entertainer*

6

I found out that acting isn't too hard. You knock on the door and somebody says, "Come in." If you walk in, you're a great actor. If you stay out in the hall, you're an idiot. When you come inside, the man says, "How do you feel?" If you say, "Fine, thank you," that's good acting. If he says, "How do you feel?" and you say, "Look on the floor. Maybe it fell down,"

# WHAT THEY SAID IN 1975

that's bad acting—that means you're not listening.

*At annual ball of Hollywood chapter, National Academy of Television Arts and Sciences, Los Angeles, Nov. 23/ The Hollywood Reporter, 11-25:9.*

## Ellen Burstyn
*Actress* 1

The first review that came out on [her film] *Alice Doesn't Live Here Anymore* was in *Variety* . . . [The reviewer] said it was boring and terrible and awful, but what bothered me was he said it was a film about little people that made you hate little people. It was such a repulsive thing to say and I said, "I don't know who this man is or anything about him, but he's a terrible snob!" And that tortured me for weeks. A friend said that next time I read a good review it would make me feel twice as good as normal. So I started thinking about that and decided, "No, because that means I have to get up and read the papers to determine how I'm going to feel that day. Am I in a good mood or a bad mood? Let me see my reviews!" There's something wrong with that. So I don't read reviews any more. I don't think critics have any more important opinions than anyone else and I refuse to let them affect my life in any way.

*Interview, New York/ The Washington Post, 3-10:(B)6.*

2

I worked in Hollywood until I attained a peak of mediocrity. I was sitting on the set of *Goodbye Charlie* the first day and felt like I had just come off the production line. Someone had done my face. Someone had done my costume. I was put together by all different departments. I was sitting there being a container for all departmental efforts. Vincente Minnelli acted my scene so I could copy it. What I was doing had nothing to do with what I had been trained to do in acting class.

*Interview, New York/ The New York Times, 3-31:38.*

## James Caan
*Actor* 3

I don't like sitting around talking about all that acting crap. But I've always wanted to be respected by the people I respect. My goal is to do good work and not quit trying. And I never refuse an autograph. These stars who say, "It's awful. I can't go anywhere," they're full of crap. They get in the business in the first place for recognition, and then they complain.

*Interview, Los Angeles/ People, 3-10:40.*

## Michael Caine
*Actor* 4

[On his film, *The Man Who Would Be King*]: The thing about this Kipling film is that it's so big that it is something people can't see on television at home. And that's what the film industry needs—big, spectacular, worthwhile pictures that will bring people away from that box in the living room and out into the cinemas. The cinema has become terribly cerebral, and now may be moving into a different cycle.

*Interview, Tagardirt-el-Bour, Morocco/ The Dallas Times Herald, 4-18:(G)13.*

5

[On nudity in films]: For myself, I am not going to take off my clothes. The only picture I've done in which there was female nudity was *Get Carter*. And two things happened. The moment Geraldine Moffat took off her clothes, I forgot all my lines. And it shortly dawned on me that, as soon as she was nude, everyone stopped looking at *me*. I'm against it . . .

*At San Francisco Film Festival/ San Francisco Examiner & Chronicle, 10-26:(Datebook)13.*

## John Calley
*President, Warner Bros., Inc.* 6

There was a time when somebody could decide who was a star. There was no TV to compete with. Studios making a hundred pictures a year could put a guy in 15 movies back-to-back and develop a recognizable personality and name. The audience had no place else to go. But now the audience tells you. I can't describe what a star is today. If I could, I would buy a station wagon, round up a batch of them and make a fortune.

*"W": a Fairchild publication, 7-11:11.*

**Frank Capra**
*Director*
1

I'm amazed at the impact of my [old] pictures on the [college] kids. What they like best about my films is the dignity and the divinity of the individual. I'm astonished to see these youngsters leave the theatres with tears streaming down their faces. They are touched by the characters in *Mr. Deeds Goes to Town, Mr. Smith Goes to Washington* and *It's A Wonderful Life.* There was no sex or violence in those pictures or any of the others I directed. It's middle-aged people who tell themselves they want to see what they suppose their children are watching in movies. Well, I can tell you this: University students are tired of explicit sex; they strongly oppose violence. God knows, sex and violence are a part of human nature, but it's unnecessary to dwell on them in movies. There's no question you can make good pictures today without either one . . . What audiences love most is an appeal to their hearts and emotions. The formula is still effective because I see it work on college kids today.

*The National Observer, 5-17:21.*

**Leslie Caron**
*Actress*
2

An *avant garde* film is understood and appreciated by a minority. Like Orson Welles' pictures. At first they are not accepted by the masses. But 20 years later they are copied and played so often they make as much money as commercial films. Audiences are limited because they point out styles of behavior that are not yet understood by the lower classes who don't want to be enlightened.

*Interview, Los Angeles/*
*The Dallas Times Herald, 3-30:(F)7.*

**John Cassavetes**
*Actor, Director, Screenwriter*
3

[On his ideas for films]: The good ideas are things that mean something to you. If it's

worth something, it's worth talking about. A lot of bad movies are made because people are just trying to earn a living. There's plenty enough to say without having to be dishonest and making a movie you don't care about . . . I don't resort to vulgarizing myself for a film. I won't get a laugh at the expense of anything I care about. I'm not shocked by nudity or bad language, but I won't use them to be a success. I won't kiss the behind of public opinion. I won't listen to 19 guys in a front-office telling me about what kids will like, or what blacks will like, or what women will like. I figure most people are like me—they don't know what they'll like until they see it.

*Interview, New York/*
*Tulsa Daily World, 5-8:(D)11.*

**Lee J. Cobb**
*Actor*
4

[On acting]: Strange thing: When you're young, you look for the romance of it all. You set out to slay the dragon. You're like a young medic who knows he's going to find the cure for cancer. Much later, when you're in it and it's too late to get out, you find the romance has flown out the window. There are just two kinds of films: the good films and the other kind. That's lesson Number 1. Lesson 2 is that an actor hardly ever gets the opportunity to do what he really wants. When it does happen, it relieves a terrible personal hunger. The greatest prize you can give others is to fulfill your own artistic needs . . . It's presumptuous and erroneous to think that [an actor] has given anything. It's just as self-indulgent for me to think that as it is for a lover to say: "Look what I've given her!" Love is a process of taking. So is all creative work. The poet doesn't bequeath his work as a blessing. It's simply taken by others and recognized for what it is.

*Interview, Brussels/*
*San Francisco Examiner & Chronicle,*
*2-23:(Datebook)15.*

**Bing Crosby**
*Actor, Singer*
5

There's an old saying in show business, particularly the movies and the legitimate stage,

# WHAT THEY SAID IN 1975

## (BING CROSBY)

that the film-makers and stage producers give the public just what the public wants. It sounds like a logical theory, but it is somewhat misleading. Take the movies as a prime example. What's actually happening is that Hollywood studios, as well as the foreign film-makers, are turning out pictures that are wanted by only a minority of the potential movie-going population—a ridiculous situation that could be changed by the film fans if they asserted themselves in volume. With exception of the handful of intensively promoted "blockbusters" such as *Love Story, The Godfather, The Exorcist, The Towering Inferno, Jaws,* and the few others that come along each year, sometimes by pure accident, the average motion picture draws less than 15 per cent of the people who are basically movie fans. This has been going on for so many years now that you would think the producers would wise up and learn more about what movie-goers want by studying what they *don't* want—and do something about it.

*The Dallas Times Herald, 7-15:(E)3.*

## George Cukor
*Director*

1

There is nothing easy in this business, but that's part of the hazard of being in it ... Nothing with Kate [Katharine Hepburn] is difficult because she's an artist and a distinguished person. When I did *Love Among the Ruins* with her, she said, at 7 o'clock in the morning, "Aren't we lucky to be in such a marvelous business?" She had been up since five and instead of complaining, she was alive with the joy, excitement of [the] privilege of working, and I think her words should be engraved on a pin and all actors forced to wear it. There are inconveniences and sometimes you don't feel like doing it, but part of the actors' job is to behave themselves.

*Interview, Leningrad/*
*San Francisco Examiner & Chronicle,*
*8-17:(Datebook)13.*

2

In the early days, people were "given" careers. There was law and order. Studios pro-

duced and managed these women [actresses] and, therefore, they had longevity. Stars at Metro went on for years. A girl like Joan Crawford, lovely and gifted, played with every leading man around—Tracy, Gable, Stewart. Today, a girl makes a success and immediately is in charge of her own career. Few are capable of managing themselves, so their careers are short-lived. There's a curious death wish they have. They aren't the good ol' girls who wanted to succeed. Occasionally, they bitch themselves up in a strange, masochistic way.

*Interview, Los Angeles/*
*"W": a Fairchild publication, 11-28:14.*

## Robert Culp
*Actor*

3

There are a half-dozen to a dozen genius actors in the world. You have to put your whole left arm and a portion of your thigh and all of your guts into it for that. You have to be crazy. Really great actors look into themselves and observe things that terrify them. They have nothing to look at but the mirror. The audience, too, is a mirror for them. I don't want to be crazy. I guess everybody is a little mad. But you better hang on to your sense of humor.

*Interview, Los Angeles/*
*Los Angeles Herald-Examiner, 2-3:(A)11.*

## Tony Curtis
*Actor*

4

Acting isn't as complicated as [acting teacher] Lee Strasberg thinks. I've listened to that Method thesis. Instinctively, you do these things. You do it naturally—I mean, digging into your own experiences. What no instruction explains is that indefinable something, the reason why the eye of the audience is on one person in a scene. That quality, the one that singles out a particular person's interpretation of an emotion, can't be taught.

*Interview/*
*Los Angeles Herald-Examiner, 7-6:(TV Weekly)5.*

## Dino De Laurentiis
*Producer*

5

You must never set out to make a masterpiece, a work of art. Maybe you make one by luck, like *La Strada;* but [Federico] Fellini and I did *La Strada* for only two reasons—to entertain and to make money. Period. Only once in my life I consciously attempt(ed) to produce a masterpiece. I got the greatest story I could think of, *The Last Judgment,* and I hired Vittorio de Sica to direct and Cesare Zavattini to write the script. We all agreed, it was to be our masterpiece, our ultimate film statement. We'd win first prize at Venice, at Cannes, an "Oscar." So we made the goddamn picture. *The Universal Judgment.* It has never been seen outside of Italy. You know why? It was a piece of junk.

*Interview, New York/*
*The New York Times, 7-27:(2)9.*

**Angie Dickinson**
*Actress*

*1*

I guess I did come up the hard way in movies. But I do laugh when I dig out some of my old interviews, in which I pompously announce that I want to be an *actress* and not a pinup girl or a sex queen. I was nuts. I've learned that you use what you've got to the best of your ability. It took me a while to realize that it's okay just to be there and be glamorous. I'm not an actress in the sense that Geraldine Page or Anne Bancroft is. I'm realistic about the difference between the dedicated actress and the glamor-girl. There are usually a lot of holes in motion-picture scripts and you have to fill them with personality, not acting. Right now, I'm very happy about being a sex symbol.

*Interview, Los Angeles/*
*TV Guide, 1-4:24.*

**Kirk Douglas**
*Actor*

*2*

I think every film is a reflection of our times . . . There was a time in Westerns when the bad guys wore black hats and the good guys white hats. Now the white hats are not so white and the black hats are not so black. But if you have a statement to make it should be secondary to the entertainment.

*Interview, Dallas/*
*The Dallas Times Herald, 5-22:(G)9.*

**Richard Dreyfuss**
*Actor*

*3*

People unconsciously go to the theatre [films, stage, etc.] to experience and understand humanity. Actors express the common denominator of human experience. In real life, children and lunatics are the only ones allowed to express these things.

*Interview/U.S. News & World Report, 5-19:58.*

**Irene Dunne**
*Actress*

*4*

Popularity is a curious thing. The public responds to a dimple, a smile, a giggle, a hairstyle, an attitude. Acting talent has less to do with it than personality. That's why I am angry with actors who say they owe nothing to the public. It is true that you work your way up the ladder by yourself. Nothing is handed to you. But we do owe gratitude to the public. It's they who make the hard work pay off.

*Interview, Beverly Hills, Calif./*
*Los Angeles Herald-Examiner, 3-23:(E)7.*

**Clint Eastwood**
*Actor*

*5*

I always think an actor ought to treat himself like a sports figure, for example a boxer who has to keep an eye on sudden and unexpected retirement. You've got to be a realist and think of the time when you want to quit or when the audiences don't dig you any more.

*Interview/People, 6-2:22.*

**Blake Edwards**
*Producer, Director*

*6*

For me, movie-making is the ultimate form of expression. It encompasses all of the senses—sight, sound, and maybe eventually touch and smell. Who knows where it is going to lead? I find making movies a means of expression that transcends writing or painting or any of the three-dimensional forms. Moviemaking also is good for the ego. It allows one to play God or dad or something Oedipal like that, which, I guess, is another need of mine. And it's also great fun to make a movie. I enjoy the

*(BLAKE EDWARDS)*

fairytale aspect of it. I guess that's the child in me, or the child in most film-makers.

*Interview/*
*The Dallas Times Herald, 7-18:(A)21.*

1

[I never aim a movie] at any group or any thing. I aim it at myself, and hope that what I've done is acceptable to the audience. I think the biggest problem is when people start saying, "Aha, I know how to do this and what groups I'm gonna go for." That's very non-productive and non-creative . . . In the final analysis, you make them for yourself.

*Interview, Carlsbad, Calif./*
*The Christian Science Monitor, 7-25:23.*

### Robert Evans
*Producer*

2

[James] Cagney once said to me, "Listen, kid, I want to give you a tip. I'm 5 feet 4 inches tall and I play opposite guys 6 feet 3 . . . By the time the scene's over, I'm 6 feet 3." It's not size or looks, it's presence. That's what makes the star—when you can't take your eye off that person up there on the screen.

*"W": a Fairchild publication, 7-11:11.*

### Peter Falk
*Actor*

3

. . . I think there's a level of intimacy and subtlety and complexity in films that you don't get on stage. I felt the opposite way when I came out here [to Hollywood]. I thought with all those lights and stops and changes it was artificiality. But if you're going to do something realistic, do it on film. Theatre is for theatrical pieces, stylized. Becket, O'Casey. A proscenium with 2,000 people up front—I don't even like watching it.

*Interview, Beverly Hills, Calif./*
*Los Angeles Times, 1-19:(Calendar)27.*

### Freddie Fields
*Producer; President, International*
*Creative Management, theatrical agency*

4

I remember seeing a very old picture where Joan Crawford was in the chorus line. She just

popped out at you. That's what a star is—somebody who carries his own set of lights.

*"W": a Fairchild publication, 7-11:11.*

### Melvin Frank
*Producer, Director, Writer*

5

Hollywood may have had its faults in the old days, but the studio "Golden Circle" system did build professionalism. They took plenty of kids, signed them for a hundred and fifty a week, and built their careers over a long span of time. A lot of them became fine actors and actresses. And a lot of others became stars. But people are in too big a hurry in motion pictures today. There's no time for long-haul professionalism. Too many people have become instant successes and institutionalized too soon—and I am thinking of people like Liza [Minnelli] and [Barbra] Streisand when I say that.

*Interview, New York, Feb. 17/*
*The Dallas Times Herald, 2-19:(G)8.*

### John Frankenheimer
*Director*

6

With 20-20 hindsight, I think I know something now: People want to be entertained. That's what they really want—something that takes them out of the 7 o'clock news. They want *not* to be reminded of their day-to-day lives. They want something that is an event, something they can talk about, something they can lose themselves in one way or another.

*Interview, New York/*
*The Christian Science Monitor, 9-15:23.*

### James Garner
*Actor*

7

We're actors. We ply our trade wherever we do it. This is what we sell. We're the court jesters. That's our function, to entertain people. It's a hell of a lot better than laying carpet.

*Interview, Los Angeles/*
*TV Guide, 2-1:14.*

### Lillian Gish
*Actress*

8

When D. W. Griffith was with us, he used to say, "Let's make this film as intelligent as we

can. Out there are many intelligent people."
Movies started going down when they forgot
that. . . . in most new films I find so much
unnecessary vulgarity. Now, if you are portray-
ing vulgar people, I suppose you have to do
them as they are. But why take normal people
and make vulgarians out of them? I move about
the world and I've seen all kinds of people, but
in my life I've never been around vulgarity such
as they show in films today. Perhaps there are
such people. But you don't want them near
you. You don't have to listen to them. It is
playing down to the public. There are more
intelligent and tasteful ones than ignorant and
vulgar ones. Mr. Griffith always said that.

*Interview, New York/*
*The Christian Science Monitor, 7-31:22.*

## Edith Head
*Motion picture fashion designer* 1

The superstars are men now. I've dressed
more men than women in the last five years. We
used to get stars like Lake, Lamour, Kelly, who
were made into superstars; some burst on the
screen quickly—Bette Davis, Norma Shearer,
Garbo, Hepburn. Now we've got Al Pacino,
Jack Nicholson, Steve McQueen, Newman and
Redford . . . all men. The public likes action,
disaster, thriller pictures—things that make you
sit on the edge of your seat. Years ago, it was
"Will the cavalry save the beautiful girl from
the Indians?"

*Interview, Beverly Hills, Calif./*
*"W": a Fairchild publication, 9-19:22.*

## Richard D. Heffner
*Chairman, Code and Rating Administration,*
*Motion Picture Association of America* 2

[On his organization, which determines film
ratings]: Some people consider us censors.
We're not. We don't ban anything, or demand
that changes be made in films. We don't make
judgments about the value or quality of films.
If you're over the age of 17, nothing we do
affects what you can see in a movie theatre.
Our obligation is toward a strictly limited constituency—the parents of young children who
want to know whether a film contains material

that they might consider unsuitable for their
children. Our job is to reflect public opinion.
The only question we're supposed to ask ourselves when we sit down to watch a film is: Will
most American parents of young children think
that the appropriate classification for this film
is G, PG, R or X? . . . Our society places a high
value on freedom, but we also believe that
young children must be treated with special
care. Minors can't be held to contracts, or serve
in the armed forces, or vote, or drink or drive a
car. And a majority of Americans seem to feel
that their young children should be shielded
from certain experiences such as watching explicit sexual acts or seeing brutal murders on
the screen. You may or may not agree. But if
you don't give public opinion some credence in
areas like this, if you don't respond positively
to the will of the majority, you may quickly
turn it into a tyranny of the majority.

*Interview, New York/*
*The New York Times, 5-11:(2)13.*

## Audrey Hepburn
*Actress* 3

It's always frightening to start a picture. I
think I'm basically an introvert. It's always
been hard for me to do things in front of
people. And it's not like riding a bicycle; it
doesn't just come back. Even with a lovely
script and fine actors and director. In the end,
you're always alone.

*Interview, Pamplona, Spain/*
*Los Angeles Times, 7-20:(Calendar)1.*

## Katharine Hepburn
*Actress* 4

Movies have changed so much. They call
movies "honest" because they can use every
word and can photograph people rolling around
and carrying on in an idiotic way. THEY'RE
NOT HONEST AT ALL! To photograph love!
You can't do that, can you? And friendship—
you can't photograph that! Not that way. If
you *underplay* it and use your imagination, the
audience will do all the acting for you. I don't
have to leap on you and groan and carry on,
you know! I mean, surely, they can get the

413

# WHAT THEY SAID IN 1975

message, can't they? What do you think has happened to our taste? It's agony. To me, it is.

*Interview, New York/*
*Ladies' Home Journal, August:108.*

1

Pornography is all you see any more [in films]. That's not true drama. It has nothing to do with true love or emotion. Love is something you can't show. It can't be described. It's in the imagination ... Can anyone describe what happens inside of someone to make him or her want to love another, to sacrifice, to do heroic, life-risking things for another person? Even to die? That's what love is and that's what good drama is made of ... Maybe pictures do reflect times; maybe people have these needs [for pornography]. But it's the weak ones making pictures who don't fight against this trend, who cater to low tastes. When they could be doing fine, dramatic things with their talent, they're making all physical stuff, and little else ... Of course, it's all money in films nowadays, don't you know it? Humor is gone; everything is gone. It's all money.

*Interview, Bend, Ore./*
*San Francisco Examiner & Chronicle,*
*10-12:(Datebook)18.*

**John Houseman**
*Actor, Producer, Director*

2

[On his recently becoming an actor]: In a way, I enjoy the novelty of acting. It's not as anxious-making as producing and directing. I was apprehensive at first about memorizing lines but found it easier than I anticipated. Certainly, acting isn't as time-consuming. You have only one thing to worry about—a performance. Producers and directors are concerned with budgets, time limitations, actors and all the rest ... Becoming a celebrity is fun and interesting. I think I enjoyed the final evidence of fame on my airplane flight out here ... The cabin attendant approached me and asked, "Aren't you sometimes mistaken for John Houseman?" That sort of thing never happens to a producer.

*Interview, Los Angeles/*
*Los Angeles Times, 12-27:(2)6.*

**John Huston**
*Director*

3

A well-made film transcends intellectuality and truth. The process of creativity in motion pictures establishes a true medium that the written word cannot attain. It is closer to the thought processes. At their very best, pictures are reels behind your eyes and you are projecting them yourself to see what you want to see. Three fairly recent films which achieved that for me were *McCabe and Mrs. Miller, Midnight Cowboy* and *Bonnie and Clyde.* As I watched them I thought I was there, not watching it happen but taking part.

*Interview, Los Angeles/*
*The Dallas Times Herald, 12-25:(F)9.*

**Wilfrid Hyde-White**
*Actor*

4

[On why he hasn't made a film in four years]: They keep making the bloody things on street corners or in public lavatories. I couldn't get excited about films like that. It doesn't appeal to me in the slightest. Besides, I can't keep walking up and down those stone steps ... I'm used to the comforts of the studios, and the kind of glossy pictures that used to fill cinemas and give people an entertaining night out. Not this sordid street-corner stuff ... Mind you, it was hard work. But when you see the results, it was worth all the sweat. Just look at the success of *That's Entertainment!* [a compilation of old musicals] —it must mean something.

*Interview, Palm Springs, Calif./*
*San Francisco Examiner & Chronicle,*
*1-12:(Datebook)12.*

**Glenda Jackson**
*Actress*

5

[On nude scenes she has played]: I think I've gone as far as I can on the screen. I can't conceive any purpose that would make me go further. But I don't feel anything, no embarrassment, at the time. It's only work, after all ... The point is, there's no emotional involvement. It's a character, that's all. You're not enjoying yourself. It would be different if

93 film technicians walked into your bedroom at a crucial moment. But it's not as if they're being shown the secrets of your home life. I tell you, nobody ever cleared a set for me! The only criterion I've always had is this: Is it necessary, or is it merely being slapped in for sensation? If it's an integral part of a script or character, then it has to be done. Just as lines have to be said. You know what you're in for when you read the script—and if you're not prepared to go all the way with it, then don't accept it.

*Interview, London/*
*San Francisco Examiner & Chronicle,*
*3-2:(Datebook)14.*

1

I've been working steadily in films for the past six years, and the depressing thing is the scripts they send me don't get better. Nine out of 10 scripts I get are rubbish, and you're lucky if one out of 10 is even readable.

*Interview, London/*
*The Dallas Times Herald, 12-21:(E)2.*

**James Earl Jones**
*Actor*

2

... the more film I do, the more challenge I feel. In film, you've got to be more expert. On stage, you might be able to give a false cry and people can't see if you're really crying. But on film you've got to cry.

*Interview, Washington/*
*The Washington Post, 3-21:(B)4.*

**Jan Kadar**
*Director*

3

[Comparing film-making in the U.S. with film-making in Czechoslovakia where he built his career]: In Czechoslovakia it is basically a state enterprise, as in all those kinds of countries—the government takes the money and gives the money, taking more away, giving less back ... You are dealing with an establishment that sees the purpose of a film much more in political terms. Here in the U.S. it is a private enterprise, so the picture has sometimes a different purpose, a different character ... [In the U.S.] a film is more or less a commercial com-

modity, and someone gives the money as a commercial venture. That makes a lot of difference. [But] the obstacles are similar. In Czechoslovakia you had to convince the political people to give you the opportunity and the money, as I did with *The Shop on Main Street* and other pictures. In the U.S. you have to convince the studio and the producers that the film will be commercially valuable. In film you are always depending on somebody. You can't just go home and open your piano and do a composition.

*Interview, New York/*
*The Christian Science Monitor, 11-28:43.*

**Howard W. Koch**
*Producer*

4

[Referring to his new film, *Once Is Not Enough*]: The fact that it has done so well, despite a negative reception by the critics, just goes to show that today's audiences make up their own minds. This isn't the first film that has illustrated this ... By the same token, some films which are critically acclaimed often end up as disappointments in terms of box-office returns ... [One reason is] because the critics have been proven wrong picture after picture. They've lost their credibility. [Another is that] very often critics engage in showboating. They try to be humorous instead of serious, and as a result they are no longer taken seriously. [In some cases], negative reviews can even help. Pictures panned by critics with reputations for knocking good movies often do very well—it's a case of reverse psychology ... [Critics] seem to go for intellectual message films. Some critics also have favorite directors or producers whose works they always lavish praise on—even if they just film somebody shooting a telephone book, their admiring critics will produce paeans to commemorate the event.

*Interview/The Hollywood Reporter, 8-7:3.*

**Stanley Kramer**
*Producer, Director*

5

[On the motion-picture ratings system]: It has worked better than any other kind of self-censorship yet devised by man. Whatever its

*(STANLEY KRAMER)*

flaws, I compare the censor code to the United Nations: It doesn't work perfectly, sometimes it doesn't work at all, but it's the only thing so far that has stopped things from getting out of control on the major scales.

*At University of Southern California/
Daily Variety, 10-29:6.*

**Fritz Lang**
*Former director*
1

Sometimes I wonder what kind of films I would make today if I were able. With the world the way it is, I think they would be very critical—very aggressive. I would want to show how television has robbed the young people of their imagination. But that would only be a small part of all I would have to say.

*Interview, Beverly Hills, Calif./
Los Angeles Times, 12-5:(4)29.*

**Cloris Leachman**
*Actress*
2

I'm only as versatile as the people I play. All the people I play are out there somewhere. All I do is hook into a character's mentality with the limitations and excesses of that particular person at that time in that situation . . . The key to everything is that we're all each other. This is as true of actors playing people as the people watching them. We're all each other—jealous, loving, frightened, hungry, needing, blind, limited.

*Interview/
Los Angeles Times, 11-30:(TV Times)2.*

**Jack Lemmon**
*Actor*
3

The trouble [with acting] is that, unlike a painter or a writer, there's nothing an actor can do without an audience. You need other actors, too, and a director. If you stand in front of a mirror acting out Shakespeare, you're wasting your time. That's the one tough thing about my profession: The only reason you're there is to evoke a response; and not just by saying the lines—that talent is the last thing you use. Acting is an intellectual process of divining some-thing, finding out why a character says what he says, does what he does.

*Interview, Beverly Hills, Calif./
San Francisco Examiner & Chronicle,
1-19:(Datebook)13.*

4

[Comparing stage and screen]: When you're on stage you have to play it broadly—you have to get to the man in the back row of the balcony. But on screen the camera catches every little nuance. You have to bring it down—'way down. I remember when I did my first film with Judy Holliday; George Cukor was directing, and he kept telling me to hold it down. It got to be very frustrating, and I finally said, "You mean, stop acting." "That's right," he said.

*Interview, New York/
The Dallas Times Herald, 2-20:(B)8.*

**Richard Lester**
*Director*
5

Making movies is like playing a game of chess: You move the pieces around and make sure you get them on the right squares. I don't enjoy making films. Usually I'm working against the clock, cramming a quart of action into a pint of time. And movies are never simple. Mine certainly aren't.

*Interview, Cork, Ireland/
San Francisco Examiner & Chronicle,
7-6:(Datebook)16.*

**Art Linkletter**
*Entertainer*
6

[On pornography in films]: Warren Beatty in *Shampoo* is an example of a young man who, at the height of his star powers, has debased the whole business . . . Marlon Brando—a star of that caliber doing *Last Tango in Paris* is to me disgusting . . . [But] when anybody asks me, "Why is Hollywood doing this?" my answer is, "Why are you people going to them?"

*Springfield (Mass.) College/
Los Angeles Times, 5-9:(1)2.*

**Louis Malle**
*Director*

1

Film has not yet had its Impressionist revolution. The approach of audiences is still very 19th-century—they want to be told a story, to have a dramatic construction with the exposition in Act One and the climax in Act Four. Impressionism was a shock, but now it's accepted that when you look at a painting you don't ask what did he want to say. A painter can go as far as he wants, which is not yet accepted in film. On the other hand, we live in an anguished and chaotic world and not everyone is satisfied with film-makers giving them the same material. I hope, I think, that people are ready for something else.

*Interview, Paris/*
*Los Angeles Times, 10-5:(Calendar)25.*

**Rouben Mamoulian**
*Director*

2

. . . the movies are the most powerful of the arts everywhere in the world. We must realize that they're not a toy. They can add to or diminish the quality of life. But for the last 10 years the movies have existed only, only, only to make money. One can say that the movies always existed to make money, and that's true. Yet the moguls, whether they began by selling gloves or insurance or scrap metal, were ambitious men and proud men, and they wanted not only to make money but also to make fine films. And in some cases they made the fine films even when it was obvious they might not earn much money at all.

*Interview/Los Angeles Times, 7-25:(4)1.*

**Joseph L. Mankiewicz**
*Writer, Director*

3

. . . never in my experience has the American or the world film business been so single-mindedly dedicated to the making of a fast, hot, quick buck as it is today. The carpetbaggers have taken over. The pimps own the profession. There is no sense of building personalities or properties or tomorrow. Can we run *Jaws* next month? No, everyone must see it tonight . . . I do not know how to write for films as they are right now. There is a kind of visual violence that is expected that I don't think I can cope with. The people that are being written about and seem to attract the interest of the audience, I am not interested in. Not all human problems should be solved by automobile crashes and burning buildings, nor should a man's problems be solved by clouting someone on the chin or by a woman's stripping herself. Too often I am taken by the fact that young film-makers are directing lenses instead of actors, directing effects, not content. Audiences will tire of the special effects and want to get back to performances, content and those little concerns that make up most of the big things in life.

*At San Francisco Film Festival, Oct. 19/*
*The Hollywood Reporter, 10-21:3,11.*

4

Sensitivity and intelligence are the qualities I look for in actors. I put far down my list an actor who says, "I feel it." I don't care if he or she feels it; I am just interested if the audience feels it. I hire actors to play a part; I don't want writing-and-directing actors.

*At San Francisco Film Festival, Oct. 19/*
*Los Angeles Herald-Examiner, 10-22:(B)1.*

**George Marshall**
*Director*

5

A good director is part psychiatrist. One of my trademarks is never to sit down on the job. I work closely with my actors, going over each line so they don't need an idiot board. I remember one time I couldn't get Susan Hayward to react properly when we were doing *Tap Roots.* I simply told her co-star, Van Heflin, so she could hear, that I didn't think she could do the scene. The next take I got perfection. Simple psychology.

*Interview, Los Angeles/*
*Los Angeles Herald-Examiner, 1-18:(B)6.*

**Walter Matthau**
*Actor*

6

. . . I am primarily an introvert. In order to become an actor, you have to sublimate that

417

*(WALTER MATTHAU)*

introversion. You have to push outward so that people can see you. You can't ask someone for a job and say, I want to be an actor but I'm too shy to read for you. Yet introverts do become good actors, and they have the capacity to observe as introverts and project what they've observed in the form of acting. It's the hardest job known to man, because you must bare whatever you are, however painful it may be. Because the audience will know if you're a phony. You've got to be what you are. And sometimes it can be very, very painful. Yet it can also be extremely satisfying, so it's worth all the pain. But it is tough. I know, because I've worked as a lumberjack, a ditch-digger and a fire-fighter. I've worked for 12 hours a day fighting a fire; take a nap and a shower and you're fine. Try to learn a tough role and know that your livelihood depends on it, with all kinds of scorpions sitting out front. See what happens to the brain and the body.

*Interview, New York/*
*Los Angeles Times, 9-12:(4)22.*

1

I think you become a better actor with age, because you're learning more. As long as you're physically equipped to walk and talk and think, you must become better ... When I think of some of the parts I played when I was going to high school, and when I just got out of high school, I have to laugh, because I didn't have enough experience to be an actor; I didn't understand about the behavior of certain classes of people. I think I understand it a little better now. Gee, I hope so.

*Interview, New York/*
*The Christian Science Monitor, 10-30:23.*

**Alec McCowen**
*Actor*

2

I like to have my cake and eat it, which you can do if you have enough cake. I love the notoriety of being in the theatre and then of having the complete reverse, of wandering among strangers ... I don't see how you could do a real job of acting if you cut yourself off

from the tiresome ordinary business of living—the vulnerability, the nervousness, the dire necessity of thinking about the laundry, the exasperation of standing in line at the post office. It couldn't be good to be too protected from the common daily round ...

*Interview, Washington/*
*The Washington Post, 3-5:(B)6.*

**Roddy McDowall**
*Actor*

3

[Acting is] a heart-breaking profession, it really is. It's the only profession I know of where the accumulation of one's work ultimately counts for very little, as far as continuance is concerned. People are discarded right, left and center, continually, without validity ... because it's a profession that's trying to guess what the public wants. The performer is constantly a possible victim of that game. Who knows what's going to be successful? ... So much of it depends on the social need of a nation. That's what makes stars—being there at the right time, being able to perform that which is subconsciously needed.

*Interview, Los Angeles/*
*The Christian Science Monitor, 8-21:27.*

**Ron Miller**
*Executive producer, Walt Disney Productions*

4

There's no such thing as a Disney formula. There are the obvious things we can't do, but basically it's entertainment. Our comedies have to be visual. Our adventures have to have a lot of action. We don't really ever find ourselves getting involved in long dialogue scenes; that's when the kids go and buy popcorn. As long as it's entertainment up there it's fine. But if you've got a turkey, They can smell it. We've made several. We're human.

*Interview/*
*Los Angeles Herald-Examiner, 7-22:(B)6.*

**Walter Mirisch**
*Producer*

5

A maker of movies is dealing with a mercurial creation and a mercurial audience. He has to recognize that a film can be disappointing, in one way or another, despite all the good intentions of the writer, director, cast, crew and producer. But what's most important is to know that you have done your best, and, having done it, that you will go on to a new challenge. In a business where rejection is a constant possibility, that's the only way to survive.

*Interview, Los Angeles/*
*Los Angeles Times, 3-23:(Home)30.*

1

...an excellent film is a combination of elements—a great director and actors telling a great story on a great location. But even though technically you know what is great, you can't just put it all together and come up with a great film. And that's because film is an art, not a science.

*Los Angeles Herald-Examiner, 10-13:(A)6.*

**Franco Nero**
*Actor*

2

I don't believe any actor can be a young man. You look in a mirror. You can't be just pretty. Your face must show many experiences. I was a thief, so I can play a thief. I've ridden a horse, so I can ride a horse. I have been a dancer, so I can play a dancer. It shows in the eyes, in the face, always so grown up.

*Interview, Los Angeles/*
*Los Angeles Times, 8-20:(4)21.*

**Paul Newman**
*Actor*

3

[On awards and testimonials for actors]: An actor can get more and go further with the least conceivable education than any professional in the world. Once you remember that, you can't really get conceited about it.

*Interview, New York/*
*San Francisco Examiner & Chronicle,*
*5-18:(Datebook)12.*

4

[On giving autographs to fans]: I don't do it. People are really offended when I say, "I'm sorry but I don't sign them." I simply don't know why anybody should be required to put his name on a piece of paper or be interrupted while he's eating dinner. It's part of that Hollywood bull and the whole sense of royalty. I don't want to nurture that philosophy. People think you are public property. You get some lady who comes up and says, "Oh, you're so cute," and she pinches my cheek. What kind of arrogance does that person have, to violate my privacy?

*Interview/Ladies' Home Journal, July:66.*

**Jack Nicholson**
*Actor*

5

Most good acting comes from the unconscious. All you really do is dredge it up.

*Interview, Salem, Oregon/*
*San Francisco Examiner & Chronicle,*
*3-30:(Sunday Scene)8.*

6

A "star" on a movie set is like a bomb. That bomb has got to be defused so people can approach it without fear. Because if a living reality doesn't exist between the players in a scene, the scene won't play. For instance, I never think of the actors I'm playing with as actors. I think of them as the people they're pretending to be. That way, if an actor makes a mistake, I don't feel it as a mistake. I see it as a quirk in that person's behavior, and I react to that quirk.

*Interview, New York/People, 12-8:53.*

**Carroll O'Connor**
*Actor*

7

[Humphrey] Bogart once said that all an actor owes the public is a good performance. I say an actor owes the public as many good performances as possible.

*Interview, Los Angeles/People, 7-14:43.*

**Laurence Olivier**
*Actor*

8

...the craft of the actor can be rewarding and happy. The basic inclination toward the work is to pretend to be or feel like someone else. You feel like a king, or you feel like an

# WHAT THEY SAID IN 1975

## (LAURENCE OLIVIER)

archbishop. That can be better than being a real king or a real churchman because they are stuck with that. Next month you, as an actor, can be somebody's uncle, and the month after that a Chinaman, and that's an advantage. There are times when your life is suffused with bitterness and misery so that you can hardly endure to wear this particular uncomfortable garment called life. I have been so wretched at times that I felt completely out of contact with reality. When I went on in a part in the nighttime, that was the only time I really felt like myself.

*Interview, Los Angeles/Time, 12-29:58.*

## Sidney Poitier
### Actor
1

[On opportunities for blacks in the film industry]: Today, if you have the wherewithal to seduce the studios into the knowledge that you can make money for them, they don't care what you look like any more. It's problematical for everyone, of course, and it's somewhat more difficult for blacks because we are new, but we are no longer completely excluded. There are some of us that can deal from a fairly substantial track record for making money, and therefore we are listened to. There is a different attitude about blacks operating in this area. These are new times. Now you will begin to see more of a substantial input by these film-makers because it is only now that some of us are able to exercise this authority. How we succeed will determine how many more blacks will hold this position in the future.

*Interview/*
*Los Angeles Times, 12-28:(Calendar)29.*

## Sydney Pollack
### Director
2

Working intimately with the same people helps the creative process. There is a reason that rep companies are successful. It saves so much time. Actors are private; it takes a long time to get them to open up. It's a painstaking process to go through this on each film. If I had my choice I would do all my films with people I know ... This kind of teamwork lets you get

back to what is really important—making the picture.

*Interview, Los Angeles/*
*Los Angeles Times, 9-10:(4)15.*

## Robert Radnitz
### Producer
3

The trouble with too many of us who make pictures is that we remain in some kind of filmic cocoon, never talking to the people we're making the films for. That insulation breeds some wild misjudgments. Too many people in the film business think of a person in a small town in the Midwest as a hick, a rube—with the result that there is often a tendency to "talk down" to audiences. I maintain there is no difference in sophistication between Davenport, Iowa, and Los Angeles or New York. I know that because I've been to Davenport, and lots of small towns, and talked with the people.

*Interview, Los Angeles/*
*Los Angeles Times, 1-19:(Home)36.*

## Charlotte Rampling
### British actress
4

I'm not dependent on Hollywood for my work. I never have been and I never want to be. I can't fight against what Hollywood is: It's more of a factory than anything else. It's just an industry. Americans make you feel you can't do without American films. They don't really recognize me in America. The European market has 500 million people. The money I get over there is far bigger. I'm also more acknowledged in Europe as an actress. Now suddenly I'm learning how to be a big star.

*Interview, Beverly Hills, Calif./*
*Los Angeles Times, 5-18:(Calendar)33.*

## Gena Rowlands
### Actress
5

[The creation of a role is] always the actress' job ... You take a script and read it, and read it again and again—about 10 times. Then you put it down and start thinking about it ... You start remembering. You remember someone who got on the subway. Or you remember something about yourself. And, finally, a very mysterious thing starts to happen. It starts coming together within your mind and your emotions ... The inside of you starts to become true to the character, and then the outside starts doing things on its own.

*Interview, New York/*
*The Christian Science Monitor, 3-25:7.*

1

[On her being nominated for an Academy Award]: There's a certain amount of personal vanity involved ... I think every actor practices an acceptance speech from age 17.

*Interview/*
*"W": a Fairchild publication, 4-4:2.*

**Ken Russell**
*Director, Writer*

2

By the time I finish writing the script, I've got the picture in my mind. I can see it very, very clearly. I can sit and run it, if you will, reel by reel, scene by scene. It won't be exactly like that when I make it, because a film's a difficult thing. It takes on a life of its own. And if you fight against it too much you destroy its own natural growth ... The most exciting part ... is the conception ... Then [the] heart-sinking feeling that now I've got to physically *do* it. And that is very, very hard work. But if it's vivid enough in your own mind to start with, then it's no problem—if you have enough technique to bring it about ... You can't do it all in a blinding flash ... But it's an odd thing; I can almost think of the whole film as one flash in my mind. And if you can get that onto the screen, that's what you have to try to achieve. It's really as simple as that.

*Interview, New York/*
*The Christian Science Monitor, 6-2:31.*

**Roy Scheider**
*Actor*

3

People are always asking me why I didn't have a [financial] piece of *Jaws* [his recent film which is now the biggest grosser in history]. It wasn't that kind of picture. If you'd read that script and knew the difficulties and dangers ahead, the seeming impossibility of it working

out, you'd have taken the salary and headed for the hills, the way *I* did.

*People, 11-24:80.*

**Maximilian Schell**
*Actor, Director*

4

[On directing]: I believe you can get the best out of people by letting them alone as much as possible. I rewrite around the people and the situations, and there comes a point at which the roles take over and begin to have a life of their own. The director's real job is to know when this happens and record it.

*Interview/*
*"W": a Fairchild publication, 5-2:8.*

**Lalo Schifrin**
*Composer*

5

[On composing music for motion pictures]: There are two kinds of composers—those who come from the conservatory and those who come from the street. I believe a film composer has to come from both. To use a literary analogy, he must be both poet and reporter.

*The New York Times, 5-25:(2)11.*

6

[Comparing music for TV with music in motion pictures]: A television theme is like a telegram—short and snappy, a quick message to stimulate an instant response. If people are in the kitchen while the TV set's in the living-room, the theme music lets them know that a certain program is about to begin. A movie score is not a telegram but a long letter. Instead of jarring an audience into action, the objective is to underline certain dramatic passages, sending off melodious signals that comment on character and situation.

*Interview, Los Angeles/*
*Los Angeles Times, 11-30:(Home)67.*

**John Schlesinger**
*Director*

7

[On Hollywood]: I do love this place; but at the same time I realize the problem, the problem that comes when you believe it all too much. That's why I try to keep out of it all, the

# WHAT THEY SAID IN 1975

rat-race part of it, when I'm here. I do like Hollywood. It's very easy to meet people here and I like that. Perhaps it's because I come from England—where we are much more regimented, where we have much more tradition and permanence—that I love the informality of the place. The barriers are not up. And I do like the fantasy itself. For instance, I *love* Disneyland. Disneyland to me is the most wonderful place imaginable. But then you have to remember the other side of things—that the fantasy here [in Hollywood] is so extreme, and the promise so extreme, that the truth behind it can be very sad, very savage. That's what interests me, what's behind the facade. It's all facade. The whole city looks like sets that will be torn down the next day.

*Interview, Beverly Hills, Calif./*
*The Washington Post, 5-4:(M)5.*

### George C. Scott
*Actor*

1

You can't "act" in a movie. You can pose and perform but you can't act. To me the greatest accolade for an actor in a movie is to make the audience think you're acting when, in fact, you're working under extreme circumstances. The lack of continuity is indescribably unassailable; also the slavish mercy to technology. You're absolutely the pawn of technology. I love to do a quiet scene well, but there's trouble afterwards when people start fooling with it. Here every time you see a script change you get scared because you don't know what you're doing. It's like pro football—a new playbook.

*Interview, Kauai, Hawaii/*
*Los Angeles Herald-Examiner, 11-30:(D)1.*

### Irwin Shaw
*Author*

2

I'm too old to fool around with Hollywood any more. When you are a young writer, screenwriting can be a great experience, but you have to get away from it. I began my career writing radio soap operas, stuff like *Dick Tracy*. I had to write lines that people could handle with

maybe 20 minutes of rehearsal. Each voice had to be recognizable as the style of a particular speaker. That was marvelous experience, even though I was writing absolute junk. Later, I wrote plays. Every time a play of mine flopped, I had to come out here [to Hollywood], write a movie and make enough money to write another play, to have a flop. But the final result of Hollywood was always terribly disappointing, because every good thing I put into a script was either elongated, erased, changed or betrayed. That was the system in those days.

*Los Angeles/*
*Los Angeles Times, 11-23:(Book Review)3.*

### Robert Shaw
*Actor*

3

I've been asked . . . "How do you give it [acting] life?" My answer is "out of my nerve-ends." I don't know why I care so much, but I do. I believe acting's a craft, not an art, and I try, with some sense of humor, to practice my craft as best I can.

*Interview, Pamplona, Spain/*
*San Francisco Examiner & Chronicle, 9-21:21.*

### Martin Sheen
*Actor*

4

People think acting is an accident. It's not. It's calculated, planned, scrutinized, rehearsed. A performer has to know what he's doing every instant, to invent and improvise and feel, to bleed a little—or else there's no growth . . .

*Interview/TV Guide, 10-25:22.*

### Stirling Silliphant
*Screenwriter*

5

In *Towering Inferno* we have a 140-page script and 14 major stars. If you wanted to give each actor five minutes of screen time, half of the film would be gone right there. It's not *Lacombe, Lucien*, where you concentrate for two hours on a few main characters. The people in disaster movies have to be recognizable right away—written with bold, broad strokes.

*Interview/*
*"W": a Fairchild publication, 1-10:2.*

**Sam Spiegel**
*Producer*

1

[Film-makers] are trying to outdo each other in shock, imagining shock therapy will cure the ills of the movie business. But it really is like electroshock therapy. The danger is that the treatment has to be stronger every time. You've got to keep scaring them [the audience] more, and where's the limit? It's really all an outgrowth of *The Exorcist.* Violence makes the appetite for violence voracious. It's not sour grapes for me; my films have done well. But it is sad that *Jaws* will outdo [at the box office] movies we all thought of as landmarks. It's like being brought up on humanist literature and then having to start reading schlock.

*Interview, Los Angeles/*
*Los Angeles Times, 9-16:(4)1.*

**James Stewart**
*Actor*

2

I've heard people say, "Look at James Stewart. He's natural." Well, I'm *sorry.* That's not an accurate way of describing what an actor does. I try to perform without letting the acting *show.* The idea, whether it's comedy or drama, is to be so persuasive that when people leave the theatre they will say, "Gee, I almost felt it was actually happening." How is that effect achieved? There aren't any rules or methods, at least not for me. John Ford, a really great director, always said it was all done by accident. I think he was probably right; but there's also some work and experimentation mixed in, and perhaps a few physical tricks.

*Interview, Beverly Hills, Calif./*
*Los Angeles Times, 2-2:(Home)27.*

3

The Western is the true movie. It is the best example of how to use the medium because it uses it visually. It does not depend on the spoken words, a catastrophe or an enormous number of stars. It treats a complicated subject in an uncomplicated way and it is truly an original. There is no other country like ours [the U.S.], and no other type of film depicts our uniqueness better. We are recognized for the Western all over the world.

*Interview/Los Angeles Times, 12-20:(2)4.*

**Lee Strasberg**
*Artistic director, Actors Studio*

4

All my life has been dedicated to one purpose: the service of talent. It's a rare commodity. In our country [the U.S.], we have more of it than any other country in the world. But less attention is paid to talent in this country than in any other. Talent needs to be nurtured and helped at all times. But nobody makes stars, least of all Lee Strasberg. Producers don't make stars. The audience makes stars.

*At dinner in his honor sponsored by*
*Masquers club, Los Angeles, June 6/*
*Daily Variety, 6-9:3.*

**Donald Sutherland**
*Actor*

5

The failure of most political movies these days is that they have such a loyalty, such a legitimate loyalty, to their points of view that they fail to communicate. The people who would like the film like it; the others are turned off.

*Interview, Parma, Italy/*
*Los Angeles Times, 1-12:(Calendar)22.*

**Lana Turner**
*Actress*

6

[On the old "studio system"]: If I didn't like a script at MGM, I cried, begged and pleaded to get my way. I'm sorry for young people today. They don't have a home place for counsel and training. In one movie they're a "star." Six months later, people say, "Whatever happened to so-and-so?"

*Interview, Beverly Hills, Calif./*
*The Dallas Times Herald, 4-13:(2)15.*

**Liv Ullmann**
*Actress*

7

Hollywood entertains, it does not communicate. If only the big producers here [in the U.S.] would give Americans the opportunity, as they do in Europe, to see sophisticated pictures, they would not want to see the fake and

*(LIV ULLMANN)*

the phony and the perishable glorified in film all the time.

*Interview, New York/*
*The New York Times, 1-29:24.*

## Roger Vadim
*Director*
1

To be a director is to be a painter in a way. You train your sense of aesthetics, of color, objects, volume and light. Most of the time when I was making my last movie, I was acting like a painter.

*Time, 5-5:52.*

## Jack Valenti
*President, Motion Picture*
*Association of America*
2

When people are fearful about the future, they look for escape. In a darkened theatre, with a 65-foot screen, you lose yourself for two and a half hours. People find this beneficial.

*U.S. News & World Report, 3-17:52.*

3

[Arguing against film censorship]: Under a free system, there is a trade-off in the society. In return for your freedom, you allow freedom for others, whether you like what they do or not. We use our freedom to provide entertainment through satire, suspense, comedy, drama or whatever it is that is entertaining . . . The real censorship of movies in this country lies in the audiences. The audience really determines what happens on that screen. If the audience won't come, the picture won't get made . . . I have a two-part philosophical rostrum: First— the artist must be free. He cannot be censored, bludgeoned, bullied, threatened or infringed upon. Second—the price he must pay is that the nature of his work may cause it to be restricted from viewing by children . . . Movies are not the custodians of children. Decisions must be made by parents . . . Mom is the censor. It's up to the parent. The parent is the one person who in actual fact directs the path of our society.

*Interview, Beverly Hills, Calif./*
*San Francisco Examiner & Chronicle,*
*8-17:(A)21.*

## Jack Warden
*Actor*
4

A good actor is the sum total of his background. So if I get a good part that is a little "stretchy," then I can go back and somewhere along the line I've been in that position or I've seen someone who has. You have to be aware of yourself and the situations you've been involved in. No matter how good an actor you are, you're never better than the situation. You have to be willing to expose every facet of yourself, even if people don't like you. When you start working on a part, all kinds of fantasies and images come to you and you can pattern the role this way or that. Usually, there's only one way to go: to hit right on!

*Interview, Malibu, Calif./*
*San Francisco Examiner & Chronicle,*
*4-13:(Datebook)13.*

## John Wayne
*Actor*
5

I really try to stand by the theory of making motion pictures [on the assumption] that people go in there to escape their everyday problems. They like illusions, and I think that, by illusion, you can portray what is to be portrayed without the vulgarity of a continous four-letter-word program.

*Interview/The Hollywood Reporter, 2-6:18.*

6

[On Westerns]: The form is not going the way of all flesh. I've been in this business 46 years and I've heard it said Westerns are on the way out every six or seven years. It's our American folklore, and folklore will never die out.

*The Washington Post, 5-11:(F)1.*

## Orson Welles
*Actor, Producer, Director, Writer*
7

[On his independent ways of making films]: There are a few of us left in this conglomerated world of ours who still trudge separately along the lonely, rocky road . . . What we do come up with has no special right to call itself better. It's just different. And if there's any excuse for us at all, it is that we simply are probably the old

American tradition of the maverick, and we are a vanishing breed . . . The maverick may go his own way, but he doesn't think it is the only way or ever claim it is the best way. And don't imagine that this raggle taggle gypsy is claiming to be free. It is just that some of the necessities to which I'm a slave are different from yours. As a director, for instance, I pay myself out of my acting jobs. I use my own work to subsidize my work. In other words, I'm crazy. But I'm not crazy enough to pretend to be free. Yet it's a fact that many of the films you've seen tonight would never have been made otherwise. Or if otherwise, well, they might have been better—but certainly they wouldn't have been mine.

*At American Film Institute tribute*
*to him, Los Angeles, Feb. 9/*
*The Hollywood Reporter, 2-11:1,17.*

### Billy Wilder
*Producer, Director, Writer*
*1*

Movies are such an expensive gamble. A painter who paints a painting and doesn't like it can throw away $2.12 worth of canvas, stretcher and paint. But if a film costs $2-million, it's going to be hanging on some screen whether you like it or not. And then, 10 or 15 years later, it comes back to haunt you on TV. We can't bury our dead. Our mongoloids live with us forever.

*Interview/*
*"W": a Fairchild publication, 1-10:2.*

### Gene Wilder
*Actor, Director*
*2*

I don't want to think of myself making great pictures. You start thinking in terms of great and you start thinking of yourself, or your own ego. I want to make people laugh and cry and say, "Wasn't that wonderful?"

*Interview, London/*
*The New York Times, 6-8:(2)17.*

### William Wyler
*Director*
*3*

I guess I could be accused of having no particular style [in making films], but looking back, the ones that were the most satisfying were not the financial successes, or the ones that won "Oscars," but the ones that had something to say socially or politically, the so-called message pictures—which is supposed to be a dirty word. I like for audiences to go away with something, although I have nothing against pure entertainment.

*Dallas/The Dallas Times Herald, 3-19:(G)7.*

### Michael York
*Actor*
*4*

[On his success]: I'm not sure I know if I have any secret. I think I've just been luckier than most. I can't explain it any other way. I do know an actor has to work very hard at keeping a career alive today. When there was a studio to protect an actor under contract it was easier to sustain a career. It was not fatal for him to appear in a couple of flops as long as he starred in just one good film every 18 months or so. I've hardly stopped working since I began. That way, the misses are quickly forgotten and the hits are what people remember me by.

*Interview, Los Angeles/*
*Los Angeles Herald-Examiner, 4-20:(E)1.*

*5*

There's a lot of phony nostalgia about movies. Essentially, the movies are—or should be—what Shakespeare said: "the mirror held up to nature," something immediate that you identify with and from which you find out more about yourself, that basically ennobles mankind. I think movies do all this. They are the art form of our time.

*Interview, Dallas/*
*The Christian Science Monitor, 11-24:38.*

# MUSIC

**Claudio Arrau**
*Pianist*
1

A real musician should have enough sensitivity to enter into any [musical] world. They call me sometimes a "romantic" pianist, but I don't believe in words like that—there is not one single piece of music that is entirely "classical" or entirely "romantic." The capacity to form yourself into something else is the secret of real interpretation. You shouldn't play only what is akin to you; you should be able to play things that are psychologically different, that in life would be foreign to you. The interpreter has in him many elements that in life don't come to the fore, but that he can use, that will be awakened in him by the music as he plays.
*Interview, Vermont/*
*The New York Times, 11-23:(2)19.*

**Tony Bennett**
*Singer*
2

When I grew up, all the idols I admired—Stan Laurel, Clark Gable, Durante, George Burns, Fred Astaire—worked hard. All were individualists. But today, for whatever reasons, it's changed. Everyone has conformed. They're all in the same musical bag. And on top of that, most of it's full of anger and protest, which I don't think have any place in music. We're all trying to better ourselves. So why can't our music and painting be beautiful and optimistic?
*Interview, Beverly Hills, Calif./*
*Los Angeles Herald-Examiner, 3-15:(B)9.*

3

Singing Top-10 hits is selling out. In boxing lingo, it's like taking a dive. But I won't sing a song unless I really like it and really feel it. Singers who sing the Top-10 may be doing okay now; but if they carry on like that for too long, the public will turn its back on them. To me,

that's watered-down music. It's silly for me to sing Top-10 songs note for note, the same arrangement and in the same key . . . If I had to sell out like that, I would probably go to a bar and get drunk. When I hear my songs played somewhere, I have to feel proud that they're my songs. I would fall apart if I heard myself singing some song I didn't want to sing. It would haunt me.
*Interview/Los Angeles Times, 3-18:(4)8.*

**Anthony Bliss**
*Executive director, Metropolitan*
*Opera, New York*
4

[On cutting opera expenses]: You can't cut the size of the orchestra, the size of the chorus, or the number of leading singers. You can do things a little more efficiently. Over the long pull, probably we can get a lighter concept for the productions and reduce the stage support cast. But that will just keep up with future inflation. And you can't just do that over one year. I think the pendulum of over-production has swung too far. One hopes any production we replace will be lighter than the one it replaces, and it will be a gradual process. First of all, I think, although some of the public cry out for less-ornate productions, if you give it to them, they don't like them. So it is a public education.
*Interview/*
*The Christian Science Monitor, 12-24:22.*

**Sammy Cahn**
*Lyricist*
5

I write endlessly. But I can't help it. If someone walks into my house right now and plays a melody that I like, I'll write a lyric for it. My typewriter and the experience of putting words on paper is a natural process, like breathing. If I'm not writing lyrics, I'm writing letters ... The [typewriter] keys open doors, and for me it's just like walking into Shangri La. In an incredible way, that has been happening to me all my life. Who could ask for anything more?

*Interview/*
*Los Angeles Times, 8-10:(Home)31.*

**Johnny Cash**
*Singer*

1

That's what my kind of music is to me: It's a romanticizing about Americana. That's what country music is to me. I wrote a song last night, kind of a weeper, called *Mountain Lady.* ... it's about a mountain lady who used to sit on the front porch in the cool of the day, wondering where her children are—that kind of thing. That's what my music means to me.

*Interview/*
*Los Angeles Herald-Examiner, 11-27:(B)6.*

**Aaron Copland**
*Composer*

2

I've lived through about 50 years of American musical history now, and the scene is much better than it was when I began in 1920. There's a matter of many more composers working now, for one thing, and many more schools having classes in composition. There is much more activity, more orchestras, everything. So we're well on the way to playing a major role, I think, in the world of music. But all Americans suffer a bit from the fact that we connect serious music with Europe. We're late-comers on the scene, and in the minds of the "big public" serious music is Beethoven, Bach and Brahms and so forth. It takes a little while for them to get used to the idea that we here in America, with the late start, are ready to be paid attention to.

*Interview, Dallas/*
*The Dallas Times Herald, 5-4:(F)1.*

**Frank Corsaro**
*Director, New York City Opera*

3

The chief reality in opera, I think, is the emotional plot. I try to go to the psychological realities. Even the music has to come after the psychological realities that impelled it. Opera is not complete until it gets onto the stage. Music alone, text alone aren't complete when it comes to the projection of idea and emotion. The director has to understand what needs to be done to complement, describe, amplify what the orchestra and voices are doing. You know the famous story about Gluck. After a performance of his *Iphegenie en Tauride*, someone asked him why Orestes sings "Now calm possesses my heart again" to an agitated accompaniment. "That is to show Orestes is lying," Gluck said. Why should the stage director be denied similar powers of amplification? When do I know I have amplified something too much, that I've gone too far? I pull away when I see that the imagination doesn't need to be led any farther. I don't like to hear about "tact" and "taste" in productions; that usually means someone's had a failure of imagination—like in the Met's Roxy version of *Tristan*. And what did tact and taste ever have to do with the theatre anyway?

*Interview, New York/*
*Los Angeles Times, 11-23:(Calendar)64.*

**Colin Davis**
*Musical director, Royal Opera, London*

4

Of course conducting has changed lately, and very much in relationship to the players. There are all these players' committees and governing bodies now. The conductor no longer has the power to threaten their livelihood as he once did. That's probably all for the best, I suppose, at least from a humane point of view. But as humans, musicians can be as lazy as anybody else. So it becomes a matter of getting them to do their best, without threats. Not always easy, let me tell you.

*San Francisco Examiner & Chronicle,*
*2-16(This World)22.*

**Mac Davis**
*Singer, Composer*

5

To an extent, people like my music because it don't make them think. They don't like music with hidden meanings. When I write something, I don't write it so poetically and so

# WHAT THEY SAID IN 1975

*(MAC DAVIS)*

heavily that the listener has to sit down and ponder over it and ask what I meant here or what I meant there. I just come out and say it as simply as possible so people don't have to think hard about what I'm trying to say. We should recognize that there is this segment of the population that just wants to listen to music and not think about what they're listening to . . . I want to make people have a good time, that's all. I don't care about being a significant artist or writing something that will change the course of pop music. If that's being "commercial" or copping out to the establishment, then that's where I'm at.

*Interview, Los Angeles/*
*Los Angeles Times, 7-3:(4)12.*

**James DePreist**
*Conductor-designate, Quebec*
*Symphony Orchestra* 1

Shifting from guest to permanent conductor is like shifting from lover to husband—you lose the privileges of an affair.

*Interview/People, 11-24:72.*

**John Dexter**
*Artistic director, Metropolitan*
*Opera, New York* 2

People dribble on about the wonderful casts at the Paris Opera. Those all-star casts only stay for about six performances. The average casting at the Metropolitan Opera in New York is on a much higher level than Paris or Covent Garden or Hamburg, especially when you consider the Met is the only opera house in the world that gives eight performances a week. I've worked at the Paris Opera, but I won't do it again—it's technically chaotic. I'd rather earn my ulcers in New York. Paris is for eating, not for working.

*Interview/*
*"W": a Fairchild publication, 11-28:11.*

**David Diamond**
*Composer* 3

[Today's young conductors have] an odious combination of human indifference and simple ignorance. Conductors today are appallingly lazy. If they have established reputations as interpreters of new music, it is usually for playing the same few contemporary works wherever they go—and they go everywhere! They expend enormous time and energy fabricating their own glamorous images off and on the podium rather than seriously and fairly equating the music of our epoch . . . Today it is the performer [conductor] who keeps the composer waiting. The performer today earns far more than the composer, who is the lowest paid in the music profession; and yet it is the composer who supplies the performer with his earning materials—year after year, century after century . . . These arrogant young men exert an unhealthy power over the composer. Not long ago, I attended a terribly distorted performance of Leonard Bernstein's *Age of Anxiety*, conducted by Seiji Ozawa. Bernstein greeted the man cordially, if not enthusiastically, after the performance, and actually had to restrain *me* from speaking my mind to him. What has caused such an unhealthy situation to come about? Very simple factors: personality, publicity and authority—but not the composer's authority! What a sad fact that these rude young men are inheriting the finest orchestras!

*Interview/*
*The New York Times, 7-6:(2)11.*

**Sixten Ehrling**
*Conductor; Head of orchestral*
*conducting, Juilliard School* 4

[On conducting at the Metropolitan Opera]: When you're in my position in the pit, you hear mostly orchestra. I think that I'm entitled to hear the singers and that the audience should be able to hear the words distinctly. I've been accused of holding down the orchestra too much, for this reason. I believe now that if I can barely hear the singers, the audience gets the right balance. I think what happens on-stage can affect what people think of the performance in the pit. A badly staged production and bad singing is reflected in how one hears the orchestra, even if it's playing perfectly. But, in another way, certain singers can create a feeling of excitement that makes myself and the orchestra do better than we might have done.

*Interview, New York/*
*The New York Times, 4-6:(1)53.*

**Eugene Fodor**
*Violinist*
1

I can feel a communication with an audience. There's something created—something living, like a tree. It's so real you can almost touch it. It grows and grows during a performance. That's the real measure of enjoyment in the communication of music.

*Interview/U.S. News & World Report, 5-19:59.*

**Carlo Maria Giulini**
*Principal conductor, Vienna*
*Symphony Orchestra*
2

I cannot just conduct. After a month of work, I need three weeks to rest, to think. I give everything to music when I do it. I cannot give everything every day. I cannot make music the way some people make breakfast. To me it is a wonder every time. A miracle. And I'm always so afraid. It is such a great mystery that a tone comes out at all . . .

*Interview, Los Angeles/*
*Los Angeles Times, 3-23:(Calendar)64.*

**Woody Herman**
*Band leader; Jazz musician*
3

The caliber of young, serious, dedicated musicians is so far above what it was 25 years ago, it's not even funny. And that's because of the musical education system. Until recently, "jazz" was a dirty word as far as musical education was concerned. It's the other way around now. Places like the Eastman School, which was always a preparatory school for young symphony musicians, has a large jazz department now.

*Interview, San Francisco/*
*San Francisco Examiner &*
*Chronicle, 1-5:(Datebook)9.*

**Jerome Hines**
*Opera singer*
4

It's a fact that when we began [at New York's Metropolitan Opera 30 years ago], the

*Interview, New York/*
*The New York Times, 12-30:27.*

**Henry Holt**
*Musical director, Seattle Opera Company*
5

We are to a great extent a populist company. Opera got started in America as an elitist art form, and it still is in some places; our mission has been to change this. When we got started in [the] '60s, some people thought we were running down the price of opera real estate by the way we promoted it; but we got people here and we found an audience.

*The New York Times, 7-17:20.*

**Vladimir Horowitz**
*Pianist*
6

The most important thing [in performing] is to transform the piano from a percussive instrument into a singing instrument. Every composer, from Beethoven to Chopin, kept hoping that one day there would be a piano that could be made to sing. Now we have wonderful pianos. But *because* we have wonderful pianos, it is necessary to find the color that will represent a singing tone, and a singing tone is made up of shadows and colors and contrasts. The secret lies mainly in contrast. Contrast is what I call technique. For example, I never play the same piece in the same way. This just happens. When I sit down at the keyboard, I never know *how* I will play something. I play the way I feel at *that* moment. The head—the intellect—is

# WHAT THEY SAID IN 1975

only the controlling factor in music-making; it is not a guide. The guide is your feelings. Of course, feeling without control doesn't work at all. If you *only* feel, you're a dilettante. It's true that control can also get out of hand. Artists must know instinctively how to strike a balance between control and feeling. For me, the most important thing is to convey to the public what the composer wanted to say. I am only an intermediary between the composer and the public.

*Interview, New York/*
*The New York Times, 11-23:(11)8.*

*1*

I've made lots of recordings, but I never listen to them because I don't want to influence myself. If they are played on the radio, I turn it off. I can listen to other people's recordings, but not my own. They bother me. I hear things. I ask, why did I play like that? I imagine things differently. Even from day to day, my ideas change. I don't know how I will play next week. I am not interested in how I played something in 1965.

*Interview/*
*Los Angeles Times, 11-30:(Calendar)70.*

**Robert Irving**
*Principal conductor, New York City Ballet*

*2*

In an opera, you're for the most part trying to keep the orchestra down so as not to drown out the singers. In ballet, you need the maximum brilliance and vitality to support the dance. In fact, the more you drown out the chattering feet, the better.

*Interview/The New York Times, 1-19:(2)8.*

**Jose Iturbi**
*Pianist*

*3*

[I] practice religiously, every day or evening. Usually two hours. I travel with a mute that I put in the piano so nobody in other hotel rooms can hear it. I believe in regularity. I don't believe in practicing six hours one day, and the day after zero. I have heard musicians say: "I am going on vacation, and for six happy weeks

I don't open my violin case"—or cello case or whatever. Human beings have different reactions. And when I practice every night there is no sacrifice on my part. This story about the difficult life of an artist—I don't like. My answer is, if you don't like it, don't do it. I do it because I like it.

*Interview, New York/*
*Los Angeles Times, 11-28:(4)30.*

**Stan Kenton**
*Jazz musician and bandleader*

*4*

I hate country-and-western music. It is ignorant music and perverted music. As a professional musician—a jazz musician—I abhor it ... The country-and-western music is an absolute national disgrace and the lowest form of contemporary music. It's a lot of whining and crying, and I cannot understand why the American public is buying it. I guess because it is being crammed down their throats ... I hate almost everything Nashville stands for. Country music has no charm whatsoever. It is music for the masses. This should be no secret. Just listen to the contents of the music, the lyrics. There's nothing in them. They have no taste.

*Interview, Cedar Lake, Ind./*
*The Dallas Times Herald, 7-3:(C)6.*

**Dorothy Kirsten**
*Opera singer*

*5*

... I think that is what is missing today—discipline—in [opera] singing, in learning how to sing and not coming in [to the pros] too soon. How can a young artist with no experience—you're thrown on the stage, and if you don't know by that time your technique so well that it doesn't make you nervous to know where the next note is coming from—how can you possibly portray a role, or be a pro? And there should be only pros at the Met [New York's Metropolitan Opera].

*Interview, New York/*
*The New York Times, 12-30:41.*

**Gladys Knight**
*Singer*

*6*

The artist is usually on the bottom of the record industry's totem pole. You often end up with fame and nothing else. You sing for the recognition, but you do it for security, too. That's what a job is for. You end up broke and a has-been. There are no has-been managers. The managers and the producers get the bread if not the fame, while the singers run up and down, knocking themselves out. Everybody gets paid before us. The record companies get theirs and then won't do things for you ... People look at us and say, "Oh, they're rich!" But it's those who run the business end who have the mansions and stuff and roll around in Rolls-Royces. I don't think that's fair. They get all that only because of us. [Singing is] such an enjoyable kind of work. And it's lucrative, too, if you can get the bulk of what belongs to you. It's when you're trying to make it that they take it all. If they give you so much, you think of how much more you really must have made.

*Interview, Los Angeles/*
*Los Angeles Herald-Examiner, 6-19:(C)8.*

**Peggy Lee**
*Singer*
*1*

When the first hard acid rock came out, I was terrified. It seemed that everything was over. I would listen very carefully to rock lyrics ... and if you broke it down and analyzed it and brought it down inside of you, you found it wasn't saying anything ... Because I enunciate clearly and think deeply, it didn't suit me at all. If I sing something, people listen to the words very clearly. So I have to be very careful ... I have a feeling that everything is changing back again ... but often with progress we have an upheaval. If you are going to repair a highway, you have to have some of those big machines to tear it all up and start over again ... And there seems to be a trend toward studying. Several of the young men in my orchestra are Juilliard graduates, or come from other fine music schools. I think they're suddenly realizing that there's more to music than making a lot of noise and excitement ... There's really a great longing for people to hear something that touches the heart.

*Interview, New York/*
*The Christian Science Monitor, 12-2:23.*

**Lorin Maazel**
*Musical director, Cleveland Orchestra*
*2*

If we get the word out soon enough to a lot of people who don't know yet what classical music has to offer, I think our institutions will become financially sound, which means we'll go on making music in a variety of ways. In short, if our profession will be peopled by artists aware of the world about them, in the social sense, and if the institutions are broadened in base to the extent that they can become responsible to the needs of that ever-growing audience, not only in times of readjustment but in very good times, then I think it's here to stay. I feel very positive about it. There's a great era coming up.

*Interview, New York/*
*The New York Times, 2-2:(2)17.*

**Lotfi Mansouri**
*General director-designate, Canadian*
*Opera Company, Toronto*
*3*

[On whether opera is "relevant"]: I hate that question. It's such a lazy question. Of course opera is relevant. I agree that we sometimes prompt it by overdoing things a little, by spending foolish amounts on idiotic stage sets. Opera is singled out for attack because it happens to be an expensive art form. But to ask if Mozart's *Cosi Fan Tutte* is relevant to the Hamilton [Canada] steelworker and his upcoming contract negotiations is the same as asking whether Shakespeare's *Hamlet* or Tchaikovsky's *Fifth Symphony* has meaning for him in terms of his wage claims. They do not, in a direct sense. But each of them opens a kind of a vista on human experience and human emotion. *Cosi Fan Tutte* says something universal. It's a story of love, of human feelings, of the constancy of our love. How lasting are the feelings of intense love? Are we fickle, when we love our wives and still feel attracted to other women? This is the universal message coming through to the Hamilton steelworker. He, too, has felt emotion. He, too, has loved and been loved; and he will have wondered, as Guglielmo does, whether his wife or girl friend does or does not love him.

*Interview, Amsterdam/The Toronto*
*Globe and Mail, 9-6:29.*

# WHAT THEY SAID IN 1975

## Zubin Mehta
*Musical director, Los Angeles*
*Philharmonic Orchestra*
1

The worst thing [for an orchestra] is an uninvolved player... You don't make music by engaging the best people—the best people don't make the best music. The Israel Philharmonic is a case of a not overwhelming orchestra that has great success, and it's because it has a personality. Some of my first concerts in Montreal were fantastic, and I want to tell you that was not a great orchestra.

*Interview, New York/*
*The New York Times, 11-26:18.*

## Robert Merrill
*Opera singer*
2

I'm worried about opera audiences. I hope they're not accepting mediocrity, less quality, and going to the opera anyway. In other words, they're not looking. If I buy a product in the department store, I look at the ingredients and what it contains. I don't think the audiences are doing that. I think they're just going to hear *Carmen, Rigoletto, Trovatore,* without even concern about who is in the cast. In other words, they're going *anyway,* and perhaps applauding and so on *anyway,* even without the quality. That, I hope, is not developing.

*Interview, New York/*
*The New York Times, 12-30:41.*

## Stefan Minde
*General director and conductor,*
*Portland (Ore.) Opera*
3

Music is not easy, godammit. But that is *my* problem, no one else's. The public is entitled to a good performance. You can never make everything right for everyone. Everyone wants something else. In order to do anything with this difficult job, you must be very stubborn. It is better to know what *you* want and be a no-man, than to know what *they* want and be a yes-man.

*Interview, Portland/*
*Los Angeles Times, 12-7:(Calendar)77.*

## Kiril Molchanov
*Artistic administrator,*
*Bolshoi Opera, Moscow*
4

The most distinctive feature of the Bolshoi in comparison to all the other major opera companies of the world is that it is a permanent company. At La Scala they plan productions around guests, and each artist has his or her own plans. A production is performed five or six times, and then it drops out of the repertory. Our principle is completely different. Both our *Boris Godunov* and our *Eugene Onegin* were done before the Second World War; *The Queen of Spades* was produced around 30 years ago. Naturally, these productions have been renewed; we are not interested in museum rarities. The singers change; the scenery is repainted or rebuilt; the plans of the stage director are reconsidered. But always we try not to destroy the original conception of the director as new artists bring something new, something of their own, into these productions.

*Interview, New York/*
*The New York Times, 6-29:(2)22.*

5

As far as I can see, American audiences have received the Bolshoi Opera with tremendous enthusiasm, despite the critics. It seems to me that differing with audiences is a characteristic of critics in general. At the least, critics ought to be urged to delay their account of a performance sufficiently to allow them to see and hear how the audience has responded. Otherwise, the reader who picks up the notice the next morning may be quite misled as to what occurred.

*Interview, New York/*
*The Washington Post, 7-20:(H)3.*

## Peter Nero
*Pianist*
6

I don't feel that there's anything creative about performing classical music; it's *re*creative. You're playing someone else's music and you have to be faithful to his wishes. There are restrictions in jazz, too, imposed by jazz audiences and other jazz performers. You're supposed to improvise constantly, but after a while you see jazz players who always improvise the same way, within a very restricted style. Is that improvisation?

*Interview, Washington/
The Washington Post, 8-20:(B)6.*

### Olivia Newton-John
*Singer*

1

I know I'm pretty. This may sound silly, but being pretty can create problems and doubts for a female singer. Some people don't take you seriously because they think you're a model who is just playing at having a career. In one review, someone said I couldn't sing, but that I would make a terrific model or air hostess. That really hurt and upset me. Though I was doing fairly well, my music wasn't taken seriously for a long time. Some people don't even bother to listen to you because they assume you can't be pretty and be a good singer at the same time. Not to be taken seriously when you're a serious artist is very frustrating. I went through that for a long time. If a pretty singer gets popular, there's another problem. Is it you or your looks that got you where you are? When you don't know whether people like you for your singing or your looks, it really shakes your self-confidence.

*Interview, Los Angeles/
Los Angeles Times, 7-21:(4)1.*

### Buddy Rich
*Jazz drummer*

2

I hate country music. In a time of sophistication, when people are trying to elevate music, particularly jazz, we're inundated with bad country music. Most of what is recorded is junk—it appeals to the lowest form of intellect.

*Interview/Variety, 2-5:77.*

3

. . . jazz is the art form this country [the U.S.] invented. We must do something for the jazz artist. Maybe we could start by giving honorary degrees . . . We ought to get a government that will do something about the jazz artist. When a ballplayer has to give up, he becomes a sportscaster or a manager. A trumpetman loses his "chops," what does he do?

There should be some provision for him so he doesn't have to go drive a taxi or shine shoes.

*Interview, New York/
The Christian Science Monitor, 4-4:26.*

### George Rochberg
*Composer; Professor of music,
University of Pennsylvania*

4

Every time you write a serious work, you are in effect laying your life on the line. But I can't think about that or worry what my message is. My job is to convince the performer . . . His job is to convince the audience. If we both do our jobs, then maybe we have something.

*Time, 5-5:57.*

### Glynn Ross
*General director, Seattle Opera Company*

5

Our audience is indicative of what I call the "new economy." In the last 10 years, more and more dollars in the gross national product have been shifted from commodities to experiences—to tourism, sports, education. These are people seeking new experiences; and that's why we have more people discovering opera. We are developing a new generation of "operaholics," and I warn people: Opera can be physically addicting.

*The New York Times, 7-17:20.*

### Mstislav Rostropovich
*Cellist*

6

Inside of every musician there exist two people. One is the technician, the other the interpreter. Until the first person is in total control, the second cannot start to have a full life. Finally, it must be the spirit that rules. . . . it is the *music* that I love, not the fact that I am *making* it. In that way, I feel like a priest who, when he speaks, only repeats the words of God. I am not being modest here. But I consider myself a bridge between the spirit of, say, Tchaikovsky or Prokofiev and the people. I am a channel, an instrument, a transmitter. My aim is always to bring the composer as close to the public as possible.

*Interview, Washington/
The New York Times, 3-23:(2)18.*

# WHAT THEY SAID IN 1975

**Julius Rudel**
*General director and conductor, New*
*York City Opera*
*1*

Unless you have really adequate rehearsals—
working from the ground up, laying stone on
top of stone—you are much better off without
them. Of course, people have to be prepared
before they go on, but you can work spontane-
ously this way. You have the attention of
everybody. For a new conductor, I find such a
performance works as an exciting audition. One
rehearsal does no good. The orchestra then
knows what to expect, and the tension is lost.
New productions are another matter. But even
here, if you don't seem to get to the crux of the
problem in rehearsal, you have to go on
anyway.
*Interview, New York/*
*The New York Times, 2-20:40.*

**Gunther Schuller**
*Musician*
*2*

I believe very much in a pluralistic, global
view of music. It seems to me that music, as a
creative and recreative activity, stems from and
involves people of all kinds from all over the
world. For too long in this country we've accorded recognition only to certain traditions
imported from Europe. Hence my interest in
our really indigenous American music, ragtime
and jazz, which have been "segregated" from
our concert halls until recently for lack of the
right credentials. Reversing this trend, as in my
own ragtime ensemble, still shocks proper Bos-
tonians even today. So it's ironic that it's precisely American jazz and ragtime which have
gained universal acceptance by the rest of the
world, rather than the music of our so-called
"serious" composers.
*Before Wolf Trap Associates, Washington,*
*Feb. 17/The Washington Post, 2-18:(B)5.*

**Beverly Sills**
*Opera singer*
*3*

I resent talk of a "meteoric" career. I never
bought or slept my way into an opera house.
Some singers make it with 10 roles. I learned

100. If mine was an overnight success, it was
the longest day's journey you ever saw.
*People, 4-7:16.*

*4*

[On her performing at the Metropolitan
Opera]: I guess every American singer wants
the Met in her obituary. It's nice for my
mother, a dream come true. And I'll never have
to answer that question again about why I'm
not singing at the Met. I was raised believing
big-league ballplayers played for the *Yankees*
and big-league singers sang at the Met. But I'm
here to tell you there are great ballplayers on
the *Mets* and great singers at the New York City
Opera.
*New York/Newsweek, 4-21:86.*

**Paul Simon**
*Singer, Composer*
*5*

... the staple of American popular music is
all three- or four-chord, country- or rock-
oriented now. There's nothing that goes back to
the richest, most original form of American
popular music—Broadway and Tin Pan Alley—
in which sophisticated lyrics are matched by
sophisticated melodies.
*Interview, New York/Newsweek, 12-15:98.*

**Gerard Souzay**
*Concert singer*
*6*

Singing is a sport because it involves muscles,
and therefore what an athlete does is what a
singer must do. You have to eat reasonably and
you have to sleep a lot ... The more young
singers are gifted, the less they are aware of the
fragility of their voice; when they come across
problems, they are not equipped to fight with
them. If you have a less natural voice, you are
used to fighting for what you have—which is a
good thing.
*Interview, New York/*
*The New York Times, 2-16:(2)19.*

**Isaac Stern**
*Violinist*
*7*

[On accompanists]: I look for solidly based
musicianship. A person who does not let the

ego-inspired frivolities of the soloist take away from the music. Someone with whom you work hand-in-glove to build a repertoire.

*The New York Times, 3-2:(2)21.*

1

I have never been willing to play work I don't believe in. If *I* don't believe in it, I will never be able to convince *you.* If in 30 minutes or so there is only five minutes that convinces me, that is not enough. I personally do not care for the Schoenberg Concerto. But I have heard Zvi Zeithlin in performances of it that have fully persuaded me because he believes in it thoroughly.

*At Kennedy Center Symposium, Washington, April 23/The Washington Post, 4-24:(C)15.*

**Vladimir Viardo**
*Pianist*

2

When I make a recording, I feel as if I'm playing in a coffin . . . Without the audience it's not a "live" performance. To be on a record, something in the performance has to have died.

*Interview/ "W": a Fairchild publication, 12-12:11.*

**Dionne Warwicke**
*Singer*

3

Lyrics are more important today than they ever have been in popular music. They must be listened to. Most of them have this in common: They pull at the heartstrings and they reach every listener.

*Quote, 8-17:97.*

**Arthur Weisberg**
*Conductor, Contemporary Chamber Ensemble; Founder, New Orchestra*

4

Music is a language that is constantly being added to. Performers don't keep up with the composers in this respect, not to speak of audiences. It requires study. Orchestra players, comfortable with traditional works, develop an antagonism to new idioms. The result is that new music doesn't have a chance. It gets played badly. Audiences, faced with this as well as radical styles, are doubly hindered from understanding what they hear.

*Interview/The New York Times, 9-15:13.*

**Lawrence Welk**
*Musician, Bandleader*

5

To me, [showmanship] means variety, constant movement, a good strong rhythmic beat, recognizable tunes. It means timing, in terms of knowing when to cut it off. Too many entertainers, especially before a live audience, seem to forget an all-important rule: Always leave the audiences wanting more. I'm reminded of this every summer when we go out touring, and I watch others who are reluctant to leave the stage. I want people to feel that I've ended my show too soon, but never that I've stayed around too long.

*Interview/Los Angeles Times, 6-22:(Home)28.*

**Frank Zappa**
*Rock musician*

6

The only difference between so-called serious music and rock is that one is written out and the other isn't.

*Interview, Los Angeles/ Los Angeles Herald-Examiner, 9-19:(B)3.*

**Pinchas Zukerman**
*Violinist*

7

[On what he looks for in an accompanist]: A partner with personality, musical conviction and a little ESP. The kind of accompanist who was available 25 years ago, someone who just played the notes, is not good enough for me.

*The New York Times, 3-2:(2)21.*

435

# THE STAGE

**Edward Albee**
*Playwright* 1

One part of the writing of a play which gives me particular pleasure is the moment when I test my familiarity with my characters—my knowledge of them—by improvising scenes for them in my mind. I will invent a situation unrelated to the play I am writing, and I will place my characters in that scene and let them have their heads. If they move freely, speak with assurance, and behave more like flesh than wood, then I feel fairly sure I know my characters well enough to begin writing them down.

*Interview/*
*The New York Times, 1-26:(2)1.*

2

The public awareness of theatre as an art form has been increasing over the past decade, and while the result of this has been a raising of broad public taste—which is good—a distressing correlation has been the firm entrenchment of mediocrity as the standard of excellence—which is not good. It is true that the level of mediocrity has risen as the public awareness of theatre around the country has risen, but the public education has not been sufficient to provide proper appreciation of what is best in our theatre, with the result that misinformation is being widely spread. And while there are more plays than ever being performed Off Broadway—plays by new, young writers—this work and its environment has, with exceptions, of course, a curiously dogged quality to it—the entrenchment of a rather high level of mediocrity, of something far less stimulating and creatively valuable than the excitement and excellence of our experimental theatre of the early 1960s.

*Interview/*
*The New York Times, 1-26:(2)7.*

**Lindsay Anderson**
*Director* 3

When you're working in the theatre, I feel that the director is working for the author and for and with the actors. This is a different balance from the cinema, where the director does have—or can have—the primary creative role. At the same time, I would never do a play that I didn't respond to personally, and therefore which couldn't also carry my own kind of sensitivity or emotional commitment, and commitment of ideas, too. So I don't think of my work in the theatre as being "not personal." I tend to be a very personal, subjective director whatever I'm doing . . .

*Interview, New York/*
*The Christian Science Monitor, 8-29:23.*

**Michelangelo Antonioni**
*Motion picture director* 4

[Comparing film directing with stage directing]: [I] wasn't satisfied with the theatre. I remember that I was fed up with the fact that I was forced to use only one "shot," this "long shot" which is the stage . . . When I directed someone on the stage, I would sit in the audience part of the theatre, and I would have just that one shot. But as soon as I got up and approached the actor to tell him something, I would see another shot. But I couldn't *do* it. So I got bored with this.

*Interview, New York/*
*The Christian Science Monitor, 5-30:26.*

**Gerald Arpino**
*Choreographer; Associate director,*
*the Joffrey Ballet, New York* 5

. . . I'm a choreographer who will use what serves him best. I have no barriers. I make no stylistic separations. To me, dance is dance. I see no difference between ballet, modern jazz or ethnic dance. I look at all of dance and simply say, "This is my language!" Of course, I'm a classicist at heart. You see, the classic dance is a science. Ballet is a great science of the body, and I feel that the classic technique is the true form of dance. But once you have trained in it, and have fully absorbed its disciplines, then you can move on to explore every other kind of dance form.

*Interview/*
*The New York Times, 10-5:(2)6.*

**George Balanchine**
*Director, New York City Ballet*

1

[On why many men, as opposed to women, have to be dragged to the ballet]: It's because men are taught that the real thing in life is to promote yourself and become something. "Art" is supposed to be silly. The main thing is to be somebody: First of all, you must try to become President of the United States; if not, then Vice President; and if not, then at least a Senator or something, a lawyer, maybe, or an assistant to somebody. If you like ballet, you're silly.

*Interview, Washington/*
*The Washington Post, 9-4:(B)13.*

**Ingrid Bergman**
*Actress*

2

The theatre is difficult because you have to repeat yourself every evening—and you have to watch yourself all day. Even this noon when I was eating a wonderful lobster, I had to tell myself, "Be careful—not too much wine because of the evening performance." I love the contact with the live audience in the theatre, but I love the camera too—it is one eye instead of a thousand eyes. That one eye sees everything and it comes so close to you that you don't have to do anything! You have to bring everything out a little more for the thousand eyes in the theatre. It's very nice that I've had both kinds all my life.

*Interview, New York/*
*The New York Times, 4-20:(2)5.*

3

Now I am coming into an older age. I cannot be in the movies and play a romantic person. If I want to continue on the screen, I have to go into character parts ... But on the stage I can play a much younger woman, because the people are so far away that they don't see your age. Also, theatre-goers are not like movie-goers—they don't care what age you are, so long as you can convey an illusion.

*Interview, New York/*
*The New York Times, 4-20:(2)5.*

**Yul Brynner**
*Actor*

4

When I was playing the King [in *The King and I*] I had to ask myself, "What is my ultimate aim?" If I had a crowd of 2,000 and there was one couple who had their horizon of life being enlarged, who had an insight into another life, who looked at each other differently afterwards, who made love differently, then something had been achieved. That thought colors everything I do.

*Interview, New York/*
*Los Angeles Times, 6-8:(Calendar)65.*

5

Different audiences do not react the same. That's the refinement of acting—to handle difference audiences. It's just the same as when you relate differently to various people you meet during the day. A Saturday night audience is very good in Los Angeles, but not good in Boston. It is a question of booze. In Boston, they will have gone to a cocktail party before the theatre, had six martinis and no food. At the beginning of the play they are rambunctious and don't hear you. Then, in the second half, the liquor starts dying and you have to kick them.

*Interview, San Francisco/*
*"W": a Fairchild publication, 9-19:21.*

**Ellen Burstyn**
*Actress*

6

[Reflecting on how, in a part she once played, she learned how to weld]: You scrape until it sparks, and then you pull the spark up.

# WHAT THEY SAID IN 1975

## (ELLEN BURSTYN)

It's called "striking an arc." If you pull it too far away, you break the arc. As I was welding, I thought, what does this remind me of—in another system? [Later, I realized] it's the same experience as being on stage. The actor strikes an arc with the audience. Then there's a flame between you. You move around the stage taking the audience with you. If you drop the connection, you have to strike the arc again.

*Interview, New York/*
*The New York Times, 3-31:38.*

## Michael Caine
*Actor*

1

One of my stage acting problems was that I was doing screen acting ... I see stage as a picture, films as a mirror. On the stage you are saying, "Look at *my* Hamlet!" On the screen you are saying, "Look at *you.*"

*At San Francisco Film Festival/*
*San Francisco Examiner & Chronicle,*
*10-26:(Datebook)13.*

## Arthur Cantor
*Producer*

2

Broadway [financing] is getting worse every year and the London theatre is also now beginning to feel the strains of growing costs that have hit New York. Broadway is a boom-or-bust business and London is also getting that way. If you have a hit, great; but it costs so much. And the age of the entrepreneur is quickly drawing to a close in that he will at least have to shift interests from a commercial base to a partially or wholly subsidized area.

*Interview, Los Angeles/*
*The Hollywood Reporter, 10-28:9.*

## Richard Chamberlain
*Actor*

3

My fantasy about an actor is being able to move people in a particular performance in a theatre and not be recognized walking down the street the next day.

*People, 1-13:60.*

## Paddy Chayefsky
*Playwright*

4

In the foreseeable future, I see nothing for me on Broadway. It's really because there are no audiences. The theatre has become a kind of unnecessary institution.

*Interview, New York/*
*The New York Times, 1-12:(1)29.*

## Henry Fonda
*Actor*

5

I don't get weary of any part I like. Some actors get bored after two months. That's them. On stage they don't listen. They're thinking about where they're going to have supper. I had long runs in *Mister Roberts, Point of No Return* and *The Caine Mutiny Court-Martial.* I know that in *Roberts*—after four years—it was better the last night. I enjoy the extra challenge of a long run. By God, you must make it fresh for every audience. If it becomes mechanical, you should change your business, or at least get the hell out of the play. I'll do a play as long as they come to see it.

*Interview, New York, March 4/*
*The New York Times, 3-5:28.*

## Martha Graham
*Modern dancer*

6

The war [between ballet and modern dancing] has ended. I don't think the war was against ballet. The war was against the frivolity of ballet. It was the ballerinas in Paris who represented "the spirit of champagne"—that was the thing that triggered us off.

*New York/The New York Times, 4-18:22.*

## Yuri Grigorovich
*Artistic director, Bolshoi Ballet, Moscow*

7

When you start creating a new ballet, you must like the music, the plot or the subject. The ballet should be the way you want it. Nobody makes us do anything; we ourselves try to find our themes. But whatever I do is a continuation of the past. I build on old traditions, and at our theatre we have great traditions. After all, it's very easy to be an innovator where there has been nothing before.

But if I can bring something new to the traditions of my theatre and my art, that's very good.

*Interview, New York/*
*The National Observer, 5-17:22.*

1

What I am trying to project in my choreography is a specific image or character. At the same time, I always bear in mind the fact that a given role may be performed today by one dancer, and tomorrow by quite another. So my first thought is always for the image, and my effort is to try to make the dancer subservient to this image. Inevitably, however, the dancer with whom one works exerts an influence of his own. To conceive an image is one thing, and to see someone actually perform it is quite different, usually. That is why whenever a ballet undergoes a change of cast, perhaps as much as 15 per cent of the work is transformed. The mere physical difference between dancers accounts for some of this. And each one is an individual. Some dancers turn more easily to the right, others to the left—even as insignificant a fact as this can alter the substance of the choreography.

*Interview, New York/*
*The Washington Post, 5-25:(L)5.*

**Alec Guinness**
*Actor*

2

I suppose I start from the outside of the character and work in. It's wrong, but I can't stop my imagination . . . I always *see* the character first. There's bound to be an exterior. And the exterior things gives you a clue to the interior. Sometimes you can get considerably into the run of a play before you discover the interior in full. A change of wig can give it to you in a flash.

*Interview, Burbank, Calif./*
*Los Angeles Times, 11-30:(Calendar)37.*

**Oliver Hailey**
*Playwright*

3

I go to the theatre to be, first and foremost, entertained by being moved to laughter or tears. It has to reach me on at least one of those levels, and, ideally, they will both come together at one point.

*The Hollywood Reporter, 5-6:6.*

**Helen Hayes**
*Actress*

4

Audiences are the most abused element in today's theatre . . . Hopefully, the period of the "liberated" playwright will be brief. The non-structured play, of which we see so many these days, dissipates the emotions, leaves the audience empty and distracted. An audience simply cannot go on reacting indefinitely to a play that doesn't know where it's going.

*Interview/*
*"W": a Fairchild publication, 7-11:10.*

5

The day I really retired from the theatre was the day I saw some tapes I had done of some scenes in *Victoria Regina*. Phony, totally overdone. I think it was the touring that did it. All those Shrine auditoriums where you worked so hard to reach the balcony. A star had to stay with a role in those days; you couldn't drop out after six months. I think over-conscientiousness kept a lot of us from developing into real artists, instead of being performing . . . objects.

*Interview, North Hollywood, Calif./*
*Los Angeles Times, 8-10:(Calendar)48.*

**Charlton Heston**
*Actor*

6

The stage is actors' country. You have to get your passport stamped every so often or they take away your citizenship.

*Los Angeles/Newsweek, 2-10:35.*

**Adela Holzer**
*Producer*

7

Theatre has to be a combination of business and art, but I think I give priority to art. If I don't *feel* for a play, I don't want to do it just to make money. For example, I don't want to do more revivals. I want to do *new* things, experimental things, things that are relevant to

# WHAT THEY SAID IN 1975

the times, and in that way I'm not too commercial. I'm very daring.

*Interview, New York/*
*The New York Times, 5-4:(2)5.*

**Glenda Jackson**
*Actress*                                                        *1*

... the theatre is a totally asexual world. No one is male or female; one is simply good or bad. But still, the theatre has certain built-in strictures. There really are fewer good parts for women than for men. In what way should women be portrayed? A truthful way would be nice.

*Interview, Beverly Hills, Calif./*
*The Washington Post, 4-20:(G)2.*

**Deborah Kerr**
*Actress*                                                        *2*

... I'm petrified just before I am due on-stage. Every night is a new challenge. A new audience must be convinced. I'm incapable of walking through a performance. With me, it's everything or nothing at all. When I read reviews which mention my "severe presence" or "calm self-control," I am startled. I may look serene or calm, but on the inside I'm terrified. Perhaps the secret of my success as an actress is an ability to make it look easy though it is extremely difficult.

*Interview, Beverly Hills, Calif./*
*Los Angeles Herald-Examiner, 4-3:(B)1.*

**Gelsey Kirkland**
*Ballerina*                                                      *3*

The reason ballet in America is getting better is that dancers are beginning to think for themselves. Teachers—*good* teachers—are beginning to make dancers realize that it really is the mind, and not just the body, that brings life to dancing.

*Interview/*
*The New York Times, 12-21:(2)10.*

**Eva LeGallienne**
*Actress*                                                        *4*

You can't teach acting. You are a *born* actor. You can help out, you can point out ways, but you can't teach it. There is no method to acting. The most important thing is imagination. But actors today are not well trained. For one thing, they start too late. In the past, actors went into the theatre very young; nowadays they all go to college. The sooner you get on the stage, the quicker you earn your living before a paying audience, the better. Become a professional as early as possible.

*Interview, New York/*
*The New York Times, 12-29:32.*

**Cornell MacNeil**
*Opera singer*                                                   *5*

To me, the over-publicizing of certain [opera] singers is one of the most unbalancing things that happens in our business. With the public they get such clout; then companies mount productions for them which then are over-publicized to the degree that the public will not accept that production without that singer. In our delicate ecology, this is enormously dangerous ... It would be fine if stars always glittered, if they weren't some synthetic gem thought up in a press-agent's office.

*Interview, New York/*
*The Christian Science Monitor, 12-29:22.*

**Natalia Makarova**
*Ballerina*                                                      *6*

American public is very enthusiastic, not discriminating. They eat everything exciting. They like tricks and cheap effects. They want beautiful things as well but they don't always understand subtleties. We cannot build art only on technique. It helps, but it is not all. Not just technique for technique. If I have strong technique, I have to disguise this. I don't say to public, "See how hard this is to do!" I work to make it look effortless, to make it look easy.

*Interview, New York/*
*The Christian Science Monitor, 9-22:27.*

**Walter Matthau**
*Actor*

1

... I was at the Winter Garden [Theatre in New York] recently to present [a Tony] Award to [playwright] Neil Simon. It's very depressing to be backstage in an old, dank, dark, dingy, dirty, drab theatre. My dressing room was four flights up ... In addition, the dressing room was dirty and cold, and we were at that theatre for six, seven hours rehearsing. It was the most depressing time, and I thought to myself, why do actors allow this? Why do they allow producers to continue in this barbaric, demented way? Actors have always been relegated to the dungeon in theatre, the same way the scalawags, rogues and vagabonds have in the past.

*Interview, New York/*
*Los Angeles Times, 9-12:(4)22.*

**Alec McCowen**
*Actor*

2

[Comparing Broadway with the London stage]: The importance of what you're doing in New York is 10 times as important as whatever you might be doing in London. If it succeeds, you're the toast of the town; and if it fails, everybody knows about it. Sometimes it's nice to go home [to England] where it really doesn't matter much one way or the other.

*Interview, Washington/*
*The Washington Post, 3-5:(B)6.*

**David Merrick**
*Producer*

3

If today's playwrights have any talent, they go into the film world where some really exciting work is going on. They can also make a lot of money on television. But there simply isn't much top-quality material available for Broadway.

*U.S. News & World Report, 8-11:45.*

**Arthur Miller**
*Playwright*

4

There is no reason to assume that the theatre is any different from any other aspect of

American life. Fundamentally, it was affected by the destruction of middle-class security. For the theatre audience is middle-class. I am surprised that no one has attempted a cultural history of the American theatre in terms of its relation to the nature of the audiences. Either there is a relation or there isn't. I think there is ... In this country, the theatre is regarded as an isolated phenomenon, when, in truth, it is one of the most sensitive to economic and social surroundings. This applies even more to comedy than to tragedy. The theatre is a leaf that changes with the passing season.

*Interview, New York/*
*The New York Times, 6-26:32.*

**Jason Miller**
*Actor, Playwright*

5

A play that is "not successful" can still be a good play, and in the long run is infinitely more valuable than the critics that panned it ... The fact that a man sits down and writes his own statement of the human condition, and gets it on-stage—which is tantamount to a miracle anyway, with the egos involved and money problems and lack of good directors—that's the important thing. "Success" is really not the final end ... The only real value of success is that it allows you to expand—to say "no" once in a while, to "say" yes to your own ideas, to what you want to do. The money is for the most part a problem. The work is what's really important.

*Interview, New York/*
*The Christian Science Monitor, 3-14:(B)10.*

**Robert Morley**
*British actor*

6

The trouble with the American [Broadway] theatre, at least from the actor's standpoint, is that every night is an opening night. People are in town from Cincinnati and tickets have been bought for them. Each night it is a brand-new audience. In London, I play every night to Londoners. It's infinitely easier.

*Interview, London/*
*Travel & Leisure, March:21.*

# WHAT THEY SAID IN 1975

**Cathleen Nesbitt**
*Actress*                                        1

There was great formality between people in the theatre in my youth, backstage as well as in the audience. People almost always dressed up. And there was always music before the play and at the intermission. I rather liked all that. I cannot really get to like this new thing of the open theatre—either as audience or as actor. I think it takes away some of the glamour.

*Interview, Los Angeles/*
*Los Angeles Times, 10-21:(4)13.*

                                                2

Actors and actresses go on feeling young more than most people, I think, because it's a sort of great democracy of age, the theatre. If I weren't on the stage where, thank God, there's no retiring age even if you dodder about, I'd probably be an old lady sitting at home playing bridge, which I hate!

*Interview, Los Angeles/*
*Los Angeles Times, 10-21:(4)13.*

**Bob Newhart**
*Actor, Comedian*                                3

. . . the American public is nicer to a comedian than to any other performer. If an actor fades at the box office, his career is washed up. If a singer's voice begins to crack, he might as well quit. If a baseball pitcher loses his fastball, they don't even return his telephone calls. But a comedian is lucky. He can be feeble-minded or stooped with age, and it doesn't matter. He can always crawl out on the stage for more laughs and more applause.

*Interview, Los Angeles/*
*Los Angeles Times, 9-14:(Home)36.*

**Rudolf Nureyev**
*Ballet dancer*                                  4

In a way, I'm learning to dance all over again. At the age of 30-plus, you don't have the strength and energy of a 25-year-old, so you have to learn to use your muscles differently. I still do the same steps I have always done, but now I am learning how to waste less energy doing them. Early in your career, you can do pirouettes very, very fast. You can gather force very quickly, and your balance is strong. Well, later on you cannot gather that same kind of force and energy. And if you try to, you will look terrible—like a monster. So you have to sacrifice quantity for quality. You learn to use less strength, different kinds of muscles, a different kind of balance. Now I am perfectly happy with four or five pirouettes instead of 10—in good shape and well phrased. And instead of jumping two meters high, I'll jump only 1.5 meters high. I can't over-strain my muscles as I did before; but, with proper phrasing, I can still look young and fresh and give the impression of ease. It's like bel canto—it's "bel dancing," if such a thing existed.

*Interview/The New York Times, 11-30:(2)10.*

**Laurence Olivier**
*Actor*                                          5

When I was running a theatre, I had only one consideration always: is it a good show and one that the audience can enjoy and respond to? That goes for *Hamlet* or *Flea in Her Ear*—or anything. And that's my criterion.

*Los Angeles Herald-Examiner,*
*3-2:(TV Weekly)6.*

**Joseph Papp**
*Producer*                                       6

Theatre is more immediate than film. It has danger, like gambling. The writer bets on the director and the director bets on the actor. At every performance, everyone is at risk. But Stanislavski was wrong. When actors take creative control, or directors for that matter, theatre is in trouble. The writer is the key man. Without playwrights, theatre cannot begin to exist.

*Interview, New York/People, 7-28:67.*

                                                7

We live in a time of monsters. Most people can't bear to look at the realities of our world. We need playwrights who can hold the mirror up to horror. Theatre like that is a force. It can hurt you and change you. Maybe it can change the world.

*Interview, New York/People, 7-28:67.*

*1*

I can bend, backtrack, switch directions, do this or that, whatever is necessary—in order to survive. My tactics, out of necessity, keep changing, but my direction has never changed: new plays, new audiences. A newspaper article appears catching me in the midst of change and a great hue and cry is raised: I have sold out, changed my course. While the shouting is still going on—"Sellout at Lincoln Center"—I am already planning to produce five new American plays.

*The New York Times Magazine, 11-9:18.*

**Vanessa Redgrave**
*Actress*

*2*

Shakespeare is so exciting to be in. It's not like a lot of TV and film material that purports to be naturalistic, though it doesn't make much difference how you play it provided a certain sense of reality is engendered. Most of the time you are doing poor material that you are trying to make into something better. But with Shakespeare there is immense potential for bettering your own work. It's rather like good hi-fi equipment. You can begin to penetrate the different pitches and levels, the different tones and values.

*Interview, Los Angeles/*
*Los Angeles Times, 1-26:(Calendar)44.*

**Ralph Richardson**
*Actor*

*3*

I always think I don't like the work when I haven't got it. When I do get it, it's like being an engine driver when he climbs into the cab and thinks, "My God, I've got to drive this bloody train to Scotland." He has a difficult job . . . requires intense concentration . . . intense. You've got to be on your toes. You've got to know, not where each foot is . . . [but] each toe! At the same time, you must make believe. The people watching believe, and you must believe it yourself . . . partly. You cannot believe the whole thing from start to finish. But you must believe bits. Not the same bit in each performance. But some bits in every performance. If there's no actor belief, you never

hold the audience. I believe this. You must force yourself. You must dream to order.

*Interview, London/*
*Los Angeles Times, 4-20:(Calendar)24.*

**Diana Rigg**
*Actress*

*4*

[Repertory] "stretches" an actor, whether one's role is large or small. It's true that specialization creeps into even the freest of milieus, but the artist should fight against that. We should be able to do *everything*.

*Interview, New York/*
*The New York Times, 3-9:(2)5.*

**William Saroyan**
*Author, Playwright*

*5*

[On theatre today]: It's become overexploratory, undisciplined, forgetful of form. And there's this preoccupation with pornography. You can't violate esthetic decorum; there has to be a little of the garment of culture. When you try for figurative nakedness, you're a supergenius or you come off shabby.

*Interview, New York/*
*The New York Times, 7-14:19.*

**George C. Scott**
*Actor*

*6*

I feel American actors have much to contribute to Shakespeare. Over 300 years English actors have refined their playing so much that they've taken the fire, the blood, the passion out of it. They've turned Shakespeare into an elocution class. It sounds beautiful, but it isn't exciting any more. I think American actors put the fire, the blood and the passion back into it—it may not be beautiful but, damn it, it sure is exciting.

*Interview/*
*Continental Airlines Flightime, February:G.*

**Peter Shaffer**
*Playwright*

*7*

. . . ideas for plays are like sirens. They call out, "Write me! Write me!" and you have to listen to them all. Eventually you make a com-

**443**

# WHAT THEY SAID IN 1975

## (PETER SHAFFER)

mitment, but it isn't easy. It has to be worth two years of your life, you know.

*Interview, Washington/*
*The Washington Post, 1-31:(B)3.*

1

When you first do a play, the actors tend to eye you [the playwright] ingratiatingly, with a kind of respectful hope, as if you are the repository of some great secret which they must have. Three weeks later, these roles have been reversed. It is you, the author, who is sliding up to *them* rather nervously and saying in a low tone, "I wonder if you'd mind putting in this line, or saying that to her." And quite often the erstwhile timid actor is staring at you and saying, "Oh, no: He [the character] would *never* say that!" Being a playwright in rehearsal involves a necessary if faintly saddening process of being gutted and then discarded. You are first welcomed, and then shown the door. It has to be this way. The actor has to take it all away from you ... People who condescend to actors, who regard them as children or amusing neurotics, can never be friends of mine.

*New York/*
*The New York Times Magazine, 4-13:38.*

## Neil Simon
### *Playwright*
2

It's hard to know how to proceed sometimes. If the critics like you, they say you should try more, and stretch. If you do, they then say, "But where are the wonderful jokes?" Frank Loesser, one of the best songwriters ever, stretched himself with *Most Happy Fella*, an absolutely brilliant piece of work. "Where are those nice little tunes?" the critics said. What you do is disregard it and get on with your work. I've been depressed by favorable reviews and I've learned from negative ones. Some critics have helped shape my growth because I've tried to live up to their hopes and wishes. I haven't been upset by bad reviews if the critic felt I didn't live up to what he'd expected. But the critics who don't think I can do anything ... another matter. But every time at the typewriter, I start with the slate clean. No one

has ever seen anything of mine before. This has to stand on its own.

*Interview/*
*Los Angeles Times, 4-20:(Calendar)27.*

## Isaac Bashevis Singer
### *Author, Playwright*
3

[On playwriting]: You must start out with a person, a hero or heroine with an address. By that I mean a spiritual address. The audience must know where this person lives, what language he speaks. Once the audience is interested in the person, you can develop action that keeps them in some sort of tension. There are many plays in which there is interesting action, but somehow the writer didn't succeed in giving us a real person. Then the play is a failure. When I see a play, I want to see a person's spiritual fingerprints.

*Interview, New York/*
*The New York Times, 10-26:(2)5.*

## Maggie Smith
### *Actress*
4

[On acting on the stage]: You'd be amazed. You can go on and on finding new things. And suddenly everything becomes clear and you say, "Oh, yes! That's the way to do it!" Onstage, you get so many chances to get it right.

*Interview, New York/*
*People, 3-10:56.*

## Tom Stoppard
### *Playwright*
5

While writing a play, the style and idiom of the play, the form and everything else tend to impose themselves on you. You start off with a kind of half-baked idea for a play and tend to work it out to its best advantage without worrying too much about an over-all view of one's entire work ... One's whole existence often comes out in a play. It consists of unconscious collecting of possible material and the elimination of most of it. There's an element of fortune, coincidence, and a sort of unconscious selection going on. There's enough mystery in the process for me not to wish to disturb it too much.

*Interview, London/
The New York Times, 10-19:(2)5.*

## Lee Strasberg
*Artistic director, Actors Studio*

1

There is so much waste in our theatre today. We don't even *have* theatre; we have "productions." Our actors become typed; and those who are the richest, our jewels, fade out because there are no parts for them. A man like Marlon [Brando]—my God! The parts he should be playing. Or Lee Cobb. Oedipus! Macbeth! Our actors fall into a pattern which is terrible to see.

*Interview, New York/
The New York Times, 2-2:(2)13.*

## Glen Tetley
*Artistic director, Stuttgart Ballet*

2

[I look for dancers who are] articulate, fluid, intuitive, musical—with the right kind of ego. I like dancers who are not bound up by themselves, but who have an absolutely devouring appetite for dance. I was brought up to believe that dancing is your whole life. It isn't something you do for a few years that is entertaining. You sense this attitude intuitively in a dancer. That's what I like about Stuttgart. You can see it in their eyes.

*Interview, New York/
The New York Times, 6-8:(2)8.*

3

There's no question of it: The situation in the United States is an explosion of dance. There has been an increase in dance audiences that is unbelievable . . . With the advent of television, the younger generation has been reared in a much more graphic, a more visual-oriented, way. That is the essence of dance, which is a very visual art . . . We're coming out of an age in which we were in love with computers. We've passed our love affair with machines [and are now paying attention to the human body].

*Interview, Washington/
Los Angeles Times, 8-11:(4)12.*

## Galina Ulanova
*Ballet coach, Bolshoi Ballet, Moscow;
Former ballerina*

4

I made lots of mistakes when I was young. Now I try to help my young dancers not to repeat those same mistakes. At the same time, I remember in my youth when an older teacher told me that I shouldn't do such-and-such or I wasn't ready for this or that. I used to insist, let me do it my way. It's the same with these young people. I can help them, but sooner or later they must find their way . . . I show them and I speak to them. A lot of telephoning, too. To explain how to express a role, how to penetrate to the dramatic heart, needs a lot of talking. Eventually, the young artist must get there himself. My task is to "wake up the idea," that's a Russian expression we have. But one's teaching systems can never be rigid; it changes all the time. Everything depends so much on the nature of the role, and the character of the dancer. Working with a mature dancer like [Vladimir] Vasiliev in *Ivan the Terrible* and working with a young ballerina like [Ludmila] Semenyaka in *Swan Lake,* those are two very different things. But it is true that in each case the main purpose is to go beyond technique, to awaken thought, to make the role come wholly alive.

*Interview, Washington/
The Washington Post, 5-31:(C)3.*

## Liv Ullmann
*Actress*

5

It's true that some actresses work by fantasizing details in the life of their character. Well, I think the fun of acting is not to make fantasies but to depict something that is real, to ask oneself, what would a real woman do here, and here? The fun of it is building a character, as if you were writing about a person. It is the closest you can come to writing if you are an actress—you "write" a person through your interpretation of her character and your actions on stage. Your performance can't be based on emotions alone. You might be fantastic one evening, but if it's all emotion and you don't

# WHAT THEY SAID IN 1975

*(LIV ULLMANN)*

really know what made you laugh or cry, how can you go back and do it again the next night?

*Interview, Philadelphia/*
*The New York Times, 2-23:(2)7.*

**Vladimir Vasiliev**
*Dancer, Bolshoi Ballet, Moscow*     1

Today there is certainly a greater emphasis on dance over mime. I like it, but there is a great danger there, and that is to forget about dramatic art altogether. The two must be combined. I love pure, abstract dance, but not if *all* the dance is abstract. It is as if you eat the same food day after day, no matter how delicious. You get sick and tired of it.

*Interview, New York/*
*The New York Times, 5-4:(2)8.*

**Gwen Verdon**
*Actress*     2

[On the current musicians strike which has closed all Broadway musicals]: It really would rock the whole city [if there were an extended strike]. I wish New York would accept the fact that we're [the Broadway stage] an attraction—like topless dancers and gambling are in Las Vegas. You come to New York to see the Empire State Building, crime in the streets and the Broadway theatre.

*New York, Sept. 19/*
*The New York Times, 9-20:19.*

**Edward Villella**
*Ballet dancer*     3

A dancer shouldn't be talking. We are "poets of gesture"—a Balanchine phrase . . . The fact is, I was always a very physical type. I liked dancing immediately. It went beyond athletics; it had all that, plus discipline, line, form. To this day my greatest joy is throwing myself around the stage with what seems like total abandon.

*Before Wolf Trap Associates,*
*Washington, Feb. 24/*
*The Washington Post, 2-25:(B)2.*

**Max von Sydow**
*Actor*     4

[On why he chose acting as a career]: . . . whatever motive I *thought* I had was probably totally false. I thought through acting I would get to know myself and my fellow man better; that the stage would be the right place for me, where I could play such magnificent messages for mankind, and so on and so on. I realized later on that this was a little bit false . . . It's so rare that you can control the parts you play or the plays you get to be in. If you would like to put forward a consistent message, according to a consequent program, it's very difficult.

*Interview, New York/*
*The Christian Science Monitor, 2-27:12.*

**Nancy Walker**
*Actress*     5

I never wear shoes in California. Except I'll put them on to go to somebody's house. I forget until I'm in New York that all shoes hurt my feet. You know, I think that's a real reason why a lot of theatre people who've made it big in Hollywood don't want to go back to the Broadway stage. Their feet won't stand for it.

*Interview, New York/*
*The Washington Post, 4-13:(F)3.*

**Tennessee Williams**
*Playwright*     6

If you're an artist, everything except your art is auxiliary—a supplement. I don't care about sex any more. I used to think it was important to eat and drink. I'm obsessed with bringing to New York one more beautiful play. I have no fear of death—except as it might intervene before my accomplishment of that. This is all! And I *will* live for it.

*Interview, New York/*
*The New York Times, 7-15:39.*

7

[Saying it is more difficult to write for the theatre now than it was 20 years ago]: For one thing, there's much less theatre to write *for,* and everybody's afraid to take the risks that are implicit in writing and producing plays today.

Producers insist on all kinds of safeguards. And audiences have changed. TV has made more and more of an assault on people's sensibilities. Granted, a certain percentage of those people will always welcome theatre, after the bang, bang, bang of TV, but not nearly enough of them. So theatre doesn't have the kind of audience support it used to have ... A lot of our younger playwrights are castrated by the system in which they work. The public isn't conditioned to have the patience to allow them to develop as artists. One must be permitted to have his failures if they are brave, creative adventures.

*Interview, New York/*
*The New York Times, 12-21:(2)5.*

## TELEVISION/RADIO

**Eddie Albert**
*Actor* 1

Television . . . is a marvelous medium of education. It would have sent Thomas Jefferson into ecstacies. If used well, TV could cure many ills of the human race. But TV's highest purpose is to sell merchandise, to move out bars of soap and boxes of cornflakes . . . I don't think I'm being unfair. Possibly one-tenth of one per cent of the material on TV is worthwhile. The rest is junk. Sometimes I'm mesmerized because *I'm* acting in the stuff, but it's still a disappointment, considering the potential of the medium to do good in the world.
*Interview/Los Angeles Times, 6-8:(Home)33.*

**Alan Alda**
*Actor* 2

It hurts me as a citizen, as an artist and as a father to see unfelt violence on television. By that I mean violence where the effects of it are not shown—stabbings, rapes, murders that are done for our grotesque or bizarre enjoyment. I find that lacking as entertainment. There's plenty of murder in Shakespeare, but it's all felt. You're invited to understand the human implications of it. But casual violence on television is awful. I hate to see it. [But] I hate even more to see it censored . . . If you censor that, you can censor anything. We have to deal with this as adults. We can't deal with it as children have been traditionally dealt with—in kindergarten. You can't let people say to us, "Oh no, not that! No, no." They can't say no-no to us if we're exercising the rights of free speech.
*News conference, Los Angeles, Oct. 30/*
*The Hollywood Reporter, 11-4:11.*

**Leon Botstein**
*President, Bard College* 3

For many children, TV has to a large extent replaced reading aloud, a good deal of physical activity with other children and the conversation, communication—implicit in dealing with others—and the use of the child's own imagination in creating his own entertainment.
*San Francisco Examiner & Chronicle,*
*10-5:(A)14.*

**Lloyd Bridges**
*Actor* 4

Early television was treated more like a play. An actor and crew rehearsed. You had time to get acquainted with your character, the director, the crew and your fellow cast members. Today, you arrive on the set and are immediately asked to fill out your character. It's barbaric!
*Interview/*
*Los Angeles Herald-Examiner, 5-1:(B)6.*

**George Burns**
*Entertainer* 5

[Performing on] radio [in the 1930s-50s] was like stealing money. You didn't even have to open a door. You just stood there, held a piece of paper in your hand, and you read it. You wouldn't even open a window. You'd say, "How's the weather?" and a sound man would open a window and you'd say, "Oooooh, it's cold out, close the window," and the man would close the window. You did nothing and you got paid for it. And everybody was in the Top 10 because there were only eight acts.
*Interview, New York/*
*"W": a Fairchild publication, 5-16:2.*

*1*

Audiences are very tough when they get it for nothing. When you go to a theatre and pay $12 a seat, you get dressed up and go and applaud and laugh. But they can do the same thing [on television], and you're sitting there in your underwear, and you're not having a good time . . . Everybody's a critic when they have a TV set long enough.

*Interview, Culver City, Calif./*
*The Christian Science Monitor, 8-25:17.*

**Richard Chamberlain**
*Actor*

*2*

There are such built-in limitations to a [TV] series—trying to feed enough good material into that machine which gobbles it up an hour a week. If you end up with three good scripts a season, you're lucky. The rest is treading water. I loved doing the *[Dr.] Kildare* series even though it was terrifically hard work. It was immensely exciting—and, even more important, wonderfully secure. But it was a mixed blessing career-wise. After five years, people, and casting directors, thought of me as Dr. Kildare. *I* thought of myself as Dr. Kildare. So jobs were hard to find at first. However, because it made me an international "star," I was allowed to work in England by British Equity. Would I do another series? I don't think so. But, you never can say. Somebody may come up tomorrow with a wonderful idea and $10-million and I might very well say yes.

*Interview, New York/*
*The Christian Science Monitor, 1-8:6.*

**Victor Cline**
*Professor of psychology, University of Utah*

*3*

In all media we have a glorification of extreme violence, overt sex and anti-social behavior, particularly on television and perhaps even more so in commercial motion pictures. All the time, we and our children are watching, learning, absorbing, gradually being conditioned. Such constant exposure to violence "desensitizes" our conscience, blunting our empathy and concern for other human beings . . . I don't want to knock TV totally. What I am pleading for is that the massive saturation, the intensity, the prurient appeal and the magnification of sex and violence be reduced to a sane level, making it something that we—and our children—can emotionally handle.

*Interview/People, 6-16:58,61.*

**Bill Cullen**
*TV game-show host*

*4*

There's a movement to sex in all areas [of television]. In the soaps [soap operas], everything is sex, but very serious. Game shows—almost everything has a sexually titillating direction. Cops? Eunuchs with badges. Doctors? Eunuchs in white coats. But the patients—no matter what is wrong with them, there's a sexual undertone. Comedies? They've gone all-out for sex—far, far past what we used to call the innuendo. Variety shows? A big stress on sex. Talk shows? A lot of sexual references and shocking stories. Actually, almost every type of show is getting sexy. It's always that way. One thing begins to click, and everybody hops on the bandwagon.

*Interview/TV Guide, 10-18:6.*

**Clint Eastwood**
*Actor*

*5*

[On feature films shown on TV]: I watched *The Good, the Bad & the Ugly* on television last week, and I think it plays okay. But an essential concept of the Western is the little-man/big-land contrast; and if you see it on a tiny screen with the fireplace going and the kids screaming in the background, you're just not drawn into it the way you are in a theatre. And, of course, there's the problem of [TV] censorship. Nowadays they not only delete dialogue and action scenes, they [also] tone the gunshots down in my movies until they sound like little pops, and they mix the slam of a punch down audio-wise and what you wind up with is very limited. I guess there's only so much you can tell on television. Here you're doing an action show and you can't really show action. If that's what people want in a Western, it's possible that they're not finding it on TV.

*The Washington Post, 5-11:(F)1.*

# WHAT THEY SAID IN 1975

**Michael D. Eisner**
*Vice president, program planning and
development, American Broadcasting
Company Television*                                    *1*

The goal of television in this country is to
entertain and inform. But entertainment need
not be synonymous with amusement, and information is not restricted to the evening news.
Drama has been a source of enlightenment and
understanding for centuries, but it remained for
television to provide the dramatist with an audience of millions simultaneously.

*Upon acceptance of Torch of Liberty Award
of Anti-Defamation League, Los Angeles,
Dec. 7/The Hollywood Reporter, 12-9:3.*

**Peter Falk**
*Actor*                                               *2*

[On the TV Emmy Awards]: There are too
many Emmys given out. It dilutes an Emmy's
value. A rare coin is valuable. But if too many
are issued, the worth of each one becomes
insignificant. Frankly, the only reason I show
up is because NBC wants me to.

*Los Angeles Herald-Examiner, 5-21:(B)6.*

**Jules Feiffer**
*Playwright, Cartoonist*                              *3*

. . . the problem of [TV] situation comedy,
outside of the fact that it goes on every week,
which is a pressure and also a diminishing return, is the fact that a writer never controls it. I
think most of us stay in the theatre because of
the control you have over your work. It doesn't
exist anywhere else. The money is better in
Hollywood. To the author, control is everything.

*Panel discussion, New York/
The New York Times, 4-6:(2)25.*

**John Kenneth Galbraith**
*Former professor of economics,
Harvard University*                                   *4*

Writing for television, I've learned in the last
year or two, is an exercise in relentless conden-
sation. It has left me with the feeling that even
brevity can be carried to extremes.

*Interview, Cambridge, Mass./
The Christian Science Monitor, 12-9:19.*

**Huge Greene**
*Former director general, British
Broadcasting Corporation*                             *5*

Giving the public what it wants [on TV] is a
loaded phrase—linked with "democracy" and
with "trusting the people"; the simple faith,
preached by many men who are not at all
simple, that what most people want all people
should have. To use the word "freedom" in this
connection is an abuse of language. What we are
in fact concerned with at this point is tyranny—
the tyranny of the ratings or the mind machines . . . Does democracy really triumph if we
merely give some mild soporific to people too
indifferent to switch the program off? Are we
not going more for democracy if we sometimes,
even quite often, give pleasure to a few people
even at the cost of provoking many into switching off?

*Los Angeles Times, 8-28:(4)23.*

**Hartford Gunn**
*President, Public Broadcasting Service*              *6*

UHF broadcasting has failed to meet its
potential. It has been branded as an also-ran in
the race with VHF. It has failed to attract the
needed attention of government officials who
are in a position to effect change. And, most
tragic of all, it has evoked apathy from the
countless viewers who, for one reason or
another, experience great difficulty in obtaining
satisfactory reception.

*Before PBS membership/
TV Guide, 11-8:32.*

**Arthur Hailey**
*Author*                                              *7*

[Saying he prefers not to write for TV]: . . .
television is so ephemeral. You work for
months; the play goes into rehearsal; it's on the
air one night, and it's gone. A friend sees you
the next day and says: "Say, I heard you had a
play on TV last night. Too bad. The wife and I
were out to dinner."

*Interview, Chicago/
The National Observer, 5-3:21.*

**Arthur Hill**
*Actor*
1

There's a place for escape entertainment. But there's more to the mind than that. It needs to concern itself with real things. Regardless of some opinion, I believe television is dealing more with this sort of material than in the past. Even in comedy programs, there are matters presented that would never have been dealt with a few years ago. I don't mean four-letter words. I mean looking at real things.
*Interview, Los Angeles/*
*Los Angeles Herald-Examiner, 1-31:(B)10.*

**Morton A. Hill**
*Chairman, Morality in Media, Inc.*
2

[Criticizing TV violence]: Many of the new programs impart a psychological horror in viewers—the kind of thing that gives people nightmares. You may see vicious dogs chasing people, or women being dragged down dark alleys by assailants, or families being held under siege by unseen and nameless attackers. It paints the world as a terrifying, dangerous, wicked place.
*U.S. News & World Report, 1-13:33.*

**Benjamin L. Hooks**
*Commissioner, Federal Communications Commission*
3

Public television [in the U.S.], without the legal or moral right to do so, has become the Caucasian intellectual's home entertainment game . . . By styling itself, preponderantly, as an electronic Harvard liberal-arts course, public broadcasting has foresaken those less privileged and influential whose cultural and educational needs are far more on "street academy" or community-college scale . . . It throws these disadvantaged people a few token bones and, aloofly, turns its back, not wanting to mingle with the masses.
*The Dallas Times Herald, 2-26:(A)22.*

**Robert T. Howard**
*President, National Broadcasting Company Television*
4

[Television] informs, entertains, provides a means of public discussion. The better it does

these things, the better society will be served. Through information, understanding and communication, the better equipped society will be . . . to find its own solutions [to its problems].
*Before Citizens for Law Enforcement*
*Needs, Los Angeles/*
*Los Angeles Herald-Examiner, 7-25:(B)1.*

5

[On the forthcoming new "family hour" concept for television]: We are in the business of being responsive to audience preferences—and to audience sensitivities. The family viewing hour concept comes in response to public concern about television programming, particularly during the early evening when children are a sizable part of the audience. Whether this concern is justified is not really the point. The concern exists . . . and broadcasters have done something about it.
*San Francisco Examiner & Chronicle, 8-3:(C)8.*

**David Janssen**
*Actor*
6

You start out with something. You try it. You eliminate or tone it down. That's the exciting part of working in television, in spite of all its frustrations. Building a character. Making it work and grow. Unfortunately, some shows don't have that chance. The economics of the industry often demands instant success.
*Interview/*
*Los Angeles Herald-Examiner,*
*7-13:(TV Weekly)4.*

**Norman Jewison**
*Motion picture director*
7

I came to America from non-commerical broadcasting in Canada and found myself in the middle of a big power structure. The air is free, but everything is controlled by three major [TV] networks. Those were the days when Arthur Penn and Paddy Chayefsky and John Frankenheimer were all working out of New York, and we all left because of disillusionment. Television used to be great. People really stayed home to watch it. Now it's just trash. Quality was paramount, but there was always this thing in the background creeping in—that

*451*

# WHAT THEY SAID IN 1975

(NORMAN JEWISON)

TV had really been devised and invented to sell deodorants and toothpaste.

*Interview/*
*San Francisco Examiner & Chronicle,*
*7-13:(Datebook)16.*

## Nicholas Johnson
*Chairman, National Council for Better*
*Broadcasting; Former Commissioner,*
*Federal Communications Commission*     *1*

Everything on TV, the programs as well as the commercials, are selling one thing above all else. And that is really a doctrine of theology: the doctrine of materialism. It says, in effect, that there is nothing in you of any value, that where you get your value is in the products you consume. Like the beer that you drink or the soft drinks you consume, the aspirin you take, the underarm deodorant you use or the breath freshener—that's what's going to make you successful; that's what's going to make you happy; that's what's going to get you a husband or help you to hold one; the measure of your life is in the things you have, not what you are. We have sold people on the notion that if they need help in any way it's not to be found in cooperating with other people, or in love, or in interpersonal relationships. It is to be found in some product!

*Television interview, Los Angeles/*
*Los Angeles Times, 8-10:(Calendar)30.*

## Danny Kaye
*Entertainer*     *2*

There are many subjects you can do today [on TV] that you couldn't do 10 years ago. Archie Bunker in *All in the Family* was the first different kind of TV show we had in years—but now every channel has its own version. Never forget that trends are not made by anybody—they are reflections of what is happening in a society.

*Interview/Los Angeles Herald-Examiner,*
*6-1:(California Living)5.*

## Ellwood Kieser
*Producer, "Insight" television series*     *3*

I have mixed feelings about the "family hour" [TV concept beginning in the fall]. There's a human way to treat sex and violence. I don't see the point in throwing them out categorically. If they were to be treated crassly, glibly and superficially, I'd rather not see them treated at all. But they shouldn't be eliminated—they should be dealt with in a sensitive, profound human way . . . Sex and violence aren't the two worst things on television. There can be too much worry over them. The two worst things are that most of the prime-time programs are escapist and that many TV commercials are exploitative of human beings. Too much of prime-time programming is done in the belief that people want to run away from reality. The commercials tell you you've got to have this product or you can't be a full human being. You get it and find you're not a full human being. Or you don't have the money to get it. Then, you're nothing. This creates violence. This creates anger.

*Los Angeles Herald-Examiner, 7-16:(D)6.*

## Cloris Leachman
*Actress*     *4*

. . . I'm so proud to be part of the one medium that has made a difference—television. Women and other minority groups are finally being treated fairly. I think the commercials did it first and set the pace for dramatic shows to follow. They showed women of all kinds and colors doing things, not just fixing breakfast in housecoats and curlers. Television explored areas in our society that films never bothered to do . . .

*Interview, Los Angeles/*
*Los Angeles Herald-Examiner,*
*5-25:(California Living)6.*

## Norman Lear
*Writer, Producer*     *5*

What leadership does in this country everywhere is to constantly underestimate the American public. Don't forget it is leadership that once said the average mentality of the average

American is 13 ... They also used to say that the working man, especially in bad times, doesn't want to come home and be made to face his problems ... that he wants escapist entertainment only. Well, everything we [his company] do asks the viewer to face his problems. It's done with humor. People are laughing. But they're also observing the human condition in which they are surviving ... The working-man loves to be stimulated.

*Interview, Los Angeles/*
*The Dallas Times Herald, 4-13: (TV Times)5.*

*1*

[TV's new "family hour" concept] is against the best interests of the American viewer because it is hypocritical and dishonest. Certainly, television has problems; but anyone in a position of leadership within the industry, with all the demographics available to them, knows that children are not asleep by 9:00, 9:30 or even 10:00 p.m. Furthermore, when it is 9:00 in some time zones it is 8:00 in the Bible Belt. Therefore, it is dishonest because, rather than dealing with the actual problems, by setting up the "family hour" the networks are succumbing to pressure from the FCC which in turn has acceded to pressure from Congress. This is the greatest violation of free speech.

*The Hollywood Reporter, 12-30:3.*

### Sheldon Leonard
*Actor, Producer*

*2*

[Television is] not like the theatre, where reality or fantasy is contained within the confines of the proscenium arch. It's not like watching people in a movie on a 14-foot screen, where they are enormously magnified, where people like Harlow and Gable are more like symbols than people. Television makes people more grainy and real than any other medium. Characters on television are expected to be comprehensible. The people watching them must be able to relate to them, to place them in the environment they are seeing them in and relate to them in that environment.

*Interview, Los Angeles/*
*The Washington Post, 8-3:(H)2.*

### Robert M. Liebert
*Psychologist, State University of*
*New York, Stony Brook*

*3*

The more violence and aggression a youngster sees on television, regardless of his age, sex or social background, the more aggressive he is likely to be in his own attitudes and behavior. The effects are not limited to youngsters who are in some way abnormal, but rather were found for large numbers of perfectly normal American children ... It is a pseudo-issue for broadcasters to claim that they have a right, by reason of Constitutional guarantees of freedom of speech, to give kids any sort of junk they want to on the argument that if the broadcaster isn't free and unmonitored, then democracy will be endangered. That isn't so. There is no precedent whatever for believing that adults' freedoms are endangered because a society enforces policies that are necessary for the welfare of its youth.

*TV Guide, 6-14:10,16.*

### John V. Lindsay
*Former Mayor of New York*

Television is certainly the most fascinating means of communication today. So many more people look at TV news than read books or newspapers. But I must admit that a good book sticks to the ribs more. And a newspaper report does, too, mainly because they can go into depth. The instant nature of TV is a problem.

*Interview, New York/*
*The Christian Science Monitor, 7-29:13.*

### Jack Lord
*Actor*

*5*

[On doing a TV series]: The single most difficult thing to come by is a good script. You can get marvelous actors, marvelous directors, fine producers, great production people, skillful cinematographers—and what's the use without a good script?

*Interview, Honolulu/*
*Los Angeles Times, 5-4:(TV Times)2.*

*453*

**Torbert H. Macdonald**
*United States Representative,*
*D—Massachusetts*
1

The bloodshed and killing in [TV] shows like *S.W.A.T.* is the worst thing to hit the United States since the plague.

*TV Guide, 6-7:8.*

**George Marshall**
*Motion picture director*
2

I object to the ritualistic speed with which TV is produced. The medium doesn't afford the actor time to digest or understand his part fully, or give the director sufficient time to chart the action . . . And I'm sorry TV looks so much alike. TV production is a factory, and you're lucky if a show turns out well.

*Interview, Los Angeles/*
*Los Angeles Herald-Examiner, 1-18:(B)6.*

**Quinn Martin**
*Producer*
3

There's a tendency among makers of feature films to shoot far more than they need and then to attempt to solve their problems by editing. I believe in tight editing, but I've been an editor long enough to be aware of a major risk: It's easy to be carried away, to lose the original point of view you started with. That hardly ever happens in TV, because we can't afford, for example, to shoot 180 minutes of film for a 60-minute show. To be tied down by a tight budget is a problem for many people, but for anyone involved in the production and editing of film, it can be a positive blessing.

*Interview, Beverly Hills, Calif./*
*Los Angeles Times, 7-27:(Home)30.*

**Anthony Newley**
*Actor, Singer, Composer*
4

My generation of performer must understand the revolution that has occurred in show business, and how the media has brought it on. It's incredible how everyone is fighting for a spot on the box [television]. Not only must I compete with my generation of entertainer, but also the neophyte, the drag queens and the sequined artists. I do my job as well or better than the younger people, but I can't compete within the glitter department. I'm of the dinner-jacket crowd, but I've still got to keep an eye on the new trends . . . I look at these young performers who are instant smashes, and they can't even keep their own TV shows when they're signed as "the new stars." The poor darlings burn up within minutes. Our lust for new faces in entertainment is almost, well, decadent. While the true professional like myself plods along, making money, and keeps his audiences.

*Interview/*
*Los Angeles Herald-Examiner, 10-12:(E)5.*

**Jack Nicholson**
*Actor*
5

I hate it when my movies are on television. [The screen is] too small. And the commercials befoul and overwhelm. The over-all concept of a film is the story, the pace at which it's told, the progressions, the aesthetic viewpoint. The object is to make all of that a part of an audience's life, for that period of time. But on television, you are turned on and off. They can make you different colors. They can relate you to potato chips.

*Interview, New York/*
*Los Angeles Herald-Examiner, 11-21:(A)12.*

**Carroll O'Connor**
*Actor*
6

[On TV actors' salaries]: An actor who is starring in a hit series must be conscious of the amounts of money that he is generating, particularly for the network. An insurance salesman who brings in a great deal of business activity and sells large numbers of policies during the year is rewarded with bonuses. Any executive who precipitates substantial business is given shares or stock options because he, himself, has generated large amounts of money. That is the American free-enterprise way that encourages talent in any field of endeavor. Ergo, the actor realizes that he's generating many, many millions of dollars in gross advertising revenues. He looks at his own gross income and finds that, although it seems large to the average person, numerically it's really a tiny percentage of the amount of monies that he's bringing to his employers. So he wants more.

*TV Guide, 4-12:5.*

1

[Saying that government intrudes in broadcast programming]: The government's wrong. Congress has no right whatsoever to interfere with content in the media—whether it's our [broadcast] media or your [written] media. And you guys and gals [of the press] out there ought to be very conscious of that. I think maybe you're not—and should be . . . At issue is the Congress moving in and interfering with the freedom of communication in this country for whatever reason . . . Instead of taking the responsibility of going back to their constituents and explaining the way this country should run and explaining the freedoms we have, the Congressmen find it much easier to put pressure on the FCC. They [the FCC] turn around and put pressure on the networks . . .

*News conference, Los Angeles, Oct. 30/*
*The Hollywood Reporter, 10-31:17.*

**Jack Palance**
*Actor*

2

Most of the [TV] cop shows are pointless. They have a beginning, a middle and an end, and they fill in an hour and a half . . . I think it's awful that so much of crime is glorified. I was horrified at how [the motion picture] *The Godfather* was accepted. Marlon Brando was a hero. Al Pacino was a hero. The public is given no choice. It's presented with the evil or the eviler. To identify with the criminal as a hero—what a sad comment on why we do TV shows.

*Interview, Los Angeles/*
*Los Angeles Herald-Examiner, 3-31:(B)6.*

**John O. Pastore**
*United States Senator, D—Rhode Island*

3

Of course there is a causal relationship between violence on television and the behavior of young people. The same thing that sells soap sells an idea. If an idea is good or bad it can be sold. As a matter of fact, if television were not that [influential] it would not be as effective as

it's considered to be. And it's become a way of life in America.

*The Christian Science Monitor, 3-5:5.*

4

[On obscenity on TV]: The tendency today is to say anything and everything. Everything has to be in the raw . . . I'm not a prude, but television was invented for the purpose of serving the family; the sets are in the home. Do you want to have on TV or radio language you don't permit at your dinner table? . . . Talk shows are blooped out here and there . . . it's very annoying. Now it's the fashion at certain hours to use the four-letter word. Now, that's going too far in my humble opinion. We need to protect the decency of our society. If we're going to become a vulgar society, Supreme Court or no Supreme Court, we're on our way down.

*Before Federal Communications*
*Commission, Washington/*
*The Christian Science Monitor, 4-24:3.*

5

[Supporting the new TV "family hour" concept and criticizing those among the producers, writers, etc. who claim their creative freedom is being violated by it]: A particular segment of the television-program production industry claims that "family viewing" violates their First Amendment right "to do their own thing." "Their own thing" appears to be peddling violence for profit while poisoning the minds of our children and grandchildren with total disregard for the obvious social and psychic costs to our nation. Except for the fact that the First Amendment has actually been invoked on the side of mindless violence, I would not address this incredible callousness . . . The threat of excessive televised violence has been too well documented and too long ignored for us to listen to the carping of a self-interested few who would oppose any attempt at meaningful reform . . . If current television fare is bland [as some who criticize the "family hour" have charged], then this is a sad commentary on the creative genius of the established American television-program production industry. If the only way our commercial program producers can capture and hold audience-interest is with

# WHAT THEY SAID IN 1975

*(JOHN O. PASTORE)*

murder, mayhem and other sordid acts of human degradation, then broadcasters should re-examine their programming sources.

*Before the Senate, Washington, Dec. 18/*
*The New York Times, 12-19:79.*

## Michael Peacock
*Executive vice president for network*
*TV, Warner Bros. Television*
1

[On TV programming]: We are too much occupied with stories and story-telling. We ignore other elements of the cultural spectrum, music and art. I think in the propagation of the species there is the responsibility of propagation of culture, that with our genetic inheritance must come our cultural heritage. With TV's means of reaching people at our disposal, that responsibility should be ours, not relegated to the back drawer of PBS but in the forefront of our thinking.

*Interview, Los Angeles/*
*Los Angeles Times, 1-14:(4)11.*

## George Peppard
*Actor*
2

I know decisions [in TV] depend on the ratings. But to me the ratings are a silliness built into the television system. I've been in important plays in small theatres on Broadway and elsewhere. When I consider that an audience of 10 million on television is supposed to be small, what is there to think? You're a failure when 10 million people watch you! It's laughable.

*Los Angeles Herald-Examiner,*
*11-16:(TV Weekly)6.*

## Frank Price
*President, Universal (Pictures) Television*
3

[On why it is difficult to attract new creative talent to work in the TV medium]: There apparently is something demeaning about having your show broken up by commercials. Most creative people who can avoid it do so, preferring the wholeness of a movie which doesn't have the appearance of existing to sell products. There's also another reason. With a

movie, the artist gets the credit. With a television show, the network does.

*The New York Times, 10-5:(2)27.*

## Jose Quintero
*Theatrical director*
4

[On his idea for a TV show about playwright Eugene O'Neill]: . . . I had a meeting with one of the network executives and he asked me if it were a Virginia Woolf sort of project. I discovered he meant—was it too intellectual? I told him it was not but he didn't seem too enthusiastic. Somehow, we must erase the notion that anyone who excels at something ceases to be of interest to television audiences.

*Interview, New York/*
*The Christian Science Monitor, 5-22:26.*

## Lee Rich
*Producer*
5

Unlike feature films, where the rating system controls the audience, TV production carries with it a strong responsibility factor. At least I [as a producer] feel the burden of it on my shoulders—I've got two daughters of my own. Of course, the responsibility extends to the parent as well. But TV is the strongest medium ever devised; it's often stronger than the parent. So you can't always rely on parents to be the watchdogs. You have to question your own judgment and conscience [as a TV producer]. You can misuse your power, or you can work to put it to the best and most proper use.

*Interview, Burbank, Calif./*
*San Francisco Examiner & Chronicle,*
*4-27:(Datebook)20.*

## Jason Robards, Jr.
*Actor*
6

The television audience accepts a lot of non-talent. Sometimes it's unbelievable—the kind of junk that's given them. Actors dependent on television have to live with it. I don't choose to do so. Fortunately, so far I haven't had to. If I were in it and really working at it, I might not talk that way. I may end up in TV—you have to stay alive. [But] you've got to do what's real for yourself. Over the years, I've been offered many [TV] series and big sums of money. People have thought me terribly mad to refuse. I still stay basically in the theatre. It's impossible to give it up. It's a part of me.

*Interview, Los Angeles/*
*Los Angeles Herald-Examiner,*
*5-25:(TV Weekly)6.*

**Artur Rubinstein**
*Pianist*

1

I won't play for television, in spite of some very big offers. I imagine a fellow listening to me while shaving, and his wife in the kitchen saying, "Turn that damn music down."

*Interview, Lodz, Poland/People, 6-30:6.*

**Roy Scheider**
*Actor*

2

[On why he will not act in television] : TV is poison to a guy who's clawing his way up. And I'm still clawing. If you give it to them [the audience] for nothing, they won't come to the theatre. And not only that, the [movie] producers won't hire you for their films. They figure, if the audience can get it for nothing [on TV], why should I make a $4-million picture with this guy? . . . The more you play hard-to-get on TV, the more they want you. Then, once they capture you on TV, once you're nailed, then the movies don't want you any more. And I do think that the most interesting writing and directing is being done in the movies these days.

*Interview, New York/*
*The Christian Science Monitor, 8-15:31.*

**Herbert S. Schlosser**
*President, National Broadcasting*
*Company*

3

Television must strike the delicate balance between following public taste and leading it by offering new forms and styles of entertainment . . . We do not seek through entertainment to create a new morality. But we must serve the millions of viewers who want at least part of their entertainment to relate to experience of the real world with which they can identify. In keeping pace with the times, we do not intend to leap too far ahead of what viewers

will accept, but we cannot lag so far behind that they leave us and turn elsewhere.

*U.S. News & World Report, 1-13:32.*

**Robert Stack**
*Actor*

4

You have to be a realist to work in television. You have to know the ground rules and be willing to follow them. Attitude is important. TV is a merchandising business. Products must be sold, ratings must stay up. And if you get yourself into a series, you had better understand that you'll never get 27 good scripts in a season.

*Interview/*
*Los Angeles Herald-Examiner, 11-28:(B)8.*

5

I disagree with those who would censor television violence because it might have some effect on some people. No two psychiatrists agree on any two things, anyway. The only censor should be the head of the household. And you have to distinguish between "violence" and "action." The latter is what *The Untouchables* was. We used guns to document a violent era, not to get ratings.

*Interview/*
*Los Angeles Herald-Examiner, 11-28:(B)8. .*

**Arthur R. Taylor**
*President, CBS, Inc.*

6

To some extent, our [TV] industry has not met its responsibilities as fully as it should. We cannot escape the fact that many people believe that television entertainment has too often been characterized by a sameness, a reliance on stale formulas and on an overuse of violence. But we have recognized that change is the law of the creative process—as it is the law of life. As a result, television is changing . . . There is a desperate need in this country for humor that is not divisive but unifying. There is also a need for action and adventure that do not espouse and elevate brutality and sadism. Despite the appetite for violence among certain segments of the public, we must discover new and imagina-

# WHAT THEY SAID IN 1975

tive approaches for sustaining action, adventure and jeopardy without resorting to brutality.

*Before Hollywood Radio and Television Society, Beverly Hills, Calif., Dec. 11/ Los Angeles Herald-Examiner, 12-12:(B)3.*

## Dick Van Dyke
*Actor*

1

[On TV's "family hour" concept] : The idea of a family hour is good, but, as they do it, they don't have anything to talk about. It's sugary; it's pap. Kids know what is real. They're not going to buy that. They know violence and sex exist. It all depends on how you use them. The way it is now, there are no crises, nothing grabs you.

*Interview/ Los Angeles Herald-Examiner, 10-16:(B)5.*

## Ralph Waite
*Actor*

2

California and *The Waltons* [TV series] allowed me the time, the space and the money to settle down a little bit and not be so driven; to come to sort of a personal understanding with life. I had to give up a lot of my ego trip–that I was one of the great American actors destined for great things on the stage— and come to an appreciation of the fact that I'm in a business, that I have to make a living and that television is giving me good work to do. The New York actor would say that I've sold out. But I can't live with that kind of arrogance any more. My whole attitude has shifted to a great deal of gratitude for simply being alive and having honest work to do. My ego is in much better shape.

*Interview, Los Angeles/TV Guide, 8-23:21.*

## Barbara Walters
*Co-host, "Today" show, National Broadcasting Company*

3

When I first went on the air, all of my friends' mothers used to think, "So how come my Marylin can't do it?" There is the feeling that it is the easiest thing in the world to be a television interviewer. Every time the wife of

someone important wants to do something, she wants to be a television interviewer, right? Every time an actress decides that she is no longer going to make movies, [she says], "I think I'll have my own talk show." Everyone thinks that it is terrifically easy. But you have to do your homework and you must have something that makes you special . . . I resent the fact that, while nobody thinks that anybody can just sit down and be a lawyer or write a newspaper column, they automatically think: oh, television, that's the easiest thing. Well, I *worked* and I never complained about the hours. I was able to *keep* those hours. I don't drink. I don't run around. I'm not on pills. I'm not a crazy lady. I don't look for excuses. I have a reputation for getting interviews that are hard to get because if *I* didn't get those important political people *myself* I would never have been allowed to do them on the air.

*Interview, New York/ Ladies' Home Journal, November:172.*

## Vincent T. Wasilewski
*President, National Association of Broadcasters*

4

Broadcasting is being assaulted by so many governmental bodies, from so many different sides, that we feel like we are being nibbled to death by ducks . . . There seems to be a determined and unremitting search for ways to get at broadcasting–to cut it down, tie it up, restrict it, inhibit it–using the Antitrust Division, using the Federal Communications Commission, the Federal Trade Commission, through consumer laws, through the Fairness Doctrine, the imposition of heavy fees, through a complex, controlling license-renewal procedure, through intrusions into programming.

*At National Association of Broadcasters convention, Las Vegas, Nev., April 7/ Daily Variety, 4-8:1.*

## David Webster
*Director for the United States, British Broadcasting Corporation*

5

[Comparing British and U.S. TV]: Your competitive system follows a sort of crude version of the laws of economics. If you get a police show that is successful, you will soon have eight other police shows. Our two-network BBC system and the independent system comprise a mixed economy; so it's not a straightforward competitive thing. It saves the commercial operators from the worst excesses of the market laws. And it saves the BBC from the worst excesses of paternalistic monopoly. The two systems interact, and, funnily enough, some of the areas in which BBC is strongest are light entertainment and sports, while ITV [the independent network] does extremely good serious drama. If you had three directly competitive commercial networks, they would all become prisoners of the economic laws, and the programming would reflect that. In the U.S., the problem is that all networks are competing for the same large numbers of viewers. Anything less than a 30 per cent share of the sets in use has had it. That doesn't mean it is a bad program, or that perhaps 20 million people don't like it. Just that not enough, according to the business figures, are watching. So it gets chopped. This sort of thinking leads to a similarity of programming—and to such a high-risk industry that you can't really do anything unusual at all.

*Interview, New York/*
*The Christian Science Monitor, 12-17:16.*

**Richard E. Wiley**
*Chairman, Federal Communications*
*Commission*
1

On the one hand, it is imperative that the [TV] medium act to protect children from objectionable programming—or at least to aid concerned parents in providing that protection. On the other hand, I also feel that television—if it is to achieve its full maturity—must continue to present sensitive and controversial themes which are appropriate, and of interest, to an adult audience . . . In my opinion, adult programs can be presented with taste, discretion and decency—and frankly, I expect the industry to make programming decisions in this area in a sensitive and responsible manner . . . I believe in freedom of the press, and I also believe that the personal interests, tastes and viewing habits of

Dick Wiley—and those who serve with him at the FCC—must never be permitted to dictate to the American public what it can see on the television screen. By all odds, ours is the finest broadcast system in the world. But like any human institution—including, incidentally, the FCC—American broadcasting has its shortcomings, excesses and oversights. One of these has been—to use the words of your [NATPE] president—"vulgarity for vulgarity's sake, violence for violence's sake and sex for sex' sake" in television programming.

*Before National Association of Television*
*Program Executives, Atlanta, Feb. 10/*
*Daily Variety, 2-11:1.*

2

Television is directed by law to serve the public interest, and I believe the "family hour" agreement [whereby the networks will program family-type shows in early evening] will test whether the industry is capable of self-regulation. I expect to see a new balance in programming that will replace much of the gratuitous and excessive violence . . . I believe that the pendulum is now swinging back to where we will have good program balance, which does not mean blandness. It isn't reasonable, either, to expect the television industry to accept the responsibility parents should exercise over what their children watch. Yet it's my theory that the networks have truly made a new commitment to their public-interest obligations.

*The National Observer, 4-19:17.*

**Jonathan Winters**
*Comedian*
3

As a performer, I look at a man's head as his own private movie camera. His eyes are the lenses and his ears are the most fantastic piece of sound equipment in the world. That also makes him the editor of anything he watches or hears. And that's why timing and clarity are so important to an actor. If he misses on either one, he's lost his audience to the refrigerator. In fact, staying on top usually is tougher than getting there. For example, TV rarely forgives a bad show and it almost never gives a second

*(JONATHAN WINTERS)*

chance to young comedians who don't make it their first time out. It's entirely possible for a kid to blow his entire career within the space of an hour.

*Interview, Los Angeles/*
*The Christian Science Monitor, 11-17:35.*

**Robert D. Wood**
*President, Columbia Broadcasting*
*System Television*                                    *1*

[On his job]: You can do everything else beautifully: run a fine sales department, a super technical staff, a superb publicity operation. But if you fail in programming, it all doesn't mean a damn. Get the programs right and the rest tends to fall in line . . . I don't think there's

any particular mystique about programming. There's a certain quality I like to see maintained and extended; most programming decisions come out of your belly, anyway.

*Interview, New York/*
*Los Angeles Times, 4-7:(4)13,16.*

**Vladimir K. Zworykin**
*Inventor of the television tube*                      *2*

[Television is] in its infancy. I don't mean technologically. I mean socially. Television could be a terrific value for human purposes. But it is not used that way. There is too much violence, too much crime. People are hypnotized by it. It's contaminating our society.

*Interview/*
*Los Angeles Times, 2-24:(1)2.*

**Muhammad Ali**
*Heavyweight boxing champion of the world*

1

Whole nations beg me to visit. I've been invited to dine with kings and presidents. Those who once scorned me now want to shake my hand and kiss me. Imagine me, an uneducated Negro, doing all this. To this day, I can't even read very well—but I hire people who can.

*People, 7-7:6.*

**Richard Armour**
*Author; Professor emeritus of English,
Scripps College*

2

I carry a little notebook with me constantly—while I'm doing the gardening or flying somewhere on a plane—and I jot down whatever comes to me, words and ideas. I'd be more embarrassed if I forgot to carry my pen and pad than if I forgot to wear my pants.

*Interview, Claremont, Calif./
Los Angeles Times, 5-8:(4)16.*

**Elizabeth Ashley**
*Actress*

3

I'm not strong enough to say, "No, my private life is private." I'm a blabbermouth. I love telling people about myself. It's my Achilles heel. Even if I know I would be much better off if I kept my mouth shut, I still can't. It's just a compulsion. I need to expose myself. There are an awful lot of people who like parts of me and find other parts intolerable.

*Interview, New York/
The Washington Post, 2-9:(F)3.*

**Brigitte Bardot**
*Actress*

4

I am a woman who has doubtless succeeded in her career, but surely not in her private life . . . Perhaps in five years I will be forgotten, perhaps not. I will be 45, and I will not have lost my beauty. And I will be able to live, perhaps, like everybody. No longer just a beautiful object, you see, but a human being.

*Interview/
Time, 3-24:61.*

5

I find my equilibrium in nature, in the company of animals. I hate humanity—I am allergic to it.

*Quote, 11-23:433.*

**Candice Bergen**
*Actress*

6

I need peace inside. That's why I'll never be a great actress. You've got to be a little mad to be a great actress, and I just don't want the madness.

*Interview/People, 7-28:50.*

**Jorge Luis Borges**
*Author*

7

Once, long ago, I saw happiness as unattainable. Now I know that happiness can be achieved at any time. As for success or failure, they seem irrelevant to me, and I never worry about them. What I seek is peace, the pleasure of thinking, and friendship; and although it may be too ambitious, a sensation of loving and being loved.

*Interview/
The Christian Science Monitor, 1-23:9*

**Charles Bronson**
*Actor*

8

I'm not a Charles Bronson fan. I don't think I turned out the way I thought I would turn out when I was a kid. It's a disappointment to me. My image, my sound, everything else. A big disappointment.

*Interview, Los Angeles/
Los Angeles Times, 11-2:(Calendar)34.*

461

# WHAT THEY SAID IN 1975

**Mel Brooks**
*Writer, Director*

1

[On the financial rewards of his new success in motion pictures]: I don't buy too much, but I can say "no" to jobs. I can say "no"! A great relief. My throat doesn't lock with anxiety when I pick up the check . . . But money means, to me, walking by a sporting-goods shop, I see a nice pair of sneakers, I buy it.

*Interview, Los Angeles/*
*The New York Times Magazine, 3-30:22.*

**Yul Brynner**
*Actor*

2

People ask me whether I have trouble stopping to play my character when I go home. Ha! I have never played a character which is even remotely like me. A human being has limits and inhibitions, but my imagination does not. So I would rather work with my imagination.

*Interview, San Francisco/*
*"W": a Fairchild publication, 9-19:21.*

**George Burns**
*Entertainer*

3

So I'll be 80 in January, so what? There comes a time when they knock on your door and give you back your pictures and you leave. I'll take my music with me because I don't know where the hell I'm going and I want it in my key. Meanwhile, I'm having a nice martini, I live in a nice house and the soup is hot. I go out with young girls and some of their youth rubs off on me, but I'm no [George] Jessel. I don't go to dark restaurants; what the hell, I got nothing to hide. I go to my office an hour a day, and I'm writing a book about how to be 80 years old and enjoy it. If I had my whole life to live over again, I'd do everything the same way. The only difference is, I'd do everything twice.

*Interview/*
*San Francisco Examiner & Chronicle,*
*5-25:(Datebook)13.*

**Ellen Burstyn**
*Actress*

4

People ask me, "How could you have been nominated for two Academy Awards and still not have been very well known?" Well, it's simple. I did it on purpose. I avoided doing the things that would make me well known. I don't want to be. I like walking the streets, shopping, being part of the crowd, being able to observe people around me. Now I'm the one who's being observed, and I don't like it and I don't hope it lasts. I've always had a lot of other things going on in my life that are much more important to me.

*Interview, Boston/*
*"W": a Fairchild publication, 3-21:9.*

**James Caan**
*Actor*

5

You know the kind of actor I am? I'm the sort who says before each movie, "Oh God, give me a break."

*Interview, New York/Time, 4-7:80.*

**Truman Capote**
*Author*

6

I'm not really jarred by anything except a certain kind of middle-class pretentiousness. I've always said I can go first class or third. But I could never go second.

*Interview/*
*"W": a Fairchild publication, 11-14:26.*

**Oleg Cassini**
*Fashion designer*

7

I'm a loner . . . an outdoor man. I'm the John Wayne of the dress business, and I'm still Number 1 whether they like it or not. I have star quality. All the things in my personal life have made me an image, while some designers remain faceless blobs.

*Quote, 6-8:530.*

**Dorothy Chandler**
*Assistant to the chairman, Times*
*Mirror Company*

8

I am a strong woman. I've had to be. **Sur**vival is the whole thing in life. But I'm **not** a dominant person that must have my way, nor do I want people to agree with me always. I don't like everybody. People are jealous and resentful because I'm a woman who's accomplished a lot. Much is said about me that isn't true. I'm bothered by it, but I'm secure enough not to let it affect me. I'm no different from any other person with a leadership role. I'm an independent thinker, not a follower, and always a rebel.

*Interview, Los Angeles/*
*"W": a Fairchild publication, 3-21:11.*

**Jacques-Yves Cousteau**
*Explorer*
1

[On being 65 and still actively participating in strenuous expeditions]: I don't feel old at all; aging is only in the head. I expect to go on this way as long as I can. Then, when I am no longer able to participate, I would simply like to be switched off during an operation. None of this business of trying to sustain the life forces . . . When it is over, it is over.

*Interview, Los Angeles/*
*The Washington Post, 12-10:(G)2.*

**Tony Curtis**
*Actor*
2

At the beginning of my career, I was mindless, almost like the shark in *Jaws.* Satisfying physical needs, like eating and/or an affair with the leading lady of the moment, were my major concerns. What time has done is simplify my feelings about things. They're not as opulent as they used to be. Not so overt. By the time you reach 50, and you begin to see the final curtain and realize that today is not forever, you'd better have reconciled your excesses or you're dead already.

*Interview, Los Angeles/*
*TV Guide, 11-29:27.*

**Bette Davis**
*Actress*
3

Work keeps me healthy. It keeps me active and I hope it keeps me young. To stay young you must stay young mentally, and I'm a 14-year-old half the time.

*London/Los Angeles Times, 10-3:(1)2.*

**Catherine Deneuve**
*Actress*
4

[On her beauty]: This is a very difficult thing to live with. Everyone I see appears to be judging my appearance. "Is she the most beautiful woman in the world, or not?" I can read it in their eyes. It is not important to me. It makes me uncomfortable. I would prefer to have people think of me as a person, not as a thing of beauty.

*Interview, Los Angeles/*
*San Francisco Examiner & Chronicle,*
*2-16:(A)16.*

**J. P. Donleavy**
*Author*
5

I suffer from being overly courteous and extremely shy and retiring. I am not aware of my own importance. I did have it when I was an unknown author, but lost it with success.

*Interview, Levington Park, Ireland/*
*People, 12-15:60.*

**Bob Dylan**
*Singer, Composer*
6

It was never my intention to become a big star. It happened, and there was nothing I could do about it. I tried to get rid of that burden for a long time. I eat and sleep and, you know, have the same problems anybody else does, and yet people look at me funny.

*People, 11-10:24.*

**Henry Fonda**
*Actor*
7

I can't be an activist. Both [of my] kids are extroverts; I'm an introvert. To this day I die inside making personal appearances without a character to hide behind.

*The National Observer, 6-21:6.*

**Gerald R. Ford**
*President of the United States*
8

I'm a determined person. And if I've got an objective, I'll make hours of sacrifice—whatever efforts are needed. Some people call it plodding. The word is somewhat downgraded, but

# WHAT THEY SAID IN 1975

*(GERALD R. FORD)*

I'd rather be a plodder and get some place than have charisma and not make it.

*Interview, Washington/*
*The Reader's Digest, August:94.*

**Ava Gardner**
*Actress*
1

. . . I could be married 20 times but I'd still knock before going into someone's room. I respect other people's privacy and I want them to respect mine. That's why I get so angry reading articles which portray me as a lonely, bored woman, sitting at home on her own. In an odd way, I actually prefer the other version—the one where I was supposedly endlessly romancing bullfighters. Why can't they show me as a fairly normal human being who just sits here enjoying her privacy . . . ?

*Interview, London/*
*Los Angeles Times, 7-6:(Calendar)39.*

**Vasco dos Santos Goncalves**
*Prime Minister of Portugal*
2

I am a common man, and I get emotional about things. I have my heart near my mouth, but, with all of this, I have a cool head. Emotion is not incompatible with lucidity.

*Interview/Time, 5-5:40.*

**Cary Grant**
*Actor*
3

I have never been more myself than I am today. I pretended to be a certain kind of man on the screen, to be Cary Grant, and I more or less became that man in life. Now I can be Archie Leach [his real name] again. I'm really more like that scrubby character I played in the movie *Father Goose* than that fey character called Cary Grant. But I earned a living being him.

*Interview, Beverly Hills, Calif./*
*McCall's, October:92.*

**Andy Griffith**
*Actor*
4

With pictures, you are lucky if you do three or four a year; the rest of the time you are sitting around the house. I like to stay busy even if I enjoy working around the house. I'm like an uncle of mine back in North Carolina. They always said he spent one hour working and seven hours looking for his tools. That's about the way I am.

*Interview/*
*The Dallas Times Herald, 10-26:(F)1.*

**Gene Hackman**
*Actor*
5

I operate on the assumption that I'm 21. When I see myself on the screen, and I look like my own father, there's a great disparity between what I feel and how I look. I never think of myself as successful. I still feel the way I did when I was in New York, thrashing around. I'm disappointed that success isn't a Himalayan feeling.

*Interview/People, 11-3:56.*

**Arthur Hailey**
*Author*
6

I'm a rather dull person. I enjoy waking up with the birds, taking walks. I like movies like *Tora! Tora! Tora!* . . . Anything mechanical, and engines—because I trust them . . . housewives in shopping centers . . . Jacqueline Bisset . . . tinkering with stereo sets with my son. To me, the apex of life is to have dinner with a beautiful woman—my wife, preferably.

*Interview/People, 3-31:40.*

**H. R. Haldeman**
*Former Assistant to the President of*
*the United States (Richard M. Nixon)*
7

[On how former President Nixon used to let off steam by issuing orders he clearly didn't intend to have carried out, such as when he was trying to plug information leaks]: The President called me into his room between meetings—he was in a rush—and he said, "I want lie-detector tests given to . . ." and he listed categories of people. He said, "I want them done today. I don't want any arguments back," and he put in some of his . . . blunter expletive-type language, I guess. I said, "Yes, sir," and left because he was mad. I went out and did not do what he told me to do. And so he blew up. He said, "I told you to get it done and I expect you to get it done"... The next day he said, "What have you done on that?" and he kind of laughed and I said, "I haven't done anything." And he said, "I knew you wouldn't." And I said, "Well, I knew you knew I wouldn't . . ."

*Television interview,*
*Los Angeles, March 30/*
*The New York Times, 3-30:(1)24.*

**Katharine Hepburn**
*Actress*

1

Paradise to me is getting up at 4:30 or five o'clock in the morning. The house is absolutely quiet, and I'll have a big roaring fire, and I'll just stay in bed and have a great big breakfast: bacon, chicken livers, steak and eggs, that kind of food. And orange juice and a big pot of coffee. Then I just stay in bed and do my script-reading and my typing or whatever I have to do. Then I watch the sun rise. Oh, golly, Paradise!

*Interview, New York/*
*Ladies' Home Journal, August:106.*

**Bob Hope**
*Actor, Comedian*

2

[Reflecting on his life] : I play golf every single day; now, how many people can do that? How could I complain? I've enjoyed all of it, all the years; and the military thing has been a wonderful part of it. If I die tonight, I'll die with a smile on my face.

*Interview, Washington/*
*The Washington Post, 2-14:(B)11.*

**Trevor Howard**
*Actor*

3

I read about pop [music] groups and people I've never heard of who own eight cars each. They've got homes and farms and big estates— and I realize it's not my world any more. It's their world. It isn't sour grapes, just a fact of life. But, as far as I'm concerned, I'm happy just to keep working as long as they ask me, to

watch cricket and find some chums to chat with. That's living.

*Interview, London/*
*San Francisco Examiner & Chronicle,*
*6-15:(Datebook)14.*

**John Huston**
*Motion picture director*

4

I marvel at the foolishness of my past. I think I must have been rather retarded, because my youth went on for a hell of a long time.

*Interview, Marrakesh, Morocco/*
*San Francisco Examiner & Chronicle,*
*5-18:(Datebook)17.*

**Danny Kaye**
*Entertainer*

5

I do things which please me—no matter whether there is a great deal of money involved or not. If it stimulates me, I do it. But I never know what I am going to be doing three months from now. Once I said to Artur Rubinstein as a joke, "Where will you be on July 12 four years from now?" He took out his little book and told me precisely where he would be. Well, if I had to live that kind of carefully structured life, it would drive me up the wall. If something challenges me or excites me, I'll do it.

*Interview, New York/*
*The Christian Science Monitor, 4-24:26.*

**Cloris Leachman**
*Actress*

6

When I want attention, I get it. I make it happen wherever I go. I can do anything. I paint. I sculpt. Whatever it is, I get the job done and make it fun. I dance around and sing all the time. Acting is 10 per cent of what I do; the rest of the time I'm sort of a mobile social worker.

*Interview, Beverly Hills, Calif./*
*The New York Times, 2-23:(2)29.*

**Peggy Lee**
*Singer*

7

I've been singing for a great many years, and something in me—pride or ego or simply a debt

# WHAT THEY SAID IN 1975

to the audience—keeps me on a busy search for improvement. If I don't improve with each passing day and with each new song, I'll be standing still. But if I stand still, I'll actually go backward. I'd rather retire before then. Right now I have no intention of retiring, and people tell me that I never will. But when the time arrives, I know I can do it, because I've saved up enough painting, sculpting, writing and reading adventures for several lives. With that, and my gift of laughter, I'll get by.

*Interview, Los Angeles/*
*Los Angeles Times, 10-19:(Home)67.*

## Rod McKuen
*Poet, Songwriter*

1

Having been born a bastard, I feel it has given me a head start on all those people who have spent their lives becoming one.

*Time, 12-29:30.*

## Mary Tyler Moore
*Actress*

2

. . . basically, what you see is who I am. I'm independent and I do like to be liked. I do look for the good side of life and people. I'm positive and I'm disciplined. I like my life in order and I'm neat as a pin.

*Interview, Los Angeles/*
*Los Angeles Times, 4-2:(4)1.*

## Ron Nessen
*Press Secretary to President of the*
*United States Gerald R. Ford*

3

[In my job], I've had to get used to being held up to extreme public scrutiny, and it leads to a touch of paranoia. I'm very high-strung, don't take criticism well and vacillate between fits of depression and euphoria. [President Ford is] even-tempered, hides his feeling when he's angry. I'd like to be more like him.

*"W": a Fairchild publication, 9-19:10.*

## Bob Newhart
*Actor, Comedian*

4

I was never the guy who put on a hat at a party and made a lot of noise. I've always been somewhat unsure of myself. For years I've been afraid that at any moment people would discover I'm a fraud, merely pretending to be a comic. I keep a rolltop desk here in my office at home, as a sort of grim reminder that—if my career as a comedian goes up in smoke—I can always return to working as an accountant.

*Interview, Los Angeles/*
*Los Angeles Times, 9-14:(Home)34.*

## Paul Newman
*Actor*

5

I'm prepared to work in any category, if the work is distinguished. Only two things I won't do—something pornographic or violent. Joanne [his wife] says I'm not Victorian; I'm out of the Stone Age.

*Interview/The New York Times, 4-28:36.*

## David Niven
*Actor*

6

. . . I guess I am a lucky man. I mean, Christ, I'm a mini-talent, really. No one's going to put up a monument to my acting after I've gone. I once described my face as a cross between two pounds of halibut and an explosion in an old clothes closet. And yet, here I am, 40 years later, still finding work. Marvelous, isn't it?

*Interview, New York/*
*The National Observer, 11-8:23.*

## Joseph Papp
*Stage producer*

7

I know where I'm going, and I usually get there. Personal conflicts don't get in the way. Any need for fame has long since been satisfied, and I never did care about money. Power I don't take personally. It's something I need to get the job done. My job is building theatre, and my job is my life.

*Interview, New York/*
*People, 7-28:64.*

## Valerie Perrine
*Actress*

8

You know what I really want? To be a simple country girl—live on a ranch with a couple of horses, some ducks, my dogs . . .

and a helicopter in the backyard to take me to Gucci. No, make that Hermes—it's classier.

*Interview, Los Angeles/*
*"W": a Fairchild publication, 7-11:14.*

**Oliver Reed**
*Actor*

1

Sometimes when I've had six or seven Scotches and as many beers, I often feel like beating the hell out of someone. But I'm careful never to be a drunken lout. It's just that I enjoy people who like a good fight and who talk about important things like women and booze, not art and politics.

*The Dallas Times Herald,*
*3-9:(Sunday Magazine)2.*

**Henry S. Reuss**
*United States Representative,*
*D—Wisconsin*

2

I'm not a back-slapper, but I'm not a recluse, either. I love friends, I love to be somebody's friend, and I like to kid around.

*The New York Times, 3-2:(3)5.*

**Artur Rubinstein**
*Pianist*

3

When I was young I used to have successes with women because I was young. Now I have successes with women because I am old. Middle age was the hard part.

*Lodz, Poland/*
*People, 6-30:6.*

**Bill Russell**
*Basketball coach, Seattle*
*"SuperSonics"; Former player*

4

I try to live my life so that every day I can look a man in the eye and, if I choose, say "Go to hell" . . . I like to think of myself as independent. I am not nice to people just to be nice. I don't smile just to smile. I don't cooperate just to cooperate. I owe nothing to nobody, except myself. I must be my own man.

*New York/*
*Los Angeles Herald-Examiner, 3-2:(B)7.*

**Adela Rogers St. Johns**
*Author, Journalist*

5

When I was younger, bringing up my five kids on what I earned as a writer, there were always bill collectors breathing down my neck. That might not seem artistic or inspirational, but it provided a sizable incentive to get my stories done. There was no time for agonizing reappraisal or even prolonged self-analysis. I had to keep pumping out those stories. Today I don't have those bill collectors chasing me, but I'm plugged in to the same busy switchboard.

*Interview, Los Angeles/*
*Los Angeles Times, 2-16:(Home)23.*

**Telly Savalas**
*Actor*

6

[On his success]: The only thing that's happened is my fan club has grown. Once it was just my mother and my immediate family. Now it's 50 or 60 million people. I love it. The [TV] series is my hiatus. It gives me time to rest up for the important moments of my life—my family, my friends, my intrigues . . . I was prepared for the applause. Just as I am prepared for the applause to stop. That is my security. If I believed all this [success] nonsense, I'd be in trouble. Any day now I expect to be exposed as a fraud. I enjoy success, but I also enjoy failure.

*Interview/*
*TV Guide, 2-22:18,19.*

**Helen Thomas**
*White House correspondent, United*
*Press International*

7

[On President Ford]: He is amiable, likeable, easy to be with, uninspired, but seems to be growing in the job. He is not as unflappable as he is pictured. But he does have an inner security and confidence in himself that is refreshing after the personality hangups of the recent past. But he also is one-dimensional, and there seems to be little planning in his future. In short, where are we going? . . . [After Richard Nixon's resignation last year, Gerald Ford] was a President who spoke of truth and honesty: "Truth is the glue that holds government together"; "Honesty is the best policy."

# WHAT THEY SAID IN 1975

Homilies, but the country loved it. What's more, he toasted his own English muffins in the morning, put his feet up on the desk in the Oval Office, likes to ski, golf, party and to have a martini or two, even when we are looking.

*Before Texas UPI*
*Editors Association,*
*San Antonio, June 7/*
*The Dallas Times Herald, 6-8:(A)15.*

**Gore Vidal**
*Author*

1

I am, at heart, a tiresome nag—complacently positive that there is no human problem which could not be solved if people would simply do as I advise.

*People, 1-27:29.*

**Mae West**
*Actress*

2

I've been so absorbed in myself since I've been a child. I've never been interested in anybody but myself. Just me, me. What other woman in the world has done what I've done? I've never done anything that wasn't a success.

*San Francisco Examiner & Chronicle,*
*3-9:(This World)2.*

**Tennessee Williams**
*Playwright*

3

Once upon a time, I thought of calling my memoirs, "Flee, Flee This Sad Hotel," which is a line from a poem by Anne Sexton who did kill herself. But then that's really quite false. I don't really regard my life as a sad hotel any more than a merry tavern. I certainly don't intend to vacate it until I'm kicked out.

*Interview/*
*Los Angeles Herald-Examiner, 10-20:(B)4.*

# Philosophy

**Mortimer Adler**
*Author, Philosopher*
1

. . . there aren't many wise men and women. Still, there is wisdom. In all the enumerations of major virtues, wisdom is one. Wisdom is a virtue of the intellect; it is not a science that can be taught.

*Interview, London/People, 3-31:34.*

**George Allen**
*Football coach, Washington "Redskins"*
2

I don't consider coaching work. When you get up in the morning knowing you are going to enjoy the day, then that's not work. No matter what the job, an ingredient of success is enthusiasm. Enthusiasm keeps you going.

*Interview, Washington/*
*Nation's Business, September:52.*

**Woody Allen**
*Actor, Director, Writer*
3

. . . there's something mysterious about the whole process of comedy. I think all good humor proceeds from the unconscious. Something really funny is always a complete surprise. Comics possess a funny outlook on things to begin with, but they're always taken by surprise when that funny connection occurs to them and pops out. If you've ever seen a team of comedy writers at work, you'll know what I'm talking about. They'll bat ideas back and forth, but the good stuff will seem to come out of nowhere. The less conscious comedy is, the better it probably is.

*News conference, New York/*
*The Washington Post, 6-9:(B)5.*

4

The structure of the joke is a psychological reflection of the concern. The juxtaposition of the trivial and the mundane—laundry, expenses, travel—functioning against the background of cosmic, major concerns. We have to reconcile the paradox of it all. The joke mirrors that paradox.

*Interview/Los Angeles Times, 10-4:(1)19.*

**Jean Arthur**
*Actress*
5

. . . they tell us we have three primitive needs—food, clothes and sex, and that's it. My God, I can live without any of it. I could live on roots in the ground. There's more to us than that. Feeling is the most important thing in life. And the need to expand and evolve. A tree overcomes and endures everything to be as beautiful as it can. That's what we should do. Become as strong and beautiful as we can.

*Interview, Carmel, Calif./*
*Los Angeles Times, 3-30:(Calendar)30.*

**Lauren Bacall**
*Actress*
6

I really do believe that work is the most important thing in your life. It keeps you going. It keeps you alive, active, interested. It keeps the juices going. I have a horror of being dependent on my children. I think women are more and more finding they've got to do something—not to compete with men—but to have something for themselves. Everything works better when you're working.

*Interview, Washington/*
*The Washington Post, 1-21:(B)3.*

**William S. Banowsky**
*President, Pepperdine University*
7

There are a number of qualities which contribute to personal success in life. Some, like being born with good parents or in a favorable country or social class, or with natural physical and mental endowments, are completely out of our control. But the ones that really count are the ones that we can do something about. And,

# WHAT THEY SAID IN 1975

## (WILLIAM S. BANOWSKY)

among these, nothing is so important as the quality of persistence. You may pick at random from a library shelf the biography of any man or woman who has made a lasting contribution to humanity. Some were extremely brilliant, others showed uncommon courage. But one characteristic will be present in every case. Every person who achieved greatness has shown uncommon persistence ... Nothing in the world can take the place of persistence. Talent will not; nothing is more common than unsuccessful men with talent. Genius will not; unrewarded genius is almost a proverb. Education will not; the world is full of educated derelicts. Persistence and determination alone are omnipotent.

*At Pepperdine University, Jan. 6/*
*Vital Speeches, 3-1:308,310.*

## Baudouin I
*King of Belgium*
1

The existence of different ideologies inside one country, as in different nations, can result in healthy competition. But in our view the success of any concept of life is not measured by its geographical spread, if it is not an expression of the free will of the population concerned.

*Moscow/*
*The Christian Science Monitor, 6-25:30.*

## Candice Bergen
*Actress*
2

People who have it think beauty is a blessing. Actually, it's a kind of sentence, a confinement. It sets you apart. People see you as an object, not as a person, and they project a set of expectations into that object. When I was younger, I tried to fulfill them, if only as a vendetta. Most men are such jerks about beautiful women, it's hard not to despise them. Commercially, of course, beauty gets you through the door.

*Interview/*
*People, 7-28:48.*

## Ingmar Bergman
*Motion picture director*
3

If you live calmly, or just sit down calmly every day for about an hour, gradually you discover your own rhythm. But most of us don't, and that's unhealthy—spiritually and physically. The important thing is not to let other people, other situations or conditions or circumstances hurt this rhythm too much. Sometimes, of course, it's healthy to be stressed. Sometimes it is good for me to get away from the island [where he lives] and live a more hurried life. But only sometimes. If you can find your own rhythm, you find a lot of other things at the same time.

*Interview, Stockholm/*
*The New York Times Magazine, 12-7:104.*

## Abram Bergson
*Professor of economics, and former*
*director of the Russian Research*
*Center, Harvard University*
4

We think of Communism to a great extent as an economic system, but it represents a political system as well, and the two are very closely interconnected. Indeed, it may be more important as an innovation in politics than in economics. What is involved, in effect, is a new technology of power, which has turned out to be fantastically successful. Communism provides an ideology through which the group in power can virtually blot out almost every conventional kind of opposition. As it nationalizes property, it eliminates the middle class as a source of opposition. The government becomes the employer of all workers, directly or indirectly. No section of the population willing to oppose the government can find an economic base on which to support political opposition. It is gone. Furthermore, you have a government monopoly of education, communication and means of production, not to mention control of the armed forces.

*Interview, Cambridge, Mass./*
*Los Angeles Times, 4-22:(2)7.*

**Tom Bradley**
*Mayor of Los Angeles*
1

During my years on the police force, I learned that hostility breeds hostility. I saw that every man was looking for some kind of warmth, whether he would admit it or not. People, all people, are looking for respect, for human dignity. This is something we all nourish. I have faith in this element of human nature, faith that there is an underlying decency in every man.

*Quote, 8-10:73.*

**Marlon Brando**
*Actor*
2

Intelligence is such a broad word. It's a measure, but only one kind. Henry Moore has an intelligence for space. Frank Lloyd Wright had it for structure. Others have it for feelings. There are different intelligences. It's how to use these differences to our advantage that interests me.

*Interview, Billings, Mont./*
*Los Angeles Times, 8-10:(Calendar)1.*

**Leonid I. Brezhnev**
*General Secretary, Communist Party*
*of the Soviet Union*
3

The community of socialist states is one of the remarkable products of our epoch, a factor which leaves an increasingly vivid and indelible mark on the whole of international life today. The socialist community is a voluntary alliance of equal, sovereign and independent states, which, being socialist ones, draw for strength and well-being only on the free work of their peoples, knowing no exploitation at home and not exploiting the labor or riches of other countries and peoples. The socialist community is an alliance of an absolutely new type. It is based not just on the community of state interests of a group of countries but represents a fraternal family of peoples which are led by Marxist-Leninist parties and which are forged into a single whole by a common world outlook, common lofty ideals and relations of comradely solidarity and mutual support. This is an alliance that rests on the permanent identity of positions and actions, which gives additional strength to every one of its participants for tackling national tasks and multiplies manyfold their combined weight and influence on world affairs. The socialist community is the most reliable support of the forces of freedom and progress in the whole world. That is precisely why imperialist reaction is so frenziedly trying to smear it. Using ideological infiltration and economic levers, the bourgeois world stubbornly but unsuccessfully is trying to weaken our unity, trying to undermine the mainstays of socialism, now in one fraternal country, now in another. Traitors to the cause of socialism are slinging mud at our community, are straining to distort both the nature of our mutual relations and our common policy.

*At Polish Communist Party congress,*
*Warsaw, Dec. 9/*
*The New York Times, 12-10:20.*

**Edmund G. Brown, Jr.**
*Governor of California (D)*
4

I have a feeling that in life we will always have to live with less than we need, otherwise it would be harmful to our personal psychology.

*At University of California*
*regents meeting/*
*Los Angeles Times, 3-25:(1)3.*

**Yul Brynner**
*Actor*
5

It's terribly important to be well in your skin. The French have that expression. I've reached the age where I'm well in my skin. The next thing to your skin is friendship. Friends come to save you in your own problems. Love affairs and marriages go up and down. Friends save you.

*Interview, Los Angeles/*
*Los Angeles Times, 8-10:(Calendar)31.*

**Art Buchwald**
*Newspaper columnist*
6

Now we seem to be going through a period of nostalgia, and everyone seems to think yesterday was better than today. I personally don't think it was, and I would advise you not to wait

# WHAT THEY SAID IN 1975

*(ART BUCHWALD)*

10 years from now before admitting today was great. If you're hung up on nostalgia, pretend today is yesterday and just go out and have one hell of a time.

*At Vassar College commencement,*
*The Wall Street Journal, 6-20:8.*

**William F. Buckley, Jr.**
*Political columnist; Editor,*
*"National Review"*
1

If it is perceived that there is a great challenge to what we know of as Western civilization, and the question is what we can do about it, the answer is mostly not to ask what we can do about it; it's simply to acknowledge that it's impossible to know what single question, which book, which speech, which encyclopedia is actually going to deflect history. And, that being the case, it's important simply to write the books, make the speeches, ask the questions—always with the hope that one of them, or all of them cumulatively, will twist the rudder a little bit.

*Interview, New York/*
*The National Observer, 11-29:24.*

**George Burns**
*Entertainer*
2

People are always asking me why I don't retire. What earthly sense would it make to retire at my age [79]? Retire to what? The time to retire is at age 35 or 40, if you can afford it. That's when retirement would be fun, when you could do anything you want. But if I retired now, I wouldn't relax, I'd collapse. There's quite a difference.

*San Francisco Examiner & Chronicle,*
*11-30:(This World)2.*

**Alexander P. Butterfield**
*Administrator, Federal Aviation*
*Administration; Former Deputy Assistant*
*to the President of the United States*
*(Richard M. Nixon)*
3

Special emphasis ought to be placed on individual honesty and personal integrity; for it's my opinion that in today's world—in govern-

ment and out—there's a surprising lack of it, certainly significantly less than 50 years ago. Suffice it to say that these virtues mean just about everything.

*At St. John's Military Academy, Wisconsin/*
*The New York Times Magazine, 7-20:18.*

**Vera Caspary**
*Author*
4

. . . some young people today, despite all their education and free lifestyles, don't look as if they'll ever find what it is they want from life. They look totally and completely lost. They still need someone to tell them what to do, what is wanted. They still dream of something happening to them, rather than making it happen. You have to do what you want to do. Not that you want to offend anybody; but you do have to stop worrying about what your mother and family and friends are going to think every time you feel that you need to do something. It's your life; you must live it the way you want. All those relatives and friends aren't going to be able to give you another life.

*Los Angeles/*
*Los Angeles Herald-Examiner, 4-7:(B)2.*

**Van Cliburn**
*Pianist*
5

"Quality" is the totality of heart, intellect and soul. It is simplicity and beauty according to each person's perception. But it is not a material thing. Real quality exists in thought.

*"W": a Fairchild publication, 2-21:13.*

**Alex Comfort**
*Author, Biologist*
6

Sexual freedom is a measure of political freedom. A society with great political freedom will not develop arbitrary sexual taboos. People enjoying sex at home would rather do that than go out to war or be the goons of society. People with less sexual spontaneity are more docile and willing to listen to those in power. And the ruling classes always seem to have the most sexual freedom. In Victorian England, sexual taboos were based on a conception of gentility, but also on fear of the influence of the French

472

Revolution. In Communist countries, sexual freedom is associated with revisionism.

*Interview, Los Angeles/*
*Los Angeles Herald-Examiner, 11-23:(A)8.*

**Paul Costa**
*Associate professor of psychology,*
*University of Massachusetts*

1

An unexpected bonus of old age is the ability to be analytical and rational and at the same time be concerned with past experiences. We don't want to give the impression that all old people are wise, but with age comes this integration of emotions and experience which adds to wisdom.

*Los Angeles Herald-Examiner, 3-16:(F)4.*

**Jacques-Yves Cousteau**
*Explorer*

2

. . . I don't think you can learn a lot about animals by observing men. But you can learn about men from observing animals. You learn, first, that behavior is not as simple as some behaviorists believe. In the simplest creature there is quite a degree of independence and unpredictability. And this unpredictability is precisely what we have developed in the characteristic of the human superiority. So we feel very clearly that we are made of the same building blocks, that we have developed more of consciousness, of what we call intelligence. We have developed that far more than any other animal. But, basically, we find the sources of our own behavior by studying the animals' behavior. There are general rules that we are not going to escape.

*Interview/The Washington Post, 1-4:(D)3.*

**Carl T. Curtis**
*United States Senator, R—Nebraska*

3

. . . the most nutritious food you can eat is meat. It makes for stronger bodies. In the whole history of the world, whenever a meat-eating race has gone to war against a non-meat-eating race, the meat eaters won. It produces superior people. We have the books of history.

*Before the Senate, Washington/*
*The Wall Street Journal, 10-7:24.*

**Catherine Deneuve**
*Actress*

4

In life, we are all hustlers . . . for anything—to have a table in a restaurant, to get a job or a man. It's a social game. Either you hustle or are hustled.

*Interview, Los Angeles/*
*"W": a Fairchild publication, 3-7:9.*

**Colleen Dewhurst**
*Actress*

5

. . . I once said that acting comes from the groin, not the brain. I think I meant it's instinctual. Someone once told me that if you watched people you would learn, when you went to play a part, that there are three areas only that characterize people. One is the groin, one is the heart, one is the head. Haven't you noticed at parties? Some people talk from the head, some from the heart, some from the groin.

*Interview, Malibu, Calif./*
*Los Angeles Times, 1-12:(Calendar)17.*

**Rene Dubos**
*Professor emeritus of microbiology,*
*Rockefeller University*

6

Diversity is at the origin of many conflicts and it tends to make the world of things and the world of men inefficient and inconvenient. But I believe that in the long run diversity is preferable to efficiency and convenience, and perhaps even to the serenity of absolute peace. Without diversity, freedom is but an empty word, persons and societies cannot continue to evolve. Human beings are not really free and cannot be fully creative if they do not have many opinions from which to select.

*At opening of New York City's American*
*Bicentennial celebration, May 22/*
*The New York Times, 5-22:39.*

**Will Durant**
*Author, Historian*

7

Youth insists on freedom long before maturity today. The liberty they enjoy contains in

# WHAT THEY SAID IN 1975

itself the seeds of chaos, and the chaos will compel the return of order.

*San Francisco Examiner & Chronicle,*
*11-9:(This World)2.*

**Loren C. Eiseley**
*Professor of anthropology and history*
*of science, University of Pennsylvania*      1

Callousness will increase as population multiplies. [If weapons are so deadly] that they cannot be used, then terror will be substituted and we will all find ourselves hostages. Already, promoted by forged papers, terrorism is passed from nation to nation. The time is not distant when it will become a way of life.

*Before Encyclopaedia Britannica*
*contributors, New York, Jan. 14/*
*The New York Times, 1-15:19.*

**John Fairchild**
*Publisher, "W" magazine*      2

There is no such thing as good or bad taste, except in the eyes of a snob. The real thing is quality. For instance, the Swiss Federal Railroad has quality because it's clean and it works. Quality people are people who do things, not people who lead idle lives. Sure, we [at *W*] do write about a dream world sometimes. But there are real things in the world that are beautiful and civilized, and people want to know what those are.

*Time, 4-21:47.*

**Richard A. Falk**
*Professor of international law and*
*practice, Princeton University*      3

... the "world-order activist" must reject realism as the basis for action. It is essential that those of us committed to eliminating war reject what sensible men who plan arms races and wage wars and run states define as "realism." The realist has no capacity to envision the kinds of major changes by peaceful means that are both possible and essential. The "realist" regards the nation-state system, with its propensity for war and its increasing tendency toward repression, as inevitable. He accepts and toler-

ates poverty and misery as immutable aspects of the human condition. The world-order anti-realist, in contrast, regards these self-styled realists as crackpot realists who seek primarily to pacify the passengers of a sinking vessel of state. World-order realists believe that political and behavioral mutations are possible and necessary, that we must work to embody them in history, and that the utopians of yesterday and today are the realists of tomorrow.

*At University of Pennsylvania/*
*The Center Report, October:19.*

**John H. Filer**
*Chairman, Aetna Life & Casualty Company*      4

Consider, if you will, that the recognition of an unsolved problem is not necessarily the recognition of failure, but just may be the necessary first step to eventual success. Learn to renew your strength by enjoying partial successes. When you have the river clean enough to swim in it, jump in and swim around instead of despairing that the water is not yet clean enough to drink. As intelligent, educated people, you have an enormous opportunity to bring balanced judgment and comment to the world rather than just the shouting of a zealot.

*At DePauw University commencement, June 1/*
*Vital Speeches, 7-1:576.*

**Gerald R. Ford**
*President of the United States*      5

Hard work should be rewarded ... I enjoy material things. I enjoy nice clothes, not flamboyant or extravagant. I enjoy doing nice things. But I enjoy doing these things because I worked for them.

*Interview/The National Observer, 7-26:5.*

**Jay W. Forrester**
*Professor of management, Massachusetts*
*Institute of Technology*      6

Growth is a temporary process. Physical growth of a person ceases with maturity. Growth of an explosion ends with destruction. Past civilizations have grown into overshoot and decline. In every growth situation, growth runs its course, be it in seconds or centuries . . . Any growth that repeatedly doubles will, in time, overwhelm its host environment. At some time, growth produces its own termination.

*The Washington Post, 6-8:(C)4.*

**Daniel X. Freedman**
*Chairman, department of psychiatry,*
*University of Chicago*

1

Our society and this "openness" have created adjustment problems for the individual. There are fewer of these problems when a society has widely accepted standards for morals and manners. Today, we don't have such a situation. This is a burden on the individual who, more than ever before, must make his or her own decisions as to what is right or wrong.

*U.S. News & World Report, 10-13:39.*

**J. William Fulbright**
*Former United States Senator, D—Arkansas*

2

Even if we could afford our extravagant lifestyle—the overpowered automobiles, the beefsteak diet—for dogs and cats as well as for humans—the throwaway boxes and bottles, the gadgets and whimsies that clutter our surroundings from the kitchen to the Pentagon and even the moon—it would still be important to conserve and cut back, to go back to living more simply. Over and above the material waste, our high living is also wasteful and destructive in the psychological sense. We have long passed the point of diminishing returns as between our gadgets and luxuries and the human satisfactions that they yield. Like spoiled children who have had too many toys, we are always looking for new playthings—and encouraged to do so by the massive advertising industry. But the gadgets only amuse us for a moment or two, and then we are off in search of something else.

*Quote, 2-16:154.*

**John Kenneth Galbraith**
*Former professor of economics,*
*Harvard University*

3

Walking is a very important part of my work pattern because it's so boring. You have to survive the boredom of your own company and

you start the next day with an enormous volume of involuntary thought which, somehow, you have to get rid of.

*Interview/*
*"W": a Fairchild publication, 9-19:2.*

4

Humor is an intensely personal, largely internal thing. What pleases some does not please others. Where humor is concerned, there are no standards—no one can say what is good or bad, although you can be sure that everyone will. In our society the solemn person inspires far more trust than the one who laughs. Also, as [humor columnist] Art Buchwald has pointed out, we live in an age when it is hard to invent anything as funny as everyday life. And because the real world is so funny, there is almost nothing you can do, short of labeling a joke a joke, to keep people from taking one seriously.

*Interview, Cambridge, Mass./*
*The Christian Science Monitor, 12-9:19.*

**Indira Gandhi**
*Prime Minister of India*

5

Democracy cannot survive unless certain basic rules are observed. One may have freedom, but freedom does not mean walking on the wrong side of the road.

*Before business and labor leaders,*
*New Delhi, July 12/*
*The New York Times, 7-13:(1)10.*

**Francoise Gilot**
*Painter*

6

[Reflecting on her relationships with the late artist Pablo Picasso and her husband Dr. Jonas Salk, conqueror of polio] : Great men are like everybody else, except they give what they have to the world through their art. The greatest thing for an artist is his art, not his person. If he becomes immortal, it's through what he does, not through who he is.

*Sarasota, Fla./*
*Los Angeles Herald-Examiner, 10-10:(B)1.*

**Valery Giscard d'Estaing**
*President of France*

7

The world is unhappy. It is unhappy because it doesn't know where it is going and because it

# WHAT THEY SAID IN 1975

senses that, if it knew, it would discover that it was heading for disaster.

*Quote, 2-9:121.*

**Arthur J. Goldberg**
*Lawyer; Former Associate Justice,*
*Supreme Court of the United States*  1

I'm not much bothered by problems. I have a sense that you do the best you can, that you mustn't hold yourself to impossible standards. In life we better learn, and we learn very hard, that you won't make a home run every time you're up at bat.

*Interview, San Francisco/*
*San Francisco Examiner & Chronicle,*
*2-2:(Sunday Scene)4.*

**Billy Graham**
*Evangelist*  2

If I didn't have my spiritual faith, I would be a pessimist. But I'm an optimist. I've read the last page in the Bible. It's all going to turn out all right.

*Interview, Hong Kong/People, 12-22:27.*

**Cary Grant**
*Actor*  3

No one is delighted about getting old, but you have no real choice. If one is too eager to pursue his lost youth, it becomes immediately evident.

*Interview, Beverly Hills, Calif./*
*McCall's, October:92.*

**George Hamilton**
*Actor*  4

Problems bring with them their own strength. Most of the fear is in facing the thing.
*The Dallas Times Herald, 2-25:(C)1.*

**Denis Healey**
*Chancellor of the Exchequer of the*
*United Kingdom*  5

The senseless accumulation of material goods of exactly the same type as the Western world has been producing since the war can no longer be regarded as the only guarantee of human happiness or the only measure of economic success.

*Quote, 2-9:122.*

**Herbert Hendin**
*Director of psychosocial studies,*
*Center for Policy Research, New York*  6

Today, much more than 20 years ago, people are much more egocentric, more into their own gratifications and satisfactions. They don't want to sacrifice. Before, they were willing to sacrifice too much perhaps. Now it is too little. Today there is a sense that anything that doesn't do things for them immediately is resented.

*Interview, New York/*
*Los Angeles Times, 8-12:(2)7.*

**Katharine Hepburn**
*Actress*  7

We are enormously impressed by success because there's so much failure. The margin of difference is often so tiny. Everyone has a breaking point that defeats and destroys him. Luckily, I haven't met mine yet . . . Even when things were going badly for me, I still turned down all kinds of offers because I didn't like them. I never had to say "Yes" when I wanted to say "No." I used to say, "Hell, I don't want to drown in somebody else's dress." If people can just keep going beyond a certain point, then they're great. But you see people constantly trying to reach that level, and just as they're about to be able to pull themselves onto the dock and sit down—they drown. And you must not let yourself drown.

*Interview, New York/*
*Ladies' Home Journal, August:108.*

**John A. Howard**
*President, Rockford (Ill.) College*  8

Terms like freedom, democracy, morality, human dignity and civil rights now lack much of the precision they once carried. They have become cheap banners that all opponents now carry into the fray of public discussion. I believe that the prostitution of our language now

constitutes a major impediment to the successful operation of society.

**Leon Jaworski**
*Lawyer*

One of the great misfortunes of today's relationship between the older and younger generations is the failure to take the time and make
the effort to engage in constructive dialogue—
the use of logic and reason and the experiences
of history. The simple truth is that all too many
of the older generation have failed, and failed
dismally, in one of the greatest privileges of the
home—that of visiting objectively with the
younger members of the family to ascertain
their concerns . . .

*Before school administrators,*
*Dallas, Feb. 24/*
*The Dallas Times Herald, 2-25:(B)1.*

**Danny Kaye**
*Entertainer*

I don't look back. I was in London recently
and someone said to me: "Why don't you come
back and play the Palladium like you used to?"
Somebody else said: "Why not make movies
like you used to?" They meant well, but I don't
want to turn around, go back 20 years and try
to recapture a time and an era and a frame of
mind I had long ago. That is really stepping
backwards. Movies are not what they used to
be, the times are not what they used to be and,
most important, I am not what I used to be. It
doesn't mean that I am forsaking my talent.
Talent doesn't change. What you have is a different attitude toward what you do. I'll do
what I need to do now. The only reason I'm
doing *Peter Pan* [for TV] is because it's something I've never done before, and it is nice to
try it.

*Interview/*
*Los Angeles Herald-Examiner,*
*6-1:(California Living)4.*

**Red Kelly**
*Hockey coach, Toronto "Maple Leafs"*

The only gracious way to accept an insult is
to ignore it. If you can't ignore it, you try to

top it. If you can't do that, you laugh at it.
And if you can't laugh at it, it's probably
deserved.

*Los Angeles Times, 10-14:(3)2.*

**Henry A. Kissinger**
*Secretary of State of the United States*

No social system, ideology or principle of
justice can tolerate a world in which the spiritual and physical potential of hundreds of millions is stunted from elemental hunger or
inadequate nutrition. National pride or regional
suspicion lose any moral justification if they
prevent us from overcoming this scourge.

*Quote, 2-2:97.*

**Polykarp Kusch**
*Professor of physics, University of*
*Texas, Dallas*

I believe that knowledge deteriorates if it is
not continuously re-examined, amplified, re-
formulated and enlarged. Unexamined knowledge ultimately becomes superstition which
has a life of its own, quite independent of its
source in human experience and of its struc-
turing by the human mind. The superstition of
today is the knowledge of a former time.

*At Nobel Conference on the Future*
*of Science/*
*The Dallas Times Herald, 11-16:(B)3.*

**Ann Landers**
*Newspaper Columnist*

Trouble isn't all bad. It's the great equalizer,
the common denominator of living, and it can
even be a blessing. Each of us is destined to be
unhappy at some time in our lives. Anyone who
is happy all the time has got to be nuts. Life is a
dynamic, moving process that produces one
problem after another. And these problems act
like a grindstone to smooth and polish us
thoroughly.

*At University of Utah/*
*The National Observer, 4-19:13.*

**Philip Lesly**
*Public-relations counsel*

How often we have heard that if we just set
our minds on solving our human problems—if

# WHAT THEY SAID IN 1975

*(PHILIP LESLY)*

we appropriate enough money and assign enough manpower—we can achieve whatever objective we set . . . we can solve the human problems on earth just as we were able to send men to the moon on schedule. But the moon is a fixed target. Scientists could predict in 1960 exactly where it would be on July 20, 1969. No circumstances would change the nature or the scope of the challenge. However, all the problems involving human attitudes are not absolutes that retain exact identity for as long as we want to deal with them. Their interrelationship is not predictable like a chemical formula or a mechanical action. The problems are part of a complex of human vagaries and sensitivities. Measurable and tangible challenges such as a flight to the moon lend themselves to organized and specific solutions. Problems that deal with human matters and attitudes do not.

*At Midwest Public Relations Conference, Madison, Wis., Sept. 13/ Vital Speeches, 10-1:752.*

**David E. Lilienthal**
*Chairman, Development and Resources Corporation; Former Chairman, Atomic Energy Commission of the United States*
1

We have a whole philosophy of life developing which is based on lack of belief in anything. I think it goes back to those people who have implanted the seeds of doubt simply because they have statistics or computers and recognize that they can get the headlines with negative talk. It is time we stopped making heroes of people who talk about things we can't do and honor those who believe there is no limit to human creative ability--political, economic and technical. Nothing that has happened justifies this negativism we have been passing through. I think you can trace the beginnings of what is still called the recession to the implanting of fear that we have reached the end of the road.

*Interview, New York/ Los Angeles Times, 5-27:(2)7.*

**Russell B. Long**
*United States Senator, D-Louisiana*
2

Democracy is like a raft: It won't sink, but you will always have your feet wet.

*The Wall Street Journal, 10-16:20.*

**James B. Longley**
*Governor of Maine (I)*
3

I admit to being a fiscal conservative and an old-fashioned guy in many ways. But I think there's a relationship between people who want something for nothing—the people who want society to support them—and a system that pays people more for not working than for working. I happen to think that a certain type of liberal is tearing this country apart. They've taken prayer out of the schools, they've burned flags, they run away from the draft, they don't face up to their responsibilities, and then they tell America on what terms they'll come back rather than pay the price for breaking the law. I think they're all interrelated—the people who want something for nothing. I just think we need to return to some very basic disciplines.

*Interview/ U.S. News & World Report, 8-18:63.*

**Michael Manley**
*Prime Minister of Jamaica*
4

Money is not the only thing in life. Money can't make your soul rich.

*Los Angeles Times, 4-23:(1-A)2.*

**Stanley Marcus**
*Chairman, Neiman-Marcus stores*
5

[His definition of "style"]: The innate or cultivated understanding of what is right; being adventuresome; knowing your limitations and social appropriateness; and having good judgment.

*The Dallas Times Herald, 7-16:(G)1.*

**Luis Martin**
*Professor of history, Southern Methodist University*
6

Many people here [in the U.S.] seem more concerned about individual freedoms than the duties that go with keeping freedom. Europeans looking from across the ocean are confused with the American obsession of individual rights. They know that such obsessions can destroy whole groups. Those people also wonder why convicted criminals are turned loose because of a technicality when everyone's convinced they're guilty. Freedom is a condition of our actions. When we lose sight of what we're doing and are more concerned about the way we're doing it, then we lose freedom.

*Interview/*
*The Dallas Times Herald, 11-11:(C)1.*

**Chaytor D. Mason**
*Clinical psychologist, University*
*of Southern California*

1

At one time we [in the U.S.] needed heroes. We didn't value ourselves very highly and could find glory only in identifying ourselves with local or national heroes. In the past, a hero was often someone involved in a black-and-white controversy that the majority of people saw as one-sided. Today we know there are two sides to most controversies, so we can't set up the image of a victorious hero who will be accepted by the large majority. Once, the press built heroes. Now it unmasks them. Television has been especially important in adding visual impact to information about the clay feet of our heroes. We can develop "heroes" like [football player] Joe Namath, but we don't worship them unreservedly.

*U.S. News & World Report, 7-21:17.*

**Margaret Mead**
*Anthropologist*

2

[The time has come] to phase out the nuclear family. We will go back to communities so the children will grow up among large groups of people. The future lies in the community-family of people of different ages and economic levels living close together.

*At women's seminar, Manila, Philippines/*
*The Christian Science Monitor, 8-8:2.*

**Takeo Miki**
*Prime Minister of Japan*

3

My first trip to America was as a student in 1929. Japan was already under the shadow of militarism. And when I went on from America to Europe, I saw Fascism in Italy and the growing strength of Nazism in Germany. I passed through Stalin's Russia on the way to Japan. The freedom I experienced in America, compared to what I had known in Japan and the totalitarian systems I saw in Europe, left an overwhelming impression on me . . . I gained the conviction that democracy is what politics should be all about. That conviction has never left me. People talk these days about a crisis of democracy. Well, we have to defend democracy. There is no alternative.

*Interview, Tokyo/*
*Los Angeles Herald-Examiner, 8-6:(A)6.*

4

Democracies stagnating in the status quo will not last long. But to democracies moving forward with the times, no crisis is insurmountable.

*Paris/*
*The Christian Science Monitor, 11-20:6.*

**Salvador Minuchin**
*Director, Philadelphia Child*
*Guidance Clinic*

5

Those who are studying the problems of the family know that the ones who make it are not those with a romantic view of marriage; they are people who see that the process of life is a process of working through and continuously readapting to new problems and new situations. The point is that even when we marry through emotional commitment—romance—we still marry strangers. We still have to work at mutual accommodation, support and growth. We can love each other and still be strangers, and there is a need to begin to know each other. So we have to debunk the idea that because we love each other the marriage is automatically going to work.

*Interview/*
*U.S. News & World Report, 1-13:45.*

**Daniel P. Moynihan**
*United States Ambassador/Permanent*
*Representative to the United Nations*

6

Liberal democracy is not an ascendant ideology. There aren't many of us left in the world.

# WHAT THEY SAID IN 1975

*(DANIEL P. MOYNIHAN)*

Democracies seem to disappear. I don't notice any new ones emerging. I don't want wholly to associate myself with what he said, but I think we might mark the words of [exiled Soviet author Alexander] Solzhenitsyn, who said in Washington: "The situation is not dire; the situation is not threatening—the situation is catastrophic."

*Interview, New York/Newsweek, 7-14:45.*

## Malcolm Muggeridge
*Author; Former editor, "Punch" magazine*  1

How I envy the Gibbon who, looking back across the centuries at the decline and fall of our Western civilization, as Gibbon himself did on that of Rome, will remark on how, as we systematically destroyed or allowed to be destroyed all the values and restraints of the Christian way of life which we had inherited, we remain convinced that each innovation, each new assault on marital fidelity, on the sanctity of the home and the responsibilities of parenthood, was bound to be conducive to our well-being and enlightenment. There is a nightmare which from time to time afflicts me. I find myself in a BBC studio deep underground, while up above the mushroom cloud gathers and the last vestiges of civilized life disappear. In our studio the discussion proceeds, and a lady participant with a particularly shrill voice is insisting that if only the school age might be raised to 20 and the age of consent lowered to 10, if only birth pills could be distributed to Brownies with their morning milk and extended to tiny tots in the play-schools, if only marriage counseling might begin with the cradle and *Lady Chatterly's Lover* get into the comics, all would yet be well. The barbarians who overran Rome came from without, but ours are home products, trained and suitably brainwashed and conditioned at the public expense. In the light of these antics, it is difficult to resist the conclusion that Western man, having wearied of the struggle by himself, has decided to abolish himself—creating his own boredom out of his own affluence, his own impotence out of his own erotomania, his own vulnerability out of his own strength; himself blowing the trumpet that brings the walls of his own city tumbling down; convincing himself that he is too numerous, and laboring accordingly with pill and scalpel and syringe to make himself fewer in order to fall an easier prey to his enemies. Until at last, having educated himself into imbecility and drugged and polluted himself into stupefaction, he keels over, a weary, battered old brontosaurus, and becomes extinct.

*At Pepperdine University, Oct. 30/*
*Vital Speeches, 12-1:111.*

## Paul Newman
*Actor*  2

One of the great qualities a person can have is to give up things gracefully. I mean, you have to give up your youth, you have to give up your superstardom, you have to give up your children, and finally you have to give up your power. What's tragic is the people who desperately try to hang on when it's simply gone past their time.

*Interview/*
*Ladies' Home Journal, July:94.*

## Pat O'Brien
*Actor*  3

People say you shouldn't dwell on the past, but you can't put a price tag on memories. There are great things that happen to you and you glory in them. You burn incense at the shrine of memory.

*Interview, Los Angeles/*
*Los Angeles Times, 1-19:(Calendar)30.*

## Farah Pahlavi
*Empress of Iran*  4

. . . I always say that in everybody's life there is a good side. Life is not easy. In Iran we say if you have more roof you have more snow. I have the positive things—happiness, friends, all the fantastic things life can give you. I have a large amount of that. At the same time, the negative side exists. One has to find a philosophy of life, to try to stay human and keep the spirit. Modern life has become difficult. It starts with your own personal character problems, feelings and sensibilities, children, husband, friends, family. And then country. And then, after that, there's the whole world . . . There is no limit; and, when you think about it, sometimes it becomes too much. But the thing is to try to come back to your own little self and then to do something . . . to act instead of just worrying and feeling depressed; to try to say, "here I am and I will do whatever I can." You have to try not to let the problems of life dominate you. Because it's a fight, always a fight between light and darkness, evil and good.

*Interview, Washington/*
*The Saturday Evening Post, November:12.*

**Paul VI**
*Pope*

*1*

Technological society has succeeded in multiplying the opportunities for pleasure, but it has great difficulty in generating joy. [The lack of joy in today's life] is perhaps a matter of loneliness, of an unsatisfied thirst for love and for someone's presence, of an ill-defined emptiness.

*San Francisco Examiner & Chronicle,*
*5-25:(This World)2.*

**Charles H. Percy**
*United States Senator, R—Illinois*

*2*

The emphasis in this country is still placed on youth. Or perhaps I should say still *mis*placed.

*Quote, 8-3:49.*

**Peter R. Pouncey**
*Dean, Columbia College, Columbia University*

*3*

. . . progress is made whether *you* contribute to it or not. It is a relatively easy thing to make one's way in the world leaving it where it is; the harder thing is to carry the world forward to a better age.

*San Francisco Examiner & Chronicle,*
*12-7:(This World)2.*

**Ayn Rand**
*Author, Philosopher*

*4*

[On "good" and "evil"]: Since I regard thinking, rationally, as the good, evil is evasion, the refusal to know, the refusal to think. And the refusal to think means the refusal to see

reality, and nothing could be more destructive. A man who has abandoned his tool of perception, his mind, can only destroy himself; he cannot achieve anything. Destruction is easy; anyone can do that. But to achieve, you need thought. Construction cannot be done accidentally; you have to know what you are doing, and that's real power. But that cannot be imposed on anyone by force. And when evil wins, it is because the good people—for whatever reason, usually their philosophical conviction—are afraid to fight, or feel hopeless and feel that it is no use fighting, and they bring on their own destruction.

*Interview, New York/*
*The Christian Science Monitor, 1-6:7.*

**Henry S. Reuss**
*United States Representative, D—Wisconsin*

*5*

I think the country prospers best when the distribution of wealth and income is not too unequal, when power is decentralized, when institutions—government, business, unions—are of a size and not so big that they lose human scale.

*The New York Times, 3-2:(3)5.*

*6*

I believe that there is no defect of democracy which more democracy can't cure.

*The New York Times, 3-2:(3)5.*

**Warren Robbins**
*Director, Museum of African Art, Washington*

*7*

The most difficult thing to deal with today, in our efforts to rediscover national values, is the fact that there are no longer any hard and fast rules to go by; authoritarianism, whether in the home or in the classroom, is passe. Absolutes are out. "Doing your own thing" is the logical extreme of democracy. But even as we are learning not to discriminate in regard to human rights and social opportunity, we must at the same time learn to discriminate more in terms of merit, of judgment, of standards of excellence. Everything may be relative, as Einstein and the cultural anthropologists tell us, but there have to be measures to go by. Even

*481*

# WHAT THEY SAID IN 1975

*(WARREN ROBBINS)*

Einstein had to establish a fixed reference point for his theory of the Universe. Therefore, if general rules are no longer imposed from the top to govern our social behavior and define our responsibilities, then we must apply them ourselves through the individual reassertion of our collective national values, our traditional values as a people.

*The Washington Post, 11-26:(A)10.*

**Yves Saint Laurent**
*Fashion designer*       1

"Quality" in life is the continual question of the value of everything you have or do and the permanent refusal of the facile.

*"W": a Fairchild publication, 2-21:13.*

**Jonas Salk**
*Director, Salk Institute for*
*Biological Studies, San Diego*     2

What is needed now is to draw attention to the nature of man, not merely as a destructive but as a constructive animal, to recognize that men *do* associate for constructive purposes as well as for destructive purposes; that both potentialities coexist. We need to understand the conditions and circumstances for bringing out in man what I prefer to think of as the best—the best in an evolutionary sense. I am not now making a personal judgment as to what I regard as the best—I am referring to Nature now, and saying to Nature, "This is what I would like to do"—and then see how Nature marks my papers.

*Television interview/Center Report, April:22.*

**John Scanzoni**
*Professor of sociology, Indiana*
*University*       3

Divorce doesn't destroy marriage, it preserves it. If there were no divorce, dissatisfactions would build up until suddenly, and perhaps violently, people would simply repudiate the whole institution, much as governments are overthrown.

*Boston, Nov. 15/*
*San Francisco Examiner & Chronicle,*
*11-16:(A)18.*

**Helmut Schmidt**
*Chancellor of West Germany*     4

I think the greatest danger to the Western world today lies in a state of mind. Too many of our people have come to look upon affluence and a democratic, free society as rights guaranteed for all times. They take it for granted that income, living conditions and social justice will automatically improve every year. They fail to appreciate that freedom and prosperity must be constantly earned and renewed through work, vigilance, risks and even sacrifice. When people believe that their well-being and liberty are permanently guaranteed, they feel that they themselves don't have to do anything. I think this attitude is our greatest danger.

*Interview/*
*The Reader's Digest, September:84.*

**Eric Sevareid**
*News commentator, Columbia*
*Broadcasting System*      5

One of the troubles with [Karl] Marx was that he lived before [Sigmund] Freud; human psychology was not his strong suit. The socialists persist in thinking that a worker in a nationalized factory will feel he owns it and will joyously work the harder. The opposite happens, for everybody's property is nobody's property and is so treated. Their emphasis is on sharing wealth over producing wealth, or equality over liberty. The end of this is almost certainly the loss of the wealth and, less certainly, the loss of the liberties.

*CBS News commentary/*
*The National Observer, 5-17:21.*

    6

[On the pioneers who emigrated to the U.S. from Europe and pushed westward across the plains] : You believed that hard work was what a man and woman did in order to matter. Some speak of this now as the "work ethic," as if it were some curious, irrelevant quirk or cult. You were at ease with the word "duty." You knew there could be no rights and privileges without responsibility. You found it natural to teach probity to your children, and self-denial, so that others, too, could have elbow room in which to live. You blamed yourself for misfortune, not others, not the government, not society itself. You knew what was known by ancient philosophers you never read—that civilized life cannot hold together without these values. Now some speak of them as the "Puritan ethic," as a curious outmoded illusion. But you were not wrong.

*At observance of 150th anniversary of organized Norwegian immigration to the U.S., New York/ The New York Times, 10-9:41.*

### John R. Silber
*President, Boston University*

1

Consider a society in which artificially aged and worn blue-jeans sell for more than new ones . . . The younger generation finds a special value in the costumes of poverty and disarray simply because these aspects of life have become far scarcer for children of the middle class than good clothes and comeliness. Just as French aristocrats at the time of the French Revolution took great delight in dressing as peasants and cavorting in bucolic roles, our young people affect the costumes of poverty; in their horizon, the poor are little more than a romantic abstraction.

*Interview/ The Wall Street Journal, 7-23:14.*

2

The intellectual community requires academic freedom. John Milton defined this essential freedom as "liberty to know, to utter, to argue freely according to conscience." This liberty is as necessary to the life of the mind as food to the life of the body . . . There is no need to protect academic freedom to say what is popular, what is generally perceived to be true, and what pleases the government; this last freedom, especially, has never been under challenge. The freedom that is challenged and that must always be defended is the right to study and expound an idea without regard to its orthodoxy. Doctrines, in order to have access to the marketplace of ideas, must not be judged on whether they are liberal or conservative,

progressive or reactionary, revolutionary or counter-revolutionary.

*Before International Association of University Presidents/ The National Observer, 12-13:11.*

### Isaac Bashevis Singer
*Author*

3

For me everything is still mysterious, even the most natural things. When I throw a stone and it falls back to the earth I know that it's gravity, but isn't that a great mystery? Just because you've seen a thing ten times, should it stop being mysterious? A writer gave me once a story about a man with a chopped-off head who talks. I said, "Isn't it marvelous enough that a man *with* a head can talk?"

*Interview, New York/ The New York Times, 10-26:(2)5.*

### John J. Sirica
*Chief Judge, United States District Court for the District of Columbia*

4

We have inherited the great principles upon which liberty is based, but we have not inherited liberty. That must be secured and maintained by every new generation.

*San Francisco Examiner & Chronicle, 6-15:(This World)2.*

### Alexis Smith
*Actress*

5

I think being a great beauty is an enormous disadvantage—like an Elizabeth Taylor who from childhood was being told how beautiful she was. Beautiful girls never have to extend themselves beyond their mere physical presence.

*Interview, New York/ The Dallas Times Herald, 11-2:(F)2.*

### C. P. Snow
*Author*

6

People need a purpose, and purpose—a purposeful life—is one thing an affluent society hasn't been able to provide. Religion gives purpose, but, in a secular age, that is gone. What replaces religion? "The pursuit of happiness" is

# WHAT THEY SAID IN 1975

*(C. P. SNOW)*

a most ridiculous phrase: If you pursue happiness you'll never find it. A great many men and women are desperately trying to find a purpose for themselves. Without it, life is peculiarly empty.

*Quote, 10-5:266.*

## Alexander I. Solzhenitsyn
*Exiled Soviet author*      *1*

Communism is as crude an attempt to explain society and the individual as if a surgeon were to perform his delicate operations with a meat-axe. All that is subtle in human psychology and in the structure of society—which is even more delicate—all of this is reduced to crude economic processes. This whole created being—man—is reduced to matter. It's characteristic that Communism is so devoid of arguments that it has none to advance against its opponents in our Communist countries. It lacks arguments and hence there is the club, the prison, the concentration camp, and insane asylums with forced confinement . . . Communism has never concealed the fact that it rejects all absolute concepts of morality. It scoffs at any consideration of "good" and "evil" as indisputable categories . . . Communism has managed to instill in all of us that these concepts are old-fashioned concepts and laughable. But if we are to be deprived of the concepts of good and evil, what will be left? Nothing but the manipulation of one another. We will decline to the status of animals.

*Before AFL-CIO, New York, July 9/*
*The Wall Street Journal, 7-18:8.*

## Lawrence E. Spivak
*Former producer and moderator,*
*"Meet the Press," National*
*Broadcasting Company*      *2*

I feel strongly about a lot of things—I'm pretty old-fashioned—loyalty, family, parents, respect. I've never had any regard for people who refer to their parents as "my ol' man" or "my ol' lady," or people who call their parents by their first names. I believe strongly in the so-called generation gap. There ought to be a generation gap.

*Interview, Washington/*
*The Washington Post, 11-13:(B)11.*

## Margaret Thatcher
*Member of British Parliament; Leader,*
*British Conservative Party*      *3*

You will not be disappointed in life if you don't get the next thing you have set your heart on. You mustn't, because then you will become bitter. You must still do what you have managed to do as well as you can, because that might offer you even more opportunity in the long run than the way in which you wanted to go. It is much better that way because people who sometimes set out to go from the bottom to the top in a certain time can be rather ruthless in their human relationships, and that can make them very hard. My way, no. Take the opportunity as it comes, but never, never, never ride roughshod over other people. Be thoughtful of them, too.

*Interview, London/*
*San Francisco Examiner & Chronicle,*
*2-23:(B)2.*

## Alvin Toffler
*Author; Former associate editor,*
*"Fortune" magazine*      *4*

We obviously need experts. But experts are very narrow people. They can't be trusted to make policy. They have disciplinary limits. They have territorial self-interest. Their careers, their egos are at stake. An energy expert, for instance, can't help seeing the future as an energy problem, and it isn't; it's so much more. I like the analogy of the eye. An expert focuses, looks deeply. But the layman performs the function of peripheral vision.

*Interview/*
*The Christian Science Monitor, 4-28:30.*

## Gus Turbeville
*President, Emerson College*      *5*

When individuals have been polled on what they believe the purpose of life is, the most frequent response has been "happiness." The second most prevalent answer has been "procreation." Personally, I cannot accept either of these. I think the purpose of life is to achieve morality. And since I think an institution is but an extension of the individual, I think the purpose of a college should be the development of morality coupled with a diligent search for truth. I see no contradiction between these two, since truth sets us free of ignorance and superstition, and morality liberates us from fear and hatred . . . When we see all the evil around us, we become overwhelmed and wonder what one person can do. The answer is plenty. Although it is true that one bad apple will destroy a barrel of fruit, it is equally true that one human being of sterling character—a Gandhi, for example—can influence an entire world. When final judgment is made on us, I do not think a single question will be asked about how others behaved or followed the laws of the universe. In the last analysis, we are going to be held responsible for what we ourselves do. It is only in striving that we grow; it is only by overcoming temptation that character is built; and frequently, it is only by suffering that we get values in perspective. If we can give witness to our beliefs by living a moral life, it must follow as the day the night that others will want to emulate us. If we change one person for the better as a result of our stay on earth, then a major purpose of our existence will have been fulfilled.

*At Emerson College, Nov. 1/*
*Vital Speeches, 12-1:122.*

**Morris K. Udall**
*United States Representative, D—Arizona* 1

If democracy means anything, it means that sooner or later the majority gets its way.

*Washington, June 10/*
*The Washington Post, 6-11:(A)1.*

**Jose Veiga Simao**
*Portuguese Ambassador/Permanent Representative to the United Nations* 2

Democracies may call themselves direct, representative, Western, socialist, organic, bourgeois or popular. They are, however, only democratic when they respect human rights and fundamental freedoms such as liberty of conscience, the right to choose one's religion, one's associates, and to participate in political life at the local and national level by means of free elections, enabling each people to choose periodically its own government.

*On 30th anniversary of UN Charter signing, United Nations, New York, June 26/*
*The Wall Street Journal, 8-19:12.*

**William Van Dusen Wishard**
*Executive Director, Federal Advisory Council on Minority Business Enterprise* 3

For the past several hundred years, the pursuit of freedom has been man's principal preoccupation—freedom from political domination, freedom from hunger and want, freedom from hard physical work, freedom from ignorance and intellectual limitation, freedom from confinements imposed by religious or social dogma. Obviously, in most of the world this search for freedom continues. But in the Western nations, the search for freedom as an overriding preoccupation may have reached its peak in the 1960s, and now the dominant need seems to be for an understanding of order. Order in this sense does not mean restrictive control. Rather it implies the proper balance in life, a sense of proportion. Nature has its own order, its own balances. When that order is distorted, then breakdown occurs. The same is true for human societies. Everywhere today the search is for new patterns of order—social order in the face of unprecedented individual liberties, economic order in the face of new levels of material development and growth, environmental order as human activities threaten to upset nature's balance of the biosphere, international order as additional nations emerge with increased degrees of power, and inner personal order as the pace of change causes dislocations in the inner balance of life.

*At University of California, San Diego, April 9/*
*Vital Speeches, 5-15:463.*

# WHAT THEY SAID IN 1975

**Walter B. Wriston**
*Chairman, Citicorp*
*(First National City Bank,*
*New York)*                                    1

One thing that keeps us all going is that we view our own means of earning our daily bread as in some way making an important contribution to our world. Without bankers, the economy would not function. Without bakers, the world would starve. Without teachers, there would be ignorance. Without politicians, there would be anarchy. Make the list as long as you like and fill in the blanks with any known occupation.

*Vital Speeches,*
*6-15:542.*

**Keenan Wynn**
*Actor*                                        2

[On his late father, Ed Wynn]: My father was not a comedian. Bob Hope is a comedian. Jack Benny was a comedian. My father was—and Red Skelton and Jackie Gleason are—something else again. They are clowns. The difference is this: A comedian can only make you laugh. A clown can make you laugh, but he can turn around and make you cry, too. Nobody made them cry the way my father did.

*Interview/*
*Los Angeles Herald-Examiner, 11-9:(F)3.*

**Allen Yarnell**
*Professor of history, University*
*of California, Los Angeles*                    3

Some historians argue that history can be predictive, like a natural science. But it simply can't. No matter how much history you know, you're not going to be able to predict the future. With all the knowledge I have about contemporary U.S. history, I thought [former U.S. President] Nixon would survive Watergate. And if history can teach us any lesson, it's that historical knowledge doesn't necessarily make political leaders wise—as we saw during the Kennedy Administration. So I tell my students not to come to me for historical insights that will automatically solve the problems they expect to face in their future . . . As long as you realize that history offers no guarantee of wisdom, you then can look upon it realistically as one way to help you understand the present. What any individual does with that understanding depends entirely on that person.

*Interview, UCLA/*
*Los Angeles Herald-Examiner,*
*4-13:(California Living)15.*

**Reubin Askew**
*Governor of Florida*

1

To claim to be a Christian or Jew who loves God and neighbor and not to take an active part in the formation of just social policies affecting those neighbors would seem to deny complete fulfillment of one's faith.

*Quote, 4-27:386.*

**Ralph Bohlmann**
*Acting president, Concordia Seminary, Clayton, Mo.*

2

[On the dispute in the Lutheran Church over whether or not to interpret the Bible literally]: In this dispute it's not simply a case of some creative, bright interpretation of Scripture pitted against some literal, wooden interpretation. It's not that clear-cut. We really *do* agree on the main point of Scripture. The Bible is good news. It proclaims the redemption of man. In the life of Christ, his miracles—walking on water, raising the dead—are not at issue. We believe them. But when Scripture says Herod was a "fox," we're not trying to teach our people that he had four hairy legs. Some of the Bible's language is figurative, some poetic. Why, there's a flexibility in our language even today. We say the sun "rises" and "sets" when we know it really doesn't.

*The National Observer, 6-28:6.*

**Frederick Donald Coggan**
*Archbishop of Canterbury, England*

3

Let us say to our young men today: "There is no finer life than that of a parish priest. Covet this calling. Train for it. Pour your best into it. Glory in it. Count yourself thrice-blessed if you hear God calling you to it."

*At his enthronement, Canterbury, Jan. 24/
The New York Times, 1-25:3.*

**Dan Dodson**
*Scholar-in-residence, Southwestern University*

4

What can be said about our religious institutions? They make the loudest protestations concerning the "brotherhood of man and the Fatherhood of God." Yet they are the most segregated segment of community life. Congregants speak of this church or temple over here as "ours" and the one over there as "theirs." If religion is to be more than tribal, these places of worship have to be God's houses, not sanctuaries belonging to people who want to hide from encounter.

*At symposium, Dallas/
The Dallas Times Herald, 6-5:(B)3.*

**Avery Dulles**
*Professor of theology, Catholic University of America*

5

The Christian cannot be allowed to think that he is living up to his religious obligations if he scrupulously observes all the feasts and fasts of the church without doing anything on behalf of the poor, the sick and others who need his help . . . Large segments of the Catholic clergy and laity have practically no realization of the intimate connection between the province of faith and morals on the one hand and that of social involvement on the other. In examining their consciences, the faithful ask themselves almost scrupulously how many times they have used curse words or entertained what are called "bad thoughts"—meaning almost invariably temptations against sexual purity—but they rarely accuse themselves of having fallen short in contributing to the common good of the society in which they live.

*At religious convocation, Catholic University/
The Washington Post, 4-18:(B)6.*

6

There is no dogmatic or scriptural bar to marriage of the clergy. It is a man-made rule, or

# WHAT THEY SAID IN 1975

discipline. The question gets to be whether you can work it out practically, whether you can get a sufficient number of priests who will accept celibacy and be contented with it . . . We don't have half as many seminarians as 10 years ago, and the ranks of the clergy are somewhat depleted. A number have left the active ministry partly because of celibacy. We are going to feel it 10 years from now. So that is a consideration. There are, however, certain advantages to celibacy. More mobility, not only in foreign missions but in the ministry to the poor and under conditions where there is minimum salary. Priests are more at the disposal of the church to move around. Celibacy is a greater sign of dedication to Christ and the church, and many lay people feel that a priest can be more at their disposal if he isn't at the beck and call of his family all the time. There are things on the other side. Some of the lay people feel that priests would understand them better if they were married priests. But then, too, there are economic reasons to consider. These would cause a real problem because the clergy are not well paid, you know. A husband generally feels an obligation to support his wife and children as well as he can. Churches would have a very difficult time meeting higher payrolls. All the dioceses that I know about are reporting budget deficits now. So unless giving to the churches is sharply increased, we couldn't support a married clergy. One way around this might be to have priests take a second job. But then you would have a part-time clergy, and that leads to difficulties of its own.

*Interview, Washington/*
*Los Angeles Times, 6-4:(2)7.*

## Jay W. Forrester
*Professor of management, Massachusetts*
*Institute of Technology*                                    1

Through his religious concepts, man has established for himself, in his own mind, a unique position at the center of the universe. At one time, this meant literally the physical center, with the sun and stars revolving around the earth. Far more recently, it has meant man as a uniquely chosen creature in nature, with special rights and privileges over the natural surroundings. But that egocentric view of man at the center, with nature at his disposal, is becoming as untenable as the geocentric theory of the world at the center of the universe . . .

*The Washington Post, 6-8:(C)4.*

## David P. Gardner
*President, University of Utah*                              2

The religious dimension is an inseparable part of our tradition. No "higher" learning is conceivable without the discipline of faith, a discipline devoted to searching out and testing value and first principles as other disciplines search out and test empirical fact. Religion is not a "gimmick," no trusty golf club to turn to only when you're in the rough. It is a daily companion and critic asking us to take off our blinders rather than putting them on, daring us to confront often hard realities . . . Hope is the anchor of life. Religious hope is that and, we might add, also the wind and the sail.

*At prayer breakfast, March 7/*
*Vital Speeches, 4-15:414.*

## Billy Graham
*Evangelist*                                                3

[Being a religious leader is] a responsibility of leadership that I was really not prepared for by way of formal education. I'm called upon to answer questions on every conceivable subject, and I feel terribly unqualified. I run scared all the time that I'll say something or do something that will bring reproach to the Kingdom of God and to the church . . . I have to think: How's this going to sound in India where I minister? Or, how's it going to sound in Africa? Now, when it comes to biblical issues and moral issues I take a strong stand. But if it's an issue of who's right and who's wrong in about 45 wars going on around the world, it's pretty hard for me to make these decisions.

*Interview, Hong Kong/People, 12-22:22.*

## James Gustafson
*Professor of theological ethics,*
*University of Chicago Divinity School*                      4

I question the competence of many pastors to make moral judgments about everything. I also question the competence of church bodies, at their annual conventions and convocations, to deliver moral pronouncements on everything that's mentioned in the morning paper—with little or no connection with moral principles, without dissent, without adequate research, without careful argumentation, without stating any reasons that are related to theological grounds. Churches have a moral obligation to combine their ethical theory and theology with an understanding of the technicality of the issues on which they pronounce. In many cases they're moving beyond their competence in making moral judgments from the pulpit or the platform.

*The National Observer, 12-27:12.*

**Jesse A. Helms**
*United States Senator, R—North Carolina*
*1*

The physical and moral strength of the American republic rests upon our religious heritage. We believe in the ethic of hard work and a just reward for our labors. This is one of the reasons why we are such an industrious and prosperous nation. We are guided by religious principles that underlie our political and legal system. This is one of the reasons why Americans are a generous and humane people. We are indeed a religious people, and this is why we are free. Throughout the world today, tyranny reigns where the free exercise of religion is prohibited by government. In the totalitarian dictatorships, religious prayer has been replaced by the cult of the personality. The modern utopian regimes, which hold their citizens in bondage, cannot tolerate the existence of religion, and they fear its influence among the people. Indeed, they promote secularism as the state religion.

*Quote, 2-23:185.*

**Ralph W. Lewis**
*Professor, department of natural science,*
*Michigan State University*
*2*

When a religious person contemplates the greatness of his religion, all the products of the scientific world seem small. And the presumed contradictions with religion will be seen as mi-

nor items of trivial consequence in the large panorama of his religious view.

*The Christian Science Monitor, 9-10:25.*

**Edgar F. Magnin**
*Rabbi, Wilshire Bouelvard Temple,*
*Los Angeles*
*3*

People ask if I have any objection to women rabbis. Of course not. It is not traditional, but we have dropped many traditions. I am not concerned with the sex of the ministry, but only with its brains and dedication. The first requisite of a rabbi, or, for that matter, any minister, is sincerity; but sincerity without judgment can be utterly futile and sometimes even bad. Leadership demands a sense of realism combined with idealism; or, if you prefer, idealism mixed with a sense of what is practical.

*Los Angeles Times, 1-4:(1)21.*

**Robert Marshall**
*President, Lutheran Church in America*
*4*

We need to know what the church stands for, and we want to hear it again and clearly . . . We have come to the time when these assumptions about Christianity are so eroded that there is increased need both for clarity and simplicity.

*The New York Times, 3-9:(1)33.*

**Humberto Cardinal Medeiros**
*Roman Catholic Archbishop of Boston*
*5*

The church is not here to be popular, but to proclaim the good news of the gospel to those who like it and to those who don't.

*Quote, 2-9:121.*

**William Lee Miller**
*Professor of religion, Indiana University*
*6*

Religion's prime role is as the shaper of public persons and not in its direct interventions. That is not to say that there should not be any direct intervention. If religion's primary role is to bring the person to the transcendent, that is not its exclusive role. There is a connection between the transcendent and our ordinary secular life, including politics. Where a body of

# WHAT THEY SAID IN 1975

*(WILLIAM LEE MILLER)*

religious people—Christians, Jews, or whatever they may be—understand their religious faith in relationship to a particular issue in the political society, then collective intervention is right. The role of the American churches, for example, in the civil-rights movement was good and important.

*Interview, Indiana University/*
*The Center Magazine, July-Aug.:68.*

**Paul VI**
*Pope*

1

You young people, at this critical, historical and spiritual moment, are you also willing, like the young people of that Palm Sunday in Jerusalem, to recognize Jesus as the Messiah, as Christ the Lord, as the center and cornerstone of your lives? It is a matter of emerging from that disturbed state of doubt, uncertainty and ambiguity in which many young people today so often find themselves. It is a matter of overcoming the phase of spiritual crisis which is characteristic of the transition from adolescence to youth, and then from youth to maturity.

*Palm Sunday mass, Vatican City, March 23/*
*Los Angeles Herald-Examiner, 3-24:(A)4.*

2

[On sainthood]: We all have some idea of the meaning of this highest title; but it is still difficult for us to make an exact analysis of it. Being a saint means being perfect, with a perfection that attains the highest level that a human being can reach. A saint is a human creature fully conformed to the will of God. A saint is a person in whom all sin—the principle of death—is canceled out and replaced by the living splendor of divine grace. The analysis of the concept of sanctity brings us to recognize in a soul the mingling of two elements that are entirely different but which come together to produce a single effect: sanctity. One of these elements is the human and moral element, raised to the degree of heroism; heroic virtues are always required by the church for the recognition of a person's sanctity. The second element is the mystical element, which expresses the measure and form of divine action in the person chosen by God to realize in herself—always in an original way—the image of Christ. The science of sanctity is therefore the most interesting, the most varied, the most surprising and the most fascinating of all the studies of that ever-mysterious being which is man.

*At mass in which Elizabeth Ann Seton was*
*canonized a saint, Vatican City, Sept. 14/*
*The New York Times, 9-15:8.*

**Jacob A. O. Preus**
*President, Lutheran Church-Missouri Synod*

3

The basic problem in most churches today—and for the past 200 years—has been the use of the historical-critical method for interpreting the Bible . . . The Book is to be believed, even if it's contrary to human understanding. But lately there have been more interpretive theories and guesses about the Bible than fleas on a dog—based on a small amount of data and a large amount of speculation.

*The National Observer, 6-28:6.*

**Joe Rainey**
*Methodist chaplain, American University,*
*Washington*

4

Hypocrisy can really be destructive of a ministry. There's been an assumption by many clergy that you have to play a role and to pretend you're a success even when you're not. Only recently have some people in this profession let in doubts about their own strength. It used to be that you *never* let on if there were difficulties with your marriage, your finances or your children. Now, it seems, there's more room for a choice: Do you present yourselves as having it all together, or as a fellow pilgrim, with special training and functions but also imperfect and not morally superior? This is an issue of honesty that many clergy are just facing.

*The National Observer, 12-27:12.*

**Larry Rasmussen**
*Professor of ethics, Wesley Theological*
*Seminary, Washington*

5

Sometimes the clergy tries to create problems for people when they really don't have them. A minister can do this, often unconsciously, by saying to a parishioner with a moral problem that "only God can be the answer." It may be a way of keeping people under their control, a way to feel useful and needed. But then there's a strong temptation to exploit this dependence. Once you make religion a condition for certain answers, there you go.

*The National Observer, 12-27:12.*

**Isaac Bashevis Singer**
*Author*
1

I really believe Jewishness is not only something learned; it is already in our blood. . . . if you have lived a certain kind of life for long generations, it enters the genes. And even if it's not in the genes, it's in the soul—and the soul is even more important than the genes.

*Interview, New York/*
*The New York Times Magazine, 3-23:28.*

2

In our house [when I was young], religion was the air we breathed. Now I see there was a lot of good in it. The feeling is always there that there is a right way and a wrong way, that we have free choice every minute of our life. We are always getting from the Almighty a menu. We can always choose. That we often choose the wrong way is our fault.

*Interview/*
*"W": a Fairchild publication, 9-19:2.*

**Robert H. Smith**
*Professor of religion, College of*
*Wooster (Ohio)*
3

Religion by its very nature claims to have a higher, usually absolute, source of truth, the tapping of which will yield an abundance of strength and good-will. No other profession claims to have this. It's a unique presupposition that sometimes keeps us from hard-nosed self-examination. We pride ourselves on our personal introspection, but that can also produce some strange blind spots. It might even reinforce some negative things about the ministry because of the feeling that "I've worked it out with God." The clergy that deliberately and maliciously abuse their position are few and far between, I believe. But those who *thoughtlessly* abuse it are far more numerous. They probably do this in all innocence by compartmentalizing their ethical thinking.

*The National Observer, 12-27:12.*

**Leonard Swindler**
*Theologian and church historian,*
*Temple University*
4

To talk of God in human language always is a trap. You can't win. When you use the finitude of language to try to talk of something infinite, you're inevitably bound to speak in limited human terms. This can become idolatry, and verbal idols are more dangerous than stone images, which you can smash with your hands. You can't do that to an idea.

*Interview/The Washington Post, 6-6:(C)9.*

**John H. Tietjen**
*Former president, Concordia Seminary,*
*Clayton, Mo.*
5

[On the dispute in the Lutheran Church over whether or not to interpret the Bible literally]: The Bible is not really in dispute here. It's really a disagreement over the nature of interpretations. We recognize the reality of miracles and the reality of the Resurrection. The story of Jonah swallowed by the whale is a good example. Our opponents say that story must be taken literally, as a historical event involving an actual individual. We see it as a narrative, a story to proclaim the truth of God. No matter how you take it, the message is the same. And if you rely on literal facts from the Bible to support your belief, you can get into all sorts of trouble, especially with accounts of Christ's Resurrection. Were there two angels or one? Or two men? Or four men and one woman? It all depends on which account you read. His disciples are told Jesus will be in Galilee, then he turns up in Jerusalem. In one account the women don't tell the disciples Christ has risen; in another they do, but only John and Peter believe them. I can believe in the Resurrection of Christ, but not because of these literal descriptions, which are contradictory. It's my hope that from this turmoil can emerge a united Lutheranism.

*Interview/The National Observer, 6-28:6.*

# Space · Science · Technology

**Sydney Brenner**
*Senior scientist, British Medical*
*Research Council*
1

[On genetic engineering]: We live at a time when there is a great anti-science attitude developing in society and government. It is very important that the way we move does not offend this situation any more. Is there a chance that in this issue we can be allowed to be trusted to regulate ourselves? For if we fail, and merely adopt token regulations, we will lose. They will come in with regulations.

*At genetic engineering conference, Asilomar,*
*Calif./The Washington Post, 3-9:(B)4.*

**William Sloane Coffin**
*Chaplain, Yale University*
2

Curiously, I think the scientists often have more to teach us about humanity than the humanists because philosophy or literature professors can say, "I don't have to take a position on anything," whereas good scientists now know that they can't be neutral. A person who's about to break the genetic code, if he's a half-way decent human being, has to stop and say, "Should I be doing this?"

*Interview/*
*The Wall Street Journal, 2-25:18.*

**Loren C. Eiseley**
*Professor of anthropology and history*
*of science, University of Pennsylvania*
3

If the human race is to survive into the next century, scientific technology will have to learn how to control the devastating forces it has unwittingly turned loose on the planet—the world's exploding population, the reckless pollution of the environment, the spiraling arms race and the expenditure of irreplaceable energy. All of these disasters are rooted in the successes of our scientific technology of the past—from things like medical advances, sanitary

engineering, atomic energy and the gasoline-combustion engine. This is the great paradox of the scientific age.

*Interview/*
*U.S. News & World Report, 3-3:43.*

**Jay W. Forrester**
*Professor of management, Massachusetts*
*Institute of Technology*
4

Technology has been improving while at the same time many aspects of our social conditions have been worsening. Some people are beginning to wonder if there might not be a connection between the two. Is it possible that the time is past when better technology automatically means better living?

*The Washington Post, 6-8:(C)4.*

**Philip Handler**
*President,*
*National Academy of Sciences*
5

There is a compelling responsibility for the academic to direct to the attention of the larger society that newly acquired understanding of phenomena, processes or trends which may pose a threat to that society or which can, predictably, be utilized to enhance its welfare. Accordingly, each time that responsibility is accepted, the academic must assure his fellows that the matter he directs to public attention has been established with all of the scholarly rigor that he ordinarily brings to his personal research and that is required by the highest canons of his own discipline. It is deeply regrettable that that has not always been the case, particularly when, in recent times, various of our colleagues have cried alarm with respect to questions of the environment.

*At American University/*
*The Wall Street Journal, 12-19:14.*

**Noel W. Hinners**
*Associate Administrator for Space Science,*
*National Aeronautics and Space*
*Administration of the United States*
*1*

In the last 400 years we learned we weren't the center of the universe but only a mere speck in the scheme of things. But finding life elsewhere would finally crumble that [center-of-the-universe] image and convince the holdouts. It would be one of the most compelling arguments that man, that life on earth, is not unique ... Realizing that we're not alone would do something toward the attitudes of where we're going and what we're trying to accomplish with our lives. Some people said those things after the *Apollo* [space] flights, but I doubt it really did much. I'm pretty cynical about man ... Once people believe that life has been able to originate and evolve elsewhere in the solar system, then they may say there is probably intelligent life in other reaches of the universe. I hope we do find life. It would be so exciting.

*Houston/*
*The Dallas Times Herald, 4-7:(D)8.*

**James Jones**
*Author*
*2*

... the United States is facing a problem which has never been faced by a nation before. We have developed a truly technological society. Technology works better than non-technology. But one of the basic problems is how to save some small breathing space for the individual to have his say, to develop his own thoughts in a society that's becoming increasingly technological. That's the basic problem we have to cope with.

*Interview, Sagaponack, N.Y./*
*"W": a Fairchild publication, 7-25:15.*

**Polykarp Kusch**
*Professor of physics, University of*
*Texas, Dallas*
*3*

We, the scientists, find pleasure in scientific knowledge. We are exhilarated when we learn of a new discovery or of a new formulation of science; we are exalted when the discovery is our own. If our constituency shares, in a modest way, the pleasure and stimulation we find in science, the satisfaction in understanding the order that pervades the universe, the future of science would be more certain. The future of science cannot be separated from the future of civilization. If my hopes for the future of mankind and his civilization are realized, then I am confident of a bright future for science.

*At Nobel Conference on the Future of Science/*
*The Dallas Times Herald, 11-16:(B)3.*

**Alexei Leonov**
*Soviet cosmonaut*
*4*

[On the experience of traveling in space]: It is difficult to communicate. What would your impression be if you found yourself alone with stars above you, stars in front of you, stars everywhere? That was my impression. You can look at the earth through the spaceship window for an entire day and night and never get tired of it.

*The Christian Science Monitor, 10-2:2.*

**Joseph T. Ling**
*Vice president, 3M Company*
*5*

Many people ... blame technology for several of society's present problems, including pollution, congestion, accidents, certain occupational hazards and more. But I look at it differently. I do not believe technology by and of itself is responsible for these problems. I believe the problem rests with those who apply technology—and, in so doing, fail to recognize or control the undesirable side effects. It's somewhat like the child who cuts a finger with a knife while slicing an apple. He doesn't throw the knife away because of this misfortune. Rather, the child learns to control his use of the knife, and it becomes a helpful instrument. Recently, I think we have learned to be much more thoughtful with technology. We are applying technology with greater care. As a result, I think technology can provide creative and effective solutions to many current problems. But, like any other discipline, technology has its limitations. For instance, in addition to the side effects, development of successful technology often requires substantial initial

# WHAT THEY SAID IN 1975

*(JOSEPH T. LING)*

investment and adequate time frames. I am not a blind worshipper of technology. But when everyone understands its strengths and weaknesses, technology can be applied wisely.

*Before American Water Works Association, Minneapolis, June 9/Vital Speeches, 8-1:614.*

**Bernard Lovell**
*Director, Nuffield Radio Astronomy Laboratories, Jodrell Bank, England; President, British (Science) Association* 1

Modern science is a blessing—and a curse. A very clear example of this duplicity is the use of the rocket. The rocket was developed for warlike purposes in World War II, although, of course, it already had a long history. Since that time, the rocket has been a vital part of the military arsenals of the world. But the rocket also is used to launch scientific instruments into space, and this has enhanced our knowledge of the universe in a very remarkable way. With relatively minor changes, a rocket today can either carry warheads to destroy mankind or scientific instruments for the investigation of the remote parts of the universe. This is a clear example in the physical sciences, but other scientists, almost without exception, can give similar examples of this thin dividing line between the good and evil results of science.

*Interview, Jodrell Bank, England/ U.S. News & World Report, 12-1:53.*

**Margaret Mead**
*Anthropologist* 2

At the end of World War II we [the U.S.] thought we just had to spread our technology all over the world: Everybody would have plenty to eat and lovely skyscrapers and schools just like ours, and the whole world would be saved. And we've discovered it doesn't work like that, and that if we tried to spread our technology over the whole world we'd simply devastate the world. We'd cut down every tree, we'd use up every single resource and we'd leave a desert.

*Before Simmons College graduating class/ Parade, 6-29:4.*

**Farah Pahlavi**
*Empress of Iran* 3

. . . the environment is being rapidly degraded by the thrust of an unbridled technology that has lost sight of the ultimate aim of progress, namely, man and his total well-being . . . Should one, under the circumstances, condemn, as some would suggest, the acceleration of technological progress? Or even proclaim a moratorium on scientific research? I do not believe so, because scientific discoveries are man's creation, and therefore cannot be held responsible. In my opinion, the basic cause of our present dilemma lies elsewhere. The human race today is at the mercy of the unchecked capabilities of its own inventions— inventions that are blind to their own consequences, or to the means to rectify them. Therefore, a pressing task lies before us if we seek to avert a catastrophe upon future generations. This task is nothing less than correcting the detrimental effects of technology while at the same time restoring the balance between men of science and ordinary people . . . Thus, the problem before us is how to reconcile the computer with the demands of a spirituality that underlines the very substance of human life. How to harness the resources of science and technology without depriving mankind of his human heritage—this is the challenge that we face and must surmount.

*Before board of trustees of Aspen (Colo.) Institute for Humanistic Studies/ The New York Times, 7-26:23.*

**William Proxmire**
*United States Senator, D-Wisconsin* 4

The National Science Foundation continues to pour its support into the academic oligarchy of the large universities. The so-called advisory panels that review NSF programs and projects are, in turn, packed with representatives from those universities that get the grants. I think it is high time the NSF looked past the East and West Coast academic monopolies to find other important contributors to our basic and applied research technology.

*The Dallas Times Herald, 3-2:(A)16.*

**Muammar el-Qaddafi**
*Chief of State of Libya*
1

Soon the atom will have no secrets for anybody. Some years ago we could hardly procure a fighter squadron. Tomorrow we will be able to buy an atom bomb and all its parts. The nuclear monopoly is about to be broken.

*The Washington Post, 2-7:(A)22.*

**Carl Sagan**
*Professor of astronomy and space sciences, Cornell University*
2

What I see about the space program that pays many times over for its cost is the scientific perspective it provides. My favorite example is meteorology. An accurate weather forecast—especially, let's say, a week in advance—is unheard-of. Meteorology is a tough field. The physics of fluid dynamics is an extremely difficult subject. Now, where you have a science such as this which presents theoretical difficulties, you usually try experiments. But how can you experiment on the weather? On a small scale you can, but certainly not on a global scale. An instructive experiment on global weather would be to stop the rotation of the earth. Well, that is expensive, it has certain undesirable side effects, and there'd certainly be people complaining! So what do you do? It turns out that right next door to us in space is a planet with the same mass and the same radius. But it essentially does not rotate. It's called Venus. Here is a natural experiment which nature has kindly provided for us. So let's try to understand the simpler meteorology of Venus.

*Interview/*
*U.S. News & World Report, 5-19:73.*

**Jonas Salk**
*Director, Salk Institute for Biological Studies, San Diego, California*
3

One needs to build the case for the value of scientists to our society and point out that it is the use to which scientific knowledge has been put by people who want power and wealth for themselves and who—ostensibly for the public good—have at times gone too far. That is self-evident. The province of science is to find reme-

dies for social problems... The scientist has become the scapegoat. We are told that if the scientists will go away, if the scientists would stop working, everything would be fine. Someone recently talked seriously about a moratorium on science "to make everything better."

*Television interview/Center Report, April:23.*

**Vitali Sevastyanov**
*Soviet cosmonaut*
4

Cosmonautics, when its goals are creative, has a great deal to offer. It has already made a genuine contribution to the terrestrial economy... With the help of cosmonautics, new deposits of oil, gas and numerous other minerals have been discovered. And what about the long-term weather forecasts, the instant information on typhoons and forest fires, the many other solutions contributed by artificial satellites? All this saves effort, energy and material resources. In the not-too-distant future, freight spaceships will be carrying minerals from the moon, Mars and Venus to the earth. I think no one would object to such trips.

*Interview, Moscow/*
*Los Angeles Times, 7-21:(2)7.*

**Irving S. Shapiro**
*Chairman, E. I. du Pont de Nemours & Company*
5

... it is important for all us non-scientists to come to understand that, while the scientific method is impartial and circumspect, it does not follow that all who profess to be scientists can pass the test of objectivity when scientific issues become a matter of public interest. It is especially important for people in positions of public responsibility to understand that scientists, too, are subject to common temptations. A desire for publicity or recognition, or some other subjective consideration, can lead anyone to an advocate's position, and that does not always produce a full disclosure of the facts on the other side of the question. It is not likely that this will change—even for scientists—but there is reason to hope that knowledgable people will develop enough sophistication to see that conclusions on public-policy issues are not always correct merely because

# WHAT THEY SAID IN 1975

*(IRVING S. SHAPIRO)*

someone with a Ph.D. has pronounced a judgment.

*At Weitzmann Institute of Science, New York, Oct. 13/Vital Speeches, 12-1:109.*

## H. Guyford Stever
*Director, National Science Foundation*
1

We as a nation must engender a sense of urgency in our science policies—not because we face any immediate crisis, or because we are in danger of running out of any particular resource or running into any major environmental disaster within the next few years, but because—to put it bluntly—time is not on our side in many of the things we have to do for the future and many of the transitions we have to make. These transitions, in energy, in industry, in institutional and social changes, and in our international activities, will take time, particularly if they are to be made in a thoughtful way based on sound research.

*At conference sponsored by Franklin Institute, Philadelphia, Oct. 29/ The New York Times, 10-30:32.*

## Wernher Von Braun
*Former Deputy Associate Administrator, National Aeronautics and Space Administration of the United States*
2

Science tries to understand nature, and religion tries to understand the creator. Science doesn't have a moral dimension to begin with. It is like a knife: If you give it to a surgeon or a murderer, each will use it differently.

*San Francisco Examiner & Chronicle, 3-9:(This World)2.*

## Muhammad Ali
*Heavyweight boxing champion of the world*

1

Horses get old, cars get old, the Pyramids of Egypt are crumbling. I want to retire while I'm still on top. As of now, this [his upcoming title fight with Joe Bugner] is the last time you will see Muhammad Ali in a fight . . . My wife is tired. I don't see my children. My life with them means more to me than boxing. My schedule was to fight Joe Frazier and George Foreman this year, then retire. But I looked at my bank account. I got $2-million cash, $3-million in property. I got a movie to make, college speaking engagements. I want to go into the Muslim Islamic ministry. Fighting, it's impossible for me to do my religious work, it's impossible for me to make the movie coming up.

*News conference, Kuala Lumpur, Malaysia,*
*June 23/The New York Times, 6-24:27.*

## Dick Allen
*Baseball player, Philadelphia "Phillies"*

2

The main thing he [the baseball manager] has to do is put the best nine men on the field. You would think this is simple, but it really isn't, for several reasons. First is the human factor; a manager will play favorites. Second, a manager may play favorites of the fans and the press. And third, he may be restrained by outside elements. Color quotas, for instance. I don't know if it's still this way in the majors, but we know in the past it was the unwritten law that no team would put more than five blacks on the field. Maybe five blacks weren't good enough to be on the field, and maybe seven should have been there. But these are the kind of things that have given managers problems.

*Interview, Los Angeles/*
*Los Angeles Herald-Examiner, 8-28:(C)1.*

## George Allen
*Football coach, Washington "Redskins"*

3

I like rookies if they have enough ability. I have found out over the years that many, many people do not evaluate youth properly. They make a mistake. Just because a man is 22, 23 or 24 years old doesn't mean that he is a football player, or a hockey player, or a basketball player, or a baseball player. I appreciate the type of rookies like the Dick Butkuses, the Gale Sayers, the Tom Macks. I haven't had any rookies play here because we haven't had any who have had that type of ability. I think that if you have to play too many rookies, too many young people, that you are not going to win a championship, you are not going to be in the playoffs. I would hope that we have a rookie play, but I found that many young people make the squad and two or three years later they are gone. So that makes me know that somebody has made a mistake in evaluating them. And that's my responsibility.

*Interview, Washington/*
*Los Angeles Herald-Examiner, 1-26:(B)5.*

4

I think we need some sort of a reserve rule. You just can't throw open the game to the highest bidder. Actually, the players have a pretty good deal right now. Where in industry does anybody have a better deal—pension, insurance, good salaries, fringe benefits? You can't continue to keep doing things for the players. The fans can't continue to afford to pay increased prices. If we have no reserve clause, I think eventually we'd kill pro football.

*Interview, Washington/*
*The Dallas Times Herald, 2-18:(D)3.*

5

Salaries in professional sports right now are astronomical. We have had a situation where one of our players was paid at a rate of about $90,000 for each hour he was in a ball game

# WHAT THEY SAID IN 1975

over a four-year period. I don't mean his salary called for that, but that's what he got . . . Every player has an agent. We recently liked the looks of a player who showed up uninvited at a tryout camp. We offered him a contract. You know what he said? "I'll have to show that to my agent." This is the age of attorneys. Every time you make a decision, you have to check it with an attorney.

*Interview, Washington/*
*Nation's Business, September:46.*

## Walter Alston
*Baseball manager, Los Angeles "Dodgers"*
1

Perhaps the truest axiom in baseball is that the toughest thing to do is repeat. The tendency is to relax without even knowing it, the feeling being, "we did it last year, so we can do it again."

*Interview, Vero Beach, Fla./*
*Los Angeles Herald-Examiner, 2-27:(C)1.*

## Sparky Anderson
*Baseball manager, Cincinnati "Reds"*
2

[On being a manager]: Communication [with the players] is the most important thing. You've got to talk to them; you've got to work at it. There's not enough time spent talking. Power should never be used. The manager who uses power has lost control. Common sense— that's the key. It's what I talk to them about. I have no rules, but they know how I feel about long hair and a number of other things. I can't count how many times I've told them that I think it's a disgrace when you see a guy who's a hell of a player who isn't also a hell of a person.
*Los Angeles Times, 8-1:(3)8.*

3

[On the manager's job]: Get the players and then let them go play ball. Don't build it up into something bigger than it is. This is the easiest game in the world . . . There are no guidelines as to who is a good manager. Is Walter Alston dumber this year than he was last because we beat the *Dodgers* this time? Am I smarter? Why all this fuss about big-league managers anyway? I'm no smarter now about base-

ball than I was in 1965, but nobody wanted to talk to me then because I was in Rock Hill, South Carolina.

*Interview, Cincinnati/*
*The Christian Science Monitor, 10-16:11.*

4

There's a lot of people I'm very disappointed in because [success] has changed their whole life. I think the major leagues have hurt a lot of people. A lot of them have never been able to cope with it. There's a lot of heartaches. There are people who got everything they dreamed of, had success and turned it into failure. You can't tell me a guy who acts like that is really enjoying himself. I know a few guys who had one year of success and all of a sudden they're somebody else. But it's funny, when they're fired, how humble they become. This game has taken a lot of guys over the years, who would have had to work in factories and gas stations, and made them prominent people. I only had a high-school education and, believe me, I had to cheat to get that. There isn't a college in the world that would have me. And yet in this business you can walk into a room with millionaires, doctors, professional people and get more attention than they get. I don't know any other business where you can do that.

*Interview, Los Angeles/*
*Los Angeles Times, 12-26:(3)8.*

## Richie Ashburn
*Former baseball player, Philadelphia "Phillies"*
5

[On pitchers]: After 15 years of facing them, you don't really get over them. They're devious. They're the only players in the game allowed to cheat. They throw illegal pitches and they sneak foreign substances on the ball. They can inflict pain whenever they wish. And they're the only ones on the diamond who have high ground. That's symbolic. You know what they tell you in a war: "Take the high ground first."

*Los Angeles Times, 6-16:(3)2.*

## Arthur Ashe
*Tennis player*
6

Who knows how much another man wants to win? It isn't something you wear on your sleeve. But sometimes I find myself just dangling on the court—loose mentally as well as physically—and asking myself: "What am I doing out here in front of all these people?"

*The New York Times, 2-2:(5)17.*

1

There is a difference between the Latin temperament and the Nordic temperament. I am aware of that when I play [Italy's Adriano] Panatta and when I play [Sweden's Bjorn] Borg. Their temperaments come out in their tennis, and all this has to be remembered by their opponents when planning tactics. I think of it all the time.

*Interview, Stockholm/*
*Los Angeles Herald-Examiner, 12-6:(B)3.*

### Red Auerbach
*General manager, Boston "Celtics"*
*basketball team*

2

I ask the player, "Are you happy with this contract?" He'll say, yes, he is. "Fine," I tell him, "I'm happy with it too. We're both happy. But I have one provision before we sign this contract. There will not be any renegotiation, because I want you to be aware that if you get hurt, we take care of you, we pay the full contract; and if you have a bad year, we're still obligated to pay. Remember, you have security and peace of mind for two-three years. You have everything. I'm the one taking the big gamble, not you. I ask only one thing. Don't ever ask to renegotiate a term contract with me. Remember, you're the one who asked for it in the first place."

*Los Angeles Times, 2-4:(3)2.*

### Ernie Banks
*Former baseball player*

3

[On why he never wanted to be a manager]: I feel it's the type of job that would change your personality unless you're geared for it. I never wanted anything that would affect me as a human being. Being a manager can make you a very bitter person. You lose—the fans boo and you're fired. You develop a bitter personality the rest of your life and don't know why. You're bitter toward everybody. Unless you make up your mind to do the best you can with

the players you have and realize all managers get fired, which is thinking negative to begin with, it can change your personality. That's the reason why I never pressed it.

*Interview/*
*The Dallas Times Herald, 4-17:(D)1.*

### Jim Barr
*Baseball pitcher, San Francisco "Giants"*

4

An umpire is a human being. That is simple enough to say, but go a step further and we will agree the mind of a human being is a complex mechanism. In my experience, a typical umpire behind the plate tends to favor the pitcher with control. If you do not give up many walks the umpire will say to himself, "This guy knows where he is throwing . . . so if he thinks he has hit the corner of the plate, he probably has." But a pitcher who lacks control will not be given the benefit. Therefore, a pitcher should be both able and wise. He should know when to argue a little bit, when to let the other guy fall into a trap by arguing, and when to simply say nothing.

*San Francisco Examiner &*
*Chronicle, 7-13:(Sunday Punch)8.*

### Frank Beard
*Golfer*

5

A slump in golf is worse than one in baseball or basketball or football. It's exaggerated. In baseball, basketball and football you have the rest of the team to pick you up until you come out of your slump. In golf, you're in it all by yourself. I have no one to pick me up.

*Interview, Philadelphia/*
*The Dallas Times Herald, 6-12:(B)5.*

### Johnny Bench
*Baseball player, Cincinnati "Reds"*

6

. . . I think we've [the *Reds*] probably been the best team in baseball during that period [the past five years]. Our problem is that we haven't always had the best pitching. Rival teams with good pitching have been able to stop us in a short series. Look, we were part of two World Series recently and that means we had to go through a playoff to get there. But

# WHAT THEY SAID IN 1975

*(JOHNNY BENCH)*

the only thing people remember about us is that we lost. Two years ago we went to seven games with Oakland. To me, that means the *Athletics* beat us in a one-game World Series. I'm not knocking winning. I like to win. But any time you get to the finals of something that originally involved 24 big-league teams, I think you've done something special. In a way, I feel the *Reds* are a lot like the Minnesota [football] *Vikings*. Minnesota has been to the Super Bowl three times recently, which is a pretty good indication of their over-all balance. But a lot of fans will tell you the *Vikings* are losers. That kind of reasoning turns me off.

*Interview, Tampa, Fla./*
*The Christian Science Monitor, 3-12:7.*

1

[Rebutting complaints that he is over-paid at $175,000 a year]: Jimmy Connors plays two tennis matches and winds up with $850,000, and Muhammad Ali fights one bout and winds up with five million bucks. Me, I play 190 games—if you count exhibitions—and *I'm* over-paid!

*The New York Times, 5-25:(5)4.*

## George Blanda
*Football player, Oakland "Raiders"*

2

I don't believe in strikes [by football players]. I work for an excellent organization in the *Raiders*—excellent coaches and ownership, and I get excellent pay. My obligation is to my ownership, not to Ed Garvey [of the NFL Players Association] ... Sometimes I think that the only thing that will come out of these negotiations between the owners and the players is that we'll be keeping the incompetents and the malcontents. What seems to be overlooked by many of the players is that we owe something to the fans who have made the pro game possible. Let's give them a break once in a while. They have problems enough of their own in these times. I'm not knocking unions. But sometimes people abuse the privilege. Maybe it's old-fashioned, but I'd like to see a little more loyalty by the players.

*Interview/The Washington Post, 9-26:(D)4.*

## Vida Blue
*Baseball pitcher, Oakland "Athletics"*

3

I know it sounds silly, and maybe it is, but now when I start seeing stories in the newspapers about the pro football teams getting ready to go to camp, I get that old feeling. I see myself in a uniform playing quarterback for a team in the NFL. I see myself in a tough game situation wondering what play to call, and then the coach sends in the play and I'm off the hook except to execute. We run the play off perfectly, and a little later we win the game and I'm feeling good all over. The guys come over to shake my hand and say, "Good game, Vida," and while my body aches from that banging I took on the field, there is nothing in the world to compare with the satisfaction of having done a good job ... This is the true sport. Baseball is fine and it's been good to me and my family; but honestly, the only sport that gets me really fired up is football. It's ridiculous to think some club would give me a tryout, but I'll tell you this: If one came along with an invitation, I wouldn't turn it down. That's right; I'd walk right out of here and give it my best.

*Interview, Oakland/*
*Los Angeles Times, 7-13:(3)2.*

## John Bosacco
*Owner, Philadelphia "Bell" football team*

4

[On the poor first year of the World Football League]: I liken our situation to what happened in the canned mushroom industry. There was a problem with botulism, and it was quickly found and controlled. But it got to the point where people wouldn't buy the stuff.

*Los Angeles Times, 9-26:(3)2.*

## Lou Brock
*Baseball player, St. Louis "Cardinals"*

5

I don't think about goals and records. Competition is what keeps me playing—the psychological warfare of matching skill against skill and wit against wit. If you're successful in what you do over a period of time, you'll start approaching records, but that's not what you're playing for. You're playing to challenge and be challenged.

*Interview, Boston/*
*The Christian Science Monitor, 1-20:5.*

**Heywood Hale Broun**
*Sports commentator, Columbia*
*Broadcasting System*

1

[On athletes in general] : History may not remember any of them, but history is not such elevating reading that it should be all that proud of the neglect. All I want from an athlete is that by living as fully as he does while he is competing, he shows me something briefly of importance, that through his work he makes us feel intense aliveness.

*The New York Times, 8-10:(2)23.*

2

I talk about the philosophy of sport, the assumption that excellence in sports is a splendid thing to achieve. But those of us who cannot achieve it should not continually attack ourselves on the grounds that we are not going to run the four-minute mile; and a goal slightly above your previous accomplishment is triumph enough. I think we've taken the fun out of sport by insisting that everybody be a champion or a failure.

*Interview, Los Angeles/*
*Los Angeles Times, 12-13:(2)2.*

**JoAnne Carner**
*Golfer*

3

The hardest thing in golf is controlling your emotions. You're facing a dead, still object, something you can only address with your golf club after a long wait between shots. Your hands are tied in knots, your mind begins to wander and you've got to find a release from tension.

*Interview, New York/*
*The Dallas Times Herald, 2-23:(C)5.*

**Rosemary Casals**
*Tennis player*

4

You meet so many people in this business. You have to go places you don't want to go. It is your job and you have to play the role. Well, sometimes you get tired of that role. Sometimes people come up and ask stupid questions. "Why don't you smile?" is one of them. You've just come off the court and just broke your goddamn ass and lost a match and they want to pop a flashbulb in your face and say, "Smile!" They don't understand, you see? You can't turn it on and off like that. After the [Bobby] Riggs thing the writers said, "See, she is just like that on court. Doesn't smile." But that's just the way I play tennis. Billie Jean King might have to laugh and talk when she plays tennis. Evonne Goolagong might have to act like she is not awake. I do what I have to do. Off court I'm laughing all the time, but I can't when I play tennis.

*Interview, Los Angeles/*
*Los Angeles Times, 6-4:(3)9.*

**Frank Cashen**
*General manager, Baltimore "Orioles"*
*baseball club*

5

The way I see it, the first thing you want in a catcher is ability to handle the pitchers. Then you want defensive skill, and, of course, the good arm. Last of all, if he can hit with power, well, then you've got a Johnny Bench. Very few good teams that win year after year have done so without a top catcher.

*The New York Times, 3-9:(5)3.*

**Bobby Chacon**
*Featherweight boxing champion*
*of the world*

6

What heavyweights get away with slays me. First, they don't have problems with weight. For me to make 126, I have to pound the road. I have to starve myself. Second, heavyweights never get into the kind of shape that we do. I watched that fight from Zaire. [George] Foreman was so badly conditioned that he could hardly stand up after six rounds. [Muhammad] Ali wasn't overly strong, either. He saw the other guy was getting tired and he just waited for him to drop. If featherweights put on that kind of fight, they would throw us in jail.

*Interview/*
*Los Angeles Herald-Examiner, 1-29:(B)1.*

# WHAT THEY SAID IN 1975

**Brad Corbett**
*Owner, Texas "Rangers" baseball club*

1

I think it takes a hell of a lot more skill to play baseball than it does football. It's natural for a man to run with a ball. It's natural for a man to tackle another man because since the start of civilization there have been people wrestling. I don't think it is natural for a man to pick up a bat and hit a ball that is coming at him at 100 miles an hour. I don't think it is natural for a man to pick up an object and with all his strength throw it through the air.

*Interview/*
*The Dallas Times Herald, 4-6:(C)4.*

2

They say in business that timing is everything. In baseball the same is true. I'm startled to see what happens if you trade a baseball player too late or if you trade him too early. The most important thing I've learned is that baseball is a game of opinions. Sometimes experience is not the only attribute to success. There is a great deal of luck involved. But there is a great premium on the ability to make the right moves at the right time. That also is true to a great extent in business.

*Interview/*
*The Dallas Times Herald, 4-6:(C)4.*

**Don Coryell**
*Football coach, St. Louis "Cardinals"*

3

... the thing that means the most in football is winning the close games. We went down to the wire 11 times last year and won eight. This year we were in six close games and won five. The teams with the most impressive records in football aren't really all that dominant. They just win the close games. It's that kind of sport, and it's that way every year.

*Interview/*
*Los Angeles Times, 12-26:(3)6.*

**Howard Cosell**
*Sports announcer, American*
*Broadcasting Company*

4

One of the reasons I am looking for challenges outside of sports is I know of no world so small as the world of sports. The people who inhabit it live in a closet-like world, virtually unaware of anything that happens outside in our society. Their horizon becomes the outfield fence. I find it utterly tiresome to hear grown people arguing about whom Yogi Berra should have put up to pinch-hit, when his major contribution to society is a guttural illiteracy. Yet he has been glorified in the sports press. I see nothing to sanctify any sports event. I consider the presentation of the game as an entertainment on one hand and journalism on the other. If a game stinks, I am going to say it.

*Interview/Los Angeles*
*Herald-Examiner, 6-15:(B)5.*

5

I think big-time college sport is corruptive and hypocritical. When a great university spends a good deal of its time and money—which they almost all do—on the importation of a 6-foot 11½-inch young man because he can drop a ball through a hoop, it's a distortion of emphasis and values that rebounds to a school's discredit. Young people are corrupted at the very beginning by college recruiters who descend upon them offering blandishments—many of them illegal under NCAA rules. So why should the country be surprised when athletes, thus corrupted, take the highest bid and engineer basketball scandals?

*Los Angeles Herald-Examiner,*
*12-10:(A)14.*

**Larry Csonka**
*Football player, Memphis "Grizzlies"*

6

In our society today, it's hard sometimes to separate the reality from the bull. But it's not like that in football. There's no bull on the football field. It's very real out there. I really enjoy being challenged out there. It's different from the day-to-day lives of most people. Only the players can go to the chalk line in the stadium. But other people have the opportunity with their lives to be challenged . . . an army officer, an Alaskan pipeline worker or a guy who works on an ocean-going tanker . . . For me, it's football. This sounds corny, but I enjoy the action and the excitement. Honors or trophies don't mean much. Hey, I got a sterling-silver cup once for some honor that I don't even remember. Today that cup is a water dish for my best friend's dog.

*Interview, Memphis/*
*Los Angeles Times, 10-9:(3)4.*

**Alvin Dark**
*Baseball manager, Oakland "Athletics"*
1

I've been on the top and on the bottom as a manager. And I've known as long as I've been managing that to win I've got to have the players. The difference between managing a championship team and a losing team is that on the championship team you've got to have championship players. When [former Oakland manager] Dick Williams went with the *Angels* last year, I heard people say he'd turn the team around. All I said was, "Has he got the players to do it?" Where did the *Angels* finish? And I'm not saying anything against Williams. All I'm saying is that you've got to have the players.

*San Francisco Examiner &*
*Chronicle, 8-17:(B)1.*

**Gary Davidson**
*Founder, World Football League*
2

[On the financially poor showing of the WFL]: I've always been interested in forming new businesses, and in sports. The World Football League has been a labor of love because it combined both of my major interests. I'm not convinced it is a failure. Getting it off the ground in the first place was the major accomplishment of my life. No one could have predicted how badly the economy was going to go. I don't feel I defrauded anyone. Quite the opposite. I explained the risks involved. Funny thing about finance and sports—when one operator loses $2-million, there's always another guy waiting with $2-million more.

*Interview/*
*The New York Times Magazine, 1-12:57.*

**Willie Davis**
*Baseball player, Texas "Rangers"*
3

I consider myself better adjusted than anyone else in this game. That's because nothing

can make me unhappy. If we win, I am happy for myself. If we lose, I am happy because of the happiness it has brought the other guy. There is no way that baseball can upset me.

*Interview, Pompano Beach, Fla./*
*Los Angeles Herald-Examiner, 3-6:(C)1.*

**Jimmy Diamond**
*Director,*
*Women's Tennis Association*
4

Some people ask if tennis has peaked and if we are just riding the crest. Others say the game will not peak for three more years. I don't know if we have reached the pinnacle. But golf did, and it has been going down. Baseball has been declining for years. In football you get the problem of over-exposure: Where once you had 12 teams there are now something like 25; and every week there are about three games televised . . . The economy hasn't hurt us at all. In a time of depression or recession sports survive. But you can't make your ticket prices so high that it is almost impossible for the blue-collar worker to come in. In an economy like this it is important to scale your prices so that the best seats are a little higher, but the not-so-choice seats remain low, and that's what we're doing.

*Los Angeles Times, 4-4:(3)8.*

**Joe DiMaggio**
*Former baseball player*
5

When I started, a kid never got his chance in the majors until he had spent five, six, even seven years in the minors learning his trade. He didn't get called up until he was trained and ready. I don't say this is right or wrong, but most big-league rookies today are about as advanced as our old B-league players. Most of them have learned only half their trade and some of them haven't learned that much. So what happens is that you've got a whole lot of kids learning and playing at the same time. Baseball's over-all product isn't as good as it used to be, and everybody knows it.

*Interview, Palm Springs, Calif./*
*The Christian Science Monitor, 2-5:6.*

# WHAT THEY SAID IN 1975

**Lefty Driesell**
*Basketball coach, University of Maryland*       1

If you've got the players who can dribble better, block out better, shoot better and move better, you're going to win. It's the mastery of the fundamentals. If there's one thing I know I can do, it is coach. A bench coach hoping to project that image [of an innovative tactician during a game] is not a good coach. I would never put in a new play in the middle of a crucial game. Motivation is far more important than sitting on the bench and changing plays.
*Interview/The Washington Post, 2-28:(D)1.*

2

If the pros keep taking our best players, college basketball will go the route of college baseball in the near future—a dead spectator sport. We won't be able to fill our gymnasiums; there will be no national television. Right now the pros have a beautiful farm system going, and it's free, and they are milking it dry.
*The New York Times, 9-30:46.*

**Leo Durocher**
*Former baseball manager*       3

. . . I'm not one of those old-timers who says everything was better in my day. I think ballplayers today are better than the players were when I played. But whatever happened to "sit down, shut up and listen"? God forbid you talk to a player that way today. And if players in my day talked to managers the way players today do, well, they were gone in a hurry. In the old days, you never talked to the manager. You heard from the traveling secretary. And if you didn't like it, well son, you could just go home. But today, what's a manager going to do about a player who doesn't listen or gives you lip? Fine them $1,000? What do they care? They're making $90,000.
*Interview, New York/*
*Los Angeles Herald-Examiner, 6-1:(B)3.*

**Chris Evert**
*Tennis player*       4

It's tough being Number 1. Everyone wants to beat me. Every time I walk out on the tennis court I'm expected to win and I can feel it. If you do lose, it's a shock—especially if you're Number 1 and not used to losing. But every once in a while I think it's good to lose to keep you eager. Because if you win all the time, there's no challenge, which is bad because you have no goals.
*Interview, Merrifield, Va./*
*The Washington Post, 1-31:(E)4.*

**James A. Farley**
*Former New York State*
*Boxing Commissioner;*
*Former Postmaster General*
*of the United States*       5

The greatest fighter I ever saw before, during and after my years as New York State Boxing Commissioner? Jack Dempsey. There were many other great heavyweights, of course. Gene Tunney, naturally. Max Schmeling, if you will. Jersey Joe Walcott was underrated. So was Jack Sharkey. As for Joe Louis, he would have given any fighter who ever lived a lot of trouble—including Dempsey. Muhammad Ali? Oh, he's a fine boxer and an entertaining guy. But I was talking about real fighters.
*Los Angeles Herald-Examiner, 6-4:(C)12.*

**Bob Feller**
*Former baseball pitcher*       6

I don't like these anti-anti sports heroes. Some of them get an award or achieve some acclaim because of the freedom and opportunities we have in this country and then use them as launching pads to brag about how great it is to be a Communist or a socialist or an anti-anti—something you couldn't do in those countries. All I can say to them is there is a plane leaving every day for those areas. If they like it that well, I'll be glad to pay their way. In fact, I'll arrange for their tickets. I feel there are many athletes taking a lot but not giving enough back to the fans. There are too many loudmouths around rapping the business that made them what they are.
*New York/San Francisco Examiner &*
*Chronicle, 4-20:(C)5.*

**John E. Fetzer**
*Owner,*
*Detroit "Tigers" baseball club*
                                                    1

Baseball is not in the big-business class of General Motors or ITT or some of the other giant companies, but it has all the headaches of big business. There are all the tax laws, inflation, the unsound economic picture of our country, labor unions, contracts, the Sherman antitrust laws. A baseball owner has to live the life of a riverboat gambler, because he can either make a lot of money or lose a lot of [money] in one year. You have to learn to live with that. You have to look at baseball as a love of accomplishment more than just a monetary reward. From that standpoint, I'm not your average businessman. I never have been interested in money *per se*. I've always believed in producing a better product. If that meets the public demand, then money becomes a residual result.

*Interview/San Francisco Examiner*
*& Chronicle, 5-18:(C)4.*

**Charles O. Finley**
*Owner, Oakland "Athletics"*
*baseball club*
                                                    2

Just because a team like the Chicago *White Sox* is stupid enough to pay a Richie Allen $250,000 doesn't mean *I* have to be stupid . . . There's an old saying that pigs get fat and hogs go to market. Well, some of the players these days aren't even pigs or hogs—they're gluttons. We have to keep salaries within reason. If we just rolled over and gave them what they wanted, we'd price ourselves out of business.

*San Francisco/*
*The New York Times, 2-16:(5)9.*

                                                    3

I've never seen so many damned idiots as the owners in sport. Baseball's headed for extinction if we don't do something [to spark up the game]. Defense dominates everything. Pitching is 75 per cent of the game, and that's why it's so dull. How many times have you seen a fan napping in the middle of a football or basketball game? Hell, in baseball people nap all the time. Only one word explains why baseball hasn't changed: *stupidity!* The owners don't want to rock the boat.

*Time, 8-18:42.*

**Gerald R. Ford**
*President of the United States*
                                                    4

Amateur athletics has developed much of [the] muscle that has built and defended and will continue to defend America. No youngster grows up today in America without participating in competitive sport. Sports not only prepares them for life, but that spirit is part of America's competitive spirit . . . As a nation, we have to be physically and mentally fit because these difficult times demand that we not only compete but that we must excel.

*Before National Collegiate Athletic*
*Association, Washington, Jan. 7/*
*The New York Times, 1-8:45.*

**A. J. Foyt**
*Auto racing driver*
                                                    5

Every time you race, the object is to win. When you lose that desire to win, I think that's when you should retire. You can accomplish a lot with hard work. Hard work is when you take a 24-hour day and make a 48-hour day out of it. When a lot of people are out in bars having a ball, I'm usually in there with that race car trying to figure out something. That's the difference between A. J. Foyt and a lot of the other guys.

*Interview, Los Angeles/*
*The Dallas Times Herald, 3-13:(F)8.*

**Joe Frazier**
*Baseball manager,*
*New York "Mets"*
                                                    6

I stress fundamentals, real fundamentals. I want my players to be aggressive. I want to see them go from first to third base and from second to home on base hits. That's how you win games.

*New York, Oct. 3/*
*Los Angeles Herald-Examiner, 10-4:(B)2.*

# WHAT THEY SAID IN 1975

**Ed Garvey**
*Executive director, National Football League Players' Association* 1

[On the striking down of the NFL Option Compensation Clause by a Federal judge]: We are gratified by the court's decision. The National Football League has said that the . . . case was a test because it was the first fully litigated case on the reserve clause in the history of professional sports. In 1974, the NFLPA struck for freedom. Today, the Federal courts have said that players deserve the rights guaranteed other citizens in our country. Professional football will continue to flourish under this ruling.

*Dec. 30/Los Angeles Times, 12-31:(3)4.*

**Sid Gillman**
*Football coach, Houston "Oilers"* 2

[On coaching]: It's such a challenge. It's a challenge, for example, to take the *Oilers*, a team that had done nothing, and try to do something with it. Taking a man and trying to improve him technically, try to make a player out of him. Trying to make a team out of a group. With some [coaches], of course, it's an ego kick. Some appreciate seeing their names in the paper. But I'm very happy if they forget about me, just leave me alone. No, the main thing is when you accomplish something, when you coach a team well and they win.

*Interview/Los Angeles Times, 1-6:(3)1.*

**Pancho Gonzales**
*Tennis player* 3

Tennis is probably the toughest, most demanding sport to learn. And because it's so difficult to play right, people have always been timid about taking it up and looking like a fool. Then tennis began to get popular as a spectator sport. Prize money and open tournaments grew and spread, and the media—especially TV— began covering tennis. So more people started playing it, and those that worried about looking foolish didn't worry so much any more because lots of other people were doing it, too . . . Tennis is a great conditioner without being

boring. That's why I'm sure it isn't a fad. I don't think the growing interest in tennis is going to change. There are about 20 million tennis players in this country today, and I can't help believing that tennis is going to gain momentum at the rate of a million new players each year. Especially since it's one game where there is a place for everyone to play. It's the world's most exciting way to get rid of all your frustrations. And there seem to be plenty of frustrations around to get rid of.

*Interview, Las Vegas, Nev./
Los Angeles Herald-Examiner, 2-2:
(California Living)13.*

**Tom Graham**
*Football player, San Diego "Chargers"* 4

I think violence is one man imposing his will against another, against the will of that man. In football, we all have the same chance. I don't call that violence. I call that competition.

*Los Angeles Times, 9-1:(3)2.*

**Bud Grant**
*Football coach, Minnesota "Vikings"* 5

[Saying pro football should hire full-time officials]: The thing that amazes me watching baseball is, on plays at first base and third base that are shown on television replay, it seems like the umpires never miss. The reason is, they see it every day. But because pro football officials work just once a week, there's no way they can be as sharp, traveling halfway across the country the way they do, working [other] full-time jobs all week. What we have now is a multi-million-dollar operation being handled by amateurs on Sunday afternoon.

*Dec. 10/Los Angeles Times, 12-11:(3)2.*

**Woody Hayes**
*Football coach, Ohio State University* 6

I never want to get to the point where people start calling me "good old Woody." You know, I used to look at Bud Wilkinson at Oklahoma and wonder how it was he could be such a nice guy and win. There are coaches who can be nice and still win, guys like [Southern California's] John McKay. Me, I can't be nice and win. It's not my way.

*The New York Times, 1-12:(5)8.*

**Edmund Hillary**
*Explorer*

1

[On mountain-climbing]: Nobody does it for scientific reasons. Science is used to raise money for the expeditions, but you really climb for the hell of it. We climbed [Mount Everest, in 1953] because nobody climbed it before—it was a mountain to climb. But even now, the danger adds something to it. If Everest were just a mountain that you plugged to the top without any danger, it would be the world's biggest bore ... I've always hated the danger part of climbing, and it's great to come down again because it's safe. But there is something about building up a comradeship—that, I still believe, is the greatest of all feats—and sharing in the dangers with your company of peers. It's the intense effort, the giving everything you've got. It's really a very pleasant sensation.

*Interview, New York, June 2/*
*The New York Times, 6-3:31.*

**Gordie Howe**
*Former hockey player,*
*Detroit "Red Wings"*

2

All pro athletes are bilingual. They speak English and profanity.

*Los Angeles Times, 5-23:(3)2.*

**Al Hrabosky**
*Baseball pitcher,*
*St. Louis "Cardinals"*

3

What I do is mentally picture myself pitching to a batter and striking him out. Then I work myself into a hate mood and make it a personal battle between me and the batter. When my adrenalin is really flowing, I try to channel it into something positive—like getting the s.o.b. out ... A lot of guys even question my sanity. But that's good. I want them to know I'll do anything it takes to win. I want them to think I'm crazy.

*Newsweek, 9-15:71.*

**Reggie Jackson**
*Baseball player, Oakland "Athletics"*

4

[On California *Angels'* pitcher Nolan Ryan's fastball]: Every hitter likes fastballs, just like everybody likes ice cream. But you don't like it when someone's stuffing it into you by the gallon. That's how you feel when Ryan's throwing balls by you. You just hope to mix in a walk so you can have a good night and only go 0-for-3.

*Newsweek, 6-16:56.*

**Phil Johnson**
*Basketball coach, Kansas City-Omaha "Kings"*

5

The key to winning is having players who all feel like they are making a contribution. You rank the worst and best teams in this league, and talent-wise there isn't that much difference except in the things you can't put your finger on. And those factors are teamwork, the player personalities, and getting the players to fit a particular style or system.

*Interview, Kansas City/*
*The Christian Science Monitor, 2-21:6.*

**Roger Kahn**
*Sports columnist, "Esquire" magazine*

6

Are athletes making too much money? Who thought up that one? Some $11,000-a-year school teacher working in a ghetto? Or a publicity executive who knows what "straw man" really means? ... I believe we should reform the society and bring rationality to our economics. But does anyone mean to start with Walt Frazier? Sport is free enterprise. Sport is *laissez-faire*. It is not a life-and-health service. Let's address newspaper attention to $150-a-day hospital rooms, without nursing care, before we worry about Walt Frazier's price per shot. Surely we can afford Walt Frazier before we can afford another 50 hydrogen bombs ... I do not know of a single legitimate league or franchise—I stress the word legitimate—that has found trouble by paying high salaries. I know of many that have approached receivership through incompetent management. The Pittsburgh *Penguins*, in hockey, failed to promote and failed to succeed a few hundred

*(ROGER KAHN)*

miles down the Pennsylvania Pike from that gold mine, the Philadelphia *Flyers*. The San Francisco *Giants* built a ballpark in a wind tunnel, and the wind blew against Willie Mays' high drives. The *Giants* now are close to bankrupt *not* because they paid Willie, but because management failed to think. With better wind currents, Willie ultimately could have fractured Henry Aaron's fracture of Babe Ruth's record. Not even a superstar can survive a tornado.

*Panel discussion before Associated Press*
*Managing Editors, Williamsburg, Va./*
*The New York Times, 11-23:(5)2.*

**Billie Jean King**
*Tennis player*                                                   *1*

This [the U.S.] is the only country in the whole world that cheers for the underdog, no matter who it is. The *only* country. You should go to Europe. They cheer for their own players no matter if they are rated first or 101st. Americans should be for Americans. We need Americans to root for us. We play over there [in Europe] and get booed; then we come home expecting to feel good and get the same treatment.

*Lakeway, Texas, April 19/*
*The Dallas Times Herald, 4-20:(C)5.*

**Bill Kinnamon**
*Former baseball umpire*                                          *2*

[On the qualities needed to be an umpire]: If you're not an extrovert and you're not at least 5-feet 10-inches tall, you probably won't make it [as an umpire]. Most ballplayers figure they can intimidate any small man and they act that way. If he [the umpire] doesn't put them down early and gain their respect right away, he's gone. That's the personal side of it. Mechanically, an umpire must have agility, stamina and be able to run. He's also got to be willing to umpire with pain, because men working the plate often get hit with foul tips going 100 miles per hour. That's the physical side of it. An umpire is constantly being tested by man-

agers, coaches and players, so he can't have rabbit ears. Quick decisions aren't that hard if the man is in position. What's hard is making sure they are based on reason. When an umpire throws someone out of the game, 99 per cent of the time it's for abusive language and is specifically covered in the rule book. But a player, coach or manager can also be sent to the showers for fighting, throwing a bat or deliberately bumping an umpire. That's the mental side of it.

*Interview, St. Petersburg, Fla./*
*The Christian Science Monitor, 3-3:9.*

**Bobby Knight**
*Basketball coach, Indiana University*                           *3*

I love long hair and beards and mustaches. Yes, sir. If you want to look like you want to look, dress like you want to dress, act like you want to act, play like you want to play, shoot like you want to shoot, do your own thing, I say "great." But you're sure as hell not coming to Indiana to play basketball. At Indiana, we're going to do *my* thing.

*Interview, Bloomington, Ind./*
*The National Observer, 2-8:14.*

**Chuck Knox**
*Football coach, Los Angeles "Rams"*                             *4*

... the main function of a head coach is to make those he's responsible for as successful as they can be ... A successful person is one who works up to or near his full potential. The only thing you can ask any man to do is his best ... There are others involved in a consistent-winning team—trainers, equipment men, film men, scouts, public-relations men, executives, doctors, lawyers and the guy who lines the field, among others. My job has three parts: to organize the division of labor, to make sure everybody knows his precise responsibilities, and to give recognition to a job well done.

*Interview, Fullerton, Calif./*
*Los Angeles Times, 7-23:(3)1.*

*5*

A Can-Do player requires relatively little coaching. He's a natural—so good that you're not really going to improve him. He's rare—one of the Jimmy Browns of pro football. Can't-Do players lack the great physical skills necessary for pro football. Coaching will improve them. But, at the same time, you can only take them so far before the law of diminishing returns takes over and you have to drop them. Question-Mark players often have the physical skills, but for some reason aren't getting the job done. Maybe the problem is psychological. Maybe it's motivation. It could be one of several things. But if you are going to put together a winning football team, you have to get that player out of the Question-Mark category and into the Can-Do section.

*Interview, Fullerton, Calif./*
*The Christian Science Monitor, 8-14:21.*

1

[On whether a football quarterback can be compared with a baseball pitcher in judging effectiveness] : No, because in baseball a pitcher is out there by himself. You can see he's being hit hard. That's a measure of his effectiveness. Or you can count his pitches and know he's thrown so many he should be getting tired. It's an individualistic thing completely. A football quarterback is working much more as a team player. For him to do well, his runners have to run, his blockers have to block, his receivers have to run the right routes. When you decide what you do with a quarterback, your decision is based on how well *all* those factors are working. After all of that, if the team still isn't moving, then you make a change.

*News conference, Long Beach, Calif.,*
*Sept. 22/Los Angeles Times, 9-24:(3)9.*

**Bowie Kuhn**
*Commissioner of Baseball*

2

[Arguing against legalization of betting on major-league baseball] : I do not think I exaggerate one bit when I say that legalization could jeopardize the very existence of professional baseball and other professional team sports. It is our position that any form of gambling on professional baseball games, legal or illegal, poses a threat to the integrity of our game, exposes it to grave economic danger and threatens a disservice to the public interest . . . I have no doubt that legalization would adversely affect baseball's reputation for honesty by creating suspicion in the mind of the betting and non-betting public.

*Before National Gambling Commission,*
*Washington, Feb. 19/*
*Los Angeles Herald-Examiner, 2-19:(C)2.*

3

. . . you get a very strong, upbeat feeling about baseball. I think you pick it up almost everywhere. Some people say baseball is benefitting from the movement toward nostalgia. I don't know if that's right or not, but I get a very upbeat feeling. And if you look at our attendance the last two years, we've gone over 30 million both of those years for the first time in our history. It's quite an achievement when you hit a level like that. It means we're averaging 1¼-million per major-league club. That vastly exceeds the attendance of any other sport. It's hard to put into perspective how big an attendance that is, but it really is enormous. Roughly, it's as much as all the other team sports put together.

*New York/*
*Los Angeles Herald-Examiner, 4-6:(D)4.*

**Tom Landry**
*Football coach, Dallas "Cowboys"*

4

. . . I don't agree that you have to have passes to have excitement in football. When a pro game is close on the scoreboard, it's tremendously interesting if you understand it—if you fully understand how the offenses are trying to break open this complicated thing. My answer to those who think football is dull is to try to understand it better. If you do, it will be very rewarding. You have to appreciate it if you know what the battle is all about down there.

*Interview/*
*Los Angeles Times, 9-26:(3)11.*

**Gene Littler**
*Golfer*

5

I never have been able, as some fellows have, to make golf an obsession. To me, it's just a job—like going to the office from 9 to 5. I never have felt a great compulsion to have to win. I

509

# WHAT THEY SAID IN 1975

play the game. I enjoy it. I don't let it devour me.

*Interview/The New York Times, 2-2:(5)17.*

**Ron Luciano**
*Baseball umpire, American League*

1

There's no redemption for the umpire, you know. There's no thrill of victory. It can become a real rut. We're always on the road. This year I'll get home about three times. Two years ago I got home once. Big deal. Just long enough to change suitcases . . . Some umpires tend to pull into a shell and build a fence around themselves. I'd rather get it out. It's like admitting when I make a mistake. There's no way I can keep it in. It helps me relax to admit that I was wrong. People only remember the one mistake, but who the hell is right all the time? I've never met the perfect man and I know I'm going to miss one now and then. You just pray it doesn't happen in a big moment. The umpire who makes a bad call to blow a no-hitter is going to cry himself to sleep for the next 30 nights.

*Interview/Los Angeles Times, 6-27:(3)8.*

**Mike Marshall**
*Baseball pitcher, Los Angeles "Dodgers"*

2

I really enjoy pitching because, every time I go out there to the mound, I'm facing the top talent in the world. It really becomes an emotional involvement. I'm just tickled to death to be out there. There can be no greater thrill.

*Interview, Los Angeles/
The Washington Post, 4-16:(E)2.*

3

I don't know anything about ballet, but I wish people would watch baseball the way ballet fans watch the dance—not to see who wins but to see how well each player performs his part.

*The New York Times, 7-28:13.*

**Billy Martin**
*Baseball manager, New York "Yankees"*

4

Everything looks nicer when you win. The girls are prettier. The cigars taste better. The trees are greener.

*Los Angeles Times, 9-17:(3)2.*

**Willie Mays**
*Former baseball player*

5

I suffered with baseball a lot, more than most people believed. When I went 0-for-4, I would go home and brood. Then I would start worrying whether I had lost it. The next day I would go to the park early and start getting in work. It isn't hard to be good from time-to-time in sports. What's tough is being good every day.

*Interview/
Los Angeles Herald-Examiner, 2-5:(D)1.*

**Mike McCormack**
*Football coach, Philadelphia "Eagles"*

6

[On pro sports]: I don't know any other profession that affects you so much personally. You get in a losing streak—you don't want to go out of the house, to see anyone. In professional sports, people pay to see a winner.

*Los Angeles Times, 11-5:(3)1.*

**John McKay**
*Football coach, University of
Southern California*

7

. . . I suppose a lot of coaches like the thrill of the hunt, the excitement of putting a team together and seeing it do well. And I think we all have ego. But I think the biggest reward I've had is watching players come through here and maybe seeing a guy who was very shy being able to get up and make a good talk and get his degree and do other things besides play football. And most of our players get their degrees, all reports to the contrary. I think that's probably the biggest thrill you have.

*Interview/
Los Angeles Times, 1-6:(3)1.*

**Jack McKeon**
*Baseball manager,
Kansas City "Royals"*

8

Let's face it, baseball is show business. Some of us take it too seriously, especially the umpires. People come out to enjoy the game, but they want a little pepper in their soup. Arguments with umpires are part of the tradition. Yet some umps are so tight they'll throw you out before you take two steps out of the dugout.

*Interview, Fort Myers, Fla./*
*Los Angeles Herald-Examiner, 3-16:(B)5.*

**Don Meredith**
*Sports commentator, National Broadcasting*
*Company; Former football player, Dallas*
*"Cowboys"*

1

If football is evaluated properly, it's a tremendous spectator sport. If it's played with the right attitude, it's a tremendous experience for the player. I've seen pro football changing, and not necessarily in the right direction. The emphasis has been shifting further, since I played, toward primarily selling a product and away from the emphasis on the person and his talent. There's a great distortion taking place. There's so much money in pro football now. You're buying more wrapping than what's in the wrapping. Everything is packaged. The player fills one space in the package.

*Interview/Los Angeles Times, 7-30:(B)8.*

**Andy Messersmith**
*Baseball pitcher, Los Angeles "Dodgers"*

2

I don't look at baseball as a life-and-death proposition as I once did. I try not to take it home with me any more. If I win, I feel great and then try to forget about it. And if I lose, I feel bad and also try to forget about it. Baseball is just a game and I try not to take it too seriously. I try not to let it rule my life. When I'm off the field, I want to be treated just like a normal person. I don't want people reacting to me because I'm a baseball player.

*Interview/*
*Los Angeles Herald-Examiner, 4-16:(D)2.*

**Johnny Miller**
*Golfer*

3

Playing crummy is easy. Playing good and winning is tough. It takes a lot out of you. It puts pressure on you. You get tired more quickly. If I'm playing bad, I can play 40 weeks in a row and not get tired. Nobody bothers you. But if you're playing good and winning, there's a lot of demands on your time. People

are always around you. They want to talk with you. There are television interviews and newspapers and everything. Then, if you don't win, there's the letdown. You always have a letdown. But people expect you to keep on going, to keep on winning. When you win a lot, you establish a reputation. Then you have to live up to the reputation, or try to live up to it. If you win by 10 or 12 strokes in this tournament, they expect you to win by 12 or 14 next time. It can get to be a monster on your back.

*San Diego/*
*The Dallas Times Herald, 2-13:(C)4.*

**Joe Morgan**
*Baseball player, Cincinnati "Reds"*

4

I'm kind of proud to play second [base]. That position requires an extra dimension. You've got guys gunning for you. You have to learn to take care of yourself . . . [The second-baseman] can make the base-runner worry. If the second-baseman makes the relay and throws in the direction of the runner's head, that runner is going to do something that isn't in his best interest. He is going to start his slide prematurely. You must remember that intimidation in baseball isn't a one-sided proposition.

*Interview/*
*Los Angeles Herald-Examiner, 4-16:(D)1.*

5

[On his being named the National League's Most Valuable Player for the 1975 season]: Personally, I'm happy for baseball that I [as a "complete ballplayer"] won. What I mean is that kids should strive to be complete players. With the designated-hitter rule in the American League, I hear some kids saying, "Well, I can hit, so I guess I can be a designated hitter." But there's more to baseball than doing just one thing.

*Cincinnati, Nov. 18/*
*The New York Times, 11-19:46.*

**Rogers C. B. Morton**
*Secretary of Commerce of the*
*United States*

6

Athletic competition can be one of the richest educational experiences a child can

# WHAT THEY SAID IN 1975

*(ROGERS C. B. MORTON)*

have. For one thing, the goal is not only victory, but, even more, participation. While victory cannot always—or, perhaps, even very often—be achieved, the striving for it sets a standard we would do well to adopt for other endeavors. The task of motivating our children to engage in regular sports activities is quite a challenge. Studies show that children spend 15 to 30 hours a week watching television, compared with only about two hours in planned physical activity. One American child in five fails to pass a simple test measuring the minimum strength and skills necessary to master and enjoy ordinary games. This sorry situation poses a threat to children's present enjoyment of life, and to their future health.

*Quote, 10-12:291.*

## Thurman Munson
*Baseball catcher, New York "Yankees"*  1

I've had a lot of writers ask me about my batting average this year. You can always count on that when you're hitting well; that's what writers notice and that's what they think people want to know about. But let me tell you something! I win a lot more games for the *Yankees* with my glove than I do with my bat. It's something you'll have to take my word for, because there are no statistics on how well a catcher runs a game, handles pitchers, blocks that plate or digs balls out of the dirt. There is only one way to tell whether a catcher is any good: Go ask his teammates and his rivals about him. If they respect him, they'll talk about him. And it won't be about his hitting; it will be about his defense and the way he gets along with pitchers. Look, I like hitting fourth and I like the good batting average. But what I do every day behind the plate is a lot more important because it touches so many more people and so many more aspects of the game.

*Interview, Anaheim, Calif./*
*The Christian Science Monitor, 8-25:25.*

## Bob Murdoch
*Hockey player, Los Angeles "Kings"*  2

People think we [in hockey] lead an exotic life. We go to all these different cities and

airports. Little do they know that all we see is the airport and the rink most of the time. There is waiting and aggravation and irritation. Of course, it's a good life; I would recommend it to anyone. But they'd have to realize it's not what they think. We play 80 games a season and that means 80 highs or lows. When you win you're on top of the world; but when you lose you're really down, and everybody gets on your nerves.

*Los Angeles Times, 11-20:(3)10.*

## Mike Murphy
*Hockey player, Los Angeles "Kings"*  3

[On the violence in hockey] : I'm not a good fighter and I don't like to fight. But if somebody hits me on the ice I have to hit back. It is a matter of the law of survival. To survive, you whack somebody back when he whacks you. If you don't do it immediately, he will whack you back harder. That's the way it is. Great players have been chased out of the league for not fighting. The first two years you are tested. You have to prove yourself, prove you are there to stay. You have to gain respect.

*Los Angeles Times, 11-20:(3)1.*

## Danny Murtaugh
*Baseball manager, Pittsburgh "Pirates"*  4

The more patient you are, the better manager you'll be. When I first came up as a manager I was too demanding. I had to learn never to expect a man to do something that he is not capable of doing. Now I try to analyze and find out their capabilities and then never ask them to exceed them.

*Interview, Bradenton, Fla./*
*The New York Times, 3-23:(5)4.*

## Joe Namath
*Football player, New York "Jets"*  5

More games are lost on confusion than on execution. When you think you have done enough preparations, that means you've got to do more ... You would be surprised how many teams with good talent beat themselves. In talent, there is little to choose among the pro teams. Games are won and lost on mistakes.

*Hempstead, N.Y./*
*Los Angeles Times, 11-7:(3)1.*

### Jack Nicklaus
*Golfer*

**1**

The major tournaments have always been the measure of greatness, and I assume they always will. With so much money at stake from week to week, some players may think the majors are losing their luster, but I'm not one of them. Nobody will remember golfers who make a lot of money but don't win the important events.

*Interview, Augusta, Ga./*
*The Christian Science Monitor, 4-15:19.*

### Peter O'Malley
*President, Los Angeles "Dodgers"*
*baseball club*

**2**

I don't think any man can predict what form sports will take in the next 100 years, and I don't think it matters. I wouldn't object to pink baseballs or orange balls or more innings or fewer, or more balls and strikes or fewer, or designated second-basemen. The details of competitive games aren't really important. What is important is the idea of a competitive pasttime. I expect that to survive.

*Interview, Los Angeles/*
*Los Angeles Times, 1-26:(3)1.*

### Walter F. O'Malley
*Chairman, Los Angeles "Dodgers"*
*baseball club*

**3**

It is the future of the game that concerns me. Salary demands are making instant millionaires of the players. Add to that their World Series cut, then the Superteam competition, and that's another $30,000 . . . Why, we had one player ask for a million-dollar contract for five years. This thing is getting out of hand—not just in baseball, but all sports.

*Vero Beach, Fla./*
*Los Angeles Herald-Examiner, 3-19:(D)2.*

**4**

In vertical cities, such as New York and Chicago, you might get away with a little more home TV [broadcasts of baseball games] than in horizontal cities, such as Los Angeles and Cincinnati. Imprisoned in tall buildings, people in vertical cities are sometimes glad to get out and go to a game, even though it's on television. But if we televised home games in a spread-out place like Los Angeles, where our patrons drive miles, no one would come except the players' wives. And a lot of them might stay home, too.

*Interview/TV Guide, 4-5:17.*

### Tom Origer
*Owner, Chicago "Fire" football team*

**5**

[On why the new WFL hasn't prospered]: There were three basic mistakes. Believe me, I learned something new every day. First of all, [1974] was the worst year for the economy since World War II. We couldn't have picked a worse time to start a football league. When you hear guys saying they dropped $1-million or $1.8-million in this league, they aren't talking about book losses. They are talking about cash losses, and that just about kills you. Second of all, it's just possible that the sports boom is over in the United States. I'm willing to believe that the pro-football hysteria has at last peaked. Third of all, we put too much trust in [WFL founder] Gary Davidson and his associates. We took a look at their record in other sports and figured that, if anybody could pull this deal off, they could. They seemed to have everything figured out down to the last little detail. Trouble is they were so over-confident they couldn't see anything disastrous happening.

*The New York Times Magazine, 1-12:48.*

### Jesse Owens
*Former Olympic track champion*

**6**

It bothers me when I hear a former athlete—one going back a number of years—suggesting that today's competitor couldn't compete with the old-timer. That's a lot of baloney. The present-day athlete is superior for many reasons. He is stronger physically, he uses better equipment, he competes on better playing sur-

# WHAT THEY SAID IN 1975

*(JESSE OWENS)*

faces and has more knowledgeable instruction . . . If an athlete doesn't progress today, it's his own fault. If he has a strong body, motivated by a dedicated discipline, he'll succeed. It's as simple as that.

*Interview, Phoenix/*
*The Christian Science Monitor, 4-16:19.*

1

[Saying victory-stand ceremonies and the playing of national anthems at the Olympics should not be discarded]: People who say the Games are [too] nationalistic are the ones who never had the opportunity of standing atop the victory stand. It's a tremendous feeling when you stand there and watch your flag fly above all the others. For me it was the fulfillment of a nine-year dream. And I couldn't forget the country that brought me there.

*New York/*
*Los Angeles Times, 12-3:(3)2.*

**Alan Page**
*Football player,*
*Minnesota "Vikings"*
2

[In pro football], management has complete and absolute control over your body. This is the only business in which your employer is called your "owner." Think about it.

*Interview/People, 12-22:49.*

**Arnold Palmer**
*Golfer*
3

It is contrary to nature for a man to say that he shot a lousy round. This is especially the case with a pro, who isn't supposed to shoot lousy rounds. So when he comes up with an embarrassing score, he can place the blame on one of two things. He can blame his body, claiming an injury to his wrist, his shoulder or his back. Or he can blame the course, pointing to poor maintenance, poor planning or poor location. It is easier to blame the course, because if you claim an injury, and come back the following week to win a tournament with an 18-under-par score, it gets a little sticky.

*Interview/TV Guide, 3-22:15.*

**Joe Paterno**
*Football coach, Pennsylvania*
*State University*
4

The fun of coaching for me is the week-to-week preparation for an opponent. Each week is different, a new struggle. You try to plug up holes, hide problems, put in a gimmick or two. That's where my satisfaction comes.

*Interview, University Park, Pa./*
*The Washington Post, 10-30:(B)1.*

**Richard Petty**
*Auto racing driver*
5

To win the Daytona-500, or any other automobile race at a major speedway, you've got to tailgate—and I don't mean at freeway speeds. You've got to stick the nose of your car under the rear end of the one in front of you, and you've got to run that way, at 185 miles per hour or better.

*The Christian Science Monitor, 5-15:25.*

6

Maybe it depends on what you think of as an athlete, but I'll put a race-car driver above any other athlete because he's got everything on the line. He does it all by himself. He's got no teammate to rely on. It's a combination of mind and body. You go five hours with no relief sometimes, handling a 3,800-pound car that takes all you can do to muscle it through the corners, plus the mental strain of knowing that one mistake and you done busted your dad-gum head. That's sure more than a football player does, resting every few seconds between plays. In a football game, the ball's in play only six or seven minutes, and there's two squads to split the time—offense and defense. A race driver's working with no time outs, either. Football players may get bunged up, but when a race driver gets bunged up, he really gets it.

*Interview, Ontario, Calif./*
*Los Angeles Times, 11-23:(3)6.*

**Steve Prefontaine**
*Track runner*
7

To hell with love of country. I compete for myself . . . People say I should be running for a gold medal for the old red, white and blue and all that bull, but it's not going to be that way. I'm the one who has made all the sacrifices. Those are *my* American records, not the country's.

*Interview, Denver/*
*The New York Times, 3-28:32.*

### Bob Pulford
*Hockey coach, Los Angeles "Kings"*

1

There's a great deal of pride in the makeup of a hockey player. It is not a joking matter to go out on the ice. They are dead serious. The basic thing is, you cannot show fear. It is a contact sport and there is intimidation. If a player shows fear he knows other players will take advantage of that.

*Los Angeles Times, 11-20:(3)1.*

### Jerry Quarry
*Former boxer*

2

The boxing world needs changes, and the first thing it needs is more white boxers. There are too many blacks. And the only way you're going to get white boxers is for the nation [the U.S.] to have a major depression. I know that's a horrible thing to say, but it's true.

*The New York Times, 6-29:(5)19.*

### John Ralston
*Football coach,*
*Denver "Broncos"*

3

The highs and lows in coaching are—well, I just couldn't draw a parallel with any other line of work. I stay in it because I want more of the highs. This is something I wanted to do when I was 11 years old. I haven't worked a day yet. It's all fun. It's a hobby. It's an all-encompassing thing. If you're worried about outside pressure, that's the wrong approach. The guy in the mirror is the one you have to satisfy. We start out about the first week of July and probably work 15, 16 hours a day—seven days a week, right through till the draft. But listen, I thrive on it. I'm not doing anything I don't enjoy.

*Interview/*
*Los Angeles Times, 1-6:(3)1.*

### Lance Rentzel
*Football player, Los Angeles "Rams"*

4

I'm sick and tired of hearing athletes put down sports. It's getting to the point where athletes are forgetting just how made they have it. All you hear about these days are guys not wanting to pay fines, guys wanting to be traded, guys suing their bosses, guys defying rules. It's gotten out of hand.

*Interview, Beverly Hills, Calif./*
*Los Angeles Times, 4-23:(B)2.*

### Brooks Robinson
*Baseball player, Baltimore "Orioles"*

5

I've always said when I broke in [to baseball 20 years ago] I was an average player. I had an average arm, average speed and definitely an average bat. I am still average all of those.

*Interview, New York/*
*The Dallas Times Herald, 5-4:(C)11.*

6

I hate to hear a player say he's a $100,000 slave or that he's a prisoner. That doesn't set well with me. But, in a sense, that's exactly what he is. When I signed with Baltimore in 1955, the choice of club was mine. Today, a prospect doesn't have that option. He is drafted and must sign with that club or not play ball at all . . . Somewhere along the line there should be some kind of modification.

*Los Angeles Times, 5-30:(3)3.*

### Frank Robinson
*Baseball manager, Cleveland "Indians"*

7

I hope that my being the first black manager will create some excitement and some participation in the black community. I hope they can point to me with pride and say, "He is black and one of us and we're happy for him." But I don't want them to come out to see me because I'm a black manager. I want them to come out because they want to see a ball game and they want to see the Cleveland *Indians* as a team do well, not just to see me do well. If the ball club does well, it will reflect on me. And if it does poorly, it will reflect on me. But I also look at it the other way: If the ball club doesn't do

515

*(FRANK ROBINSON)*

well, it doesn't mean that a black man can't be
a manager in the major leagues.

*Interview, Cleveland/*
*The Dallas Times Herald, 2-23:(C)1.*

**Fred B. Rooney**
*United States Representative,*
*D—Pennsylvania*     *1*

I am . . . concerned . . . that boxing remain
an honest sport—one which pits strength, agility
and endurance of one boxer against the
strength, agility and endurance of his opponent.
This competitive sporting profession should not
be permitted to be run into the ground by
racketeers. However, because boxing can be a
very profitable business venture, it is [an] inviting target for the racketeer. The unscrupulous
promoter can make himself a fortune on a
single contest . . . [My bill would] maintain the
integrity of professional boxing by having the
authority to prevent the interstate broadcast or
telecast of boxing matches in which there is
evidence of illegal efforts to influence the outcome of the event.

*Interview, Washington/*
*Los Angeles Herald-Examiner, 3-23:(B)5.*

**Pete Rose**
*Baseball player, Cincinnati "Reds"*     *2*

[On pitchers] : I don't think enough of them
are good athletes. They can't hit, can't field,
can't bunt, can't run. I wouldn't want a job
where I played only once every fifth game.

*The Christian Science Monitor, 3-11:8.*

**Carroll Rosenbloom**
*Owner, Los Angeles "Rams" football team*     *3*

The only time I want to be congratulated for
a successful season is when we win the Super
Bowl. I don't consider anything less as being a
successful season. We now feel we have the
finest players, the finest coaches, the finest
trainers, the finest equipment men, the finest
doctors and . . . the finest general manager in
the NFL. As surely as day follows night, we
should win the Super Bowl this season. I'm not
interested in being one step closer. The name of

the *Ram* highlight film next season will be "The
*Rams* Took It All."

*Los Angeles, April 28/*
*Los Angeles Herald-Examiner, 4-30:(B)1.*

    *4*

American fans will come to see a Pele, a
[Kareem Abdul-] Jabbar, or an O. J. Simpson.
But when you settle down to the hard grind,
the teams better be winning, or the superstars
lose their impact.

*Los Angeles Herald-Examiner, 6-19:(C)1.*

    *5*

The need to charge as much as we do [for
tickets to football games] is the fault of the
owners themselves, myself included. We are
making the public pay for our stupidity . . .
First, an average team wastes from $300,000 to
$500,000 a year on bonuses. And for what
purpose? In what other industry, including the
entertainment field, does an apprentice receive
a bonus for the opportunity to prove himself?
If a man makes your team, give him a fine
salary. But why we got started on this bonus
business is beyond me. The fans could care less,
and it's bad for morale among your vets . . . It's
just a custom. Why did guys use to take off
their hats when ladies got into the elevator?
That made no sense, either. But it was a
custom. So everyone did it.

*Interview/*
*Los Angeles Herald-Examiner, 6-20:(C)1.*

**Darrell Royal**
*Football coach, University of Texas*     *6*

I can't think of a glamorous position, a position of any significance, that doesn't put pressure on you. What makes football coaches stay
with what we do, I suppose, is not all that
different from what keeps people in the entertainment field. I have a lot of friends in that
field and I can't think of anything more heart-
breaking, more gut-wrenching, than making an
appearance before an almost-empty house. It's
the same thing for us [coaches] when we do
our number and we get no applause or maybe
get raked over the coals a bit. I think the

applause is a part of it. All of us have a little ham in us. Now, that's not popular for a jock to say. You know, folks think you're supposed to do it all for the good of the team: "It doesn't matter about me." That's a bunch of b.s. As I said, a lot of us are no different from entertainers. What makes a guy want to entertain when he's had one heartbreak after another? Well, every now and then you get accepted, you hit a hot button and you get recognition.

*Interview/Los Angeles Times, 1-6:(3)1.*

## Pete Rozelle
*Commissioner, National Football League*

1

[Defending the draft, reserve clause, etc.]: The major goal of any team sport is to have competitive balance. I think that the rules of the NFL promote this successfully. I cite as an example the fact that half our games this season were decided by seven points or less. Our rules promote cycles, wherein rather than having a team down forever and certain teams dominating, you have teams able to improve themselves even if they don't have a great financial edge.

*Interview, New York/*
*Los Angeles Herald-Examiner, 2-11:(C)3.*

2

If team-sport betting were legalized, there would be a serious erosion of the public confidence on which our sport is built—and without which it cannot survive. We firmly believe that government-sponsored team-sport betting would soon create a generation of cynical fans, obsessed with point spreads and parimutual tickets and constantly prone to suspect the motives of players and coaches alike. These persons will inevitably become skeptics rather than supporters, adversaries rather than advocates of our game.

*Before National Gambling Commission,*
*Washington, Feb. 19/*
*The Dallas Times Herald, 2-20:(D)3.*

3

[Arguing against making permanent the lifting of blackouts on televising home games when they are sold out 72 hours in advance]: We're not saying the league is suffering millions of

dollars of losses because of the lifting of the blackout. We're calling it an erosion. This year, season ticket sales are down all over the league, and we attribute that to television saturation of games in the home market. That makes football a studio sport. And each year we are going to hurt a little more.

*Interview, Sept. 22/*
*The Washington Post, 9-23:(D)5.*

4

[On the striking down of the NFL Option Compensation Clause by a Federal judge]: The National Football League is, of course, disappointed with the decision of the Minneapolis court. We had hoped that the court would find the antitrust laws to be sufficiently flexible to accommodate the unique and special needs of a professional football league. Such leagues depend on competitive balance . . . We continue to believe that collective bargaining offers the best solution to the broad range of labor-management issues in professional football, and that team-equalization rules have served and will continue to serve the interests of fans, players and clubs alike.

*Dec. 30/Los Angeles Times, 12-31:(3)4.*

## Derek Sanderson
*Hockey player, New York "Rangers"*

5

Salaries are just too much now. The economy is on a downer and fans are just getting tired of the kind of money athletes are getting. It's all getting out of proportion. Things have to be put in perspective. Like, are plumbers really worth $92 an hour? We [in sports] shouldn't be getting that kind of money, either. It was this kind of financial structure that ruined Hollywood with all those big production things.

*Interview, New York/*
*Los Angeles Times, 3-9:(3)11.*

## Bo Schembechler
*Football coach, University of*
*Michigan, Ann Arbor*

6

[On his coaching priorities]: First, I want them [his players] to have the same kind of experience I had when I played. The game must be satisfying and worthwhile ... The second priority in justifying the existence of a football program is its ability to serve as a rallying point for the student body. Students today may be a little more reserved in showing their feelings, but they still enjoy coming out to the games on Saturday afternoon and supporting the team. A third consideration is the alums. Michigan has the largest alumni group of any university, and football is often the activity that does the most to cement ties among the school and its former students. We may have an excellent chemistry department on campus, but you can't expect to pick up a paper in California and read about what's happening in our labs. But you can turn to the sports page and read about the Michigan football team.

*Interview, Ann Arbor/*
*The Christian Science Monitor, 9-10:20.*

**Mike Schmidt**
*Baseball player, Philadelphia "Phillies"*     *1*

[On Philadelphia fans]: They read their sports pages, know their statistics and either root like hell or boo our butts off. I love it. Give me vocal fans—pro or con—over the tourist-types who show up in Houston or Montreal and just sit there.

*Los Angeles Times, 3-31:(3)2.*

**Tex Schramm**
*President, Dallas "Cowboys"*
*football team*     *2*

[On using TV instant replays to help settle disputed field calls]: Obviously, you cannot allow every play to become a film study; some coaches would protest them all. One alternative is that each team would only be allowed "X" number of challenges. But then it really kind of gets away from the game: Should you use your challenge now? Then there could be booing because you didn't challenge. But if you use them all up, you don't have any challenges left at the end of the game. It just gets to be a circus and detracts from the game. Then there's the problem of how many cameras and how many viewing locations do you need. It would probably take 10 or 12, but I know we're not going to buy 10 cameras for each club. And, even if we did, how are we going to get enough people to watch them? If you're going to get into this, you better be sure it's right. The worst thing you can do is reverse a call and then the next day find that another angle shows it was right. And how do you use the equipment fast enough to render a decision without interminable delays? The rules we've adopted to get more offense into the game have added about seven more plays this year and five minutes have been added to the length of the game. We don't want to make the games longer without increasing the number of plays.

*Interview/*
*Los Angeles Times, 12-9:(3)1.*

**Sam Schulman**
*Owner, Seattle "SuperSonics"*
*basketball team*     *3*

The high-priced players, because of the nature of things, are prima donnas. The so-called superstars destroy the younger players—they take away the initiative and desire. We [owners] just have to take a whole, entire new look and re-evaluate, and make every effort to sit down with the players and get to an understanding that they are going to kill the goose that laid the golden egg.

*Interview, Seattle/*
*Los Angeles Times, 4-27:(3)7.*

**George Schwartz**
*President, Philadelphia City Council*     *4*

We ought to legalize betting on everything—the fights, basketball, baseball, football, hockey ... Gambling is something that has been with us since the beginning of time. We have a natural tendency, all of us, to gamble on something. That should be the future.

*Before National Gambling Commission,*
*Philadelphia, May 28/*
*The New York Times, 5-29:25.*

**Tom Seaver**
*Baseball pitcher, New York "Mets"*     *5*

Whenever a player raises the top salary in any sport, it has to help everybody below. The owners might not want to admit it, but it's absurd to think it won't help. The one thing it definitely does is give us a better understanding of our worth. Pitchers with comparable records and ability have a valid point in seeking a comparable salary.

*Interview/Los Angeles Times, 1-12:(3)9.*

1

I don't aim to be another Sandy Koufax or another Bob Gibson. I am a self-competitor. I pitch against myself. I set my own standards of excellence. Ten years from now, when I look back on my career, I won't measure myself by records or by other men. I only want to know that I was the best pitcher I could possibly have been.

*Interview, St. Petersburg, Fla., March 4/*
*Los Angeles Herald-Examiner, 3-9:(B)5.*

**Bill Sharman**
*Basketball coach, Los Angeles "Lakers"*
2

Every week in the NBA you see increased use of hands. There is more pushing, more shoving, more grabbing. The skill factor is diluted when great players like Jabbar, McAdoo, Cowens, Lanier and others must fight merely to get clear. Pro basketball isn't supposed to be shuffleboard, but it shouldn't be football and hockey, either. The game is getting dangerously away from the officials . . . We have had a lot of fights and a lot of near-fights this season. When players hang on each other, elbow each other and harass each other during the early part of the game, they are setting up a sure-fire beef later. It isn't visible to all spectators, but these things are slow-coming in a game. You torment a guy long enough and you are soon going to see fists.

*Los Angeles Herald-Examiner, 11-23:(B)1.*

**Fred Shero**
*Coach, Philadelphia "Flyers" hockey team*
3

My team comes first. I'd do anything for my players. I'd lie, cheat, steal for them, and they know it. That's why everyone works so well together on our team. There are things I would do for my players I wouldn't do for my own family.

*Los Angeles Times, 4-10:(3)1.*

**Jimmy (the Greek) Snyder**
*Odds-maker*
4

It's always the great athletes who get injured the most, and this is what makes sports so unpredictable. The mediocre athletes seldom get hurt because they don't extend themselves. What happened to Ruffian [a race horse that injured its foot and had to be destroyed] is like what happened to [football's Joe] Namath and what happened to [baseball's] Mickey Mantle.

*Interview/*
*"W": a Fairchild publication, 7-25:2.*

**Willie Stargell**
*Baseball player,*
*Pittsburgh "Pirates"*
5

[On whether he would like to become an American League-style designated hitter]: I think the way we [in the National League] play baseball, the old-fashioned way, is better. It [the DH] takes away the strategy of the game—whether you should bat for a pitcher who is doing well late in the game in which you're trailing, or the skill of bunting up a player to score a run. Then you struggle all game long to get one run up on a team to force their starter out of the game and get a reliever. With a designated hitter, the starter can stay in the game . . . I know I've said I may like to become a designated hitter when my legs finally give out. It can prolong a player's career by several years. But, right now, I like getting involved with both the offensive and defensive sides of this game.

*Interview, Pittsburgh/*
*San Francisco Examiner & Chronicle,*
*6-8:(C)4.*

**Casey Stengel**
*Former baseball manager, New York*
*"Yankees" and New York "Mets"*
6

The trouble with women umpires is that I couldn't argue with one. I'd put my arms around her and give her a little kiss.

*Time, 8-11:37.*

**Hank Stram**
*Former football coach, Kansas City*
*"Chiefs"*
1

. . . excitement in all sports is going to come from offense. In baseball, it's the home run; in boxing, it's the knockout; in basketball, it is shooting the eyes out of the basket; in football, it is the long pass . . . the long run. That is why soccer is not a big hit in the United States—not enough scoring.

*Interview/The Washington Post, 4-1:(D)2.*

**Jim Sweeney**
*Football coach, Washington State*
*University*
2

I think there are values in football which are perhaps more important than the game itself. I look at football as a way of life and as a vehicle for teaching. Therefore, I think you [the coach] can live with the pressures and maybe even divorce yourself from winning and losing to some degree—to try to treat winning and losing as impostors. You know the poem *If,* by Kipling? ["If you can meet with Triumph and Disaster/And treat those two impostors just the same . . . Yours is the Earth and everything that's in it . . ."]

*Interview/Los Angeles Times, 1-6:(3)4.*

**Lee Trevino**
*Golfer*
3

I'd be satisfied with $2-million, and that's my goal. Other guys have goals like winning a lot of championships. I'd like to win the Masters so I'll have all four major titles, but the name of the game is money.

*Augusta, Ga./*
*The Washington Post, 4-13:(D)10.*

4

Golf is like fighting. When you're ready to strike the ball, your stomach gets hard. In other words, your stomach helps you when you hit a shot. You tighten your stomach. Have you ever tried to hit a golf shot with your stomach relaxed? It's not going to go any place.

*Interview/*
*The Dallas Times Herald, 5-4:(I)2.*

**Bobby Unser**
*Auto racing driver*
5

Luck is everything. If you don't have luck on the racetrack, you can't win. Luck controls everything we do in our lives. I've always tried to have it on my side.

*Interview, Indianapolis/*
*Los Angeles Herald-Examiner, 5-26:(B)5.*

**Bill Veeck**
*Former baseball-club owner*
6

Sports are becoming increasingly more important as our world becomes more disordered, as society seems to be based on such shifting sands. It's the one thing in which there is a clearly defined area of play, rules and penalties that apply to all. Three strikes and you're out— even if [attorney] Edward Bennett Williams defends you.

*Interview, Easton, Md./*
*The Washington Post, 8-31:(H)3.*

**Virginia Wade**
*Tennis player*
7

If you play professionally, you train to play as well as you can and you accept what happens. I'm no longer afraid of losing. I spend more time preparing and less regretting.

*The Christian Science Monitor, 7-22:18.*

**Bill Walton**
*Basketball player, Portland "Trail*
*Blazers"*
8

Through circumstances, like in professional basketball, there are a few of us who make very large incomes. Still, we wouldn't be paid these salaries unless the owners felt it was in their best interest. The salaries we receive are a reflection of the extraordinary emphasis placed on spectator sports in this country, and the huge sums of money our labor generates. There are tremendous amounts of money being made in the world of sports today. Unfortunately, the people who are participating in the sports . . . are not receiving the profits. It's going other places.

*Interview, Garden City, N.Y./*
*Los Angeles Herald-Examiner, 1-15:(B)5.*

**Dick Williams**
*Baseball manager, California "Angels"*
1

Team pride is doing the best for your club no matter what sacrifice it entails. If you don't have self pride, you can't have team pride.

*Interview/*
*Los Angeles Times, 4-3:(3)4.*

**Ralph Wilson**
*Owner, Buffalo "Bills" football team*
2

They [the NFL Players Association] want pensions, health policies, special meal allowances, special working conditions and all the other fringe items. Then they want to turn around and operate free-style in those areas that would protect the owners. I'm not opposed to unionization. I welcome it. But if the players are going to drift from place to place, I feel the working scales should be fixed. It is that way in the automotive industry, in the steel industry, in mining and the like.

*Interview, Palm Beach, Fla./*
*Los Angeles Herald-Examiner, 3-7:(C)1.*

**John Wooden**
*Basketball coach, University of*
*California, Los Angeles*
3

If you'll look, over the years, it's the great offensive performers who got all the headlines. Jack Dempsey, Babe Ruth, Ted Williams. But in most sports, *defense* produces championships. People say the Super Bowl is dull. I don't think it is. It's just that usually the teams are so strong on defense. The Boston *Celtics* were breaking all sorts of records in the 1950s, but they weren't winning championships until Bill Russell came. His defense made them invulnerable. And the Oakland *Athletics* in baseball this year—look at their defense: Green, Bando, Rudi, Campaneris. Just great.

*Interview, Los Angeles/*
*Los Angeles Times, 1-31:(3)6.*

**John Wooden**
*Former basketball coach, University of*
*California, Los Angeles*
4

. . . there's far more over-coaching than under-coaching. We try to make a complex thing out of something that is really not all that complex. If we'll just get the athletes in good condition, if we'll teach them to quickly and properly execute the fundamentals, and if we'll insist that they play together as a team and not for themselves, there's not much left. Just do those things and the X's and O's aren't going to make much difference.

*Interview, Los Angeles/*
*Los Angeles Times, 9-6:(3)6.*

5

In my opinion, the money pro basketball players make is way out of perspective. The average salary in the NBA is $100,000 and look at all the side benefits he gets. Look at the retirement benefits of a basketball player and compare them to the retirement benefits of a teacher in our society. I have no sympathy when I hear a pro athlete complaining of the amount of travel he has to do. Not the way he's getting paid. Compared to other occupations, he has it made. He can make enough money in five years to retire for the rest of his life. I can't see where there can be any motivation problems, either. Not at what they're making.

*Interview, Los Angeles/*
*The New York Times, 10-19:(5)10.*

**Carl Yastrzemski**
*Baseball player, Boston "Red Sox"*
6

I should know something about hitting by now. I've been around long enough. But sometimes I don't think I know anything about it. To me, it's the most frustrating part of being a baseball player. I say that because I've had days when I've gotten up five times, hit the ball well five times, and had nothing to show for it. But I've also had days when I couldn't get the ball out of the infield and wound up with two hits. The biggest thing I've found in hitting is not to get discouraged and change something that gets you completely messed up—even though the tendency is often overwhelming. But you just can't do it and survive. I was a lousy hitter in May doing exactly the same things that made me a great hitter in June.

*Interview/*
*The Christian Science Monitor, 8-20:25.*

# WHAT THEY SAID IN 1975

**Andrew Young**
*United States Representative,*
*D–Georgia*

1

Our entire athletic programs in our major institutions, from almost junior-high up, have gradually been geared toward a kind of professionalism in our athletics so that if a person has not grown to be 7-feet-tall or does not weigh 200 pounds they are shunted off and given a ball and told to go for themselves. The major physical-education intelligence of this nation is directed toward less than one-tenth of one per cent of the population who will become professional athletes.

*Quote, 9-7:171.*

**Bella S. Abzug**
*United States Representative,*
*D–New York*
1

We are not interested in ripping off a piece of power for women in a society that has no soul. We want to change the society completely. The odds are that we will change power, but power won't change us.

*Quote, 4-13:337.*

2

I've spent a good part of my adult life as wife, mother, lawyer and member of Congress. I have both a happy marriage and a happy life. And it's due to the fact that I could make choices and change roles and mix them. The question of choice is the big issue–to be whatever you want to be. If a woman wants to be just at home, fine. I'm a great champion of the home-woman.

*Quote, 10-5:266.*

3

. . . there is still an enormous cultural conditioning which influences men and women. Women are still conceived in the television and radio as being creatures of consumption who run around squeezing toilet paper and worrying about the shine of their floors and the taste of their coffee. And that's the role that many of them are prepared to believe they still have to carry forward.

*The Dallas Times Herald, 10-22:(A)20.*

**Jessie Bernard**
*Scholar-in-Residence, United States*
*Commission on Civil Rights*
4

Women are subjected to put-downs all the time [in the business world]. Sometimes they're mild ones, such as calling them all "girls." Often, men will make fun of women in a semi-humorous way. When the women don't laugh, they're told: "Why don't you have a sense of humor about this?" This is especially true when there is only one woman in a group; she gets clobbered. Women in this male world are at such a disadvantage–they have to overcome so many hurdles–that sometimes they don't think it's worth the effort. The result is that women are excluded when important decisions are being made–often in the men's restroom, in fact. In addition, a lot of women who are very opposed to the women's movement say [to women's-rights advocates]: "Please pipe down. Don't be so aggressive. You're ruining my position in my office. I'm way up there." The truth is that, even if it's true that she's "way up there," she's not really in "the club." She thinks she is, but she's not "in."

*Interview/*
*U.S. News & World Report, 12-8:71.*

**Antonia Brico**
*Orchestra conductor*
5

I am not a feminist–that word that means rah-rah for women–women this and women that. I've never linked myself up with just the women's movement; but when interviewers say, "Are you a feminist?" and "Are you a Women's Libber?"–ye gods, I battl~d for women way back in the 1930s when there was no such thing as "Women's Lib," or whatever. I just believe in anybody's getting a chance–irrespective of whether it's a man or a woman.

*Interview/*
*San Francisco Examiner & Chronicle,*
*5-18:(California Living)32.*

**Ellen Burstyn**
*Actress*
6

I'm not aligned with any feminist group. I am a woman in 1975, dealing with my, and the world's, consciousness. We're all going through an enormous change, but you don't have to be

# WHAT THEY SAID IN 1975

a feminist to be a part of it. I'm certainly not anti-feminist—I'm all for the change. But I don't like to be narrowed in my identity.

*Interview, Boston/*
*"W": a Fairchild publication, 3-21:9.*

## Jacqueline Cochran
*Aviatrix*

**1**

I have never been discriminated against in my life. I think the women complaining they've been discriminated against are the ones who can't do anything, anyway. Baloney.

*The Washington Post, 1-13:(B)1.*

## Jill Ker Conway
*President-designate,*
*Smith College*

**2**

The whole structure of higher education for women was built without any attempt to relate the educated person to the occupational structure of society outside. That's why the whole first generation of educated women has nervous collapses. So, instead, they created the service professions. That's been the accommodation, educating women for a service role. Always applying knowledge, not creating it . . . We have to change the perception of employers that women have certain kinds of skill(s), and something must be done to make women realize what skills they have.

*The New York Times, 3-18:42.*

## Luis Echeverria (Alvarez)
*President of Mexico*

**3**

It is imperative that every woman should be valued for herself, for the work she does, for the ideas she upholds, for the causes she defends, and not solely for the support she gives to the world of her husband. It is imperative to replace the stereotyped image of the female sex as merely the sum of suffering, tolerance, patience, generosity and prudence by another image which includes intelligence, courage, independent judgment

and firmness—qualities which women possess but which they have had to suppress, to their own detriment.

*At International Women's Conference,*
*Mexico City, June 19/*
*Los Angeles Herald-Examiner, 6-20:(A)9.*

**4**

Only a critical, radical effort will make possible the true liberation of women, that is, human liberation and the transformation of the world economic order. If women remain aloof from the great, global revolutionary process, they will not advance substantially. Women will get more rights, which the system cannot deny them, but they will be confined for another century in the same citadel of isolation.

*At International Women's Conference,*
*Mexico City, June 19/*
*San Francisco Examiner & Chronicle,*
*6-29:(This World)2.*

## Harlan Ellison
*Author*

**5**

The question of whether women have a different approach to writing is profound, and the answer is yes and no. No, in that women are human beings who've existed on this planet along with us in many shared experiences, so the analogues, the paradigms are pretty much the same. Yes, in that they have lived like the blacks lived in the South for many years. The blacks' view of the South is utterly different from the whites' view, and if you read about it you'd find it was two different worlds. Women have been a slave cadre in our midst for thousands of years. Their experience comes from constantly looking at the world from the viewpoint of someone who's had to wash dishes and cook food and bring up babies. But the slaves have been unshackled and, damn it, they're going to tell us what the world looks like from their point of view. And what they tell us—good, bad, indifferent—must be listened to.

*At discussion sponsored by University*
*of California, Los Angeles/*
*Los Angeles Times, 6-9:(4)9.*

**Sam J. Ervin, Jr.**
*Former United States Senator,*
*D–North Carolina*

1

When I first came out and made a speech against the [Equal Rights] Amendment, a lobbying group in Washington for women, called the National Women's Party, wanted to send up a committee to my office to point out the error of my ways, and I told them I'd be glad to see them. I told them why I opposed it and I told them that, under a radical interpretation, it would deprive Congress of the right to draft or enlist men for combat service without drafting or enlisting women for combat service. And they said, "Why, that's what we want. We want to be drafted." Well, they were about my vintage, and so I said, "Now, ladies, I've always tried to be a very gallant gentleman and never referred to a lady's age under any circumstances, but, notwithstanding your youthful appearances, I am bound to observe that you are about a month after the draft age. If you are going to convince me that women want to be drafted, you had better send up some of those young women of draft age to tell me so."
*At University of San Francisco/*
*San Francisco Examiner & Chronicle,*
*3-23:(California Living)12.*

**Millicent H. Fenwick**
*United States Representative, R–New Jersey*

2

I am not one who blames men for sitting on women. We are mutually responsible. I blame myself. I held back at times when I should have acted. Women can't expect men to change until they do. We are all prisoners of the culture.
*Interview/*
*The Saturday Evening Post, September:6.*

**Janet Flanner**
*Writer*

3

[On Women's Lib]: Hurray for it, I say! Anything that will advance women to something more than equality calls for my full applause. Women need to have their superiority acknowledged. I'm not speaking about things like weight-lifting. But it's the women who have the babies, who keep their little noses dry, run the home. I know of an ideal couple—there

should be more of them today—he makes the beds and she's a carpenter.
*Interview, New York/People, 2-24:63.*

**Betty Ford**
*Wife of President of the United*
*States Gerald R. Ford*

4

We have to take that "just" out of "just a housewife" and show our pride in having made the home and family our life's work. Downgrading this work has been part of a pattern in our society that has undervalued women's talents in all areas . . . [Ratification of the Equal Rights Amendment] will not alter the fabric of the Constitution or force women away from their families. It will help knock down those restrictions that have locked women into old stereotypes of behavior and opportunity. It will help open more options for women.
*At Greater Cleveland Congress of International*
*Women's Year conference, Oct. 25/*
*The Dallas Times Herald, 10-26:(A)11.*

**Francoise Giroud**
*French Secretary of State for the*
*Condition of Women*

5

[On the election of Margaret Thatcher as leader of Britain's Conservative Party]: It's a wonderful and funny success at the same time. I've got the impression that it has created panic amongst men. But they are wrong. What I rejoice in is that Mrs. Thatcher is a Conservative elected by Conservatives. It shows that progress for women is not related to politics.
*The Christian Science Monitor, 2-24:4.*

**Germaine Greer**
*Author; Women's-rights advocate*

6

I see more conspicuous degradation of women in America than anywhere else. Planes in America are a completely masculine environment. On the plane the stewardesses can't see me and some address me as "Yes, Sir." They have such a sexual thing going with the male passengers that if you cut across it you're likely to get backlash. In predominantly male environments like bars, the men don't even size up a woman before grabbing her and shouting, "Let me buy you a drink." I had to practically beat a man senseless in a Peoria hotel bar where I'd gone to buy a can of beer to wash my hair with. And there's still a nervousness in hotels when a single woman checks in—why is she alone? And it kills me why you have to be half-naked in this country to serve drinks. Why don't women say I'm not going to wear this crap? I'm speechless when I see the waitresses dressed that way. It's too humiliating to ask, "Why are you wearing that rubbish?" Why is there no trade union making rules that say **people** don't have to dress like Jackanapes? There's a terror of growing old here, too. Women grow old more gracefully in Europe.

> *Interview, Detroit/*
> *The Dallas Times Herald, 11-9:(D)7.*

**Martha W. Griffiths**
*Former United States Representative,*
*D–Michigan* 1

It is a myth that women can't handle high public office, and I wouldn't drop dead if we had a woman Vice President in 1976. Before this century is out, there will be a woman President . . . The biggest error of women after they got the right to vote was not to become interested in politics. More women should run for office, and all this stuff that people won't vote for a woman is bunk.

> *At panel discussion before American*
> *Association of University Women, Seattle/*
> *The Dallas Times Herald, 6-25:(A)25.*

**Elinor R. Heller**
*Chairman, board of regents,*
*University of California* 2

[Objecting to the use of the term "chairperson"] : I want to be addressed as "Madam chairman." The regents' bylaws and standing orders refer to the "chairman" of the board and that's what I want to be called . . . I believe in equal access. I believe that women should have equality of pay and job opportunities, within the limits of their physical strength. But calling someone a "chairperson" is reaching for something that just doesn't mean a thing.

> *Interview/*
> *Los Angeles Times, 7-21:(2)1.*

**Annie Jiagee**
*High-court justice of Ghana* 3

I don't think this world will be destroyed by an atomic explosion. I think it will be destroyed by the explosion of injustice, and that is why the question of the liberation of women is very basic: It is a manifestation of injustice . . . When we are fighting for women's liberation, we are fighting to release a dormant part of humanity . . . If women succeed, we have a hope.

> *At United Nations, New York/*
> *The Christian Science Monitor, 6-12:17.*

**Jacqueline Levine**
*Director, national women's division,*
*American Jewish Congress* 4

If women's liberation is to have real meaning, it must include freedom of choice and how we spend our time, including the right to choose to work at careers, to work at home or to serve as volunteers. The NOW rationale seems to be that if a job is done for pay it is acceptable, but that if it is done for love or compassion or just plain neighborliness, it is somehow inferior or demeaning. We reject this approach entirely.

> *Before American Jewish Congress women,*
> *Philadelphia, March 2/*
> *The New York Times, 3-3:34.*

**Sophia Loren**
*Actress* 5

Women are fighting for emancipation. Yes, I agree with the fight they make. But sometimes they go too far. And they forget all those wonderful qualities that are typically feminine—that make us the right complement for a man. What would women do without men? Why, we couldn't even be mothers!

> *Interview, Paris/*
> *McCall's, September:30.*

**Ida Lupino**
*Actress* 6

I have not too many women friends. I'm not particularly a woman's woman. I'm not a group type. In fact, there's very few women I really like. I don't like to see women behaving in a masculine manner and ordering men around. That's why I don't have too many women friends, because my sex is inclined to go through the back door to get to the front door.

*Interview, Durango, Mexico/*
*Los Angeles Herald-Examiner, 3-6:(B)2.*

**Imelda Marcos**
*Wife of President of the Philippines*
*Ferdinand E. Marcos*
1

The demand for equality has too often had overtones of revenge, the venting of grievances, the acquisition of advantage, the aggression of concealed hatred and envy. [The feminist movement] should not and need not be anti-male. Women are not adversaries, the enemies of men, but their equal partners. [The Oriental woman] has not sacrificed her femininity to individualism but has rather enhanced it with participation. She has not striven for a sterile status but has preferred to play her true role in nature and human society.

*At International Women's Conference,*
*Mexico City, June 20/*
*Los Angeles Herald-Examiner, 6-20:(A)9.*

**Margaret Mead**
*Anthropologist*
2

Every time we liberate a woman we liberate a man. As civilization has developed, we have progressively freed more and more people to contribute as individuals rather than just as parents to the culture of the world.

*The Christian Science Monitor, 6-12:17.*

**Davidson Nicol**
*Director, United Nations Institute for*
*training and redevelopment*
3

At present, women's minds are conditioned from birth. They are forced to relate everything to the male, to their family and even to society. Women's minds must be liberated to think of themselves as persons just as the male child and the adult male are trained to think and lead. Women can then . . . become more useful members of society and more effective members of their families. They can then also be contrib-

utors to original thought and civilization instead of supportive members.

*At San Francisco International Women's*
*Year Conference, Oct. 25/*
*San Francisco Examiner & Chronicle,*
*10-26:(A)11.*

**Ewald B. Nyquist**
*New York State Commissioner of Education*
4

Equality is not when a female Einstein gets promoted to assistant professor. Equality is when a female schlemiel moves ahead as fast as a male schlemiel.

*News conference, Albany, N.Y., Oct. 8/*
*The New York Times, 10-9:50.*

**Estelle R. Ramey**
*Professor of physiology and biophysics,*
*Georgetown University Medical School;*
*Women's rights advocate*
5

The women's movement has been greatly misunderstood. It's not a cause but a symptom —a symptom of social changes instituted by men. Three things: Men control the educational system, and this country has educated more women than any in history. Men send their daughters to college, but they don't realize that these days college is goal-oriented and no mere finishing school, so the daughters learn skills that enable them to fight the system. Two, it was male scientists who found the [birth-control] pill. An affluent people always seek population control. So you have women who are educated and not pregnant, with new mobility and sexual freedom, and they're asking themselves questions about their role in life. Three, it was men who developed the machines that made muscles obsolete. Technology brought the need for more people to do the work, people not just muscular but with intellectual powers, staying power and physical skills.

*Interview/The Washington Post, 9-28:(E)3.*

**Ayn Rand**
*Author, Philosopher*
6

I'm against Women's Lib . . . It's making an issue of an anatomical feature of your gender. I'm against that for the same reason I am against racism. I am against classifying anyone on anatomical, physiological grounds ... What makes you human is your mind, and that is in your control; that's what you are to be judged on.

*Interview, New York/
The Christian Science Monitor, 1-6:7.*

**Annemarie Renger**
*President, West German Bundestag
(lower house of Parliament)*
1

I would say my office shows that indeed a woman can gain such a position in today's society, that a woman may even rise to the highest of offices. But that does not mean a breakthrough has been achieved ... The number of available women is very small. They make up one-fifth of the membership in our political parties, of which only a few can engage in an active political role. We have to ask ourselves where we can find qualified persons to fill jobs that still are held mostly by men. We have to look all over the Federal Republic. There would be more chances if the women themselves made an effort. It is certainly true that there still are not the same training or educational opportunities for women. Every young girl should know that she should plan an occupation to go with her life's vocation. With several children, I do not think it makes sense that one give the children to third persons to raise. But one must recognize that marriage does not solve all the human problems of life.

*Interview, West Berlin/
Los Angeles Times, 3-9:(1)4.*

**Jill Ruckelshaus**
*Women's-rights leader*
2

The ERA is necessary to require legal recognition of the economic contribution of the homemaker, to insure equality of opportunity in public education, governmental "manpower"-training programs and recreation programs; to insure that labor laws restricting women's job opportunities are repealed and never again enacted; to insure equal opportunity, privileges and benefits in all aspects of government employment, including admission to the military services and military-training schools; to require that married women be permitted to maintain a separate legal domicile from their husbands' domicile; to insure that the families of women workers receive the same benefits as families of men workers under the Social Security laws, government pension plans and workmen's-compensation laws, and numerous others.

*Interview/
U.S. News & World Report, 12-1:39.*

**Jihan Sadat**
*Wife of Egyptian President Anwar el-Sadat*
3

I believe in [sexual] equality, but at the same time ... the man should be the head of the family, for the sake of family unity. I don't like ... neglecting the main things for a woman, which are the children, the husband. [In Egypt], we don't want to make it such a confrontation. I need my husband and he needs me. Equality in salaries, in jobs, this is what I want. But if the relationship between the husband and wife is good, he will not sit there and tell the wife to do everything. He will help.

*Interview, Bonn, West Germany, Feb. 19/
Los Angeles Times, 2-20:(1)20.*

**Phyllis Schlafly**
*National chairman, Stop ERA
(Equal Rights Amendment)*
4

... the overwhelming majority of women do not want ERA. They recognize it as a fraud which will do absolutely nothing for women, but which constitutes a big take-away of the rights that women now have ... ERA would take away the right of a young woman to be exempt from the draft and from military-combat duty. It would take away the right of a wife to be supported by her husband and provided with a home by her husband. It would take away the right of a mother to have her minor children supported by the children's father. It would take away the right of a woman who does manual labor to have the benefit of protective labor legislation. Furthermore, there is no end of mischief that ERA, if ratified, could cause in the hands of its proponents ... ERA will take away our right to attend single-sex colleges because, by definition, such colleges discriminate. It would take away the right to maintain fraternities or sororities on college campuses, because they discriminate on the basis of sex. ERA will most probably legalize homosexual marriages, too, and enable these couples to file joint income-tax returns, adopt children and get other rights that now belong to husbands and wives ... There is no gain in ERA for women. It won't give women any rights in employment. It won't give them any rights in education. It won't give them any rights in credit. There is no way that ERA can add anything to the effect of the Equal Employment Opportunity Act of 1972, the education amendments of 1972, and the Equal Credit Opportunity Act of 1974.

*Interview/*
*U.S. News & World Report, 12-1:39,40.*

## Dinah Shore
*Singer*

1

A female performer in television walks a perilous line. Being a female star, and yet not being a dominating woman, is to walk on eggs; for there is nothing less attractive than a woman who has lost sight of the fact that she is first a woman.

*The Washington Post, 5-4:(TV Channels)5.*

## Gloria Steinem
*Editor, "Ms." magazine*

2

If we can judge from history, sex-based prejudice is the most intimate and deep-rooted; the last to go. Even now in corporate board rooms, minority men are usually invited to join the board before women of any race. White men affirm their masculinity by having a minority man on the board—providing, of course, that there are only one or two and can't outvote them. But to have a woman enjoying the same position, especially at upper levels, just devalues the work. Why should a man be honored by a job that "even a woman" can do? If there *is* a woman President, it obviously won't change

everything magically overnight. Still, it would be a major change, because at least we would have before us the image of a female person being honored in authority. At a minimum, it would set the dreams of our children free. Girls could then dream of becoming President. And boys could see that human talent comes in all forms.

*Interview/*
*U.S. News & World Report, 7-7:47.*

## Virginia Y. Trotter
*Assistant Secretary for Education,*
*Department of Health, Education and*
*Welfare of the United States*

3

[On women's rights]: Legislation can support equality, but without the involvement of men and women together to give the law life and momentum, meaning and action, then nothing we can do in Washington can make a real difference. The task of teaching, reorientation and facilitation are the primary tasks for women and will remain so until the goals we seek have become interwoven into the fabric of social consciousness. How do we begin? First, by listening to ourselves, listening to our experiences, by listening deeply and humbly—but with a sense of trust and confidence that we can understand what our experience shows we require, for that is what the new image must incorporate. The old model of a "good woman" has become insufficient for life today. The old image has grown so small and narrow—and if women are not prepared to believe and to understand their own lives better than do men, they will not have the courage and stamina to change them ... A new image of women as active participants and leaders in society does not mean women will desert the emotional validity of personal relations as we move into the world of action. We will bring it along with us to a place where it is badly needed. What we need is the gift of a new image—one that shows men and women honestly and realistically interrelating and active in all phases of life.

*At Academic Woman Conference,*
*Kansas State University, Feb. 15/*
*Vital Speeches, 4-1:375.*

# WHAT THEY SAID IN 1975

**Liv Ullmann**
*Actress*  1

All women should have the right to find out who they are, what they want and the freedom to choose and live accordingly, like men have had for so long. Of course, women will experience new problems and responsibilities with the new freedom—so far women have enjoyed the advantages of unconsciousness. Women's Lib is fine if it teaches women their rights and possibilities. But it is harmful if it orders everybody to wear red stockings or put away their kids in day institutions, regardless of the actual need to do so.

*People, 1-27:57.*

**Beryl Vertue**
*Television producer*  2

I've never been that aware of [the feminist movement]. I just do what I have to do. If you think something is easy or difficult just because you're a woman, you'll start to believe it's a rule. As a woman, perhaps the only difference in dealing with men in business is if they say "no," they say it more politely.

*Interview/"W": a Fairchild publication, 9-5:4.*

# The Indexes

# Index to Speakers

# WHAT THEY SAID IN 1975

# Index to Subjects

## A

Aaron, Henry, 507:6
Abdul-Jabbar, Kareem, 516:4, 519:2
Abortion—*see* Medicine
Abu Dhabi, 355:4
Achievement, 481:4
Acting/actors/stars, 405:2, 405:5, 406:5, 406:6,
    406:8, 407:1, 407:6, 408:2, 408:6, 409:4, 410:1,
    410:2, 410:3, 410:4, 411:1, 411:3, 411:4, 411:5,
    412:2, 412:4, 412:5, 412:7, 413:3, 413:4, 414:2,
    415:2, 416:2, 416:3, 416:4, 417:4, 417:6, 418:1,
    418:2, 418:3, 419:1, 419:2, 419:3, 419:5, 419:6,
    419:7, 419:8, 420:2, 420:4, 420:5, 421:1, 422:1,
    422:3, 422:4, 422:5, 423:2, 423:4, 423:6, 424:4,
    425:4, 437:2, 437:3, 437:4, 437:5, 437:6, 438:1,
    438:3, 438:5, 439:2, 439:5, 439:6, 440:2, 440:4,
    441:1, 441:6, 442:1, 442:2, 442:3, 442:6, 443:2,
    443:3, 443:4, 443:6, 444:1, 444:4, 445:1, 445:5,
    446:4, 448:4, 449:2, 451:6, 454:2, 454:6, 456:6,
    457:2, 458:2, 459:3, 461:6, 462:2, 462:5, 473:5
    autographs, 408:3, 419:4
Advertising, 29:6, 202:5, 373:1, 475:2
    credibility, 35:1
    drugs—*see* Medicine
    factual aspect, 45:1
    false, 56:3
    lawyers—*see* Judiciary
    a tool, 34:3
    *See also* Television
Aerospace industry, 54:4, 204:2
Africa, pp. 267-273, 488:3
    African National Council (ANC), 271:2
    British aspect, 267:2, 336:5
    Chinese (Communist) aspect, 267:2
    colonialism, 129:1, 267:2, 268:2, 269:1, 270:2,
        270:3
    Communism, 113:5, 271:5
    Organization of African Unity (OAU), 270:3
    Soviet aspect, 267:2, 271:5
    U.S. aspect, 116:3, 267:2, 268:1, 268:2
    *See also specific countries*
Age, 462:3, 463:1, 463:2, 467:3, 472:2, 473:1,
    476:3, 477:1
    *See also* Youth
Agriculture/farming, 193:1
    aliens, illegal, 175:1
    costs, 49:1
    environmental aspect, 91:1
    exports, 31:2, 132:6, 179:5, 182:2
    food, 95:5, 132:6
        meat, 473:3
        prices, 179:5, 191:2
        as weapon, 128:5, 129:5

Agriculture *(continued)*
    scientific/mechanized, 31:3
Air transportation—*see* Transportation
Alabama, 227:1
Albania, 326:4
Albert, Carl, 228:3
Alcoholism—*see* Medicine
Algeria, 293:2, 355:4
    French aspect, 267:2
Ali, Muhammad, 500:1, 501:6, 504:5
Allen, Richie, 505:2
Allende (Gossens), Salvador, 32:1, 116:2, 142:4,
    276:2, 277:6
Alston, Walter, 498:3
America/U.S., pp. 10-19
    apathy and euphoria, 12:1
    apex of history, 14:1
    aspirations, fulfillment of, 14:4
    Bicentennial, 11:4, 18:3, 27:4, 280:5
    boredom, lack of, 12:1
    can do anything, 173:2, 173:4
    challenge, acceptance of, 12:4
    change, 10:4
    citizen, average, 18:1
    confidence in, 15:4
    confused purpose, 14:3
    decadence, 17:3
    defeatism, 15:3
    degradation of, 16:2
    dream, American, 17:6, 58:2, 192:3
    European appreciation of, 15:1
    the flag, 17:5
    heritage, worthy of, 11:4
    impatience, 14:5
    incentive to excel, 17:4
    ingenuity, 16:4, 18:4, 18:5
    life-style, 13:5
    limits, 10:3, 17:6
    materialism, 13:5, 17:6
    mood, 13:2
    morality, 17:2, 63:3
    negativism, 15:4
    optimism, 17:1
    past, contempt for, 18:2
    patriotism, 14:6, 18:3
    perfection in, 10:1
    revolutionaries of our time, 13:3
    sins, national, 12:2
    uniqueness, 12:1
    vitality, 17:3
    winning, used to, 11:3
American Airlines, 32:1
American Society of Architects, 30:1
Americans for Democratic Action (ADA), 59:1

Broadway—*see* Stage
Brown, Jimmy, 508:5
Buchwald, Art, 475:4
Bugner, Joe, 497:1
Bunker, Archie, 452:2
Burns, Arthur F., 181:5, 186:3, 194:3, 252:2, 257:5, 259:1
Burns, George, 426:2
Business—*see* Commerce
Busing—*see* Civil rights—education
Butkus, Dick, 497:3

# C

Caetano, Marcelo, 270:2, 326:2
Cagney, James, 412:2
Calcutta (India), 136:5
California, 263:2
Calmness, 470:3
Cambodia:
    Communist take-over/military success, 291:3, 296:5, 297:2, 300:1, 303:2, 304:4, 305:4, 306:2, 308:1, 308:4, 309:3, 310:3, 310:5, 310:6, 311:1, 311:2, 311:3, 315:3
    Constitution, 309:1
    democracy, 296:2, 309:1
    U.S. aspect, 298:6, 310:5, 311:1
        aid, 296:2, 297:2, 298:2, 299:2, 299:3, 299:4, 303:2, 303:3, 306:2, 309:2, 310:1, 312:1, 313:4, 314:1, 315:3
        *Mayaguez* incident, 303:1, 304:2, 305:2, 307:3, 307:5
        pull-out, 296:4
    Vietnamese (North) troops in, 312:2
Campaneris, Bert, 521:2
Canada, 341:2
    economy, 283:1
    government budget, 164:3
    oil exports, 107:5
    television aspect, 451:7
    United Nations aspect, 361:2.
    U.S. aspect, 279:3, 280:2
Cancer—*see* Medicine
Capital punishment—*see* Crime
Capitalism, 37:5, 47:1, 48:6, 50:1, 122:3, 185:2, 187:5, 195:1, 317:3, 322:2, 326:1, 335:1
Caribbean—*see* Americas
Carli, Guido, 181:1
Carnegie, Andrew, 18:4
Castro, Fidel, 71:5, 277:4, 277:7, 364:6
Central Intelligence Agency (CIA), U.S.—*see* Intelligence/spying
Chad, 361:2
Chancellor, John, 379:4
Chanel, Coco, 375:6
Charisma, 463:8
Chayefsky, Paddy, 451:7
Chekhov, Anton, 392:5
Chicago (Ill.), 249:5
Chicanos—*see* Civil rights

Chile:
    Communism/Marxism, 281:2, 282:1
    coup of 1973, 116:2, 276:2, 277:6, 281:6
    elections, 281:3
    military government, 281:4
    repression, 281:5
    U.S. aspect:
        CIA involvement in, 32:1, 116:2, 138:1, 142:4, 276:2, 281:6
        coup of 1973, 116:2, 276:2, 277:6, 281:6
        ITT aspect, 32:1
China (Nationalist)/Taiwan, 131:4, 311:1
China (People's Republic; Communist), 286:2, 363:5
    African aspect, 267:2
        *See also specific countries*
    Angolan aspect, 273:2
    Asian aspect, 290:5
        *See also specific countries;* Indochina, below
    detente, 130:5
    economy, 291:1
    foreign affairs, 130:1
    Indochina aspect, 297:1, 302:4, 308:5, 312:1, 314:5
    Korea (South) aspect, 290:1, 290:4, 294:4
    Mao Tse-tung aspect, 293:6
    Philippines aspect, 286:4
    Soviet aspect, 285:4, 288:3
    suppression/regimentation, 16:3, 285:5
    Thai aspect, 286:4
    United Nations aspect, 359:6, 361:2
    U.S. aspect, 18:5, 71:5, 116:2, 117:4, 121:2, 137:1, 137:4, 287:1, 295:3, 336:1
Chopin, Frederic, 429:6
Christianity—*see* Religion
Church—*see* Religion
Churchill, Winston S., 80:3
Cigarette smoking—*see* Medicine
Cinema—*see* Motion pictures
Cities—*see* Urban affairs
Civil rights/racism, pp. 20-28, 476:8, 527:6
    bills, 22:2
    blacks/Negroes, 20:1, 20:2, 20:3, 21:1, 21:5, 22:3, 23:1, 23:4, 23:6, 24:4, 25:4, 26:1, 26:3, 26:4, 27:1, 28:1, 235:5, 524:5
        in baseball, 497:2, 515:7
        Bicentennial (U.S.) aspect, 27:4
        in boxing, 515:2
        crime aspect, 70:1
        employment/unemployment, 22:4, 23:5, 25:1, 26:2, 182:6
        gains, 23:7
        Mayor, 259:5
        in motion pictures, 420:1
        quotas, 497:2
        strategic role, 23:2
        university faculties, 25:2
        whites, common interests with, 24:1
    Chicanos/Spanish-speaking, 20:3, 23:5, 25:2
    Chinese-Americans, 26:4
    church, role of, 489:6
    class aspect, 22:3, 23:4

# F

## S

# WHAT THEY SAID IN 1975

Soviet Union *(continued)*
U.S. aspect, 18:5, 113:4, 115:5, 118:1, 119:5,
119:6, 121:2, 124:1, 125:2, 126:5, 127:4,
133:1, 133:3, 134:1, 134:2, 134:3, 135:1,
135:2, 137:1, 137:4, 205:2, 206:2, 211:3,
269:3, 319:3, 320:2, 323:6, 326:3, 328:1,
329:7, 330:3, 336:1, 336:2, 341:1, 343:1,
363:1, 364:6
Berlin agreement, 327:4
CIA raising of submarine, 378:3
comparison, 10:2
defense/military:
ABM treaty, 206:2
nuclear test-ban treaty, 206:2
strategic-arms (SALT) treaty/talks, 117:4,
119:6, 206:2, 327:4
U.S. vs. Soviet—*see* defense, above
Vladivostok agreement, 206:2
Middle East confrontation, 119:6
trade, 116:2
wheat/grain sale, 45:3, 55:5, 122:2, 135:4,
174:5, 331:1
World War II, 143:5
Space, 240:1, 493:4, 495:2, 495:4
*Apollo,* 493:1
life on other planets, 493:1
moon landing, 477:7
*Sputnik,* 363:5
Spain, 320:2
defense/military/Army, 320:5
Communism, 318:3, 320:5
democracy, 320:5
Fascism, 320:5
Franco, Francisco, 320:5
Juan Carlos assumption of throne, 327:1
reform, political, 317:4
Speech, freedom of 380:5, 383:4, 385:2, 453:1,
453:3
Sports, pp. 497-522
amateur, 505:4
anti-heroes, 504:6
athletes, importance of, 501:1
college—*see specific sports;* Education—college
criticism by athletes, 515:4
European aspect, 508:1
excellence, 501:2
fans, 497:4, 500:2, 504:6, 505:3, 517:2, 517:4,
518:1
future of, 513:2
gambling/betting, legalization of, 509:2, 517:2,
518:4
importance, 520:6
injuries, player, 519:4
language, player, 507:2
mountain-climbing, 507:1
old-time athletes, 513:6
Olympic Games, 514:1
salaries/benefits, player, 500:1, 505:2, 507:6,
513:3, 515:6, 517:5, 518:3, 518:5, 520:8,
521:5
small world, 502:4

Sports *(continued)*
superstars, 516:4
television coverage, 513:4, 517:3, 518:2
underdog, 508:1
U.S. aspect, 505:4, 508:1, 513:5
winning/losing, 498:6, 499:6, 503:3, 505:5,
505:6, 506:2, 506:6, 507:5, 510:3, 510:4,
510:6, 511:2, 511:6, 512:2, 512:5, 516:4,
520:7
*See also specific sports*
Stage/theatre, 422:2, pp. 436-447, 466:7
democracy of, 442:2
an art, 436:2, 439:7
audience, 409:5, 437:5, 437:6, 438:4, 439:4,
441:4, 441:6, 442:1, 442:5, 443:3, 444:3,
446:7, 449:1
British, 443:6
London, 438:2, 441:2, 441:6
Broadway/New York, 371:1, 434:5, 438:2, 438:4,
441:2, 441:3, 441:6, 446:2, 446:5, 456:2
Off Broadway, 436:2
Winter Garden Theatre, 441:1
comedians, 442:3
critics/reviews, 441:5, 444:2
directing/directors, 436:3, 436:4, 441:5, 442:6
entertainment, 439:3
financing/costs, 438:2
formality/glamour, 442:1
long runs, 438:5
mediocrity, 436:2
motion pictures compared with, 412:3, 415:2,
416:4, 436:3, 436:4, 437:2, 437:3, 438:1,
441:3, 442:6, 443:2, 446:5
non-structured plays, 439:4
open theatre, 442:1
playwriting/playwrights, 370:7, 436:1, 438:4,
439:4, 441:3, 442:6, 442:7, 443:7, 444:1,
444:2, 444:3, 444:5, 446:6, 446:7, 450:3
political, 374:2
pornography, 371:3, 443:5
realism, 442:7
repertory, 420:2, 443:4
strike, musicians, 446:2
success, 441:5
television compared with, 441:3, 443:2, 446:7,
450:3, 453:2, 456:6
touring, 439:5
U.S. aspect, 441:4, 441:6, 443:6
unnecessary institution, 438:4
waste in, 445:1
women in, 440:1
*plays:*
*A Flea in Her Ear,* 442:5
*Caine Mutiny Court Martial, The,* 438:5
*Hamlet,* 431:3, 442:5
*King and I, The,* 437:4
*Mister Roberts,* 438:5
*Most Happy Fella,* 444:2
*Point of No Return,* 438:5
*Victoria Regina,* 439:5
*See also* Acting

# U

# V

# W

## X

Xerox Corp., 47:2

## Y

Yeats, William Butler, 330:1
Youth, 463:3, 465:4, 467:3, 472:4, 473:7, 476:3, 477:1, 480:2, 481:2, 483:1, 490:1
   *See also* Age
Yugoslavia, 286:3

## Z

Zambia, 268:2
Zavattini, Cesare, 410:5
Zeithlin, Zvi, 435:1
Ziegler, Ronald L., 382:5
Zionism—*see* Middle East
Zola, Emile, 387:5